STRATEGY AND COMMAND

STRATEGY AND COMMAND
The Anglo-French Coalition on the Western Front, 1915

ROY A. PRETE

McGill-Queen's University Press
Montreal & Kingston · London · Chicago

ISBN 978-0-2280-0576-6 (cloth)
ISBN 978-0-2280-0664-0 (paper)
ISBN 978-0-2280-0769-2 (ePDF)
ISBN 978-0-2280-0770-8 (ePUB)

Legal deposit third quarter 2021
Bibliothèque nationale du Québec

Printed in Canada on acid-free paper that is 100% ancient forest free
(100% post-consumer recycled), processed chlorine free

Funded by the Government of Canada | Financé par le gouvernement du Canada | Canada | Canada Council for the Arts | Conseil des arts du Canada

We acknowledge the support of the Canada Council for the Arts.
Nous remercions le Conseil des arts du Canada de son soutien.

LIBRARY AND ARCHIVES CANADA CATALOGUING IN PUBLICATION

Title: Strategy and command. The Anglo-French coalition on the Western Front, 1915 / Roy A. Prete.
Other titles: Anglo-French coalition on the Western Front, 1915
Names: Prete, Roy A. (Roy Arnold), 1943– author.
Description: Includes bibliographical references and index.
Identifiers: Canadiana (print) 20210101849 | Canadiana (ebook) 20210101873 | ISBN 9780228005766 (cloth) | ISBN 9780228006640 (paper) | ISBN 9780228007692 (ePDF) | ISBN 9780228007708 (ePUB)
Subjects: LCSH: World War, 1914–1918—Campaigns—Western Front. | LCSH: World War, 1914–1918—France. | LCSH: World War, 1914–1918—Great Britain. | LCSH: France—Military relations—Great Britain. | LCSH: Great Britain—Military relations—France. | LCSH: France—Military policy. | LCSH: Great Britain—Military policy.
Classification: LCC D544 .P743 2021 | DDC 940.4/144—dc23

Set in 10.5/13.5 Minion Pro
Book design & typesetting by Garet Markvoort, zijn digital

CONTENTS

Illustrations vii
Maps ix
Abbreviations xi

Preface xiii

1 Setting the Stage:
The Political and Military Background 3

2 Trench Warfare:
Strategic Re-Evaluation and the Zeebrugge-Ostend Coastal Plan,
December 1914–13 January 1915 34

3 Conflicting Strategies:
The 29th Division and Neuve Chapelle,
14 January–13 March 1915 65

4 Planning the Spring Offensive and the Command Issue,
14 March–21 April 1915 99

5 Second Ypres and Joint Planning for the Artois Offensive,
22 April–8 May 1915 134

6 Operations: The Artois Offensive, 9 May–25 June 1915 152

7 Catalyst for Change: Impact of the Artois Offensive 170

8 Strategic Conflict: The Calais and Chantilly Conferences, July 1915 195

9 Objections to Loos and British Strategic Reversal, July–August 1915 218

10 Operations: The Loos and Artois-Champagne Offensive, September–October 1915 242

11 Salonika, Egypt, and the Western Front, September–December 1915 271

12 Preparation for 1916: Leadership Changes and Strategic Coordination 301

13 Reflections and Conclusions 324

Notes 343

Bibliography 403

Index 423

ILLUSTRATIONS

Raymond Poincaré 16

René Viviani 16

Alexandre Millerand 17

Herbert Henry Asquith 17

Horatio Herbert Kitchener 18

Kitchener on recruiting poster 19

Winston S. Churchill 20

Joseph J.-C. Joffre 24

Joffre, profile, in ceremonial headdress 24

Ferdinand Foch 25

John French 25

Henry Wilson 26

Joffre and Foch 40

Joffre bids farewell to Kitchener, 29 March 1915 118

David Lloyd George 178

Kitchener, greeted by French leaders, 6 July 1915 206

Political-military conference at Calais, 6 July 1915 207

Maurice Sarrail 244

Aristide Briand 291

Joseph-Simon Gallieni 291

Anglo-French conference in Paris, 17 November 1915 294

Douglas Haig 312

William Robertson 312

Allied military conference, Chantilly, 6–8 December 1915 320

MAPS

Western Front trenches, 1915 38

The Anglo-French theatre, 1 January 1915 67

Battle of Neuve Chapelle, 10–13 March 1915 95

Battle of Ypres, April/May 1915 136

The Anglo-French theatre, 9 May 1915 148

Anglo-French offensives, May/June 1915 154

Anglo-French troop dispositions, September 1915 257

Anglo-French offensives, September/October 1915 262

The eastern Mediterranean 270

The defeat of Serbia, 1915 281

Anglo-French front, 19 December 1915 313

ABBREVIATIONS

A	Annexe
AE	Archives des Affaires Etrangères, Paris
AFF	Archives of Fournier-Foch (private collection, now in Archives nationales, Paris)
AFGG	*Les Armées françaises dans la Grande Guerre*
AG	Archives de Guerre, Service historique de la Défense, Vincennes
AN	Archives nationales, Paris
BN	Bibliothèque nationale, Paris
BEF	British Expeditionary Force
CA	Churchill Archives Centre, Cambridge University
CAB	Cabinet Papers, National Archives, London
CGS	Chief of the General Staff
CT	Cipher Telegram
FO	Foreign Office, London
GQG	Grand Quartier Général (French Headquarters)

HGW *History of the Great War based on Official Documents*

IWM Imperial War Museum, London

LHMA B.H. Liddell Hart Centre for Military Archives, King's College, London

NA National Archives, London

PA Parliamentary Archives, London

RA Royal Archives, Windsor Castle

THW *Times History of the War*

T Telegram

WO War Office, London

PREFACE

MORE THAN ONE HUNDRED YEARS after the end of the First World War, its long shadow still hangs heavily over the collective memory of the Western world. As one of the great defining events of the twentieth century, the First World War has continued to attract widespread scholarly attention as scholars have combed the archives and revisited the issues in quest of new and more satisfying interpretations.[1] The arrival of the war's centenary sparked heightened interest, witnessed, among other things, by the launching of a new journal, new studies on traditional political and military topics,[2] and a vast number of books on varied aspects of the human drama related to the war.[3] The centenary celebrations of 2014–18, including media programming and special commemorative events, have brought into focus the popular thirst to better understand this cataclysmic event of unheralded proportions.

The battlefield history of the Western Front has been of sustained interest, with books focusing on the great drama of the Battle of the Marne in 1914,[4] the Canadian and British roles in the Second Battle of Ypres in April 1915,[5] French tactics in the Battle of Artois in the spring of 1915,[6] and the trial by fire of the British "New Armies" in the Battle of Loos in September 1915.[7] There have been several recent volumes detailing the huge slaughter and seeming futility of the Battle of the Somme in 1916 – which has left a lasting scar on the British psyche[8] – while the controversial generalship of Sir Douglas Haig is still being reappraised.[9] The contribution of General Ferdinand Foch has been more fully appreciated and the performance of the French Army reassessed more favourably.[10] New battlefield accounts written from the eyewitness experiences of participants have been particularly poignant.[11]

There has also been continued interest in Anglo-French military relations during the war. In well-received scholarly studies, William James Philpott has explored Anglo-French command relations on the Western Front largely from a military point of view and Elizabeth Greenhalgh has made an important contribution to the broader aspects of Allied coalition warfare, especially after 1916.[12]

The argument presented here is that, as a pivotal year in the evolution of Anglo-French command relations, 1915 warrants its own specialized treatment, based on in-depth research in the political and military archives of both Entente powers. The agonizing and unsuccessful battles of 1915 provide the vital link between the "War of Movement" in 1914 and the great attrition battles of 1916. The clash of traditional French and British strategies was exacerbated in 1915, when stationary trench warfare and deadlock assumed new proportions and the mobilization of resources loomed larger in Allied planning. Many new issues had to be resolved as the two governments and their military leaders attempted to come to grips with the new reality of total war.

Based on a close interaction between political and military leaders in the pre-war period, French strategy remained relatively constant in 1915, with heavy reliance on allies, whose support had been carefully nurtured prior to the war. As Robert A. Doughty has observed, throughout the entire conflict "French grand strategy rested on the idea of waging a multi-front war against the Central Powers."[13] In addition to their own military engagement, the French consistently relied throughout the war on the success of their allies for their own success. Chief among these allies were the Russians, whose participation formed the touchstone in French strategic planning. To a large degree, French strategy and planning depended on the participation of the Russian Army, whose ability to engage the forces of the Central Powers in a two-front war was vital to France's success on the Western Front. That the war was fought in France and Belgium and involved the devastation of the French homeland added a particular urgency to the need to drive the Germans out of France.

For the British, on the other hand, the year 1915 marked the transition from limited to total commitment to the continental war, fully evidenced by the middle of 1916 with the Battle of the Somme. In the pre-war period, the primary focus of British defence planning was on the defence of empire, with sea power being its main underpinning. Confronting the growing strength of the German empire, the British had entered into the Entente Cordiale with France a decade before the war and had engaged in military-staff talks with the French as a contingency plan in the event of a European conflict. It should be remembered, however, that with the dawn of 1915, the European war (as it was then called) had been underway for just five months and the British had not yet committed themselves completely to the war on the continent. It was in the course of 1915 that the British, reassessing their strategic interests, became a full coalition partner in the continental land war.

British strategic planners were less committed to the immediate needs of the Russians on the battlefront than were the French. While the British eagerly awaited the Russian "steamroller" to swing the war in favour of the Entente, they were more suspicious of the Russians than were the French. France's alliance with Russia dated from 1894, while Britain had signed the Triple Entente with Russia much later, in 1907, and this agreement only regulated long-term colonial competition and was not a binding alliance. In the eyes of British planners, Russia was a great power, a vital ally with preponderant military resources, boasting an army greater than that of Germany and the ability to determine the outcome of the war. The great imperative, therefore, was to bind the Russians to the Entente diplomatically, as witnessed by the Straits Agreement of March 1915, while at the same time meeting their financial needs and supplying them with arms and munitions in order to obtain a maximum contribution from their efforts in the field.[14] A major concern of the British was to keep open the sea lanes with Russia. The British assessment of Russia provided them with greater flexibility in their strategic thinking for a time. But, ultimately, the need to support their French and Russian allies by a maximum military contribution on the Western Front would trump all other considerations.

British and French policy and strategy were thus at loggerheads through much of the year. With stalemate on the Western Front, British global strategy for the defence of empire, with its preference for operations peripheral to the main European theatres, was at odds with the strategy of French commander-in-chief, General Joseph J.-C. Joffre, for offensive action on the continent aimed at driving the Germans out of France and giving aid and assistance to the Russians. This strategic difference lay at the root of much of the conflict between Joffre and Sir John French, the commander-in-chief of the British Expeditionary Force (BEF) in France and Belgium.

In the broad perspective, it should be remembered that the European powers had not waged a large-scale war involving the entire continent since the end of the Napoleonic wars a century earlier. Nor had any of them waged a war with the entire panoply of increased firepower which led to trench warfare and deadlock. The long drawn-out industrial warfare that resulted, which would require the mobilization of all of the resources of the state, was a different kind of war, for which the nineteenth-century experience and training of the generals had left them ill-prepared,[15] and for which the perception and practices of the politicians proved inadequate. In this new kind of war, largely experimental in nature, there was a constant "groping at the wall" at every level of leadership. Wedged between the period of movement ending in November 1914 and the great attrition battles of 1916, 1915, the first full year of trench warfare, was thus a watershed, with major new challenges. As the war dragged on, the Allies' lack of success began to undermine the public's confidence in its leaders, both political and military.

With the advent of stalemate on the Western Front and the indeterminant lengthening of the war, the vast potential of Britain's contribution to the war effort in France loomed larger in French eyes. At the beginning of the war, the French were able to field 72 regular divisions and the Russians 102; hence, the great reliance on the Russians in French strategic planning – a fact often obscured in historical literature as a result of the Russian withdrawal from the war following the Bolshevik Revolution. By comparison, in 1914, the Belgians had 7 divisions, the Serbs had a force of 11 divisions, and the British had an expeditionary force of 6 divisions, of which 4 initially went to France, followed by a fifth. By the end of 1914 that number had increased to 10 regular divisions and 2 territorial divisions, and an initial cavalry division had expanded to 2 cavalry corps.[16] Belgium and Serbia, and later Italy, were also part of the French calculus, according to their military strength, in what was inexorably a multi-front war. The British, given the disparity between the size of their forces and those of Russia, played a far lesser role than the Russians in the early stages of the war. Because of the relatively small size of the BEF in 1914, the British were inevitably the junior partners in joint planning with the French on the Western Front, and despite an increase of more than 20 divisions in 1915, they remained so throughout the year.

For the French, the relative significance of British military participation increased dramatically when the British, under the leadership of Secretary of State for War Lord Horatio Herbert Kitchener, created massive New Armies and began mobilizing necessary military resources. With a population of thirty-nine million, equivalent to that of France, and as the greatest commercial and naval empire in the world, Britain had an unrivalled potential for growth in the mobilization of men and the production of arms. From this stemmed the French desire in 1915, as the war stalled in France and the Russians suffered reverses on the Eastern Front, to have the British contribute more and more of their military resources to the war effort in France – rather than to allocate them to the pursuit of imperial interests elsewhere.

Despite the entry of Italy into to the war on the side of the Entente in May 1915, the year 1915 was a very bad one on the battlefield for the Entente powers, marked by stalemate on the Western Front, a succession of major defeats on the Russian front, the Gallipoli disaster, and the defeat and occupation of Serbia. Because of the critical nature of the situation for the Entente, the British were inexorably drawn deeper and deeper into the European conflict. The question was what form their increased participation should take. The limited success of the French Army on the battlefield in 1915, coupled with the disastrous retreats of the Russians on the Eastern Front in the spring and summer, with no end in sight, proved to be the chief catalyst for increased British commitment to the continental war. The needs of the Entente coalition thus took precedence over other interests in British strategic planning.

Understanding this process requires that attention be paid to important aspects of Anglo-French military relations in 1915 with regard to operations and operational planning. Accounts of the 1915 battles on the Western Front, for example, often treated from a British perspective, frequently neglect the background in Anglo-French relations. Yet these Allied political-military and strategic discussions are the thread that links the high drama of 1914 with the bloodletting of 1916, marked by the transition from limited British commitment to defence of the continent in 1914 to that of total involvement in 1916.

The treatment of several unresolved issues, within the political and military framework of the two countries, is thus crucial. Various twists and turns in the relationships between Sir John French and his government, between Joffre and the French government, and between Sir John and Joffre during the planning of the stillborn Zeebrugge and Ostend coastal operation in early 1915 bear further scrutiny. While it is well documented that the conflict between British peripheral strategy in the Dardanelles expedition and French operational strategy led to the breakdown of Anglo-French command relations and the isolated British attack at Neuve Chapelle in March 1915,[17] the pathway to renewed cooperation in the Artois offensive has not been fully explored.

Nor has the impact of the Second Battle of Ypres in April on joint planning for the Battle of Artois the following month been examined in detail. The Anglo-French Artois offensive in the spring of 1915, though an operational failure, was particularly heavily laden with political and military consequences, yet many of its repercussions have only been partially appreciated.

Several other aspects of Anglo-French command relations and coordination in 1915 have been explored in only a limited way. The findings of detailed research, particularly in French archives, confirms that the intricacies of the political-military background in each country and Allied command relations in 1915 warrant additional in-depth discussion. What was the impact in joint planning of the state of arms production and supply in each country? Why did the British decide at the end of June to send the New Armies to France, and what actually was said and agreed upon at the first Anglo-French political-military conference held at Calais on 6 July 1915?[18] To what extent did Joffre circumvent these strategic directions? Why were the British so slow in accepting the need for a unified command, given the many difficulties experienced in the coordination of joint offensives?

There are still other questions. What was the interaction between Joffre and his government in the formulation and execution of French strategy? What was Joffre's role not only in Anglo-French command relations but also in Allied coordination in 1915, and what impact did this have on the British and other allies? Did the British act contrary to their interests in September 1915 in giving their full support to Battle of Loos and the Artois-Champagne offensive in France? What was the impact on the Western Front of the Salonika expedition launched in September during the battle of Loos and the Artois-Champagne offensive? What were the repercussions for Allied military relations on the Western Front as a result of the British build-up of forces in Egypt in anticipation of the evacuation of the Dardanelles at year's end? To what extent did the experiences of 1915 and the special leadership of Joffre set the stage for the 1916 Allied campaigns and the major battles in France in 1916? Finally, what was the cumulative impact of Anglo-French strategic decision making and battlefield experience on joint command relations? Such questions invite further research and investigation.

While not a comprehensive treatment of all aspects of Anglo-French wartime relations in 1915, this volume is intended to fill the gap in terms of the policy and strategy of the two Allies and their joint command relations. There are various interpretations relating to the nature of the Anglo-French coalition on the Western Front: that interpersonal relationships were the single most important factor in the functioning of that coalition[19] or that the British northern-flank military strategy, based on the British interest in defending the Channel ports, was the key element and the chief source of discord in the operation of the coalition.[20] The argument presented in this volume and the one preceding it, *Strategy and Command: The Anglo-French Coalition on the Western Front, 1914*, which forms the background to the present study, is that the political and strategic aims of the belligerents were the main determinant in Anglo-French command relations.[21] This derives from the fact that the military commanders, despite their independent-mindedness, were ultimately subordinate to the civil authority. Even though the military chiefs sometimes functioned independently, in a general way they carried out or were affected by the policy and strategy of their respective countries. The long view would suggest the primacy of policy in Anglo-French command relations in the First World War.

Indeed, in August 1914, once the British entered the war, the chief issues, as detailed in the earlier volume, were limited British commitment to the continent and the British desire for freedom of action in the face of Joffre's desire to obtain maximum British participation on the battlefield. Several crises, some of a very serious nature, followed in Anglo-French command relations in 1914 in consequence of these differing approaches.[22] The advent of hostilities consolidated British commitment to the alliance but left open many issues as to the extent of British participation and the day-to-day conduct of the war.

In addition to reaffirming his leadership of Anglo-French operational planning, Joffre began progressively in mid-1915 to play a more prominent role in the coordination of strategic planning for the entire Entente coalition. By situating Anglo-French command relations with reference to the larger political-military context and the internal politics of each state, the author has sought to get behind the scenes and to understand more fully the dynamic of Anglo-French decision making – with all its implications for command relations and the conduct of the war.

In sum, although many factors affected Anglo-French command relations in 1915, including the technological and tactical challenges of trench warfare, questions of armament and supply, the politics of each country, civil-military relations, linguistic and cultural difference, and the personalities of the commanders, the most basic factor, it is argued, was the differing strategic approach of each country, which reflected its differing political objectives. The field commanders, each with a specific point of view, were left to coordinate their efforts, which often resulted in severe conflict. In a number of instances, however, particularly in requesting more British troops for the front and in their opposition to the peripheral operations, they colluded against their political masters, leading to strained civil-military relations in both countries.

Ultimately, in the course of 1915, as in the first months of the war in 1914, both the operational preferences of the British commander and the strategic aims of the British government had to yield to the exigencies of the coalition, whose maintenance represented a higher goal than any immediate interest. The British, to support their French and hard-pressed Russian allies, thus sent their New Armies to France in mid-1915 and engaged them fully at Loos in September, signifying an increased commitment to the war in France.

The great irony was that, as the British evacuated the Dardanelles at the end of 1915, liquidating that costly external venture, they found themselves engaged in a new peripheral expedition in Salonika at the insistence of the French. As British strategy in 1916, largely under military direction, focused on the Western Front, a significant source of conflict with the French – in a complete reversal of roles – was French adherence to the Salonika expedition.

The terminology in this volume, as in its predecessor, draws on traditional British usage rather than the current American breakdown of warfare into strategic, operational, and tactical levels. The basic idea of military strategy common to both traditions – involving the deployment of resources for the accomplishment of a political or military objective – remains constant. But what in current American parlance is termed strategy, which includes the deployment of national resources and is a function of governmental direction, is here termed "grand strategy." Also, what in current American usage is termed the operational level of warfare, which has to do with the planning and execution of campaigns and major operations, is referred to here as operational strategy (or just strategy) and includes the deployment of large units in the field. The deployment of large units falls under the title of tactics in American usage, while tactics, as here discussed, involves the deployment of small units and their method of engagement in combat in the field.[23] One of the great strengths of General Joseph Joffre was that, both as French chief of the General Staff prior to the war and as commander-in-chief during the war, he was cognizant of the diplomatic situation and the needs of French allies and, as a result, pursued a strategy which may be termed "grand strategy" in its fullest expression.

The current volume is the second in a trilogy of books on Anglo-French command relations on the Western Front during the period 1914–16, when Joffre was French commander-in-chief. The third volume in the sequence, yet to appear, will complete the series by examining the events of 1916. This final volume, in addition to focusing on treatment of Anglo-French command relations on the Western Front, will explore the wider context in which Joffre attempted to coordinate the military offensives on the several Allied fronts. Within the Anglo-French military context, this volume will be largely devoted to joint planning prior to and during the Battle of the Somme, the relationship between the Battle of Verdun and the Somme, and execution of the joint offensive. While Joffre had dominated the military side of the Anglo-French coalition from the outset of the war, by mid-1916, as the number of British divisions mounted to the benchmark of fifty, Sir Douglas Haig, who had replaced Sir John French in December 1915 as commander of the British Army, assumed much greater independence of the French chief. An important ongoing subtheme will be conflict over the Salonika expedition. Joffre's removal from office at the end of 1916 led to the dissolution of the Allied framework of cooperation he had established and dashed even the semblance of Entente coordination.

The author owes a debt of deep gratitude in the preparation of this volume to the kindly services of the numerous keepers and archival personnel in France and Britain who have so graciously made available the rich holdings of their repositories; and to the numerous copyright holders who have allowed the quotation of excerpts referenced in the notes. In particular, the author wishes to express his appreciation to Her Majesty the Queen for permission to consult files in the Royal Archives at Windsor Castle. The author also wishes to express his appreciation to the Royal Military College of Canada, which has provided funding in the form of several research grants and a sabbatical leave for the pursuit of this project. Stuart Daniel drew the maps. James Kenny and Alayna Jay assisted in the research of English documents. Brian Jevons aided in the preparation of three chapters. Keith Neilson read parts of the manuscript and provided helpful advice. The peer reviewers assigned by McGill-Queen's University Press have helped make this a better book. Editor Curtis Fahey has greatly improved the text. Kyla Madden, senior editor at the press, deserves special recognition for her patience and ongoing support, which have assisted in bringing this work to fruition. Lastly, the author wishes to express his appreciation to his wife, Carma, whose support and thoughtful reflections have been invaluable and who has proofread and refined the text. In fond appreciation, this book is dedicated to her.

Roy A. Prete
Kingston, Ontario
29 October 2020

STRATEGY AND COMMAND

CHAPTER ONE

Setting the Stage: The Political and Military Background

THE HARD-FOUGHT BATTLE OF YPRES, which drew to a close in mid-November 1914, marked the end of the War of Movement on the Western Front. The French, British, and Belgian armies, in a concerted effort under French leadership – despite the difficulties of Allied coordination – had fought the German Army to a standstill. Each side having failed to outflank the other in the "Race to the Sea," manoeuvres in the field gave way during this battle to "entrenchments, barbed wire" and "bullets from automatic weapons," accompanied by unprecedented loss of life.[1]

As the lines of trenches stabilized from the Alps to the North Sea, the western Allies gradually began to realize that the short war of manoeuvre, for which all the belligerents had prepared, had resulted not in victory but in trench warfare and deadlock; and that the conflict would be long and costly, involving all the resources of the state. Adapting to the changed conditions of the war would be the major challenge of the next three and a half years, for the impasse on the Western Front could not be broken, despite the vastly increased size of attacks, until the German offensive in the spring of 1918.

The French and British governments responded quite differently to the new challenges of impasse and trench warfare, creating further tensions in their relationship. To understand the strategic conflict experienced between the two governments in 1915 and its implication for Anglo-

French command relations, it is necessary to consider not only the origins of their conflict in the pre-war period but also the legacy of the first campaign season in 1914. While these questions have been treated at length in *Strategy and Command: The Anglo-French Coalition on the Western Front, 1914*, the first volume in this series, they will be reviewed here briefly in order to lay the groundwork for a discussion of the 1915 Allied experience.

By the end of the 1914 campaign season, the politics of fighting the war in each country began to have a decided impact. In Britain, there was an attempt to strengthen the machinery of wartime decision making, while France saw a parliamentary challenge to the authority of the cabinet and the High Command. The last weeks of 1914 thus marked a new period, characterized in both countries not by the glorious return of the troops but by adjustments in the political-military structure and also in the military leadership. And most importantly, as treated in the next chapter, the dawn of the new year marked the Allied quest for a grand strategy better adapted to the changed conditions of the war.

FRENCH POLICY AND STRATEGY PRIOR TO 1914

The roots of Anglo-French strategic conflict in 1915 hearkened back to the pre-war policies of France and Britain, the Entente Cordiale partners, and provided the framework for their military strategies prior to the war and during the initial phase of the conflict in 1914. Military planning in each country and the initial conduct of operations derived from these strategies.[2]

French pre-war defence policy had relied on the support of coalition partners, particularly the Russians, and the strength of the French Army. As the great battles of the war unfolded on the Western Front, France's strategy continued to rely on the support of its allies. For the French, the successful operation of the Entente coalition remained a vital key to victory.[3] While France possessed an empire of fifty million people and many vital resources, the main purpose of the French Navy was to keep the sea lanes open in the Mediterranean Sea for the safe passage of troops from French colonies in North Africa.[4]

The role of alliances had assumed vital importance following the disastrous Franco-Prussian War of 1870–71. Given the growing disparity between French population and industrial resources and those of Germany, it soon became apparent that France could no longer stand alone against German military might. Faced with the threats from across the Rhine in a series of diplomatic crises in the twentieth century, the French put greater and greater reliance on their allies and potential allies. The alliance with Russia signed in 1894 was the cornerstone of French defence policy as it would force Germany into a two-front war; and even with the added weight of Austria-Hungary as an ally of Germany, the French alliance with Russia would serve to right the military imbalance.[5]

French security was further buttressed by negotiation of the Entente Cordiale with Britain in 1904, which marked a significant political realignment despite its lack of formal commitments. By this arrangement, Britain was to have a protectorate over Egypt and the French a free hand in Morocco, and the two powers agreed to consult if these terms were challenged. Innocuous enough in and of itself, the Entente Cordiale was transformed into a quasi-alliance by the addition of military and naval conversations following the two Moroccan crises of 1905 and 1911. But the British resisted any formal commitment to the French, despite the close cooperation envisaged in the 1911 military conversations and also despite the 1912 naval accords, which defined the respective division of labour for the British and French navies in defence of the Mediterranean and the Channel coasts.[6]

Of the two political arrangements, France placed much greater reliance on the Russian alliance, in view of the formal Russian commitment and the vast Russian Army. General Joseph J.-C. Joffre, chief of the General Staff after 1911 and later commander-in-chief of the army, was able to adopt an offensive strategy after 1911 only because the Russians promised to deliver 700,000–800,000 men against Germany by the fourteenth day of mobilization. The non-binding Entente with Britain was useful as a contingency plan but at best would contribute only a small army of six divisions on the French left wing. Incredibly, French military leaders placed limited value on the role of the Royal Navy. Fixated as they were on a short war and the pre-eminent role of land armies, their appreciation of the navy's value in a long war was seriously impaired. The French military position was further strengthened by the likelihood of Italian neutrality following the 1902 Franco-Italian colonial accords, which would free French forces guarding the Italian frontier.[7]

Joffre fully appreciated the importance of alliances for French security; hence his efforts in 1911 and subsequently to reinforce the alliance with Russia and also the Entente Cordiale with the British. In so doing, Joffre worked hand in glove with his government and its leaders.[8]

From the onset of hostilities, Joffre understood that for France to win the war, it would need to be fought on many fronts with the support of French allies.[9] With the broadening of the coalition *union sacrée* government of René Viviani on 27 August 1914, Alexandre Millerand, a forceful personality, replaced the flighty and unpredictable Adolphe Messimy as war minister. Both Millerand and Joffre were in complete accord that a primary aim of France during the war was to obtain the maximum contribution from French allies. Millerand became the effective mouthpiece for the High Command in dealing with the British during the entire length of his ministry, which lasted until the end of October 1915.[10]

In the pre-war period, the British were the wild card for the French. Their participation in any future war was much desired, and staff arrangements had been forged to accommodate that possibility. But as the British, even after the naval accords of 1912, were unwilling to enter into a formal agreement with the French, their participation in the war had to depend on the circumstances of the moment. Happily, the German invasion of Belgium in August 1914 provided just such a circumstance, which united the main thrust of public opinion with the long-term interests of British defence policy in favour of participation in the war alongside the French.[11]

Joffre's military policy was thus a continuation of pre-war diplomatic policy with its heavy focus on alliance politics. In reading Joffre's memoirs, one is forcefully impressed that the Russians played a much larger role than generally considered in French strategic calculations.[12] In 1914 the pre-war plan for a coordinated Russian attack bore fruit in diverting two and a half German corps from the Western to the Eastern Front on the eve of the Battle of the Marne, and the French continued to rely on Russian offensive action in the Battle of Ypres to relieve pressure on the Western Front.[13] Throughout 1915, the successes or the failures of this vital ally, and the appropriate operational strategy on the Western Front – whether to take advantage of troop movements to the east or to attack in order to take pressure off the Russians – were constantly on Joffre's mind. The need to sustain the Russians and to provide for a unified Allied strategy played a major role in his assertion of the role of de facto coordinator of the Entente coalition in early July.

So far as the British were concerned, Joffre's objective from the beginning of the war in 1914 was to obtain the maximum contribution possible. The first task was to firm up the alliance relationship. As early as 12 August 1914, Joffre demanded the forward deployment of the British Expeditionary Force in the Maubeuge area in order to ensure that the British would participate in the first great battle with the enemy.[14] Then, at each step of the ensuing campaign, he insisted that the British government send all available forces to France. And finally, Joffre tried to assure maximum British participation in each joint engagement, and, as a corollary, the alignment of British forces with French strategy and operational directives.[15]

BRITISH POLICY AND STRATEGY PRIOR 1914

British pre-war strategy was quite different from that of the French. As a great commercial empire of 250 million people, covering one-fourth of the surface of the globe, the British empire relied principally on the Royal Naval for its defence. Britain's main concern prior to the war and at the outset of hostilities was to balance imperial defence with the maintenance of a suitable balance of power on the continent.[16] While the British were able to wrest control of the high seas from the Germans in the first four months of the war, their continental allies, France and Russia, proved much less able to stand up to the military might of the Central Powers, Germany and Austria-Hungary. British policy thus underwent a major transformation as the British recognized with succeeding battles the ever-growing need for increased military commitment to the continent in order to buttress their French and Russian allies.

British global defence policy prior to the First World War has often been distorted in the literature by an exaggeration of the attention given to continental defence,[17] which was in reality part of a larger strategy for the defence of the empire.[18] The British attempt to balance the defence needs of a great maritime empire with the maintenance of a suitable equilibrium on the European continent resulted in a substantial ambivalence in British policy toward defence of the continent.[19] While the British cabinet prepared for war to the extent of authorizing the preparation of staff plans for coordination with the French in the pre-war period, it was unwilling to make any firm commitment.

The British strategy to send the British Expeditionary Force to France to support the French Army, as agreed on in pre-war military conversations, was applied in August 1914. The decision to enter the war on behalf of the Entente partners was made partly because of the public outrage over the German invasion of Belgium and partly because participation in the European war was deemed essential to the maintenance of vital British interests on the continent. Clearly, it was not in British interest to have German hegemony on the continent. But entering the war still left open the question of how the war was to be conducted. The decision to send the British Expeditionary Force to fight alongside the French Army was not made without equivocation, for several political and military leaders, including Sir John French, commander of the BEF, would have preferred a strategy based on direct support of Belgium.[20]

As a maritime and commercial empire, Britain was intent on protecting vital pre-war imperial interests, its naval mastery, its commercial empire, and the balance of power on the continent, as well as, should the occasion arise, further enhancing the empire. For Britain, the war involved a limited commitment initially and was not a struggle for survival, as it was in France. As David French has demonstrated, British strategy at the beginning of the war was aimed at naval dominance of the high seas, "business as usual," and limited military intervention on the continent, where it was believed the great armies of Russia and of France would be victorious against the Central Powers.[21]

The British government, as before the war, wanted to maintain its freedom of action as much as possible in order to avoid being dragged into a military strategy contrary to its interests.[22] In recognition of this policy, Sir John French was instructed to cooperate with the action of French armies but to maintain his complete independence.[23]

Two factors intervened very early in the war to alter fundamentally British grand strategy. The first was the appointment of Horatio Herbert Kitchener as British secretary of state for war on 6 August 1914 to give the Liberal and peace-minded government of H.H. Asquith a military allure. Unlike his contemporaries, who believed that the war would be of short duration, with the troops home by Christmas, Kitchener was convinced that it would be long, at least three years. His strategy in consequence was to mobilize the military resources of the empire and to create massive New Armies in Britain in order to intervene in a decisive way at a time when the resources of the country's continental allies were partially used up and thus win the war for Britain, which would then be the dominant power at the peace table.[24] In retrospect, it is clear that, without the intervention of the British New Armies on the continent, the Entente powers would have lost the war in 1917, if not before. But, this war-winning strategy consigned many thousands of young British men – some have claimed a whole generation – to premature death.

The second element that upset the British strategy of limited military action on the continent was the relative weakness of the French and Russian allies in conflict with the armies of Germany and Austria-Hungary. Despite his long-term plans, Kitchener understood in the short term the absolute necessity for Britain to sustain its continental allies with all available means to prevent them from suffering a military disaster, which could lead to a separate peace. A pessimist by nature, he feared most of all that the German armies would be victorious, either against the French armies in 1914, or against the Russian armies and then the French armies in 1915, preparing the way for a German invasion of Britain.[25] The importance he attached to sustaining British allies, which ultimately took priority over imperial considerations, helps to explain the dynamic of the coalition, whereby the British, often against their will, under the exigencies of the war, advanced from a limited military commitment to France at the beginning of 1915 to a total war effort on the continent by year's end.

How was this possible? Did the British act contrary to their fundamental interests in so doing? To answer that question, it may be useful to reflect on the fundamental nature of state policy and its adaptation in time of war.

THE NATURE OF COALITIONS

Remarkably, historians have devoted limited study to the theory of the nature and operation of coalitions, despite the fact that the two world wars of the twentieth century were both fought as coalitions and nearly all subsequent wars have involved several belligerents in a concerted effort against a common foe. Pioneer works, mostly in articles, have focused largely on case studies.[26] Notable exceptions are Elizabeth Greenhalgh's *Victory through Coalition*, which attributes the Allied victory in 1918 to the albeit imperfect operation of the Entente Cordiale coalition,[27] and Meighen McCrae's book on the Supreme War Council, which details its role in Allied strategy and war planning during the last two years of the war.[28]

What is apparent is that broader considerations of state policy undergird the basic concepts relating to the functioning of coalitions. Foreign policy is intended to defend the vital interests of the state. As Paul Kennedy has pointed out, military alliances are "not the same as friendships" and generally are "entered into for motives of self interest, usually that of self protection."[29] According to Henry Lord Palmerston, the great nineteenth-century British diplomat and later prime minister, "nations have no permanent friends or allies, they only have permanent interests."[30] Alliances are formed, sometimes with former foes and even traditional enemies, as in the case of the Triple Entente, when vital interests appear to be threatened. In a great war, in which the defence of key interests depends on the maintenance of one's ally or allies in an alliance, the latter then becomes essential; for in the event of their defeat and withdrawal, the primary interests of the state may be impaired in a critical manner.

In a coalition, parties frequently have conflicting interests and aims. For example, Russia early in the war coveted the Dardanelles Strait linking the Black Sea and the Mediterranean; and Kitchener, imbued with the ideas of imperialism, had as his goal not only the defence of the empire but also its enhancement in the eastern Mediterranean. The French also had their eyes on the eastern rim of the Mediterranean as their post-war sphere of influence.[31] How could such conflicting interests be harmonized?

To prevent conflict between the partners, and to reduce suspicions, the wartime solution arrived at was for the Entente partners first to pledge not to make a separate peace, which they did on 5 September 1914. They then proceeded to resolve their conflicting interests by a series of secret treaties. The March 1915 Straits Agreement with Russia served not only to avoid a wartime conflict over the fate of the Dardanelles but to bind the Russians to the war effort by giving them a stake in the post-war settlement. The British and the French resolved their future acquisitions and spheres of influence in the Arab Middle East by the Sykes-Picot Agreement in 1916, by which the French would get possession of Syria, the British, Iraq; and Palestine would be held jointly, with other spheres of influence also spelled out.[32]

While such arrangements could provide a modicum of harmony at the political level, tensions often remained, with each country suspected of pursuing its own interests *sub rosa*. An additional factor, as General N.P. Mikhnevich, a late-nineteenth-century Russian theorist opined, was the belief that "allies will strive to shift the heaviest burdens on to other shoulders."[33] This was certainly Sir John French's view of the French and may to some degree explain his deep reluctance to accept unity of command under French leadership.

THE ANGLO-FRENCH ENTENTE AND COMMAND RELATIONS DURING THE 1914 CAMPAIGN

While the British had entered into the war in 1914 in defence of their vital interests, the question of grand strategy as a coalition partner – essentially how and by what means to fight that war – remained open. How much of the state's human and material resources should be mobilized and by what means? How should resources be allocated between theatres and for what purposes? What should the balance be between navy and army, and how much resources should be allocated to each? How much of British productive and financial resources should be allocated to allies? In the First World War, the question of adaptation to a long war and the need to provide guns and munitions on an unprecedented scale, both for the massive New Armies and for less-favoured allies, particularly the Russians, also raised major issues in terms of state organization. In the case of Britain, all of these issues became the subject of ongoing discussion.

Unlike the French, whose pre-war policy and subsequent strategy were defined to a large extent by their geo-political situation, Britain, as a maritime empire and as the dominant naval power, had more options and more independence of action. But the experience of 1914 brought home the narrowing of possibilities as Britain's allies fared less well in the field than expected, which shifted the vital interest from pursuing earlier goals to maintaining and supporting the coalition.

As the last volume in this series has demonstrated, the British intended to make only a limited military commitment at the outset, sending an expeditionary force of four infantry divisions, followed by a fifth in a few days, and one cavalry division, and Sir John French was cautioned against engagements unless large bodies of French troops were involved. But the circumstances of the campaign led to an ever-increasing level of commitment.

On the French side, Joffre's main goal, as indicated, was to obtain a maximum participation from his British allies and ultimately to have them conform to French strategic planning. When the war came, there was substantial friction with the British, who did not mobilize until after the invasion of Belgium on 3 August, did not declare war until the next day, and only decided to send the British Expeditionary Force to France two days later. The French were anxious to include British forces in their initial left-flank operation, which they delayed a few days for that purpose. Ultimately, under pressure from Joffre, Kitchener pushed the British Expeditionary Force forward to engage with the French in the operation, but he did so contrary to his better judgment, preferring to have the BEF maintain a contingent position in reserve. His instructions to Sir John French on 9 August to avoid major engagements unless the French were fully engaged and his affirmation of Sir John's independence of command were reflections of those misgivings, and of the limited British commitment to continental defence.[34] As a result of Sir John's full liberty of action, cooperation with his Gallic counterparts would depend to a large degree on the level of confidence between the two.

The results are well known. The BEF, in a forward position at Mons, was outflanked by the German First Army on 24 August as a result of bad strategy on the part of the French, whose Plan 17 did not allow for a wide German sweep across Belgium. The result was a major rift between the two commands. And a further drubbing of British forces at Le Cateau on 26 August resulted in Sir John's headlong retreat to the Seine, where he hoped to find safety. While his armies pulled back, Joffre's strategy consisted of strengthening his left flank by the deployment of troops from his right wing, the colonies, and the interior.

The conflict between the two commands deepened as Joffre, in spite of the French launching a counter-attack at Guise on 29 August, was unable to persuade Sir John French to maintain his position in the line. It was only after pressure from the British government and the dramatic visit of Kitchener to Paris on 1 September, when he instructed Sir John to stay in the line and fight with the French, that the French staff was able to implement its strategy for pulling apart the German line by a strong attack on its right flank. Vital British cooperation was restored, and the result was the successful First Battle of the Marne between 5 and 9 September, in which the British Expeditionary Force and part of the French Fifth Army marched into the gap in the German line. In addition to poor campaign strategy on the part of the French, limited British commitment to continental defence at the outset and the British desire for independence of action had been significant factors in the initial conflict in the field.[35]

Another conflict arose over the defence of Antwerp following the German attack on the outer forts on 27 September 1914. The British placed a much higher priority than the French on the defence of the Channel ports. In fact, it should be remembered that the British decided to deploy with the French in the years prior to the First World War at least in part because the Belgians, recognized as neutral by an international agreement in 1839, were unwilling to work up staff relationships.[36] And the British were very unhappy with the French because Joffre continued to pursue a strategy of outflanking the Germans (despite promises of support for the Belgians), whereas the British wished to strengthen Antwerp as long as possible. Winston Churchill, the first lord of the Admiralty, made a dramatic bid to save the Citadel by a personal visit to Antwerp but to little effect. Ultimately, the fortress fell on 10 October. Happily, Belgian, British, and French forces joined hands as they fell back and took up a defensive position on the Lys, following Belgian inundations.[37]

The conflict over the defence of Antwerp had derived from a basically different appreciation of strategic policy. When Joffre's initial strategy did not give the hoped-for results, vital British interests were exposed by the German attack on this vital port. British strategy for the direct defence of the Channel coasts, which had initially been subordinated to French strategy, took on new life, but it only partially succeeded without the support of Joffre, who continued his strategy of outflanking the German army.[38]

An interlocking conflict of major proportions occurred when the BEF, stalemated on the Aisne River, wanted to redeploy on the left flank in the Race to the Sea in order to be near to British ports. With an increase of forces to ten divisions, Sir John thought he could roll up the German flank. The French were reluctant to redeploy the three British corps located on the Aisne as they would have to be replaced in their existing position in the line. The French command also feared that the British, whom they viewed as invariably slow, late, and unaggressive, would not attack with sufficient vigour in this vital Race to the Sea.

Only reluctantly and under pressure from Kitchener, who was concerned about the defence of Antwerp, did Joffre begin the redeployment in early October. What had not been known until discovered from the diaries of Raymond Poincaré, the French president, and other sources, was that when Sir John French failed to take Lille on 19 October, Joffre requested his recall and his replacement with General Henry Wilson, the British subchief of staff, who had made the pre-war arrangements with the French![39] The call for Sir John's replacement represented a major breach in Allied relations.

In a meeting at Dunkirk on 1 November between Kitchener, Poincaré, Joffre, and Ferdinand Foch (who came late), at the height of the Battle of Ypres, Kitchener was prepared to replace Sir John French with Sir Ian Hamilton. Wilson, however, was persona non grata with the Asquith government because of his role in the Curragh affair of March 1914 involving the imposition of home rule in Ireland. The French turned down Kitchener's offer of Hamilton. In fact, they thought this would be a less satisfactory arrangement than the existing one since Foch, who had been appointed coordinator in the northern theatre on 4 October, had managed to establish a working relationship with Sir John through Henry Wilson.[40] Sir John was thus retained in his post.

This conflict also reflected the differing strategies of the two allies. At the beginning of the war, the British intended to make only a limited commitment to the war in France. But the demands of battle in the face of French inability to stand alone prompted a step-by-step increase of commitment. Despite his earlier instruction, Kitchener ordered Sir John on 1 September to cooperate with French forces, leading to the reversal of the Marne. British divisions were sent as soon as they could be readied or spared from home defence, so that, by the end of the Battle of Ypres in November 1914, there were ten regular British infantry divisions, the equivalent of two territorial divisions, and two cavalry corps in the field.

In the heat of the Battle of Ypres, Kitchener on 1 November, moreover, attempted to buoy up the French political and military leaders at Dunkirk by promising them "a magnificent English Army of a million men for July 1, 1915."[41] Now that the New Armies were being formed, it would be nigh unto impossible to deny them to hard-pressed allies. While Kitchener's pledge did not bind the British cabinet, it did show that the British were being drawn inexorably by the exigencies of the war in France to a greater commitment to continental defence.

Support of British allies was in fact looming large as a vital interest of state, for defeat would have been a disaster for Britain. And, despite vigorous attempts to escape that exigency in early 1915, whether through the Dardanelles expedition, the retention of the New Armies in Britain, or the limitation of those forces' offensive role in France, by the autumn of that year – once some of the New Armies were being deployed in France – the British were unable to escape total commitment to the continental war.

FRENCH ADJUSTMENTS IN THE POLITICAL AND MILITARY STRUCTURES

The test of war showed deficiencies in both the French and British conduct of the war effort. In France, the onset of war altered the traditional power relationships within the French government, and the government, in turn, gave a huge grant of power to Joffre for the conduct of operations. The conflict on the battlefield, in which Joffre became the "Victor of the Marne," furthered changed the relationship between the High Command and the government.

In a patriotic session of the French Parliament on 4 August 1914, all political groups, rallying to French President Raymond Poincaré's call for a *union sacrée*, agreed to set aside political differences in favour of an energetic conduct of the war. The Chamber of Deputies voted almost unlimited powers to the government for the prosecution of the war effort and then adjourned.[42] The government, in turn, granted Joffre unfettered authority for the conduct of operations. "The political direction of the war properly belongs to the Government," said a statement approved by the cabinet; "the conduct of operations is under the exclusive purview of the Commander-in-Chief."[43] On 27 August, as the military situation deteriorated, Radical Socialist Premier René Viviani, under Poincaré's prodding, fashioned a *union sacrée* coalition, joining together all of the major parties (except the far right) for the pursuit of the war effort.[44]

During the diplomatic crisis preceding the onset of war, Vivaini, who was serving as both premier and foreign minister, had had an attack of nerves, and Poincaré assumed effective control of French diplomacy. Poincaré carefully managed France's role in the pre-war crisis, spearheading the pullback of French troops ten kilometres from the German frontier to persuade the French nation and particularly Britain that

left Raymond Poincaré, president of the French republic, 1913–20. Brushing aside the traditional role of Third Republic presidents as figureheads, Poincaré revived the powers of the presidency as spelled out under the constitution and was the guiding influence in the French government during 1915. (*Times History of the War* [hereafter THW], 1:28)

right René Viviani headed the French government in 1914 at the outbreak of war and formed a *union sacrée* coalition on 27 August to shore up French support during the French retreat from the frontiers. A relatively weak leader, Viviani nonetheless brought together a team of capable ministers. His ministry fell in October 1915 as a result of parliamentary dissatisfaction over the conduct of the war on the Western Front and its handling of the Salonika expedition. (THW, 1:37)

left Alexandre Millerand, the French war minister in Viviani's *union sacrée* government from August 1914 to October 1915, was a forceful personality who considered it his main function to advocate the cause of the commander-in-chief and to shield him from criticism in the government and the Parliament. (*THW*, 1:84)

right Herbert Henry Asquith, British prime minister, 1908–16. An experienced parliamentarian, Asquith led a government of capable department heads, on the pre-war model, in which he was the chief conciliator. After the Shells Crisis in May 1915, he formed a coalition government including the Unionists but failed to provide the unity of direction and forceful leadership necessary to prosecute the war effort effectively. He was supplanted by David Lloyd George at the end of 1916. (*THW*, 5:286)

Horatio Herbert Kitchener (from painting by Angele) was brought into Asquith's cabinet as the secretary of state for war at the outset of the conflict to give the government a martial appearance, and he remained in this position until his boat was sunk by a German torpedo in June 1916. Termed the "Architect of Victory" by a notable biographer because of his recognition that massive New Armies would be required to win the war, he often ran afoul of his civilian cabinet colleagues for his non-disclosure of information and enjoyed a bittersweet and tangled relationship with Sir John French, commander of the British Expeditionary Force in France. (*THW*, 1:287)

Kitchener on recruiting poster, in July 1915, while the issue of conscription was being debated in Great Britain. Under the voluntary system, nearly 2.5 million men volunteered for service in the British Army before conscription was finally invoked at the end of 1916. (IWM)

France was not the aggressor.[45] While Viviani ensured his coalition's parliamentary majority and maintained control of internal policy, Poincaré played a dominant role in French diplomacy and revived the president's long-dormant powers of supervision of the army laid out in the constitution of the Third Republic.[46]

Despite the weak leadership of Viviani, his *union sacrée* government formed in late August 1914 included a competent team of seasoned ministers drawn from across the political spectrum, including two socialists, Jules Guesde and Marcel Sembat. Alexandre Millerand was made war minister, a position he had held previously; Aristide Briand, a former premier, became minister of justice; Alexandre Ribot, a notable financier, was brought in as finance minister; and Théophile Delcassé, author of the Entente Cordiale with Britain, resumed his earlier role as foreign minister.[47] From London, Paul Cambon, the French ambassador, wrote, "With Millerand at the War [Ministry] and Ribot at Finance, it will no longer be possible to call it a 'ministry of incompetents.'"[48]

Nonetheless, Poincaré continued to exercise general supervision over the ministry, using the powers of the presidency more fully than

Winston S. Churchill, termed the "Greatest Briton" for his role in the Second World War, was first lord of the Admiralty from 1911 to May 1915, when, tarred with the major responsibility for the Dardanelles fiasco, he was replaced in Asquith's government. In early 1915 Churchill and Sir John French planned a coastal operation for a landing at Zeebrugge and Ostend and a military advance against the German right flank, until the Dardanelles venture captured Churchill's attention. (*THW*, 1:46)

his predecessors.[49] A former premier, cool-headed, methodical, and capable of extracting the essential elements from masses of documentation, Poincaré provided overall direction and stability to the government, compensating for Messimy's lacklustre leadership.[50] Poincaré, in fact, was one of the few governmental leaders willing to stand up to the tall, massive, overpowering, unyielding, strong-willed, and authoritarian commander-in-chief.

While Vivian's coalition government's reputation had been badly tarnished by its flight from Paris to Bordeaux on 4 September, it remained intact after its return to Paris in December 1914. Faced with new problems of purchase and supply associated with the advent of industrial trench warfare and stalemate, the government assumed a more aggressive role in the administration of the war effort. The bureaucracy expanded rapidly to deal not only with industrial production but also with war-related areas such as agriculture, health, transport, and commercial obligations. In response to Joffre's urgent request, Millerand, much to his credit, had already taken an aggressive stance in the production of munitions, appealing to the private sector on 20 September while he was still in Bordeaux.[51]

Though his initial deployment had proven defective, Joffre's reputation as the "Victor of the Marne" elevated him beyond criticism and placed him in a dominant position vis-à-vis his government, making him the unchallenged master of French strategy for a time. The government's flight from Paris to Bordeaux not only weakened its authority but also hampered its supervision of the High Command. That said, failure of the military command to obtain decisive results during the War of Movement caused much surprise and disappointment in France among the populace and the government alike and soon led to a reassertion of political authority, principally by the Chamber of Deputies.

The French cabinet returned to the capital on 11 December to face a restive Parliament, many of whose members had just been on the front and were in a testy mood. After a patriotic session on 22 December, the Chamber, in view of the unhappy prospect of a long war, began to regret the vast powers conferred upon the cabinet and commander-in-chief and to reassert its traditional role. As the "Victor of the Marne," Joffre was still too popular to allow a direct attack on him. The Chamber, moreover, had also agreed not to play into the hands of the enemy by direct challenges to the government. Discontent with the government and High

Command was therefore channelled into the Army Commissions of the Chamber and Senate, which took up much of the review function normally reserved for the Parliament.

In early 1915 these two commissions reasserted their traditional right to inquire into the War Ministry's handling of supply and matériel. In the course of the year, despite Millerand's attempt to thwart their activities and shield the High Command from "civilian interference," parliamentary inspection was extended to the army zone at the front under Joffre's control. Although Joffre still enjoyed vast prestige and power, the period of unchallenged military authority had drawn to a close, succeeded by a long period of intense civil-military conflict in which the Chamber, in the absence of victories in the field, would eventually acquire renewed control over both the government and the military command.[52]

After the failed 1915 spring offensive in May–June 2011, a coterie of Radical Socialists in the Chamber moved to have Joffre, already under attack in the parliamentary commissions, replaced. For the moment, his position was secure. But, following the failed Artois offensive, the government, at Poincaré's urging – who considered Joffre abusive of his authority and unwilling to take advice – obliged him to consult regularly with his Army Group commanders.[53]

READJUSTMENTS IN THE FRENCH COMMAND

Anglo-French command relations were greatly altered in the course of the 1914 campaign with the appointment of General Ferdinand Foch on 4 October as personal assistant to Joffre and coordinator of the Allied forces in the northern French theatre. While he was given authority over French Army commanders in the theatre, his relationship with the British and the Belgians extended only to Joffre's request that they coordinate their efforts through him. Foch had been a friend of Wilson in pre-war days, and his appointment was initially resented by Sir John, who disliked being subject to Joffre's subordinate at a time of strain in his relationship with the French commander-in-chief. At the same time, Sir Archibald Murray, the chief of staff, was unhappy that coordination with the French would now pass through Wilson, the subchief.[54]

A fighting general, fully committed to the offensive, with the capacity to inspire confidence and evoke the utmost energy from his associates, Foch had a better understanding of the British military than many of his peers. He soon showed his mettle in coordinating with the Belgian king in the Battle of the Yser and won British respect for his vigorous leadership and unstinted military support in the Battle of Ypres in late October and early November. Foch, in fact, may well be credited with having averted disaster in the northern theatre during the Race to the Sea.[55] By the end of the campaign season, he had won to a considerable degree the respect and trust of the British command. In 1915 the pattern was for Joffre to issue general instruction on intended joint operations, but for Foch to work out the details of their implementation with the British command in the field.

On the other hand, Foch was not above intriguing with Wilson, over a period of more than two months, to have Wilson replace Murray as British chief of staff after the plan to have Sir John French replaced by Wilson had been foiled at the beginning of November.[56] The latter plan, with Joffre's support, also backfired for Wilson, as described below. That Joffre sought the removal of British generals whom he deemed unequal to their tasks should not come as a surprise given that he had replaced fully one-third of his senior officer corps in the first four months of the war in 1914 in a bid to toughen up French military leadership.[57] Viewing the British Expeditionary Force as an adjunct to the French Army, Joffre expected the same quality of leadership from British generals as he did from his own.

Foch's appointment as coordinator for the northern theatre on 4 October prefigured the refashioning of the French Army's command structure. On 5 January 1915 two provisional army groups were set up, the northern, under Foch, and the eastern, under General Yvon Dubail.[58] In mid-June 1915, under government pressure to engage in a more collegial style of command, Joffre created three army groups from the two provisional groups he had organized in January. Both Foch and Dubail retained their commands over their respective army groups; General Édouard de Curières de Castelanau was appointed to command the new centre army group.[59]

Significant changes were also made in the personnel of the French command at the close of the phase of movement. General Henri Berthelot, the most hearty of anglophobes, was dismissed as assistant chief of staff on 22 November and given the command of a corps.[60] His removal from Grand Quartier Général (GQG; French headquarters) represented a victory for Major Maurice Gamelin and the Third Bureau in conflict with

left Joseph J.-C. Joffre served as chief of the French General Staff from 1911 until the outbreak of the war and was commander-in-chief of the French Armies of the Northeast from the outbreak of the war until December 1915, when he became commander-in-chief of all French forces. Often criticized for the costly attacks conducted under his leadership, he was the guiding force in Anglo-French operational strategy on the Western Front and played a significant role in Allied coordination after the summer of 1915. (*THW*, 1:82)

right Joffre, profile, in ceremonial headdress. (Callwell, *Wilson*, 1 [following 216])

left Ferdinand Foch, considered a "fighting" general, coordinated the operations of the Belgian, British, and French armies on the French left from October 1914 until his replacement in December 1916. Foch had a particularly close relationship with Sir Henry Wilson, who had played a major role in preparing pre-war joint plans. (Aston, *Marshal Foch* [opposite title page])

right John French (from painting by J. St Helier Lander). Known as a "Thruster" from his South African War experience, he commanded the British Expeditionary Force in France from August 1914 to December 1915. During the 1915 campaign season, he was often caught between the peripheral strategy of the British government and the demands of the French commander-in-chief, General Joffre, for offensive action on the Western Front. On such issues, Sir John almost always sided with Joffre. (*THW*, 4:123)

Henry Wilson, who claimed to be the "ugliest" man in the British Army, was an officer of considerable talent but with a noted penchant for intrigue. He played a major role in coordination between the French and British armies during the 1914–15 campaign seasons. (Callwell, *Wilson*, 1 [opposite title page])

Berthelot's strategy of assault on the "inner" wing. The Third Bureau, having acquired the right to advise the commander-in-chief directly, had indeed demonstrated the value of its strategy in preparing the decisive Battle of the Marne. Their opponent thus became the subject of a reassignment to the field.[61]

One of Berthelot's last official acts, on 17 November, was to vent his spleen on the British. In response to their renewed request for relief of an extra 1,000 yards of trenches, he complained – echoing the criticism of Foch – that the British did not understand that "war is not played as a sport" and that the British government had failed to send the "numerous divisions ready" on British soil. "Will we soon have to be on guard against them?" he queried.[62]

The concept of "perfidious Albion," held in many political circles and by Foch, Colonel Victor Huguet (liason officer at British headquarters), and others, was still very much alive in Berthelot's mind. Britain, according to this view, manipulated the continental balance for its own interests but brought little in the day of reckoning. In effect, the prejudices and stereotypes evident in anti-British sentiment prior to the war had remained largely intact during the first months of combat. Suspicion and mistrust of British intentions remained a major impediment to effective cooperation in the field.[63]

After centuries of bitter rivalry, the British, for their part, were also very mistrustful of the French, their traditional enemy. Aristocratic British military leaders thought that their middle-class French counterparts lacked a sense of gentlemanly conduct: they were scheming, indirect, and sometimes small-minded. Most of all, British officers resented the imperious attitude of the French military leaders and their desire to dominate.[64] These attitudes were reinforced in Sir John French's mind by experiences of 1914 and early 1915, when he felt he had been unsupported on several occasions. As for British political leaders, they distrusted the instability of the French political system, with its numerous parties and frequent change of ministries. British politicians worried that French public opinion lacked the cohesion and stability necessary to fight a great war.[65] These attitudes would have a major impact on the decision making of the British government in mid-1915, when it feared that the French were beginning to wobble.

Berthelot's departure, nonetheless, removed a serious irritant in command relations and paved the way for a somewhat more accommodating attitude toward the British at Grand Quartier Général. His replacement was General Maurice Pellé, who was known for his skill as a military diplomat. General Alphonse Nudant, who succeeded Pellé as the other assistant chief of staff, also "looked a first rate man" to a British observer at French headquarters. In common with others at GQG, Nudant respected the British Army for its defensive ability but had serious doubts about its offensive capacity, preferring to retain that role for the French Army.[66]

While the long-held stereotypical image of the British as "slow, late, and unaggressive" had had a significant impact on Allied command relations during the War of Movement, it would have an even greater impact during the long period of stalemate and trench warfare that followed. Regarding the British as unsuited for offensive action, partly because of their failure to coordinate their actions closely with the French during the War of Movement, the French would attempt repeatedly to have them hold more and more of the trenches in order to free French forces for offensive action.[67]

But the British, as much as the French, were anxious to avoid the attrition of the trenches and eager for the success of offensive action. The allocation of the trenches would thus remain a basic issue throughout 1915 and 1916 when the major battles were being planned, at which time the French usually pressed the British both to relieve French trenches and to make a major contribution to the fighting. The matter would come to a head in a dramatic way under General Robert Nivelle in the spring of 1917.[68]

Joffre's one consistent objective was to obtain a maximum contribution from the British. This took the form of assuring both the maximum deployment of British troops in France and their utmost contribution on the front, but always under French strategic direction. In 1914, in addition to normal communication through liaison officers and in conferences, he had resorted to a number of ploys to accomplish these ends, including using the diplomatic channel, encasing British troops with French ones, and attempting to have personnel changed at British headquarters. In 1915 Joffre proved equally innovative in trying to assert unity of command and also in assuming a major role in the overall coordination of Entente military planning. As a result of the requirements of the coalition, coupled with the support – sometimes very reluctant – of Kitchener, he generally succeeded.

BRITISH POLITICAL ADAPTATION: THE WAR COUNCIL

In Britain, the Liberal government of H.H. Asquith continued to show many of the same strengths and weaknesses that it had at the outset of the war. Parliament had granted a wide range of discretionary powers to the cabinet for the conduct of the war. But Sir John French's freedom of action, as commander of the British Expeditionary Force, was narrowly circumscribed by Kitchener, the secretary of state for war, who remained the effective voice of British strategy. Two strong men, Kitchener at the War Office and Churchill at the Admiralty, tended to dominate strategic policy, with input from Sir Edward Grey, the secretary of state, and the prime minister. Yet the government, often functioning without adequate professional advice, followed anything but a coherent policy. Recognizing these deficiencies, Asquith adjusted the machinery of wartime government at the end of the 1914 campaign season in order to develop new plans to meet the "new situation arising out of the growing stalemate on the Western Front and the intervention of Turkey as a belligerent."[69]

A number of ill-coordinated diplomatic and military initiatives associated with Turkey's entry into the war had convinced Asquith that the existing cabinet system, with its lack of systemized contact between armed services, its lack of professional advice, and its lack of overall direction, was no longer adequate for the coordination of the war. In late November, he thus set up a special cabinet committee, the War Council, for the overall direction of the war, superseding the moribund Committee of Imperial Defence. The new body, concerned with the long-term problems of British strategy rather than the day-to-day conduct of the war, consisted initially of Asquith, Kitchener, Churchill, Grey, Chancellor of the Exchequer David Lloyd George, Chief of the Imperial General Staff James Wolfe-Murray, First Sea Lord John (Jackie) Fisher, and Sir Arthur Balfour, a prominent member of the Unionist Opposition, with the "indispensable" Maurice Hankey as secretary.[70] The growing interest and involvement of Lloyd George in military matters was a portentous development.

The War Council, however, which met for the first time on 25 November, changed little in the British power structure. Asquith lacked the energy and determination to impose a centralized direction on the war effort. Kitchener and Churchill, often in conflict, still remained dominant in the formulation of British strategy, which, while attempting to respond to the needs of their French and Russian allies, strove to maintain Britain's independent role. The advice of the technical services, as witnessed by the Dardanelles fiasco, was not always solicited or accepted. Although the War Council, sometimes expanded to include the commander of the BEF, provided an organ for the systematic formulation of policy, it proved largely ineffective owing to its ever-increasing numbers, lack of authority (except as delegated by the cabinet), and irregular meetings and agenda. That said, however, the council marked a first step toward a more effective conduct of the war at the cabinet level, which ultimately culminated in the powerful War Cabinet under Lloyd George at the end of 1916.[71]

WILSON'S INTRIGUE AND CHANGES IN THE BRITISH COMMAND

The British field command, like the French High Command, underwent significant adjustments at the end of the 1914 campaign season. The events leading to General Sir Archibald's Murray's recall as chief of the general staff (CGS) at British headquarters were to prove a painful chapter in Anglo-French political military relations which demonstrated the seamier side of the alliance. The affair, which occupied the attention of both governments and commands over a period of two and a half months from mid-November 1914, centred on the intrigue of Major-General Sir Henry Wilson, subchief of staff, conducted in tandem with both Sir John and the French, to obtain the post of his less-than-competent superior, Sir Archibald Murray.

The French command, as shown by their earlier attempt to get rid of Sir John, were convinced of the need for a more aggressive approach at British headquarters. Having failed at Dunkirk on 1 November in their bid to have Wilson, who had won their admiration in the pre-war period, take over as commander-in-chief, the French now attempted to have him installed as chief of the general staff in place of the unaggressive Murray, whom GQG had come to regard as the chief source of British caution and reserve.[72] The French command and, in turn, the French government thus gave full support to Wilson's quest for promotion. The many twists and turns in this tale, which involved both governments at the highest level, are recounted elsewhere.[73]

Asquith, soon recognizing the intrigue for what it was, thought Wilson totally unacceptable as a result of his role in the Curragh affair of March 1914, when several senior military officers had resigned rather than impose home rule on Protestant Ulster. Wilson had remained at his post as director of military operations but conspired with the Opposition against the government.[74] Nevertheless, the French government persisted over several months in its pro-Wilson efforts, the matter of Murray's recall becoming an unresolved diplomatic question. On 22 January 1915 Millerand, on a trip to London, again discussed the matter with Kitchener, who had earlier recommended Quartermaster-General Sir William Robertson as chief of staff. On the preceding day, Grey had confided to Sydney Clive, the British liaison officer at GQG, that the British government was "quite ready to accede to the wishes of the French, if a suitable man could be found." [75] In Millerand's presence, Kitchener assessed the possibilities. He considered Wilson, whom he had had on his staff in South Africa, "dangerous and impulsive." Admitting that Murray was "too slow" and therefore not acceptable, he went on to extol the merits of General Douglas Haig, commander of the British First Army in the field, who had now also become a candidate for the post.[76]

Sir John was now ready to act, having reasserted his independence of the French by refusing Murray's recall in an earlier exchange and his partial independence of Kitchener in delaying the appointment of his candidate, Sir William Robertson. An influenza epidemic, which affected several members of his staff on 20 January, provided the perfect excuse.[77] On 24 January Sir John proposed Murray's replacement by Robertson, citing Murray's poor health, which would limit his effectiveness for a month.[78] Kitchener and Asquith, of course, immediately telegraphed their approval. Robertson assumed the functions of office on 26 January.[79] The appointment would, in the long run, provide a substantial element of stability and high-quality professional advice and expertise.

The events leading to Robertson's appointment illustrated all the difficulties of senior military appointments within a coalition. The British government, because of the need to cooperate with the French, apparently felt the need to give the French satisfaction with regard to Murray's recall but was not prepared to accede to Wilson's campaign for advancement. As second-in-command, the chief of staff held much power and influence and therefore had to be politically acceptable. Wilson had too many political liabilities: he was therefore turned down in spite of repeated French representations on his behalf. Despite the fertile opportunities for intrigue offered by the diffusion of power within the coalition, Wilson failed to turn the agitation to his advantage.

The matter, moreover, was one not only of Allied relations of but civil-military relations as well. While rejecting Wilson, Sir John's favourite, the government was not prepared to impose its choice of Robertson on him at once, but, on the other hand, it gave him very little leeway to choose anyone else. Haig was finally suggested as an alternative. Yet Sir John made his own decision, albeit within very narrow limits of discretion. Joffre's attempt to obtain a more aggressive-minded British command, beginning with his earlier request for Sir John's recall, had met with partial success. According to Joffre's post-war statements, the recall of Murray was a great "relief" to the French command.[80] Robertson, moreover, in French eyes, was a "good choice in default of Wilson."[81]

But Wilson, "returning from a five-day tour round the French positions," was surprised to learn that he had not only failed in his bid for CGS but had been replaced as subchief by Brigadier-General E.M. Percival.[82] Wilson's new position as chief liaison officer with the French, contrary to Foch's expectation,[83] drastically reduced his power and influence. In effect, Robertson, who had the full confidence of the generals in the field,[84] shut him out of power, denying him access to important documents, some of which were even sent to the French without his knowledge.[85] Unlike Wilson, who sought power by intrigue, Robertson effectively wielded it through military competence and single-minded toughness, as the cabinet would find out a year later when he became chief of the Imperial General Staff.[86]

Wilson's reduced position as chief liaison officer, moreover, put him into conflict with Sydney Clive, upon whose liaison roles his new function encroached.[87] Promotion to the rank of lieutenant-general thus proved to be cold comfort to the aspiring subchief,[88] whose scheming had come to naught.

A new era in command relations had arrived. Though Sir John preferred Wilson socially and slighted the working-class Robertson, whom he even excluded from his mess, Robertson made no secret of his intent to exercise the full prerogatives of his office, and Sir John, despite attempts to assert his independence of the new chief of staff, found himself generally unable to resist his advice.[89] The vacillations of the British command, divided between the tendencies of Murray and Wilson during the War of Movement, now came to an end as a result of the aggressiveness and toughness of the new man behind the throne. But Robertson was a devoted "westerner" and an advocate of offensive action. The advent of siege warfare thus played a miserable trick on the new unity of purpose, resulting in very heavy losses.

Joffre had apparently learned his lesson. While resorting to a number of other ploys as a means of obtaining greater British participation and greater control over the British Army, he made no further attempt to influence the choice of appointments to the British staff.[90]

CONCLUSION

The close of the 1914 campaign season marked the end an era. Change of personnel in both the French and British commands – a change that, in the latter case, also affected the way the command functioned – had important consequences. The appointment of Foch as allied coordinator in the northern theatre greatly altered the relationship between the two commands, with Foch now serving as Joffre's effective voice for the coordination of operations. Berthelot's departure as French assistant chief of staff would remove a convinced anglophobe, whose suspicions of the English were ever-present. The recall of the francophobe Murray as British CGS and the installation of Robertson in his place would stabilize the British command, compensating to some degree for the variableness of its chief, which had been exaggerated with near-disastrous effects by the competing tendencies of the cautious Murray and the often reckless Wilson. Though Wilson's role as coordinator with the French would still pose problems, it was much better suited to his capabilities as an effective intermediary.

At the governmental level, both France and Britain began to adjust to the demands of a long war. In France, Parliament, through the Army Commissions, began to assert its rights and nibble away at the excessive powers of the commander-in-chief. In Britain, the War Council, the first of several attempts at the creation of institutions capable of managing the multiple dimensions for the new kind of war, was instituted in November 1914. Though ineffective, it at least marked a beginning.

While these developments were significant, they were not "game-changing." The decisive change, so far as command relations were concerned, was the re-evaluation of French and British strategies at year's end, a subject treated in the next chapter, which would set the stage for 1915 and test the mettle of the two field commanders and their governments.

CHAPTER TWO

Trench Warfare: Strategic Re-Evaluation and the Zeebrugge-Ostend Coastal Plan, December 1914–13 January 1915

AS THE 1914 CAMPAIGN SEASON DREW TO A CLOSE, the western allies began to reappraise the situation and consider future plans. In both France and Britain, the seeming failure of initial grand strategy in the first campaign season of the war raised the question of whether or not a new strategy should be sought, which would take advantage of the diplomatic situation in the Balkans and draw enemy forces to that theatre.

Since the 1980s, a number of scholarly works have shifted the emphasis from the "easterner-westerner" strategic debate among French and British military planners to the workings of the Entente coalition, which it is argued was the prime consideration.[1] While this is undoubtedly correct in the larger perspective, the vigorous debate at various times between those who preferred an "eastern" strategy as opposed to a "western" one cannot be denied, particularly in the face of trench warfare and stalemate on the Western Front. Nor should the role of civil-military relations in both countries be underestimated in the attempt to forge a strategy adapted to the new conditions of warfare. The clash of opinions and the interaction of personalities makes for a fascinating story in its own right.

Certain members of the French government such as Poincaré, Viviani, and Aristide Briand, the minister of justice, favoured a peripheral strategy, while Joffre and the French staff, buttressed by Millerand, stood by the initial strategy of fighting a multi-front war in lockstep with the Russians and in close cooperation with other French allies. The cabinet's espousal of a plan in early January to send an army to Salonika in support of the Serbs challenged Joffre's exclusive control of French strategy.

The result was a long and difficult political-military struggle between the "easterners" in the cabinet, supported by the parliamentary left, and the High Command which would mark 1915 and continue through the rest of the war.[2]

The general situation, from the British point of view, had been profoundly altered by events that occurred during the last two months of 1914. The advent of trench warfare on the Western Front, with its extreme costs and little likelihood of breakthrough, raised the question of whether Kitchener's New Armies should be deployed in France or whether a more satisfactory field of action could be found elsewhere, which would take advantage of the capabilities of the Royal Navy to deliver a surprise attack in a strategic location. The entry of Turkey into the war at the beginning of November posed special problems for British defence of Egypt[3] and made the quest for new allies in the Balkans imperative.[4] An expedition to the Balkans might rally various Balkan states to the Allied side, cut off Turkey from the Central Powers, and open a line of communications with Russia. A series of competing options thus emerged which related to grand strategy for the defence of the empire.

The Battle of the Falklands on 8 December, which resulted in the destruction of Admiral Maximilian von Spee's cruiser squadron, moreover, cleared the outer seas of German warships, giving the British full liberty of action for the use of British sea power to open secondary theatres outside of France. Although the Balkan situation was much more complicated than the British government perceived, the cabinet continued to hope to find some "territorial formula which would bring Bulgaria and Romania into the fighting line alongside Serbia and Greece."[5] A military expedition there might well be decisive. But any external operation requiring the diversion of British troops from France was bound to raise the hackles of the French and British commands in France and cause serious problems in their relations with their political masters and with each other. The stage had thus been set and the curtain about to rise on the perplexities and dilemmas of 1915.

But even before the idea of the Dardanelles attack arose, there were three competing Entente strategies relative to the Western Front. Believing the trenches could be breached, Joffre aimed to drive the German Army out of France by attacking the huge bulge of enemy trenches in northern France, from both sides, in Artois and Champagne. This he justified in terms of profiting from the numerical superiority created by the German diversion of troops to the east against Russia and the need to support the Russians who were faring badly. Underlying all was his adhesion to the concept of offensive warfare.

Sir John French and Winston Churchill, on the other hand, in a plan presented by Churchill on a visit to British headquarters on 7 December 1914, wanted to clear the Channel ports of enemy submarine bases by a combined military and naval operation against Ostend and Zeebrugge. Hearkening back to the days of Wellington, Sir John, like Sir Douglas Haig, dreamed of rolling up the German right flank in a major coastal operation.

Kitchener, who much resented Churchill's dabbling in his strategy, had yet another plan. While imperial considerations never strayed from his view, his chief concern was to keep Britain's allies in the field until the New Armies could intervene and win the war for Great Britain. The loss of Lodz by the Russians in early December indicated that the "Russian steamroller" had been brought to a halt while still in Russian Poland, and led Kitchener to ponder the likelihood of a German offensive in France and what measures should be taken to counter such an eventuality.[6] His intent was thus to allocate British resources as necessary to keep both the Russians and the French from faltering. Better than any other British leader, he understood the imperatives of coalition warfare. When all was said and done, despite his differing view with Joffre on the offensive, Kitchener was likely to endorse Joffre's operational strategy since it always had its eye on the Russians and the broader needs of the coalition.

This chapter will consider the impact of competing operational strategies on Allied command relations from the end of the 1914 campaign in December through to the second week of January 1915 when the British cabinet gave its tentative approval to Sir John French's plan for a combined operation on the Belgian coast. The interaction between various strands of the debate provides further insight into the complexity of competing strategic options facing the Entente coalition. The ensuing conflict between Britain's peripheral strategy and Joffre's operational strategy, culminating in the unsupported British attack at Neuve Chapelle in March 1915, is reserved for the next chapter.

FRENCH STRATEGIC RESPONSE TO CONDITIONS OF TRENCH WARFARE

The French command reviewed several components of its strategy as a result of the advent of trench warfare. Already in October and November

1914, as the greatly increased artillery demands of the new kind of warfare became apparent, Joffre had pressed his government for an accelerated production of guns and munitions. With a large part of French iron and coal reserves occupied and much of their industrial heartland in the hands of the enemy, the French increase in the production of war materials is nothing short of a marvel. By turning to private industry as well as government armouries for the production of guns and ammunition, French leaders pioneered a process the British would later adopt.[7] Deficiencies in coal and iron were partially made up for by "imports from Britain, the United States, and numerous other countries around the world."[8] But stocks of guns and ammunition were still in very short supply and inadequate for the new conditions of trench warfare in 1915.

As the hard fighting in the Race to the Sea drew to a close in mid-November after the Battle of Ypres, General Ferdinand Foch, the Northern Army Group commander, displayed a growing awareness of the new conditions of war, recognizing that "a large number of siege guns, with plenty of ammunition" would be required to "break down obstacles" opposed to French forces. "Our offensive has to be organized with a view to operations against fortified positions," he wrote to the commander-in-chief on 19 November 1914, "in other words, siege warfare on a large scale."[9] But he remained unshaken in his belief that "to make war is to attack."[10] The principal operational change was the demand for more heavy artillery. As noted, Joffre had already impressed on Millerand some weeks earlier the need for massive increases in the production of guns and ammunition.

In Foch's view, the Germans, having been stalemated in the west, would withdraw troops in order to take the offensive in the east. To take advantage of this situation, he recommended renewed offensive action in Flanders, an area where the trenches had not yet hardened and in which the participation of the Belgians and the British would be assured because of their special interest in the area.[11] Foch's calculation of German strategy proved to be correct. In view of the growing deadlock on the Western Front after the Battle of Ypres, Eric von Falkenhayn, the German commander, decided to transfer seven infantry divisions and one cavalry division from the Western to the Eastern Front in the hope of inflicting a crushing blow on the Russians in Poland. Although the German command did not expect to knock the Russians out of the war, it hoped to win a victory "big enough to check the enemy for a long time." To make this diversion possible, the Germans decided "to act purely on

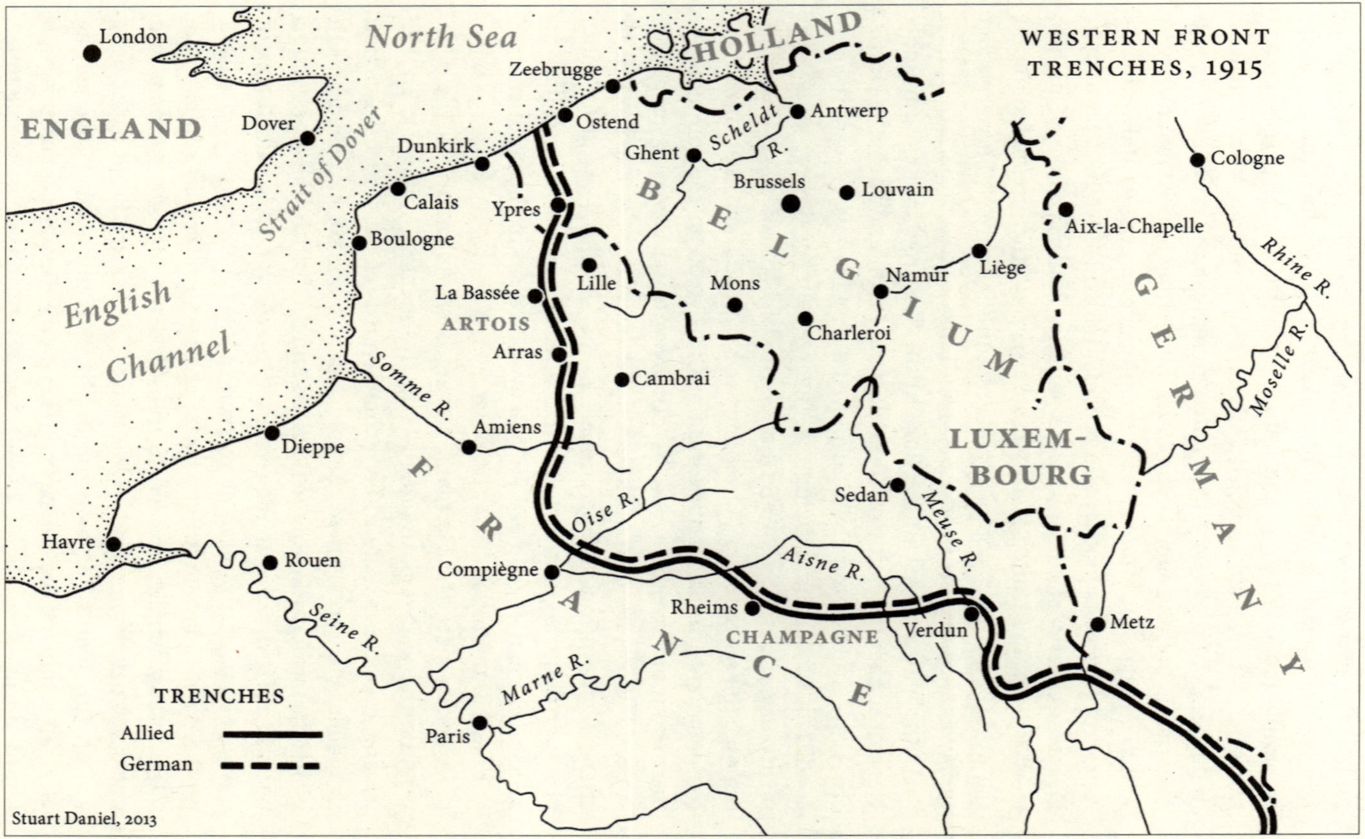
WESTERN FRONT
TRENCHES, 1915
North Sea
HOLLAND
ENGLAND
London
Dover
Strait of Dover
English
Channel
Zeebrugge
Ostend
Antwerp
Scheldt R.
Dunkirk
Ghent
Calais
Ypres
Brussels
Louvain
Boulogne
BELGIUM
Lille
Mons
Namur
Liège
Aix-la-Chapelle
Cologne
Rhine R.
Moselle R.
GERMANY
La Bassée
ARTOIS
Charleroi
Arras
Cambrai
Somme R.
Amiens
LUXEM-
BOURG
Dieppe
FRANCE
Sedan
Meuse R.
Oise R.
Havre
Rouen
Compiègne
Aisne R.
Rheims
Metz
Seine R.
CHAMPAGNE
Verdun
Marne R.
TRENCHES
Allied
German
Paris
Stuart Daniel, 2013

the defensive" on the Western Front, "with the most careful application of every technical device," thus contributing further to the growth of trench warfare "with all its horrors."[12]

Meantime, Joffre, in view of the information received on German troop movements to the east, had begun to consider renewed attack on the Western Front to take advantage of the fewer troops there and to support the Russians. As a result, on 20 November, he instructed Foch to study the possibility of an Anglo-French attack south of Ypres.[13] On 1 December, while up in the north of France to meet the British king, Joffre thus had long, informal talks on the strategic situation with Sir John French. "Joffre ... expects to have a considerable quantity of heavy artillery available in a week or two," Sir John reported to Kitchener, who had been urging an immediate French attack, "and by that time we hope that German requirements in the Eastern theatre will have caused more withdrawals from our front in the West, and that we shall be thus enabled to batter down the enemy's trenches and make a vigorous advance."[14] Given the material circumstances of the war, that was indeed an optimistic appraisal.

On 7 December, Foch presented the French plan to Sir John. It called for British relief of the French XXI Corps south of La Bassée, on the British right, and a secondary British attack toward Warneton and Messines. Aimed merely at straightening a kink in the line south of Ypres, the British attack would be accompanied by a similar French attack north of Ypres. (See map on page 67.) The French would launch the principal attacks with French forces in Artois and Champagne.[15]

Joffre's basic strategy, which he would apply consistently not only in the mud and rain of the forthcoming December attack but throughout all of 1915, was embodied in General Order no. 8, issued on 8 December to all French Army commanders. The primary goal of the French strategic plan was to drive the Germans out of France and to support the Russians on their front – now made urgent because of reported German troop movements to Poland. The strategy aimed to punch through the great bulge of German trenches extending across northern France by attacking from both sides in Artois eastward toward Cambrai and Douai, and in Champagne northward toward Attigny. Secondary attacks would be launched on other fronts to pin enemy forces to the ground, distract the enemy's attention, and prepare for later actions.[16] Such limited attacks, motivated in large part by the doctrine of the offensive,

Joffre and Foch (left to right), seen together here in mid-1915, collaborated closely as a team in coordinating the operations of the British Expeditionary Force with the strategy and operations of the French armies on the Western Front in 1915. (*L'Illustration*, 17 July 1915)

would keep up the morale of the troops and were also intended to prevent displacement of German troops to the Eastern Front against Russia. In these "partial" offensives, Joffre hoped to obtain some success until the Russians could "finish the business."[17]

In pursuance of this strategy, an initial attack was launched in Artois on 16 December, which failed for lack of artillery, followed by larger offences in Champagne from 20 December to 30 January 1915 and again from 16 February to 16 March.[18] The great spring and fall offensives of 1915 were also patterned on variations of this model. Had ample means existed to carry it out, this would have been a well-conceived strategic plan. Indeed, the same plan was revived and successfully applied by Foch in 1918. But the means for its success, particularly in artillery and ammunition and the necessary tactical innovations, were lacking in 1915, and Joffre's early piecemeal attacks, in particular, had little chance of success and proved very costly.

When Joffre received disturbing news from Maurice Paléologue, the French ambassador in St Petersburg, in mid-December 1914 on the decline of Russian offensive capability, he recognized the need for better communications with Grand Duke Nicholas Nikolaevich, the Russian commander. In mid-January, Joffre pressed his government for the right to communicate directly with Nikolaevich, rather than through Paléologue or the military attaché. When this was finally granted in early March 1915, Joffre received detailed reports from the grand duke on the condition and capability of the Russian Army.[19] The free exchange of information would be required for a close cooperation of the French with their Russian ally, from whom Joffre expected far more military support than from the British.

By the close of 1914, the French government had begun to react to the demands of trench warfare and Joffre's strategy of partial operations without significant gains. In France, as in Britain, a strategic review at the end of that year was based on the advent of stalemate on the Western Front. Members of the cabinet and the Parliament also began to consider how to curb the near total control of strategic direction of the war given to Joffre at the outset and to look for more favourable strategic options to the seemingly fruitless bloodletting on the Western Front. By 1 January 1915, Prime Minister Viviani, Minister of Justice Briand, and President Poincaré, largely at the instigation of Briand, an ardent "easterner," had begun to consider alternatives to Joffre's unsuccessful offensive in Champagne, which had begun on 20 December and was still continuing.

Faced with a war on three fronts – the Western, the Eastern, and the Serbian-Austro-Hungarian – some French political and military leaders believed that Austria-Hungary was the weak link in the Central Powers and that it could be beaten independently of Germany. In early October, General Louis Franchet d'Espèrey, commander of the First Army and a former attaché in the Balkans, had suggested to Poincaré the sending of eight divisions to Salonika to join with the Serbs. By November, Briand had devised a plan to send an Anglo-French expedition of 400,000 men to Salonika, to reinforce Serbia, bring in other Balkan allies, and attack the southern flank of Austria-Hungary. Both General Joseph-Simon Gallieni, who had played a major role in the Battle of the Marne, and General Édouard de Curières de Castelnau, commander of the Second Army, thought that a strong expedition to Salonika could induce Greece, Bulgaria, and Romania to join the Allied powers and march in an attack along the Danube toward Vienna. On New Year's Day, 1915, Poincaré, Briand, and Viviani had breakfast to discuss sending an expedition to the Balkans, which, landing in the Adriatic or at Salonika, would march to Budapest and Vienna, taking Austria-Hungary in the rear.[20]

According to Poincaré, Viviani had no faith in the success of the ongoing Champagne attack. The prime minister faulted Joffre for "lack of a plan," Briand considered him "mediocre," and Poincaré thought that he was "short-sighted and close-minded." Coming to believe in a deadlock on the Western Front, Viviani had grown favourable to Briand's plan of mounting, with the British, an army of 400,000–500,000 men which would land in the Adriatic and at Salonika, sustain the Croates and Slavs, and march on Budapest and Vienna.[21] This plan, buttressed by a plan suggested by Gallieni to Briand and Viviani the same day, was similar to one being advocated at the same time by David Lloyd George to the British cabinet, supported by key members of the War Council.[22]

A few days later, Poincaré was visited by two mobilized politicians. Lieutenant-Colonel Léonce Rousset, a distinguished military author and former deputy from Verdun, urged a Balkan offensive against Austria-Hungary as a means of breaking the stalemate on the Western Front. Lieutenant Paul-Louis Benazet, a Left-Radical deputy from Indre and an aide of General Franchet d'Espèrey, came carrying a memorandum from the general advocating an expedition to Serbia that would march on Vienna and, engaging Romania, cut off the Turks from Germany and open a line of communications with Russia.[23] That the eastern strategy, while yet in its infancy, had the support of some prominent generals in the field, was beginning to be identified with leftist politics, and had the backing of influential members of the British government foreshadowed much of its future development.

Poincaré thus arranged a dinner at the Elysée Palace with the commander-in-chief and "all the ministers" on 7 January, at which time Viviani and Briand presented the idea of the "diversion via Serbia." Joffre "argued energetically" against the plan, "declaring that he needed all his forces in France" and that only on the Western Front could victory be had. With the ammunition crisis coming to an end, he hoped, in an indeterminate length of time, to "break through the German front." Joffre, moreover, thought that supplying an army of even 100,000 via Salonika would be difficult. Both Viviani and Briand seemed convinced, and even Poincaré was impressed with Joffre's calmness, though he had reservations. Joffre also resisted a proposal for a second-line reserve army, saying he needed every available man on the front.[24] Still the master of French strategy, Joffre thus carried the cabinet with him – at least temporarily – and Millerand, the ever-willing mouthpiece of the French command, would likewise advocate Joffre's Western Front strategy in London against the growing British tendency to consider diversion of their forces to secondary theatres.

Also on Joffre's mind was the related question of having the British dispatch all available forces to the Western Front immediately. This would allow him to relieve corps of his Eighth Army about Ypres in order to create the necessary reserves for offensive action.[25]

BRITISH STRATEGIC RE-EVALUATION IN RESPONSE TO TRENCH WARFARE

The advent of trench warfare prompted an even more far-reaching strategic re-evaluation in Britain. By December 1914, most members of the British cabinet had come to realize that, contrary to pre-war expectations, the war would not be a short one but a long and costly slugging match marked by trench warfare and likely stalemate on the Western Front. To resolve the deadlock and find a cheaper way of winning the war, the quest began for a new grand strategy which would identify more productive theatres for the deployment of British resources, especially the New Armies; use British resources to attract new allies, particularly in the Balkans, which could tip the balance in the Allies' favour; and take advantage of the manoeuvrability offered by the Royal Navy.

But the Asquith government was a loosely knit pre-war apparatus. In the absence of effective decision-making bodies, British strategic formulation became largely ad hoc, and varied, depending on which dominant personality held sway in cabinet. The demands and plans of the field commander and, even to greater effect, the French ally also had to be taken into consideration. A further complication was the ever-shifting politics of the Balkan states in the face of the changing fortunes of Russia in the region.

Sir John French's preferred strategy was quite different from the emerging view of his government. As William Philpot has carefully pointed out, Sir John's predilections for British military action along the Belgian coast in defence of the Channel ports (either from France or by a direct landing in Belgium) extended back well beyond 1914.[26] His Belgian strategy was forced underground at the War Council meeting of 5 August 1914, in favour of the Wilsonian strategy of intervention on the continent alongside the French Army. But the traditional naval "blue water strategy" for direct action from the sea began to reassert itself in mid-September after the failure of French strategy to safeguard the Channel ports. Even before the German attack on Antwerp, therefore, Churchill and Sir John had agreed, during Churchill's visit to headquarters on 26–28 September while the British Army was on the Aisne, to relocate the BEF to the French left, where it would be nearer to the sea lanes, the Belgian Army, and the endangered coastal ports.[27]

With the fall of Antwerp on 9 October, Churchill, as first lord of the Admiralty, became even more alarmed about the danger posed by enemy submarine bases in the Belgian ports. On 22 November, he wrote to Sir John urging a joint naval military action along the Belgian seacoast to free Ostend and Zeebrugge; and, as the trenches had begun to harden, to take the enemy in the flank.[28] On a visit to British headquarters on 5–7 December, the assertive young first lord, acting on his own initiative, fully endorsed Sir John's strategy of deploying the BEF on the extreme Allied left in order to clear the Belgian coast. On Churchill's urging, it was agreed to launch a combined military and naval attack on Ostend and Zeebrugge, which would have the further advantage of giving Sir John's cavalry full scope of operation on the Belgian coast.[29]

At the outset, this new strategy seemingly fared very well in London. In an "immediate conference" with Asquith, Grey, and Kitchener, Churchill was able to get the new coastal strategy approved.[30] "The strongest possible telegram"[31] was then dispatched to Joffre via the diplomatic channel on 9 December giving the "very decided opinion" of the British government that British forces should be redeployed on the far left of the Allied line. In that position, they could successfully engage in an offensive in conjunction with the Royal Navy to free the Belgian coast, whose ports were now being adapted as German submarine and air bases targeting Britain. The request was buttressed by arguments intended to work on French minds. British public opinion, it was argued, would require such a measure to free the Channel ports and would be willing to sustain the necessary losses to make it successful. Failure to clear the Belgian coast, on the other hand, "could later render hazardous the transport of reinforcements sent from England to France."[32]

Kitchener, who, by his reputation as the empire's great soldier and in his position as secretary of state for war, dominated strategic planning, had conceptions based on different premises. As a British imperialist, with long years of defending the empire in Egypt and India, he took a global view of European politics. Contrary to the position of his colleagues, his initial view, tempered by his experience in South Africa, had been that the war would not be a short one, over in six months, but a long, gruelling struggle of at least three years' duration. Such a war, he believed, could be won only by the intervention of massive British New Armies. The New Armies would not only win the war but were also intended to win the peace by allowing Britain to impose terms on its allies, when their resources were weakened, that were favourable to the empire.[33]

His immediate approach was governed by his appraisals of respective Allied strengths. The French Army alone, he thought, reflecting on his experience as a volunteer in the French Army in 1871, was no match for the Germans. The Germans, he advised the Committee of Imperial Defence in 1911, would go through the French "like partridges," and in private he told Lord Reginald Esher "he was sure the Germans would beat the French."[34] Since the French could not stand alone against the Germans, only the effective operation of the coalition could prevent French defeat. Nor did he believe the Royal Navy could prevent a German invasion of

Britain in the event that the German Army should triumph over the French. Britain herself would then be subject to invasion. Even a lull in the fighting on the Western Front, he feared, might permit the Germans to launch 250,000 men in an invasion of England.[35] This possibility was what he dreaded most of all.

More than other British leaders, therefore, Kitchener was concerned with the needs of Britain's allies and placed a higher priority on the successful operation of the coalition. Not only must the French hold with the help of their British allies, but the Russians must hold to tie up German forces and prevent their diversion to the west to deliver the knockout blow to the French.

His view on the inevitable links between fronts and his deep concern about a possible invasion of Britain are summarized in a telegram he had the Foreign Office forward to Sir George Buchanan, the British ambassador to Russia, on 4 October 1914:

> It is most important that we should be kept accurately and continuously informed as to real progress of the fighting on the Eastern front of Germany in the next few weeks. Upon this will depend the critical decisions that we shall have to take in regards sending troops abroad or keeping them at home.
>
> If the Russians defeat or continue to push back the Germans we can with safety send fresh troop abroad to help French & Belgians. But if there is a deadlock between Russia & German forces and the Germans are able to maintain a defensive line, we must be prepared for an attempt to land German troops in England and if we are misled to real situation that develops between Russians & Germans and denude this country of regular troops in the winter we may suddenly be confronted with a situation at home that would not only be critical but fatal.[36]

The danger of Germany breaking through the French line and invading Britain was thus constantly on Kitchener's mind at the end of 1914 and throughout 1915. At the Dunkirk Conference on 1 November 1914, to the great consternation of the French, Kitchener, fearing a German breakthrough in the ongoing battle of Ypres, spoke "very seriously of the possibility of a German landing in England."[37] After the successful conclusion of that battle, Kitchener became anxious about German troop movements to the Eastern Front during the last weeks of November because of the danger of their fighting the Russians to a stalemate and then turning back on the French. He thus pressed Sir John at the beginning of December to urge on Joffre an immediate attack in the west to prevent further German troop movements east.[38] Kitchener's strategy, as a result, was in agreement with Joffre's projected December offensive on the Western Front.

Sir John found himself in a bind, caught between his own preferred newly elaborated strategy supported by Churchill and that earlier urged on the French by Kitchener. Joffre's December plan for the British to attack on Messines and Warneton, with a request to relieve part of the French XXI Corps south of Ypres, was in fact received on 7 December at the very moment when Churchill was meeting with Sir John. The Russians, however, having just lost Lodz, were making repeated calls for an attack in the west. Sir John was faced with little alternative but to defer his plan for clearing the Channel ports and to engage his forces in conjunction with the immediate French offensive.[39]

Sir John's frustration with the French, nonetheless, led to a sharp spat with Foch on 8 December, when he agreed to participate in the forthcoming attack but refused to relieve the French XXI Corps on his right south of La Bassée.[40] Foch was unimpressed. "How this baby likes to cry," was his sardonic observation to Wilson, who was the effective intermediary.[41]

"Of course we are disappointed here at the turn events have taken," wrote Churchill from London to Sir John on 13 December, but, referring to a request for naval support, "we shall do our utmost, to help the French in their feeble secondary 'dog-in-the-manger' attack on the left flank."[42] It should not come as a surprise to anyone that the British offensive on Messines and Warneton between 14 and 20 December turned out to be little more than a demonstration, marked by an acrimonious interaction between French and Foch and growing dissatisfaction on the part of Joffre. "Sir John is not out for fighting and heavy losses," wrote Wilson on 8 December, an attitude entirely understandable under the circumstances. Sir John's own frustration mounted as the offensive drew to a close. "The French … are very unsatisfactory people to deal with in any joint undertaking," he wrote on 18 December as the French redeployed forces elsewhere without telling him.[43]

FRENCH SUPPORT OF THE COASTAL OPERATION: THE REQUEST FOR MORE TROOPS

At French headquarters, the British proposal to move the BEF to the far left, received as the December engagement was about to begin, received a cool reception. Nevertheless, Joffre saw in it the opportunity to draw the British more fully into the war effort, which was his overriding objective. His response was thus one of acquiescence, as a means of attracting British troops, coupled with delay in its execution. While "recognizing the advantages of the proposed measure," he informed the British government that the redeployment of British troops would have to be postponed in view of the forthcoming offensive which was rendered necessary by the general military situation. A successful British attack on Messines, he added, would move British forces farther northward.[44]

Foch had serious reservations about the proposed coastal operation. While Millerand mistakenly had the impression from his discussion with the British ambassador, Sir Francis Bertie, that the coastal initiative came from Kitchener,[45] Foch (probably on the basis of his discussions with Wilson) rightly informed Joffre that the idea originated with Churchill, whose predilection for the defence of Antwerp was well known, and alerted the French commander to the possible political implications. Alluding to the recent visit of Charles de Brocqueville, the Belgian premier, to London, Foch warned that "Belgium constantly seeks political support on the British side rather than ours."[46]

Having decided to break off the December offensive, Joffre nevertheless pursued the idea of the British coastal operation with Foch on 19 December. Basing his views on a study done by the French staff, Joffre concluded that British forces, in light of promised reinforcements, were sufficient, in conjunction with the Belgian Army, to occupy all of the trenches from the Lys to the sea. This move would have the benefit of having the British relieve two corps of the Eighth French Army about Ypres which could then go into reserve with a view to either defensive or offensive operation.[47] After the experience of the most recent attack, said a further appraisal sent two days later, the theatre north of the Lys could not yield decisive results. This front therefore ought to be considered a defensive one in which French troops should be economized. As the British had on several occasions expressed an interest in being closer to the sea, the proposed move should be accepted because it would give "the

English and the Belgians a defensive role better adapted to their capacities."[48] French perception of the British as ill-suited for offensive warfare thus guided the French staff's preference to have the British occupy the trenches and reserve offensive operations for French forces.

French flirtation with the British coastal strategy, however, was short-lived. By 21 December, the French staff, in line with Foch's earlier warnings, had already begun to take a harder look at the political implications of the situation. A new appraisal of British strength led to the conclusion that, even with the arrival of the promised 27th Division, British forces would not be sufficient to take up the whole front from the Lys to the sea; and that to await further reinforcements would entail a long delay. Moreover, there were certain dangers, said the French staff, of having British forces cover Dunkirk. The proposed solution therefore was to have the British relieve immediately only the IX and XX Corps of the French Eighth Army north of the British, and to maintain French forces between the British and Belgians. This solution had the advantage of "not abruptly interrupting French collaboration with the Belgian Army, in Belgian territory," said the memorandum, "a consideration not to be neglected."[49] French competition for control over the Belgians was thus a major consideration.

Despite this change of strategy, Joffre used the British request for British redeployment as a lever for requesting more troops. On 22 December he sent an urgent message via the diplomatic channel calling on the British government to have the 28th British Division follow the 27th immediately. This would facilitate Sir John's plan to extend his left "toward" the sea, he said, and free one or two French corps. These reserve forces he required as a result of Russian failures in Poland and the subsequent risk of Germany transporting troops westward and launching another attack similar to that at Ypres.[50] Four days later, while again acquiescing to the coastal operation, he complained of British sluggishness in the last operation, and, attributing it to Sir Archibald Murray, Sir John's chief of staff, asked for his replacement.[51]

Joffre was usually well informed about British military developments, thanks either to Foch via Wilson (who was incredibly indiscreet in sharing information from London with Foch),[52] or Arthus de la Panouse, the military attaché in London. With the benefit of inside information, Joffre's continued pressure for deployment of British troops took many forms.[53] "Wily as an old peasant,"[54] according to Poincaré, Joffre used every proposed military action by Sir John or concern of Kitchener as the basis for requesting further troops. Whatever their differences on proposed operations, Joffre and Sir John French were in complete and total agreement as to the primacy of the Western Front and the need to have Kitchener send all available forces. They thus concerted their efforts to force Kitchener's hand. As was his practice in similar circumstances, Sir John called on Joffre to make representation to the British government on his behalf.

Following the British War Council meetings of 7 and 8 January, which opened up the possibility of alternate theatres for British troop deployment, Sir John asked Joffre to add his voice to the call for more British troops in France. Happy to comply, Joffre made even stronger representation to the British via his government on 12 January to have the British send immediately every available force to France. The new demand was based on Lord Kitchener's concern for the danger of a German offensive in France.[55] Likewise, on the occasion of the French president's visit to Saint-Omer to decorate British generals on 12 January, Sir John renewed his pressure on the British government via the French. "Marshal French awaits the reinforcements promised by Kitchener," wrote Poincaré, but "he fears that they will not be sent in the time announced, [and] he is fearful that the English Government is thinking of a diversion in Serbia (like Briand)."[56]

Unbeknownst to Sir John, the stage had been set for further strained relations with Joffre, on terms wholly unfavourable to Sir John. Joffre had in fact prepared a ruse to have a maximum of British forces committed to France in order to free his own for offensive action, but, as later events show, he had no intention of allowing either the deployment of British forces on the Channel coast or a coastal operation.

OPPOSITION TO THE COASTAL OPERATION WITHIN THE BRITISH CABINET

In Britain, the strategy of Sir John French and Churchill for clearing the Channel ports faced an equally stormy future. It soon became apparent that Kitchener's immediate support was more apparent than real. Indeed, Churchill's attempt to advance a combined naval and military operation was the event that set off a major quarrel between the two over Churchill's meddling in Kitchener's strategy.

The conflict had been brewing for some time on the issue of "small naval units, some of them outfitted with omnibuses," other units of naval airplane squadrons, and armoured vehicles deployed by Churchill in northern France; and the difficulty of integrating them within the army. Questions of discipline, rank, pay, and the need for officers in these forces led Kitchener to complain to Sir John, on 11 December 1914, of the "many freaks" the Admiralty were "constantly starting in the Army."[57] The Army Council, reviewing the deficiencies of the mechanical transport of the Royal Naval Division, recommended that it either be integrated into the army or discharged. Churchill in turn begged French for "the comradeship & chivalry of the Army for their treatment." "Omnibuses as military transport were a new idea in war," he wrote to Sir John. "This was the first unit of its kind; & I am sure you w[oul]d not allow the men who have served under you loyally and, as you told me, usefully, to be despoiled & dispersed at the prompting of any of these departmental jealousies against wh[ich] you & I have always warned."[58]

Indeed, Churchill was one of the most creative minds of the war, as his letter to Asquith on 2 January 1915, suggesting experiments with caterpillar vehicles with small armoured shelters to cross trenches and flatten barbed wire, fully attests.[59] As such, he may be considered the father of modern tanks. But his innovative ideas and constant meddling only served to heighten his conflict with the authoritarian Kitchener.

The straw that broke the camel's back was Churchill's plan on 17 December to visit Sir John French again with a view to pushing forward the Ostend plan since the intervening Anglo-French attack had come to a standstill. Kitchener became so upset that he went to see the prime minister. "These meddlings have in K's opinion already produced friction between French & himself, & between French's staff and his Staff," Asquith wrote to Churchill.[60] In a letter to Sir John, Kitchener complained about "Winston & his wildcat schemes which K said he could not stand any longer and asked Asquith to put Churchill in charge of the W[ar] O[ffice] and allow him to resign!"[61]

Asquith, of course, did not allow Kitchener to resign. Called upon to calm troubled waters, as he was wont to do, Asquith, the great arbiter, ruled in Kitchener's favour. "I am clearly of the opinion that you should not go to French's headquarters or attempt to see French," he wrote to Churchill. "Questions of concerted naval and military action," he said, could best be discussed and arranged in London.[62] Though Churchill persisted for a time, claiming that Kitchener had made unfair accusations, the dispute was short-lived. "Winston and Kitchener had a meeting of conciliation and fell on one another's necks yesterday," reported Asquith on 22 December. "Today at the cabinet they were on the friendliest terms."[63] But that did not stop Churchill's meddling. Though not going to the front for a time, Churchill continued to write frequently to Sir John, giving him advice on strategy and exchanging with him secret government documents.[64]

Kitchener nonetheless imposed his strategic agenda. On 18 December he received confirmation of earlier information that the Russians were dangerously short of munitions. Such a situation, Kitchener had told the prime minister and Grey the day before, could lead to Russia going on the defensive and thereby allow Germany to transfer large forces to the Western Front. In that case, Kitchener had no faith that the French front could be held.[65] The government therefore immediately requested that Sir John come over to give his appraisal of what was seemingly a very dangerous state of affairs.[66]

French, Kitchener, and Asquith met at Walmer Castle, Kent, on 20 December for a crucial review of the strategic situation. Sir John tried to alleviate Kitchener's fears. According to the calculations of French's staff, German manpower was insufficient to turn massive forces westward and break through the Western Front. Both "French's proposed movement to the extreme left flank of the coast" and Kitchener's concerns were discussed at length two days later at the cabinet meeting on 22 December. "According to K's estimate," recorded Asquith, "if the Russians lost Warsaw the Germans might bring forty divisions to reinforce the attack on the [Western] front."[67] It was thus agreed that Sir John should hold an immediate conference with Joffre "as to the best strategy" during the following few weeks "while the Polish situation is undecided."[68] The coastal operation would temporarily have to wait on the strategic requirements of the coalition.

The French field commanders were much taken aback by Kitchener's fears. In a preliminary conference with Foch on Christmas Day, Foch was "greatly amused" by Kitchener's concern that, that having pushed the Russians back to the Vistula, "the Germans would send .4 million soldiers over to this theatre & take Paris!"[69] In this cordial interview, Sir John now agreed to relieve the XVI Corps of the French Eighth Army about Ypres on his left after 10 January, when British reinforcements, the 27th and 28th divisions, had arrived.[70]

On 27 December, Sir John French met with Joffre at Chantilly as requested by the British cabinet. Joffre's response was similar to that of Foch. Sir John dutifully relayed the government's concern regarding "the possibility of a withdrawal of German troops from the Russian frontier" to allow for a breakthrough on the Western Front and the "capture" of Paris. Joffre "was astounded to hear that such a view of the situation could be seriously entertained" and assured Sir John that he had amassed troops near the railheads and made plans for any such eventuality. The Russians, Joffre thought, had sufficient ammunition for the defensive but could not go on the offensive for a period of six weeks. Their lines he considered secure.[71] His appraisal of the Russian situation thus differed greatly from that of Kitchener, probably because he thought the Russians were bluffing on their information, a conclusion Kitchener had come to himself a day earlier in view of the Russian attempt to negotiate a loan of £40 million in London.[72]

Joffre was optimistic about the opportunity afforded by the situation. Giving a very favourable appraisal of his own ammunition supply, owing to the much increased output of French industry, Joffre outlined his operational plan to break through the enemy's lines from the south at Rheims and from the west at Arras. To do this he desired to amass as many French Corps troops behind these points as possible and to economize troops in the trenches so as to spare more for "action at decisive points." Sir John was completely taken up with the plan, which included his much coveted attack on the Belgian seacoast. "Joffre consents to my working with the Belgian Army," he wrote in his diary. Sir John thus offered, on the spur of the moment, to gradually take over the whole line all the way from La Bassée to the sea as troops became available.[73]

In the exaggerated hope of carrying out his cherished coastal offensive, Sir John thus made a commitment to the French well beyond his immediate current means. But, of course, the New Armies then forming would be in the field in a few months, and there was still a belief in some quarters that the war would be over in June or July.[74] "I am seeing [Tom] Bridges [British military attaché at Belgian headquarters] tomorrow to see what can be done with the Belgian Army," he wrote.[75]

Following a suggestion from the British government, Joffre and Sir John decided on closer liaison between French and British headquarters. Wilson would thus go every two weeks to French headquarters "to receive information on overall operations and to assure the means of a closer cooperation between the French and English Armies." At the same time, it was agreed that Sir John would meet monthly with Joffre at French headquarters.[76]

The two chiefs had seemingly come to total understanding regarding future plans. Sir John's "dream," in which he "indulged from the first," of planting the British flag "in the face of the enemy on the field of Waterloo" appeared about to be realized. "But alas! like many others it was destined never to be realized"[77] – largely because neither the Belgians nor the two chief strategists on the Western Front, Kitchener and Joffre, in the final analysis, would give it their support. In this Sir John was caught between the upper and the nether millstones of Allied cooperation, his own views counting for little.

BELGIAN DEMURRAL

Sir John's enthusiasm soon gave way to the difficulties of mounting the operation. His initial plan called for incorporating the Belgian Army into the British Expeditionary Force. On 28 December he spoke with Tom Bridges at Belgian headquarters at Furnes, whom he asked, in view of the proposed coastal operation, to "approach the King with a proposal to incorporate the Belgian Army of 6 Div[isions] of 70,000 men in Brigades into our army."[78] Based on the well-understood military concept of strengthening weak forces by integrating them with stronger ones, the plan nonetheless showed a singular naiveté about the political difficulties faced by a small country trying to preserve its sovereignty and independence. It was a scheme that apparently had already been tried by the French, who had been careful in the early months of the war to encase Belgian troops at both ends of their line with French forces. The next day Wilson "discussed" with Foch "the use of, or incorporation of, [the] Belgian Army." "His opinion," noted Wilson, "is they are almost useless; they won't fight seriously alone, & they refused either incorporation or mixture with French troops; refused even the loan of a Chief of the Staff."[79]

The initial Belgian response, nevertheless, was hopeful. On 31 December, Bridges, reporting on his interview with the Belgian king on the 28th, thought it possible he might agree to Sir John's plan. By Bridges's report, 10,000 of the 50,000 available soldiers would be required to hold the inundated line, allowing Sir John to calculate that 40,000 would be available to "intermingle" with British troops. These, he concluded, would free 20,000 British troops from the trenches. With considerable enthusiasm for the new project, he immediately began to consider a deployment of British forces which would allow the British to extend to the sea at once. "If the Belgian King will consent to this [plan]," he wrote in his diary, "I shall ask Joffre to remove the 9th and 20th French Corps [of the French Eighth Army between him and the Belgians] – one to Arras and the other to relieve the 1st Corps N of La Bassée."[80] Less generous than his earlier offer to Joffre to take up the whole line from La Bassée to the sea, this plan, reflecting Kitchener's caution, would position the British for the offensive more quickly.[81]

But Sir John's specific proposal, made to the Belgian king via Bridges on 31 December, to "incorporate 4 of the 6 Belgian Div[isions] by Brigades into our 8 Divisions"[82] failed. Attempting to avoid coming under the control of either Britain or France, the small country's Great Power protectors, King Albert sent a message via Bridges on 2 January 1915 that he was "unable to fall in" with Sir John's plan but "promised to cooperate to the utmost of his power."[83] The failure of the Belgians to agree to Sir John's plan dealt it a substantial blow.

But, not to be deterred by an initial setback, Sir John then turned to Kitchener, urging at year's end that fifty-two battalions of territorial troops (the equivalent of about four and a half divisions) and some of the more well-trained divisions of the New Army, with a supply of guns and ammunition, be sent out at once to allow him to carry out his cherished scheme.[84]

At this point, French's coastal scheme fell prey to a growing feud between himself and Kitchener. The relationship, never very good at best, between Sir John and his former South African chief had been strained by Kitchener's visit to Paris on 1 September when Kitchener had forced Sir John to collaborate more closely with the French. The greater blow was Kitchener's apparent attempt to replace Sir John with Ian Hamilton at Dunkirk on 1 November. The French had carefully concealed from Sir John that Joffre had, in fact, initiated the process for his recall in an attempt to have Wilson installed in his place.[85] Of a prickly and distrustful nature, Sir John remained insecure in his command.[86]

The period after 20 December was marked by renewed strain. In his memoirs, Sir John noted that his encounter with Kitchener at Walmer Castle on that date, after which Kitchener showed him his estate at

Broome, "was the last of all the many days of happy personal intercourse which I spent with my old African Chief." Thereafter, their relations, he noted, "were always clouded by a certain mistrust of each other."[87]

There were many sources for that growing mistrust. Resentful of the secretary of state's tendency to meddle in his operations, Sir John frequently read into communications inferences that were not there. On 29 December, for example, following French's report of his conversation with Joffre, Kitchener asked Sir John if it would not be possible to have Foch replace the southernmost part of Sir John's force in order to allow him to carry out more quickly the proposed relief of French forces on his north. Sir John, as the marginalia indicate, took extreme umbrage at what he considered Kitchener's meddling in his operations. "It is impossible for me to say recently how I will deploy the Troops at the required moment! This must be left to me and I must use the available troops according to the situation at the moment!"[88] When Sir John failed to reply to Kitchener's request, the latter wrote again chastising him. "You have not answered my letter about La Bassée-Armentières."[89]

Sir John nevertheless added new fuel to his feud with Kitchener. Kitchener's plan for what was termed the "New Army" was in effect a grandiose plan to create several distinct "New Armies" of six divisions each, with each division to function under its own leadership. In "a very important memo" at the very beginning of January, Sir John "condemned" Kitchener's plans for the incorporation of new recruits into the New Armies as independent divisions and argued that partly trained troops could not be effective with regular forces in formations larger than brigades, and that integration by single battalions was even better. This was a direct challenge, "a facer," as Wilson put it, to Kitchener, who had just announced on 2 January the commanders for six of the New Armies.[90] Sir John then bypassed Kitchener on 4 January by sending copies of this memo and also his appraisal of the strategic situation (opposing that of Kitchener) directly to the prime minister and to Winston Churchill.[91]

Authoritarian and secretive, Kitchener had earlier been criticized by his cabinet colleagues for withholding information from the cabinet, and Sir John undoubtedly wished to marshal cabinet support against him. Kitchener, however, promptly reprimanded Sir John for not following established lines of communication and, with Asquith's approval, reaffirmed that documents should pass via the secretary of state.[92] Sir John's weak excuse was that he had had the document delivered directly to Asquith only "to save time" and that he had no idea Kitchener would object.[93] These personal clashes were symptomatic of deeper underlying differences.

The most fundamental cause of the growing rift between the field commander and his political chief was the basic re-evaluation of strategy then taking place in Britain over the future conduct of the war. If campaign seasons put the operational efficiency of a coalition to the test, the "down season" is frequently the time when basic political and strategic decisions are made. "Ideas which are now coming to the fore," wrote Churchill to French on 1 January 1915, "will determine the scope and character of the war in the summer."[94]

In the same vein, sometimes lesser events on the field set off major strategic re-evaluations. The abortive British attack on Messines and Warneton, in the rain and mud of December, with its loss of 5,000 men and no appreciable gain, finally convinced leading members of the cabinet that the war on the Western Front had come to a stalemate and that the French strategy of direct assault under conditions of trench warfare was futile.[95] The initial British strategy of naval dominance, token military intervention, and business as usual, while the huge continental armies of France and Russia overwhelmed the enemy, had failed.[96] The front was deadlocked in France, and, as Keith Neilson has observed, "the expected Russian 'steam roller' had not yet shown itself capable of defeating the Germans … and in fact it now appeared as if Britain would have to act both as Russia's armourer and financier."[97]

BRITISH STRATEGY REVISITED: STALEMATE AND ALTERNATE THEATRES

The British government thus undertook a basic strategic re-evaluation. This re-evaluation was of particular importance as it involved the future use of the New Armies, which Kitchener to that point had assumed would be sent to France. Indeed, the dominance of the Royal Navy, unchallenged on the high seas after the Falklands victory of 8 December, afforded new opportunities for striking on distant frontiers while also opening up new vistas for the employment of the New Armies along the lines of "traditional" strategy. Turkey's entry into the war and the diplomatic situation in the Balkans pointed to the possibility of deployment of British forces at some strategic point outside of France in order to obtain new allies and perhaps, while defending Egypt from the Turks, renew communications through the Straits with Russia.[98] The basic objective, which ultimately led to the Dardanelles expedition, was, as C.J. Lowe has so aptly pointed out, to "find some means of breaking the deadlock on the western front by employing British seapower" and "to knock out the weakest German ally, Turkey, and mop up all the Balkan neutrals by the sheer attraction of a dazzling success."[99]

On 29 December, Churchill and Maurice Hankey, the secretary of the War Council, laid their views before the prime minister in memoranda "written quite independently but coming by different roads to very similar conclusions." "Both think that the existing deadlock in West and East is likely to continue," wrote Asquith. Both agreed on the need for "finding a new theatre for our new Armies" rather than sending them to France, where, in Churchill's words, they will "chew barbed wire or be wasted in futile frontal assaults."[100] As a result, Churchill, unbeknownst to Sir John, temporarily abandoned his support for the coastal operation in Belgium.[101] Having earlier suggested a combined naval and military attack on Gallipoli, Churchill now favoured taking the Island of Borkum and then invading Schleswig-Holstein,[102] an idea that he entertained for several weeks after the Dardenelles operation had gotten underway, as a second-stage attack.[103]

Hankey's farsighted memorandum suggested the development of "a lot of new mechanical devices such as armed rollers to crush down barbed wire, bulletproof shields and armour," and favoured sending divisions of the New Army to Turkey, where, "in conjunction with the Balkan states," they might "clear the Turks out of Europe."[104] Lloyd George, who added his voice to this growing chorus in a memorandum on 1 January, argued the case for British expeditions to Salonika to join the Serbs (much as members of the French cabinet were advocating) or alternately to Syria with a view to "knocking the props under" the Central Powers.[105] "Profoundly dissatisfied with the immediate prospect – an enormous waste of life and money day after day with no appreciable progress," Asquith was very sympathetic to these proposals.[106]

Kitchener, moreover, although basing his entire strategy on the concept of a long war, was equally "baffled" by the "new kind of warfare which he did not understand." "I don't know what is to be done," he told Grey; "this isn't war."[107] On 2 January, therefore, Kitchener addressed a letter to Sir John French in which he advanced the view that, as the chances of either the Germans or the French breaking the deadlock on the Western Front were very slight, new theatres for offensive action ought to be considered. "The feeling here is gaining ground," he wrote, "that although it is essential to defend the line we hold, troops over and above what is necessary for that service could be better employed elsewhere." He asked French for his evaluations of potential external theatres of operation which might sway the diplomatic balance and take pressure off of Russia.[108]

Kitchener thus embraced competing objectives which were to prove irreconcilable. His basic view of sustaining the coalition was clear-headed and provided consistency to his efforts. But the advent of trench warfare, and the consequent quest for new fields for the deployment of the New Armies, particularly in the unstable and unpredictable Balkans, muddled his vision. While his desire to support the Russians and also advance British imperial interests in the Balkans remained constant, the quest for a suitable operational field proved illusory. Kitchener was therefore pulled in two directions: on the one hand, by the demands of the French and the need to keep the coalition together and Russia in the war; and on the other, by the demands of Lloyd George, Churchill, and others for external operations.

Nor was the War Council able to harmonize these competing tendencies. Begun only at the end of November to replace the Committee of Imperial Defence as the guiding instrument for the strategic conduct of the war, it suffered from a number of deficiencies, not the least of which was lack of authority since all its decisions had to be ratified by the full cabinet. But more fundamental was the extreme individuality of its members, particularly Churchill and Kitchener, who each carried the power to sway the council from day to day. Added to that was the lack of expert opinion to appraise strategic initiatives. There was little long-range planning. Clever, persuasive, and forceful, Churchill had a wonderful capacity for developing new ideas but failed to submit them to the crucible of expert opinion and was impatient for immediate and heroic results. As Sir John was to find, Churchill's support for any given plan continued only until he embraced another.

As a consequence, just as Sir John was attempting to mount support for his coastal operation, the British government's re-evaluation of strategy threatened that the New Armies, when ready, might be diverted to other theatres. Kitchener's letter probing the advantages of action on other fronts also carried with it an implied critique not only of the French command but of Sir John as well. The latter's reply was sharp and immediate. In a carefully drafted memorandum, he cited many of the arguments advanced by "westerners" throughout the war against deployment in external theatres. Sir John disputed the thesis of stalemate on the Western Front and postulated that the failure of the current French efforts were due essentially to unfavourable weather. "Breaking through the enemy's lines is largely a question of expenditure of high explosive ammunition," he wrote. He argued against the employment of British troops elsewhere "until the impossibility of effective action in France and Flanders is fully proved." Again arguing in favour of his Belgian coastal operation, Sir John raised specific objections to all of the possible external operations, in which he believed British troops would also encounter fortified entrenchments. The most promising of these operations, he suggested, was that of carrying aid to Serbia via Salonika, but that would depend on the attitudes of the Greek and Bulgarian governments.[109]

Sir John French's attempt to marshal the cabinet against Kitchener had limited success. "My opinion of K's capacities increases daily," wrote the prime minister on 3 November,[110] indicating that Kitchener's position was virtually unassailable. French's proposals for the coastal operation thus fared very badly when presented before the War Council on 7–8 January. Churchill, in a letter, reassured Sir John that Kitchener had placed his views fairly before the council, and that Sir John's memorandum on strategy, which had been circulated to the cabinet, had "made a profound impression." But Kitchener "demurred very strongly to sending the 52 territorial battalions, saying that their dispatch now w[oul]d dislocate all his arrangements for the future, whether in regard to the expansion of the army for foreign service, or the provision for home defence." Kitchener further argued that the required quantities of guns and ammunition for the proposed operation were not available, and that the offensive would dangerously extend the French line.[111]

Amassing a considerable body of evidence, Kitchener argued that the real danger was a German attack on the Western Front, in preparation for which he was sending reinforcements, the 28th and 29th divisions, and the Canadian Division, within six weeks, so that Sir John could relieve French troops and create French reserve forces for that contingency. "Great doubt was thrown & naturally exists here, on the ability

& even the intention of Joffre to make a really strong offensive himself," wrote Churchill to the British commander, "& even if his offensive was launched, it was said that the coast attack by the British w[oul]d not be an integral part of his plan."[112]

Churchill's concern about submarine bases at Zeebrugge and the fact that German submarines had sunk the British battleship *Formidable* in the Channel on 1 January, with the loss of six hundred lives, had not sufficiently strengthened Sir John's hand to carry his proposal. Despite Churchill's protestations of support for Sir John's plan, his advocacy of it in the War Council meetings was undermined by his concern over the stalemate on the Western Front and his growing interest in other theatres.[113] Sir John's coastal plan, following Kitchener's agenda, was about to be sacrificed on the altar of Allied solidarity. "The abandonment of the Zeebrugge project does not prevent you from cooperating to the utmost extent, compatible with your present resources, with any offensive movement contemplated by General Joffre," wrote Kitchener to Sir John on 9 January, showing his true colours.[114]

On the issue of overall strategy, Sir John's appraisal fared equally poorly. The consensus reached by the War Council would provide definition for British strategy throughout 1915. The main direction of British strategy, the council decided, was to support the French Army in either defensive or offensive operations until the German Army was driven out of France. But should an anticipated future German attack prove that the trenches were unbreachable by either side, then consideration should be given to alternate theatres for the deployment of the New Armies.[115] The door was now opened wide for the study of a whole gambit of secondary theatres of operation, which marked British strategy in 1915.

Kitchener had scored a decisive victory in "round one," since his refusal to send the fifty-two battalions of territorials requested by Sir John effectively stalled the coastal operation. In view of the open disagreement between Kitchener and Sir John on the proposed coastal operation and on the wider strategic review underway, Asquith determined that Sir John should cross over to London and attend a new meeting of the War Council.[116] Within a few days, news had spread far and wide within the inner circle of British decision makers that Kitchener and Sir John were at loggerheads, and hopes were expressed that a "rupture" could be avoided.[117]

SIR JOHN'S REBUTTAL AND RENEWED SUPPORT FOR THE COASTAL OPERATION

Sir John French did much better in the rematch. On 13 January, French attended a session of the War Council at 10 Downing Street in London. Prior to the meeting, he met with Kitchener, whom he now found "very agreeable and anxious to help," which set the tone of the meeting and allowed Sir John to get a favourable hearing. Sir John reiterated to the council his appraisal of German strength as being insufficient to make a breakthrough on the Western Front and renewed his recommendation for the Belgian coastal operation and the immediate dispatch of "as many ter[ritoria]l battalions as possible." With limited help from the government, he claimed to be able to arrange sufficient ammunition and argued that the operation would require no more than 8,000 casualties, compared with Kitchener's estimate of 10,000. Arthur Balfour thought that, given the equilibrium of forces, the most "probable condition" on the Western Front was one of stalemate," but Churchill now "strongly argued" in behalf of the joint naval and military attack on the Belgian coast. This proved decisive. Sir John had his way with the council. Swayed by his arguments and trying to be obliging, Kitchener reversed his earlier position and gave his approval for the preparation of Sir John's coastal operation, the final decision on its execution being reserved until February.[118] In support of the operation, arrangements were to be made for the dispatch of two territorial divisions, but without their guns. Kitchener, in fact, gave Sir John the schedule before he left London for the arrival dates of future reinforcements in anticipation of the operation:

9–15 January	28th Division
1–10 February	Canadian Division
10–15 February	29th Division
15–22 February	24 battalions (two divisions) of territorials
April–May	the first of Kitchener's New Armies

This schedule of troop arrivals he also communicated to the French.[119]

"Sir J. thinks great things have happened!" wrote Wilson, and "there was no quarrel with K, which was a great thing."[120] Sir John's coastal strategy appeared to have triumphed. But his victory was pyrrhic in the extreme. Having scored a seeming triumph for his coastal project, Sir John went back to France only to face the stiff opposition of Joffre to the project, as the French chief, having obtained the promise of British troops, manifested his real strategic intentions.

CONCLUSION

The grim reality of the new circumstances of war on the Western Front had become increasingly evident by December 1914 and January 1915. The advent of trench warfare and stalemate had shattered the illusion of a short war. The war would be long and require the mobilization of the full resources of the state. In both France and Britain, the new conditions of warfare led to a strategic re-evaluation, but with quite different results.

In France, the main outlines of French strategy, which relied on the strength of the French Army and close interaction with Russian forces and the support of lesser allies, remained in place, despite a challenge from key members of the government who favoured an eastern strategy which would require massive French intervention in the Balkans. Joseph J.-C Joffre, the French commander-in-chief, widely acclaimed as the "Victor of the Marne," was able to head off this redirection of French strategy in a meeting with key government leaders on 7 January 1915 in which he argued that the main thrust of French strategy should be to beat the German army in France. This would give the greatest aid to Russia, France's principal ally, and not stretch French resources in peripheral operations. Countering the argument that the trenches on the Western Front were impenetrable, he hoped for a breakthrough when he had adequate munitions. Joffre was still the master of French strategy, providing consistency of direction, and would remain so for some time, but not without a rising set of challenges.

Once the Race to the Sea had ended, Joffre had defined an important new operational strategy that involved smashing in the vast salient south of Arras by attacks in Artois and Champagne. He was very anxious that adequate munitions and matériel would be in place in time for renewed major offensives in the spring. The main thrust of the French High Command, in the interim, was to engage in partial operations, which would keep German forces on the French front as a means of supporting Russia, wear down the German Army, and keep up the morale of French forces.

In Britain, where the high seas had been cleared of German forces by the middle of December, a major strategic re-evaluation took place in the face of stalemate on the Western Front. A swirl of ideas followed, aimed at using the resources of the Royal Navy to engage in peripheral operations. An attack in the Balkans, it was argued by key ministers, would capitalize on the diplomatic situation in the Balkans and bring in new allies following Turkey's entry into the war.

Winston Churchill, the first lord of the Admiralty, and Sir John French, the commander of the BEF, favoured defending British interests more directly by an attack on Zeebrugge and Ostend, aimed at freeing the Channel ports. Churchill's role in this proved to be ambiguous. Having initiated the idea in consultation with Sir John, he flirted with other possible landing operations before giving renewed support to the coastal operation and playing a significant role in having it approved by the government on 13 January.

Kitchener, the secretary of state for war, still the dominant voice in British strategy, was perplexed by competing options. His main concern was that providing maximum military support to the French Army on the Western Front might be necessary in order to prevent a stalemate on the Russian front. Such a stalemate, he feared, would allow the Germans to launch a massive attack against France, leading to a breakthrough, which would threaten the British Isles with German invasion. Very reluctantly, therefore, he finally agreed to support Sir John French's coastal operation and promised to send the troops – five divisions in all – deemed necessary by Sir John.

To persuade the British to send a maximum number of forces to France, Joffre pretended to sustain the British-led coastal operation for a time and, in conjunction with Sir John French, requested maximum British forces for this purpose. But, as the next chapter will show, Sir John's dream of freeing the Channel coast and rolling up the German flank was crushed in its infancy by the British government's decision to launch an expedition to the Dardanelles and Joffre's strategy of coordinated joint offensives on the Western Front.

CHAPTER THREE

Conflicting Strategies: The 29th Division and Neuve Chapelle, 14 January–13 March 1915

FROM THE MURKY WATERS OF British political-military deliberations in early 1915, with their competing strategic agendas, developed renewed tensions between the French and British governments, increased strains in British civil-military relations, and a new and more acute Anglo-French command crisis. Hardly had Sir John had time to bask over his victory with the British cabinet on 13 January 1915, regarding his proposed coastal operation, than he was faced with the firm and unalterable opposition of the French commander-in-chief, who insisted that Sir John fall in line with French operational strategy. The failure of the British government to give sustained support to Sir John French's Ostend-Zeebrugge plan threw him back into the necessity of cooperating directly with Joffre's plans.

The British War Council in fact had substituted a strategy of independent peripheral operations in place of an independent operation on the Belgian coast. The council meeting on 13 January 1915 was most notable in that regard. After a wearying discussion on possible external theatres of action for British forces, the council, which had earlier approved the Ostend-Zeebrugge plan, approved a last-minute proposal by Churchill carried over from the War Council of 7 and 8 January for the naval bombardment of the Dardanelles forts. Also, a subcommittee was struck to study the future employment of British troops in external theatres.[1] The Dardanelles expedition was thus born and with it the likely diversion of British troops intended for the Western Front.

At the end of January, parallel proposals were being considered: both a naval attack on the Dardanelles and a joint military operation with the French in Greece, the latter with the hope of bringing Greece and Romania into the war on the Allied side. Very much irritated over Joffre's opposition to his coastal plan, Sir John French was even more distressed with the prospect of his government diverting elsewhere forces promised to the Western Front.

Sir John, as a result, concerted his efforts with Joffre's strategic plan, considering it the lesser of two evils, and, setting aside for the time being his idea of a coastal operation, insisted that all available British forces be concentrated on the Western Front. But his failure to obtain the promised 29th British Division, coupled with heightened French demands for the relief of French trenches, caused tempers to flare and led to a major command crisis with the French. The low point in Anglo-French command relations for 1915 was reached on 10 March 1915 as Sir John French took on the German Army at Neuve Chapelle with only token support from the French.

JOFFRE'S STRATEGY AND THE BRITISH COASTAL PLAN

Once the British had committed themselves to a schedule of troop arrivals, Joffre was free to press his true strategic preferences on Sir John. A major part of Joffre's concern with regard to the British coastal-operation plan was that it would give them too much influence with the Belgians. An internal Third Bureau memo of 7 January warned against the dangers of a too-close Anglo-Belgian military collaboration, which would lead to "the English putting King Albert in their pocket." It therefore recommended that French forces should participate in any coastal operation.[2] Joffre would have none of it and decided to scotch the entire coastal plan.

Sir John's meeting with Joffre at Saint-Omer on 17 January on future operations was thus acrimonious and the beginning of a serious rift with the French command. Joffre "doesn't like the proposed move along the coast," recorded Sir John: "He fears it will extend our line too much for our strength. He says his line is too 'thin' in parts and that a serious 'break' anywhere (say at Roye) would entail bad consequences. He would much prefer that I should relieve as many of his troops as possible and enable him to form 'Reserves' which he could use either for *offence* or *defence* according to the circumstances." Rather than have the British engage in the coastal operation, Joffre thus "pressed for the relief of the

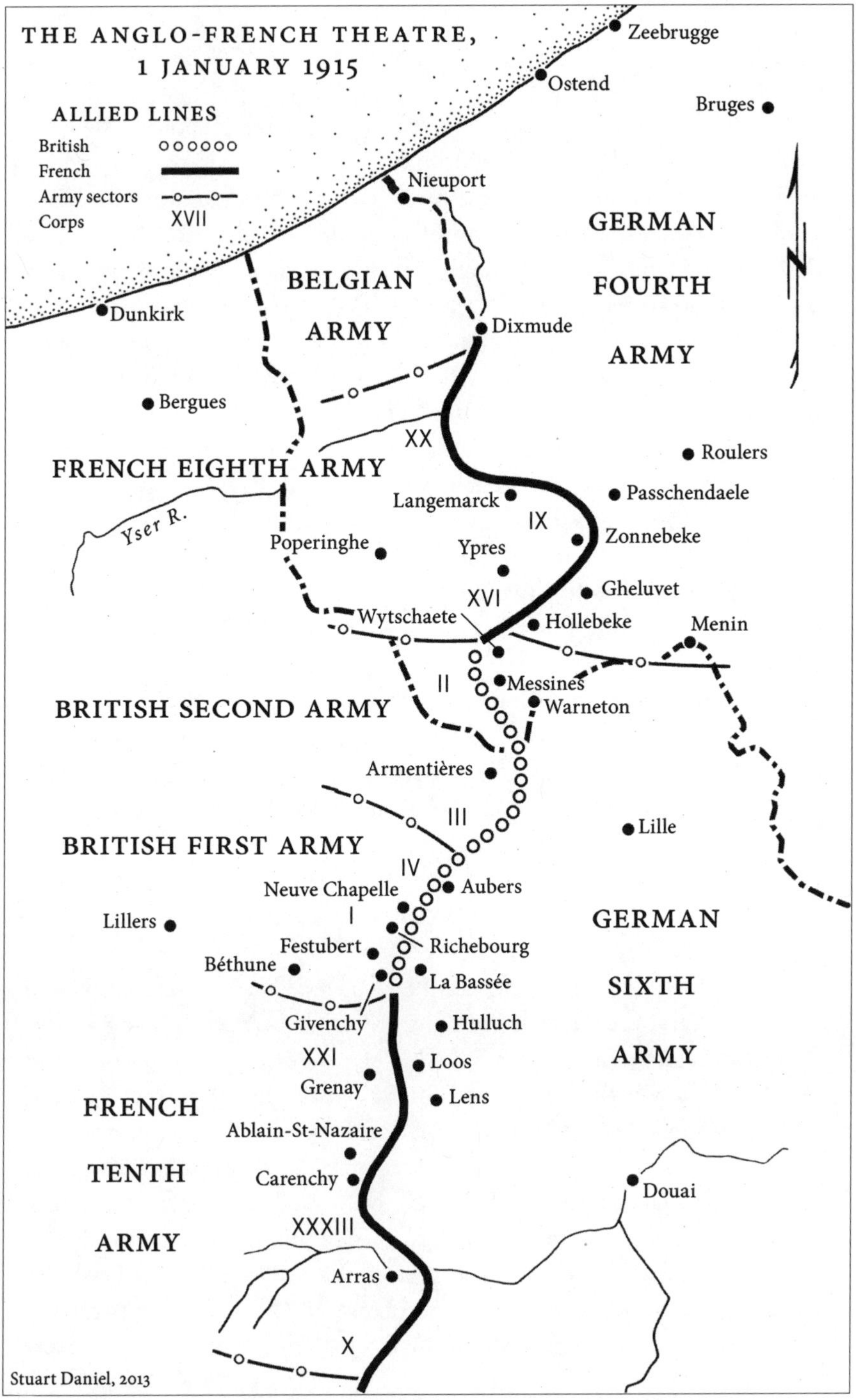
THE ANGLO-FRENCH THEATRE, 1 JANUARY 1915
ALLIED LINES
British
French
Army sectors
Corps XVII
Zeebrugge
Ostend
Bruges
Nieuport
GERMAN FOURTH ARMY
BELGIAN ARMY
Dunkirk
Dixmude
Bergues
XX
Roulers
FRENCH EIGHTH ARMY
Langemarck
Passchendaele
Yser R.
IX
Poperinghe
Ypres
Zonnebeke
XVI
Gheluvet
Wytschaete
Hollebeke
Menin
II
Messines
BRITISH SECOND ARMY
Warneton
Armentières
III
Lille
BRITISH FIRST ARMY
IV
Neuve Chapelle
Aubers
Lillers
I
GERMAN SIXTH ARMY
Festubert
Richebourg
Béthune
La Bassée
Givenchy
Hulluch
XXI
Loos
Grenay
Lens
FRENCH TENTH ARMY
Ablain-St-Nazaire
Carenchy
Douai
XXXIII
Arras
X
Stuart Daniel, 2013

IX & XX Corp opp[osi]t[e] Ypres" to firm up French reserves.[3] The future course of operations thus pitted the basic strategies of the two against each other.

A marked divergence also appeared in their appreciation of the general situation. Joffre now thought it possible that the Russians would no longer be able to take the offensive for two or three months. The Russians, he said, were "short of amm[uni]t[ion] & rifles (their output of shells is only 13000 a day & sh[oul]d be at least 40,000 & they have asked the French to supply them with 100,000 rifles a month." As a result, the Germans would be able to bring forces to the Western Front for an attack. Joffre also thought that with "fine weather & unlimited amm[unition] he could break thru at Arras," which was part of his strategy for punching in the huge bulge at Artois. Sir John disagreed with both of these assessments. No agreement being reached, it was finally decided that Joffre should place his wishes in writing and that Sir John would go to Chantilly for a second meeting on 21 January.[4]

In a letter from Joffre two days later, Joffre forcefully reiterated the French position calling for relief of French forces. While the operation on the seacoast against Ostend-Zeebrugge was "no doubt interesting," the French commander considered it of "secondary character" and "without direct relation to the principal operation." Joffre argued that such an operation should "complete" rather than precede the principal French operation and, as part of a mop-up operation, would be better considered at a later stage when Kitchener's newly organized Third and Fourth Armies arrived on the continent.[5] Joffre's attempt to squeeze out the seacoast operation therefore resolved itself into a dispute over the extent of British reliefs.

At British headquarters, where the issue was warmly debated, there was "considerable divergence of opinion" as to the French being able to mount an effective offensive with their present strength. Robertson and Wilson argued in the affirmative, Sir John and Murray in the negative. Sir John nonetheless decided, in support of the French plan, to give partial satisfaction to Joffre's request by offering to relieve his IX and XX corps during the first week in March, but only (as Kitchener had suggested earlier) on the condition that Joffre agree to relieve Sir John's I Corps at the south of his line between La Bassée and Richebourg.[6] The Ostend-Zeebrugge operation ostensibly would have to be postponed until the arrival of the British Third Army, the first of Kitchener's New Armies, in April.[7]

In a snarly letter from British headquarters on 20 January, Sir John contested Joffre's new appraisal of the likelihood of a German attack, contrasting it with his earlier appraisal on 27 December. The British, like the French, also needed to maintain adequate reserves on their front, argued the British command. Sir John would agree to the proposed relief of the French IX and XX corps only if the British I Corps on the south of the line was relieved, in turn, by the French.[8]

The dispute was temporarily resolved with Joffre at a meeting at French headquarters at Chantilly on 21 January. The day previous, on the first leg of a trip to Amiens, Sir John learned that French headquarters "truly believed" that the Germans had forward "at least 3 more corps."[9] At the Chantilly meeting, attended by Joffre, Foch, Sir John, Wilson, and Huguet, Joffre "went over all the same old ground" but "added one other important fact" of which Sir John was unaware: namely, "that several of [Joffre's] corps were holding too long a line & have been too long in the Trenches," and, given their fatigue, if they were "vigorously attacked, the line may be broken." "I still think that there is a certain amount of exaggeration in all this and that some attempt was being made to force my hand," wrote Sir John. The issue of trench reliefs, nevertheless, after much discussion, was settled largely in Sir John's favour in an agreement drawn up by Wilson and signed by Joffre and two days later by Sir John.[10]

The 21 January agreement provided for the British to relieve first the French IX Corps, and then the XX Corps, as soon as the arrival of reinforcements from Britain would permit – probably at the beginning of March. When that relief had taken place, the French would relieve the British I Corps at the south of the line. In the interim, the British would lend to Foch some cavalry units to provide a few days rest for a portion of the French IX Corps (the latter having been in the trenches since October). Joffre also agreed to allow the British to borrow artillery from the Belgians "or any other Belgian formation" deemed necessary. Sir John thus believed he had preserved his coastal-operation strategy by having Joffre agree to a paragraph allowing him to negotiate directly with the Belgians.[11] At the same time, the French agreed to maintain their current forces at Nieuport and those north of the French XX Corps next to the Belgians (one division and territorial forces).[12]

The coastal operation, as Sir John told Churchill, would be deferred until the middle of March, when the reliefs had taken place.[13] In reporting these arrangements to Kitchener, Sir John requested a timetable as to when the first troops of the New Armies might be expected.[14] In Sir

John's mind, after tough negotiation with Joffre, the coastal operation had been deferred only until the arrival of the New Armies. The operation thus seemed secure until Millerand, the French war minister, arrived in London on 22 January to argue in favour of Joffre's strategy with the British cabinet.

MILLERAND IN LONDON DAMPENS THE COASTAL OPERATION

Joffre's growing demands for British forces may have been a factor in Kitchener's reversal of his position on 13 January, when he approved Sir John's coastal plan and provided him a precise schedule for the arrival of reinforcements. So insistent were the French in their demands for reinforcements that Kitchener came to feel that they "were not fully aware" of the extent of his efforts, and so he requested on 14 January that Millerand come to London to see for himself.[15] Kitchener also wished to review with him "certain eventualities" that might arise,[16] presumably the danger of a German attack on Serbia and the possibility for action in this theatre of operation.

Fully briefed on Joffre's wishes,[17] Millerand thus became his emissary in London on 22 January, during which visit he insisted on the integral application of Joffre's strategy with all the key ministers: Kitchener, Asquith, Lloyd George, Grey, and Churchill. His first intervention, undertaken in his interview with Kitchener, concerned the Belgian coastal operation favoured by Sir John and for which Kitchener and Churchill had been making preparations. "On the use of new British forces, I refute that Joffre approves the expedition at the present toward Ostend-Zeebrugge," Millerand wrote, arguing that it "must necessarily be subordinated to the main operation."[18] This was an eye-opener for Kitchener, who "told Millerand that he had not heard a word" of Joffre's objection from Sir John.[19]

To Millerand's insistence that the scheduled arrival of British troops be hastened in fear of a German attack as early as 15 February, Kitchener objected that an earlier departure would only cause difficulties. The four divisions promised, moreover, he said, had been promised specifically for the Ostend-Zeebrugge attack and only two of them had been intended to replace French troops in the line.[20] The twenty-four battalions of territorials, he said, could not be used for reliefs.[21] Millerand continued to press the French case:

> I develop my leitmotif: above all it is essential that we be as ready as possible to withstand a strong German offensive, probably in the near future as Kitchener himself has indicated. For that, we must constitute an army of manoeuvre behind our line, which must include, according to Joffre, a minimum of six and a half army corps. But he lacks 2 (the 9th and 20th), retained on the Yser by the shortage of English forces. It is therefore of capital importance and extremely urgent that the 4 British Divisions arrive as soon as possible, and free our two corps. That is why I insist on the date 15/2 [15 February, instead of 20 February as Kitchener had intended for the completion of their arrival].[22]

Millerand was equally adamant in opposing the plan for an expedition to Greece in support of the Serbs, which was gaining ground in the British cabinet. Fearing that German forces intended for the Western Front were now being directed toward Serbia, which soon would face an Austro-German attack, Kitchener argued in favour of the expedition. Reiterating Joffre's Western Front strategy once again, Millerand indicated that some members of the French government had had a similar idea on Serbia but had abandoned it after having met with Joffre.[23] Thinking that he had dissuaded the British secretary of state for war, Millerand reported to his government that a diversion to either Ostend or Salonika, in any case, would involve only about 30,000 British soldiers. The essential point was that Kitchener was going to send three more divisions or 75,000–80,000 men to France before 20 February.[24]

At dinner, Asquith told Millerand that "it is of prime importance that we work in full agreement and [he] seemed to agree that forces indispensable for the security of the western front ought not to be diverted either for the Ostend operation or for Serbia." But Churchill "seemed disappointed" by Millerand's and Joffre's "formal opposition" to the Ostend operation. The coastal operation would not only destroy the submarine nest at Zeebrugge, said Churchill, but would serve as the prelude to a major operation in Holland.[25]

Other matters were discussed: Kitchener's efforts at creating the New Armies, the state of ammunitions, the British request for a base at Dunkirk, and the need to replace Murray as French's chief of staff. Before Millerand left England, Kitchener showed him the new formations at Aldershot, which much impressed him.[26]

Millerand, having pressed Joffre's Western Front strategy unremittingly, and with somewhat too much single-mindedness for the reluctant British, left behind a trail of resentment. To Churchill, Sir John's agreement with Joffre on 21 January to take up French trenches and to postpone the Ostend operation was, as he wrote to Sir John on 24 January, "a heavy blow." His comments on Millerand's visit signalled growing dissatisfaction. "The French are very self-centered & v[er]y much inclined to regard the British & Belgians as pawns in their game. As for the Navy, it is only the table on which the chess board stands."[27]

Millerand's trip to London delivered the *coup de grâce* to the proposed coastal operation. That Joffre was opposed to this plan had been carefully concealed by Sir John, and when it was brought to light and the true demands of French strategy were made clear – namely, that Joffre required these reinforcements to take up the trenches to free French forces – the British had second thoughts.

Churchill had already expressed his opinion to the prime minister on 11 January. In one of his frequent forays into strategy, he again wrote to Sir John on 24 January, having consulted at length with both Sir John's chief of staff, Murray, and the prime minister: "It is attempting too much to (1) take over the Ypres salient from the French and also (2) to make the coast attack. Either may be possible, but our resources do not cover both. Of the alternatives we were not at all attracted by the first. It is a bleak & dreary role for the British Army simply to take over more & more of this trench warfare so harassing to the troops & so unrelieved by any definite success."[28] Then other alternatives intervened to cloud the issue further.

THE ABORTIVE GREEK PLAN

On 28 January the Greek government indicated its willingness to intervene on behalf of the Allies, provided that Romania agreed to cooperate and Bulgaria pledged neutrality. If Bulgarian neutrality were in doubt, then Greece would require, in addition to Romanian intervention, two Allied army corps to dissuade the Bulgarians. While the major agenda item in the War Council meetings of 28 January was the proposed Dardanelles expedition, the idea of an expedition to Salonika in favour of Serbia (as earlier suggested by Lloyd George) gained ground in view of the Greek offer.[29] Recognizing the primary need of sustaining the Russians and the French, Kitchener favoured sending only a small expedition of 80,000–100,000 men to Salonika with a view to its political effect.[30] The problem was lack of available forces.

At the subcommittee meeting of the War Council on 28 January, Churchill, in view of the proposed Serbian operation, questioned the need to keep forces in England for the Ostend-Zeebrugge offensive since that operation now appeared on the point of abandonment. Approved by Kitchener, the proposal for the Serbian operation was ratified by the War Council later in the day. In the background was the deep-seated desire of the British government to safeguard the global strategic independence of Britain in the face of the continued demand for troops resulting from Joffre's strategy. "Are we truly obliged to send our troops to France, as vassals?" exclaimed David Lloyd George, chancellor of the Exchequer and supporter of a major expedition to Greece, who played an ever-increasing role in the determination of British strategy.[31]

Ironically, Churchill, co-author of the Ostend-Zeebrugge plan with Sir John French, then undertook, this time "with Kitchener's blessing," the unpleasant task of communicating "to his old friend," Sir John French, that all four divisions promised for the coastal operation – the 29th Division, the Canadian Division, and the twenty-four battalions of territorials – would either be retained in England or be subject to recall if sent to France.[32] The British War Council's desire to mount an expedition in aid of Serbia, combined with Joffre's resistance to the Ostend-Zeebrugge plan, sounded the death knell for the coastal operation.

The matter came to a head with Churchill's visit to Sir John's headquarters on 29 January 1915 at which time Churchill presented the decision of the War Council and asked Sir John if he could rearrange matters with the French in consequence.[33] Sir John, however, after a night's reflection, told Churchill that he "was absolutely opposed to the diversion of any troops from this theatre." Doubtful of the diplomatic impact of a small Balkan operation, Sir John raised the issue of the "very certain and decided resentment of France." Using his considerable persuasive power, Sir John thought he "rather brought him round," so that before Churchill left, he "promised" that no change would be made on the scheduled arrival dates of British troops but warned Sir John that once they were in France he should "be prepared for the possibility of the Gov[ernmen]t ordering 2 Divisions away."[34] Needless to say, the coastal operation had effectively been quashed. Thereafter the issue shifted to that of troop arrivals and the British promise to maintain the original schedule. The tussle took on its fundamental character as a conflict between Joffre's western strategy and the eastern approach of the British government, supported by part of a divided French cabinet.

GOVERNMENTS VERSUS COMMANDS ON SALONIKA

For a brief period in early February, the politicians of the two countries attempted to outmanoeuvre the military chiefs on the question of an expedition to Salonika. In response to Sir John French's resistance on 29 January to the diversion of promised forces, the British War Council scaled down the size of the proposed expedition to half of the force indicated by the Greeks on 28 January as essential for their entry. Thus, when Lloyd George presented the idea to members of the French government on 2 and 3 February, he spoke in terms of sending an Anglo-French corps of only two divisions, with the intent, not of having a strategic impact, but of serving the diplomatic purpose of bringing in Greece and Romania and assuring Bulgarian neutrality. Millerand considered the required French forces "indispensable" on the Western Front. But the French government, with the active support of Poincaré, decided in favour of the Greek project. The French hoped that the British could form the necessary division "in addition to the four which are to arrive in France before 15 February."[35] Delcassé, who paid a visit to London immediately after the meeting with Lloyd George, indicated his government's adhesion to the Salonika project,[36] and Millerand on 6 February obtained Joffre's approval for sending a cavalry division and a battalion of "chasseurs" for the expedition.[37] French cooperation seemed assured.

In the meantime, Joffre and Sir John, despite their recent quarrel, concerted their efforts against the British government's eastern strategy. On 26 January, after Millerand's trip to France, Sir John sent a request via Foch to have Joffre intervene with the British government (without mentioning Sir John's name) to "send reinforcements without delay, by division, by brigade or by battalion, without waiting for the formation of Army Corps or even less armies."[38]

Following Churchill's meeting with Sir John French on 29 January, Sir John sought assurances from Kitchener that "there would be no changes in arrangements for troops coming out," and added: "Otherwise joint plans of Joffre and myself will be completely upset."[39] Reassuring Sir John that he had talked with Churchill, Kitchener replied that "unless you hear from me all stands." He, however, had not heard of any joint plans with Joffre and wondered if, by the arrangement for the relief of trenches, which would give the British a line of forty miles, Sir John would "not be rather extended on such a long line, including the rather dangerous Ypres salient."[40]

In response, Sir John revealed the main outlines of his arrangement with Joffre and his intended plan for the future. His arrangement with Joffre was to relieve the French IX and XX corps north of Ypres "as soon as the 24 battalions of Territorials arrive and are drafted into Brigades. He understands that this relief cannot commence before second week in March." Joffre would then relieve the British I Corp on the right of the British line. "I shall of course adjust my length of line," Sir John assured Kitchener, "to the troops available to hold it." When these dispositions were made, Sir John planned to have "10 Divisions in the trenches and two Corps and the Cavalry in Reserve … to engage effectively in any advance which may then become possible." Such an advance he thought possible as early as middle of March, when "the drawbacks of the weather are removed and when more ammunition and heavy artillery are removed."[41]

On 5 February, Joffre visited Sir John's headquarters and had lunch. The record of that interview is very sketchy. In his diary, French indicated that Joffre "had nothing particular to put forward" but that he was "very cheery and full of confidence" and in full agreement with Sir John's assessment of the German Army.[42] Wilson added further details: "Joffre was in good form. He told us that he still meant to push thru N of Arras & E of Rheims & thought he could do it by his guns & Reserves." Joffre, moreover, was confident about the Russians "bringing up large reinforcements next month" and about Romania joining the Allies at the end of February.[43]

In the meeting Joffre expressed his firm opposition to the Salonika expedition.[44] And, as Wilson noted, "Sir J asked him to tell Mr. Millerand (whom Joffre was going to see tomorrow) to insist on K sending out more troops now, & that K had '5 or 6 Divisions' he could send if he was not afraid of invasion!"[45] Judging by the routine nature of British reports of the discussion, a recriminatory Third Bureau memorandum, which Joffre took to the meeting, complaining that the British Expeditionary force was not carrying its fair share of the load, particularly in terms of trench reliefs, does not appear to have been mentioned.[46]

Sir John had successfully laid the blame for delays in troop and trench reliefs at the feet of the government, as evidenced by the fact that three days later, on 8 February, Joffre sent a new and more pressing request to the minister of war asking Kitchener to respect the timetable for arrival of the promised divisions. Only the Canadian Division would begin to arrive on 9 February, he said, when all forces – the 29th Division and twenty-four battalions of territorials – were supposed to have arrived by 15 February. As these forces were intended to relieve troops destined for offensive action elsewhere, their non-arrival could have "serious results," he complained. He also requested the two territorial divisions Sir John had turned down in favour of the twenty-four battalions.[47] Following immediately on the heels of the French decision to send a division to Salonika as part of an Anglo-French Corps, this was a direct attack on British participation in the plan for deployment of troops to the Mediterranean.

Sir John also renewed his opposition to the Salonika expedition following the visit of Lloyd George, Edwin Montagu (the Treasury's financial secretary), and Lord Northcliffe (powerful newspaper magnate) on 6 February. Fully apprised of the Salonika plan and the French minister's support of sending a division, Sir John wrote Kitchener arguing the diversion would be "a strategic mistake" unless "something very decisive" could be gained by such a move.[48]

A conciliator at heart, Asquith, in view of the growing conflict between government and command, requested on 8 February that Sir John attend a meeting of the War Council "as soon as possible."[49] The next day at 5:00 P.M. Sir John was present in London at the War Council, having already "had a long talk" with Kitchener in advance of the meeting. "The question at issue," wrote Sir John, "was the advisability of sending a Division to Salonika to entice the Greeks to join forces with the Serbians – & indirectly to make Romania come in." The chief concern was that "150,000 German troops were now massed on the Romanian frontier, and that Germany & Austria entertained the immediate prospect of 'strangling' Serbia & carving a way thru Bulgaria to Turkey." The build-up of such a large force Sir John said was unlikely, since German forces were largely occupied in the campaign against Russia. To Lloyd George's assertion that the French ministers were in agreement with the plan, Sir John countered that "this was entirely opposite to the view expressed to me by the French C[ommander]-in-C[hief] Joffre." Nevertheless, Sir John began to yield to the apparently unanimous view of the War Council that "the dispatch and arrival in the Balkans of such a contingent would assure the neutrality of Bulgaria & compel Greece & Romania to come in at once." "I said that speaking as a strategist, I thought ... if such a result was made sure by a binding arrangement such a detachment would be justified and would be a wise movement – but if all this was not absolutely certain to result it would be a great strategic error. I further remarked that until I got the troops I had been promised and in the faith of which I had entered into certain definite arrangements with the French, I would be unable to relieve the French troops to the west of Ypres at the promised time."[50]

Sir John thus laid out carefully the implications of the non-arrival of the promised reinforcements. All the same, the decision was taken to press forward with the Salonika expedition (subject to confirmation of French support) on the supposition that it would immediately activate the Greek offer to enter the war. It was also decided to dispatch the 29th Division to Salonika and, as a compromise, to send Sir John another territorial division in its place.[51]

But the proposed Salonika expedition came to naught as the Russians suffered serious reverses in east Prussia and Poland in the Battle of the Masurian Lakes, between 7–8 February, and were also forced to withdraw from Bukovina. The state of the military situation ruled supreme. Romania held back in its offer to intervene and the Greeks, finding the offer of two divisions too meagre under the circumstances, and unwilling to proceed without Romania, turned down the Anglo-French offer on 15 February. The project was postponed.[52]

THE DARDANELLES EXPEDITION

The British War Council, meanwhile, at the urging of Churchill and with the consent of Kitchener, had opted in mid-January for a naval action on the Dardanelles which would be followed by a military action on the Turkish port of Alexandretta.[53] An Allied presence in the Balkans, it was hoped, would recruit potential allies.

The Dardanelles operation would also bring aid to the hard-pressed Russians, who had earlier requested help against the Turks, and open up a maritime communications route with them. Since Turkish entry into the war had closed the Straits, the only ports available to meet the ever-growing demands of Russia for rifles and war matériel were Archangel, ice-bound from December to April, and the far distant Vladivostok on Russia's Pacific coast. In both cases, the handling and transporting of large quantities of war supplies by rail to the Russian front was problematic.[54] But, in the mind of the imperialist Kitchener, in addition to bringing immediate aid to the Russians, the operation would allow the British to join Alexandretta with the rich petroleum fields of Mesopotamia. And in the immediate post-war period, this British band of territory would constitute a barrier against Russian incursions from the north and those of the French coming from Syria, and would thus assure British domination of the eastern coast of the Mediterranean.[55]

There was an immediate problem, however, in that the French had long considered the eastern Mediterranean as their sphere of influence. Alexandretta, in particular, was regarded as a French port, the key to France's imperial expansion in the region. Not only did trade from northern Syria, Persia, and upper Mesopotamia pass through Alexandretta, which had railways connecting it with the main Turkish system, but also it was the seaport terminus for an oil pipeline from Mosul.[56] Without knowing the whole British plan, the French government became suspicious of British intentions, particularly with regard to Alexandretta. These doubts (sustained by the facts) persisted, despite assurances from Churchill to Victor Augagneur, his French counterpart, on 26 January that no expedition would be launched on Alexandretta without full French cooperation.[57]

Warned by technical advisers that a purely naval operation against the Dardanelles fortresses was unlikely to yield decisive results, the British War Council, on Asquith's urging, began to look for a military backup. Thus, on 16 February, three days before the scheduled bombardment of the Dardanelles, Kitchener agreed to dispatch the 29th Division to the Isle of Lemnos and to send additional forces stationed in Egypt – the Australian and New Zealand divisions – plus some Royal Marine battalions already allocated to the operation, if necessary.[58] This decision was ratified by the cabinet on 17 February.[59] Whatever its destination, the 29th Division would be lost to Sir John French and the Western Front. When the 29th, the last of the regular British divisions, rather than being sent to France, was chosen on 9 February for an expedition to Salonika, and a week later was designated for the Dardanelles battleground, a significant strategic confrontation was bound to arise between the two allies.[60]

The French were also asked to send a division to Lemnos.[61] The French cabinet, which deliberated the issue on 18 February, felt obliged to contribute a division to the expedition to prevent the British from gaining a foothold in the Levant. Aware that Joffre was unwilling to release troops from the French front and that he would raise objections, the cabinet, in the interest of time, decided to proceed without consulting him. If Joffre refused later to free a division from the front, one could be made up from partially trained troops in the depots.[62] The response from Paris reflected the strategic divisions within the government and between the government and the High Command. The French government's official response was to agree to send the requested division.[63]

Frustrated in his imperialist ambitions as a result of French participation, Kitchener was irritated to learn that the French had detached one division potentially available for the Western Front in order to be involved in the Middle East in defence of their imperial interests. Informed by Henry Yarde-Buller, his liaison officer to GQG, that the French at the beginning of 1915 still had a million and a half men in their depots, Kitchener claimed that the need for reinforcements on the Western Front was not nearly as serious as Joffre had represented to him.[64] There was at least a modicum of truth in Kitchener's assertion.

The Senate Army Commission had in fact complained to Millerand on 2 February that the French front was lightly held and had only three or four army reserve groups at various places along the front available for either important defensive or offensive action at a time when "our depots and garrison cities in the interior are overflowing with troops," with reportedly little to do, and urged the creation of new formations.[65] This class of 1915, a double cohort because of the Three Year Law of 1913 – a measure providing for military conscription of all males from the age of twenty for a period of three years – would figure prominently in Joffre's optimistic plans for a major breakthrough offensive in the spring.

Millerand, for his part, was irritated that British reinforcements promised to the Western Front were late and that the 29th Division was being sent elsewhere.[66] The French government remained suspicious that the British intended to open a new theatre in the French sphere of influence in the Middle East without consulting them.[67]

The two military commanders were also thrown into conflict as a result of British strategy. Joffre was furious over the redeployment of the

29th Division and feeling the effects of it directly since Sir John, in its absence, now refused to carry out any reliefs whatever. On 20 February, Joffre again communicated with Millerand, asking him to intervene vis-à-vis the British government to have Kitchener send the 29th Division and all available territorial divisions as soon as possible to the Western Front in order to allow Sir John to relieve the French corps on the left of the British armies. The diversion of German troops to the large operations north of the Vistula, he argued, made it imperative to pierce the Western Front in several places. Sir John French, moreover, had agreed to cooperate in an action in the La Bassée region. "The question is of great importance; it is pressing, and it will not escape you," he wrote to the minister of war, "that a clear and quick solution, the consequence of which moreover will be to resolve certain objections of the Marshal, will alone be of a nature to put an end to the delays [so] highly damaging to the development of operations."[68]

Apart from the official diplomatic communication, Millerand relayed his displeasure to Kitchener on 21 February via Lord Reginald Esher, the ubiquitous semi-official liaison between the two. Kitchener, Millerand complained, had gone back on his word in the matter of the Serbian expedition, had substituted a territorial division for the 29th Division, and had not kept the schedule for troop arrivals. It was difficult to make adequate plans if the British did not keep their commitments.[69]

In fact, on 19 February, in view of the crumbling Russian frontier and mounting French resistance, Kitchener had reverted to the idea of sending the 29th Division to the Western Front; however, he was reminded by Churchill that a first-line division might be decisive at the Dardanelles, while, in view of the large forces on the Western Front, the replacement of a regular division by a territorial one would be of little significance. In view of the danger of the Eastern Front, Kitchener nevertheless decided, against the pressure of several members of the War Council, including the prime minister, to retain the 29th Division in England for use on the Western Front if necessary.[70] In Kitchener's view, the need to maintain the alliance took primacy over all other considerations.

Kitchener's explanation to the French military attaché was clear. A territorial division was being sent to Sir John French to replace the 29th Division and all four divisions promised would be in France by the end of February. But the 29th Division was being retained in England for use either on the Western Front or deployment in the Mediterranean.[71]

Kitchener's reply to Millerand's concerns was not a little acerbic. "Millerand's complaints do not seem to me to be at all well founded," he wrote to Esher. Whether or not we send the "29th Division or any other Division, seems to me to be a detail that does not come into any agreement as regards troops to be sent to France." The delays were due, he said, to "precautions of the Admiralty against the enemy's change of tactics in the matter of Submarines," which he regarded "as an Act of God and the King's enemies for which the War Office can take no responsibility." "I had not supposed," he said, with some bitterness, referring to the non-arrival of French troops at Antwerp in October 1914, that the French took such a "strict" view about keeping commitments. The letter contained a severe warning. "I hope that the French will be satisfied with what they got," he said, noting that the last allotment of territorial troops was even more than promised, and "it may be some time before they get any more."[72]

TRENCH RELIEFS, THE 29TH DIVISION, AND NEUVE CHAPELLE

Meanwhile, the quarrel in the field between Joffre and Sir John over the question of relief of French trenches reached a crescendo, for which the non-dispatch of the 29th Division became a touchstone. It proved a convenient sticking point as the British chief prepared a new operational plan, and the French upped the ante in terms of their expectation of British participation in the field.

Unlike Joffre and Haig, later commander of the BEF, Sir John French made frequent trips to the front, interacted with his troops, and had a reasonable understanding of the suffering endured by men in the trenches. Faced with the alternatives of manning the trenches or offensive action, Sir John clearly favoured the latter. In this he had the support of his government.[73]

The coastal operation having been suspended owing to French opposition and British interest in a foray into the Middle East, Sir John began to cast around for another offensive operation. "Robertson [the new chief of staff since 26 January] has submitted to me a very interesting memo with a proposal for future action," he wrote in his diary on 7 February.[74] A week later, on the 14th, Sir John took steps to implement the plan at an operational conference at British headquarters.[75] Meanwhile, Foch, in a trip to French headquarters, had arranged for a coordinated French attack. The British attack, planned for north of La Bassée and later known as the Battle of Neuve Chapelle, would coincide with a renewed French offensive at Arras and Vimy by the French Tenth Army.[76]

The origins of the Battle of Neuve Chapelle also owe at least something to the irrational and the romantic. As a remarkable series of love letters in the Imperial War Museum makes clear, Sir John French acquired a mistress (not his first) in London in early 1915. The first letter, dated 19 November 1914, to Mrs Winnifred Bennett expressed condolence for the loss of her lover killed in action; the second, of 18 January 1915, indicated that French had seen her on his recent trip to London and foreshadowed a blossoming relationship and greater personal intimacy. By 24 February, he acknowledged drawing much strength from their relationship. "With your gage in my hand and your love in my heart, there is no knightly thing I cannot do," he wrote. On 16 March he revealed that the Battle of Neuve Chapelle "was actually conducted *under your banner* and your Beloved Spirit gave the inspiration."[77] While it is hard to take at face value the romantic declarations of a man given to periodic philandering, the possibility has to be considered that men may sometimes be driven as much by emotion as by rational calculation. There can be no doubt that, whatever the role of Mrs Bennett in inspiring the battle of Neuve Chapelle, Sir John drew considerable personal strength from his relationship with her in the quarrels with Joffre and Kitchener leading up to it.[78]

The conflict between Joffre and Sir John erupted on 17 February when Joffre, reverting to the hardline appreciation of the Third Bureau that the British were not carrying their fair share of the load, attempted to have Sir John not only engage in the joint offensive action but also carry out additional reliefs beyond those stipulated in their agreement of 21 January. The letter, dated 15 February, outlining this wish had something of a reasonable tone and reflected Foch's coordination of British and French plans with Joffre during his recent trip to French headquarters. Joffre stated that, because of the German offensive against Russia and Allied numerical superiority on the Western Front, the French Tenth Army under Louis Maud'huy on Sir John's right would undertake offensives at Arras and Vimy. Sir John was asked to engage in a coordinated attack with his right in the direction of La Bassée, to be followed by a secondary attack south of Ypres toward Warneton. Following the view at French headquarters that the British were not bearing a proportionate part of the burden, Joffre suggested that Sir John not only engage in the offensive but assume a larger portion of the line. Specifically, he proposed that the agreement of 21 January be altered so that Sir John would replace the IX Corps and a part of the XX Corps but maintain the front of the British I Corps where the attack was to take place.[79]

The letter brought forth an immediate riposte from Sir John. In agreement with Joffre's appraisal of the overall situation and the need for offensive action, he indicated that he was about to inform Joffre of the attack he had been planning for a few days, which corresponded exactly to the French plan. But to carry out the La Bassée attack "vigorously," Sir John asked that the relief of the French IX and XX corps be postponed until after the operation.[80] The relief of these two corps, argued Sir John, depended not only on the relief of his I Corps but on the arrival of the 29th Division, which was now to be sent elsewhere. The territorial divisions sent in its place, he stated, would require training before being able to take up the trenches, and, moreover, one of the divisions earmarked for reliefs (the Canadian Division) would have to be sent to the First Army on the right to carry out the attack.[81] Sir John thus proposed a vigorous attack for the first part of March, whereas to carry out the reliefs desired by the French would delay it till early April.[82]

Sir John, though unobliging, was not simply being obdurate. In fact, he appears to have been following the advice of Robertson, who considered the territorials able to engage in offensive action but not take up the trenches immediately without further training.[83] Unbeknownst to Joffre, moreover, the British 28th Division of Indian troops that had been put into the trenches on 3 February to relieve French troops had performed badly and had to be relieved, creating further pressure on British reserves.[84] This apparently was not communicated to the French.

Joffre, however, in his biting reply on 19 February, insisted that Sir John carry out the relief of the French IX and XX corps by the end of February in addition to launching the La Bassée attack. Without these reliefs, warned Joffre, the French would not be able to carry out their offensive, which Kitchener had just indicated to Joffre as essential in view of Russian losses in Poland.[85] "It is thought that our officers regard the War as a sport," Bertie, the British ambassador in Paris, had written to Sir John French on 13 January, gauging the French attitude that "of the long Anglo-French lines only a very small portion is held by British Troops."[86]

Indeed, Joffre's reply reflected that view entirely. In light of the growing dissatisfaction at French headquarters with the 21 January agreement, it reverted to the earlier optimistic offer of Sir John French on 27 December to take over the whole line from La Bassée to the sea, and argued that Sir John had adequate forces in hand both to relieve the X and XX corps and to carry out the projected offensive. The British occupied a front of fifty kilometres, with a force of approximately twelve divisions, Joffre stated, while the French Tenth Army held the same length of front with eight divisions. Overall, he argued, the British had twice the density of soldiers on their front as had the French on theirs.[87]

This letter created a substantial disturbance in the British command. On 20 February, Foch and Émile Belin, the French chief of staff, visited British headquarters to decorate members of his staff; afterwards, Belin handed Joffre's letter to Sir John and made an appointment to discuss it with him the next day at Foch's headquarters at Cassel. Wilson deemed the letter "very stiff," "inaccurate in some important details & rather hectoring in tone." For his part, Sir John "showed much anger at the tone of Joffre's letter" and refused the next morning to meet with Foch and Belin.[88] In Sir John's view, the letter was "grossly inaccurate, very overbearing and is making redundant and impossible demands."[89] He thus sent Robertson, Wilson, and Huguet to tell the French generals that he "flatly refused to relieve anybody before April 1st & even then did not promise," though he reiterated his willingness to participate in the desired operation. To Foch, who had been hoping for at least the relief of one division of the IX Corps, Sir John's total refusal came as a substantial disappointment.[90]

Nor was Wilson, as in previous disputes, able to find some middle ground. His attempts to have Robertson agree to Foch's request for relief of one division of the French IX Corps, which Foch deemed essential for the success of his Arras offensive and for which Wilson thought the British had adequate forces, came to naught as Robertson reaffirmed on 23 February that "no reliefs could take place" before 1 April. When Wilson told Foch of this on February 23,

> he was distinctly upset and annoyed. He said he thought Pere Joffre would be d___ angry, that he would say the F[ield] M[arshal] did not stick to his word, did not play the game, had no soldiers instincts, etc. & that in fact to declare that no reliefs could take place till Ap[ril] when in Feb[ruary] alone the F[ield] M[arshal] had rec[eive]d 1 cav[alry] Div[ision], I T[erritorial] F[orce] Div[ision] & 24 T[erritorial] F[orce] Batt[alio]n[s] over & above the 28th

> Div[ision] was to talk like a fool & that he (Joffre) would not stand it … In short, Foch much doubts whether Sir J is worth keeping, & thinks it quite possible Joffre may say so to his Gov[ernment].[91]

The dispute had reached a boiling point, and Foch correctly anticipated that Joffre would take decisive action.

Sir John, however, did not give way, but, as Wilson suggested, simply restated "the whole case" from the British point of view. The task fell to Robertson, who, with considerable acuity, drafted a letter to Joffre for Sir John's signature and sent it without showing it to Wilson beforehand, thus cutting him out of the decision-making process.[92] Arguing on the basis of the 21 January accord between Sir John and Joffre, the letter placed the blame for Sir John's inability to relieve the French on the British government and its failure to meet the timetable of troop arrivals. The Canadian Division, which was to have arrived on 10 February, had arrived only on the 20th. "The 29th division of regulars was to have arrived on February 15, but as a result of an agreement between the French and British Governments and probably endorsed by you, it has been sent elsewhere." The territorial division that was to have replaced the 29th Division would not arrive before 28 February and would need a few weeks training before taking up the line. As these forces had been earmarked for the relief of the French IX Corps, no reliefs could now be undertaken before 1 April. Sir John nevertheless agreed to undertake the planned offensive toward La Bassée on approximately 7 March in conjunction with the French attack on Arras. Denying that he had ever agreed to relieve all the French forces north of La Bassée, Sir John contested the validity of comparing the density of British and French forces in occupying the trenches, owing to the many factors involved.[93]

The two commands were deadlocked. Rather than follow Wilson's suggestion relayed via Foch that the French commander respond in a friendly personal letter suggesting reliefs of a reduced nature, Joffre instructed Foch to arrange what reliefs he could directly with Sir John, particularly in view of the anticipated official announcement later that the 29th Division would indeed be sent to the front.[94]

Command relations were further embroiled at this point by a misstep in communications. At some point, Kitchener indicated unofficially to Cambon that the 29th Division would in fact be sent to the Western Front. "[Maxime] Weygand [Foch's chief of staff] showed me a wire," wrote Wilson on 23 February, "from GQG saying K had told Cambon that he was now sending 29th Div[ision] here & not to Lemnos."[95] The French staff was hopeful that this would resolve the conflict over reliefs. But Sir John French, when apprised by Wilson, had heard nothing of the arrival of the 29th Division through official channels.[96] The reason, as indicated, was that Kitchener, after consulting with Churchill on 19 February, had decided, against the advice of several members of the cabinet, to keep the 29th Division in Britain for deployment to either the Western Front or the Dardanelles.

This breach of protocol was only a small part of a new and more serious flare-up between Kitchener and Sir John. Having decided to keep the 29th Division in England for deployment either to France or the Mediterranean, Kitchener asked Sir John on 24 February to provide information on the "scope of the joint operations" under preparation, in view of the forthcoming discussion in the War Council on sending the 29th Division to the Near East. Missing his cue completely in not providing confidentially at least the outline of the planned offensive, Sir John refused this request, citing "the need to preserve secrecy."[97] This was a justifiable concern. "If ever these things get out they seemed to be talked about by the women in London,"[98] he wrote in his diary. But this rebuff and refusal to provide any information on the planned offensive to the secretary of state for war weakened Kitchener's case on his behalf. Sir John's request for the 29th Division, without any indication of its vital role in joint operations, fell on deaf ears.[99]

Kitchener, moreover, took a peevish attitude toward the French plan to send a division to the Dardanelles in conjunction with the British. As noted, Kitchener's hope was to acquire Alexandretta as the key to communication with the Middle East once Russia had been awarded the Straits. But the French, who considered the eastern end of the Mediterranean as their sphere of influence, had interests in Syria which they wished to defend. In spite of Joffre's opposition, the French decided on 22 February to send an expeditionary force to the Near East, consisting of two infantry brigades and a cavalry regiment, drawn from forces in the interior and North Africa.[100] On 27 February, Kitchener wired Sir John that he had difficulty preventing the government from sending the 29th Division immediately to the Dardanelles and had decided to keep it at home "pending developments there." "He also remarks," wrote Sir John, "that as the French can spare virtually a whole regular Division for service in the Near East, he does not see that we [should] waste any more troops in the trenches."[101]

But that was not the whole story. Kitchener's want of confidence in Sir John's leadership was at least part of the reason why forces were withheld. This Kitchener had conveyed to the French commanders Foch and Joffre a week earlier via the Belgian premier, Count Charles de Broqueville. Having sent for de Broqueville, Kitchener "told him that he (K) was sick of sending troop to Sir J.[,] that he never puts up a fight & so mismanaged his troops that he squandered all his reinforcements." After telling Foch this on 21 February, "de Broqueville went on to Chantilly to tell Joffre" in what was yet another unofficial line of communication with the French.[102] In addition, part of de Broqueville's task was to urge on the French, as Kitchener had on Sir John, "the idea of attacking all along the line on a given night without art[illery] fire."[103]

Sir John's dissatisfaction with Kitchener had also been mounting: "The people at home give me a lot of worry," he wrote to Mrs Bennett on 27 February. "They get so easily upset by nothing. They firmly believe all the German lies about the Russian Reverse. Of course they have lost a good many men but they are recovering themselves even now. Yet I get the most pessimistic letter & telegram warning me of every kind of disaster & suggesting the most impossible solutions of imaginary difficulties which will never arise. I have more trouble with the War Office than I have with the Germans!"[104]

Kitchener's withholding the 29th Division and his derogatory comments on wasting troops in the trenches were the straw that broke the camel's back. The height of French's fury on 28 February was recorded by Wilson: "Sir J was as usual, loud in his abuse of K; said he would gladly put him up against a wall & shoot him! & that he had told Asquith & Haldane & others what he thought of K."[105]

The dispute between Sir John and his superior in London had an immediate impact on Sir John's relationship with Joffre. Becoming totally obdurate, Sir John now not only refused to relieve any of the French IX Corps, a project that Foch and Wilson were in the process of arranging through Robertson, but, in addition, demanded that the French immediately relieve the British Cavalry Division, which had been providing temporary reliefs for part of the corps for almost a month.[106]

These decisions were particularly regretted by Foch and Wilson. Under Wilson's instigation, the two therefore devised a scheme to reverse

Kitchener's decision on retaining the 29th Division in England. "I dictated a wire which I suggested he [Foch] should send Joffre & he took it down himself," wrote Wilson. Very indiscreetly, Wilson revealed Kitchener's recent communications as the true source of Sir John's most recent obduracy. Sir John and Kitchener were not getting along. Just as Sir John had not informed Kitchener of the intended Allied offensive, so Kitchener was not aware that the 29th Division was required to relieve French forces necessary for the success of the French attack.[107] This Foch faithfully relayed to Joffre at French headquarters, citing Kitchener as the chief "object of the new crisis."[108]

At this stage Joffre took vigorous action through the diplomatic channel. His first step, relying on Wilson and Foch's information, was to place the entire dispute with Sir John before the French war minister and to ask him to intervene with Kitchener for the immediate dispatch of the 29th Division. Sir John's new refusal to relieve French troops, Joffre said, reflecting information from Wilson, was the result of a letter from Kitchener to Sir John which claimed that since the French were sending a division from their front to the Dardanelles, the French must have adequate reserves on their front. Moreover, as the British government might be required to give greater scope to the Dardanelles operation, it was retaining the 29th Division in England, "where it will be more useful than in France, immobilized in the trenches, where they do not attack." Marshal French, said Joffre, had indicated that "because of the mediocre quality of the troops he is receiving at the present," he could not relieve any part of the French IX Corps. Joffre desired to set the record straight: 1) no division had been withdrawn from the French front to participate in the Dardanelles expedition; 2) French troops, far from being inactive in their trenches, were engaged in an energetic offensive in Champagne, which was taking the pressure off of other parts of the front; and 3) the projected coordinated operation of the French Tenth Army at Arras with the British at La Bassée could be carried out only if, thanks to the arrival of the 29th Division, the French IX Corps were made available to reinforce the French Tenth Army. Joffre thus asked the minister to intervene directly with Kitchener for the immediate dispatch of the 29th Division. He concluded with the observation (leaked by Wilson) that because Sir John, for reasons of secrecy, might not have communicated to Kitchener the joint operational plan, Kitchener might not know that in retaining the 29th Division in England, he was rendering impossible any operation of any size in the north of France.[109]

Joffre's appeal to Millerand created a considerable stir in the French cabinet, before whom it was read on 2 March. The cabinet examined carefully the complexities of the feud between Joffre and Sir John, the number of British divisions received, and Kitchener's reluctance to send the 29th Division. The truth, Poincaré concluded, was that Kitchener had "no confidence" in Joffre's offensive plans or his ability to break the line and therefore was keeping in reserve divisions that might be sent to the Dardanelles or elsewhere. Sir John French, however, was faulted for not complying with Joffre's wishes and, on Poincaré's instance, Millerand and Delcassé were given the task of bringing "the dangers of this situation" to the attention of the British government and trying to obtain unity of command under Joffre. On the second point, the example the French delegates were to cite was the unity of command under the British recently worked out for the Dardanelles operation.[110]

THE FRENCH REQUEST FOR UNITY OF COMMAND

On 2 March, for the first time in Allied relations, as a result of the breakdown in relations between Joffre and Sir John, Millerand raised the issue of a unified command in a personal letter to Kitchener which also had been approved by the French cabinet.[111] In his letter, Millerand enclosed Joffre's inflammatory letter to him and made a further pitch, reiterating Kitchener's earlier commitments, for the immediate dispatch of the 29th Division as necessary for Joffre to create the reserves required for his offensive. Noting Sir John's unwillingness to take up trench reliefs as Joffre requested, Millerand made a reasoned argument for "unity of concept and execution" which could be obtained only by "unity of command." A "precise and clearly defined" relationship between the different chiefs was essential, he said, and Sir John, "who addresses Joffre as General-in-Chief of the Allied Armies," should "consider him as such in reality and receive his instructions." The Dardanelles arrangement in which French General Albert d'Amade was under the orders of British General William Birdwood could well serve as a model.[112]

Millerand's letter struck a raw nerve with Kitchener and greatly disturbed Asquith. Kitchener's response, having written Millerand on 4

March, was to forward a copy of both Joffre's and Millerand's letters to Sir John the next day for his observation. Putting strong pressure on Sir John to comply with French wishes, Kitchener raised the bogey of Allied unified command. "Millerand in his letter," he wrote, "refers to the necessity of unity of command and complains that having received reinforcements you are not prepared to carry out what Joffre requires of you as regards relieving the French troops on your left, and that this action on your part was embarrassing Gen[era]l Joffre in carrying out his projects." Kitchener then delivered Sir John a very firm slap on the wrists: "It is very important that your cooperation with Joffre should be as close as possible and that you should do everything in your power to carry out his wishes."

Kitchener also chastised Sir John – unfairly, it turned out – regarding a portion of Joffre's letter in quotation marks (actually taken from a letter by Foch) which Kitchener thought to be a misquote of one of his telegrams and asked Sir John not to quote his messages to the French without permission. The prime minister, he said, was "rather astonished after your remarks about the excellence of the Territorials at the War Council, to read General Joffre's statement on their inferior quality." "We were interested to learn that the forthcoming operations are to be at La Bassée and Arras and hope you will do your utmost to make these successful." Wilson's plan for having Kitchener reconsider the redeployment of the 29th Division, however, failed, as Kitchener merely explained to Millerand "the reasons why the Gov[ernment] had decided not to send the 29th Division to France."[113] Sir John, for his pains, had properly been put in his place.

Kitchener, however, was careful to dodge the issue of a unified command with the French by reasserting the fiction of good relations between Sir John and Joffre. "In reply to Millerand," he told Sir John, "I said that in all your reports to me you gave me to understand that your relations with Joffre had always been most intimate and cordial and expressed my astonishment that there should be the least doubt that you were always prepared to carry out his wishes to the utmost of your powers."[114] To this Sir John sang a harmonizing part in reply. "As to my relations with General Joffre," he replied to Kitchener, "they have always been of the most cordial nature." "Slight difference of opinion must of necessity arise but we never quarrel and I have no idea how it ever came to be supposed that we did. The war we have had to deal with has been most difficult &

complex and I feel sure, whatever others may think, the French Generals will be the first to acknowledge the assistance & support they have received from us throughout as we, on our part, do of them."[115]

Sir John's explanation of his comments on the quality of the territorials was more laboured. He had had to tell Joffre that a territorial division had been substituted for the 29th Division "in order to explain why it would be impossible to carry out, with only a Territorial Division, what I had promised to do with a regular one." "I have written to the Prime Minister to explain why I consider it unsafe to put an untrained Division of second line troops (on their first arrival) into a very critical & vulnerable part of the line & to assure him that such a decision on my part in no way detracts from my opinion of Territorials as expressed in the war council & in my dispatches."[116] Sir John thus tried to square the circle in an attempt not to cut off the further dispatch of territorials to the front. Indeed, Kitchener had wired on 1 March (prior to his receipt of Millerand's letter) that another territorial division, the 2nd London, which Sir John had requested on 19 February, would be sent to the front.[117] That division, despite the quarrel, began to embark on 5 March.[118]

Kitchener's long reply to Millerand on 4 March, written in comprehensible but sometimes awkward French, was recriminatory and self-assertive in tone. Important not only for what it said but for what it did not say, it made clear that Sir John French had not kept Kitchener properly informed, nor had Joffre. Kitchener expressed his surprise that "there exists a lack of sympathetic collaboration" between Joffre and Sir John and that Sir John "was having serious difficulty" keeping commitments assigned to him; he was also surprised to learn that Sir John attributed his inability to comply to the "mediocre quality of troops received." Having never been totally apprised of the arrangement for reliefs worked out between Joffre and Sir John, he asked that Joffre address him directly on the need for troops. "As to the operations designated in General Joffre's letter, this is the first time that I hear these plans formulated." His request for information to Sir John had been denied, he supposed, "on the advice of Joffre."[119]

Acknowledging that there existed "much delay" in sending troops to France, Kitchener used this as a lever to raise the issue of making Dunkirk a British base, which Joffre had earlier refused for reasons Kitchener claimed never to have fully understood.[120] In reality, as further documentation will show, apart from questions of supplying their left wing, the French command wished to retain Dunkirk as a means of exercising influence over the Belgian Army with a view to the post-war settlement and to denying the same advantage to the British. There is also some suggestion that the French were worried that, if the British obtained control of Dunkirk as a supply base, they would not give it back after the war.

Kitchener's explanation on the issue of the 29th Division was a classic. That he had not sent the 29th Division to France as hoped was justified with the observation that "in the conduct of a war, it is sometimes impossible to realize projects conceived in advance." That the question of the East had become one of great importance, he argued, was witnessed by the fact that the French had also decided to send a division. That division, though not taken from the front in France, might have been used for its reinforcements. The 29th Division was initially to have gone to fortify the partially trained colonial divisions in Egypt; however, Kitchener explained that, "in view of the serious situation of the Russian Army and the consequent possibility of a vigorous attack on the Allied line, I hesitated to send the Division to the East." He nevertheless had sent Sir John a territorial division, which was now in France and which was "perfectly competent to work in the trenches." Having himself commanded an army on the field of battle, he wrote, "I understand entirely the desire of the Generals to have the most troops possible at hand," but, he concluded, "the influence of the generals is too often limited by local and temporary circumstances."[121] Here indeed was a profound statement on the fundamental conflict that often exists between the civilian and military points of view which was basic to the whole issue.

Kitchener gracefully sidestepped the matter of a unified command, alluding to the cordial relations which he supposed had always existed between Joffre and Sir John, and his surprise that Sir John was having difficulty in complying with Joffre's wishes relative to the relief of trenches. Never mentioning directly the idea of a unified command, Kitchener pledged to use his efforts "toward an even closer collaboration and an even more devoted understanding between Field Marshal French and the Generalissimo of the Allied Armies in France." He wished the French well in their forthcoming offensive.[122]

While explaining many things, Kitchener's letter showed that a number of issues – Dunkirk as a British base, a unified Allied command, and, more central to the discussion, Kitchener's plan for the use of his New Armies – remained unresolved. Poincaré, who termed the letter "neither fish nor fowl" (moitié figue, moitié raisin), inferred from it that Kitchener "does not expect much" from Joffre's offensive plans and that "he attaches much more importance to the Dardanelles operation."[123] As Kitchener had carefully avoided the issue of a unified command, Delcassé replied on 7 March by inviting Kitchener to a conference with Millerand and Joffre at French headquarters to discuss "the necessary conditions for a greater success in military operations … notably, a more complete and fuller collaboration of the English Command."[124] The question of a unified command, a fairly dramatic approach to Allied command relations, was officially on the agenda.

JOFFRE WITHDRAWS SUPPORT OF THE BRITISH ATTACK

After he had played the diplomatic card, Joffre's second measure in response to the conflict with Sir John over the relief of the trenches was more drastic. On 2 March, the day after his appeal to Millerand, Joffre instructed Foch to make no commitment regarding the date for the French attack at Arras, citing lack of adequate men and munitions in view of the Champagne offensive underway and "various reasons of which you are not unaware." The next day he postponed it indefinitely, pending the accumulation of adequate forces in the area, and requested that Foch come to headquarters for further consultation on 6 March.[125] With only two divisions in reserve for the Arras operation, the French Tenth Army's "attack south of Arras was going to be a poor show," noted Wilson, even before Joffre postponed it.[126] By 4 March, the French intent had become clear to the British. Foch's notes on the Arras attack, wrote Wilson, "make the position perfectly plain & show that, except in synchronizing in time, we get no assistance & it was never intended we should, from the French."[127]

Indeed, Joffre's dissatisfaction with the British command reached a peak on 5 March. In his interview with Sidney Clive, the British liaison officer at French headquarters, "he said very bitter things, all the more impressive in that he was not in the least in a rage, but deliberately saying what he thought after reflection. Evidently the two things which he felt most deeply were a sentence in the last letter from GHQ which said that the non-arrival of the 29th Division was 'presumably with his approbation,' and the refusal to give his IX Corps a bit of rest by taking over a bit of their trenches with our cavalry."[128]

The crisis reached its climax on 7 March when Joffre advised Sir John that, because French forces at Ypres had not been relieved, he had inadequate reserves and therefore the French Tenth Army would not be able to carry out its offensive.[129] Returning from Chantilly to British headquarters on 8 March, Huguet reported to Wilson the depth of Joffre's irritation and discontent with the British chiefs as he made that decision. "Joffre was very angry with both Sir J[ohn] & K[itchener], calling them both liars & saying it was impossible to trust either or work with either."[130] After the British attack, Joffre confided to the minister his underlying hope that in the case of "strictly defensive results" (that is, a British failure), it would be easier to persuade the British commander to relieve the French IX and part of the XX Corps.[131] Allied field cooperation thus completely foundered as the French withdrew their support for the British attack.

The curiosity is that Sir John French decided to go ahead with his planned offensive despite the lack of French support. Joffre's communication of 20 February had been a clear warning that relief of French troops was the "*necessary condition*" (Joffre's emphasis) for the French to carry out their offensive at Arras.[132] Sir John nevertheless had carried out a review of the general situation with his staff on 23 February and decided that, given Allied numerical superiority, the situation was favourable for an attack.[133]

The idea of a British victory was on his mind. "The French are beginning to make some progress from Rheims & the Argonne," he wrote his mistress on 2 March. "It is for us in the North to make a good push and we are going to do it."[134]

And so, despite a full awareness on 8 March that the French "would be unable to give him much support in the offensive movement," Sir John proceeded with his assault at Neuve Chapelle on 10 March.[135] Despite the fact that he was being committed to an isolated attack, Sir John still harboured the view that he had the best of the argument. Joffre, he noted on 7 March, "is rather burnt that I haven't kept the cavalry in the French trenches opposite Ypres. I think I thoroughly understand French 'finesse' methods by now," he concluded, "and am prepared to meet them. This is really annoying to Pere Joffre."[136] Sir John apparently hoped to reassert his independence of both Kitchener and Joffre by a success on the field of battle and at the same time prove that the Western Front could be pierced.

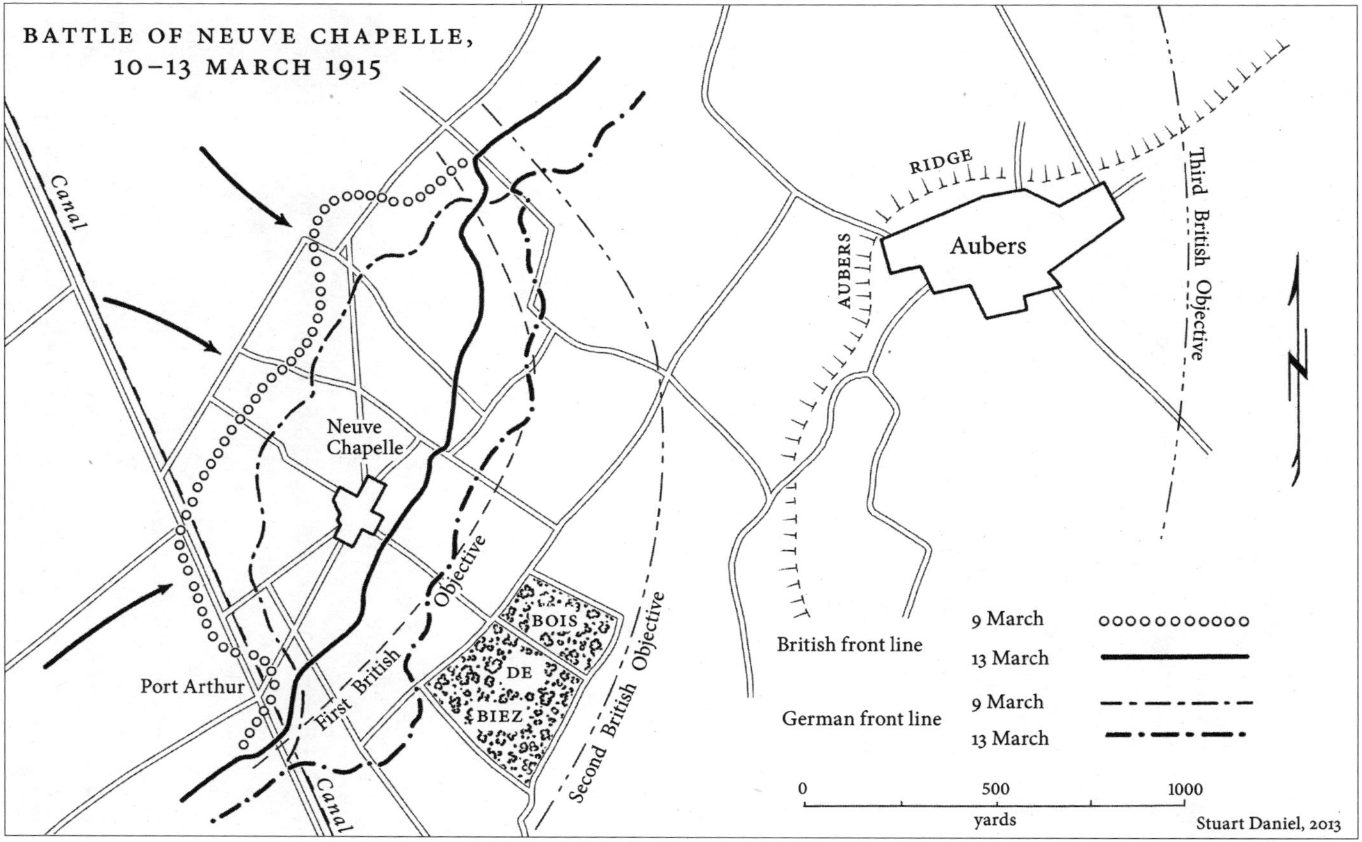
BATTLE OF NEUVE CHAPELLE,
10–13 MARCH 1915
Canal
Neuve
Chapelle
Port Arthur
First British Objective
BOIS
DE
BIEZ
Second British Objective
AUBERS
RIDGE
Aubers
Third British Objective
British front line
9 March
13 March
German front line
9 March
13 March
0
500
1000
yards
Stuart Daniel, 2013

BRITISH SUCCESS AT NEUVE CHAPELLE

The Battle of Neuve Chapelle, conducted between 10 and 13 March 1915, marked the culmination of Allied misunderstanding on the field of battle. A well-prepared and well-fought operation on the British side, the attack caught the Germans by surprise. After initial success against enemy trenches on a front of two thousand yards, the battle was broken off after three days when the British ran short of ammunition and were unable to advance. The French limited their support to adjacent artillery fire[137] and gave orders for a vigorous support on the British left and right only after the initial British advance. The battle may be termed a tactical British success, reaffirming that enemy trenches could breached, but it produced no strategic results. Total British losses in killed and wounded were about 13,000 men.[138]

CONCLUSION

The breakdown in Allied cooperation at Neuve Chapelle demonstrates the impact of the conflicting British and French strategies on Allied command relations. It also demonstrates the failure of the various mechanisms of decision making and coordination to deal with complex political-military issues. The threatened diversion of British forces first for the proposed Salonika expedition and then to support the British Dardanelles naval action set off the dispute. The problem was exacerbated by the French command's attempt to have Sir John both carry out reliefs and engage in offensive action. In this the French were pressing the British to make a greater contribution on the field.

Rendered particularly obdurate by his quarrel with Kitchener and the British government's reluctance to commit all its forces to the Western Front, Sir John refused the French demands. And, without British relief of French trenches, Joffre withdrew his support for the British attack at Neuve Chapelle. Both commands wished to have the glory of offensive operations and to have the other side carry the weight of trench warfare.

In the case of France, government and command were in total agreement on the need to draw the British into the Western Front as much as possible. British strategy for alternate theatres was thus undermined by Joffre's continual demands for troops in France. The British might well have resisted French demands for reinforcements on the Western Front, particularly after Joffre scuttled the seacoast operation for which they had been requested, had not the needs of the coalition become urgent as the Russians fared poorly in East Prussia, Poland, and Bukovina.

Faced with the likelihood of deadlock on the Western Front, Kitchener had been caught up earlier with the British cabinet in the illusory idea of a major diplomatic coup by showing "Khaki" in a symbolic force in the Balkans. The failure of the Russians both undermined Balkan diplomacy, prompting Greece and Romania to withdraw their offers of intervention, and ultimately led Kitchener, for whom the operation of the coalition was the prime consideration, to give Joffre satisfaction in reinforcing the Western Front. But his refusal to send Sir John French the 29th Division, which had become symbolic of British intentions, set off the row between commands.

None of these problems ought to have had a decisive impact on Sir John's relations with Joffre, except to cause delays. But Sir John had also been rankled by a series of British government strategic initiatives: the rejection of his Belgian coastal operation, the decision to seek alternate fronts for employment of the New Armies, and finally the decision to retain the 29th Division in Britain and replace it with a territorial division. The arrival of other British divisions was also delayed.

His testy relationship with Kitchener was frayed by these initiatives and also by personal affronts in which each seemed to take delight. Sir John was also highly irritated by the French government and command's attempt to have his chief of staff replaced, as discussed in the preceding chapter, and he was further embittered by Joffre's scuttling of his cherished coastal operation. The climate of rancour and mistrust between the two field commanders contributed to the breakdown. Sir John's decision to attack alone at Neuve Chapelle and thereby demonstrate British capabilities was apparently intended to re-establish his independence of both Kitchener and the French.

The reader cannot helped but be awed by the complexity of the interactions: on the British side, a government whose members were in conflict over strategy, and a field commander hostile to the secretary of state for war both because of his management of the war effort and because of his strategy. The zig-zag nature of decision making within each government and between them, when faced with an ever-changing diplomatic situation in the Balkans, showed that Allied leadership and institutions were wholly inadequate to deal with the fluid nature of the war. Such an imbroglio was not repeated until September 1915, when Bulgarian intervention against Serbia, and the threat of an Austro-German attack on the Balkan ally, set off another round of turmoil and confusion.

While the non-arrival of the 29th Division on the Western Front and its ultimate diversion to the Dardanelles may be seen as the cause of the breakdown of Anglo-French command relations prior to the battle of Neuve Chapelle, it was more a symptom than a cause of that breakdown and became a symbol of everything that was wrong in the relationship: the incoherence of the British decision-making process, the inadequate coordination between the two governments, the lack of communication and conflict in civil-military relations between Kitchener and Sir John, and the inability of the two field commanders to work harmoniously together.

On the French side, there was likewise conflict between government and command, but Joffre, still a force to be reckoned with, largely prevailed in his focus on the Western Front, though he was unable to prevent the French government from diverting a minimal force to the Balkans in order to represent French interests in the area. Yet he was totally incapable of managing the strategic repercussions of his strained relationship with Sir John French, as witnessed by his attempt in mid-February to have the British commander-in-chief take over more trenches than earlier agreed at a time when the 29th Division was being withheld for the Dardanelles expedition. The story might have been quite different without that inflammatory demand. Joffre's quarrel with Sir John brought command relations to a new juncture as Joffre sought satisfaction from the British and French governments and raised the issue of a unified command. At the same time, Joffre's action in refusing even the minimal support available for the Neuve Chapelle attack lacked gallantry, his frustrations and vindictiveness overcoming his sense of Allied solidarity. The event marked the nadir in Allied command relations in 1915.

CHAPTER FOUR

Planning the Spring Offensive and the Command Issue, 14 March–21 April 1915

THE ANGLO-FRENCH COALITION PROVED to be remarkably resilient, despite the sputtering nature of its operation. The turnaround in Anglo-French command relations that followed the low point marked by the isolated British attack at Neuve Chapelle was particularly noteworthy. That readjustment took place at two levels: between the French and British commands, and between the French command and the British government. Few long-term issues were resolved, particularly regarding British strategy, but enough short-term accommodations were made for all to back Joffre's next big offensive drive.

The battle of Neuve Chapelle, with its breakdown of cooperative efforts, dramatically illustrated the need for conciliation between commands. Both Joffre and Sir John took steps to improve their relationship. On 14 March, Joffre sent Sir John a letter of congratulations on the "brilliant results obtained."[1] Two days later Sir John enquired concerning future French plans and urged "the absolute necessity for arriving at some conclusion to our common action."[2] "Proud of his success," but embarrassed by his inability to continue the offensive, Sir John now recognized the need for closer cooperation with the French.[3] The conundrum that he wished resolved was how the French could be short of men to carry out their strategy of a "simultaneous advance from Arras and Rheims" if, as indicated in one of their communications, they had 2,300,000 men on the Western Front and the Germans, according to British intelligence, had only 1,400,000.[4] Why, Sir John queried, had the French been unable to move forward at Champagne and why had they demanded that he relieve their IX Corps before the battle of Neuve Chapelle if they had such a massive numerical superiority?[5] Sir John's under-evaluation of German forces thus emerged as a significant factor in his dispute with the French.

JOFFRE'S OFFENSIVE PLAN

Joffre was not long in formulating a new offensive plan. The problem was that he had to convince his government. On 17 March 1915 Joffre laid his new plan before Millerand. By this time, the shortage of French guns and munitions appeared to have been largely overcome by the unparalleled efforts of French industry under Millerand's energetic direction.[6] The manpower deficiency caused by the huge losses in the 1914 campaign season – 454,500 deaths by the end of November 1914[7] – and heavy losses in subsequent operations – 268,00 deaths in partial operations from October 1914 through March 1915[8] – would soon be made up by the double-cohort class of 1915, with several new divisions to boot.[9]

The Russians were making very good progress in their Carpathian offensive. In the course of the campaign, Przemysl fell on 22 March.[10] The news was also good elsewhere. The naval bombardment of the Straits fortresses, underway for nearly a month, appeared to be going well, but with ominous concerns about floating enemy mines. An Anglo-French force of 60,000 would soon be assembled in the area.[11]

The improved military situation raised the prospect that Italy might soon enter the war on the side of the Entente powers.[12] This would create a new front against Austria-Hungary in what was already a multi-front war. Although Joffre did not expect the Italians to tie down large bodies of enemy troops because of the mountainous terrain and narrow valleys on the enemy front, Italian entry into the war would divert Austro-Hungarian forces, thereby relieving pressure on the Serbs and Russians. Italian participation in the war on the side of the Entente would also have a salutary effect on potential Balkan allies, and with the addition of thirty-eight Italian infantry divisions and four cavalry divisions, give the Entente powers a marked numerical advantage. But, ironically, the addition of a new ally would put more pressure on Joffre to lead the coalition in a vigorous attack on the French front, in conjunction with simultaneous attacks elsewhere.[13]

The French government, in fact, had its own reasons for supporting the offensive. In the words of Robert A. Doughty, "neither they nor Joffre had any desire to go on the defensive and let the French army lapse into a passive role. The French people, they believed, would not tolerate a long period of inactivity in which military forces bided their time waiting for more favorable conditions. Political and strategic situations demanded a significant effort on the Western Front."[14]

Joffre was unduly optimistic about the results to be obtained from a big Allied push forward on the Western Front. All French offensives since the Battle of Flanders (First Battle of Ypres), he told Millerand, in a sweeping reiteration of French operations, had been directed toward the final goal, which was to break the enemy defensive line and force a "strategic exploitation." The British action at Neuve Chapelle and the French offensive in Champagne had both fallen into that category. The Champagne offensive, like the earlier operations, also had the purpose of "coming to the aid of the Russians, engaged in heavy fighting north of the Vistula," whose support was ever on Joffre's mind. In an attached memo, Joffre lauded the achievements of the Champagne offensive, now ending for want of ammunition. That offensive, he argued, had overtaken German trenches on a front of eight kilometres, obtained moral superiority over the enemy, prevented German troop movements to the east, drawn German troops from other parts of the line, and produced enormous German losses. While noting the British success at Neuve Chapelle, Joffre deprecated it on the basis that French attacks in Champagne had diverted German forces from the British front and left only inferior forces in front of the British. The British had achieved surprise, he said, because of their "previous inaction." The future seemed bright. With the support of English reinforcements, French forces brought up to strength, the addition of new French divisions being formed in the interior, and replenishment of the necessary stocks of ammunition, Joffre looked forward to the "combined action of several armies," which he was "convinced" would lead to "decisive victories" in the "main theatre."[15]

The French cabinet examined the plan the next day, on 18 March. As some members of the government were concerned about Joffre's excessive optimism, it was decided to invite the commander-in-chief to a dinner with the entire cabinet at the Elysée Palace on Sunday, 21 March, in order to allow him to explain his plan. Of the ministers, only Gaston Doumergue and Albert Sarraut objected to the government scrutinizing the plans of the High Command. Poincaré, for his part, was struck that Joffre now required the action of the new units being created in the interior for his forthcoming offensive, having declared a few weeks earlier against their formation.[16]

In the after-dinner conversation that extended till 4:00 P.M., Joffre managed to persuade the ministers to support his plan. "Clearly, but ploddingly," he explained his ideas. The Champagne offensive, which had been undertaken "because of the necessity" of helping the Russians and preventing the Germans from crushing them in Poland, had given satisfactory results but had to be broken off for want of ammunition. By 15 or 20 April, the shortage of explosives for shell fabrication would be over; and with the class of 1915 and the new units being formed, his reserves would be increased from four to eight corps. He would then attack, "pierce the German front and force the retreat of the enemy." "He was very categorical," wrote Poincaré, that the decision must be sought on the French front and would be achieved "probably before summer, certainly before autumn." Entirely Clausewitzean in his approach, Joffre aimed to beat "the best German's armies," after which the Germans would be entirely at their mercy.[17]

Implicit in Joffre's discussion was the concept that the new offensive would greatly benefit the Russians, who were very short of munitions but still making good progress on the Carpathian front. Complaints from Grand Duke Nicholas on 12 April that earlier French operations had not prevented large movements of German troops from the Western to the Eastern Front led Joffre to promise a strong offensive on the French front within three weeks. He emphasized to the ministers the importance of a simultaneous offensive by the Russians, Serbs, and possibly the Italians, which would have a considerable impact.[18]

So optimistic was Joffre and so confident of a French victory that he did not wish that Kitchener should send to the French the "totality of the new Army being formed." Rather, Joffre considered that the current British force with immediate reinforcements would be sufficient. "But he believes it essential that the Marshal be under his command," recorded Poincaré. "That is the point we must raise with Kitchener on his next trip.[19]

While Kitchener at the outset of the war had wished to raise massive new armies to intervene when France and Russia were exhausted, and thereby win the war for Britain, Joffre's remarks provide evidence that in the spring of 1915 he thought that he could bring the war to a successful conclusion in conjunction with the Russians – then doing very well in their Carpathian offensive – without the full weight of the British New Armies, and thereby secure better terms for French security at the conclusion of the war. So confident was Joffre in the success of the spring offensive and an early conclusion of the war that he commissioned another, harsher study of future armistice terms at GQG in April 1915, well in advance of the Artois offensive, which called for the Rhine to be the future military frontier with Germany.[20]

Joffre also spoke "with bitterness" with the ministers about the British request for Dunkirk as a base. Despite Kitchener's warning that without Dunkirk he would "not be able to supply his troops," Joffre refused to yield on this matter. In view of Joffre's recalcitrance, Poincaré worried that failure to come to an understanding would lead the British to seek other theatres of operation and not send the New Armies to France. "This perspective does not displease [me]," Joffre replied to Poincaré.[21]

The verbal clash then went from bad to worse as Poincaré raised the scenario of Britain sending forces to Italy in the case of Italian intervention and France being obliged to do likewise to defend its interests. In reply, Joffre vowed that he would never allow the diversion of any troops from the Western Front; indeed, that he would resign first, to which Poincaré insisted that as commander-in-chief he must submit himself to the civil authority.[22] "If you order me to go to the trenches to get shot, I will go," Joffre retorted, "but if you order me to uncover the heart of France I will disobey."[23] Unwilling to open a breach in civil-military relations, Poincaré did not press the issue before the embarrassed ministers; and, as calm returned, Joffre acknowledged that after his forthcoming victory it would be possible, "if the general interest required it," to divert some forces to other theatres.[24] The general, despite his insubordination, thus carried the cabinet with him, getting carte blanche until May for his offensive, at which time "the situation would again be reviewed."[25]

In retrospect, Joffre was unduly sanguine in his belief in victory, especially in view of his repeated failures to break the German line. The partial successes of the two recent attacks by the French and British had only encouraged the French staff. The myth, in fact, prevailed at French headquarters that "we can get through where we like; whether we go through depends on what we have ready handy, and whether we can push it in at the right moment."[26] With adequate reserves and ammunition, it was therefore thought possible to break through and win the war. The necessary means Joffre hoped to have by the end of April, even without the British New Armies. It was, of course, a mirage.

But his conviction that he could win without the support of Kitchener's New Armies helped diffuse for the moment one of the most fundamental issues dividing the French and British: that of British peripheral strategy and limited commitment to the alliance. With a new clearly defined offensive plan, moreover, Joffre would be in a much better position to eliminate the drift in his relationship with Sir John French, while the forthcoming visit of Kitchener would allow discussion of the command issue and Dunkirk. Clearly, the mandate of the French cabinet for Joffre's spring offensive allowed him to relate more positively with the British command and government.

On the question of peripheral theatres, Joffre had made his point. Unprepared to provoke Joffre's resignation, Millerand gave way on the subject and turned over to Joffre four of the five new divisions being created in the interior, with the caveat that he might need to recall them at a later date[27]; however, he knew full well that it would be nigh impossible to extract them from Joffre's command, and that Joffre had requested them, at least in part, to block any French tendency toward external theatres of operation.

RANCOUR AND CONCILIATION

The question of British relief of French trenches proved less tractable. The Battle of Neuve Chapelle had removed the basic issue, underlying Sir John's quarrel with Joffre prior to the battle, of fighting or guarding the trenches. Having learned, however, of the forthcoming arrival of the South Midlands Division, another British division of territorials, Joffre took up the question once again with Sidney Clive, on 15 March, as to "when the IX Corps is to be relieved." Clive in turn raised the matter with Robertson two days later on a trip to British headquarters.[28] "Reassured" by his success during the Battle of Neuve Chapelle, Sir John was now in a more obliging frame of mind.[29] He thus indicated his willingness on 18 March to relieve a division of the French IX Corps prior to 1 April, providing the French would leave behind their guns.[30] The reason the British required the French to leave behind "some 75's & some Heavy guns," Wilson noted, was because the British had "no amm[u]n[ition] to spare" for their regular guns, and they were unable to "trust" their territorial guns.[31]

But the Battle of Neuve Chapelle had ended on a sour note on 13 March when Sir John refused to reveal his intentions to Foch, who by this time had made preparations to aid him in the attack.[32] Still smarting from that incident, Foch refused to leave behind French guns, and he also refused to increase the ammunition for the Belgian guns in British service since "they were getting their full allowance as it was."[33] However, after a more formal request by Robertson through Huguet, Foch relented, and on 20 March he agreed to the terms of the British offer.[34]

The arrangement nonetheless broke down on the 22nd, when Sir John tried to get Foch to leave French artillery "sine die." "He, of course, refused," wrote Wilson. "He offered to leave them till the 10th Ap[ril]; but Sir J. would not have this."[35] As a result, the agreement foundered amidst mutual recriminations, Foch claiming that Sir John had adequate artillery in the unused cavalry of the First British Army to make the reliefs, and Sir John asserting that these were to be held in reserve for the future attack. Finally, it was agreed, on Wilson and Robertson's advice, that the entire relief action should be delayed until the British had received sufficient artillery from England to allow the simultaneous relief of both the French artillery and infantry.[36]

Noteworthy was Wilson's interpretation that Sir John's renewed intransigence in dealing with the French was due to the visit of Winston Churchill, who on 17 March had come over for a few days and seemingly convinced Sir John of the importance and likely success of the Dardanelles operation.[37] News of the loss of several British and French ships at the bombardment of the Dardanelles forts on 19 March reached British headquarters a day later. Thereafter, in order to undercut the Dardanelles venture and get rid of Churchill, Wilson intrigued assiduously over the next two months with several senior leaders of the Opposition to bring down the government.[38]

Both Foch and Wilson nevertheless took steps to improve the attitude at French headquarters, where, on 20 March, Foch "found Joffre very ready to quarrel" with Sir John. "Foch tried & thinks he succeeded," Wilson reported, "to persuade Joffre not to quarrel with Sir J, but to insist on more amm[u]n[i]t[ion] & more troops being sent to us" during Joffre's forthcoming visit with Kitchener.[39] But, as Clive reported on 22 March, "Gen[eral] J[offre] was very angry about the non-relief of his corps."[40]

On the British side, Wilson played the major role in laying the groundwork for renewed cooperation between the two commands. On 23 March he had a wide-ranging discussion with Joffre at Chantilly. Rising fully to the occasion, Wilson managed to allay much of the ill will between the two commands. To Wilson, always persona grata at French headquarters, Joffre confided his new offensive plan and recounted his confrontation with the ministers. In reply to Joffre's bitter complaints that Sir John "calls me C[ommander]-in-C[hief]" but "disobeys my orders," Wilson "insisted on the importance of dispelling the poisonous idea in Sir J's head & at home that the French had 800,000 more men in the line than the Germans," which he argued was the source of much of the misunderstanding. Joffre promised to draw up a statement on the subject for the British. Relating the difficulties of Sir John's personal relationship with members of the British government, Wilson indicated that the British commander's "own idea was to collect amm[uni]tion & men for another attack" but that this must be coordinated with the French offensive. Sir John, Wilson said, had trouble in finding out what his government and Kitchener intended to do, that is, "whether this was going to remain the principal theatre." Wilson also advised Joffre of the low state of British ammunition shipments. "By degrees," wrote Wilson, "I got him to look at the picture in a different way."[41] In fact, Wilson managed to persuade Joffre that the field commanders had a basic community of interest and that the real problem was the British politicians and British strategy.

On the affirmative side, Wilson gave Joffre positive advice on how to get on better with the British command: to keep them informed of any change of plans and not to repeat confidential things to "chattering politicians like Millerand," as the matters always got back to Sir John. Wilson also advised him on how to manage the British: "I told him to give us orders without appearing to do so, not to refer to our numbers, or dispositions, etc., which always led to explosions, but to refer to Sir J's known loyalty & leave the rest to his good heart – and to me."[42] Here indeed was a thoughtful reading of Sir John's temperament, and how to obtain British cooperation through leadership and not compulsion.

An essential part of the interview was Joffre's confidence in the success of his plans; "he calculated that by the end of Ap[ril] … he would have enough men, amm[uni]tion, [and] trench mortars, which are now being made by the 1000."[43] Ultimately, full British cooperation would depend on renewed confidence in French leadership and operational planning.

The session was, as Wilson recorded, "a very important meeting in a critical moment."

On his return to Saint-Omer two days later, Wilson delivered a letter from Joffre outlining his plan of attack. The French Tenth Army would launch the decisive attack (in Artois) in cooperation with the British Army toward the end of April. To constitute the necessary forces for the attack, Joffre asked that the British relieve his IX and XX corps about Ypres. In the meantime, secondary attacks could be engaged in only if ammunition and troops were available and "so long as the decisive operation is not weakened."[44] The presentation of a new offensive joint plan refocused British perspectives and won their renewed confidence and support. Sir John indicated that "he was satisfied" with the letter, and Robertson, who was present, "left the room at once to study the relief of the XX Corps."[45] On 26 March, Robertson advised Foch that the British would relieve the French IX Corps as soon as possible, since new artillery was in the process of arriving.[46] Sir John, moreover, expressed his general agreement with Joffre's plan but cautiously deferred his final response until after the conference with Kitchener on 29 March.[47] The two commands were thus well on their way to a mutual understanding before that meeting.

BRITISH MUNITIONS

A third factor leading to improved Anglo-French command relations was Sir John's attempt to come to a better understanding with Kitchener on the issue of ammunition. That issue was a long-term bone of contention between the two. The traditional nineteenth-century military doctrine, accepted by all at the outset, prescribed that artillery should serve merely as a support to infantry attacks. That concept, under conditions of trench warfare, gave way to the idea of artillery playing the key role in preparing the attack of the infantry. This realization, however, took place much more quickly at the front than it did at the War Office.[48] Kitchener, it must be acknowledged, was very slow to understand the imperatives of technological warfare, particularly with regard to the role of artillery and high-explosive shells. "Kitchener *knows nothing* about European warfare," Sir John French had written to Churchill on 3 September 1914.[49] Sir John's opinion apparently never varied. On 3 January 1915 he argued that breaching the Western Front was dependent on the availability of high-explosive ammunition.[50] Kitchener, on the other hand, was prone to assume that the trenches on the Western Front were unassailable, and, in view of the difficulties of ammunition production, to seek other theatres of operation where less ammunition would be required.

The difference of opinion was exacerbated by the fact that, on 13 March, Kitchener had cut to three-quarters the delivery of shells to the Western Front in order to increase supplies for the Dardanelles expedition.[51] The dispute took on new proportions following the Battle of Neuve Chapelle. Kitchener, Asquith recorded following their interview on 18 March," was distressed & preoccupied with the reckless way in wh[ich] our men expend their ammunition – particularly shells – last week," amounting to "2 shells per square yard gained!"[52] By one calculation, as much ammunition had been expended at the Battle of Neuve Chapelle as during the entire South African War.[53] The following day Kitchener sent a reproof on behalf of the War Council to Sir John regarding the excessive expenditure of ammunition at the Battle of Neuve Chapelle.[54] Sir John French was even more adamant in his views. "Robertson has given me a private letter he has received from Wolfe Murray on the expenditure of am[muni]t[ion] at Neuve Chapelle," Sir John recorded in his diary on 23 March 1915. "It is said to have been dictated by K. The only comment I have to make upon it is that whosever['s] idea [that] it expressed the author of it is completely ignorant of the conditions under which modern war is carried on."[55]

To ease the tension between the two, Winston Churchill, on his trip to the front on 17 March, suggested a private meeting between them, which Sir John then proposed to Kitchener.[56] As a result, on 23 March, Kitchener had dinner and a long talk alone with Sir John aboard HMS *Attention* at Dover. "I noticed that K looked tired & worried," Sir John recorded. "We first talked about ammunition & K told me that the shortage in manufacturers was so accentuated that he had no hope of bringing the supply up to what we asked for a considerable time to come. He said if we were unable to make progress on this front with less expenditure he would have to consider the possibility of employing the 'New Army' in a theatre of war where so much amm[unition] was not required."[57] For his part, French "strenuously denied that he had let off too much ammunition from his big guns in the fighting at Neuve Chapelle."[58]

Sir John attempted to convince his superior of the need for more ammunition on the French front by lecturing him on the requirements of the modern battlefield. "I told him quite bluntly that neither he or his advisers had any conception of what modern war was really like. This trench warfare … was the inevitable outcome of the deadly nature of modern rifles & m[achine] guns. The old forms of attack & defense were of the past. Wherever we put the new armies they would find the same conditions prevail. And a free & stupendous expenditure of amm[uni]t[ion] was the only way by which the infantry attack could be prepared. The enemy trenches must be broken down, his wire entanglements torn up, & the M[achine] G[un] resistance reduced by art[illery] fire & an unlimited amount of amm[unition]."[59] Modern armchair generals would have applauded. "I think he was partly convinced," Sir John concluded, observing that Kitchener "seemed brighter and more hopeful & cheerful when he left."[60]

The issue of French command relations was also discussed. "K complained very much that the French so completely failed to support me in the recent operations," recorded Sir John.[61] In this he was reflecting the entire cabinet's "strongly expressed opinion" that there had been "a regrettable want of cooperation between the French and British Armies" at the Battle of Neuve Chapelle and also its belief that Sir John had been left to attack unsupported.[62] Sir John replied quite correctly that he "had every reason to believe that this absence of support was by *Joffre's special order.*"[63] Sir John also noted the inequality in his relationship with Joffre, who "was too apt to treat him 'like a Corporal.'"[64] But no solution was offered on either side.

The discussion covered other issues: the invitation of Kitchener to visit Millerand and Joffre at French headquarters, Kitchener's disinclination to go, Asquith and Grey's insistence that he should, and the need for Sir John to be present; the question of Dunkirk as a British base; possible Italian entry into the war; and the Dardanelles attack, of which Kitchener "was not hopeful of success."[65] Altogether, the interview cleared the air between the two,[66] although Kitchener, beset by very serious labour problems in the munitions industry and under heavy attack by Lloyd George and others at home on the matter, was unlikely to give much satisfaction on the supply of munitions for some time to come.

KITCHENER'S VISIT TO FRANCE

Kitchener's visit to France at the end of March 1915 was the final event that contributed to restoring a semblance of harmony within the coalition. The visit originated with Millerand's request of 7 March that Kitchener be invited to France to consult with him and Joffre in order to resolve the command question. Other issues outstanding since January included the British request for Dunkirk as a base and the French refusal, which loomed relatively large in Kitchener's eyes. But the fundamental question that concerned the French government was that of British strategy and the future employment of the New Armies. As Poincaré had observed repeatedly since early January, the British thought that little would come from Joffre's offensives on the French front and were therefore prone to seek other theatres for deployment of the New Armies.

The French were therefore flabbergasted to learn on 9 March that, although Kitchener was personally quite happy to consult with the French, on the prime minister's instruction, he was not to discuss either the question of British use of troops in the Levant or the future deployment of the New Armies. This question Asquith considered premature in view of the possible need to deploy troops in support of the naval bombardment of the Straits.[67]

The French government responded by expressing astonishment that the major issues were excluded from the agenda and making representations to the British government to have these omissions rectified.[68] In the background, however, not immediately visible to the French, was the question of power relations within the British cabinet. According to Esher, the real reason Asquith limited Kitchener's powers in dealing with the French was that he had become too authoritarian in the cabinet; and, without the discretionary powers to decide the future deployment of the New Armies, Kitchener had little interest in talking with the French.[69] Kitchener thus stalled on 22 March, claiming his inability to leave the War Office.[70] His strong leanings, moreover, were toward an expedition in the Middle East, particularly at Alexandretta in support of British imperial ambitions, once the Dardanelles had been forced, an idea that had the support of key members of the War Council including Winston Churchill.[71] He was thus unwilling to make commitments to the French regarding the New Armies.[72]

By 20 March, however, the French had become wary of British interests, and, following an interview between Augagneur and Churchill, they came to suspect that a British Alexandretta expedition was in the offing, despite avowed British plans for an expedition to the Dardanelles.[73] The question of the timing of Kitchener's visit therefore became all-important to them. "I had a longish interview with Cambon, who is rather nervous about an approaching interview between Kitchener & Joffre & Millerand," reported Asquith on 22 March. "He wanted to hurry it up, as his Government are apparently afraid K may plan out the disposition & theatres of operation of his New Armies without due consultation with them."[74] Although Kitchener was reluctant to go, Asquith insisted that he should in order to reassure the French as to the "ensemble" of British operations "both East and West."[75] The use of Dunkirk and the question of unity of command would be on the agenda; the use of the New Armies would not.[76] On the French side, the French military attaché in London expressed the opinion that Kitchener should come even if major items were excluded from the agenda. According to this view, a discussion with Joffre on the strategic needs of the Western Front could in itself yield the desired results.[77]

POSITIONS ON THE QUESTION OF A UNIFIED COMMAND

The position papers prepared by the French government in preparation for Kitchener's visit were most illuminating. On the question of the unified command, the records of the French Embassy in London and the Ministry of War were searched to identify any pre-war arrangements that could serve as the basis for subordination of the British command to the French. Cambon in London offered an optimistic initial appraisal on 22 March that the question of "supreme command" ought not to raise any problem, since, according to pre-war arrangements, command "ought to belong to the French General."[78] Upon searching the archives, however, he was obliged to dispel the reigning assumption that such an agreement existed. "I found no trace of this disposition," he wrote. "However, in the course of discussion between the Staffs, it was verbally agreed that command would belong to the British admiral at sea, to the French general on land." It was regrettable, said Cambon, that adequate technical arrangements had not been made either at the military or political level in the pre-war period.[79] Cambon nonetheless hopefully reported to Millerand that on several occasions Kitchener had told embassy staff that English troops were under the orders of General Joffre and that Kitchener addressed Joffre as "General Commander-in-Chief of Allied Armies" when he wrote to him.[80] Those indicators implied that conceptually, at least, Kitchener understood the need for unity of command.

In support of the French case, the only document that the French Army staff at the Ministry of War could find was a secret report addressed to the president of the republic in March 1912 on the eventual cooperation of British military forces with those of the French armies of the northeast. "The coordination of operations of the English Armies with the French Armies of the Northeast will be assured by directives emanating from the Commander-in-Chief of French forces operating on this theatre and addressed to the Commander-in-Chief of English troops."[81] None of these directives provided any more than general guidelines, let alone the basis for a firm understanding, despite the optimistic hopes of the French War Ministry.

The French General Staff at Chantilly was equally firm in its view. The question of command having been settled for other theatres – the North Sea, the Mediterranean, and the Dardanelles – it ought now to be resolved on the French front at a time when operations were becoming "more active" and required "a more rapid execution." "In the French theatre of operations, that direction must belong to General Joffre," affirmed a staff memorandum.[82] There followed a nine-page statement documenting incidents since the beginning of the war in which Sir John's independence of mind had caused problems in Allied coordination.[83] There could be only one conclusion.

Kitchener's attitude toward Allied coordination took on broader dimensions. As early as 22 January, following Millerand's visit, Esher suggested to the British secretary of state for war that "Joffre should be given a chance of considering the broader strategy," to which Kitchener heartily agreed.[84] At the War Council on 28 January, Kitchener expressed concern that Germany's "central position" allowed it to "coordinate" the efforts of the Central Powers, while "the Allies, on the other hand, were acting independently." Accordingly, Kitchener expressed his opinion that "there should be some central authority where all the Allies were represented and full information was available" and "attacks should be arranged to take place simultaneously."[85] The council decided that, in his forthcoming trip to Paris, Lloyd George should "avail himself of any favourable opportunity which may present itself … to start the idea of a central body to provide the Allies with facilities for consultation with a view to greater coordination of effort."[86] That idea was presented by Lloyd George to Poincaré on 3 February, but with no apparent follow-up.[87]

On the command issue, Kitchener, however, remained reluctant. Clearly, the independence of action implicit in Kitchener's original instruction to Sir John French reflected the very nature of limited British involvement in the continental war and British determination to maintain control of their own forces in their own interests. Kitchener's most trusted adviser on relations with the French was Esher, who was commissioned as a special envoy by Kitchener on 23 January, first to meet Millerand and then "occasionally to go over and discuss matters with him."[88] As with many autocratic individuals, Kitchener was suspicious of officially established bureaucracies and frequently relied on an unofficial network for appraisals from the field, such as those of Henry Rawlinson, his former aide-de-camp in South Africa, rather than those of Sir John French[89]; and those of Esher rather than those of the Foreign Office.[90] Esher's frequent visits to France generally included both the French War Ministry and British headquarters at Saint-Omer, and during these visits he attempted to soothe over not only Anglo-French relations but relations between Sir John and Kitchener.

On 21 March, after consulting with Millerand and Sir John French in succession, Esher wrote his appraisal to Kitchener: "If this war ends in an unsatisfactory peace, it will be on account of mishandling of the French Alliance and a misunderstanding of the French character."[91] Esher attempted to define French character for Kitchener: "With these people an ounce of sentiment goes further than a pound sterling. Finesse is of no use with a nation whose patriotism is rooted in an ideal and not in self-interest. Besides, the French can out-finesse anyone."[92]

Both Millerand and Joffre, he observed privately, "complain of want of candour in us."[93] In Esher's view, the failure of the British to define command relations was a "grave misunderstanding which was bound to create dangerous situations, political and military." Esher urged Kitchener to approach the French with greater frankness. "Either you desire Sir John and his army to be under the orders of Joffre or you don't. If you do not, (which I hope is the case), you should, I venture to think, say so in the plainest and most unmistakable terms, and explain that our system of Government makes it impossible, quite apart from military sentiment; – for this is the truth. I am confident that they will understand."[94] The results of Kitchener's meeting with the French show that he paid attention to Esher's views, being willing to define the Anglo-French command relationship but, for the moment, unwilling to alter it.

The British command, with the most at stake, also began to position itself. On 20 March, Esher had an interview with Sir John French and found the difference of perception between Joffre and the field marshal as to their respective positions "embarrassing and absurd; all the result of want of frankness," with Sir John claiming an independent command and Joffre taking the view that he was "Generalissimo over both armies." "The Field Marshal says that the English army would never yield its best under such circumstances" and "that the Government holds him responsible and no one else."[95] In a communication directed to Millerand, Esher indicated on 23 March that Sir John's instructions from the British government assured him the command of his army "alongside" General Joffre and that the government would oppose the subordination of the British to the French command. The British government, argued Esher, would have much difficulty understanding why Sir John, whose independence of command had been unquestioned when he had "only a handful of soldiers," should be placed under French command now that he had an army of 400,000."[96]

Wilson was even more blunt and ultimately very effective in presenting the viewpoint of the British command at French headquarters. On the eve of the conference, Wilson learned from Pellé, Joffre's chief of staff, that Joffre was indeed going to raise the question of command at the meeting, with the intent that "he should be able to give Sir J. orders." In the interview with Joffre and Pellé that followed, Wilson told Joffre that, in order to have "power to command" British forces, "he *must* have the power" to dismiss their commander, and, as the British government would not grant that, a unified command could not be conceded.[97] Amazingly, with this argument, Wilson was able to persuade Joffre to keep the subject off the formal conference agenda.[98] In a last-minute memo, Pellé advised Joffre that the question of the subordination of the British field marshal should not be raised at the conference since "his obedience was unlikely" and he had "too much prestige" to be replaced. British subordination could be obtained, Pellé argued, reflecting Wilson's views, not through Sir John's obedience but through assigning him objectives and convincing him of the necessity of achieving them.[99]

DUNKIRK REJECTED AS BRITISH BASE

On the issue of Dunkirk, the French staff was less willing to compromise than the government, but, ironically, more for political than military reasons. The question apparently had been dealt with previously at a technical level between the two armies. Bertie, however, advised Sir John on 13 January 1915 of French political concerns: "that Havre, Rouen and more particularly Boulogne are in appearance more English than French"; and that the British showed a tendency to "take possession" wherever they go.[100] It is not clear from this communication whether the fear about the British refusing to relinquish Dunkirk after the war was widespread in French political circles. Yet it certainly was a concern in some quarters, showing how incredibly suspicious the Allies were of each other.

The question arose at the ministerial level on 22 January during Millerand's visit to London, at which time Kitchener, broaching the subject, attached considerable "importance" to the need for Dunkirk as a British supply base. Millerand, in any case, was familiar with Joffre's objections. Dunkirk, Millerand said, could not be turned into a British supply base since it was a French port of trade, and, as a counter-measure, he suggested the creation of large supply depots between the existing ports and the troops.[101]

Millerand nevertheless left the door open, and Kitchener asked him on 2 February if a decision had been made on the question. Immediate troop movements, said Kitchener, would increase British forces in France to 410,000 and existing bases would be insufficient for their supply. Millerand's inference was that Kitchener wished Dunkirk to be a large permanent base of supply for the time when the New Armies would arrive in France. But Millerand, in his reply to Kitchener on 6 February, on Joffre's advice, stated that adequate facilities already existed for British supply in the ports of Le Havre, Rouen, Boulogne, and Dieppe, particularly in view of the efforts being made to create large depots between the ports and the troops.[102]

Kitchener, not easily dissuaded, had the War Office raise the issue again on 19 February with the French, this time also seeking use of the port of Calais, which would be of "great value for the debarkation of troops and the evacuation of the wounded."[103] Consulted by the war minister on this new request, Joffre became even more strident. As Dunkirk was a fortified place near the front, he argued, no Allied installation could be authorized, nor could the British be installed at Calais since that port was essential for the supply of the Belgian Army. In any case, there was no need for further British bases, he asserted; existing ones were sufficient to supply an army of 450,000 men and 180,000 horses.[104]

Millerand sent his renewed rejection on 28 February. Though couched in suitably diplomatic language, it brought forth "the wrath of the British Government," which "insisted in the most pressing way" on 3 March that

Dunkirk be made a British supply base and added that failure to do so could "compromise" the sending of new troops to France.[105] Kitchener's ire was reserved for Millerand, who had complained in a personal letter on 2 March of delays in British troop arrivals. In his reply on 4 March, Kitchener used the delay in British troop arrivals as the signal for raising the issue of Dunkirk. "It is with surprise," he wrote, "that I hear that General Joffre has persistently opposed my request for facilities in this port," a decision for which "I have never been able to understand the precise reason." Even with the new arrangements, the existing ports, he argued, were barely adequate for maintaining current forces, and unless Joffre was prepared to remove his objections, the British would have "the greatest difficulty" maintaining present forces "without speaking of a substantial increase." "I must add," he concluded with some bitterness, "that Her Majesty's Government is greatly surprised that this hospitality has thus been refused."[106]

The issue was squarely on the agenda for Kitchener's meeting with Millerand and Joffre. In a secret and personal memo to Millerand on 13 March, Joffre showed his hand. The basic political reason why Dunkirk and Calais could not be given to the British was that this matter involved the question of influence over Belgium. The British, argued Joffre, had shown a marked tendency to take Belgium under exclusive protection and to lead it to believe that Belgian territory could be liberated only by British forces. In support of this view, he cited the siege of Antwerp, the transport of the British Army into Belgium, and the "attempt to put their hands on the Belgian Army." This had aroused the suspicions of Premier de Broqueville and the king, which had drawn them closer to the French. "As much from the point of view of the required liaison for military operations as that of maintaining our influence in Belgium at the time of peace negotiations," concluded Joffre, "we must maintain a close connection with the Belgian Army." He thus desired to have the Belgian Army "encased with French forces capable of giving them support and of representing France at the time of the march into Belgium."[107]

The French staff, in fact, was in the process of formulating French military war aims and had visions of integrating Belgium in a post-war French military security arrangement extending to the Rhine,[108] and thus wished to limit British influence over Belgium. Both Calais and Dunkirk were fortified places, Joffre argued. Joffre considered Calais less sensitive than Dunkirk, and, if absolutely necessary, he was prepared to allocate to the British its excess capacity, beyond what was required to supply the Belgians. But Dunkirk, on the French left flank, near the Belgians, could not be surrendered to the British.[109]

These political considerations aside, Joffre thought that military reasons alone were sufficiently convincing to satisfy the British. As a fortified place, Dunkirk required large numbers of French troops, leaving no space for British cantonments. The argument about railway disruptions he thought even more convincing. As Calais was the supply base for the Belgians via Dunkirk, British use of Dunkirk would disrupt the railway communications for supply of French troops on the Yser, the Belgian Army, and the French Eighth Army about Ypres. In the event of further British troop build-ups on the continent, requiring additional port facilities, Joffre was prepared to offer the British Cherbourg and Saint-Nazaire, in addition to Boulogne, Dieppe, Le Havre, and Rouen already in their service.[110] As shown at his meeting with the ministers on 21 March, his intransigence on the issue had become the source of considerable concern to his government, which took a much more flexible approach.[111]

THE CHANTILLY CONFERENCE, 29 MARCH 1915

The preparations for the conference took on the character of a tragicomedy when the British discovered that a serious breach of protocol had been committed – namely, Sir John French had not been invited.[112] The prime minister thought that Sir John should attend,[113] and Kitchener, at his meeting with Sir John at Dover on 23 March, agreed that Sir John "might be of help to him" in his discussion with the French. It was accordingly decided that Sir John should "wire to Joffre" asking if he wished him to be present.[114] As the conference was being set up by Millerand, Joffre was somewhat embarrassed, not knowing even the items to be discussed. He therefore said he had no personal objection to Sir John's presence but enquired as to Kitchener's desires.[115] A flurry of telegrams passed between embassies until it was agreed that Sir John should attend and that Kitchener would arrive for the conference on 29 March.[116]

Indicative of the improved climate between the two commanders, Sir John renewed the old game of the two commanders concerting against Kitchener by sending Wilson on ahead of the meeting to "work" Joffre on points to impress on Kitchener. These included: the material demands of the modern battlefield and the need for unlimited ammunition; the folly of seeking other theatres where less ammunition would be required; "the necessity for a great prolonged battle in the western theatre to clear

Joffre (far left) bids farewell to Kitchener, with Millerand (far right) observing, after an Allied political-military conference at French headquarters on 29 March 1915. Following the breakdown of Anglo-French cooperation in the Neuve Chapelle offensive, 10–13 March 1915, Kitchener came to France to meet with French political and military leaders and restored harmony through the promise of additional territorial divisions. (*Miroir*, 11 April 1915, Service historique de la Défense, Vincennes)

France & Belgium"; and the willingness of Sir John to relieve the French IX and XX corps if Kitchener would send out another territorial division.[117] This mission Wilson carried out on 28 March on the eve of the conference, to good effect.[118]

The Chantilly Conference on 29 March 1915 was the event that cemented Anglo-French understanding and laid the basis for the Anglo-French spring offensive of 1915. Present were Millerand, Jean César Graziani, the chief of staff at the French War Ministry, Joffre, Pellé, Kitchener, Sir John French, Huguet, and Wilson. Kitchener chaired the meeting. The conversation, during the three-hour session, was essentially between Joffre and Kitchener, reflective of the true bases of power in the coalition, with some participation from Sir John and, to a lesser extent, Millerand. A wide range of issues was discussed, but the essential item was Joffre's new offensive plan.[119]

The meeting began with Kitchener expressing concern over a possible German offensive in Holland, a fear generated by recent German depredations against Dutch shipping and an alarm in Holland on 26 March.[120] Reflecting his continued backing of a British coastal strategy, Kitchener argued that in such an event Holland should become the principal theatre of the war. Joffre, however, "wouldn't hear of it"[121] and maintained that the principal theatre must "always be in *France & Belgium*." In his view, the Allies were at last in a "position to do something decisive." "An enormous quantity of ammunition," he said, ostensibly for Kitchener's benefit, was "the special requirement of such a war." "His conclusion was – we must wait until about May 1 until we were completely ready in men, guns & amm[unition] & then break thru the enemy line."[122]

Lord Kitchener then bared his soul regarding the dire circumstances of the British munitions situation. Production had tripled since the beginning of the war, but that was not nearly enough. And, though plant space had been increased ninefold, the workmen could not be had, with newly recruited employees having fallen off from five thousand in December to six hundred in March. Even Wilson was unaware that Kitchener's "labour troubles … were so bad." "The Frenchmen" were very much shocked by this revelation of what Sir John considered "in reality a very grim state of affairs." In Kitchener's view, compulsory service was the only way out.[123]

A discussion then arose as to what constituted an adequate stock of ammunition, with Joffre asserting that seventeen rounds per field gun per day and five to six rounds for heavy artillery would be sufficient, although he would prefer more. Kitchener obliged Sir John to agree, but with evident bad grace, that these ammunition levels would suffice. However, Kitchener, under the circumstances, was not prepared to guarantee that these figures would be met.[124] "We are getting 6–7 rounds a day; the French are getting 17–20," recorded Wilson, "but with our small number of guns we should be getting 30."[125]

The bargaining then began on the question of reinforcements. Sir John carefully recorded the results:

> In order to carry off his big offensive, Joffre said he must get the 9 & 20 Corps from East of Ypres and asked K to let me have troops to enable me to relieve them.
>
> Lord K said he would send 2 Terr[itorial] Divisions as soon as possible: within 3 weeks.
>
> Joffre asked if in this circumstance I could promise him to relieve the 20 Corps by April 20. I agreed.[126]

The question of smaller operations in the meantime was raised, with Joffre asserting his intention to launch one (the Woevre offensive) in a week in order to prevent German troop movements to the Russian front and inviting the British to do likewise. For the French, how to aid the Russians was always a consideration. But Kitchener objected that such attacks would only delay the principal operation. As a result, the question of a preliminary British action was left open, with both Kitchener and Joffre agreeing that it ought not to delay preparation of the main offensive.[127]

Also discussed at the conference was the issue of the British request for Calais and Dunkirk as bases, an issue on which Kitchener was very insistent. Joffre agreed to let the British use Calais but refused them the use of Dunkirk, indicating that it was a French fortress and hence an integral part of the French front, and that British use of the fort would disrupt the French railway system for supply of the Belgians and the French forces at Ypres. Finally, after an acrimonious discussion, it was agreed to have John Cowans, the British quartermaster-general in London, and Camille Ragueneau, Joffre's director of support services, meet to resolve the issue on a technical basis. Kitchener, however, fired a parting bolt. The promise of his sending the two divisions might depend on the British getting use of the facilities at Dunkirk, if these two officers thought it necessary.[128]

The issue of the Dardanelles was raised by Kitchener, who indicated the British had no strategic plan except to "seize the heights of Gallipoli overlooking the Narrows." To Sir John French, who enquired if it was intended to send more men to the Dardanelles, Kitchener replied that there were now 67,000 British soldiers there and that was sufficient. The final statement of British policy, however, came from Kitchener, who said that "after dispatch of the 2 Divisions [to the Western Front], he could not send any more troops until & unless we broke the line or showed that substantial headway could be made on this theatre."[129] In the final analysis, the basic question of the use of the New Armies had simply been deferred until after the spring offensive; Kitchener's attitude was one of "wait and see." The timing of the spring offensive raised the related issue of Allied coordination, with Joffre asserting that, in selecting the date, "Russia must also be considered."[130]

Kitchener took advantage of the occasion to present his view on the subject of Allied coordination and to say that he would soon set out his ideas to Joffre on the overall conduct of the war. The French command, he said, could serve as intermediaries to discuss the coordination of military efforts with the Russians. If the offensive for the end of April could be executed simultaneously on the two fronts, it would greatly impress the Germans and serve as a tangible evidence of the agreement of the Allied armies. The moral effect on the enemy, he thought, would be considerable.[131] The initiative for Joffre's later role as Allied coordinator thus began, curiously, with Kitchener himself.

In short, the conference was significant both for what it discussed and what it did not. The prospects of Italian intervention and strategy were considered, but no one asserted, as was later claimed by the French command after the fact, that the French spring offensive was planned as a means of bringing Italy into the war. The proposed military expedition to the Dardanelles was discussed, but the use of the New Armies was not, except for Kitchener's observation that no new forces would be sent to France unless the front could be broken. The question of Allied coordination was examined, but the command issue – the reason for which Millerand had invited Kitchener to France – was never mentioned.[132]

Millerand, after lunch on 29 March, however, raised the question privately with Kitchener of Sir John French's subordination to Joffre. Kitchener, according to Millerand, agreed in principle. "Lord Kitchener raised no objection" to the principle of "unity of command" and "necessity [of] subordination," Millerand reported to Delcassé later in the day.[133] To the French cabinet the next day, Millerand noted that "Kitchener had declared himself in agreement with Joffre in considering unity necessary." Since the beginning of the war, he had given instructions to Sir John French and "he is ready to communicate them to Cambon, so that Joffre could invoke them if need be."[134] "They are of a nature," reported Millerand, "to give complete satisfaction to General Joffre."[135] But, observed Kitchener, "why do you not name Joffre a Field Marshal? French never ceases to observe that he is a Field Marshal and Joffre is only a general."[136] The question of rank appeared to assume significant proportions, although Poincaré feared that even if promoted to field marshal, Joffre would be junior to French.[137]

Millerand's handwritten notes of the conversation offer a substantially different picture. "There can be no question of giving orders directly to English troops," Kitchener had responded when "the question of command and of the subordination of Field Marshal French" was raised.[138] Kitchener thus showed considerably more reserve on the issue than Millerand had reported to the French cabinet, and in fact was prepared only to communicate to the French his instructions to Sir John French, "without speaking of it to his colleagues."[139] Did Millerand misrepresent Kitchener's true position to the cabinet? Or did Kitchener, tongue in cheek, claim that communication of Sir John's instructions would satisfy the French, as the matter was raised again at the train station?[140] The answer is not entirely clear, but it is obvious that the differing appreciation of what was said would lead to yet further misunderstanding.

The conference ended on a pleasant note, with Kitchener declaring himself happy with his visit.[141] The French were surprised to find him "singularly 'genial,' a mood which was new to them and astonishing" after the "shivers" he inspired in Millerand during his visit to London. On the other hand, they found Sir John French "rather grumpy,"[142] and "Field Marshal French and his Minister rather irritated with each other."[143]

For his part, Kitchener went away with a less than favourable impression of Joffre.[144] The focus of his strategy on the Western Front and his unwillingness to consider other options, contrary to the British mindset, was the apparent cause. "It is impossible to get the French Generals & Staff to look at anything but their own trenches & what lies in front of them," Asquith observed after Kitchener's report to the cabinet on 30 March. "As soon as their ammunition is in full supply they are going in concert with [Sir John] French to make a great push, and seem to be confident they can drive the Germans back to the Meuse," he summarized.[145]

The Chantilly Conference, in the words of William Robertson, "passed off exceeding well" as the basic issues of the joint offensive and the allocation of trenches had been resolved. The British command, at least, went away feeling that important work had been accomplished. "The air has been well cleared and we know where we are and what is intended," Robertson wrote to Charles Callwell on 31 March. "The general situation here between ourselves and the French has never been better than at present," he observed. "I have never been so hopeful as at present, subject, of course, to the ammunition question."[146] What is certain is that the conference laid the basis for planning the Anglo-French spring offensive and cleared the way for renewed short-term understanding between the French and British commands. It in no way resolved the basically divergent strategic approaches of the two allies.

With the improved climate of opinion between the British and French commands, a number of issues were disposed of quickly between them. The issue of Dunkirk was quickly resolved almost with a stroke of the pen. Upon his return to British headquarters after the conference on 29 March, Sir John "discussed the question of Dunkirk as a base" with Robertson and decided "not to press for it but to manage with Calais for the present." John Maxwell, the quartermaster-general on French's staff who joined the discussion, reaffirmed that he could "manage 8 new Division with Calais." If the dispatch of further British divisions required additional port facilities, British headquarters were prepared to ask for Cherbourg.[147] "Yesterday's difficulties about Dunkirk have been got over by Maxwell, saying he doesn't want it," wrote Wilson on 30 March.[148]

RENEWED COOPERATION: GROUNDWORK FOR THE SPRING OFFENSIVE

There was still a bit of sputtering, nevertheless, as Cowans, the quartermaster-general in London, "apparently" continued to think Dunkirk was necessary.[149] Sir John French as a result sent Maxwell to London on 6 April to explain his views to Kitchener. "I have heard something which leads me to think the French have a rooted objection to our establishing ourselves at Dunkirk," Sir John wrote to Kitchener on 8 April. "If it is true it is rather amusing, but I will tell you what it is when I see you."[150] The allusion was evidently to the French suspicion, noted by Bertie, that once the British were installed at Dunkirk, it would be impossible to dislodge them after the war.

The conflict between Kitchener and Joffre over the appropriate response to a German offensive in Holland evaporated as the prospect waned. By 30 March, Kitchener was "weakening" on the danger,[151] "no longer attaching any importance to it."[152] Churchill, however, continued to support the idea of a British offensive in Holland until Grey and Kitchener "put their foot down firmly" in early April.[153] But rumours circulated in mid-April that Churchill and First Sea Lord Jackie Fisher were again toying with the idea of launching eight divisions at Rotterdam since the Dardanelles naval bombardment had fared poorly.[154]

The questions of the relief of the French IX and XX corps, which had agitated command relations for so long, was likewise resolved with remarkable celerity and relative harmony in anticipation of the new offensive plan. On 1 April 1915 Sir John wrote a letter to Joffre in which he indicated that he had given orders to have British forces take up the whole of the line of the French IX and XX corps by 20 April; that secondary actions were being prepared with Foch to harass the enemy; and that he hoped to be ready to "cooperate" with Joffre's offensive at the end of April with his entire First Army, consisting of eight divisions. He observed with caution, however, that these arrangements had been made in view of the forthcoming arrival from England of two territorial divisions toward the third week in April.[155]

Not incidental to Sir John's resolution of his difficulties with the French was his establishment of a better understanding with Kitchener. On 31 March, Sir John, following the suggestion that he cross over and discuss the results of the Chantilly Conference with Kitchener, had breakfast and a "long talk" with him in his residence at York House in London. The night previous Sir John was assured by the "full investigations" of F.E. Smith of Kitchener's staff that "there was no immediate intention of looking for any other theatre of war." Kitchener nonetheless made his position perfectly clear regarding the forthcoming offensive, stating definitely that he considered Joffre and Sir John on "trial." If they showed within the next month or six weeks that they could make a "substantial advance" and "break the German line," he would back them up "with all the troops he could send." But if they failed to do so, the government "should look for some other theatre of operations."[156] "K added that they had no fear on our account but were inclined to doubt the French. He said he had not been very favourably impressed by Joffre." These assurances, despite the bluntness of Kitchener's message, seemed to satisfy Sir John. "I told him I thought he had put the matter very fairly," he wrote, "& that I was content to accept what he said." "We had, on the whole, the most satisfactory talk we have had yet," he concluded.[157] The next day, as indicated, Sir John threw his full support behind the French plan.

The reason, of course, that Kitchener's strictly conditional pledge of support was music to Sir John's ears was that the field commander had unbridled confidence in the success of the proposed operation. This became abundantly clear on 5 April, when Sir John and Robertson met with Foch to plan the offensive. Foch began by telling the British of his plans for the attack of the French Tenth Army north of Arras at the end of the month, with 6 corps supported by 210 heavy guns and 800 75-millimetre field guns. Sir John explained his plans for the attack of the First Army at La Bassée with 4 Corps and 580 guns. The weight of the attack was impressive. The French promised full support of the British. "Foch hopes to have 5 heavy batteries & 2 Divisions to cooperate with Haig in an attack on La Bassée," Sir John observed. Foch then "explained on a big map the course which he expected the operations would take" following the anticipated breakthrough. Sir John's offensive would veer north of Lille and fulfill a much cherished dream. "It seems likely that we may once again traverse the field of Waterloo,"[158] he observed hopefully. To Mrs Bennett in London, he wrote on the same day that he expected his visit on 14 April would be "the last chance" he would have to see her "before the end of the war – if as I believe it will finish in June or July."[159]

That optimism was not in the least shared by the War Office. "What struck both Lord K and Fitzgerald [his secretary]," Callwell wrote to Robertson regarding the Chantilly meeting, "was the extraordinary confidence of the French side and also G.H.Q. … that the war would soon be over. So soon as June was frequently mentioned. We over here can see no signs of this and do not believe that the Germans, even when they begin to give way, will be found easy to defeat."[160] Kitchener's statement to Sir John on 31 March assuring his support in the event of a breakthrough was in reality an expression of his disbelief in the operation, rather than one of backing for Sir John, as the latter supposed.

The greatly improved relationship between the two nevertheless continued to blossom for a while. "It was a good comfort and help to me to have a quiet talk with you," Sir John wrote to Kitchener on 2 April. "I have always been most anxious to keep you in close touch with everything, but writing is difficult ... and telegraphing is worse." He thus offered to "run over to London for a few hours" in about ten or twelve days when the joint plans would be complete and lay them all before Kitchener "one morning early (whilst we are fresh – without anyone knowing)."[161]

Sir John's secret breakfast appointment with Kitchener at York House on 14 April, without the knowledge of even the prime minister or Churchill, produced salutary short-term results.[162] Several outstanding issues began to dissipate in the course of Sir John's two-hour talk with Kitchener. "He is much more helpful about the amm[uni]t[ion]," recorded Sir John, noting Kitchener's difficulties with the cabinet on the question. Sir John then confided his "future plan of operations" to Kitchener "and explained everything to him on the map." Kitchener, in turn, "promised absolute secrecy," to the satisfaction of Sir John, who earlier had refused to confide his plans for the Battle of Neuve Chapelle for fear of a breach of secrecy. Even the most thorny and divisive question between them – how the New Armies should be integrated into the expeditionary force – was resolved. "He is quite prepared to acquiesce in any method I may think best to adopt as regards their employment," Sir John recorded, "but he wants me to look at them and try them before finally directing whether to keep them in corps or not."[163] All outstanding issues seemed to be resolved and mutual trust restored. "I have had a talk with French," Kitchener wrote to the prime minister on 14 April. "He told me I could let you know that with the present supply of ammunitions he will have as much as his troops will be able to use on the next forward movement." Even Kitchener had grown more optimistic about the offensive. "I think the next move will be much better than the last with cooperation from the French forces which failed last time."[164]

Sir John's private visits with Kitchener, it might be noted, also allowed him to pursue his personal interests. After his 31 March meeting with Kitchener, Sir John wrote to his mistress thanking her for "the blessed 2 days" he had spent with her, which had "filled" him "full of courage & strength." "You, my Darling, have raised me up from what I think is Much worse than Death."[165] On his return to Saint-Omer on 16 April, Sir John again wrote to Mrs Bennett of the salutary effect of his time with her. "My one Sweet Darling (at last I can call you my own!) I was heart broken to part from you to-day. But *Darling, Darling*, my Spirit is with you every moment. – I can see you now so clearly kissing me a good-bye – your beautiful face & form standing beside the fire when I was going out! God! How I love you!"[166] Mars and Venus had made at least a temporary accommodation in the pursuits of the British chief.

THE COMMAND ISSUE UNRESOLVED

The command question proved much more complex and capable of no ready solution. As promised to Millerand, Kitchener, upon his return to London, read to Cambon "the instructions approved by the Cabinet" and given to Sir John French on 9 August 1914. These instructions, Cambon reported, recommended that Sir John "strive to cooperate as sympathetically as possible with the plans and wishes" of the French commander. But, as British forces were very small in comparison to French forces, the British chief was not to engage his troops against superior enemy forces without the assurance of being supported by the French Army. He was to understand that his command was "independent" and that "he could not escape responsibility in any way" by following an order from General Joffre. These instructions had never been changed.[167] The nature of Sir John's instructions came as a great surprise to the French cabinet. Poincaré gave voice to their disappointment. "What Kitchener said to Millerand on the unity of command does not correspond with the instructions given," wrote Poincaré, "and these instructions entirely justify the attitude of French." Delcassé, as a result, was given the responsibility of "showing the English Government all the difficulties implicit in this arrangement."[168]

Millerand also raised the issue the same day in conversation with Esher, arguing that it was "indispensable" that "Joffre's supremacy" be established.[169] Kitchener, Esher noted, had been "amiable but unaccommodating." Esher therefore argued that Sir John French "*alone* could put the relation on a sound basis; he could not be forced." Millerand countered that the British government should have the moral courage to insist" on Sir John's subordination to Joffre, citing the example of General Albert d'Amade having been placed under Hamilton in the Middle East. In Millerand's view, Joffre should not give orders to the British Army, but, in order to assure victory, "every strategical movement should be imposed by Joffre upon French and accepted by him as orders."[170] Esher then undertook the unpleasant task of explaining the French point of view to the British commander; however, he made clear that the resolution of the matter rested with Sir John,[171] whose hand could not be forced.

Esher's subsequent attempt to have Sir John voluntarily submit himself to Joffre fell on unreceptive ears. Sir John had been informed by Wilson prior to the Chantilly Conference that "the question of command" was "prominent in the minds of the French military authorities." Wilson, following his discussion with Joffre on 28 March, had informed Sir John that the idea emanated largely from Millerand, and that, as a result of Wilson's talk with Joffre, the latter would drop the issue. "There can however be no doubt," Sir John noted, "that Millerand – the French War Minister – has pressed it with K and our Government," which, he affirmed, "entirely refused to listen to it."[172]

Sir John was brought up short on 31 March, therefore, to learn, in his discussion with Kitchener, that the French were still pursuing the issue. Sir John, Wilson reported on 2 April, "is again very angry with Joffre who, with Millerand is … trying to get him (Sir J) under his command." Sir John's ire was punctuated with the statements that "he had no opinion of Joffre as a soldier" and that that sentiment was shared "at home."[173]

Brought into the discussion on 2 April by an appeal from Sir John,[174] Esher attempted to resolve the issue on a voluntary basis. Writing to Sir John on 3 April, he expressed his opinion that the "misunderstanding" on the command issue was "the cause of everything unpleasant in the atmosphere of the Allied Armies." "Joffre," he said, "has been allowed to think from the beginning, that you had been instructed to act under him, and that the refusal to do so came from you, and that the *Government* were too weak to insist!" Millerand, likewise, had been "thunderstruck to learn" (from Esher prior to the conference) that Sir John "had received implicit instructions to act as the Commander-in-Chief of an Allied Army," having earlier received "quite the contrary impression." Esher nevertheless maintained that it was now too late (in view of the strength of British forces) to subordinate Sir John officially to Joffre, and that any move in that direction would be misunderstood by the British Army and the British people. Esher's proposal, therefore, was that Sir John write a personal and confidential letter to Joffre pledging his support. While noting the independence of his command, Sir John would also indicate his willingness to subordinate himself voluntarily to French leadership for the Allied cause. Establishing such an intimate relationship would redound to the "supreme military advantage" of the Allies.[175]

On 4 April (Easter Sunday), Esher presented his plan in person to Sir John. With obvious reluctance, Sir John "agreed in principle" to sending a "conciliatory" letter to Joffre, and commissioned Esher to write a draft of it in French, but made no promise to send it.[176] Having the upper hand on the issue, at least momentarily, and with the apparent backing of Kitchener, Sir John was unlikely to give way.

Esher's project in the final analysis proved to be stillborn. While Kitchener dealt privately with the French on the command issue, without involving his cabinet colleagues, it was now Esher's turn to talk privately with the prime minister and to speak "much more freely" than he had with Kitchener. "I told him what I did not tell K," Esher wrote to Sir John on 12 April, "that I hoped you would write a nice letter to Joffre. He was keen about it and said it might do good, and could do no harm."[177] The draft letter that Esher forwarded to Sir John on 12 April as the basis of his letter to Joffre reaffirmed Sir John's independence of command but assured Joffre of British cooperation in the forthcoming offensive and "unity of action." Effusive, even garish, in its attempt to be French, it contained extravagant expressions such as "I embrace you with all my heart." In Asquith's words, it was "a fine full-blooded composition suited to the digestion of those for whom it was intended."[178] But the project does not appear to have been endorsed by Sir John. That no copy of the letter is found in Joffre's "strictly personal" file provides circumstantial evidence that it was never sent,[179] suggesting that in both content and language it was unacceptable to Sir John.

Nor was any progress made on the diplomatic front, as Delcassé "continued to discuss the question of the command through Cambon, the French ambassador in London. Growing impatient with the lack of results, Millerand wrote a personal letter to Cambon on 14 April in which he urged that "in the interest of common operations" the question be resolved "according to logic and good sense by the end of the month."[180]

The benefits of a unified command, which would provide greater effectiveness in the planning of operations and closer coordination in their execution, were all too apparent. The disjointed nature of Anglo-French operational planning and the lack of integration of forces on the battlefield had been clearly demonstrated, adding to the philosophical arguments in favour of a unified command. But having a unified command under French leadership, as a means of resolving disputes between the two commands, raised immediate fears of French domination and control of the BEF, which the British were not willing to countenance at this point. The question was very sensitive.

Both Kitchener and Sir John rejected the notion of a unified command, each for his own reasons. Sir John's ongoing mistrust of the French was a significant factor. If for no other reason than preservation of the independence of his command, a unified command under French leadership was anathema to him. Kitchener's reasons were more political, outweighing the benefits of a unified command for joint operation, which he acknowledged. Only slowly did the French begin to realize that the demand for Sir John's subordination ran counter to the whole idea of limited British commitment to the continent and British independence of action, particularly at a time when the British were planning a major diversion to the Dardanelles. Nor did Kitchener, as indicated in his discussion with Sir John French, have any confidence in the success of the joint spring offensive to break through the German line. Neither Kitchener nor Sir John, in the final analysis, was willing to relinquish even partial control of the British Expeditionary Force to the French. Joint military planning and the conduct of combined operations thus continued on an ad hoc consultative basis and were denied the benefits that a unified command would have provided.

PLANNING THE JOINT OFFENSIVE

The discussions on the question of a unified command, however, do not appear to have materially hampered the effectiveness of joint military planning. While Sir John French was "again suspicious of Joffre" on 1 April,[181] by the 5th he was fully prepared to cooperate with Foch's plan. To a high degree, a clear understanding between Kitchener and Sir John materially benefited the latter's relationship with the French. With the requisite definition of support from Kitchener, who ultimately controlled British grand strategy, Sir John was able to make firm commitments to the French regarding operational plans. In agreeing fully to the French plan, Sir John, moreover, despite his reluctance to admit the principle, effectively subordinated himself to French operational direction.

The planning process thereafter went relatively smoothly. There were minor irritations. On 3 April, for example, Foch was somewhat disappointed that the partial British attack in support of the French attack at Woevre, then beginning, would be limited to an artillery action of the First Army about Neuve Chapelle.[182] Though Sir John readily acceded on 5 April to Foch's plan for the spring offensive,[183] planning the details of its execution led to a minor squabble as Wilson objected to having the French and British attack side by side, fearing that a breakdown in the timing of the attacks could foil the plan. Foch amended his plan accordingly to have "a portion of the French XXI Corps sitting quietly in its trenches doing nothing" between the contiguous attacks.[184]

But neither Robertson nor Sir John were happy with the troop dispositions in Foch's plan. "It seems to be impossible to arrive at any satisfactory joint plan of attack with the French," wrote Sir John in his diary on 8 April. "I suppose, as usual, "we shall have to do our best *in our own way* & 'take our own line' and trust to them to co-operate with us to the best advantage."[185] But a further explanation by Foch convinced the British chief that the French plan was "quite satisfactory."[186] Thereafter nothing more serious than Foch's complaints about the slowness of the British preparation[187] and Sir John's fears of French delays until Italian entry into the war[188] would mar the planning process. Given the previously failed state of joint command relations, these were minor irritants of limited importance.

The basic solvent in Allied command relations was Joffre's unbounded confidence in the success of the new offensive plan. That expectation ran equally rampant at British headquarters, where Robertson and Wilson expressed their mutual delight on 10 April at the strength of the forces to be engaged. "We have 10 divisions and 600 guns of which 100 are heavy," wrote Wilson. "Foch has 14 divisions and 950 guns, of which 230 are heavy. I can't help thinking we ought to succeed." According to British intelligence, there were only 180,000 Germans on the line "from Ypres to the southern point of the Tenth Army," while the British and French planned to attack with 300,000 men on a small portion of this line" and, according to Wilson, "had ample men over to hold the rest."[189] In a long talk with Foch, Wilson opined that, once the line was broken, the fighting might become "one of localities" and cavalry might be "pushed through" to seize Douai or even Valenciennes and thereby oblige a "general retirement" of that part of the German line.[190]

CONCLUSION

Following the low point in an Anglo-French command relations, resulting in the unsustained British attack at Neuve Chapelle, the two commands took steps to improve relations. In this instance, Wilson, who understood both points of view, played a significant role in mediating the conflict. Both commands, despite their differences, were united in their demands for more British troops on the Western Front and in their opposition to the Dardanelles adventure.

With Kitchener's promise of two more territorial divisions in a conference between Kitchener, Millerand, and the military commanders at French headquarters on 29 March 1915, Sir John agreed to fulfill his commitments to relieve the disputed French trenches, effectively defusing the conflict that had led to the isolated British attack at Neuve Chapelle. Sir John and Kitchener, in a series of private meetings, also resolved in large measure the misunderstanding that underlay Sir John's uncooperative attitude toward the French. One of Sir John's tasks was to persuade Kitchener regarding the need for unprecedented quantities of ammunition in trench warfare, at a time when British productive capacity was hampered by labour shortages.

Other issues remained more intractable: the British request for the use of Dunkirk as a port and the French demand for a unified command to eliminate British independent-mindedness and resistance to Joffre's plans. The port issue, which turned on Joffre and the French government's secret desire to hold onto Dunkirk as a means of maintaining control of Belgium and the Belgian Army, was resolved on the basis of military considerations and the technical shipping needs of the British, who were granted a larger portion of Calais' capacity and promised other more remote bases, if needed.

Out of sensitivity to Sir John, the question of a unified command, which appeared to have Kitchener's initial support, involved a long discussion between Kitchener and Millerand in which Kitchener finally revealed his initial instructions to Sir John to act in cooperation with the French but as an independent force. Always mistrustful of the French, Sir John, who was implicated in the discussion through Wilson and Esher, proved very jealous of his authority and was wholly resistant to the idea of a unified command. Kitchener understood the benefits of an overall Entente strategy, which he suggested Joffre try to implement. He also understood the benefits of unified command on the Western Front in terms of a coordinated action. But he was obviously more anxious to retain strategic control of British forces, especially with the looming deployment of British troops to the Dardanelles. As his discussion with Sir John indicated, Kitchener had no confidence in Joffre and Sir John's joint offensive to break through. This undoubtedly further dampened his initial support for a unified command.

The most fundamental question, that of the future deployment of the British New Armies, which Asquith had forbidden Kitchener to discuss with the French, remained unresolved. All that Kitchener was able to promise was that he would not send to the Dardanelles more than the 67,000 British troops already earmarked for that purpose.

The most powerful ingredient for improved Allied command relations was Joffre's new plan for a combined spring offensive, which he averred, with unbounded optimism, would pierce the German line and lead to a decisive victory. But the bubble of enthusiasm on which joint cooperation was based would be dampened by the German gas attack at Ypres. And the grim reality of trench warfare in the joint Artois offensive in the spring would shatter the dream of a strategic breakthrough and once again imperil the very fragile state of Anglo-French command relations and Sir John's improved relationship with Kitchener. Failure in the spring offensive would likewise raise anew, with greater poignancy, the question of Anglo-French command relations and bring to the fore the broader issue of Entente strategy and the overall direction of the war.

CHAPTER FIVE

Second Ypres and Joint Planning for the Artois Offensive, 22 April–8 May 1915

THE LONG PERIOD OF ALLIED PLANNING from the middle of December 1914 through to the spring campaign season of 1915 had yielded significant conflict – mainly because the British quest for a more effective place to deploy their growing forces than in the trenches of the Western Front clashed with the French strategy of driving the Germans out of France and supporting the Russians, their prime ally. The independent British action at Neuve Chapelle on 10 March marked a low point as Sir John refused to relieve French trenches and the French Army gave only token support to his offensive. But a visit by Kitchener to France with the promise of reinforcements, and an unduly optimistic assessment by Joffre that he could break through the German lines without full British support, paved the way for renewed cooperation in planning the major joint offensive in Artois for the spring.

However, there was an unforeseen disruption. Prior to the proposed offensive, the Germans launched a gas attack at Ypres that lay raw old wounds in command relations in advance of the major offensive in Artois, which itself proved singularly unsuccessful. The vast readjustments at multiple levels that followed the failed Artois offensive changed much of the Allied political and military landscape of the war, as subsequent chapters will show.[1]

According to Clausewitz, the immediate aim of battle is to destroy the enemy's "centre of gravity," which he defined as any object the loss of which would necessitate capitulation. The "centre of gravity" could be the main army in the field, public opinion, vital territory, the enemy's capital, or, in coalition warfare, the opposing coalition. In the latter case, the "bond uniting the enemy alliance" was a "legitimate military objective" which might be imperilled by an attack on one of the enemy armies or at the juncture of Allied enemy armies.[2] The German offensive on the Somme in March 1918 will readily be recognized as a nearly successful application of this dictum. The Second Battle of Ypres, on the other hand, has been dealt with largely in terms of the first major application of chemical warfare[3]; and Canadians have been particularly proud of the tenacious resistance of the First Canadian Division in this baptism of fire.[4] But the full impact of the battle on Anglo-French command relationships has not been fully considered.[5]

To what extent did this attack at the juncture of Anglo-French forces, like the later one in 1918, place important stresses on Anglo-French command relations? And what was its impact on the planning of the joint spring offensive in Artois and the ability of the Allied commanders to carry it to a successful conclusion? This chapter will address both questions.

THE GERMAN GAS ATTACK AT YPRES

On the afternoon of 22 April, clouds of greenish-yellow chlorine gas released from thousands of storage cylinders floated over the French lines on the northern arc of the Ypres salient between Steenstraat and Langemarck. Taken with panic, the French 45th Division of Algerian troops and the French 87th Territorial Division between the Belgians on the left and the British on their right abandoned their trenches on a front of four and a half miles and fell back more than three miles, leaving a gaping hole in the line.

Fortunately for the Allies, German use of the experimental gas had only the limited objective of taking the Pilckem heights overlooking Ypres, with the possibility of reducing the Ypres salient. The breach in the line was not vigorously exploited. The German High Command had a few days earlier decided to go on the defensive in the west and to launch a major offensive in the east to assist the Austrians, hard pressed by the Russian advance in the Carpathians. The gas attack at Ypres was intended primarily to mask the diversion of eight German divisions to Galicia.[6]

Ypres, an historic Belgian cloth-making town with several ornate stone buildings, was an important communications centre for the Allies. A railhead of several lines converged at Poperinghe, eight miles to the west.

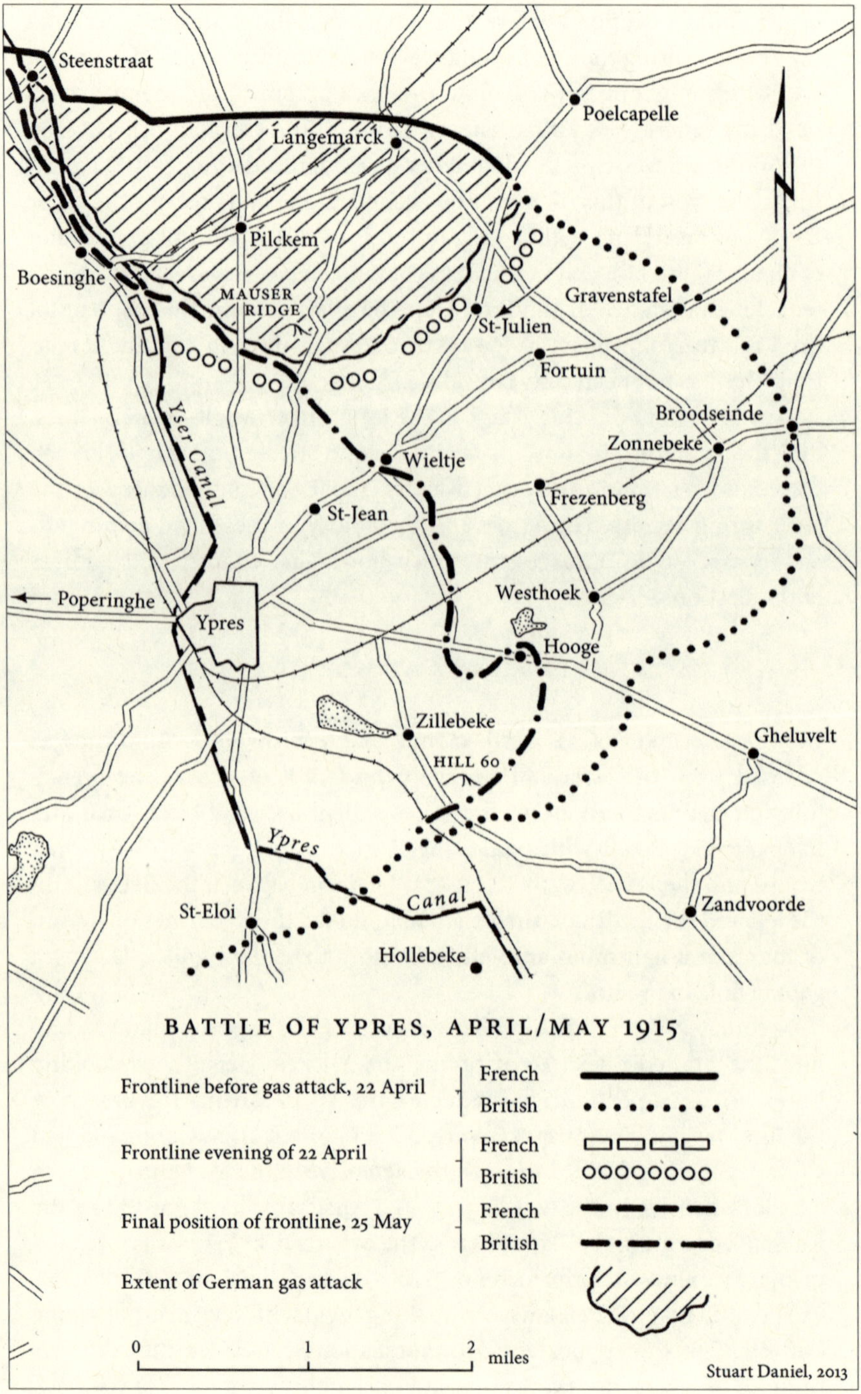

BATTLE OF YPRES, APRIL/MAY 1915

The preservation of the Ypres salient was thus of considerable importance to the Allies throughout the war. Its loss in the first Battle of Ypres in 1914, it was feared, would open the doorway to a German advance to the English Channel.[7]

The German use of gas at Ypres on 22 April 1915 came as a short, "sharp surprise" to the Allies,[8] a "bolt from the blue," in Sir John's words,[9] as previous warnings from intelligence information on an impending gas attack, mostly from Belgian sources, had been largely discounted.[10] "The troops are all scared with these 'gas' rumours," Sir John wrote to Mrs Bennett after the first gas attack. "The Germans have used it and stupified all the men in the trenches before they came in. What infernal Devils they are." The use of gas, he contended, was "quite contrary to the Hague & Geneva Conventions."[11]

The breach in the French line left British forces in a dangerously exposed forward position. The adjoining Canadian Division of the British Second Army had only one week earlier taken up the line from the French in the salient. The Canadians launched counter-attacks in the night toward Saint-Julien to cover the exposed British left flank.[12] By next morning, both British and French commands had prepared counter-offensives with available forces to stabilize the front, demonstrating the underlying military solidarity that almost always prevailed among the Allies in a crisis.[13]

At 11:00 A.M. on 23 April, Sir John went to see Foch, who told him that he had ordered in forces from Nieuport and one division (153) from the French Tenth Army at Saint-Pol. During the day, Horace Smith-Dorrien, commanding the British Second Army, sent in units of the 5th and 28th divisions "between the Canadians & the French" and made "some little progress," while Sir John ordered the British Cavalry Corps to the area as a reserve.[14] By the end of the day, Foch was able to report to Joffre that "we now have at present all the means to take a vigorous offensive tomorrow with the aim of seriously retaking the lost terrain." "A perfect and active understanding has not ceased to reign between all the Allied armies."[15]

RECRIMINATIONS

Sir John French, on the other hand, took a much less generous view of the situation. On 24 April he "complained" to Huguet of the "horrible mistake which had been made by General Foch & [Victor] d'Urbal with General Joffre's sanction – in leaving the line so weak and unguarded."

Thinking the French mission, which had no new information on what "steps were being taken at once to restore the situation in the line held by the French and to secure the ground between me and the Belgians," was "treating the whole thing very casually," Sir John "got really angry" and "spoke [his] mind fully." As a result, Huguet hurried off to see Foch, who himself came by later in the day to see Sir John and told him that an additional division (152) had been ordered up and a third (18) "was held in readiness to come if wanted." These divisions, he said, would be in a position to attack the next day, or the day after at the latest.[16] Sir John, in addition to being "annoyed with the French (with reason)," noted Clive, was "also afraid they will ask him to take back the ground they have lost; he says he won't do this, & if they insist he will take troops away from his right [designated for the forthcoming attack]."[17]

The breach in the French line reopened all the old wounds in Sir John's relationship with the French dating back to the rejected Zeebrugge plan and the subsequent quarrel over taking up the French trenches. "Although the gas, no doubt, had something to do with the panic, this would never have happened," Sir John reported to Kitchener, "if the French had not weakened their line a great deal too much, and it was in the fear of something of this kind that I was so averse to relieving their 9th and 20th Corps until I am stronger." He also expressed fears that the coming offensive would, as a result, be delayed "by several days."[18] Yarde-Buller reported to Kitchener from French headquarters in a similar vein. The French "made a great deal" of reports of six hundred French soldiers being suffocated, but he suspected that this might be only an excuse for the failure. The real problem, he said, was French failure to leave adequate support behind the lines taken over from the French IX and XX Corps.[19]

On 24 April the Germans launched a gas attack on the Canadians, who, under heavy artillery fire, gave some ground but maintained the forward British position.[20] Canadian losses were "very heavy" – already "over 5000," Wilson noted on 25 April, out of a total of 11,000 engaged.[21] In Wilson's view, the British also had made the mistake of not maintaining sufficient reserves in the northern Ypres salient.[22] They therefore had few forces available to bring to the immediate aid of the Canadians. As Robertson noted, "the Canadians got well hit before we could help much, & we had to put in anything we could scrape up."[23]

Sir John French's anger with the French thus reached a crescendo on 25 April. "He is furious with *Foch* & Joffre & all Frenchmen!" Wilson recorded. "He says they always let him in [down] (at Mons, on the Aisne & now) & that our Ministers are right & we ought to clear out of France bag & baggage & go elsewhere! Where he did not know!"[24] In this outburst, Sir John would have agreed totally with Mikhnevich's dictum that, in a coalition, "allies will strive to shift the heaviest burdens on to other shoulders."[25] Ironically, Sir John's statement was made on the same day Sir Ian Hamilton successfully launched British troops on the Gallipoli peninsula.

Robertson, who, unlike his chief, was not noted for intemperate outbursts, expressed views similar to those of Sir John on French performance. In a letter to Callwell of the same date, he summed up the entire experience: "We have been terribly let down by those d—d Frenchmen," he wrote. "2 whole divisions on a front of 4 1/2 miles went back – straight 4 or 5 miles. Some went nearer 20. One lot bagged an officer's motor in Ypres and went off in it! Complete debacle & panic of the worst kind." This, he said, left the British line "entirely exposed." "The Canadians had to pull out to their left & hold what they could of the vacated front and bear the full brunt of the attack until the next day. We were not in a position to reinforce them with much until the next day, as of course we had not spare reserves to make good French fugitives." His further complaint was that "the French as yet have done *nothing* to regain the lost ground or help us except send up 2 Divisions which as yet have not been in action." "We have had the choice of d—d hard fighting to get back what the French lost," he concluded, "or of retiring out of the salient," a dilemma he viewed as "disgusting."[26]

In Sir John's view, the responsibility to recapture the lost trenches lay with the French alone. "I saw S[mith] D[orrien] this afternoon," he wrote on 25 April, "and gave him full instructions. He is to understand it is the role of the French *entirely* to take back the lost trenches. Our role is to support and assist them in doing so, whilst we also insure the recovery of *our own line*."[27] Smith-Dorrien, however, indiscreetly relayed this message to French General Henri-Gabriel Putz, commanding the French forces in the salient, "in language which seemed to imply" that the British "should not give the French effective support," and when Foch heard of this he asked Sir John "to put it right."[28] Two days later, for this indiscretion and other operational deficiencies, including promoting the idea of withdrawing from the salient, Sir John removed the troops in the salient from Smith-Dorrien's command and put them in a special group under

Herbert Plumer, commander of V Corps in the British Second Army, which would report directly to British headquarters.[29] A few days later, on 7 May, Smith-Dorrien was sent home and Plumer replaced him as commander of the Second Army.[30]

PLANNING THE JOINT OFFENSIVE

The German gas attack at Ypres put considerable stress on Anglo-French planning for the Allied joint offensive. On 22 April, before learning of the gas attack, Sir John recorded that Foch, who came to see him that afternoon, was "very sanguine about the coming operation & hopes for great things."[31] Foch, who found Sir John "in very good humour," in fact had just returned from seeing the Belgian king, who was already considering possible actions to aid the Allied offensive. "Excellent intentions, but hell is paved with them," wrote Foch to Joffre, with some cynicism. [32] The purpose of Foch's visit to British headquarters was to relay Joffre's suggestion that the joint offensive be delayed for a few days so as to accumulate the means to strike "bigger and harder" and also to arrange for a conference between Sir John and Joffre on 26 April. In reporting his efforts, Foch further requested an additional army corps from Joffre for the attack of the Tenth Army under d'Urbal, whom he lauded for the cogency of his ideas and his "discernment," "judgement," and "authority."[33]

Joffre's response to the German attack at Ypres on 23 April was first to congratulate Foch on the rapid measures taken to restore the situation and to authorize use of the newly formed units of the Tenth Army reserves to retake the lost trenches and, if possible, go beyond.[34] On 24 April Foch was told "he could have all the men and ammunition he wishes." The next day, Clive found "GQG quite happy about the French attack, and ready to alter their plans to suit the German convenience."[35] The view was apparently gaining ground that the offensive was now becoming more costly than the defensive, and that attacks were now proving more costly than the measures taken in response.

Despite the strains in Allied relations introduced by the German gas attack at Ypres, the meeting of 26 April passed off relatively well as the commanders focused their attention on the forthcoming joint offensive north of Arras. The meeting consisted of Joffre, Foch, Huguet, Sir John, and Wilson. First of all, Joffre soothed the ruffled feathers at British headquarters by thanking Sir John "for the support" the British "had rendered to the French troops in their recent troubles." As a result of the German offensive at Ypres, Joffre thought that "the Arras-La Bassée attack" would now have to be delayed, but "as little as possible," and put forward 6–8 May "as tentative dates." Sir John indicated his willingness to engage in the attack "at any time after the Ypres situation was restored."[36]

For the British, guaranteeing the future security of the Ypres salient had become an important issue. The three divisions sent to the Yser, Joffre asserted, were those he had intended to send to Castelnau for his attack. To satisfy the English need for security, he proposed "leaving 1, 2, or all 3 of these Divisions up North." On the immediate strategy at Ypres, "Foch said he considered it absolutely necessary to regain our old line of trenches ... to retain the Ypres salient," to which Sir John agreed. Joffre also relayed the happy news from Poincaré that "Italy was on the point of coming in" and mistakenly that Romania "would also join."[37] The discussion thus came to a seemingly happy meeting of minds. What had not been resolved, as Wilson ruefully observed, was how to proceed if the French attacks of that afternoon and subsequently were to prove unsuccessful.[38]

SHORTENING THE LINE

The crisis came on 28 April. On that date, following a day of unavailing French and British attacks,[39] Sir John French decided that he was not going to commit his reserves to regain the salient, and that if the French were not able to advance, he would withdraw from the exposed British salient and assume a shorter line in front of Ypres. That alternative had been on Robertson's mind since 26 April[40] and had entailed "a good deal of discussion" at British headquarters on the use of British reserves,[41] with Wilson advocating their engagement and Robertson being opposed.[42] On 27 April, "Smith Dorrien wrote a long and pessimistic letter about the situation," noting that "he didn't expect to get on," that the German line was "too strong," and that "he was contemplating a retirement to a short line ... in front of Ypres."[43] That report apparently tipped the balance at British headquarters. Not only did French failure to retake their lines make the forward British position difficult to hold and maintain, it raised for Sir John French the additional bogey that if the French were driven out of their new positions, the British would risk being cut off.[44]

The issue led to a considerable row with Foch and Wilson on one side and Robertson and Sir John on the other, and a serious fallout between Robertson and Wilson. While Foch, whom Wilson saw in the evening of 27 April, agreed that the Germans needed to be pushed back to their old trenches, he ultimately was not prepared to commit "the heaps of guns & ammunition" of the Allies and "attack everywhere" along the front as Wilson proposed, but continued to focus on the future joint offensive north of Arras and on small offensives with limited objectives in the Ypres salient.[45] Wilson, nonetheless, argued at British headquarters on the morning of the 28th that "as long as the enemy remained where he was on the N., no shorter line was tenable, as it would be raked from end to end & the Poperinghe-Ypres road would be useless to us." In his view, a shorter line would lead to the loss of Ypres. But neither Sir John nor Robertson was convinced; the latter, particularly, thought a shorter line could be held and favoured "retirement if the French don't get success today or tomorrow."[46] Robertson, of course, was right and made a good judgment call on the issue, not falling prey to the German trap by committing major forces to repel a secondary attack. Wilson, more French than the French, found himself advocating a stance beyond that which Foch was prepared to take and was marginalized at British headquarters.

The dispute came to a head at a meeting between Sir John and Foch at Cassel on 28 April, attended by Robertson, Wilson, Foch, Weygand, Foch's chief of staff, and Huguet. Sir John "complained of the delay the French were making in their forward movement to retake the line" and that his troops were tired and his logistics difficult, and warned Foch that "unless a substantial advance was made immediately," he would be obliged to withdraw from the forward line he was holding to a shorter line, Fortuin-Frezenberg-Westhoek.[47] In Sir John's view, the "big business" was the forthcoming battle north of Arras, and he did not wish to "compromise it in using up his reserves around Ypres." Foch, on the other hand, resisted any idea of British withdrawal to a shorter line, arguing that the withdrawal would expose the Ypres-Poperinghe road to enemy artillery fire and that the new line would be subject to enemy fire from the crests to the east and northeast of Ypres and could not be held. While acknowledging that the major priority was the forthcoming battle north of Arras, he argued that "it is a deplorable tactic to accept losing a first battle, in order to win a second one." He therefore would mount new attacks the next day in the French sector from west on the Yser Canal to the east toward Langemarck, using heavy artillery, and asked Sir John to assist him. Non-committal on the amount of support he could give, the marshal nonetheless agreed to delay his retreat a day pending the French attack.[48]

Following the conversation, Foch sent Sir John a note describing in the darkest terms the consequence of British withdrawal to the shorter line. In his report to Joffre, Foch described his ploy. Even if the projected attack toward Langemarck failed to yield any serious success, his tactic was simply to "buy time in maintaining the English on their current line," and later as long as possible on the line to which they planned to retreat, until the joint offensive north of Arras began. Foch, in fact, acknowledged to Joffre that he had painted the consequences of the British retiring to a shorter line "darker" than he actually thought, since the Germans, except for the use of gas, were not pushing their attacks.[49] Rather than request further French reinforcements to retake the salient, Foch planned "to try to convince the Marshal of the necessity for the English to make a violent effort to reestablish the situation."[50]

The tentative arrangement worked out on 28 April was compromised in the evening, however, when Wilson brought word from Foch that delays in the arrival of heavy field artillery would postpone the French attack for yet another day, until 30 April.[51] That news, as Wilson recorded, led Sir John to "one of the worst explosions ag[ains]t the French I ever heard."[52] Perplexed as to his future course, Sir John, accompanied by Wilson, went to see Foch again the next day at Cassel, and "once more pressed on him the absolute necessity of an immediate and successful movement."[53] Sir John's initial stance had been to order the withdrawal of his line at once. But more amenable to Foch's arguments in the absence of Robertson, Sir John agreed to participate with the French in the attack on the 30th, and to postpone his withdrawal until the results of that engagement were known.[54]

Kitchener, for his part, expressed his satisfaction on 28 April that Joffre did not intend to delay the joint offensive and was mainly concerned that the French, wanting to recover the troops engaged at Ypres, might delay their big offensive and thus lose the initiative to the enemy, who might again attack elsewhere.[55] With that urging, Sir John hardened his position toward the French and, on the morning of 30 April, spelled out his position in a letter to Foch. "In effect," wrote Wilson, "it amounted to this[:] that the French broke because they had too few troops, although he (Sir J) had constantly pointed this out; that the French had said they would attack before yesterday & yesterday but had not done so, and that if the attack today was not successful he would commence his retirement tonight."[56]

"Unless a substantial advance is made to-day, I must commence to withdraw from the Salient," Sir John wrote to Kitchener. "The troops there are in the most exposed and dangerous situation which has caused me deep anxiety." "What angers me so is that all this might have been entirely avoided if Joffre had not withdrawn so many troops and left the line so weak." This he considered unacceptable. "I warned him over & over again about it," he continued, "and I hear Foch did also, but he wouldn't listen." Astutely, Sir John used the occasion of his misunderstanding with the French to request New Army reinforcements from Kitchener. "I am eagerly looking forward to the arrival of the new Army, which will enable us to do something solid and substantial without having to depend upon their caprices & delay."[57] But a visit by Foch at 4:00 P.M. and glowing reports of initial French success caused him to delay his retreat yet another day.[58]

The breakdown came on 1 May 1915, when the French failed to join in a planned joint attack at the juncture of their forces. "I am very much inclined to think that it was never intended by him [Foch] that they should attack and that the French have been playing a game of theirs over all this time," Sir John wrote in his diary. Thus, despite a further note from Foch urging that the British retreat be delayed as much as possible, Sir John notified Foch in writing of his intention to withdraw to the new line.[59] Foch, however, did not seem to be terribly upset when they met at 5:00 P.M. on 1 May. "After some display of apprehension as to the effects of our retirement (which I think was rather assumed for effect), he seemed to agree and proceeded to discuss seriously our joint plans for the big attack."[60] The British withdrawal to the new line was carried out in stages on the nights of 1–2 and 3–4 May.[61]

Sir John's letter to Kitchener on 2 May described the pain in the relationship as the focus now shifted to planning the details of the forthcoming joint offensive north of Arras. The fighting at Ypres, Sir John said, had been limited to German shelling since 29 April, and in his opinion the Germans had abandoned their main thrust in the theatre. "The French have practically ceased to make any further serious attempt to regain the old line of trenches," he reported. He thus indicated it had become necessary to retire his forward line, a move that was then in progress, some 2,500 yards on the east end of the salient (to the line Fortuin-Hill 60). "In view of the supine attitude adopted by the French, no other course is possible for us," he wrote. "Altho they moved 3 Divisions up here from Arras they have done very little with them" beyond stabilizing the line north of Ypres and pushing the enemy back about a mile east of the Yser Canal. His explanation of French performance showed the lack of confidence in the relationship. "I think when their troops lost the trenches in the first instance they didn't think that the British troops would be able to make so firm a stand: This, and the fact that they felt rather ashamed of themselves, caused them to make a show of trying to do a thing which they never really intended. They are really most difficult and unsatisfactory people to work with."[62]

RESERVE FORCES TO GUARD AGAINST A FUTURE EVENTUALITY

The aftermath of the Ypres imbroglio was that on 2 May, when Foch and Sir John met to plan details of the Arras attack, Sir John strenuously resisted Joffre's plan to go on the defensive at Ypres and to divert troops from the Ypres salient for the Arras offensive. The British government, Sir John told Foch, "was much disturbed with the recent fighting & were anxious about our left." Sir John thus made adequate French reserves at Ypres a condition for his engaging in the forthcoming offensive.[63] "I have spoken very seriously to [Foch] about recent events," he reported to Kitchener, "and have warned him that if this part of the line to the North of us is in my opinion not left sufficiently strong (with a good deal 'to spare' in view of possible 'gas' annoyances), I shall abandon my support of *him* in the big crunch and reinforce my left. I have told him emphatically that I shall do this without a moment's hesitation, without any further warning to him, if he let me in again."[64] While Foch insisted on directing one division toward Arras, he promised to leave three regular divisions in addition to the 87th Territorial Division in reserve in the salient.[65] On this point, Sir John was so anxious that on 3 May he spelled out to Foch in writing that, as condition for British participation in the joint offensive, three regular French divisions would need to be maintained to secure the British left flank at Ypres and the division next to the British could not be a colonial one.[66] The latter provision reflected Sir John view, reinforced by the previous experience, that French colonial divisions were less reliable than regular French divisions. Joffre formally agreed to these conditions on 5 May.[67]

By the beginning of May, as the first phase of the hard-fought Second Battle of Ypres drew to a close, much of the goodwill and trust that had prevailed between the French and British commands ten days earlier had evaporated with the renewal of acrimony and distrust in the relationship. The timing could not have been worse for allies preparing a major joint operation. The practical result was that French forces in reserve behind Ypres were lost to the forthcoming offensive. In retrospect, Sir John French did not need to draw on French reserves to repel successive German attacks on British trenches. These, however, prolonged the battle of Ypres until 25 May, making it the longest British battle on the Western Front in 1915.[68] Given the lack of French aggressiveness in retaking lost ground in the sector, and the repeated German attacks on the British sector of the line, one can well appreciate Sir John's concern about guarding the salient without French troops in reserve.

At British headquarters, working relationships between Wilson and Robertson were also badly strained. For several days the two had been at loggerheads over the question of engaging British reserves to retake the Ypres salient or withdrawing to a shorter line. Another irritant was Wilson's suggestion in the meeting with Foch on 2 May that the British extend their line about 2,400 yards to the Yser Canal as "a better point of juncture" with the French, a suggestion "not at all approved by Sir J[ohn] or by R[obertson]."[69] "Almost openly hostile" in his attitude to Wilson, Robertson considered him "pro-French and anti-English," while Wilson considered Robertson "openly anti-French."[70] The relationship was further aggravated by what Wilson considered Robertson's unfair treatment of Lieutenant-Colonel Frederick Cavendish, a British liaison officer at French headquarters, "for having told" Wilson of problems relating to what Wilson considered "bad liaison work with the French."[71] The issue of Wilson's subordination came to the fore in a clash between the two on 6 May in which Wilson asserted that, following the terms of their appointment in January-February, neither one was subordinate to the other.[72] Their relationship remained strained for some time to come, each regarding the other with suspicion, and was a further source of difficulty in Anglo-French coordination.

Starting on 22 April and extending in its various phases until 25 May, the Second Battle of Ypres was the longest and second most expensive British battle of 1915, costing nearly 60,000 casualties – falling just short of the Battle of Loos with 62,000. The Germans had 35,000 casualties. It was largely a British battle, with limited French support; the French had 40,000 casualties on all fronts in April 1915.[73] With sixteen divisions in the Ypres salient, the British rendered considerable service to the Allied cause in opposing eleven and a half German divisions. The evidence would suggest that Foch's admittedly half-hearted support in the battle came at a very high cost in Allied relationships, in what for the British command was a very serious situation, leading to the immobilization of three French divisions in the forthcoming Artois offensive.[74]

ARTOIS: LAST MINUTE GLITCHES

The usual problems in the field, irritating but of no great significance, arose as the Allied attempted to synchronize their attack plans for the Artois offensive. On 5 May, Joffre, while praising British action at Ypres, confirmed his intention to attack on the 7th and asked the British to proceed with their attack on the 8th. To this the British command agreed, despite the loss of Hill 60 near Saint-Eloi on 5 May.[75] At the same time, Joffre asked the Belgians to engage in military activity on their front during the offensive, which they agreed to do.[76] On 6 May 1915 Joffre left Chantilly for temporary headquarters at Doullens, near the front, to supervise the offensive personally.[77]

But a series of delays set in as the French on 6 May postponed their attack to 8 May because of fog in the Arras area, which prevented them from firing their artillery and observing the results to make further corrections. The British and the French would thus attack simultaneously on the 8th.[78] Despite two visits of Foch to Sir John's forward headquarters at Hazebrouck on the 7th to deal with the delay,[79] a misunderstanding arose on the British part over the precise nature of French orders regarding the length of bombardment and preliminary operations. Wilson soon settled the issue by having Foch reaffirm his revised plan to engage in one day of bombardment, and then have all of the Allied infantry attack, rather

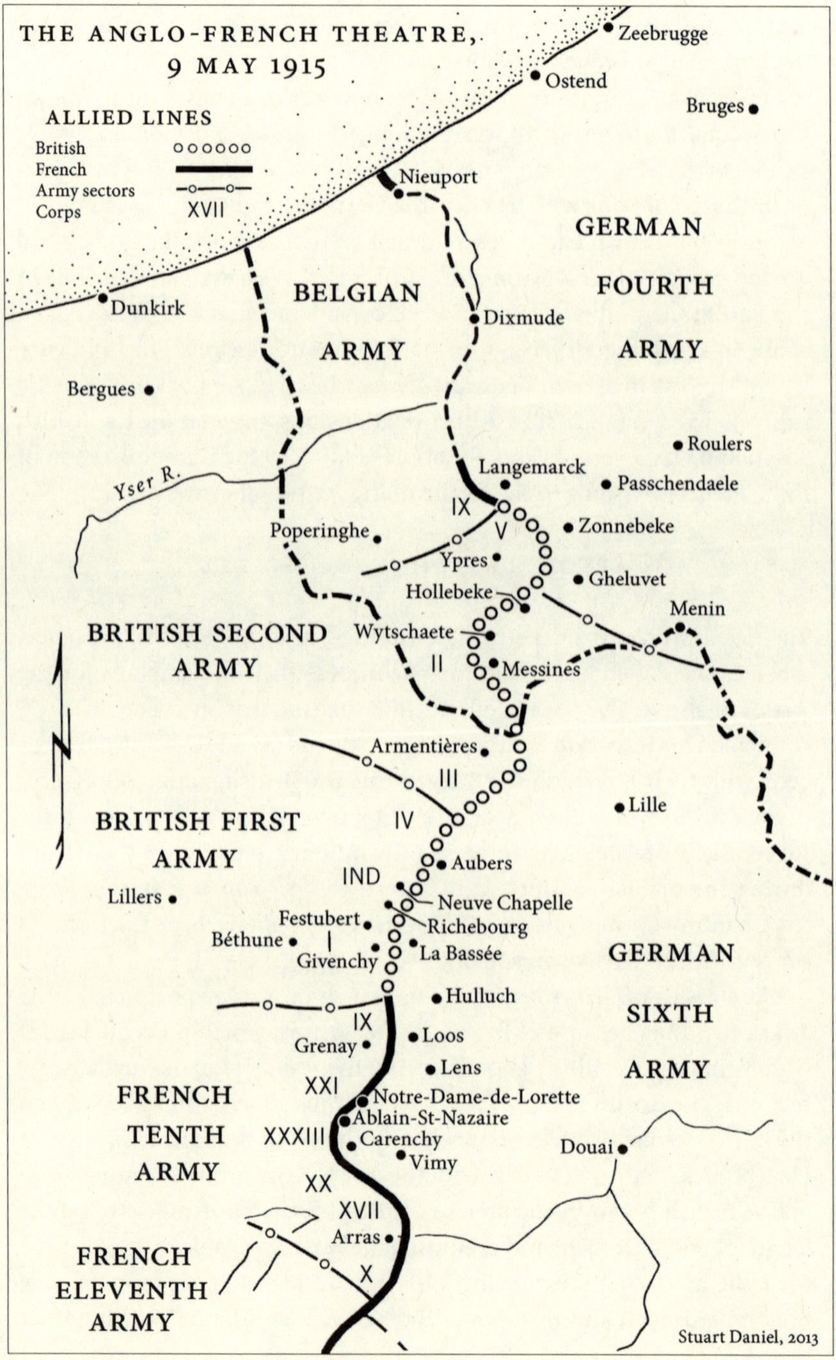

THE ANGLO-FRENCH THEATRE,
9 MAY 1915
ALLIED LINES
British
French
Army sectors
Corps
XVII
Zeebrugge
Ostend
Bruges
Nieuport
GERMAN
FOURTH
ARMY
BELGIAN
ARMY
Dunkirk
Dixmude
Bergues
Yser R.
Roulers
Langemarck
Passchendaele
IX
V
Zonnebeke
Poperinghe
Ypres
Gheluvet
Hollebeke
Menin
Wytschaete
BRITISH SECOND
ARMY
II
Messines
Armentières
III
Lille
BRITISH FIRST
ARMY
IV
Aubers
IND
Lillers
Neuve Chapelle
Festubert
Richebourg
Béthune
I
Givenchy
La Bassée
GERMAN
SIXTH
ARMY
Hulluch
IX
Loos
Grenay
Lens
FRENCH
TENTH
ARMY
XXI
Notre-Dame-de-Lorette
Ablain-St-Nazaire
XXXIII
Carenchy
Vimy
Douai
XX
XVII
Arras
FRENCH
ELEVENTH
ARMY
X
Stuart Daniel, 2013

than have an intervening French attack on Notre-Dame-de-Lorette, as originally envisioned. But, owing to thundershowers and mist, the combined Allied attack had to be delayed yet another day to 9 May.[80]

RELATIONSHIPS AND EXPECTATIONS ON THE EVE OF BATTLE

As the great battle approached, Anglo-French command relations seemed to be on the mend. "We continue to act in total accord with our friends," Foch reported to Joffre on 7 May, noting at the same time that Joffre's complimentary letter to Sir John of 5 May, following the strained relations of the Second Battle of Ypres, had "produced an excellent effect."[81] There remained a deep undercurrent of mistrust at British headquarters, however, with Robertson deeply suspicious of French intentions, and he and Wilson still not having totally resolved their spat over their approach to the French and still eyeing each other warily.[82]

While Kitchener and Sir John had been at each other's throats over the employment to be made of Kitchener's New Armies in early January 1915[83] and Kitchener's actions in support of the Dardanelles, and while other issues were the subject of frequent explosions on the part of Sir John French, relations, as indicated in the last chapter, had begun to improve markedly between them in March and April 1915. They had met in a series of secret meetings, the first for dinner aboard a ship at Dover on 23 March, and then for breakfast twice in York House, London, on 31 March and 14 April.[84] These meetings had led to growing confidence between the two, a point not generally appreciated in the literature.

The rapprochement worked to the extent that Sir John, in a meeting with Kitchener on a ship in the English Channel on 6 May, laid out fully his plans for the immediate combined Anglo-French Artois offensive, having assured Kitchener four days earlier that his stock of artillery shells was satisfactory. This growing openness was in sharp contrast to Sir John's usual tendency to withhold information. Kitchener was sufficiently impressed that he dropped his earlier condition – made in the meeting on 29 March 1915 with Joffre and Sir John – that success in the field would have to be achieved before he would send more than the agreed minimal reinforcements, and promised Sir John the deployment in France of all six divisions of his First New Army.[85] The schedule for their arrival was communicated to the French. The 9th Division, the first to arrive, was to come on 9 May.[86] As the British approached the Artois offensive, Sir John had thus established quite satisfactory working relations with Kitchener and had his full support. Yet the Artois offensive would dash all that and lay the basis for Sir John's eventual recall.

Expectations among both French and British generals before the offensive were generally very high. Joffre was hopeful that the attack would "break the line beyond mending" and lead to the conclusion of the war in three months.[87] Foch, Sir John recorded, "is full of hope of success."[88] There were a few dissenting voices. Robertson, for example, "seemed to think it doubtful that the French would get through with 16 Divisions, saying [to Clive on 5 May] that Divisions disappear like water."[89] Viviani, the French premier, "thought the war would not finish this year" and that Russia, whose offensive in the Carpathians had stalled toward the end of April, "would not be in a position to make much more progress for several months, owing to lack of rifles and & ammunition."[90] But Sir John French's optimism was unmitigated. "Personally I think they are all wrong about Russia," he wrote on the eve of the battle. "If we get forward on this side and Italy now gets on the move, Russia will play her part in the summer & we shall have peace in the autumn."[91] The new wine of Neuve Chapelle had gone to his head!

CONCLUSION

One might have supposed, at first glance, that after the re-establishment of better relations between Joffre and Sir John French at the end of March, the planning process for the mutually agreed combined spring offensive would have gone forward without a hitch. But the conduct of war entails many unforeseen exigencies, not the least of which, in this case, was the German gas attack launched at Ypres on 22 April on French and then Canadian and British forces. Sir John attributed the retreat of two French divisions in the line northeast of Ypres, between the Canadians and the Belgians, not so much to the gas attack but to the massive withdrawal of French troops from the sector in the weeks previous. This brought forth all of his old rancour about not being properly sustained in 1914 at Mons and on the Aisne.

Sir John's anger intensified when, in a carefully conceived ploy to keep the British in their advanced position as long as possible, Foch promised renewed offensives to retake the lost territory but failed to do so in sufficient strength to succeed. The lack of trust was evident on both sides. Foch's main concern was to husband French resources for the forthcoming offensive in Artois, a concern shared by both Kitchener and Robertson at British headquarters. The final blow for Sir John came on 1 May, when, for want of French advances on their line, he decided to retreat to a less exposed line at Ypres.

Despite the acrimonious atmosphere created by this situation, Joffre and French were able to concert their efforts for their major offensive in Artois in May, albeit with a few days' delay. The price of Sir John's participation, nonetheless, was that Joffre maintain three division of French regulars in the sector as a strategic reserve, a condition to which Joffre acquiesced on 5 May. As a result, these three division were lost to the joint offensive.

Yet, despite all these strains, expectations, both at French and British headquarters, ran very high as the final preparations were made for the joint offensive. Notwithstanding the incoherence of Anglo-French command relations, which came with a significant cost in efficiency, the two commands were united in their desire to deliver a decisive blow to the enemy.

CHAPTER SIX

Operations: The Artois Offensive, 9 May–25 June 1915

THE HIGH EXPECTATIONS OF the French and British high commands for the joint Artois offensive began to melt away by degrees as the battle progressed. While the French got off to a good start with an impressive forward advance of two to three miles in Artois on 9 May, following a sustained artillery bombardment, they were unable to exploit that victory and soon found their onward thrust stymied by new German trenches and lateral enemy fire. Within two weeks, the hope of a breakthrough had dissolved. As the grand hope of an immediate victory slipped through their hands, they then had to decide whether to continue the offensive in a second phase and how to develop a new strategy for ultimate victory. The political fallout from the failed offensive also had to be confronted.

For the British, who were suffering from a greater penury of munitions than the French, the bubble of high expectations began to burst almost immediately with the lack of success at Aubers Ridge within the first few days. The story of Anglo-French command relations during the battle is largely one of Sir John's attempt to make the largest possible contribution, given his lack of munitions, while preserving his freedom of action in his interaction with Foch and Joffre. In these interactions, Sir John's soured relationship with Kitchener was a significant factor. Allied command relations were shaken as a consequence of difficulties in execution and the failures of the joint offensive.

But none of these things was done in a vacuum. At each stage, the circumstances on the battlefield triggered political-military responses of long-term significance in both countries. Sir John's early appraisal that the lack of high-explosive shells was the principal reason for his initial failure led to the Shells Crisis, the fall of the Asquith government, and the formation of the Unionist coalition. A newly discovered appraisal written by Robertson at the end of the battle prefigured the major political military changes undertaken at year's end.

On the French side, Joffre's initial failure led to a continuation of the battle without the hope of decisive victory, partly to support the Russians who were driven to the San River. The failure of the first phase of his attack also led the French General Staff to undertake a major strategic re-evaluation, which called for massive new offensives in two locations on the Western Front, one to draw in German reserves and the other to break through the enemy's lines. This new strategy would require the support of the British New Armies, despite their possible allocation to the British-led Dardanelles venture. Much of the future of the war in France would thus be determined as these issues, raised in the wake of the failed Artois offensive, were dealt with at the political-military level. For the sake of exposition, however, this chapter will focus on the military interactions between the two commands during the battle, and shortly thereafter. The wider political-military ramifications of the failed offensive will be treated in the next two chapters.

INITIAL FRENCH SUCCESS AT VIMY RIDGE, BRITISH FAILURE AT AUBERS RIDGE, AND THE BRITISH SHELLS CRISIS

With the class of 1915 fully incorporated, Joffre was able to allocate to General d'Urbal's Tenth Army six corps and three divisions for the attack on Vimy Ridge, with a corps to follow once the attack began. The French attack from the junction of Haig's First Army at Notre-Dame-de-Lorette was to extend south on a wide front of twelve miles, with the objective of "breaking through enemy lines." A breakthrough would give access to the Douai plain beyond, opening the potential for open warfare, and cutting German supply lines as far south as Rheims. The German line opposite the French was lightly held with only four divisions. Following a massive artillery barrage of four hours beginning at 6:00 A.M. on 9 May, Henri-Philippe Pétain's XXXIII Corps in the centre broke through enemy lines on a wide front and by 11:00 A.M. was in possession of Vimy Ridge, having advanced two to three miles. Open country lay ahead. The

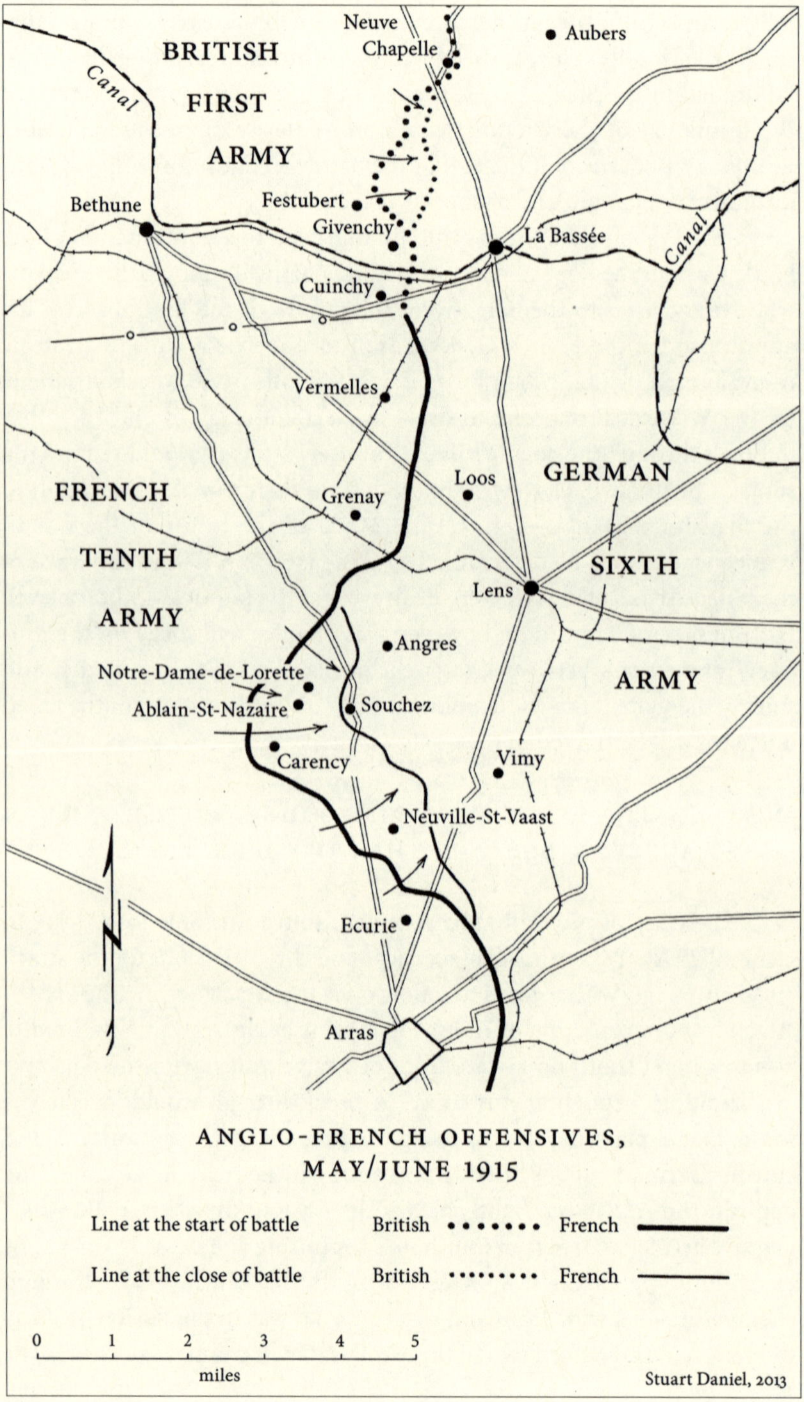

ANGLO-FRENCH OFFENSIVES, MAY/JUNE 1915

initial success was stunning, but German enfilade fire, counter-attacks on the French centre, and French inability to move reserves forward over broken ground before new German trenches could be dug stymied further advance.[1]

The results for the British, on the other hand, were a miserable failure as the British First Army under Haig attacked with three divisions at Aubers Ridge on 9 May. Only the British 8th Division carried the first line of German trenches. The French, as Sir John learned from a visit by Joffre at 5:00 P.M. and a letter from Foch in the evening, had "been most successful North & East of Arras ... At some point they have got on 5 kilometers. They have captured over 2000 prisoners & 11 guns."[2]

For Sir John, the disappointment of the British failure was all the more keenly felt in the light of French success. In fact, that success at the outset became the foil against which Sir John and others at British headquarters made their appraisals. Writing in his journal on 8 May, even before the attack, Wilson differentiated between the lavish French expenditure of munitions in the preliminary attack and the short English bombardment. "It is curious the difference in the method of attack. The French bombarded against houses, farms & villages with 310 Heavy guns all to-day, & at 5 A.M. they let go all their guns for 5 hours & then the Inf[antry] attacks. We have no previous bombardments, but at 5 A.M. all our guns go for 40 minutes & then the Inf[antry] attacks. We shall see which is the best plan. At last this great attack of 100,000 English bayonets & 600 guns & 210,000 French & 1100 guns is off."[3]

The British failure in contrast to French success was a sharp slap in the face for Sir John, who had pinned so much hope on the joint offensive. Already insecure in his position, he attempted to put the blame for the failure on other shoulders – notably those of Kitchener. The May 1915 Shells Crisis, which led to the collapse of the Asquith government, was the result. The failed attack on Aubers Ridge on 9 May became the catalyst for change in the British government as the hard realities of twentieth-century warfare were driven home.

In the meantime, failure of the British attack on Aubers Ridge led to a change of battle plan at British headquarters and renewed difficulty with the French. As Sir John recorded on 10 May: "During the day Haig heard that 8 Div[ision] had been driven out of the positions they had won by art[illery] fire during the night. He also learnt that there had been considerable losses in the attacking troops *and* that the enemy entrenchments were especially strong. He *therefore cancelled the above ord[er] &*

reconsidered the situation. He came to me this afternoon with another plan which he put in writing later. I am going to consult Joffre & Foch in the morning about my *future plans*."[4]

That change of plan would involve Haig's transfer of the 7th Division south and an attack on his right at Givenchy in three days.[5] "Haig has miscalculated the whole thing from start to finish, so has Robertson," wrote Wilson. "We now appear to [have] 15,000 casualties & have done *nothing*."[6] Under these conditions Wilson suggested to Sir John that "if we are up ag[ains]t something we can't solve we had better go South & help the French,"[7] an attractive idea.

For the moment, Sir John supported Haig's new plan "to drop the left attack, move 7th Div[ision] to the right to attack by his right about Givenchy either tomorrow or Thursday [12 May] – with previous heavy art[illery] preparation." To Wilson, Sir John "admitted" regarding the method of attack that "the French were right & he and Haig were wrong."[8] Haig's new plan, however, would entail a night attack in an attempt to capture the element of surprise, after three days of intensive artillery preparation. The ensuing battle extending north through Festubert to Neuve Chapelle became known as the Battle of Festubert.

The plan was relatively well received when Sir John and Wilson presented it to Foch at Bryas on 11 May. While Foch "had to refuse" the loan of some 75s as Sir John requested[9] (though these were later granted), he seemed amenable to the new British plan of attack provided it was delayed as little as possible.[10] In his interview with Foch, Sir John was shown evidence that "very strongly fortified and entrenched" positions had been weakened by French high-explosive shell fire "so *intense* and so *accurate* and *continual* that they were rendered practically harmless before the infantry attacks were launched."[11]

Later in the day, on 11 May, Joffre came by Sir John's headquarters and they discussed Haig's new plan. Sir John, now more cognizant of his dire predicament owing to lack of heavy artillery and high-explosive shells, suggested as an alternate plan that British forces be used as a French reserve – "sending troops south to support the French in & when they succeeded in really breaking thro' the German lines."[12] This option was later withdrawn, presumably in order for Sir John to preserve his freedom of action.

By the morning of the 12th, Sir John, after a discussion with J.P. DuCane, a major-general of the Royal Artillery at British headquarters, who affirmed that the initial success of the French was "almost entirely due to their profuse expenditure" of high-explosive ammunition,[13] was also fully convinced that the British lack of high-explosive shells was the cause of their failure. The same day, as recorded in his diary, Sir John decided to send aides Brindsley FitzGerald and Frederick Guest back to England the next day to see Kitchener and Asquith respectively to convey personally his "ideas on the general situation, [his] views and impressions."[14] Sir John's aides also had the mission to talk to key Unionists Andrew Bonar Law and Arthur Balfour and to convey vital information to Lloyd George. The *Times* military correspondent, Charles à Court Repington, likewise received his information on that day, which resulted in a lead article on the 14th attributing the British failure at Aubers Ridge to the lack of explosive shells.[15] This set off the Shells Crisis, more fully described in the next chapter, with all its attendant consequences.

FESTUBERT

In the days following, optimistic after the initial gains on 9 May, Joffre continued to press attacks, which made few gains in the face of strong enemy defences, while the German Army hurried to bring up reserves. Part of Joffre's motivation was to aid the Russians, who were in full retreat after the German breakthrough at Gorlice-Tarnów on 2 May. Nor did he wish to appear weak before the Italians who were about to enter the war on the behalf of the Allies. On 15 May, after several days of unsuccessful attacks, however, Foch decided that, to be successful, a new attack had to be better prepared with a new base of departure similar to the 9 May operation and that the German strongholds of Souchy and Neuville-St-Vaast had to be reduced to prevent enfilade fire. French attacks were launched against these strong places until the general offensive was resumed on 16 June.[16]

As French offensive actions continued, the British command's shortage of high-explosive shells put them on an unequal footing in bargaining with the French on future actions on 12 May, when Sir John again discussed the matter with Joffre and Foch at Foch's headquarters at Bryas. Sir John had three possible courses of action in view of his shortage of high-explosive shells: 1) "to stand altogether on the defensive"; 2) to send infantry to aid the French in their hoped-for breakthrough opposite Loos – which Wilson and Robertson favoured; or 3) to proceed with

Haig's attack from Givenchy to Neuve Chapelle. Sir John's account of the meeting, attended also by Wilson, Huguet, and Weygand, is illuminating:

> I stated my case that if I elected to attack in accordance with Haig's proposal it would not be commenced before Friday night (14). Joffre at once said he thought this would be "trop tard" [too late].
>
> Joffre asked me to relieve his 58 Division which holds the French line of trenches immediately south of our line – and also another division N of Ypres.
>
> I proposed to send troops down to support the French along the present line of attack.
>
> It is evident to me [Sir John observed quite correctly] that Joffre's idea is to get us to do all the "trench" work and release as many of his troops as possible for attack.
>
> As I did not agree with (& rather resented) his attitude the discussion became rather acrimonious.[17]

Wilson's quasi-comic version of the negotiations indicates that, at least tentatively, "Sir J agreed to the relief of the 58th [Division], but would not hear of relieving up at Ypres, said he had no troops, that it was dangerous to change *troops there even* if this strengthened the force there, then the next minute he produced 4 Div[ision]s for an attack on Loos which the French don't want. Joffre pointed out that we should be doing very little if we only relieved the 58th Div[ision]; & hinted at Gov[ernmen]t action which luckily Sir J did not quite catch & I got the chance of interpreting wrong, but as both were getting hot I got Sir J to go away saying he would send an answer by me later."[18]

In the final analysis, Sir John only partially acceded to the French request for taking up more trenches and agreed later that day to relieve their 58th Division, if he could, but turned down the role of any further relief of trenches and decided to continue with Haig's attack as planned.[19] When faced with the thankless job of manning the trenches or attack, even with the impediment of shell shortage, and ultimately only one division of the New Armies as reinforcement, Sir John clearly preferred to attack. The resulting British attack north of Givenchy extending through Festubert to Neuve Chapelle on the night of 15–16 May met with an initial success, breaching the German second line on a front of 800 yards and the first line on an additional front of 1,800 yards.[20]

WITHHOLDING TROOPS: THE SHELLS CRISIS AND THE NEW ARMIES

Sir John's offensive capacity was much diminished as an unexpected consequence of the Shells Crisis. Although Kitchener refrained from striking back publicly, as a result of the press attack on him, and did not seek to cashier Sir John,[21] he had other very effective ways of punishing the British field commander. On 14 May, the day the lead article in the morning edition of the *Times* blamed the lack of success in the field on the lack of high-explosive ammunition, Kitchener wired Sir John informing him of his decision to stop the dispatch of the remaining five divisions of the First New Army, including the 14th, which was to have arrived on 18 May. The reasons cited were the Allies' failure to break the German line, the lack of ammunition, and the increased danger of invasion following Russian defeats.[22] Prior to the offensive, Sir John had told Kitchener that his ammunition supplies would be sufficient. The grand meeting of the minds prior to the battle, in which Kitchener had promised the entire First New Army, had simply gone up in smoke.

Kitchener was not acting totally out of vindictiveness, although that appears to have been a significant factor, but also in light of his assessment of the Allied strategic situation. In the War Council on 14 May, he pessimistically reviewed the military situation with his colleagues. The Russian defeats in which the Russian Army was driven back nearly to the San River gravely concerned him and raised new fears of a German invasion of England. Noting the huge Russian setbacks, and their severe penury in ammunition, he again raised the spectre of a massive German diversion to the west and a huge assault on the French of a million men, which, following a failed French offensive, he thought "would be successful[,] as against [the] Russians." Fear of a prior enemy landing in Great Britain to prevent British support of the French was also on his mind. Kitchener thus decided, in view of the depleted condition of his territorial forces, to keep all remaining divisions of the New Armies in England for defence against an enemy landing and as a strategic reserve to send to France in case of a major German attack.[23] He undoubtedly also had his eye on possible reinforcements for the floundering Dardanelles expedition.

From Sir John's point of view, the decision to renege on sending the First New Army to France was disappointing enough, but even more galling was Kitchener's assessment, which was sent to Sir John via General Edmund Allenby, returning to the field, to the effect that the British failure to break through was the result of the deficiencies of the British command.[24] This led to further acrimony in his strained relationship with Kitchener.

The quarrel between Sir John and Kitchener played out on several levels. On the strategic level, Sir John adamantly resisted Kitchener's plan of withholding forces of the First New Army. "An important advance has been made by the French during the past week," he wired to Kitchener on 15 May, "and the Germans have already brought up a great part of their available reserves." Pointing to the renewed British attack, Sir John reminded Kitchener that "the plan now being executed was prepared in conjunction with the French on the assumption that the First New Army would be sent as promised." "The whole Allied plan will be seriously affected if it is withheld," he argued, and "our relations with the French will also be strained." He therefore "earnestly" urged that the 14th Division "should be sent as arranged!"[25] Kitchener has again "played me false," Sir John wrote in his diary, noting that his agreement with the French to relieve the 58th Division had been based on the arrival of the 14th English Division from England.[26]

Kitchener's reply was caustic and self-justifying. "I promised that if the German lines were really broken through I would send the 1st New Army to carry on the advance," he replied. "Until I am assured of it, I cannot send the only reserve we have." Turning the ammunition question and Sir John's critique "about both gun and rifle ammunition and our capacity of production" on him, Kitchener said that "further troops sent now to the front could not be supplied with all you require."[27]

But Sir John pressed the issue, chiding Kitchener for having given him "official notification that the XIV Division would be dispatched on 18th May." Reiterating that "it was with that understanding that I entered in engagement with the French Commander-in-Chief," he argued that failure to honour this commitment "may possibly make my position very difficult."[28] On 16 May, Sir John further observed regarding the success of his new attack north of Givenchy: "The enemy have been broken on a front of 2 miles and a maximum depth of about 1,500 yards."[29]

Encouraged by a further report on 17 May of Sir John's success,[30] and impressed by the need to honour Sir John's commitment to the French, Kitchener relented. "I hope the advance you report will be maintained," he wired on 17 May, and "as you appear to have entered into some arrangement with General Joffre regarding the 14th Division, this division will be sent to you tomorrow, 18 May."[31]

The repercussions of this dispute in British civil-military relations were immediately felt in relations with the French. The reasons explained by Kitchener for withholding further troops did not sit well with Foch and Joffre, who, when apprised of the situation in an interview with Wilson and Sir John on 17 May, agreed that Kitchener was "mad," apparently with regard to his fears of a possible disaster on the Western Front following the defeat of Russia.[32] Wilson, however, learned a few days later how grim the Russian situation was as the Russians were forced to retreat behind the San River in mid-May. They reportedly "were down to 3 r[oun]ds a gun" and would not be able to take the offensive for two to three months as "the state of their contracts was hopeless."[33] In response to a query sent directly in a wire from Hanbury Williams, the British military attaché in Russia, as to what his "strategic policy" was, Sir John sent Wilson on 22 May to confer with Joffre. Joffre's stand-pat answer was "'active and aggressive operations'" and that "the real decision must be *here*, it will not be in Russia, nor Servia, nor Italy."[34] Joffre's attitude on this question prefigured much of his military strategy for the rest of the year.

The British continued their attack on Festubert on 18 May, but withering fire from German machine guns slowed their progress. Rainy weather then brought operations to a virtual standstill for three days.[35]

PLANNING THE SECOND PHASE: THE JUNE ATTACKS

Despite these setbacks, an optimistic Foch visited Sir John's headquarters during the afternoon of 21 May and said that he entertained hopes of the French Tenth Army, under d'Urbal, seizing Vimy Ridge by the end of the month.[36] D'Urbal unleashed a massive artillery bombardment during the night of 21–22 May. But the barrage of shells and methodical infantry advances that followed achieved almost nothing, German defenders having yielded very little ground by 25 May. Foch's vision of capturing Vimy Ridge turned out to be a mirage.[37]

The BEF fared no better than the French Tenth Army. Wilson complained on 25 May of British attacks becoming "increasingly feeble."[38] Sir John recognized this fact. He therefore ordered Haig's First Army to stop trying to break through the German lines and instead to conduct a "holding attack." Even though Foch told him that the French intended to make another big push two or three days hence, Sir John felt he had no other course of action, as the First Army was rapidly exhausting its supply of shells and the French High Command continued to press him to have the BEF occupy a longer stretch of the Allied trenches.[39]

Twenty-four hours later, Sir John finally agreed to relieve the French 58th Division with a British division. The motivation for his decision, he told Foch, lay in his respect for the courage of French soldiers and in his recognition that the attainment of French military objectives was vital to the overall success of the Allied coalition. Sir John imposed two conditions on Foch, nonetheless: that the French division in question be withdrawn from the areas south of the BEF's positions; and that the division's artillery remain in its present location. Foch readily accepted these terms.[40]

Meanwhile, Joffre had decided on 25 May to delay his main offensive toward Vimy Ridge until 31 May on account of fierce fighting at Souchez and Neuville-St-Vaast, which anchored each end of the Vimy salient and which d'Urbal had been unable to take.[41] Two days later, on 27 May, Joffre advised Wilson that he wanted the BEF to attack in the direction of Loos. Joffre argued that a golden opportunity now presented itself thanks to the entry of Italy into the war on the Allied side and to the transfer of German troops to Russia. These developments, Joffre urged, made German manpower on the Western Front "very thin." If the French and British threw every available soldier and cannon into the fray, positive results were bound to follow.[42] Italian entry into the conflict, creating a new front with significant potential, had thus begun to play a role in Joffre's strategic calculations.

On 30 May, Foch visited British headquarters and informed Sir John that the French now planned to make their main assault on 3 June[43] and suggested that the British could best assist the French by advancing toward Loos. To this Sir John replied that he would attack between 5 and 7 June, but only if the French had punched a hole through the German defences.[44]

The French High Command subsequently postponed d'Urbal's offensive on five occasions[45] and Sir John changed the beginning of the British attack three times, always selecting starting dates that were one to four days behind those of Joffre.[46] In spite of their differences, Joffre and

Sir John belatedly settled on 15 June as the date for the beginning of the Allied offensive.[47] But mist forced Joffre to postpone his offensive by twenty-four hours.[48] Sir John agreed to follow suit.[49]

JOFFRE'S SCALED-DOWN EXPECTATIONS

By 27 May, the French General Staff had come to the realization that the Artois offensive would not produce decisive results and had begun to plan for new and more powerful offensives, which would require the participation of the British New Armies.[50] Joffre himself was shaken. Before the renewed joint offensive on 16 June, he had reached the conclusion that it would produce only limited results and that the war would drag on for a long while. On 13 June he had lunch with Poincaré, Viviani, Millerand, and Delcassé at the Elysée Palace. Joffre struck Poincaré as looking pale, thin, and tired. Even more worrisome to Poincaré than Joffre's physical appearance was his attitude. He seemed much less confident. Joffre indeed declared that a successful general offensive was now impossible. In order to dislodge the strongly held trenches, he had amassed three hundred heavy guns along a nine-mile front around Arras. Even so, he dared not promise a breakthrough. He now predicted a long war that would drag on through another winter campaign.[51]

Poincaré countered that, if local offensives did not accomplish anything more than getting soldiers killed unnecessarily, perhaps Joffre should go on the defensive until he had a greater quantity of artillery pieces. Joffre resisted this stricture for two reasons: he had to keep his troops in fighting trim, and he needed to force the Germans to keep a maximum number of units on the Western Front in order to prevent transfers of more formations to the Eastern Front, where they would make life even more difficult for the already beleaguered Russian army.[52] Offensive doctrine and loyalty to his Russian allies were his touchstones and determined his stance on this occasion, as on many others.

Part of the reason for Joffre's downcast mood, Poincaré opined, may have derived from his dissatisfaction with the performance of prominent British generals and politicians thus far in the war.[53] As noted above, Joffre had to spend much of his time trying to persuade Sir John to advance at the same time as himself. Even worse from Joffre's perspective was the ongoing struggle over the future dispatch of the British Second New Army – whether to France or the Dardanelles. Joffre, of course, wanted Kitchener to send it to the Western Front. But to his regret, the British cabinet had already decided to send the Second New Army to the Dardanelles.[54] Kitchener, among other things, had reasoned that since British munitions were limited and the French Army did not have any 75-millimetre guns to lend to the BEF, there was no point in sending fresh troops to the Western Front.[55]

In marked contrast to Joffre, Sir John was in an upbeat mood as the date of the renewed Anglo-French offensive approached. On 9 June he told Wilson that he foresaw the end of the war in October 1915 – a mere four months away – because the Germans would no longer have the capacity to replace their manpower. The enemy, Sir John claimed, would be forced to sue for peace when the number of its casualties exceeded the number of its replacements. While waiting for the inevitable victory, Sir John remained convinced, however, that the best strategy for the BEF was to capture the Channel ports.[56]

The British night offensive finally got under way during the evening of 15 June. A systematic artillery bombardment preceded Haig's advance at Givenchy. Three divisions of the British First Army overwhelmed the first German trench and captured part of the second line of defence. An enemy counter-attack later that night, however, forced the British to retreat to their original jumping-off point. The following morning, Haig's troops recaptured the Germans' first two lines of trenches and claimed to be on the verge of seizing their third line.[57] But British success proved short-lived owing to the weakness of their later attacks that day.[58]

To the south, an initial French success at Arras was also of brief duration. Joffre had prepared well according to the tactical art of the day, with Neuville-St-Vaast having been reduced and d'Urbal's forces now increased to twenty-three divisions (three of which were territorials) and three cavalry divisions against nine German divisions, with three in reserve. Supplied with ample artillery, d'Urbal bombarded a variety of targets from 10 through 15 June as a way of disguising his main objective, and on the morning of the 16th he brought down overwhelming firepower on the first German trench. But his offensive achieved little. The Tenth Army gained only two miles of terrain in three days because the Germans answered with massive bombardments, enfilade fire, and furious counter-attacks. Foch consequently ordered a stop to the fruitless assault on 18 June. Additional attacks to take Soucy continued until these were finally stopped on 25 June.[59]

IMMEDIATE FALLOUTS

On 18 June, before the final conclusion of the battle, Colonel Marie-Jean Penelon, one of two official liaison officers travelling daily between Chantilly and Paris, informed Poincaré that Joffre's offensive had failed completely, with high loss of life, because German fire from the flanks rendered French positions untenable along a narrow front. The failure greatly undermined Poincaré's confidence in Joffre's ability to succeed on his own. A troubled Poincaré thereafter regarded it as indispensable for the foremost French politicians and commanders of army groups to have consultations about military planning and operations.[60]

Poincaré's reaction to the news of the failure at Arras was mild compared to the reaction of the Parliament. The Chamber of Deputies and its Army Commission loudly castigated the government and GQG. Fortunately for Joffre, the deputies aimed most of their barbs at Millerand.[61] By fall, the agitation would gain enough steam to bring down the Viviani ministry.

There was immediate fallout on the British side as well. On 19 June, Esher wrote Sir John that Joffre's latest failure could result in a decline in French national morale. Asquith's cabinet, Esher further warned, might perceive the wiser course as one of dispatching more troops to Turkey instead of to France. He advised Sir John that only he had the power to prevent this scenario from unfolding.[62]

The thought of not receiving reinforcements galvanized Sir John. Upon receipt of Esher's letter, he sprang into action, paying a visit to Foch's headquarters the same day. Foch having called off the offensive, Sir John nonetheless expressed the hope that the French would capture Vimy Ridge and, as a result, break through the German lines. Foch replied that he expected to take Vimy Ridge by the end of the month but doing so would still not be enough to pierce German positions. When Foch asked Sir John what he proposed to do in order to assist the French, Sir John pleaded that insufficient ammunition precluded a British offensive, but that he would contribute artillery support. He went on to promise that the BEF would maintain sufficient pressure on the Germans to keep them from transferring units to French sectors; and he would have fresh units ready to throw into the breach if and when the French Tenth Army broke through the enemy's front. In addition, Sir John pledged to support the French in the new general offensive in July, about which Joffre had spoken informally on 4 June, by attacking along the line La Bassée-Arras.[63]

The recent experience raised both for Esher and for Joffre the issue of unity of command, dormant since earlier discussions in March. In response to the troubled command relations during the offensive, Esher, writing in his diary, identified the chief problem as lack of unity. He added an ominous warning: the Allies might lose the war unless they created unity of command on the Western Front.[64]

FORCING KITCHENER'S HAND

Kitchener also had his misgivings, particularly about future operations and another major joint offensive for which Joffre had requested on 27 May the dispatch of the British New Armies to France.[65] On 15 June, Kitchener wrote to Sir John reminding him that during their last meeting Sir John had said that Joffre's offensive at Arras would last only until around the end of June. Afterward, Kitchener and Sir John would have the opportunity to discuss the policy of the current campaign before making any decisions about their future course of action. However, Sir John's latest letter had indicated his desire to collaborate in a proposed French offensive in July with all the men and material that the government could provide. A puzzled Kitchener asked Sir John to clarify his remarks, since he found them "rather upsetting to [his] calculations."[66] Kitchener was obviously not in favour of another grand offensive.

Collaboration between leading French and British generals as a result increased dramatically during the second half of June as the two commands joined hands in a manoeuvre designed by Wilson to force the dispatch of British troops to the Western Front. Their common interest was to oppose the Dardanelles strategy of the British government, which diverted troops from the Western Front, and to resist Kitchener's desire to go on the defensive in France. On 22 June, when in a meeting with Joffre Wilson expressed concern "about strain on France, about Dardanelles, about Russia," Joffre agreed to meet Sir John at Chantilly two days later to draw up a joint plan to present to the British government.[67] Sir John told Clive that he was pleased with Joffre's decision to consult him before GQG communicated, through diplomatic channels, with the British government.[68] Two very closely coordinated messages followed.

On 23 June, Sir John advised Kitchener that he needed more troops and shells for several reasons: to cooperate in Joffre's offensives, lengthen the line of trenches held by the BEF, maintain high morale among the Anglo-French armies, keep French defeatists from signing a separate peace treaty with Germany, relieve German pressure on the Russian Army, and force the enemy to use up its manpower reserves.[69] Joffre wrote a letter in much the same vein to Millerand on the morning of 24 June. He appealed to Viviani's cabinet to convey his concerns to the British government.[70] By launching a joint British and French initiative, Wilson, who had worked up the initiative after consultation with Foch, calculated that the request would reach the entire coalition cabinet and not be stalled by Kitchener.[71]

Joffre and Sir John met on the afternoon of 24 June, with Robertson, Wilson, Pellé, and Huguet in attendance, to consult on future plans. Joffre said that the French Army would soon cease its offensive at Arras. Instead, efforts to capture Vimy Ridge would be limited to "constant small enterprises with the double objective of gaining ground and pinning down the enemy." He would launch another major offensive to the right of Arras in five or six weeks – or even later.[72]

Sir John advised his French colleagues that Asquith's cabinet might try to oblige him to adopt a defensive posture on the Western Front. In that case, Sir John made it clear that he would oppose his government's policy. Joffre responded that a defensive strategy would result in the defeat of Russia and, in turn, the defeat of France and Britain. Consequently, he would never consider such a strategy for even one instant. Both field commanders were of one mind on their desire to maintain solidarity with the beleaguered Russians, their hostility toward the Dardanelles expedition, and their striving to obtain all available divisions in Britain for service in France.[73]

After the cordial meeting, which an exuberant Robertson praised as "by far the best conference yet held and a great advance was made,"[74] Sir John told Joffre that he planned to inform the British cabinet of his views in person in the near future and requested that the French government support him. Joffre eagerly complied with his request, contacting Millerand about the matter later that day.[75]

Joffre and Sir John were now working in harmony, largely because of common strategic interests. On the evening of the 24th, Sir John wrote to Mrs Bennett asserting: "We [he and Joffre] are both hampered by our respective governments. They are the 'greatest thorn in the side' a general in the field can suffer from. They are suggesting all kinds of impossible moves and plans!"[76] Relations between the supreme commanders had clearly improved at the strategic level, but much rancour persisted at the operational level.

The day after the meeting at Chantilly, Joffre ordered an end to the Arras offensive. His secondary attacks elsewhere proved even less successful. Overall, what little ground the French Army managed to capture during the Artois offensive came at a very high price in blood: 140,000 casualties from 3 May to 25 June.[77] For their part, the British, in the battles between 9 May and 18 June, which were equally unavailing, suffered 26,000 casualties.[78]

The field commanders followed through on their representation in support of their joint operational plan. On 26 June, Sir John informed Kitchener that he and Joffre shared the views Sir John had communicated to the government three days earlier with regard to the need for troop reinforcements in view of a forthcoming offensive. Kitchener forwarded Sir John's telegram to Asquith, with the editorial comment that he found the meeting of 24 June between the two field commanders to be "curious."[79]

On 29 June, Huguet advised Joffre that Sir John would be leaving for London on 1 July in order to present his demands to Asquith's government. Sir John, reported Huguet, hoped to return to France with a promise from Asquith that the Second New Army would be dispatched to France.[80] The following day, Joffre, in a letter to Millerand, underlined Sir John's full agreement on future plans and the need for Viviani's ministry to intervene with Asquith's cabinet for the purpose of obtaining the New Armies to serve alongside the French Army on the Western Front.[81] Joffre and Sir John's appeals to their respective governments were attempts to overturn Kitchener's decisions regarding where to dispatch the New Armies. Their efforts would be a significant factor in having more British units sent to France.[82]

CONCLUSION

The course of Anglo-French command relations was anything but smooth during the first half of 1915. Hardly had the fallout from the breakdown of relations from the Neuve Chapelle incident been smoothed over than the German gas attack at Ypres presented new challenges and threatened to upset joint planning for the Artois offensive. Those difficulties were partially overshadowed by enthusiasm for Joffre's new plan, which promised not only to achieve a decisive breakthrough on the Western Front but also to aid the hard-pressed Russians, whose offensive power was very much eroded by extreme shortages of rifles and ammunition.

Joint coordination of the offensive itself, especially in its later stages, produced new challenges in a relationship that was often frayed at the edges. But the field commanders found it in their interest, despite their own differences, to combine against the peripheral strategy of the British government, to work together to have a large British force sent to France, and to resist Kitchener's defensive strategy for the Western Front. While the strategic conflict between French and English at the beginning of the Dardanelles adventure had pitted the two staffs against each other, their common interests now brought them together. The driving force in both cases was the differing strategies of the two coalition partners.

The Artois offensive was a painful experience for both the British and the French, as initial success and high hopes were dashed against enemy trenches. Sir John was more hampered than the French by a shortage of shells, which had two main effects: his attempt to lay the blame on Kitchener and the government, and their quest for a field of action that would produce greater results. While he and both Foch and Joffre made some effort toward mutual support during operations, acrimony arose in planning the second-phase June offensive, making well-coordinated joint action impossible. The aftermath of the battle, to which we now turn, was crucial for both allies in a wide range of areas.

CHAPTER SEVEN

Catalyst for Change: Impact of the Artois Offensive

FROM THE STRATEGIC POINT OF VIEW, the great Allied offensive in Artois, which began on 9 May 1915 and continued in successive waves until 25 June, was anything but decisive. An initial French breakthrough on Vimy Ridge was soon stopped by a German counter-offensive, and a second major assault on 16 June failed completely. Successive British attacks on Aubers Ridge (9 May), Festubert (15–16 May), and Givenchy (16 June) proved equally ineffective. The line of trenches had not budged significantly, despite the loss of 140,000 casualties on the French side and more than 26,000 on the British, as opposed to 74,000 Germans. But, as additional research in French and British sources has shown, the battle had much more extensive repercussions in the Allied conduct of the war than heretofore known and indeed became the catalyst for nearly all the major political and military changes of 1915.

The failed Allied offensive brought home to the Allies the full implications of trench warfare and dispelled once and for all the mirage of a short war and a quick victory. The British failure in the field precipitated a crisis in the British government which led to the fall of the Asquith ministry and the formation of the first coalition government. The sweeping changes in military leadership that took place in December, with Sir Douglas Haig replacing Sir John French as commander of the BEF and Sir William Robertson becoming chief of the Imperial General Staff, were also prefigured. The Artois offensive led as well to a major British strategic re-evaluation and, despite the Dardanelles venture, a much greater commitment to continental defence, as the British government took the fundamental decision to send the New Armies to France, as a result of the political fallout in France from the failed offensive and Russian defeats in Poland.

The French government, which faced an outcry on the conduct of the war, managed to weather the storm until after the fall offensive. Millerand's powers nonetheless were reduced by the appointment of four under-secretaries to the War Ministry, one of which was Socialist deputy Albert Thomas, in charge of munitions. Joffre also found his powers limited somewhat as the government obliged him to consult with his army group commanders. Faced with the failure of its existing strategy, the French General Staff was forced to make a basic strategic re-evaluation which led it to seek in Kitchener's New Armies the one hope of victory. Joffre therefore requested the immediate dispatch of twenty divisions of the New Armies to France. The immediate result was a major strategic conflict with the British in the spring and summer of 1915. Apart from the need to reinforce the floundering Dardanelles offensive, the main sticking point for the British was French operational strategy on the Western Front and the use to be made of British New Armies in the field. Following the Artois offensive, the French also sought once again to obtain the subordination of the British High Command. The failed Artois offensive thus triggered major changes as the Western Allies attempted to cope with the new realities of industrial warfare.

This chapter will focus on the political and military impact of the Artois offensive on the two governments and commands. It will treat the crises within both the British and French governments on the question of munitions, the adjustments within the two High Commands, and the divergent effect of the failed Artois offensive on French and British strategic planning. Prominent in that regard was the French request for the immediate dispatch of twenty divisions of the British New Armies.

The next chapter will focus on additional impacts of the failed Artois offensive. The grand overarching strategic issues were the ultimate destiny of the British New Armies, whether they were to be dispatched to France or the Dardanelles, and the clash between Joffre and Kitchener on their intended usage, if sent to France. The result was the first full-blown Anglo-French political-military conference at Calais on 6 July 1915.

The French command likewise came to realize that the fragmented Allied military actions were ineffectual. Italy's entry into the war, coupled with the failure of the Anglo-French attack in Artois in May 1915 and the continued retreat of the Russian Army, raised the question of Allied coordination with greater urgency in the summer of 1915. Joffre thus called an Allied military conference for 7 July, in an effort to engage all of the Allies in an "energetic, concerted offensive."[1] These two landmark conferences are detailed in the next chapter.

THE BRITISH SHELLS CRISIS

In his memoirs, Sir John gave an account of his radical decision to appeal to the public and leaders of the Opposition with regard to the dire shortage of high-explosive shells at the front, to which he attributed his initial failure in the Artois offensive. He wrote that, during the battle on 9 May, he was in close observation of the operations for several hours from the "tower of a ruined church," a vantage point that allowed him to see on Aubers Ridge the "great inequality of the artillery duel of the two forces." "As attack after attack failed," he stated, "I could see that the absence of artillery support was doubling and trebling our losses in men." He thus attributed the failed offensive to the shortage of munitions, as only "8 per cent of our shells were high explosive, and we had only sufficient supply for about 40 minutes of artillery preparation for the attack." "I therefore determined," he continued, "on taking the most drastic measure to destroy the apathy of a Government leading the Empire to the brink of disaster," namely, to reveal to the public the shortage of ammunition.[2] He took this action, a gross violation of the normal rules governing civil-military relations, even though a friend, presumably Winston Churchill, who was with him at the observation point,[3] counselled him "that it meant my certain recall from the Command in France."[4]

Sir John's resolve was stiffened, he said, by a telegram from Kitchener, awaiting him on his return to headquarters, ordering that 20,000 rounds of ammunition, "20 per cent of our scanty supply," be shipped immediately to the Dardanelles.[5] Though the movement of ammunition from France to the Dardanelles was only a time-saving device and the ammunition was replaced in twenty-four hours, thus having no effect on the battle, the timing of Kitchener's demand was most inopportune.[6]

Sir John recounted that "I immediately gave instructions that evidence should be furnished to Colonel Repington, military correspondent of *The Times*, who happened to be then at Headquarters, that the vital need of high-explosive shells had been a fatal bar to our Army success on that day." He also sent an edited copy of correspondence between himself and the government on the ammunition question via his aides, Brindsley FitzGerald and Frederick Guest, to David Lloyd George, who was in conflict with Kitchener over the supply of munitions. Similar copies were sent to the leader of the Opposition, Andrew Bonar Law, and to Arthur Balfour, a senior member of the Unionist Party.[7] The list clearly shows who Sir John believed would have an interest in using the information against the government.

The intent of these actions, however, was not so much to overthrow Asquith's ministry as to secure the removal of Kitchener as secretary of state for war. "I devoutly wish we could get rid of Kitchener from the War Office," Sir John wrote to his mistress on 21 May 1915. "I'm sure nothing will go right while he's there. It is so hard to have enemies both in *front* and *behind*!"[8] What Sir John apparently failed to appreciate was that the principle of cabinet solidarity would channel the attack more against Asquith's handling of the war effort than against Kitchener.

The picture that emerges from the first-hand accounts of the time, Sir John French's diary and that of Henry Wilson, differs slightly from the one in French's memoir as to the sequence of events. These sources show that Sir John resolved on his "drastic" measure only gradually. In his diary account of 9 May, Sir John reports that the unsuccessful attacks ran up against machine-gun fire, but he says nothing of his impression of the artillery battle he witnessed, nor of his immediate plan to "go public" on the question of the ammunition shortage.[9] The latter omission is not necessarily significant, however, as his diary, written with an eye to the future history of the event, did not necessarily contain material that would later reflect poorly on him.[10]

But Wilson, who was at Sir John's evening meeting with Joffre on 9 May, describes circumstances which would suggest that the real motivation for Sir John's outrage was his own failure in face of French success. "Joffre came at 6 o'c[lock]," Wilson reported.

> He was also well pleased [with French success] but none of the French were the least boastful. Sir John was quite nice to Joffre, and this was difficult as Haig's attack had been a complete failure. Neither the 1st Corps, Indian Corps nor IV Corps could do anything, we lost some 10,000 men and never gained a yard. Now whose

> plans were right? Foch or Haig? I heard later that the French fired 176,000 rounds of '75' shell and in the last ten minutes of bombardment they were firing 46 shells a second. We fired 50,000 rounds.
>
> Kitchener wires wanting us to send some ammunition to the Dardanelles. Whew![11]

Sir John's pique at French success in the face of his own failure was thus exacerbated by Kitchener's request for ammunition for the Dardanelles, and these factors together provided the background to French's attempt to shift the blame for the failed offensive on to Kitchener and the shortage of ammunition.[12] But the final decision came only three days later as Sir John grew to appreciate more fully the impact of his shortage of high-explosive shells.

The gravity of Sir John's plight with regard to ammunition, as detailed in the last chapter, was fully driven home only when he began to plan with Haig and the French the next offensive action. Haig's new plan to renew the offensive by a night attack north of Givenchy was relatively well received when Sir John and Wilson presented it to Foch at Bryas on 11 May.[13] In his interview with Foch, Sir John, as he recorded in his diary, "saw plans of the ground which had been won by the French in the last few days. It is very strongly fortified and entrenched, numerous works and redoubts being included in the various trench lines. The French high explosive fire had, however, been so *intense* and so *accurate* and *continual* that they were rendered practically harmless before the infantry attacks were launched."[14] This diary entry of 11 May was Sir John's first mention of the role of high explosives in the French success, suggesting that he came to a full realization of the reason for French success only at this interview two days after the British attack.

Later in the day, on 11 May, Joffre came by Sir John's headquarters and they discussed Haig's new plan. Sir John, who was now beginning to get a more complete picture of his predicament on account of his lack of heavy artillery and high-explosive ammunition, suggested as an alternate plan that British forces be used as a French reserve. "I suggested also the possibility of my sending troops south to support the French in & when they succeeded in really breaking thro' the German lines,"[15] he wrote.

There can be no doubt that, by the morning of the 12th, Sir John was fully convinced that the initial French success on 9 May and the British failure both revolved around the supply of high-explosive shells. As

Sir John recorded: "DuCane told me that the success of the French was almost entirely due to their profuse expenditure of H[igh] E[xplosive] amm[uni]t[ion]. He showed me figures that they used in their attack of 9 & 10 [May] – four or five times as much as we did or *could*. It is to my mind, a great question whether we ought not to stand altogether on the defensive till an adequate supply of H[igh] E[xplosive] is available."[16]

It was only on 12 May that Sir John recorded that he was sending home FitzGerald and Guest the next day to see Kitchener and Asquith to convey personally his "ideas on the general situation, my views and impressions."[17] They also had the mission, earlier described, to talk to Balfour and Bonar Law and to convey vital information to Lloyd George. On the same day, Repington received his information from which the front-page article in the *Times*, attributing the British failure at Aubers Ridge to the lack of explosive shells, appeared on 14 May, beginning the attack of the newspapers owned by Alfred Harmsworth, 1st Viscount Northcliffe, on Kitchener.[18] The sustained comparison between the failure of the British attack and that of the French success due to heavy artillery shows it to be Sir John's conclusions of 12 May.[19]

In short, the original sources reveal a growing conviction on Sir John's part, between the attacks on 9 May and 12 May, that the lack of British success resulted from a lack of high-explosive shells. It was therefore on the 12th, not the 9th, that French decided to launch his campaign against the government on the issue.

FALL OF THE ASQUITH MINISTRY

Meanwhile, in London, the conflict-riven Liberal government of H.H. Asquith was entering the final crisis of its existence after ten months of war.[20] "I don't suppose there is in the Kingdom a much more unhappy man," Asquith wrote to Sylvia Henley on 12 May 1915,[21] but not in regard to the looming crisis in the government. Rather, he was lamenting that Venetia Stanley, a young woman of twenty-seven with whom he was in love, and who had been his confidante for three years, had announced her engagement the day before to Edwin Montagu, a Jewish member of his cabinet, and, to make matters worse, her forthcoming conversion to Judaism. The irony of it, he wrote to Sylvia, Venetia's older married sister, was that the two people he trusted the most should "combine to deal a death blow to me," which "leaves me sore and humiliated." His hope was that he could weather this personal crisis "without any external sign of disquietude or impotence."[22]

The political crisis grew worse the next day. "Thank God," he wrote to Henley, "I have had & am having, a very full distracting day; every kind of horror and difficulty; Winston quarrelling with Fisher: Kitchener is quarrelling with both." [23] It is almost certain that, pained as he was by his breakup with Venetia Stanley, Asquith reacted more rashly in the ministerial crisis than he might have otherwise done[24]; but, as a middle-class socialite known for his fondness for beautiful young women with a penchant for politics, Asquith was not long in replacing Venetia with her married sister Sylvia as his new, though less intimate confidante, to whom he was affirming his intense love less than a month later.[25]

Apart from his personal misfortunes, Asquith had to face the reality of his government's less than successful conduct of the war. The twin issues that forced his hand in the formation of a coalition government – that of the Dardanelles and the ammunition crisis – were reflective of two of its main shortcomings. The resignation of First Sea Lord Fisher (his ninth), on 15 May, resulted from a three-cornered dispute with Churchill and Kitchener over Churchill's plan to increase the naval support of the Dardanelles, an action that Fisher thought would expose Britain's shores by diverting ships from the North Sea.[26] That such a dispute should arise mid-way through the venture was symptomatic of the weak and vacillating hand of the government on the direction of strategy.[27] The ammunition crisis, likewise, had to do not only with the supply and kind of ammunition available to the BEF in France but also with the unwillingness of Asquith's government to lay aside liberal principles and totally mobilize for war.[28]

In a circular to his cabinet colleagues on 17 May 1915, Asquith cited the need for "what is called a 'broad based' Government" to carry on "the continued prosecution of the war in order to avoid public criticism." Public criticism, he believed, was "an asset of much value to the enemy." But the Opposition's threat of exploiting the government's shortcomings was the decisive factor. "The resignation of Lord Fisher, which I have done my best to avert," he continued, "and the more than plausible parliamentary case in regards the alleged deficiency of high explosive shells, would, if unduly exploited (as they would have been) in the House of Commons at this moment, have had the most disastrous effect on the general political and strategic situation." "Such a discussion," he asserted, "might have had the result of determining adversely to the Allies the attitude of Italy."[29] That forming a coalition with the Unionists was the only way to avoid a new election within the statutory five-year limit, the last having been held in 1911, obviously was not lost on him either.[30]

He thus opted for a coalition government with the Unionists. The coalition cabinet under Asquith, formed on 25 May, had twelve Liberals, eight Unionists, one Labour Party member, and one independent, with Kitchener firmly anchored in his place as secretary of state for war. Sir John's attempt to bring down Kitchener had backfired badly, although it did have the salutary effect of installing Lloyd George as minister of munitions. The unity of the new ministry, however, was more apparent than real; it never functioned properly as a team owing to ongoing suspicions, internal divisions, and competing agendas.[31]

With the change of government there was also an adjustment in the machinery for running the war, with added complications. The War Council created in November 1914 was supplanted by a new committee, known as the Dardanelles Committee, which was enlarged from eight to twelve members, adding four senior Unionist leaders, to give an appropriate balance between the parties in the coalition. Maurice Hankey continued as secretary. The new committee, originally intended for the management of the Dardanelles campaign, soon became responsible for the overall management of the war. Too large and unwieldly to function effectively, this body, like the War Council before it, lacked authority since all its decisions had to be approved by the rest of the cabinet.[32]

In the new government, Arthur Balfour replaced Churchill as first lord of the Admiralty. Given a sinecure post in the cabinet as chancellor of the Duchy of Lancaster, Churchill continued to sit on the Dardanelles Committee until it was replaced in early November by the much smaller War Committee on which he was denied a seat. No longer able to express his views on the conduct of the war in this inner forum, he resigned from the cabinet and was eventually given the command of a battalion in France – a major step down from his earlier aspiration of leading a corps or a brigade.[33]

A complete evaluation of the munitions crisis is beyond the scope of this work and has been done elsewhere.[34] A few observations are in order, however, to appraise how Kitchener and Sir John should be seen on the issue. First, it is clear that Kitchener accomplished a major task in setting up the machinery for increased armament production and laid the basis

David Lloyd George was appointed minister of munitions in Asquith's coalition government in May 1915 following the Shells Crisis. An "easterner" in the cabinet, he worked closely with his French counterpart Albert Thomas in coordinating the production of war matériel. He succeeded Asquith as prime minister in December 1915. (*THW*, 5:287)

for the success achieved under Lloyd George, since until early 1916 nearly all of the munitions delivered derived from Kitchener's orders.[35] It is also clear that the demands of armament production among the Allies were much greater than anticipated as Kitchener had the task of outfitting the existing force and the massive expansion of the New Armies,[36] not to mention supplying the Russians.[37] Yet it is plain as well that Kitchener failed in a number of regards: 1) he did not bring in private firms to an adequate degree in 1914 on the French model, as advised by Esher and others; 2) he was very slow to appreciate the tactical needs of modern warfare, and continued to think in terms of the infantry leading the artillery into battle as late as March 1915; and 3) he was unable, without adequate government support and regimentation of the workforce, along with the disruptive effect of the volunteer recruitment system, to manage organized labour with any degree of success.[38]

While Sir John made representations for high-explosive shells as early as September 1914, the messages were somewhat mixed by a subsequent request to reduce the proportion of such shells from 50 to 25 per cent, by a field study in early 1915 that said shrapnel was more effective than high explosives in cutting barbed wire,[39] and by assurances from Sir John as late as 2 May that ammunition supplies would be adequate, despite a very low proportion of high-explosive shells. Sir John himself had badly gauged the need for this kind of ammunition.

Sir John was undoubtedly sincere in his belief, following the Aubers Ridge offensive, that its failure was due to lack of high-explosive shells, particularly in view of the French experience. But the lack of high-explosive shells did not tell the whole story. Prior to being attacked, the Germans had concealed their barbed wire in trenches, thus making it immune to British shrapnel, and had sunk their machine guns in redoubts level with the surface and were therefore able to open fire after bombardment.[40] Kitchener's failure to respond to the need for high-explosive shells, and the critical long-term shell shortages, thus became a convenient scapegoat for French's own tactical failures. The ongoing conflict with Kitchener over the Dardanelles and its drain on resources from the Western Front reached the kindling point when Kitchener requested that ammunition be diverted for the Dardanelles.

KITCHENER AND SIR JOHN

Kitchener showed "exemplary patience" in the Shells Crisis, refraining from answering further attacks in the Northcliffe press, notably the *Times* and *Daily Mail.* Rather, he relied on his own mystique and popular support to bolster him in his position.[41] But, as indicated, he took severe punitive action against Sir John French on 14 May, the day the lead article in the morning edition of the *Times* blamed the lack of success in the field on the lack of high-explosive ammunition, by cancelling the dispatch to France of the remaining five divisions of the First New Army, including the 14th, which was to have arrived on 18 May. The reasons cited were the failure of the Allies to break the German line, the lack of ammunition, and the increased danger of invasion following Russian defeats in Poland.[42]

The latter preoccupation was one that had played on Kitchener's mind since the beginning of the war. The Russians, having been broken through at Gorlice-Tarnów on 2 May, had now been pushed behind the San River. Imagining a scenario in which the Germans would launch a million men against France after the Central Powers had beaten Russia, Kitchener argued in the War Council on 14 May that the remaining divisions of the New Armies should be kept in England for defence against an enemy landing and as a reserve to send to France in case of a major German attack.[43]

Withholding the divisions of the New Army was a major blow to Sir John, whose planning for the offensive with the French had been based on their arrival, and led to three days of wrangling in communications with the secretary of state for war, as indicated in the previous chapter, until, on 17 May, Kitchener relented to the extent of sending the 14th Division, which Sir John claimed was necessary to fulfill his obligation of relieving the French 58th Division. The dispute occasioned considerable acrimony on both sides, with Kitchener protesting that he had promised to send the New Armies only if Sir John's attack broke through, and that it would not serve any purpose to send new forces without adequate ammunition; and Sir John citing recent successes north of Givenchy and his obligation to the French.[44] Sir John's conclusion was that Kitchener has again "played me false."[45]

On the personal level, the quarrel between Sir John and Kitchener took on new dimensions. The full measure of Kitchener's ire was revealed to Esher in a note. "I am deadly sick of this system of intrigue with Headquarters, and if I get an excuse, I shall take it and get out of it all,"[46] he wrote, threatening his own resignation on the issue. Suspicious that Sir John had instigated the *Times* attack on him, Kitchener sent him a letter on 14 May indicating that it had been confirmed that Repington had been at British headquarters. "Until war correspondents are allowed by the Government, I do not think it is right for you to allow Repington to be out with the Army."[47] Sir John's reply was surly in tone: Repington, he said, was an old friend who had stayed with him over "the last 10 or 12 years," and was there in "an entirely private capacity." "I really have no time to attend to these matters," he complained.[48]

Sir John outlined his case to the prime minister in a private letter on 20 May for the removal of Kitchener. While lauding Asquith's support of him, French claimed that Kitchener, "in his letters, in his telegrams, and in his formal messages, brought thru mutual acquaintances (of his entirely irresponsible people)," had been "*overbearing and unjust.*" "The climax came," Sir John wrote, "when a verbal message was brought to me (by Lord Kitchener's orders) by General Allenby – one of my own generals – telling me that the Troop[s] under my command were entirely wanting in 'go' and 'dash' – that if the men were only led properly they would be able to charge over the enemy trenches and posts without any great artillery preparation and that he hoped soon to see me taking example by the conduct of the Troops in the Dardanelles." "It was the grossest insult to me and the army I command." While "determined to ignore" the insult, Sir John continued: "To speak the truth I feel most strong that the presence of Lord Kitchener at the War Office is most detrimental to the successful conduct of operations in this theatre of war so long as I remain in command."[49] There can be no doubt that Sir John hoped that the cabinet crisis would result in Kitchener's replacement. Indeed, when Lloyd George, who had been in a long-running feud with Kitchener over munitions, complained to the prime minister on 19 May that Kitchener had deliberately withheld information from the Munitions Committee, his source was Sir John.[50]

But Kitchener, who, in Asquith's initial negotiations with the Unionists, was to be superseded by David Lloyd George at the War Office, was far too strong in the country to be replaced, as evidenced by the burning of the *Daily Mail* on the floor of the London Stock Exchange on 20 May, in reaction to the attacks on Kitchener in the Northcliffe press.[51] At the same time, however, Asquith was unwilling to consider the dismissal of French, with whom he maintained very good personal relations, on the basis only of rumours of his direct role in the affair.[52] He therefore chose to arbitrate between his quarrelling chiefs; and, on 30 May, four days after forming his new cabinet, he took a trip to the field "to discuss [with Sir John French] the whole strategic, political & personal situation in all its aspects."[53] At the conclusion of that trip, he reported to Sylvia Henley that he was "satisfied" that, after two long talks with French, he had "dispelled the miasma of doubt & suspicion between the 2 Field

Marshals."[54] But that proved to be only a temporary relaxation of tensions in an ongoing conflictual relationship.

Kitchener, for his part, while deciding against any punitive action against his surly subordinate, called on the ubiquitous Esher on 21 May to act as a go-between with Sir John, to counter the rumour then circulating that he himself intended to replace French. In addition, Esher's mission was to help French more fully understand Kitchener's assessment of the strategic situation, which he as a field commander might not be fully qualified to appreciate, and to assure him of his support. "I am out to fight the Germans and not Sir John French," he asserted.[55] Esher also delivered a rebuke to Sir John on the involvement of the field staff in political matters. "From what Sir John said," however, Esher was deceived into believing that the press campaign against Kitchener derived from Sir John's intriguing entourage, and "that he had been a very unwilling participator in this newspaper intrigue," a conviction that he communicated to Kitchener.[56]

As a result of his trip to the field on 22 May, Esher was able to convey Sir John's displeasure at not receiving the whole of the New Army as promised, to sooth Sir John's hurt over Kitchener's critique via returning generals, and to relate French's raw nerves over "a certain tone of coldness or lack of appreciation that he seems to detect in your telegrams and letters towards his operations and Troops."[57]

To prevent further misunderstanding, Esher suggested, on the advice of William Robertson, Sir John's chief of staff, that all communications between the Kitchener and Sir John French should pass between the secretary of state for war and the commander-in-chief; that is to say, as official communications, with the advice of their respective staffs, rather than personally between the two.[58] This Kitchener approved, which relaxed tensions to a certain degree, smoothing the rough edges of the personality conflict that existed between the two men. While not apparent at the time, the main result of the measure was to strengthen the position of the wily Robertson as the controlling voice at British headquarters, and to aid him in his vertiginous climb to power as chief of the Imperial General Staff at year's end.

While the appointment of Lloyd George as minister of munitions went a considerable way to resolving the munitions problem, both Kitchener and French suffered a loss in stature in the fracas: Kitchener, in the reduction of his powers; and French, in his loss of political capital, as well as in his reduced control of headquarters. Aware of his weakened political situation, he would be less willing thereafter to challenge the government on matters of grand strategy. As will be shown below, by the end of the Artois campaign, the decisions he had taken in the field and his relationship with his superiors had placed his command in a precarious situation and prepared the way for his eventual fall.

Sir John French's decision to blame the failure of his offensive at Aubers Ridge on 9 May on the shortage of high-explosive shells, and his action in "going public" and appealing to Opposition leaders and Lloyd George on the matter, have been well known since the publication of his memoirs in 1919, and have been commented on variously. Yet there remains some uncertainty over the primary cause of Asquith's decision to rework the ministry,[59] whether it was the Shells Crisis or the resignation of Lord Fisher, the first sea lord, over the Dardanelles strategy, and even over the role of Asquith's heartbreak after the loss of his girlfriend, Venetia Stanley.[60] But one is obliged to give at least some credibility to Asquith's own explanation, quoted above, that "the alleged deficiency of high explosive shells, would if unduly exploited (as they would have been in the House of Commons at this moment) have had the most disastrous effect on the general political and strategic situation," particularly with regard to Italian entry into the war.[61] While additional research has served to clarify the relationship between Sir John French and Kitchener prior to and during the crisis and the impact of the initial French success in Sir John's growing awareness of the benefits of high-explosive shells, the major fact that emerges is that Sir John's fundamental aim in the Shells Crisis was to have Kitchener removed from office.[62]

As noted earlier, however, what Sir John failed to realize was that his attack on Kitchener, because of the principle of cabinet solidarity, was really an attack on Asquith's government and its failure to mobilize the resources of the country,[63] a fact Asquith was not likely to forget. Acting on the advice of the king, Asquith, it must be remembered, not Kitchener, was solely responsible for the removal of Sir John French in December 1915 after the failure of the Loos offensive.[64]

ROBERTSON'S BLAST TO THE KING

Sir Douglas Haig's complaint to the king after the Loos offensive in September regarding Sir John's failure to bring up reserves in time after an initial breakthrough has long been credited with having been the major factor in his recall.[65] But there was another player in the story. A piecing together of documents shows that Sir William Robertson, Sir John's chief of staff, launched a powerful attack, immediately following the failed Artois offensive, on Sir John in critical comments to the king's secretary and also laid out the plan for the British political-military restructuring that was adopted at year's end.

In the Robertson Papers located in the B.H. Liddell Hart Centre for Military Archives in King's College, London, is a copy of a letter from Robertson to the king's secretary, Lord Stamfordham, dated 23 June 1915, in which Robertson comments on the recent campaign and the general strategic situation.[66] By this time, the British had suffered further defeats at Givenchy on 16 June and then had to break off effective action for want of munitions. A handwritten folio follows in the file that gives the appearance of an internal undated memo, which, among other things, proposes certain structural changes in the Imperial General Staff in London.[67] But an enquiry to the Royal Archives confirmed what this author had suspected: namely, that the handwritten folio was an integral part of Robertson's letter of 23 June 1915 to the king's secretary.[68] When the two are put together, they make plain that Robertson played a major role in laying the groundwork for Sir John's recall and the later restructuring of the Imperial General Staff.

So far as British relations with the French were concerned, the attached handwritten pages indicated that Robertson was very unhappy with Sir John's leadership and complained of the constant bickering between Kitchener and French. He also complained that French and Joffre had never properly concerted their efforts. Robertson then blasted his chief, stating that he suspected the government "pay[s] no heed to his (Sir John's) opinion" because he is "a discredited nonentity" in their eyes. He argued that, "if they do *not* trust him they should replace him. If they *do* trust him, they ought to take his advice," or at least solicit his opinion. Moreover, Robertson was of the opinion that Sir John French had never fully placed his own views before the government and had either suppressed or watered down staff documents. Robertson thus sent the uncut originals of three of his recent memoranda for distribution. Not sparing Kitchener in his critique, Robertson went on to recommend major structural changes in London: that the British Imperial General Staff should be restructured with a "trusted & competent head" to provide effective staff work and strategic control of the war, a task the secretary of state for war was not able to perform for want of staff advice.[69]

This was an amazing document for the time. Here in fact was not only a major broadside against Sir John French by his closest adviser but also the blueprint for the staff reorganization that would later take place in December. Sir John's conduct of the Artois offensive and Robertson's appraisal of it provided the bombshell which was poised to explode after one more misstep. French's mishandling of Loos was that event.

FRENCH POLITICS AFTER ARTOIS: CRITIQUE OF MILLERAND AND JOFFRE

In France, as in Great Britain, the military failures in Artois in the spring of 1915 gave rise to a barrage of criticism, focused, in the French case, on the conduct of operations and the management of the war effort. Despite the impressive success of the French X Army in its attack north of Arras on 9 May, subsequent French failures on Vimy Ridge erased all hope of immediate victory. While governmental leaders had been critical of Joffre's strategy of partial operations prior to the Artois offensive, which had proven costly and to little avail, they were now shocked and disappointed when they learned in a cabinet meeting on 22 June that the Artois offensive, on which they had placed high hopes, had to be halted. This was in contrast to the German success in Galicia after the Gorlice-Tarnów breakthrough on 2 May. As a result, ministers and parliamentarians began to lose confidence in the High Command.[70]

In May, Gaston Doumergue, the minister of colonies, wanted to take Millerand's post himself and to install Gallieni as commander-in-chief in place of Joffre.[71] At the beginning of June, a "campaign against Joffre became very violent" in the Chamber.[72] An agitation, centred on Senator Paul Doumer, an influential former premier, and the Radical Socialists arose to have Gallieni replace Millerand and to have Foch installed in place of Joffre.[73] At the same time, another project involving General Charles Lanrezac, former commander of the Fifth Army (replaced by Louis Franchet d'Espèrey before the Battle of the Marne) sought to replace Millerand with General Pierre Dubois and Joffre with General Maurice Sarrail.[74] But these efforts did not have enough support at that moment to succeed.

One of the consequences of the Parliament having voted to remain in session in its meeting on 12 January, as mandated by the constitution, was that the Commissions also continued to function. In the absence of regular sittings of the Parliament, the commissions took on the role of parliamentary watchdog of the war effort, and insisted on inspections in both the interior and eventually the zone of the army, a wide band of territory at the front reserved for the army's administration. Millerand resisted their efforts to oversee the work of both the War Ministry and the High Command. As for Joffre, jealous of his authority and unwilling to have politicians interfere with his strategy and management of the war effort in the operation zone, he engaged in a long-running battle to restrict members of the government and the parliamentary commissions from engaging in inspections. He was sustained by Millerand, but little by little Joffre was obliged to enlarge the scope of inspections. The commissions considered it their role not only to oversee the government's conduct of the war with regard to the production of armaments and provisions but also to monitor the living conditions, health services, and a host of other concerns related to the soldiers both in the interior and at the front. In consequence, the ministers were obliged to spend a vast amount of time responding to the queries of the commissions.[75]

While the French staff was very sparing in its sharing of information, the government and commissions had access to a series of unofficial channels. In addition to information gleaned in the parliamentary inspections, various mobilized deputies, such as Abel Ferry and others, shuttled back and forth from the front to report on the conduct of operations,[76] and some generals had links with politicians with whom they shared their views on strategy and the conduct of operations. While the government had essentially no staff to evaluate information from the front, the General Staff having left with Joffre at the beginning of the war, the cabinet and the commissions were often informed by these unofficial channels.

Before the spring offensive, Millerand was already under attack by the Senate and Chamber's Army Commissions with regard to shortfalls in munitions production.[77] One of the criticisms voiced in the Parliament was that he had too heavy a workload to attend to the multitudinous burdens of his office and needed additional support. As the May attack drew to a close, Millerand was obliged to accept a reduction in his powers on 20 May through the appointment of Albert Thomas, a Socialist deputy, as under-secretary in charge of armaments. Later he was forced to accept three additional under-secretaries to attend to the medical service, the supply service, and aeronautics.[78] Thomas, who later became the minister of munitions, had remarkable success in his position and his appointment went a long way toward resolving the munitions crisis.

The munitions crisis in France was less severe than that in Britain, however, in that the French recognized earlier than the British the huge requirements of trench warfare. Despite the impediment of having the Briey coalfields and Lille industrial region in enemy hands, the French system of enlisting the private sector worked better for armament production than the British model of reliance on state armouries. As early as 20 September 1914, Joffre had urged on Millerand the need for large quantities of munitions, and he repeated this call with more urgent requests, as the needs of trench warfare became more apparent, for an increased stock of munitions and more field guns, heavy artillery, and machine guns. Adding to the productive capacity of state munitions factories, Millerand, as early as September 1914, ordered French industrialists to engage in the manufacture of munitions and left the allocation of resources and share of the market to the powerful Comité des Forges. Prices were fixed at the pre-war level to avoid inflationary competition. Iron and steel deficits were made up by importations from the United States, Britain, and several other countries. As in other countries, troops were recalled from the front to work in munitions factories and women became involved in large numbers.[79] While the results were remarkable, they were insufficient to meet the demands of the front, especially in the area of heavy artillery, for which there were serious shortfalls in the spring of 1915.[80]

There were many complaints from commanders in the field on Joffre's autocratic conduct of operations. Under the influence of Poincaré, who agreed that Joffre failed to listen to his subordinates, lacked flexibility, and abused his authority, the government obliged him to meet with his army group commanders periodically to consult them with regard to future attacks.[81] The first such meeting was held on 23 June and attended by Poincaré, Viviani, Millerand, Joffre, and Joffre's three army group commanders: Foch, commander of the Northern Army Group, Castelnau, commander of the newly created Central Army Group, and Dubail, commander of the Eastern Army Group. Poincaré and Viviani criticized Joffre for "creating false hopes for a breakthrough." Joffre's plan for launching new large offensives after a brief delay was supported by Foch, but both Dubail and Castelnau favoured delay – Dubail for two months or more, and Castelnau until sufficient means had been amassed for two large attacks.[82]

Though he was not obliged to follow the advice of his subordinates, Joffre's authority had been seriously eroded, and the government thereafter would play a more important role in the decisions of the High Command. In this charged atmosphere, success on the battlefield became more and more crucial. At the same time, issues related to the political landscape in France would occupy a much larger place in British strategic deliberations.

STRATEGIC RE-EVALUATION AT GQG AFTER ARTOIS

At GQG, lack of success in the Artois offensive, starting with the failed May attack, led to a major strategic re-evaluation. So optimistic and confident of a French victory was Joffre before the Artois offensive that he had told the assembled cabinet ministers on 18 March that he did not wish that Kitchener should send to the French the "totality of the new Army being formed." Rather, Joffre considered that the current British force with immediate reinforcements would be sufficient. "But," recorded Poincaré, "he believes it essential that the Marshal be under his command."[83]

In its new appraisal after the Battle of Artois, the French General Staff recognized that French armies alone, without the active participation of the British New Armies, could not beat the German Army on the Western Front. Already, on 27 March, a Third Bureau memorandum asserted that growing British forces ought to serve as a reserve for the French Army.[84] After initial failures on the field, the idea was taken up with renewed vigour. In a key memorandum on 25 May 1915, which would serve as the basis for Joffre's strategy for the rest of the year, the Third Bureau placed victory against the German armies conditional upon the arrival, as soon as possible, of twenty divisions of the British New Armies, to allow for the planning of larger attacks. In the reckoning of the Third Bureau, the experience of 9 May had demonstrated that one could always break through enemy lines, but it was impossible to exploit the breakthrough because the enemy could easily bring up his reserves to plug the breach. To resolve this problem, it was necessary to attack in depth in two places: the first to use up enemy reserves, and the second in order to press the breakthrough.[85] This was to become the settled view for the next offensive.

To have available the necessary forces for such attacks, it was essential, reasoned the French General Staff, to have a major increase in their *masse de manoeuvre* (mobile forces). Only the British possessed the necessary resources in the form of Kitchener's New Armies. Of the fifty-eight divisions constituted by the British, only twenty-one were in France. Even if the British New Armies did not have a "significant offensive capability," they could nevertheless relieve French divisions in the trenches (such as the troops of the II Army south of Arras) in order to free them for the attack. It was within this optic that Joffre decided that the British must send their New Armies to France "as soon as possible."[86] After the failed spring offensive of 1915, it was no longer possible to deny the widening gulf of strategic opinion between French and British planners. Thus began the debate that led to the Calais Conference of 6 July 1915.

Kitchener drew other strategic conclusions from the Triple Entente's overall military situation and the Allied failures in Artois in May. Before the Artois offensive, when his confidence in the success of the operation was at its high point, and his relations with Sir John French were still cordial, he withdrew his earlier condition that the French would have to break the German line before he would authorize the departure of the New Armies to France. Hence, on 6 May he promised to Sir John the sequential dispatch of the six divisions of the First New Army, according to an established timetable.[87] But on 14 May, Kitchener changed his mind, following Sir John's failure at Aubers Ridge and the press campaign directed against the London chief on the subject of munitions. Despite the fact that the first division promised had already left for France, Kitchener cancelled the departure of the others; and in spite of Sir John's protests, he received only two divisions more in order not to default on his promises to relieve French trenches.[88]

On 14 May, Kitchener explained to his colleagues in the War Council his concerns about the overall situation which had motivated his decision. Very pessimistic, following Russian defeats in Poland, he was afraid that the Germans would launch a great victorious offensive against France and then invade Britain. He therefore wished to keep the First New Army in Britain to guard against any eventuality and, if necessary, to boost the Dardanelles expedition, which also was going badly. To achieve these purposes, it would be necessary to adopt a defensive strategy in France.[89] In fact, on 7 June, the War Council decided to send three divisions of the First New Army to the Dardanelles to allow Hamilton to take the offensive.[90]

Thus, contrary to Joffre, Kitchener, after the breakdown of the Artois offensive in May, advocated a defensive strategy on the Western Front.[91] This strategy held sway until Joffre demanded the dispatch of the New Armies to France. There followed a month of negotiations and various meetings before the two allies attempted to resolve the difference at the Calais Conference on 6 July.

JOFFRE'S APPEAL FOR THE BRITISH NEW ARMIES

From the beginning of the war, Joffre had used a variety of methods to insist that the British send more troops to France. He had acted through his government on a number of occasions; he had coordinated demands with Sir John French; he had taken advantage of Millerand's visit to London on 22–23 January 1915; and he had intervened directly with Kitchener during conferences on 1 November 1914 and 29 March 1915. Frequently, he linked his demands with the immediate needs of the battlefield or future operations. Sometimes, even, he couched his demands within the framework of Kitchener's fears or preferred operational plans.[92]

This time, Joffre led off on 27 May by asking the French war minister to appeal to the British government for the dispatch of twenty divisions of the New Armies.[93] In addition, anxious to tighten his direct communication links with Kitchener, Joffre wrote Kitchener a personal unofficial note which he had delivered by Yarde-Buller, British liaison officer at GQG.[94] Joffre would speak directly with the man who had the greatest influence over British strategy and who would be the most likely to give him satisfaction.

In preparing his overall strategic evaluation, as this note indicated, Joffre was anxious about the global situation of the Allies following Russian defeats in Galicia. The strategic situation required that "the main allied effort must take place in France," he wrote, since the Russians will be "unable for some time to carry out an offensive" and questions of terrain would prevent the Italian armies from "debouching in the plain." "The events at Arras," he continued, "prove that tactically we can break the German line" if the Allies made a larger-scale effort and attacked "simultaneously on several fronts." His message to the British was simple and unequivocal: France, which had "engaged 2,200,000 men on its northeastern front, was at the limit of its resources in men." The solution to the problem was now "in the hands of the British." He therefore asked that "the dispatch of the British new armies take place with the least possible delay," according to an established timetable, so that he could plan with Sir John French new offensive operations from which he anticipated decisive victory.[95]

Kitchener interpreted Joffre's note as a trial balloon because it had not been signed, and thus gave only a vague verbal reply through Yarde-Buller. He avoided mentioning any date for the dispatch of the New Armies to the Western Front.[96] In the background to Kitchener's reticence was the idea, reinforced by the recent press criticisms, that these armies ought not to go to the front without having at their disposition an adequate stock of munitions.[97] Kitchener, moreover, had very little faith in large-scale French offensives, which would cause enormous losses without bringing significant advantages. In his opinion, any troops sent to France would be used to undertake new offensives. Kitchener's strategy for the moment, therefore, was to fight a war of attrition in the hope that the Germans would continue to break themselves against Allied trenches.[98]

Immediately after this exchange of communications between Joffre and Kitchener, a conference of considerable importance took place, almost by chance. On 30 May, Prime Minister Asquith, once the new coalition government had been formed, went to visit the French front. He spent some days at Sir John's command post in Saint-Omer to resolve differences between Sir John and Kitchener, and to visit the troops. He also met Joffre, Foch, and Millerand there on 2 June 1915.[99] During this conference, Asquith came under strong pressure from Joffre, Foch, and Sir John to authorize the sending of all available British troops to France.[100] In this regard, as previously noted, Joffre and Sir John concerted their efforts. But Asquith, knowing the position of Kitchener,[101] avoided any firm commitment on the subject.[102] In the absence of Kitchener, who, according to Poincaré, preferred to keep the New Armies "for another theatre of operations,"[103] Asquith focused the discussion on "technical matters"[104] and avoided the vital questions of British strategy and the eventual allocation of the New Armies between the various fronts. The French emerged from their encounter with Asquith disappointed that, for "want of rifles and munitions," there could be no question of receiving the twenty divisions they had requested. In fact, Asquith said, with respect to the "5 or 6 divisions" that the British might send in the near future, the French would have to "share with them a portion of the munitions reserved for French's army."[105] According to Foch, Asquith even requested "that we furnish 75 caliber guns to the British Army, which has neither an equivalent gun nor quantity of munitions."[106]

Even though this preliminary conference did not give immediate results, Asquith was much impressed by the "imperturbable optimism" of Joffre and Foch, who were "absolutely convinced" that they had "the Germans in the palm of their hand" and that they would make a breakthrough "without delay" which would lead to the conclusion of the war. That attitude he contrasted with "the unease and forebodings" in London[107] and the reservations of his colleagues toward the Western Front. As a consequence of the marked strategic difference between the military commanders at the front, including the commander of the BEF, and the military authorities in London, Asquith came to the conclusion that major steps had to be taken to resolve the matter. Returning to London, Asquith thus urged on Kitchener the necessity for Sir John French to come to London "as soon as the operations in progress would permit" to discuss "the general strategy for the months to come." And after this British strategic reappraisal, "there should follow a conference between the English and the French in which that strategy should be determined between them."[108] The British prime minister, having found that the vast difference in the strategic appreciation of the two allies was unacceptable, had taken the initiative to solve the problem.

The Battle of Artois resumed on 15–16 June with a British attack at Givenchy and a new French attack on Vimy Ridge, both of which gave very little in the way of results. French attacks continued until 25 June.

In the meantime, Joffre, who did not anticipate decisive results from these actions, was planning two new large-scale offensives, to take place about 15 July. According to the French General Staff, in order to exploit the breakthrough, it would be necessary to attack on a much wider front in order to avoid artillery fire on the flanks, as occurred at Vimy Ridge on 9 May. This time, the primary large-scale attack (to include twenty-one new French divisions) would consist of forty divisions on a wide front about Arras, while the secondary attack in Champagne would consist of ten divisions. On 4 June, before the conclusion of the Artois attacks, Joffre communicated unofficially to Sir John French his plan for these new operations. For Joffre's plan to work, the British would need to relieve the twenty-five-mile front of the Second French Army between Hébertune and Chaulnes, which would free two French corps for the attack. The British would also be asked to attack alongside the French in Artois, either to the north or the south of the French attack.[109]

But these plans depended on the British. For the British command to be able to carry out the necessary relief of the Second French Army, Kitchener would have to send several divisions of his New Armies to the Western Front. To persuade the British chief, Millerand sent a delegation to London a few days later, which consisted of three French officers: Colonel Edmond Buat, Millerand's *chef de cabinet*, an aide, Nobel, and Colonel Renouard of Joffre's Third Bureau. These officers had an interview with Kitchener on 8–9 June, during which they outlined Joffre's new plan and, following up on the conference with Asquith on 2 June, asked Kitchener to send his new divisions to carry out the desired reliefs.[110] But Kitchener, who had just approved the departure of the last three divisions of his First New Army for the Dardanelles on 7 June, raised as an objection the lack of munitions for his Second Army, the only one now available, which he did not think could be sent to France before 15 August. "In his view," wrote Buat, "success will be achieved through the organization of more strongly reinforced fortifications on every front. It is against these that the Germans will break themselves, after which, but only after which, the offensive will be taken."[111] The results of this mission were therefore, according to Lord Esher, Kitchener's confidant, "a lamentable failure," Kitchener being "in the least sympathetic humor."[112] The confrontation of strategic views had arrived at a complete impasse.

In effect, following this interview, Kitchener took the counter-offensive by sending General Sir Arthur Paget on a special mission to Sir John's headquarters in order to suggest to him that he carry out the reliefs desired in Joffre's plan with forces in hand and adopt a defensive attitude.[113] In addition, Paget was sent to Joffre to make the same suggestion.[114]

Sir John French's reply to the Paget mission underscored his disagreement with the strategy of his chief in London. According to Sir John, the only solution compatible with "the military situation and the honor of the British armies" was his cooperation with a French attack planned for the month of July, "with all the resources that His Majesty's government could put at his disposition." At the same time, Sir John stated his decided opposition to the role of "passive defensive" for the British Army, which he believed would be "disastrous" for its morale and offensive spirit.[115]

Apparent to observers, both then and now, was that the resolution of the conflicting strategies around the deployment and use of the New Armies would require consultation among the highest political authorities of both countries. Herein lay the genesis of the first Anglo-French political-military conference on 6 July 1915.

CONCLUSION

The evidence now available would suggest that the Artois offensive of 1915 was the event that finally opened Allied eyes to the true nature of trench warfare and crushed the hope of a quick and easy victory. In retrospect, one is obliged to acknowledge that, although the Artois offensive in the spring of 1915 had little strategic value, it served as the catalyst for major changes in the Allied conduct of the war in an effort to break the impasse.

On the British side, the establishment of the first British coalition government on 26 May was the immediate result. Balfour replaced Churchill at the Admiralty and, with the appointment of Lloyd George as the minister of munitions, Kitchener's powers were reduced. The important political and military structural changes that took place in December 1915 were the long-term consequence of the re-evaluation sparked by the failed spring offensive and Robertson's recommended structural changes. In the event, Robertson, a committed westerner, was placed in charge of a much more powerful Imperial General Staff, and Haig, his ally in the field, was appointed as commander-in-chief of the BEF. The Western Front strategy was thus bound to prevail in 1916. The failed Artois offensive was decisive in the political-military sphere, though producing very little in the way of tangible results in the field.

The Artois offensive produced equally dramatic results for the French. Owing to disappointment within the government and the Parliament on the conduct of operations, both Millerand's and Joffre's powers were circumscribed. GQG's strategic re-evaluation led to Joffre's urgent call for the dispatch of the British New Armies to allow him to engage in a major new offensive, which pitted his strategy against that of Kitchener. That conflict led to a major revaluation of British strategy and the political-military conference at Calais on 6 July 1915. Also, following the Artois offensive and in light of the overall military situation of the Entente powers, Joffre took the lead to coordinate Allied military efforts at the Chantilly Conference the following day. A new era was dawning in Allied conduct of the war. To these two important conferences and their consequences we now turn our attention.

CHAPTER EIGHT

Strategic Conflict: The Calais and Chantilly Conferences, July 1915

THE YEAR 1915 WAS NOTEWORTHY FOR, among other things, the strategic conflict between the French and the British relative to the conduct of the war on the Western Front.[1] That conflict derived from the differing political aims of each country, from the divergent attitudes between political and military leaders, and, above all, from a different assessment of the military situation by the French and the British. To resolve these strategic differences, and to maintain the concerted operation of the coalition, the highest-ranking political and military authorities of the two countries met in Calais on 6 July 1915, in what was the first Allied conference of its kind. This was an important step forward in the otherwise fractured nature of Anglo-French military strategy.

British historians have long maintained that no minutes of the meeting were kept.[2] But research by the author has uncovered the existence of the conference notes of the British prime minister, while a colleague inadvertently came across the British summary of the meeting's conclusions in a 1917 file. Also, unknown to early British researchers for some time were the complete unofficial minutes of the meeting in the private papers of Alexandre Millerand, the French war minister. These key documents, amplified by other findings, allow us to understand the true nature of the strategic debate and the decisions taken at the Calais Conference on 6 July 1915. They also provide a better understanding of the sequence of events leading to the Anglo-French offensive in the autumn of that year.

While the pre-war arrangements for command and coordination on land and sea between the French and the British were to prove inadequate in the crucible of war, arrangements for French coordination with the Russians were even more tenuous. A military agreement had been made for immediate Russian attacks in East Prussia, but no mechanism had been set up for Allied coordination. After the failure of the Artois offensive and the continued retreat of Russia in the spring of 1915, Joffre became concerned that no instrument existed for the coordination of Allied grand strategy and the conduct of the war. The entry of Italy into the war and the creation of a second front added to the urgency for Allied coordination. To address these concerns, Joffre took the initiative in calling a conference with the military representatives of all the Allied powers on 7 July, at French headquarters at Chantilly, in which he attempted to coordinate the fall offensives of the several allies. This marked a major milestone in Allied military planning.

His plan for coordinated offensives became unhinged, however, by huge Russian defeats on the Eastern Front in the course of 1915. These reverses also unravelled the diplomatic situation in the Balkans by bringing Bulgaria into the war against the Allies, with disastrous results for Serbia. Joffre's initiative, nonetheless, could claim significant success in aiding the faltering Russian ally, though the British, for their part, soon realized that the French commander's strategy for Allied coordination made it increasingly difficult to retain their freedom of action in the Dardanelles and subsequent Salonika expeditions.

ORIGINS OF THE CALAIS CONFERENCE

As demonstrated in the last chapter, the exchange of letters on conflicting strategies and the missions of emissaries lacking authority could not resolve the strategic impasse between Joffre and Kitchener generated by Joffre's request for twenty divisions of the New Army for the launching of major new offensives on the Western Front. It was up to those in positions of power to address the problem.

Asquith had already come to the conclusion, following his trip to France in which he met with Joffre, Foch, and Millerand on 2 June, that a conference would be needed in due course to resolve differing strategic conceptions between French and British authorities. In face of the obvious failure of the Buat mission on 8–9 June, Paul Cambon, the French ambassador in London, proposed to Kitchener a conference between himself, Sir John, Joffre, and Millerand[3] as "the only means of coming to an agreement on these important points." Kitchener indicated that he was always ready to talk with General Joffre, Asquith having already envisaged such a conference. But the British wanted to wait until the end of the operation in process north of La Bassée before meeting with the French, since, in Kitchener's words, the "success or lack of success of this operation could have a bearing on what decisions to take."[4]

The French government, which gave its agreement to the idea of an Allied conference on 23 June, similarly wanted to see the results of current operations before consulting with the British. Expanding the scope of the conference, the French also asked that the naval authorities be present "in order to assure the most effective collaboration possible of allied land and naval forces."[5] The object of the conference would be "the resolution with regard to the combined action of Anglo-French forces, whether in Flanders or the Dardanelles." On Kitchener's suggestion, the conference was further enlarged to include the prime ministers of both countries so as to make the decisions of the conference "binding." And, to allow the British to complete their prior strategic re-evaluation, which was to commence at the beginning of July, the date of the conference was finally set for 6 July. Calais, also on Kitchener's suggestion, was chosen as its site.[6] Thus came into being the first political-military conference between the two allies. While the immediate initiative originated with the French ambassador in London, the process for resolving the strategic question reflected the wishes of both Asquith and Kitchener.

In the meantime, as noted earlier, Sir John attempted to force Kitchener's hand on the question of reinforcements, and also on the strategic issue, by cooperating more intimately with Joffre, despite the friction between them during their recent offensive. In order to reinforce their request for the dispatch of the New Armies to France, Sir John and Joffre addressed coordinated requests in near-identical terms to the British government on 23–24 June, asking for a fixed timetable for the arrival of the New Armies to permit joint planning of the new offensives.[7] Wilson, who masterminded the démarche, calculated that the two requests coming through different channels, in addition to reinforcing each other, would oblige a discussion in cabinet, where opinions were divided on Kitchener's strategy, and hence produce a firm commitment on the part of the government.[8]

At Sir John's request,[9] the two military chiefs met at Chantilly on 24 June to "draw up in common their future plans," which would allow them to concert their efforts in opposition to Kitchener's strategy. Accompanied by Robertson and Wilson, Sir John indicated to Joffre (flanked by his chief of staff, Major-General Pellé) his support of Joffre's plan for a new large-scale offensive in five to six weeks. The two chiefs also agreed that Kitchener's defensive strategy, which Joffre argued would lead to the defeat of the Russians and then that of the French, should be resisted. They expressed their mutual opposition to the Dardanelles expedition. After reviewing their coordinated letters requesting British troops, they promised to work together in the future to have all available British troops sent to France.[10] This community of views of the French and British commanders was intended to put additional pressure on the British government.

The plan worked. Despite his unhappiness with regard to the method employed by Sir John French to force his hand, Kitchener felt an added obligation to send troops to France following the joint planning of the offensive, so as not to be accused of having deserted the French.[11]

FRENCH PUBLIC OPINION AND POLITICS

The most decisive factor, however, that figured in the British strategic review was their perception of the political situation in France. The failure of the Artois offensive had multiple ramifications. According to Poincaré, Joffre, following the defeats of the 16 June offensive, had "become more accessible to taking counsel."[12] The government obliged him to hold periodic meetings with his army group commanders – the first on 23 June. At that meeting, Poincaré reproached Joffre for having "given public opinion hopes which could not be realized" and stated that "the country, finding its illusions shattered, will perhaps lose part of its required strength in patience and perseverance."[13] Toward the end of June, the parliamentary agitation against Millerand and Joffre intensified, and Millerand was criticized even more severely than previously in the Army Commission of the Senate.[14] The need for victory was becoming more and more imperative in order to silence these criticisms. As Millerand later revealed, as a result of criticism in the Chamber against the war minister, and "the inactivity" of Joffre, "the Ministry had pressed Joffre to take the offensive, which he was ready to do if he obtained the necessary support from the British army."[15]

The state of public opinion in France was of considerable importance to British planners, who tended to believe that the French Army was dependable but that the French government was unstable and unreliable.[16] The British thus saw in the erosion of French public opinion the rationale for another great French offensive. As early as 12 June, Kitchener, in summarizing Joffre's reasons for wanting another large offensive, exclaimed, "The French people cannot look upon the continuation of the conflict, with equanimity of soul, nor with the total certainty that a long war of attrition requires. Therefore, an effort to win the battle must be made."[17]

In the month of June, several messages of similar portent were communicated to Kitchener and Asquith. On 20 June, Lord Esher, who carried out quasi-official shuttle diplomacy on behalf of Kitchener, wrote from Paris that the morale of the people had declined since his visit a month earlier. At the same time, Esher alleged that, if the current French offensive was unable to take the Douai plains, "there will be a more or less swift reaction among civilians and women in favour of peace. Even for what is called here 'une paix boiteuse' [a mutilated peace]."[18]

On 23 June, Sir John, in arguing the case with Kitchener for a new offensive, observed that a lack of British support at this critical juncture of the war could have a serious effect on French attitudes. He indicated that he had learned from "reliable sources" of the existence of a party in support of "peace at any price" in the centre and south of France which was slowly gaining ground.[19] Sir Douglas Haig, the most respected of the British army commanders in France, wrote Prime Minister Asquith on 25 June concerning the discontent among civilians and soldiers in France as a result of the British sending so many troops and munitions to the Dardanelles. He also observed that certain well-informed people were fearful that, if progress was not soon made "to drive the enemy out of France, the peace party could succeed, and that peace could be made before winter!"[20] This message was reinforced on 29 June by Lord Derby, who, just returned from France, was "filled with forebodings about the weakening of French spirit – both civil and military."[21]

The conclusion to be drawn was clear. Significant measures would have to be taken to reassure the French. As Ambassador Bertie wrote from Paris on 4 July 1915, "if the French do not obtain victory now, the political situation could become difficult and the possibility of a generous peace offer made by Germany to France should not be lost sight of."[22] Bertie's conclusions, unknown to the British cabinet, were based on information gleaned directly that morning by LeRoy Lewis, the British military attaché, from a conversation with Millerand. According to Millerand, neither the army nor the public could stand up to a second winter campaign without victory, and as a result, the government could fall.[23]

On the reverse side of the coin, the findings of the Boulogne Conference on munitions on 19–20 June made the case for a defensive strategy. At that conference, Lloyd George, the British minister of munitions, met with his French counterpart, Albert Thomas, along with experts from both French and British headquarters. After having examined the requirements for munitions under current conditions of war and production capabilities, they concluded that the quantity of munitions necessary for a successful offensive on the Western Front would not be available before the spring of 1916. Their suggestion was the implementation of an active defensive strategy on the Western Front in the meantime.[24]

This idea was fully endorsed by Kitchener, who, in a memorandum for the cabinet on 29 June, advocated an active defensive posture on the Western Front and adjournment of the offensive in France until the spring of 1916, when the New Armies would be better trained and more adequately supplied with munitions. The Russians, by that time, would be in condition to renew their offensive.[25]

But Esher, who dined with Kitchener that evening, argued against these conclusions, explaining that "the malaise in France" was on the increase because of criticism of the military conduct of the war. Joffre would certainly not accept inaction until the spring of next year, said Esher, in view of his offensive already planned with Sir John. As a palliative measure, Esher suggested that Wilson, who had made the arrangements prior to the war for the intervention of the BEF in France, should come to London to present the French position. For, he said, the French "would never believe that their case had been well presented to Lord Kitchener without Wilson having made it."[26]

That intervention proved decisive. Later that same evening, Wilson, in addition to Robertson, already invited, was asked to attend the special meetings of the British cabinet on 2–3 July.[27] These sessions would hammer out British strategy prior to the Calais Conference.

But by then, several messages on the uneasiness in France had already influenced Kitchener, as was evident in his interview with Wilson on 30 June. A dedicated supporter of the Dardanelles campaign – which Wilson claimed the French "hated" – Kitchener asserted that he intended to reinforce that theatre in order to obtain victory. Evacuation of the Dardanelles, he said, would cause "troubles in India, the loss of Egypt, and in addition loss of the entire force." But to Wilson's surprise and satisfaction, Kitchener was already planning major initiatives to sustain the French. Kitchener indicated that he had prepared three memoranda for the Calais meeting specifying when the New Armies would be ready to go to France, when the required stock of munitions would be available, and when the reinforcements necessary to replace losses would be in the theatre. For the time being, at Calais, Kitchener would speak to the French only of fifteen divisions of reinforcements, but he thought he could reinforce British troops in France with twenty-five divisions before the end of the year. These reinforcements would consist of three armies of six divisions, a Canadian division, and, after victory in Gallipoli, six divisions from the Dardanelles, which would also go to France. Astonished with this "programme," Wilson thought the French, both civilian and military, would be happy if, at the end of the year, the British had fifty divisions in France and could take up sixty miles of trenches (as opposed to the twenty-five that they held at the moment). On the other hand, Kitchener was still very firm on the question of strategy and insisted on the necessity for a defensive strategy on the Western Front.[28]

In an interview with Asquith on 1 July, Wilson further prepared the ground. Asquith was already aware that in France there was a "strong agitation against Millerand and Joffre" which, in his opinion, would succeed against the former but not against the latter. Upon Asquith's request, Wilson recapitulated the French grievances: the lack of munitions for recent British offensives, doubts about British strategic intentions for the autumn and the winter, French opposition to the Dardanelles expedition, and their insistence on a "programme" for the dispatch of British troops "for the months to come." To all of this, Asquith seemed very attentive.[29] Sir John and Robertson also had interviews with Kitchener and Asquith before the cabinet meeting to express the point of view of the British Army in the field.[30] The grand result of these several interventions relative to French uneasiness was that, before the cabinet meeting on 2–3 July for the discussion on strategy, several key players were already prepared to reassure their French ally by making firmer commitments.

At the first session of the cabinet on the morning of 2 July, Sir John, supported by Robertson, gave his appreciation of the strategic situation in France and "surprised" the twenty-two members of the cabinet by announcing a major new offensive planned in concert with Joffre for the beginning of August.[31] "Very divergent" opinions were then expressed, and as a result, after two and a half hours, the session was adjourned to the following day.[32] On 3 July the entire cabinet again met with Sir John and Robertson, and this time Wilson, representing the French point of view, was included as well. According to the latter, the French "were not angry, but discontented and a little suspicious." The main reasons, he said, were "the Dardanelles [and] the lack of munitions." After "much discussion," Kitchener said that, in his opinion, the Second New Army must be sent to the French right away, and that a timetable for the departure of the New Armies needed to be communicated to the French at Calais. The cabinet further decided, with some reservations in order to maintain freedom of action relative to the different fronts, that the Western Front would be the main theatre of war and that the government would send all the troops it could to France, though it continued to insist on the importance of a defensive strategy. The cabinet approved a note drawn up by Asquith giving the conclusions of their deliberations.[33]

A crucial moment in Britain's twentieth-century history had taken place with the country's decision to send the bulk of its forces to France for the defence of the continent. That decision was taken principally because of the perceived weakening of French morale and in order not to "desert" the French militarily.[34] Concern with French public opinion and Allied solidarity was thus decisive. Even before the Calais Conference, the British had decided to give satisfaction to the French with regard to the dispatch of the New Armies to France.

Asquith's note, communicated to the king, is worth analyzing as a window into the government's attitude with regard to the intended role of the New Armies in France and the strategy for their engagement. For the moment, he stated, the best service that British forces could render would be to relieve French trenches to free French troops, either for the offensive or the defensive. "In view of the imperfect state of the equipment of our new army in the area of artillery munitions," Asquith continued, "we must strongly represent to the French that they should postpone all offensive operations." But, even in this instance, the cabinet – watering down Kitchener's views – left a loophole: if the French considered such operations essential, Sir John would sustain them with "his existing forces in a helpful manner according to his judgment, but without too heavy losses in his army."[35] For this element of flexibility with regard to strategy, Esher reproached his government for "a rather weak-kneed decision."[36] In any event, the foundations had been laid for the application of Joffre's strategy even before the Calais Conference.

Historian Rhodri Williams has expressed the view that the British acted in consequence of bad information in the spring and early summer of 1915: that they confused the normal conflicts of the political system of the Third Republic with a true lowering of morale; and that during that time there was really no war-weariness in France.[37] The evidence suggests, however, that key political players in France thought otherwise, and that there were significant pockets of discontent as the population adjusted to the concept of a long war. On 16 June 1915 one historian-turned-soldier wrote from the field: "One cannot help feeling a certain weariness in the course of such a long campaign with no clear ending in sight. [This sentiment] is felt everywhere, coupled with a clear determination not to stop before victory"[38] More research is required to ascertain the breadth and depth of that sentiment. It was certainly shared by France's political leaders and fully communicated to the British. The fact remains that perception may play the same role as hard facts in the decision-making process.

THE CALAIS CONFERENCE

The political-military conference of French and British leaders, the first of its kind, held at Calais on 6 July 1915, marked a turning point in Anglo-French conduct of the war. The British delegation, in addition to Prime Minister Asquith, who chaired the meeting, included Kitchener, as secretary of state for war, Balfour, as first lord of the Admiralty, Lord Crewe, who was temporarily replacing Grey as secretary of state for foreign affairs, and Sir John French, the commander-in-chief of the British Expeditionary Force in France. Their powerful French counterparts likewise attended: Prime Minister Viviani, Millerand, the minister of war, Augagneur, the naval minister, and Joffre, commander-in-chief of the French armies of the northeast. In addition, Albert Thomas, recently named French minister of munitions, plus an unidentified aide-de-camp (perhaps Captain R. Douymayrou) from Millerand's office were present.[39] Poincaré did not attend, presumably because his analogous British counterpart, King George V, British head of state, was not present either. Nevertheless, powerful political and military leaders of the two countries, who possessed the necessary authority to formulate a joint strategy, assembled for the first time. The conference was held in recognition that the war could not be won without the effective operation of the Anglo-French coalition.

The conference was very badly planned. First, no one came to welcome the British delegation, which arrived at Calais toward midnight on 5 July.[40] On the morning of 6 July, the conference, which the French thought was to open at 9 o'clock, was adjourned to 10 to allow the British to get up and have breakfast.[41] Members of the French delegation, in the meantime, marched back and forth on the platform of the Gare Maritime, the meeting place. But, according to Hankey, all seemed in a good humour when the conference finally began at 10 o'clock.[42]

Even more serious, for reasons that have never been explained, liaison officers such as Wilson and Huguet were excluded from the meeting.[43] As a consequence, the conference took place in French, without the traditional interpreters, to the disadvantage of the British, who, with the exception of Kitchener, had a very limited command of the language. "I have never in my life heard so much bad French spoken," observed Asquith, whose own French was barely passable, while noting that "none of the French could speak a word of English."[44] Communication must have been painful under those circumstances. Even more serious, no official minutes, normally the task of the liaison officers, were kept. The result was that each side could interpret the rather ambiguous conclusions as it wished, believing that its views had prevailed.[45] This was a sure formula for later misunderstanding.

From the historical point of view, the results have likewise been obscured for a very long while. On the British side, in the absence of official minutes, historians have had to rely principally on secondary accounts, those of Maurice Hankey, the secretary of the Dardanelles Committee, Henry Wilson and Sydney Clive, the British liaison officers, Esher, and others, based on what they learned from the participants, especially the British.[46] The "draft conclusions" of the conference, drawn up by Hankey after the fact, were later misplaced and discovered only by chance, more than half a century later, by my colleague Keith Neilson in British files for 1917.[47]

But in-depth archival research has uncovered the accounts of several participants, allowing for a much fuller appreciation of the conference. Some of Asquith's descriptions of the event plus his conference notes have been located in the files of his confidante, Sylvia Henley.[48] Sir John's account and his description of the conference sent to Winnifred Bennett add further details.[49] But the richest cache of documents was found in Alexandre Millerand's private papers, including his personal notes on the conference and an unofficial set of minutes several pages in length. These documents, in conjunction with other sources, allow us to establish accurately and completely what really happened at this crucial event.[50]

Some uncertainty nonetheless remains as to the results of the hour-long private conversation between Kitchener and Joffre which preceded the official session of the conference on 6 July. We know that Kitchener arranged through Wilson this interview "all alone" with Joffre, in order to "explain all his fears and to show him his complete hand, and to come to an agreement as to what he would say in front of the politicians, which he (K) hates and of whom he is as suspicious as Joffre."[51]

Before the conference, Joffre already knew through Robertson the prior decisions of the British government.[52] But, since there is not an account in the archives of the private interview between Kitchener and Joffre, and secondary documentation remains fragmentary,[53] the precise results are difficult to nail down. George Cassar, Kitchener's biographer, has affirmed that Kitchener indicated to Joffre his intention of sending immediately to France his Second New Army and the other New Armies thereafter, but that, for want of munitions, he desired that the Second New Army should be "placed in the trenches rather than employed for active operations."[54] That desire was in fact expressed by Kitchener in his "Note on the subject of the arrival in France of English divisions," which he apparently handed to Joffre and which he honoured the next day in his discussions with Sir John French.[55]

But it is difficult to believe, as Cassar and others have affirmed, that the two chiefs came to an agreement on strategy,[56] given their vigorous confrontation on the subject during the conference and Joffre's later actions contrary to Kitchener's wishes. It should be noted nonetheless that, at the conference, Joffre spoke in terms of "attrition," rather than breakthrough, apparently for the benefit of the English, to avoid "disillusion as at Arras,"[57] when in reality his plans were still geared to seeking a strategic breakthrough.

At the conference, Asquith, as chair, opened the proceedings with a brief statement in which he reaffirmed British commitment to the Allied cause until the realization of "complete victory" and the determination of the two allies "to contribute all their forces to the accomplishment

Kitchener (centre), greeted by (left to right) Albert Thomas, Millerand, and Joffre at the Calais train station, 6 July 1915, prior to the Calais Conference. (Augagneur, the French naval minister, was also present but, standing beside Kitchener, is almost totally obscured in the photo.) An important arrangement was made in private consultation between Kitchener and Joffre prior to the conference to employ the First New Army, soon to be sent to France, in a defensive role. (*L'Illustration*, 17 July 1915)

of the common task." The purpose of the conference was simply to determine "the means most likely to lead us to the achievement of our common goal."[58] Viviani, on behalf of the French government, "replied in like terms" and "acknowledged that we only differ on use of means."[59] The solidarity of the alliance was thus reaffirmed without equivocation by the two political leaders.

Kitchener, who with Joffre dominated the conference, then made a stirring presentation in which he reassured the French by discussing his plans for sending vast new forces to France. He began by explaining that there were already three divisions of the British New Army on the Western Front, bringing the total to twenty-four. He then gave the timetable

The first full-blown Anglo-French political-military conference was held at Calais on 6 July 1915. (Four in front, left to right): Joffre, Kitchener, Delcassé, Asquith; (in background, left to right): French, Viviani, Augagneur, Balfour, Thomas, Millerand, and Crewe (representing the British Foreign Office). The conference was decisive in that the British promised their New Armies for France and established the schedule for their arrival. (*L'Illustration*, 17 July 1915)

for the departure of the other New Armies. The six divisions of the Second New Army, now ready to depart, would be in France by the end of July, followed by a Canadian division at the beginning of August. The other New Armies, each with six divisions, would follow in regular sequence. The Third New Army would embark at the end of August, the fourth on 31 October, and the fifth probably about the following April. In the spring of 1916, toward the end of April, two other armies would be ready.[60] The announcement of these massive reinforcements, thirty-seven divisions altogether, was a major victory for the French – for whatever the strategy, defensive or offensive, the promised arrival of the New Armies in France signified a very firm British commitment to the French alliance.

As to the Dardanelles, Kitchener reaffirmed his plan to score a victory, sending there three divisions of his First New Army (approved 7 June), plus two territorial divisions (approved 5 July), the latter to "remain in Egypt ready for any eventuality."[61] Despite the military failures to date, Kitchener was entirely optimistic about the future of the Dardanelles operations, based, it would appear, on a serious underestimation of Turkish military capabilities.[62] "Once the fleet gets through, everything will get through," he said. "I am counting on it for September." And, not resisting the temptation to promise even doubtful reinforcements, Kitchener unveiled his plan to send the ten British divisions from the Dardanelles to France after victory in the Dardanelles. These divisions, added to the other forces designated for France, plus three Indian divisions and an Australian one, would add up to a magnificent total of seventy-five divisions for the French front, that is to say, a million and a half men. "For a million and a half at the front, we will need a million behind them. I will have them," Kitchener declared.[63] This was an extraordinary promise! Found only in the minutes and in the personal notes in Millerand's private papers, Kitchener's extravagant declaration on future troop deployments to France, far beyond the constraint of fifteen divisions he had indicated to Wilson, was bound to lead to future disappointments.

Kitchener then outlined the British point of view on strategy. The situation with regard to munitions, Kitchener affirmed, would not be favourable before the end of 1915, "as the increase in artillery reduces the number of rounds [available] per piece." But he foresaw major improvements toward the end of the year. "When the second army will take up the line, there will be 6 or 7 rounds per gun. It will be the same when the third arrives. But, at the end of the year, despite the arrival of the fourth army, there will be 13 rounds per piece." His strategy, to wait before making a major offensive, was the logical conclusion. "We must not go too quickly," said Kitchener. He therefore counselled "caution, especially now," and urged France not to "lose people in offensives." "Passive defence is the loss of an army," he said, but he argued that there was "a major difference between a passive defensive and unlimited offensive."[64] His plan therefore was one of active defence, involving three or four offensives not to break through but to "shake the enemy," to "kill the enemy rather than to gain ground."[65] Kitchener wished to husband Allied forces, for, in his opinion, "after having pushed back the Russian armies, Germany will consider doing the same with regard to France."[66]

Millerand, on the other hand, spoke in favour of the offensive, underlining the importance of political considerations, "public opinion and the morale of the troops." He observed that the arrival of British troops would allow the Allies, "by a judicious allocation of forces," to achieve the goal of "beating the enemy in order to improve the general situation." That observation upset Balfour, who exclaimed, "Then you will lose people." An ardent defender of the war of attrition, Balfour thought the essential goal should be to "kill Germans" (tuer du boche), meaning, "to wear out the enemy in maintaining our forces for the decisive moment."[67]

Joffre, looking at the Allied situation from the point of view of a multi-front war, then countered with his argument in favour of an offensive strategy based on the needs of the entire coalition. In terms of Allied grand strategy, he insisted that "each nation must do its duty as an ally." "Russia does its in retreating," he said; Italy also does its duty, "although halfheartedly," through its attacks, while Serbia, through its inactivity, "is failing its duty." "And we [the French and the British] have as a duty to fight continually." "I want to fight; otherwise, I will not command the French army."[68]

Rejecting smaller actions as proposed by Kitchener, Joffre proposed two great offensives, one on a front of twenty-five kilometres, and the second on a front of thirteen kilometres. "In these offensives," he affirmed, refuting Kitchener's argument, "I will lose less people than in local defensives and in small actions. These … will be costly." "Defence," he exclaimed, "is impossible." In a month, he would have his infantry and his artillery ready to launch the attacks.[69] "We cannot remain 3–4 months without doing anything."[70] "My aim is to beat the enemy and to kill Germans as much as possible. But one must never say that such actions [will result] in breakthrough; [this will bring] disillusionment, as at Arras."[71] The latter observation was evidently a concession to the British point of view, for the fundamental reasoning behind the two attacks was to score a breakthrough. Joffre's ruse, it would appear, was to talk the language of attrition in order to obtain British troops.

Joffre continued his argument, affirming that "the question of effectives is entirely in our favour," stating that the French had 40 per cent effectives for reinforcements, and the Germans only had 37 per cent. To which Viviani added, "And there is the Russian army … the English Army." In anticipation of the Allied military conference the next day, Joffre again expressed his vision with regard to the solidarity of the coalition and stressed that all the Allies should attack in concert to aid the hard-pressed Russians. "In conclusion, it is vital that the British Army contribute its maximum, 6 divisions as soon as possible … and everyone, no matter what the cost, must do their duty as an ally."[72]

After these two eloquent presentations by Kitchener and Joffre on their respective strategies, various individuals tried either to find common ground between the two strategies or to point out the differences.

Augagneur observed that, since the British concept according to Balfour was to "tuer du boche," the defensive was to be excluded. The only thing therefore to determine was "how to carry out the offensive," from which he concluded, "There is not a great difference between Kitchener's opinion and that of General Joffre."[73]

But the clash of ideas was not limited to Joffre and Kitchener; it also pitted Sir John French against his military overlord. Taking up Joffre's argument in favour of the offensive, Sir John emphasized that the offensive "independent of the boost to morale that it gives to the troops … gives us the initiative as to the place of attack and the field of battle, and that an enemy under attack is not capable at the same time of attacking elsewhere." Kitchener's rejoinder to the British field commander was that he "did not share this opinion." Kitchener's chief fear was that Joffre, in order to carry out his major offensives, would be obliged to "uncover" his front elsewhere, exposing it to later enemy attack.[74]

To this argument, Joffre replied that he had two types of defence, his "mobile defence" and his "fixed defence," and that it was with the former that he would attack. He added, "To increase these mobile troops is why I am asking for the greatest number of English divisions as soon as possible." But Kitchener was unconvinced. With unflinching tenacity, he again expressed his reservations: "I am afraid that these offensives will commit you too deeply. I would like to see much caution. I am convinced that the German staff will attack you. If you are ready, it will be a great German defeat. That is certain. If you are engaged in the offensive, you will no longer be able to reply to them. They will gain the advantage."[75]

Kitchener's reasoning was shared by Viviani, who was "convinced that the Germans are going to attack us." Viviani's conclusion, based on "everything that has been said," was "that we must fight in order to retain the most Germans on our front … but he would like that we first organize the defensive."[76] That observation revealed the nascent conflict between civilians and the military among the French. Joffre's reply was sharp: "I do not want people to discuss my operations."[77]

The crucial moment of the conference had arrived from the point of view of military planning, for several, including Kitchener, Sir John, Augagneur, and Crewe, echoed Joffre's attitude toward political interference with his operations. "It is a matter for the generals," said Kitchener. "We will not discuss their operations." And Crewe added, "It is impossible at this table to define the extent of operations."[78] This consensus relative to Joffre's freedom of action, arrived at without full consideration of its implications, in fact gave him a blank cheque for planning the forthcoming offensives, as he wished.

It then fell to Asquith, as chairman of the meeting, to give a short closing commentary on the military question. As in the British cabinet, over which he presided as arbiter of disputed views,[79] he appeared to have found sufficient common ground among the various opinions expressed to draw up conclusions suitable to everyone. Here is the text of Asquith's remarks, according to the French minutes in the Millerand Papers, which correspond in detail with Asquith's conference notes:[80]

> We are almost entirely in agreement in principle and we only have difficulty with the application.
>
> Mr. Millerand has said that the purpose of the offensive is to retain Germans before us, to shake them, without the notion of breakthrough at any price.
>
> Mr. Balfour has said, "We must kill people."
>
> Mr. Augagneur has said, "We must not engage to the point of not being able to disengage."
>
> Mr. Viviani has said, "Let's fortify the defensive."
>
> I conclude that these are only details in execution, which only concern the generals.[81]

Asquith thus concluded, mainly with reference to the advice of the politicians, in favour of attrition warfare based on a strategy of limited offensives, not having given sufficient weight to Joffre's argument. In leaving the details of carrying out operations to the generals, Asquith had not anticipated that his statement, in the absence of an official agreement binding the Allies to a clearly defined strategy, would have no impact whatever on a general as independent-minded as Joffre.

The conference adjourned after three hours,[82] and everyone was pleased with an "excellent dinner" which "put them all in a very good humor."[83]

CONFERENCE AFTERMATH

For the British delegation from London, the conference was "an entire success."[84] Esher applauded the fact that, for the first time, there had been "something on the order of a true discussion relative to the strategy to follow on the western front."[85] Sir John believed that the conference helped to "dispel the clouds" in Anglo-French relations and to push back unhealthy forebodings which had rapidly grown recently,[86] while Millerand declared himself "entirely satisfied."[87]

The ambiguity relative to the conclusions of the conference, however, immediately gave rise to varied interpretations, each side believing that its argument had carried the day. The British political leaders, Asquith, Balfour, and Crewe, thought that Kitchener had been "magnificent and dominated the whole affair,"[88] and that their strategic views had been accepted. Based on their reports, Hankey had drawn up the conclusions of the conference for the British government. These conclusions reaffirmed that the general policy of war of attrition would be continued, and that no major large offensive operation would be undertaken. But that provision should not prevent attacks of a considerable scale to harass the Germans, impose heavy losses on them, or lower their morale or push back their line. The British were to take up more of the front, the trenches would be reinforced, and the British government, without "definitive obligations," planned to send the greater part of the New Armies to France. Sir John should not engage in any offensive action likely to result in major losses or to threaten Allied capacity to resist should a decisive attack from the enemy be undertaken.[89] The British politicians seemed therefore to have anchored themselves singularly on what they had said themselves, without having reflected on the attitude of Joffre to whom they had given full freedom for the execution of his plans.

Sir John French, on the other hand, believed that "Joffre's point of view was accepted by the two governments, on condition of being wise and prudent,"[90] and that "the original plan drawn up by Joffre and me remains intact."[91] In addition, he was pleased that "our government has said in a categorical manner what troops will be sent and when they will arrive."[92] He did not hesitate, therefore, to continue his planning for the offensive with Joffre.

For Joffre, the main result of the conference was that the British would dispatch immediately six divisions of the Second New Army to France, which would allow him at the Allied military conference in Chantilly the next day to confirm, with Sir John's full support, his plan for the Anglo-French offensive on the Western Front.[93] In addition, Joffre could count on the arrival of the other British New Armies,[94] which augured well for the long-term future of the campaign in France. In sum, so far as one can judge from the evidence, the discussion at the conference on 6 July had no impact on Joffre's offensive strategy on the Western Front, except that he asked Sir John French on 7 July, seemingly in response to his pre-conference understanding with Kitchener, that the new British divisions relieve a part of French forces in the trenches south of Arras, and that these divisions go on the defensive in order to economize British munitions for the offensive elsewhere.[95]

THE CHANTILLY CONFERENCE: COORDINATION OF THE ENTENTE COALITION

In pre-war planning, the French and the British had at least made tentative arrangements for the coordination of their military efforts, but no mechanism had been set up for overall Allied coordination, beyond the normal interaction through the diplomatic channel. The French had made provision for immediate Russian attacks in East Prussia, and Joffre, in his decision making, as has been shown, always had in view the role of the Russians in the coalition and their support. But, in the spring of 1915, the entry of Italy into the war, coupled with the failure of the Artois offensive and the headlong retreat of the Russians, who were being mercilessly driven back by a combined German and Austro-Hungarian offensive, emphasized the urgent need for coordination of the Allied military effort.

In the summer of 1915, Serbian inactivity and the entry of Italy into the war raised the question of Allied coordination with even greater urgency. Following Italy's entry into the conflict, Poincaré received word on 8 June that two Italians armies were beginning their advance to the Isonzo River. But two days later, he learned about a Serbian advance into Albania, rather than against Austria-Hungary, which demonstrated the desperate need for greater Allied coordination. "The larger the coalition, the less easy it will be to coordinate," observed Poincaré.[96] Italian entry into the war completed the ring of allies occupying the outer European perimeter, which included Great Britain, Belgium, France, Italy, Serbia, and Russia. Their activities risked being frittered away in isolated actions, while the Central Powers, with the benefit of interior lines of communication, could beat them, one at a time. The British tendency to divert resources to the Dardanelles, rather than to send them to reinforce the Western Front, was also of major concern to the French command.

The need for overall coordination of the Entente coalition was all too apparent. The issue had been on Kitchener's mind. As early as 29 March, while on a trip to France, Kitchener had indicated that he was quite prepared to have Joffre play a wider role in the overall coordination of the coalition, with a view to a simultaneous attack on both the Eastern and Western Fronts.[97] As the Artois offensive drew to a close, Joffre's staff took up the issue. "The war has no direction" (la guerre n'est pas conduite), said a Third Bureau memorandum on 21 June 1915. The great need, argued the Third Bureau, was for a common plan of action to take the pressure off the Russians. With an army of 2.5 million men, and the apparent acknowledgment of their leadership by their English and Italian allies, the French, it was argued, should provide that direction.[98]

On 24 June, Joffre put before his government a full-blown plan for creation of a central organ at French headquarters for the overall coordination of Allied military effort. This plan called for the assignment of Allied military representatives at French headquarters "to inform the French Command accurately ... to speak for the General-in-Chief he represents, then to transmit plans and directives drawn up by the French Command."[99] This was remarkably similar to Allied Supreme War Council created in 1917, except that the latter body had both political and military representatives and was more collegial.[100] Joffre's most immediate concern, however, was to engage all of the Allies in an "energetic, concerted offensive" to take the pressure off the hard-pressed Russians, and to combat the growing tendency within the British government to divert forces to the Dardanelles and to "rest purely on the defensive in France."[101]

Rather than wait for a theoretical demonstration of the value of the proposed new structure for Allied cooperation, Joffre recommended to his government on 29 June that the French command assume leadership at once in calling an Allied military conference.[102] Unfortunately for later Allied coordination, the creation of a new body capable of long-term Allied coordination was set aside in favour of a more immediate solution: the convening of an Allied military conference at Chantilly on the day following the political-military conference at Calais. This second conference defined Allied grand strategy under Joffre's direction and drew up plans for coordinated offensives in the fall. The Chantilly military conference constituted the first systematic effort toward unified action by all the coalition powers.[103]

Representatives from all the Allied powers were present at the Allied military conference, which met at Chantilly on 7 July 1915. In addition to Millerand, Joffre, and Pellé for the French and Sir John, Roberston, and Wilson for the English, the Chantilly Conference included the following: Major-General Félix Wielemans, assistant chief of staff of the Belgian Army; Colonel Paul Ignatieff, the Russian military attaché in France; Lieutenant-Colonel Giovanni di Breganze, Italian military attaché in France; and Colonel Stephanovitch, detached from the Serbian Army to GQG.[104] Joffre led the discussion by underlining the principle of Allied solidarity and the need for coordinated military action to prevent the Central Powers from defeating the Allies individually. He said that the war would be won on the three main fronts, the Belgian-French, the Russian, and the Italo-Serb. The Dardanelles offensive and the conflict in the Caucuses were minor theatres not likely to produce decisive results. Outlining the situation in each major theatre, Joffre indicated that the Russians had been subjected to the main offensive of the German-Austro-Hungarian armies for two months, and that the Allies, therefore, must come to their rescue as the Russian had done for the French in the 1914 campaign.[105]

The first Italian offensive on the Isonzo River on 23 June had been little more than a demonstration with limited results, while the Serbs had remained inactive on their front.[106] Joffre therefore urged the Italians and Serbs, both of whom he deemed as having limited forces before them, to engage in strong offensives as soon as possible. Likewise, the French and British would launch a major offensive after the shortest possible delay, probably in the first part of August, the British having promised the day previous at the Calais Conference the immediate dispatch of six new British divisions, with other armies to follow. To this offensive plan, Sir John gave his full support, but he reserved for later discussion Joffre's suggestion that the new divisions be used to relieve French troops south of Arras.[107] That the Allied powers, under Joffre's leadership, had devised a plan for concerted fall offensives by each of them was remarkable given their previous disunity – a landmark development in the quest for a coherent Entente grand strategy.

Following the Chantilly Conference, Joffre pressed forward in planning for the Anglo-French offensive. In a meeting held at Saint-Omer on 11 July, between Sir John French, Robertson, and Wilson, on the one hand, and Joffre, Foch, and Huguet, on the other, it was agreed between the two commanders that Sir John would relieve thirty kilometres of French trenches south of Arras with the New Army, and that the British would attack at Loos about 15 August, in coordination with a French attack around Arras. But, contrary to his earlier plan, Joffre now envisaged making his large-scale attack in Champagne (rather than in Artois, as earlier stated), where the terrain was better suited "to an action of large forces."[108] On 19 July, Joffre finalized his plan for a major French attack of thirty divisions in Champagne, and the date was put forward to 30 August to allow for stronger heavy artillery and more munitions. In Artois, to launch a combined attack, ten French divisions would make an attack on Arras, while eight or nine British divisions would attack at Loos.[109] The next chapter examines the discussion that then arose around that plan, as the British objected to their assigned terrain, and the ultimate outcome.

CONCLUSION

In coalition warfare, allied partners are not always free to follow the strategy that best corresponds to what had been their interests and strategic preferences in the pre-war era. The failure of a major ally in wartime may be disastrous. The collapse of the alliance, whose "center of gravity" in Clausewitzian terms, has been broken, can lead to the ruination of one's own country. An ally in danger must be sustained. This in part would explain the vigorous German support in 1915 of Austria-Hungary, the weaker ally.

In 1915, after the failed Artois offensive, Britain was faced with the prospect that, according to the best information, France might falter politically as a result of internal discontent. The British government in consequence sent its New Armies to France while, at the Calais Conference on 6 July, continuing to express its reluctance to engage in large and expensive offensives and its preference for attrition warfare. Joffre, with the immediate support of Sir John, paid no attention to these strictures and went ahead with his original offensive plan.

But ironically, despite the objection of Sir John French to the terrain that the French had selected for his attack about Loos, Kitchener and the British cabinet were obliged to yield to the exigencies of their French and Russian allies in August 1915 by giving maximum support to the French offensive. It was by this means that the British advanced from a limited commitment to the Western Front in the early months of 1915 to a near total commitment in the fall.

In sum, the summer of 1915 was a turning point in terms of recognition of the need for better coordination of Allied strategy and planning, not only in the consultation of Anglo-French political and military leaders at Calais, but also in the Allied military conference held at Chantilly the next day. The latter in particular marked a new initiative in strategic planning for the whole alliance, which would, if properly applied, prevent the Central Powers from using their central lines of communication to beat the Allies one at a time. While the results were less than expected, the Italians did manage to pin down greater Austro-Hungarian forces on the Isonzo River in their offensives in the fall of 1915, and, according to a French staff account, the combined Anglo-French offensives in September, in Loos and Champagne, led to the diversion of thirteen German divisions from the Eastern to the Western Front in September and October.[110]

These results were sufficient to encourage Joffre and his staff to call a second Allied military conference at Chantilly on 6–8 December 1915 to coordinate the 1916 Allied offensives. In the meantime, the Calais Conference having set the tone, French and British political and military leaders met in numerous conferences, until, after the Salonika imbroglio in the fall of 1915, it was recognized that such meetings were inadequate as a vehicle for Allied cooperation.

CHAPTER NINE

Objections to Loos and British Strategic Reversal, July–August 1915

THE SUMMER OF 1915 MARKED a number of new departures. On the international stage, this was the period, framed by the political-military Calais Conference of 6 July and the subsequent Allied military conference at Chantilly, in which the French command began to assume a larger role in the coordination of the Allied coalition. Yet it was also at this time that the Dardanelles expedition took on greater importance in terms of the diversion of men and munitions to the east, which riled French and British commanders on the Western Front and created new conflicts with their governments.

In Anglo-French command relations, the period following initial planning for the fall offensive involved a sharp clash between Sir John and Joffre over the extent of British participation in the projected British attack at Loos in conjunction with French troops at Arras. The dispute centred on Sir John's reluctance to launch a major offensive because of what he viewed as the unsuitable terrain at Loos for an attack and the competing needs of the Dardanelles for munitions.

The dispute once again raised the issue of the need for a unified command. As a means to oblige Sir John French to conform to his wishes, Joffre put forth a formula for the partial subordination of the British command to French strategic direction. It, however, was limited to the direction of specific offensives, in an attempt by Joffre to devise a remedy for ill-coordinated offensives that would be acceptable to the British government.

French domestic politics intervened to play an important role in planning the fall offensives, with serious doubts by senior military leadership and within the government as to their likely success. Against the backdrop of a mounting wave of criticism of the conduct of the war by the war minister and the High Command, Joffre's firing in late July of General Maurice Sarrail, an "easterner" with close Socialist connections, sparked a cabinet crisis that threatened to topple the ministry. This provided the background to both French and British decision making. With Millerand's assistance, Joffre, however, was able to withstand the government's resistance to the renewal of a large offensive, despite the absence of a more adequate supply of heavy artillery and the demand for more troops for the Dardanelles. Not even Poincaré, in a tense face-to-face meeting with Joffre, was able to persuade him to alter his plan.

Kitchener's visit to France on 16–19 August proved decisive. Joffre used this visit, in a carefully orchestrated plan, to build confidence in the French Army and underscore the need for full British participation in the fall offensive. Ironically, for reasons similar to those that impelled the British to send the New Armies to France – the concern regarding internal French politics and the need to prop up both their French and Russian allies – Kitchener made a major strategic reversal with regard to the employment of British forces in France. He obliged Sir John to engage fully at Loos and also approved Joffre's command formula. In the final analysis, the needs of the alliance trumped Kitchener's preferences for a more defensive operational strategy and his previous resistance to subordination of the British command to French leadership.

PLANNING THE FALL OFFENSIVE

An examination of Anglo-French planning for the fall offensive in France allows us to understand better the paradoxical results of the Calais Conference. For Joffre, the main result of the conference was that the British would send six divisions of the Second New Army to France immediately, which would allow him to pursue his offensive plan with greater vigour. Moreover, he could now count on the arrival of the other British New Armies according to a fixed schedule,[1] which promised a much rosier future for the campaign in France.

Already on 24 June, Joffre and Sir John French had agreed at a meeting held at French headquarters at Chantilly to undertake "another heavy attack" in five or six weeks on a broader front than the previous one. At that meeting both expressed their opposition to the Dardanelles offensive and rejected the strategy of "passive defence," which the British government appeared to favour, as "bad strategy" and "unfair to Russia, Serbia and Italy."[2]

On 7 July at the meeting of the Allied military representatives at Chantilly, Joffre pursued his initiative to coordinate a series of Allied offensives in order to take the pressure off the Russian front. Within that framework, he proposed that the French and the British launch a major operation of Anglo-French forces on the Western Front in early August, to which Sir John French agreed to give his entire support.[3]

The exhortations of British politicians at the Anglo-French political-military conference on 6 July, with regard to prudence in the use of Allied forces, had no impact on Joffre's offensive strategy. In compliance with Kitchener's request, nonetheless, in the note presented to him before the conference, Joffre asked Sir John French on 7 July to use the new British divisions to relieve a part of French forces in the trenches south of Arras and go on the defensive, in order to economize British munitions for an offensive elsewhere.[4]

Preparation for the joint offensive continued. As noted in the last chapter, following the Chantilly Conference, the two commands met at Saint-Omer on 11 July where it was agreed that Sir John would relieve thirty kilometres of French trenches south of Arras with his Second New Army, and that the British, in cooperation with a French operation around Arras, would attack at Loos about 15 August. But, seeking a terrain better suited to the operation of large forces, Joffre now envisaged making his large-scale attack in Champagne, rather than in Artois, as earlier planned.[5] Joffre's plan for a major French attack of thirty divisions in Champagne was finalized on 19 July, at which time he also delayed the date for the joint offensive to 30 August in order to concentrate more heavy artillery and munitions.[6]

Joffre's new plan reflected the thinking of his staff that the inability of French troops to advance in the Artois offensive resulted from failure to attack on a wide enough front to overcome the effect of enfilade fire. The Germans had also brought up their reserves too quickly, allowing them to counterattack and establish new fortified positions to counter the Allied advance. In the new plan, the Anglo-French operation in Artois would pin down enemy reserves while the wide attack in Champagne was intended to force the vital breakthrough. For the combined operation in Artois, ten French divisions would make an attack on Arras, while eight or nine British divisions would attack at Loos.[7]

SIR JOHN'S OBJECTIONS TO LOOS

But after 20 July, when Joffre's plans were firmly drawn up, Sir John and his staff became worried about the offensive as a result of a concern expressed by Sir Douglas Haig, who was to command the British operation. Haig was anxious about the strength of the German fortified positions at Loos and the difficulty of the terrain in a coal-mining area dominated by "a mass of fortified houses, buildings and slag heaps extending over many square miles." Of even greater concern at British headquarters was their lack of munitions, given the strength of the German fortified position at Loos.[8] By 17 July, Sir John had learned that five more British divisions were being sent from Britain to the Dardanelles and also that ammunition deliveries to his front were being severely cut.[9]

There were other considerations. Sir John French appears to have lost confidence in the French ability to move forward. In a conversation with Esher on 15 July, he expressed the fear that the war would end in a *paix boiteuse*, a stalemated peace. Even had the Artois offensive succeeded, Sir John argued, "we should not have got the Germans back more than 20 miles."[10] By 17 July, he was even more pessimistic. "The F[ield] M[arshal] said tonight," Esher noted, "that he was very doubtful whether it was wise to deliver violent attacks against the German lines, and that he was by no means sure that we should not wear them out more surely if we remained on the purely defensive."[11] In private, Sir John thus appears to have begun to trim his sails to Kitchener's point of view on the strategy to follow. To Esher he had acknowledged two days earlier that he "was within an ace" of having lost his command.[12] Given the precarious nature of his tenure after the Shells Crisis, it was unlikely that he could maintain a position in opposition to his government for long.

Thus, on 20 July, Sir John began to prepare Joffre for a less than energetic British attack at Loos, though in doing so he cited only the military considerations. In his journal he recorded: "I told Clive [liaison officer to French headquarters] to remind Joffre of the difficult nature of the country occupied by the Germans in front of the 1 Army – and that (particularly having regard to my shortage of amm[unition]), he must not expect me to do more than a strong 'holding' attack."[13]

The planning process at British headquarters proceeded apace as Sir John, much concerned about the future offensive, discussed the situation repeatedly with William Robertson, his chief of staff, on 22, 23, and 24 July. Sir John recorded his decision thus:

> After a careful examination of the ground at *Loos* and *Lens* and a consideration of Haig's two reports I am doubtful of the success of an attack against these places which I had arranged with the French to make.
>
> To have any prospect of success such an attack would have to be supported by an almost unlimited expenditure of Art[tillery] Amm[unition]: and our present receipt do not promise an adequate supply for this purpose.
>
> If we abandon this project it would seem advisable to choose a point of attack which offers the best tactical advantage and I do not think that is to be found on the front of the [First] Army.[14]

The preferred location for the alternate attack was to be at Wyeschaete in the Ypres sector farther north. On 25 July Sir John observed to Clive that "he was thinking of giving up the idea of attacking the Hulluch plateau [Loos], as it is too strong … that D[ouglas] H[aig] was against the plan, & would prefer to attack further north." Robertson also confirmed this stance the next day, saying that "we sh[oul]d not be helping the French by throwing away thousands of lives in knocking our heads against a brick wall."[15]

The lack of high-explosive shells for an attack against a heavily fortified position at Loos appeared to be the major consideration, for, as Robertson told Wilson, "we are getting 2000 shells a day *less* than we were a month ago, & these most of 4.5", 5" and 9.2" all H[igh] E[energy]."[16] In a letter to a member of the king's immediate entourage, Robertson elaborated. "When I was in England last [end of June], much discussion took place as to whether our policy should be offensive or defensive, but the discussion was quite unnecessary because the ammunition supply settles the question." Decrying the loss of three hundred men per day and "nearly 10000 per month" as a result of the "enforced defensive" in face of the more amply supplied German force, Robertson made a strong appeal for more munitions.[17] The shortage of ammunition, which was a key consideration in Kitchener's advocacy of a defensive offensive strategy at the Calais Conference, was thus having its impact on planning at the Western Front, an issue not unrelated to the Dardanelles offensive.

STRAINED COMMAND RELATIONS

Sir John requested a meeting with Foch at his headquarters at Frévent for 27 July to explain his concern regarding the joint offensive,[18] thereby opening a dispute of several weeks in Anglo-French planning. At Frévent, Sir John, without, however, disclosing his grave penury of ammunition, made the case for the likely failure of his part of the joint operation against any sector of the heavily fortified front between the left of the French Tenth Army and Loos, and argued for an attack elsewhere. Foch conceded that "our previous attacks show us that we cannot hope to break the line at a single blow." "What we can hope for," he continued, "is to occupy positions now held by the enemy by means of powerful and repeated attacks and that such action on our part would necessitate the enemy falling back some distance." The British Army, he offered, might attack in the northern part of the sector – not shoulder to shoulder with the French, but in near proximity – and still fulfill the role of attracting German artillery and obtain control of the Douai plain. That result, he argued, would not be obtained by the British attacking farther to the north. Though impressed by Foch's argument, Sir John French declined to give a definitive answer and asked for additional time to consider the matter, to which Foch assented but urged that his decision be not long delayed, given the need for immediate preparation.[19]

In the meeting Foch shared his evolving conception of the nature of the battlefield. "Against all strong positions it is necessary to have lots of guns and plenty of ammunition; in fact, what we are engaged now in is siege warfare and not active operations in the open field and no attack should be started until the proper means are available." The battle would thus be an artillery one of the "bite and hold" variety which Foch as an artillery officer was to pioneer if Joffre had not instructed him on 11 August to think once again in terms of a strategic breakthrough.[20]

In his private report to Joffre of this "difficult" conversation, Foch described Sir John's frame of mind as betraying "total indecision."[21]

This was not far off the mark, since Sir John oscillated between various solutions. After the conference Sir John told Wilson that "Foch had convinced him but that Haig & Robertson would oppose him heavily, still he would attack down near the French."[22] By the next day, Sir John had changed his mind and told Wilson that "he was not going to attack alongside the French," and further, that "Joffre never told him anything, that the French could not be trusted, that Foch had changed his plans, etc., & that in consequence he would attack elsewhere."[23]

Apparently, Foch's discussion of the need for successive artillery attacks had convinced Sir John that the French were planning only a limited action in Artois. "I have reached the conclusion that the French do not mean to make any *decisive* attack at Arras," he wrote in his diary. "I have to work rather in [the] dark because Joffre never gives me his full confidence or discusses plans with me," he complained. He therefore concluded that "we should do much better if we operated at part of our line which offers greater tactical advantages than the region just N. of the French."[24]

Sir John was now caught in the crossfire. His own lack of confidence in the proposed Artois offensive was buttressed by his need – given his weakened position following the Shells Crisis in May – to conform to what he believed to be government policy. In addition, Robertson, on the basis of the lack of ammunition, and Haig, because of the unfavourable terrain, were strongly opposed to the Loos attack. On the other hand, Foch and Joffre were demanding that Sir John launch a major offensive according to their previous joint plan – an attack for which Sir John had serious doubts regarding the extent of French involvement.

In these circumstances, Sir John resorted to a ploy to cover all his flanks. In a letter to Joffre, which he personally drafted after having rejected one written by Robertson,[25] Sir John put forth the British case. Rather than attack in concert with the French at Artois, against heavily fortified lines and in difficult terrain, he argued in favour of improving the British position for the winter on the Wyeschaete-Messines Ridge in the north and the Aubers Ridge in the south. But more significantly, he expressed the desire "to direct the movements of the Army under my command in loyal co-operation with you as Commander-in-Chief, and in strict accordance with your conception of the most efficient means to be adopted to secure the triumph of our common cause." Sir John

French thus placed the entire operational decision-making process in Joffre's hands and pledged to "direct the movements of the British Army in accordance with the wishes you express."[26] His desire to improve his position for the winter revealed his overall lack of confidence in the joint offensive, and his placing the decision in Joffre's hands was undoubtedly intended to transfer the onus for a failed offensive onto the latter's shoulders.[27]

Joffre's response to Sir John's letter was twofold. First, he sent Sir John's suggestions to Foch for further study, and then, having Foch's reaffirmation of the soundness of the joint venture in Artois, reasserted on 5 August the need for Sir John French to conform fully with the joint plan for a major attack, arguing that a British action "in any other part of the line would merely be a separate and divergent effort."[28]

Sir John, meantime, had spent four days in London, returning 5 August, during which time he communicated with Kitchener about the cutback of munition deliveries, a matter that Kitchener said would be rectified by 7 August.[29] Sir John's field strategy, nonetheless, remained unchanged. Caught between the views of his government and the demands of the French command, he resolved the problem with subterfuge and bluff. To Joffre, Sir John indicated that he would "endeavour to meet his wishes in any way he could." But his instructions to Haig "were to make it clear that it was only my intention to support Joffre vigorously with artillery. The infantry were to fulfil strictly a containing role." On the basis of Foch's analysis, Sir John believed that the French attacks were to be mainly "artillery battles" and was therefore prepared to do little more than make a demonstration.[30]

But Joffre was not put off quite that easily. Apprised in an additional letter from Sir John on 10 August of his continued preference to attack elsewhere, and suspecting that Sir John intended only to make a demonstration rather than a serious attack in the direction of Loos and Hulluch, Joffre reaffirmed in forceful terms two days later the need for a "large and powerful" British attack "with the maximum force you have," according to the French plan.[31] In response, Sir John instructed the British field commander to make an attack sufficient to take the first line of trenches, and then to wait and see what the French achieved.[32] On 14 August he assured Joffre that he fully understood the importance of carrying out his plan, but pointed out that he would be able to participate only according to his supply of munitions.[33] The dispute remained unresolved, despite a renewed pledge of support by Sir John to Joffre, delivered through Wilson on 16 August.[34]

THE SARRAIL AFFAIR AND THE FRENCH POLITICAL CRISIS

In France, a political crisis that extended intermittently from late July 1915 until the collapse of the Viviani government in October was triggered by Joffre's dismissal on 22 July of General Maurice Sarrail, commander of the Third Army, who was the darling of the socialist left. The crises that followed gave voice to the long-term quest for alternate theatres of war which stemmed from the onset of trench warfare and stalemate on the Western Front, and had led to a governmental strategic re-evaluation in early January. The "eastern" strategy for a major deployment in the Balkans, advocated by Briand and some generals in the field, began largely as a means to avoid the heavy losses of trench warfare on the Western Front and to rally Greece, Romania, and possibly Bulgaria to the Allied cause. This strategy aimed first to strengthen the Dardanelles operation and, when Bulgaria allied with the Central Powers in late September, to launch an expedition in Greece to come to the aid of Serbia.

The heavy losses suffered in the failed Artois offensive, with little or no advance, gave further impetus to the quest for an eastern strategy, which more and more came to be associated with the political left. The accumulated dissatisfaction of the Chamber and Senate Army Commissions with Millerand and Joffre's conduct of the war was ever in the background, with the added irritant of the long-running and unresolved quarrel over inspections.[35] Thus, the Sarrail Affair, which energized the nascent eastern strategy, must be seen in the light Joffre's struggle to keep the fall offensive alive against the mounting opposition of the French president, a growing part of the government, and the parliamentary commissions, which wished first to strengthen the Dardanelles operation and, when Bulgaria allied with the Central Powers in late September, to launch an expedition in Greece to come to the aid of Serbia.

In his memoirs, Joffre outlines with meticulous detail his role in Sarrail's dismissal. Following earlier concerns, Joffre became unhappy with Sarrail's lacklustre conduct of operations in the Argonne in June and July 1915. Fully aware that Sarrail had strong political connections with the political left, Joffre took the precaution of having Sarrail's immediate superior, General Auguste Dubail, commander of the First Army Group, conduct an investigation, which led to Sarrail's dismissal on 22 July 1915.[36] Joffre could hardly have appreciated the storm this action would generate.

Having won 100 seats in the 1914 spring elections, the Socialist Party, the largest bloc in the Chamber, was a force to be reckoned with and its support was necessary for the maintenance of the *union sacrée*. It had been planning to have Joffre replaced by Sarrail in the fall of 1914, when the war broke out and confirmed Joffre in his position.[37] The government thus made a number of concessions to retain Socialist support. To calm the anticipated furor over Sarrail's removal, an issue closely tied to discontent with Joffre's leadership, the Viviani government offered Sarrail the post of commander of the Expeditionary Corps of the Near East (Corps expéditionnaire d'Orient) in the Dardanelles on 23 July, which, to its dismay, he refused.[38]

The parliamentary crisis that followed, as Sarrail further solicited the support of his political friends, threatened to unseat the ministry and destroy the *union sacrée*, until the government landed on the expedient of increasing the number of divisions in the French expeditionary force in the Dardanelles with Sarrail as its commander. While leftist politicians in France and a handful of generals had long favoured the deployment of larger forces in the Near East, the immediate spark for the new venture came from the French government's need to find a command for Sarrail in order to allay the anger of his supporters.[39]

On 3 August, Sarrail outlined his conditions to Millerand for acceptance of the post: that the name of the expeditionary force be changed to Army of the Near East (Armée d'Orient); that he not be subordinated to a British general; and, most importantly, that he be given the command of no less than four additional divisions. In a later conversation, Sarrail refused to leave Paris until the divisions had been sent, fearing that he might in fact arrive empty-handed.[40] So began the project for an enlarged and renewed French drive in the Dardanelles – with all its implications for relations with the British – and the French government's futile attempt to detach four divisions from Joffre just as he was about to launch his fall offensive.

The main thrust of opposition to Millerand was from the Socialists and Radical Socialists who pressed for his removal. On 5 August two Socialist ministers, Jules Guesde and Marcel Sembat, threatened to withdraw from the government, a move that would trigger its fall. Tired and dejected, Viviani was ready to give way, but he was propped up by Poincaré, who told the Socialists they could always raise the issue in the Chamber. But forcing a debate in the Chamber, which no one wanted, would be bad for the war effort. On 13 August a delegation representing the Army, Naval, and Foreign Affairs Commissions of the Chamber made a representation to Poincaré on the Dardanelles. "The three commissions unanimously considered a larger expedition necessary immediately."[41]

In a session devoted entirely to the crisis on 14 August, the cabinet, after a long discussion, finally opted to stand together. Among the complaints against Millerand, elaborated by Poincaré, was that he did not keep the president or his colleagues adequately informed. Millerand's defence was that he was entirely behind the war effort, and Gaston Doumergue, the minister of colonies, expressed the concern that the Socialist agitation might well be the prelude to a campaign for peace.[42] While the worst of the crisis appeared to be over, the government remained in turmoil for nearly two weeks as it debated how its approach could best be presented to the Chamber of Deputies. The possibility of holding a secret session of Parliament was discussed. But in a regular session of the Chamber on 26 August, in which deputies cheered at the mention of Joffre, Viviani sought credits for the new under-secretaries responsible for health and munitions, in what became a vote of confidence on the general performance of the government. While reaffirming the government's solidarity with the commissions, Viviani deflected the call for a secret session of the Chamber by saying that all relevant information had already been given to the commissions, and, with the support of the Socialists, the government received an overwhelming endorsement of 535–1. For the time being, the crisis had been averted.[43]

OPPOSITION OF THE FRENCH GOVERNMENT TO THE FALL OFFENSIVE

In the meantime, the French government, in the midst of a major storm over Millerand and Joffre's conduct of the war, and the need for a strengthened Dardanelles offensive, had grave concerns about the proposed fall offensive in France. While Poincaré had been briefed in general terms by Viviani and Millerand on the results of the Anglo-French political-military conference at Calais on 6 July, he had not been apprised of the specific results of the military conference at Chantilly, nor had the cabinet. In a cabinet meeting on 5 August, Millerand read a letter from Joffre, dated 3 August, in which Joffre made the case against sending additional troops to the Dardanelles. The Russians, he said, were retreating before the Austro-German forces for want of arms and munitions and would not be able to reconstitute for months. The French Army, the only one capable of beating the Germans, was at its maximum strength in effectives and would only grow weaker, he confided, and it should therefore attack in consort with French allies as agreed at the 7 July conference.[44] Having just obtained a copy of the minutes of the latter conference, and become fully aware of Joffre's plans, Poincaré was alarmed that Joffre had arranged for all of the Allies, including the French and British, to launch major attacks in mid-September. Given Joffre's claim that the French Army was now at its maximum strength and would hereafter decline in strength, and assuming that the war would last into the next year, Poincaré thought a major offensive in the fall would be an ill-considered drain on French resources. He thus wrote Millerand asking him to sit down with him to review Joffre's plan, and to put it before the cabinet.[45]

The cabinet, it turned out, had grave misgivings about the fall offensive. In a meeting of Millerand and Joffre with the army group commanders on 11 August, Millerand advised the generals that the government had decided the night before that "it was opposed to any offensive" but that he personally "did not share this opinion," and, moreover, that the attack "had been agreed upon with the British Government." Hearkening back to the Calais Conference on 6 July, he presented a very distorted view of the proceedings – that Asquith had expressed the preference of the British government not to attack before winter, when he would have more forces and, above all, more munitions, but that Joffre had put forth his plan for a new offensive with only a brief delay, to which Asquith had finally agreed. Castelnau, commander of the Central Army Group, who was to lead the major fall offensive in Champagne, upon further assurances from the minister that the "offensive had been agreed upon with the English Government at Calais," concluded that they must keep their commitments.[46]

When Joffre complained that there had been delays in the delivery of munitions, Millerand asked Foch and Castelnau if they had enough munitions for their attacks. Reflecting his revised appraisal of trench warfare, Foch, who was to lead the secondary offensive in Artois, replied that these were really siege attacks, which required enough ammunition for sustained and methodic attacks, and that "with the limited means that we have: guns, heavy artillery [and] munitions … we can expect only limited results."[47] Castelnau spoke in terms of breakthrough and manoeuvre, to which Foch pointed out the difficulty of such operations with a limited quantity of munition. This prompted Joffre to issue a sharp rebuke to Foch, his most loyal of supporters: "We are trying to do what we have to with the means at our disposal. If we chose your system of methodical attacks, which would require a month of combat, with a maximum expenditure of munitions, when could we declare ourselves ready to attack? Perhaps next year, no doubt never. But we must act, for us and our allies. As our regulations say, only inaction is reprehensible."[48]

After the minister left, the generals decided to continue their preparations for the offensive, which was to get under way as soon as possible. Joffre's observation was, "If, when we are ready, the government forbids us to attack, we shall see."[49] Yielding some ground on the question of adequate munitions, Joffre agreed with Castelnau that the coming offensive should then be "a vigorous attack, nothing more, success or failure," and pledged that if the attack did not succeed in a few days, it would be called off. With considerable foresight, Foch confided in his journal his overall assessment of the forthcoming offensive: "It was not going to deliver what was expected [and] it would not be broken off as desired."[50]

Three days later, on the afternoon of 14 August, Poincaré, Viviani, and Millerand went to see Joffre at Chantilly to try to resolve the misunderstanding between him and the government. Aware of various complaints about his command and rendered "ticklish" by the attacks in Parliament, Joffre, who appeared tired and worn, wanted to know if he still had Poincaré's approval. Poincaré reaffirmed that he had "his entire confidence and that of the government." But on the proposed offensive, and the Dardanelles, the two butted heads. The new offensive that Joffre was preparing was to begin on the 10 or 15 September, would be on a thirty-kilometre-wide front in Champagne, and was to last four or five days. While reaffirming Joffre's right to be the "master of [his] plan," a huge concession in and of itself given the government's earlier resistance, Poincaré referred to the opposition of several army commanders to such an attack, in favour of several smaller ones. Joffre replied, "We must act because of the Russians; it is an obligation of the alliance." To this Poincaré took umbrage, saying to Joffre that questions relating to the alliance were within the government's jurisdiction and that he should judge things only from a strategic point of view. Taking a new tack, Joffre replied that, for military reasons, he could not "remain on the defensive. Our troops, little by little, would lose their morale and physical fitness." While he could not guarantee the success of the operation, he thought that, with the 900 heavy guns that he had on a front of thirty kilometres and adequate ammunition, he had a good chance of success. He was completely confident that the Germans could not break through should they attack.[51]

With the conversation shifting to the Dardanelles, Joffre complained bitterly about Sarrail. "What do we want to do in the Dardanelles?" he exclaimed. "Prepare a command for a factious general?" Joffre vigorously resisted sending the four divisions requested until after the offensive in France. Poincaré then backed off, realizing that "if we insist, he will resign."[52] In the discussion, according to Poincaré, Viviani gave him half-hearted support and Millerand said nothing.[53] With Millerand's tacit support, Joffre stood fast against the government delegation, maintaining effective control of French strategy. This he did by sheer force of will – demonstrating the tenacity that, as Poincaré acknowledged in his memoirs, made possible the "reversal" of the Marne.[54] But this was but one incident in the grand tug-of-war between government and command that would ensue until the end of the campaign season.

The next day, Penelon, the liaison officer between the government and the High Command, expressed Joffre's complete satisfaction with the meeting and communicated the latter's call for the re-establishment of the Conseil supérieur de la Défense nationale, which would meet regularly, weekly if possible, under Poincaré's presidency and in his office. This body, an inner cabinet, which had functioned before the war, would include the president of the republic, the commander-in-chief, and three key ministers (the minister of war, the minister of the navy, and the minister of foreign affairs), with other ministers as needed. Joffre indicated he would write Millerand on the subject.[55]

The need to concentrate authority in a smaller council in a government with such divergent views was all too apparent. When Joffre wrote Millerand on 20 August to suggest the revitalization of the Conseil supérieur, he elaborated on its purpose. Once this body reached a consensus, in consultation with the key ministers, its decisions would be conveyed to ministers of lesser rank.[56] Joffre also suggested the formation of a permanent secretariat, the Section d'Etudes de la Défense nationale (Studies Section of National Defence), which would function at the War Ministry under the direction of the army chief of staff, to study questions related to the war and inform the Conseil supérieur of its findings. While these proposals may have seemed altruistic, they were really a calculated attempt by Joffre, who alone with his staff possessed the requisite technical knowledge, to have his own way with the government. Millerand, not surprisingly, put his official stamp of approval on Joffre's proposal concerning the Section d'Etudes one week later.[57] This study group tendered reports on the Dardanelles in August and September 1915.[58]

On 21 August, Poincaré arranged for Joffre to meet with himself, Viviani, Millerand, Delcassé, and Augagneur for the first meeting of newly constituted Conseil supérieur de la Défense nationale. Somewhat more conciliatory than earlier, Joffre promised that, if his September offensive did not prove decisive, he would send four divisions from his reserves to the Dardanelles. Poincaré appraised the strategic situation: "It would evidently be very desirable to have the Straits opened, both to influence the Balkan states and to allow us to communicate with Russia, and to send it munitions, when winter will have closed the port of Archangel."[59] Under Poincare's direction, this group of ministers (with some minor variations) and Joffre met six more times, dealing mostly with matters related to the Dardanelles and Salonika expeditions,[60] until the body was reconstituted under Briand's ministry at the end of October. The Conseil supérieur de la Défense nationale would then play an ever-increasing role in both French and Allied strategic planning.

THE COMMAND ISSUE

While he insisted that the British command carry out the offensive as planned, Joffre also tried to use Sir John's offer of voluntary subordination on 16 August as a means to achieving unity of command under French leadership. The question, as noted earlier, had been raised by Millerand in private discussions with Kitchener on 29 March following the Neuve Chapelle dispute. Millerand reported that Kitchener "was in agreement with Joffre on the necessity of unity"; moreover, he had suggested that Joffre be promoted marshal to put him on a rank equivalent to that of Sir John. But Kitchener side-stepped immediate action on the issue by promising to communicate "unofficially" to the French Sir John's instructions of 9 August 1914, "without bringing it to the attention of his colleagues."[61] The French government therefore was dismayed a few days later to learn the true nature of Sir John's original instructions, which, while urging him to cooperate with the "plans and wishes" of the French, specified that "his command is independent." This meant, among other things, that he could not evade responsibility by sheltering himself behind an order from General Joffre.[62]

Millerand's further urgings that, in view of the forthcoming operations in May, the matter be dealt with according to "logic and good sense" fell on deaf ears.[63] The existing arrangements in the final analysis were not uncongenial to British interests as they allowed a modicum of Allied direction by Joffre, whose prestige as "Victor of the Marne" fitted him for the task, without the obligation of a binding arrangement.

Following the acerbic discussions between the two commands during the second phase of the Artois offensive in June, and the difficulties in coordinating joint actions, Joffre was again determined to raise the issue of a unified command under his direction. But he was headed off by Wilson on 22 June on a visit to Chantilly. Anxious to promote better relations between the two commands, Wilson advised that the command issue was a sensitive matter that should not be pursued at that moment.[64]

On 30 July, as the dispute over the projected Loos operation came to an impasse, Joffre renewed his request to the British government for the subordination of Sir John French to the French command.[65] But, as Joffre did not believe that "either the British government or British public opinion would agree to complete and permanent subordination of the main British forces to the French command," he proposed a formula for limited subordination, which he thought would not offend British pride. According to this formula, which would apply only during the temporary period in which British troops contributed to the liberation of French territory, "the initiative for combined actions of French and British forces will fall upon the French commander-in-chief, notably with regard to effectives to be engaged, objectives to attain, and the dates to be established for the beginning of each operation." The commander-in-chief of British forces, on the other hand, would retain "complete liberty with regard to the means of execution."[66]

In London, on 9 August, the French ambassador laid Joffre's formula before Sir Edward Grey, the British secretary of state for foreign affairs, who, considering the matter to be "purely military," raised no objection. Kitchener likewise "found it quite acceptable" but, before accepting it, wished to talk it over with the two commanders-in-chief in France.[67] As the crisis unfolded, Joffre further requested that Kitchener oblige Sir John to make a major attack according to the French plan.[68]

KITCHENER'S INTERVENTION

The visit of Kitchener to France from 16 to 19 August was crucial from a number of points of view. The key elements that would affect his perception of the situation were the shakiness of French government, the dire straits of the Russian Army, and the strength of the French Army.

Kitchener arrived in the middle of a ministerial crisis, "a strong movement against Millerand," which threatened to overthrow Viviani's government. The British ambassador in Paris, Francis Bertie, had kept the British government informed of the unfolding events. Advising Grey in early August on the unrest surrounding Sarrail's dismissal and the Socialists' call for Millerand's removal, Bertie reported on 6 August, after talking with Briand and Delcassé, on the "very persistent" rumours on the possible collapse of the ministry, "chiefly from the extreme left and from the Socialist portion of the Cabinet." In his opinion, if the ministry should fall "to get rid of Millerand," the president of the republic would ask Briand to "reconstitute the ministry."[69] In this, he proved to be correct. Yet, after talking with Delcassé on the evening of 14 August, Bertie was hopeful that the government would not fall.[70]

As early as 28 July on a visit to London, Wilson found Asquith "anxious about the political outlook of France, and the intrigues against Millerand and Joffre, and … spoke of the return of Caillaux." Wilson reassured Asquith at that point that "to date there was no sign of bad work."[71] On 9 August, Wilson had a long talk with Joffre after lunch at Chantilly. They discussed Kitchener's forthcoming visit; Wilson was asked to be a member of the British party. They also discussed the British shortage of shells and Joffre's plan for the fall offensive. Wilson then went to Paris and had conversations with Bertie with regard to the growing ministerial crisis, from which he learned that "Joffre & Millerand were safe for the present."[72] But by the time Kitchener arrived in France on 16 August, the ministerial crisis had worsened and Wilson's view had therefore become darker. But he gave Kitchener the worst-case scenario, in informing him shortly after his arrival of the French political crisis. Millerand's departure, Wilson said, would be nothing more than a prelude to an attack on Joffre. In the background were the groups led by Caillaux and Valois that favoured an end to the war and that would gain ground if the ministry should fall.[73] The latter perspective would undoubtedly feed on Kitchener's fears related to the fall of the French government.

At the same time, the situation on the Russian front was desperate as a result of the fall of Warsaw on 5 August and the subsequent loss of Kovno.[74] It was thus imperative to help the Russians by attacking on the Western Front. While Kitchener had been opposed to a major offensive on the Western Front at the Chantilly Conference on 6 July, the need was now urgent to help the French, in view of the troubled state of the French government and the perilous state of the Russian military effort.

Kitchener's itinerary, the first two days of which had been prepared by Joffre, was intended to instill confidence in the French Army and thereby obtain Kitchener's commitment for full British engagement in the fall offensive. Arriving from Boulogne on 16 August, Kitchener, after inspecting troops of the French Sixth Army, would lunch at Chantilly, Joffre's headquarters, and, in the course of the next day and a half, inspect troops of the Fifth and either the Third or First French Armies. Army Commanders Castelnau and Dubail would attend various dinners.[75] In this carefully planned endeavour, Foch and Wilson would also play significant roles. Millerand and Wilson accompanied the party.

Foch was a key player in the manoeuvre to have Kitchener commit to the French fall offensive and then to oblige Sir John to participate fully. Foch's journal entry for 16 August contained the following illuminating entry: "At Compiègne, I had an appointment to meet with Joffre and Millerand to welcome Kitchener, to visit the Sixth Army [and] observation points ... and to definitively draw in Kitchener for the offensive who will veer French in this direction, who is still undecided and reticent. The task was accomplished."[76] Wilson also made his pitch to Kitchener after the dinner on the first day (which Pétain said would be the last organized by Millerand). He recorded: "When we left I went to K's train & had a long talk with him about the French political positions. I found him very sensible. He listened to all I had to say of dangers ahead of Caillaux & Valois group [and] of degommé [sacking] of Millerand and being only a preliminary to attack on Joffre, of the Valois and Caillaux group wanting, in reality, to make peace, of the absolute necessity for our doing nothing to upset the French soldiers such as Sir J. not putting his back into the forthcoming attack, etc, and he told me he quite agreed & would speak to Sir J. … A good day's work on K's part."[77]

The cause of solidarity with the Allied partners, French and Russian, triumphed. Kitchener now agreed, in a major strategic reversal, that it was vital to sustain the French government and the French Army with full British participation in the new offensive. While the British in early 1915 had assumed that the Russian "steamroller" would allow them to focus a portion of their military efforts elsewhere, their strategy now had to be revised in light of the Russian defeats so as to provide as much military assistance as soon as possible. Impressed by his review of French troops in his tour with Millerand and Joffre, Kitchener acted decisively: he first gave full support to Joffre's offensive and obliged Sir John to launch a major attack on the unfavourable position at Loos; he also approved Joffre's formula for the partial subordination of Sir John French.[78] In doing so, he did not mention to Sir John the unified-command formula.[79]

On Kitchener's return to London, the British cabinet approved of his strategic decisions. Asquith summarized the choices facing the government in a letter to the king: "The French are resolved to launch a major offensive – for reasons both military and above all political; in order to meet the requirements of their own army and people, and to appease the Russians, who are inclined to be angry and suspicious."[80] Kitchener, "far from being optimistic that major military advantages can be accomplished, is strongly of the opinion that we cannot, without doing serious and possibly fatal damage to the alliance, refuse the cooperation which General Joffre is asking and expects."[81] Accordingly, to the question of British participation in Joffre's offensive, "there was but one answer."[82] The British cabinet approved the offensive, with only Churchill and Carson dissenting.[83]

In order to sustain the French and Russian alliances, Kitchener had cast aside his principles of attrition warfare and ironically had traded roles with Sir John French in supporting Joffre's offensive. Without this offensive, he was afraid that the French and the Russians might make a separate peace.[84] This was a very grim appraisal of the situation. Kitchener's conclusions are memorable. "We make war as we must, not as we would like."[85] Losses of over 60,000 in the Loos offensive followed automatically.

In their appreciation of the political situation in France, British politicians appear to have overreacted to the governmental crisis and the small beginnings of a peace movement. In his study of the French in the First World War, Jean-Jacques Becker has indicated that the major concern among the Paris population in August 1915 was the rising price of foodstuffs and rents, without a commensurate increase in wages, and that while there was a small peace movement, particularly among women concerned about the rise in prices, the population in general was staunchly behind the war effort and doggedly prepared for a second winter of war.[86] That the British had long-term stereotypes relative to the instability of the French government and French public opinion, as earlier indicated, may account, at least in part, for their concerns. Tapping into existing doubts about France's reliability as an ally, Wilson and possibly others appear to have exaggerated the gravity of the French situation to get full British support for the joint offensive. In the final analysis, British perception of the political situation in France, rather than the reality, played a decisive role in their decision to engage fully at Loos.

While Kitchener had long appreciated the military advantages of a unified Allied command on the Western Front, he had also displayed very considerable reluctance to give formal approval to such an arrangement, until faced with a significant crisis; and even then, he agreed to only partial subordination of Sir John French to Joffre, providing for French direction in specific operations. Undoubtedly, Kitchener was reluctant to integrate the BEF in France under Joffre's control while the allocation of troops to the Dardanelles was in question and Joffre was pursuing a strategy in France for a massive offensive of which he did not approve.

But one may surmise that in the background there was a deeper concern related to national sovereignty and the role of the army as its main guarantor. This was all too evident in the refusal in January 1915 of King Leopold of Belgium to give control of any part of his army to either the French or the British. The British appeared to have believed, when the French proposed a unified command repeatedly as a way of resolve conflict between Sir John French and Joffre, that this was merely a manoeuvre to get control of the strategic direction of the British Army and have it play a greater role which would not necessarily be in their interest. The British felt much more comfortable with the BEF being an associate army, willing to cooperate with the French but always under British control, as outlined in Sir John's initial instructions.

This attitude would account for the ongoing British reluctance to surrender the direction of their army in France to a French general, except in a dire emergency, as in the case of German spring offensive in 1918. Despite the recognized need for unified command, when Foch was appointed on 3 April 1918 as Allied commander-in-chief of French, British, American, and Belgian forces, the commanders of each army retained "full tactical control of their armies and were given the right to appeal to their respective governments if they believed the orders from Foch placed their army in danger."[87] This would indicate the ongoing concern with giving up the command of national armies to an Allied general, even in a time of emergency.

An important factor behind the right of appeal was the ongoing mistrust that was always present in the Anglo-French relationship. Recall again N.P. Mikhnevich's claim that "allies will strive to shift the heaviest burdens on to other shoulders."[88] This was certainly Sir John's view of the French. In times of crises, as during the initial battle on the frontiers, during the battle on the Aisne, and during the Second Battle of Ypres, he always feared that he would not be adequately sustained. This explains his unwillingness to take up a proportionate length of trenches in order to keep a strong reserve, his request for three regular French divisions to be stationed near his front, and his adamant opposition to unity of command under French leadership in which he would be subordinated to French direction. His *amour propre* was also a factor. It should be remembered that it was only after the lessons learned in the First World War that the British and Americans in the Second World War agreed to the immediate creation of the Combined Chiefs of Staff and the appointment of commanders-in-chief in each theatre.

That the subordination of the British command to the French command was a sensitive issue is demonstrated by the secrecy with which Kitchener treated the matter. Rather than sharing the document outlining the new arrangement with Sir John French, Kitchener merely told him to comply with Joffre's wishes. While Grey had foreknowledge of the arrangement, it would appear, from the absence of discussion of the command issue on Kitchener's return to London, that the subject was not raised in cabinet.

What has been lacking in studies based on British sources has been what Kitchener said and did when he went on repeated visits to France. In consultation with Joffre, Foch, Poincaré, Millerand, Ribot, and Cambon at Dunkirk on 1 November 1914, for example, in the midst a major crisis in the field, Kitchener promised the French "a magnificent English army of a million men for July 1, 1915," a statement not widely reported in British accounts.[89] Nor did he tell Sir John French about the unified command arrangement to which he had just agreed and, as indicated, he apparently did not mention it to the War Council on his return to Britain. The Millerand Papers, including Millerand's notes on private conversations with Kitchener, have proven a very rich source in filling this gap. As we have seen, Millerand's papers also provide detailed minutes of the 6 July meeting at Calais (including Kitchener's overly optimistic forecast of British troops arrivals), for which it was believed for some time among English authors that no record had been kept. These papers, when used in conjunction with Poincaré's diaries and other French records, provide a much clearer view of the panorama of Allied relations.

While limited in its total application, the unified command arrangement of August 1915 might have served as the basis for future command relations had Sir John remained in command of the BEF. What it did, in effect, was to regularize the informal relationship which had long prevailed between the two commanders in giving Joffre "the initiative for combined actions of French and British forces … notably with regard to effectives to be engaged, objectives to attain, and the dates to be established for the beginning of each operation." When Haig, concerned about the need for unity of command, replaced Sir John as commander of British forces in December 1915, his first act was to subordinate himself voluntarily to Joffre,[90] so the command formula had no further application. It should be observed that Kitchener's willingness to agree to this arrangement came at a time when he had finally agreed to French strategy on the Western Front, suggesting that his conflict with Joffre on strategy had been a major impediment to an earlier agreement.

Kitchener's visit to France and his full support for the French joint offensive cleared the air between the commanders-in-chief. Sir John French immediately asked to meet with Joffre at GQG on 23 August to explain what he intended to do and what resources he had at his disposal.[91] On 22 August, as the French cabinet met amidst further acrimonious debate over a speech given by Millerand in the Chamber which seemed to violate their previous understanding, Delcassé read a letter from Grey indicating that Kitchener had returned from France "very satisfied." Grey said Kitchener had indicated his agreement with Millerand on "every point" and that his visit had established "real harmony" between Marshal French and Joffre. Referring to rumours of possible changes in French leadership, Kitchener further expressed the view that a ministerial change or change of command would "compromise the intimacy which had been established between allied general staffs" through sustained efforts over a long period of time. He also noted that, in his interviews with the military chiefs, they had decided on a renewal of the offensive – the plan for which, he urged, should be communicated secretly to the Russians.[92] With British support, it would now be doubly hard for the government to cancel Joffre's intended offensive. Joffre's manoeuvre had worked wonderfully well. The support that he had carefully garnered from the British could now be used to shore up his support with his own government.

CONCLUSION

The study of the several crises in Allied command relations in 1915 lends further credence to the view that the differing strategies of the two powers were the major cause of difficulties in the field. In the case of the objections of Sir John French to the Loos offensive, the evidence presented would suggest that, within two weeks of his government's definition of strategy at Calais on 6 July, he began to adopt a similar approach. Starved for munitions, as a result of the diversion of supplies to the Dardanelles, he had few options but to protest the role assigned to him to attack against the heavily defended area at Loos. The difficulty of the terrain and the shortage of munitions became the issues around which the discussion revolved.

An even greater challenge to Joffre's plan for the fall offensive came from his government. While Poincaré and the Viviani government were generally opposed to a huge offensive, Joffre, with Millerand's support, was able to withstand their objections and proceed as planned. The presentation of his plan to Kitchener, in view of the ministerial crisis and the huge Russian setback on the Eastern Front, was critical to Kitchener's strategic reversal on the offensive. Kitchener also yielded to French demands in accepting a formula for the partial subordination of the British command to French direction.

Kitchener's response to the situation in August 1915 illustrates the point that in coalition warfare allied partners are not always free to follow the strategy that corresponds to their political preferences and what had been their pre-war interests. The initial British imperial stance, with the priority it attached to defending the empire, could not be maintained because of the weakness of their allies. When the consequences of a prolonged war became apparent after the Artois offensive, the British were obliged to come to the assistance of the French, who, according to the best information, began to waver politically in June 1915. The British sent their New Armies to France; and, in spite of the reluctance of the British government to undertake major costly offensives, and its preference for a defensive strategy, as expressed at the Calais Conference on 6 July, Kitchener and the British cabinet had to yield, in a major strategic reversal, to the demands of their French and Russian allies in August 1915 by giving maximum support to the French attack. The needs of the alliance had trumped the preferred British strategy. The British government by these means moved from a limited commitment toward the Western Front at the beginning of 1915 to near total commitment in the fall.

CHAPTER TEN

Operations: The Loos and Artois-Champagne Offensive, September–October 1915

HAVING COME TO TERMS WITH the British over the extent of their participation, Joffre faced continuing challenges – mainly from the French government and Parliament – in his attempt to mount the combined Loos and Artois-Champagne offensive. Already agitated over the failure of the Artois offensive, French parliamentarians became more restive in the summer of 1915 with Joffre's dismissal at the end of July of Maurice Sarrail, a general popular with the Socialists. Sarrail became a lightning rod for the eastern strategy, around which rallied a substantial part of the parliamentary left in a bid for an augmented French contingent in the Dardanelles under Sarrail's command. A huge wrangle ensued between the government and High Command as Joffre manoeuvred to keep all available forces under his command for the fall offensive.

Following Kitchener's endorsement of the Loos offensive, the French and British field commanders engaged in relatively cordial interactions in their planning, even though the joint offensive was postponed several times until it was finally scheduled for late September. There was, of course, the normal jockeying over the relief of French trenches, and Sir John revealed a growing mistrust of Joffre over his direct communications with Kitchener. But both commanders were united in their resistance to their governments' diversion of troops and munitions from their front for a renewed push under Sarrail on the Asian side of the Dardanelles. The principal clash was between Joffre and his government, which wished to detach four divisions from his front for the Sarrail venture just as the fall offensive was about to begin.

The joint offensive in the Loos-Arras region and the French attack in Champagne began with great expectations, after many delays, on 25 September; but, after initial successes, it became bogged down in limited engagements and ultimately led to a standstill on all fronts, with very limited results. The attempt in the latter phase of the battle to coordinate successive smaller joint operations under such inauspicious circumstances frazzled the nerves of both the French and the British.

The failed battle, however, just like the failure of the Artois offensive in the spring, had much broader repercussions. The accumulation of grievances over the conduct of the war, grievances that were especially strong among the Socialist left, brought down the French government and led to a major reworking of the French command system under Briand, the new premier. Sir John French's failure to make available British reserves after an initial breakthrough at Loos was the final event that sparked his recall at year's end. The failed offensive led to important changes not only in the field but also in the British political-military structure, with significant implications for British strategy in succeeding months. The relationship between Joffre and the French government was also revamped. And Joffre, recognizing the need for overall Allied cooperation to bring the full weight of the Allies against the Central Powers, launched an energetic initiative in early December to coordinate the efforts of the entire Entente coalition for offensives in 1916.

SARRAIL AND FRENCH POLITICS

The Sarrail Affair, as it unfolded, must be seen in the light of the French government's demand in late August for the detachment of four divisions from Joffre's command for an Asiatic landing in the Dardanelles, and Joffre's struggle to keep the fall offensive alive against the mounting opposition of the French president and a growing contingent both in the cabinet and in the Chamber of Deputies.

The French offer to increase their participation in the Dardanelles expedition came as a welcome surprise to the British government but raised serious issues in joint planning related to the Western Front. The Dardanelles expedition, which began as a naval bombardment of the

General Maurice Sarrail was dismissed by Joffre in late July 1915, but subsequently, to placate his left-wing political supporters, who were also "easterners," the French government appointed him to head an expanded Dardanelles expedition to land on the Asiatic coast. (*THW*, 2:42)

Straits on 19 February 1915 and ultimately escalated into a full-fledged military expedition, had been a British initiative to which the French had given reluctant support in order to defend their interests in the eastern Mediterranean.[1] The April landing of British and French troops at Cap Helles, British forces at Anzac Cove, and French troops at Kum Kale on the Asiatic side of the Straits, and the later British landing at Suvla Bay in early August, all proved fruitless and resulted in an entrenched stalemate just like that on the Western Front.[2] The future of the expedition, which saw two French divisions and ten British divisions pinned to the ground, was under review in Britain in the late summer of 1915.

The British government was thus quite taken aback when the French, at the end of August 1915, unexpectedly became ardent supporters for the deployment of four additional divisions to the Asiatic side of the Straits to bolster the campaign.[3] While initially delighted with the French offer to help with what was increasingly becoming a bad business, the British soon realized that there were a number of potholes in the road ahead. Immediate questions arose such as how such a deployment would affect the major Anglo-French offensive planned for September in France, and what shipping requirements would be required for the new enterprise. And where would the British find the two divisions of British troops necessary to replace the two French divisions at Cap Helles that the French wished to withdraw in order to make up a contingent of six divisions for the Asiatic deployment? Kitchener's solution was to withdraw two British divisions from the Western Front for that purpose, with the understanding that they would be replaced by two new divisions from Britain. That proposal, as one might expect, met with immediate protests from both Joffre and Sir John. To address these and other issues, Kitchener met War Minister Millerand, Sir John, Joffre, and Sarrail, now designated for the new French eastern command, in a political-military conference at Calais on 11 September 1915.[4]

With the major fall offensive in Champagne and Artois about to begin in less than two weeks, the French government continued to face the unrelenting opposition of Joffre to any diversion of troops from the Western Front, and particularly at that moment. These interests prevailed. At Calais, all agreed that the Allied offensive in France should take immediate priority. Yet, aware that French impetus for the expanded Dardanelles expedition was largely political, Kitchener supported the French plan for increased forces at the Dardanelles. Under extreme pressure from Millerand, Joffre very reluctantly agreed to make available four divisions from his front for the expedition, but not until 10 October, after the French fall offensive. In the discussion, Sir John expressed his unstinted support of Joffre's position and likewise resisted any redeployment of British troops from the Western Front to the Dardanelles.[5]

The lines of conflict were therefore drawn on the political-military front between the politicians on one side and the field commanders on the other over the diversion of further troops from the Western Front for an enlargement of the Dardanelles venture. This state of affairs remained unchanged when word of the intended mobilization of Bulgaria and its likely entry into the war on the side of the Central Powers reached Western capitals on 21 September 1915, which redirected attention from the enlargement of the Dardanelles venture to the need for an expedition to Salonika in support of the Serbs.[6]

To many, the fact that the French not only created an enhanced force for the command of a disgraced general but also adjusted their strategy to accommodate the situation may seem incomprehensible. But it must be remembered that much of French political left favoured an eastern strategy and that Sarrail served as a vehicle for its implementation; and that the parliamentary agitation in favour of Sarrail was in fact directed against Joffre and Millerand, the latter thought to be too uncritical of the commander-in-chief.[7] The expedient adopted reflected the changing landscape in terms of the reassertion of parliamentary control over the ministry and the High Command.

PREPARING THE FALL OFFENSIVE: SUPPORTING THE RUSSIANS

Kitchener's memorable remark about the British waging war as "we must" signified their full cooperation in the joint Anglo-French offensives in Loos and Artois-Champagne in the fall of 1915. To coordinate that offensive, seven of the foremost French and British military field officers met in a conference at Chantilly on 22 August. Joffre, Foch, Pellé, and Huguet represented France; Sir John, Robertson, and Wilson represented Britain. In addition to the gravity of the military situation, Joffre informed his colleagues that "there was great shakiness in civil and military circles in Russia and some assistance was urgently required." The tentative date for the beginning of the French offensive, delayed from the end of August, was now set for 8 September, as Joffre wanted to launch the attack as soon as possible owing to the dire straits in which the Russian Army found itself.[8]

The military situation was indeed disastrous on the Eastern Front. The Germans had already captured Warsaw on 5 August. They and the Austro-Hungarians then drove the Russians back another 190 miles to the east by the time that summer gave way to autumn.[9] Sir John therefore agreed completely with Joffre's reasoning that an Anglo-French offensive had to be undertaken in the near future for the purpose of preventing the collapse of the Russian Army.[10]

Joffre would postpone the date of the Champagne offensive twice more: at the end of August he postponed it until 15 September,[11] and finally, for reasons that will be explained below, he later settled on 25 September.[12] The latter was a decision of dire consequences, since it delayed the offensive into the beginning of the rainy season. In sharp contrast to Sir John's resistance to the many delays in the coordination of the BEF's forward movement with that of the French Army at Artois in May and June, there is no record of his opposing Joffre's rescheduling of the fall offensive. In addition, after Kitchener's visit, Sir John never wavered in his willingness to cooperate fully with the French Army's requests for artillery support prior to the offensive.[13]

DELAYS: MEN AND MATÉRIEL

Finding enough manpower for the offensive presented a problem for Joffre, who wished to engage as many French troops as possible. The British could help provide the answer. Reverting to what the British perceived as the French pattern of asking them to "take over a good deal more line and at the same time prepare a big offensive,"[14] Joffre requested on 20 August that the first divisions of the British Third New Army relieve French divisions for the attack.[15] To this request Sir John gave only partial satisfaction, replying two days later that the BEF, at present, could relieve just the French 56th Infantry Division.[16]

Initiating a further delay, Joffre advised Sir John on 1 September that the Centre Army Group in Champagne would not be ready to conduct operations before 25 September, and therefore that he had decided to delay his offensive until that date.[17] What Joffre did not divulge was the real reason for the postponement: that constituting the French Second Army – an important formation in the Centre Army Group – turned out to be more difficult than anticipated, and its new commander, General Henri-Philippe Pétain, insisted on additional time to plan his attack and to get to know his immediate subordinates better.[18] In the same communication, Joffre asked Sir John to relieve the French 51st and 154th infantry divisions before 25 September.[19] To this, Sir John replied on 3 September that the delayed arrival of the Third New Army prevented him from giving a definite answer.[20]

The jockeying continued. On 7 September, Sir John declined to relieve the 154th Division owing to his wish to create a reserve force for the BEF's offensive.[21] But, five days later, he advised Joffre that the BEF could take over the line for the 154th Division on 20 September.[22] Foch then told Wilson that 20 September would be too late to enable the 154th Division to reach the battlefield in time for 23 September,[23] deemed necessary for the offensive beginning on 25 September. While there was much discussion to and fro, Sir John was more cooperative in relieving French divisions before Loos than he had been prior to Artois. Ultimately the French assembled fifty-three divisions, thirty-five in Champagne and eighteen in Artois; the British, twelve before Loos.[24] That Joffre did not have as many divisions as he wanted in Champagne was only marginally affected by Sir John's inability to relieve additional French divisions.

For the British, providing enough shells for the offensive was an even more difficult hurdle than finding enough soldiers. Indeed, Sir John regarded it as the greatest obstacle to success. On 23 August he wrote a letter to Kitchener in which he expressed guarded optimism: "It is far more a question of ammunition than anything else, and I feel sure you will do your utmost to help us in that direction."[25] Kitchener responded that he would try to meet Sir John's needs to the best of his ability. On 12 September, as the battle approached, Sir John informed Mrs Bennett that, with regard to the supply of shells, "we are really better off than we've ever been!"[26]

The numbers support his statement. By 14 September, the BEF had 180 heavy artillery pieces and 720 field guns.[27] Four days earlier, Asquith had written to King George V: "Sir J. French is to be supplied during the next three weeks with an exceptionally large quantity of High Explosive ammunition; it is hoped with 350,000 shells."[28] The French, for their part, had readied 2,000 heavy artillery pieces and 3,000 field guns.[29] Yet, impressive as these numbers appeared, they would ultimately prove inadequate for an offensive faced with the demands of trench warfare.

Command relations also improved as the two commanders concerted their efforts prior to the battle during the late summer of 1915.[30] Sir John reported that he felt "very kindly" toward Joffre after the Calais Conference of 11 September, in which they both came out in opposition to diversion of troops from the Western Front.[31] But mistrust lingered: Sir John believed that the French were undermining him when Joffre set up a direct line of communications with Kitchener through Brigadier-General Henry Yarde-Buller, the British liaison officer at GQG. During the 22 August meeting of the Anglo-French military chiefs, Sir John stated to Joffre that "he thought it best for General Joffre to get all his information from him and not from Lord Kitchener, because any other procedure might easily lead to misunderstanding."[32]

Sir John's complaints about Kitchener grew more pointed in the days that followed. On 12 September he voiced his displeasure with Kitchener acting as though he was supreme commander of the operation, "whereas he really knows nothing except what the General [Joffre] chooses to tell him."[33] When Clive failed to persuade Sir John French two days later that Joffre had not been undermining him by communicating directly with Kitchener, he put it down to Sir John's poor health.[34] Sir John had in fact been bedridden from time to time on account of a prolonged bout of bronchial pneumonia and influenza. His health had been sufficiently impaired that Rawlinson thought that he should relinquish command of the BEF.[35]

On a visit to the front on 20 September, Kitchener was "amazed" at one of Sir John's outbursts against Joffre, which, he told Wilson, "simply knocked him out" – "he could not understand it."[36] The origin of Sir John's anger derived from his dislike of Kitchener holding private talks with Joffre. To make a comparison, Sir John told Wilson that he (Sir John) would never agree to speaking privately with Millerand.[37] The underlying cause of the tension between Sir John and Kitchener, however, lay in their differences over strategy. While Sir John unequivocally favoured offensives on the Western Front and opposed any eastern strategy, Kitchener, though recognizing the primacy of the Western Front, supported the enhanced French operations in the Dardanelles as a means of defending British interests in the Middle East.

In Britain, Kitchener had supported the French offer of an augmented Dardanelles expedition with his colleagues. His main motive, he told Sir John, was to win the campaign quickly so that he could get the Allied divisions in Turkey back to the Western Front.[38] On 3 September, Asquith's cabinet recognized that success in the Dardanelles would greatly benefit the Allied cause.[39] Wilson, however, recorded in his diary on 10 September: "K also told me that our Gov[ernmen]t (by which he means himself chiefly) feel so strongly about the Dardanelles that they [would] send all the troops themselves if the French cry off."[40] Kitchener had undoubtedly been the driving force behind the Asquith government's determination to stay the course in Turkey.

DIVISIONS FOR SARRAIL

Meanwhile, in France, Viviani's ministry desired to pursue an eastern strategy, while Joffre firmly believed that war could be won only on the Western Front. The debate over whether to increase or decrease the Allied presence at the Straits – or cancel the Dardanelles expedition altogether – constituted a glaring distraction for Joffre as the date for the offensive on the Western Front approached.

On the British side, the Dardanelles expedition was not going well. At the end of August, Lieutenant-General Sir Ian Hamilton had reported that his troops were tired and dispirited, and that the increase in losses owing to illness was alarming. He asked for reinforcements. If the War Office denied his request, Hamilton advised that he would be forced to cede Suvla Bay and then shorten his front even further. Wilson believed that the British either had to leave the Dardanelles or end up with a "handsome disaster."[41] De la Panouse, the French military attaché in London, seconded Wilson's bleak assessment, albeit in more tempered language. He advised Joffre that Bulgaria's anti-Entente attitude and its decision to grant passage through its territory to German and Austro-Hungarian troops made him believe that the Dardanelles operation was not worth the trouble.[42]

But the French government, like the British government, rather than pulling out of the Dardanelles, favoured reinforcing the expedition. As discussed earlier, the contest between the government and Joffre for the necessary forces continued through August, with Joffre admitting grudgingly on 21 August that he would provide four division for the Asiatic landing if his fall offensive failed to produce decisive results.[43]

The next day, Joffre requested that Millerand give him two more territorial divisions for his offensive in Champagne.[44] Millerand agreed three days later, on 26 August, but he warned that the offensive could commence only after Joffre apprised Viviani's cabinet of his definitive plan.[45] This condition undoubtedly came from the government, because the war minister made no secret that he advocated granting the army High Command absolute liberty to conduct operations.[46]

MOUNTING PRESSURE FROM THE CHAMBER AND THE GOVERNMENT

As the summer progressed, deputies were becoming more and more fed up with the way that Viviani's ministry was directing the war effort. The Army, Navy, and Foreign Affairs Commissions of the Chamber – the "Three Commissions of National Defence" – roundly criticized Millerand's performance, but many of their complaints were really aimed at Joffre. On 26 August, the commissions censured Joffre directly for refusing to relinquish divisions under his command so that a reserve army not answerable to him could be created in the zone of the interior. Its mission would be to defend Paris.[47] The three commissions, for all intents and purposes the actual voice of the Chamber, were exerting pressure on Millerand as a way of obliging him to rein in Joffre.

The following day, the commissions went beyond criticism of the government's inaction and asked Viviani's cabinet to organize, without delay and with the agreement of France's allies, an expeditionary force to seize the Turkish Straits and capture Constantinople, the capital of the Ottoman empire.[48] In consequence, a day later, Viviani decided to constitute the "Army of the Near East" by 28 September. On 31 August, Millerand instructed Delcassé to inform the British government that the French divisions serving at Cap Hellas must be relieved by British units and would be transferred to Sarrail, the commander of the Army of the Near East.[49]

On 28 August, Viviani's cabinet also unanimously agreed that, if the British suffered a setback in the Dardanelles, the dispatch of additional French troops to that area of operations would be essential. But, later that day, Joffre, meeting with key political leaders in the Conseil supérieur de la Défense nationale, attempted to renege on the pledge that he had made earlier to send four divisions to the Dardanelles if his offensive in Champagne proved indecisive. He told Poincaré, Viviani, Millerand, Augagneur, and Delcassé that he required the four divisions for his impending offensive and then to parry an eventual German attack.[50]

A spirited controversy then ensued between Poincaré and Joffre in which Poincaré reminded Joffre of his earlier promise. In remarks that reflected the worsening Russian situation with regard to munitions, Poincaré, who expected little from the Champagne offensive, stated that it was vital to open the Straits and, more important, to supply munitions to the Russian Army than to recapture a few metres of French soil. Joffre countered that he needed the four divisions until 20 or 22 September, because if French troops pierced German defences, their success would enable the Allies to cancel the operation in the Dardanelles.

The discussion then became heated. Poincaré retorted that a failure in Champagne would discourage the army, to which Joffre replied that to do nothing would be dishonourable. He assured Poincaré that the French would kill more Germans by attacking than vice versa. Millerand broke the impasse when he declared that a study by the military staff of the War Ministry indicated that the four divisions would not be ready for transport in any case before 20 September. In the end, Joffre grudgingly agreed with the politicians to put the four divisions at the disposal of the government between 20 and 22 September, ready for immediate embarkation to Turkey.[51]

On 1 September, Joffre, as indicated above, postponed the date of his offensive from 15 to 25 September. His change of plan left Poincaré to wonder what would become of his promise to send the four divisions to the Dardanelles.[52] Joffre provided the answer later in the day, following this decision. The divisions, he said, could not be dispatched to Turkey until the beginning of October for three reasons: the Army of the Near East destined for the Dardanelles had yet to consider its exact mission; operations that would soon be in progress in France would preclude their withdrawal from the front on 15 or 16 September, the latest possible date to allow them to arrive in Marseille by 24 September; and, if France sent reinforcements and the Dardanelles expedition failed, people would regard the failure as a French rather than as a British one.[53]

On 3 September, Millerand strongly reminded Joffre that a setback in the Dardanelles would be neither a British nor a French but rather an Allied setback, the consequences of which for the Entente could be grave.[54] Four days later, Millerand instructed Joffre to send four divisions from France to Turkey in early October, giving him the choice of which divisions to select.[55] This communication again shows Millerand, at the behest of the majority of Viviani's cabinet, trying to impose government control over Joffre.

Joffre wasted little time in his attempt to circumvent what he deemed to be yet one more example of civilian interference in his operations. On 8 September he replied that operations in progress made it impossible for him to comply with Millerand's request.[56] His stalling tactics demonstrated his dyed-in-the-wool opposition to sending any formations outside France.

The Allied political-military conference held at Calais on 11 September did little to allay the tension in the relationship. While all assembled agreed that the forthcoming offensive in Artois and Champagne should take priority, Joffre very reluctantly agreed under pressure from the ministers to make available four divisions from his front for the Dardanelles expedition, but not until 10 October, after the French fall offensive.

Thus, on 14 September, Millerand asked Joffre to have four divisions ready for embarkation to Turkey by 10 October.[57] But Joffre continued to defy the Viviani cabinet even more openly as the date for the Champagne offensive approached. On 20 September, he wrote to Millerand asserting that the Calais agreement made the departure of the four divisions for the Dardanelles dependent on the outcome of his offensive on the Western Front. Joffre went on to say that he therefore could not commit himself categorically to transporting the four divisions from Marseille on 10 October. In his view, the Dardanelles expedition was a risky venture that could entail such a cost in men and matériel that the French Army might end up weakened to the extent of compromising the campaign in France.[58]

The following day, Viviani lamented that the Dardanelles operation would never take place because GQG was opposed to General Maurice Sarrail being its commander.[59] While the government applied a growing amount of pressure on Joffre in the late summer of 1915, in order to persuade him to obey its directives concerning the dispatch of four divisions to the Dardanelles, its newly found assertiveness was less the product of its own willingness than an attempt to convince an increasingly restive Chamber of Deputies not to topple it in a non-confidence vote. Remarkably, Joffre was able to get away with his defiance owing to the weakness of the divided Viviani cabinet.

Another issue then threatened to weaken the Anglo-French partnership with regard to the Dardanelles. On 31 August, the Third Bureau of GQG compiled a report stating that success in the Dardanelles depended on coordination of British and French contingents there. The combined force would, needless to say, need one commander; and the commander, of course, should be French.[60] The following day, Kitchener rejected that proposal and advised Sir John that the French force in the Dardanelles would operate independently of the British.[61] It was essential that the French and British coordinate their movements and communicate their intentions, he said, but since the two theatres of operation were far from each other, it was necessary to give Hamilton and Sarrail each his complete liberty to act.[62] Kitchener was determined that Hamilton would not be subordinated to Sarrail, an attitude that he explicitly stated to Millerand on 14 September.[63] Kitchener's action was undoubtedly motivated by his lack of confidence in Sarrail's leadership, an opinion he shared with Joffre, who had cashiered him as commander of the Third Army in July. Foch, Wilson, and Huguet also shared a low opinion of Sarrail. Wilson reported in his journal on 9 September that "Sarrail has forced the hand of a weak Govt to give him a bigger command & they agreed. Joffre has temporarily stopped this business until after our attack [on the Western Front] … Joffre would crush it completely if he could but he can't do more than he has done."[64]

At the Calais Conference on 11 September, the French had admitted in private that the government had formed the Army of the Near East in order to find a post for Sarrail. Joffre confided to Kitchener that he did not like the eastern expedition in general and had no confidence in Sarrail in particular.[65] Millerand was also skeptical of Sarrail's ability. Hence, on 14 September, under pressure from Joffre, Millerand apprised Sarrail that Viviani's ministry thought that the time had come for him to submit his plans for the Dardanelles operation.[66] According to Kitchener, Sarrail's main objective was to obtain an important command and use it as a stepping stone to succeed Joffre. Kitchener added that Millerand feared Sarrail and therefore had played Sarrail's game.[67]

Millerand, in fact, had good reason to fear Sarrail. He was the protégé of the Socialists, who controlled more than one hundred of the six hundred seats in the Chamber of Deputies. They and their leftist allies had the power to bring down Viviani's government whenever they chose, but for the moment their demands were being at least partly met.

The French coalition government was indeed weakening fast in the late summer of 1915. On 28 August, Poincaré admonished members of the cabinet, divided by the differing political agendas of their parties, to set a good example of unity and strength. Viviani insisted that he and his fellow ministers were collaborating with more confidence recently, and Millerand promised to do his utmost to accomplish whatever depended on his efforts.[68]

To the extent possible, Millerand, it should be noted, supported Joffre in the latter's disputes with the politicians. Joffre himself recognized this fact. On 14 September he told Wilson that Millerand was not as bad as he appeared. Since his position in cabinet was precarious, he had to mind his "p's" and "q's." But he was doing all he could to assist Joffre.[69] Not only was Millerand's tenure in jeopardy, however; the entire Viviani ministry stood on shaky ground. In fact, it had less than one month of life left before it collapsed toward the end October.

Divisions within the government were a serious impediment to good civil-military relations. Joffre, Poincaré noted, conversed once a week with Poincaré, Viviani, Millerand, Augagneur, and Delcassé. But, according to Poincaré, Millerand – who would have preferred not to be at these meetings – rarely uttered a word during them, and spent most of his time before and afterwards attempting to protect Joffre from Viviani's ministers.[70] Joffre, moreover, helped Millerand to keep civilians in the dark about happenings at the front. One of Joffre's favourite ways of doing so, Poincaré claimed, was for Joffre to accompany him on his visits to the zone of the armies in order to prevent officers from speaking freely with him.[71]

Despite his reticence in sharing information, Joffre recognized the need to achieve better civil-military coordination. He thus played a key role in mid-August in the revival of the Conseil supérieur de la Défense nationale and the associated Section d'Etudes de la Défense nationale, which functioned at the War Ministry under the direction of the ministry's army chief of staff.[72] The Conseil supérieur, which was intended to coordinate the strategy of an inner cabinet of key ministers with that of the commander-in-chief, was a partial success, but the divisions and rancours within the cabinet often spilled over. In sum, civil-military coordination in France left much to be desired.

WEAKNESSES WITHIN THE BRITISH GOVERNMENT

Across the English Channel, Asquith's government stood on only slightly firmer ground, owing in part to competing agendas. The British cabinet was engaged in a year-long debate over the merits of conscription, favoured by the Unionists, and was rocked in October by the precipitous resignation of Sir Edward Carson, the attorney general, on the issue.[73] In the midst of this, Kitchener held a negative opinion of most of his cabinet colleagues. The exceptions were Asquith and Balfour, whom Kitchener described as the "only honest and capable ones."[74] Lord Esher complained of the government's "weakness and fear of criticism."[75] Wilson found inertia the order of the day. According to him, Asquith and Kitchener made speeches implicitly saying that they would "wait & see!"[76] Wilson's disgust and contempt for British politicians also extended to the entire House of Commons, which he claimed was "not doing much good."[77]

Certainly, at least two junior members of Parliament were not doing the army any good. Josiah Wedgwood and Robbie Harcourt, travelling to France in mid-September as Royal Naval Air Service officers, met with Esher separately. Considering whether or not to ask the House of Commons to remove Kitchener and Sir John for "incapacity and old age," they visited British formations, gathering tidbits of information from officers of all ranks. Esher, writing to Kitchener, opined that their views on the British war would be a joke except for the danger that they could become public knowledge. Fearing that all "these disgusting intrigues" might one day result in a "big explosion," he advised Wedgwood that "nothing would be more fatal than a public row" in the House of Commons. He thought that Wedgwood absorbed what he was saying. Yet, while having headed off their initiative in the short run, Esher did not seem to think that Wedgwood and Harcourt would take his advice to heart for long. He concluded with the words: "Look out for squalls!"[78]

ON THE EVE OF THE BATTLE

Allied coordination was no better. Kitchener held more frequent talks with Millerand and Joffre, and their results, de la Panouse reported from London, pleased him.[79] Unfortunately, Kitchener's direct communications with Joffre and failure from time to time to include Sir John in them, as mentioned above, actually worsened interactions among the three men. The British and French governments attempted to develop better cooperation in numerous conferences in the fall of 1915 with regard to the Dardanelles expedition and the later Salonika expedition, but these also proved to be highly ineffective.[80] Although the Allies faced a difficult time in coordinating their efforts in the fall of 1915, and set up a loose-knit advisory body of key political leaders from both countries in January 1916 (to be discussed later), the latter proved to be less than effective. Only a more desperate situation would motivate them to create the Supreme War Council in early 1917, following the Caporetto debacle in Italy. The prelude to the Loos and Artois-Champagne offensive was over. The battle itself was about to begin.

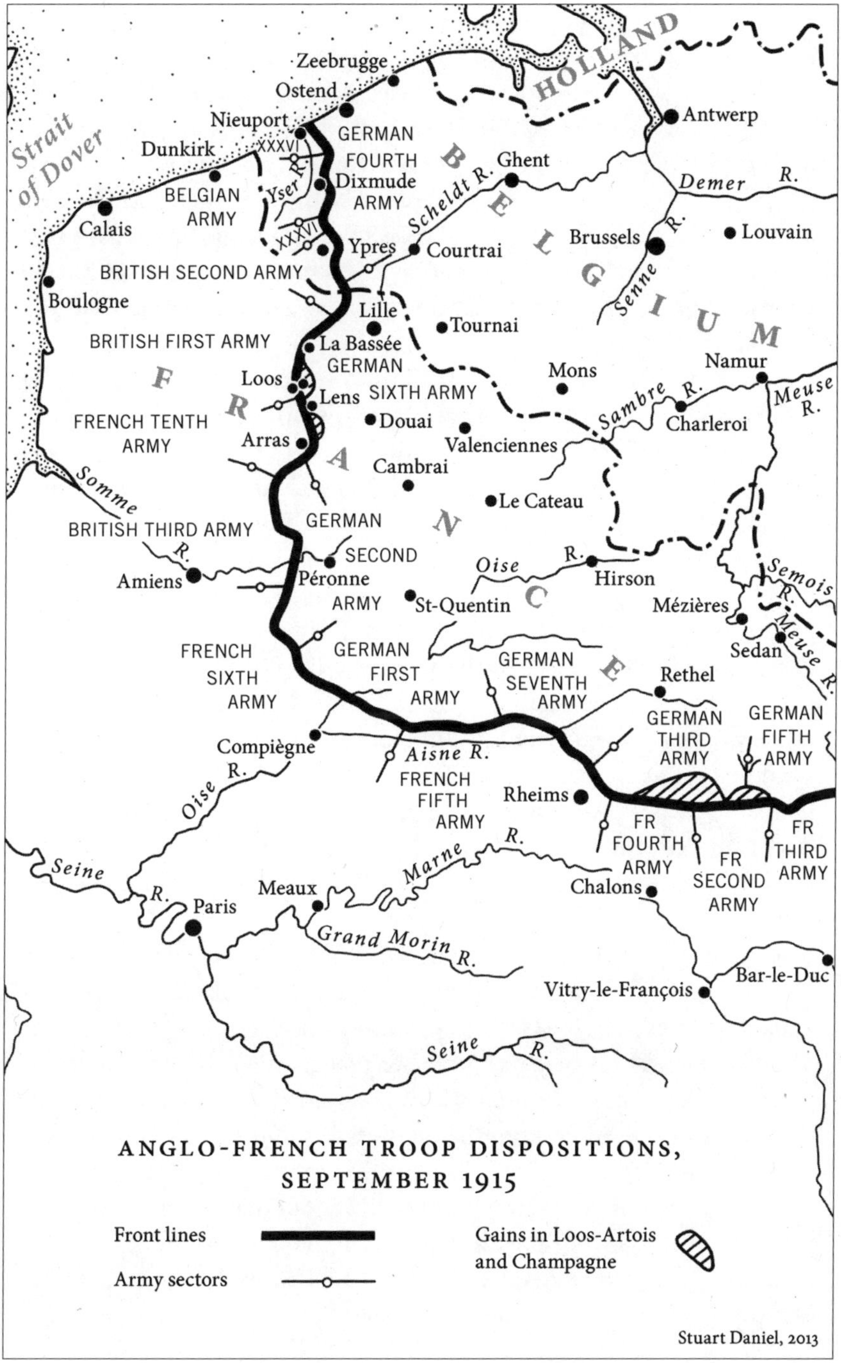

ANGLO-FRENCH TROOP DISPOSITIONS, SEPTEMBER 1915

The situation in theatres beyond the Western Front was very bleak in the summer and fall of 1915. On 22 August the Russians promised to attack the moment that Joffre unleashed his offensive in Champagne.[81] But the Russian Army was still falling back one month later. In the words of Robert Doughty, "Warsaw fell on August 5, and the Polish salient ceased to exist by the middle of August. For the next six weeks the Germans and Austrians advanced relentlessly across Russia, finally halting at the end of September on a line that ran from south of the Gulf of Riga to Dvinsk, Pinsk, and the northern tip of Romania. From Gorlice-Tarnow, the Central Powers had advanced more than 300 kilometers."[82] The Italians were already running out of shells by 9 September and admitted that they would be unable to resume offensive operations against the Austro-Hungarians until ten days after the Anglo-French offensive on the Western Front started on 25 September.[83] The French and British would have to conduct their joint offensive without much help from either the Russians or the Italians. The Serbs remained largely inactive.[84]

Still, Joffre was optimistic. On 14 September he informed the army group commanders that his objective in Champagne was "to drive the Germans out of France." In order to effect a breakthrough, the offensive would be general, consisting of several large-scale assaults executed at the same time on wide fronts.[85] But breaking through German defences would be easier said than done. The Germans had constructed a second band of trenches five kilometres behind the first and a third fifteen kilometres to the rear of the second. Each of these bands of trenches was an in-depth defensive system.[86] Undaunted, Joffre believed that he possessed the tactical formula to penetrate the German lines: "terrific violence" from artillery fire, then all available infantry units advancing simultaneously "in depth," and finally the cavalry galloping forward to exploit the breach in the German defences.[87]

Joffre also did his best to make sure that the French offensive would catch the Germans by surprise. He ordered small-scale attacks along the entire Western Front to keep them guessing about the actual site of the main assault. French intelligence reported that German intelligence did not appear to anticipate an Allied offensive.[88] But that attempt was foiled. Documentary evidence proves that the Germans knew of the offensive, since they had in their possession a copy of Joffre's order of the day to his army group commanders on 14 September.[89]

In addition to accurate German intelligence on the French plan and their strong defences, Joffre had to contend with the probability of inclement autumnal weather slowing the French offensive in Champagne and the Anglo-French offensive in Artois. Robertson regretted Joffre's two postponements of the offensive, because the British and the French were "gradually losing the good weather, days [were] becoming short and much haze and mist prevail[ed]."[90]

These obstacles failed to dampen Joffre's optimism. He wrote to his army group commanders on 14 September: "The Germans have very few reserves behind the thin line of trenches." He continued: "The simultaneous attacks, their strength and their extent, will prevent the enemy from collecting reserves of infantry and artillery at the same point as he was able to do north of Arras. They are a certain guarantee of success."[91] Amassing large numbers of troops and huge quantities of shells fuelled Joffre's high expectations but it remained to be seen whether his forces could break through strongly fortified enemy defences.

French and British units would begin unleashing their artillery bombardment not later than 23 September – two days before the infantry was scheduled to advance.[92]

POLITICAL CHALLENGES DURING THE BATTLE

No sooner had the Allied guns opened fire at the front than Joffre came under fire of a different kind from far behind the battlefield. On 23 September, Poincaré wrote a letter to Millerand reminding him that Viviani's cabinet had decided to ask Joffre to provide them with the exact number of cannons and shells that the army had stockpiled for use in its impending offensive. Joffre, Poincaré observed, feared leaks and therefore did not want to divulge the requested information prior to the beginning of the offensive. Even after the start of the offensive, he complained, Joffre was opposed to Poincaré, Viviani, or Millerand passing on the information in question to other members of the cabinet.[93]

In his letter, Poincaré further disapproved of Joffre's attitude and behaviour. He told Millerand that the two of them had the prerogative to give statistical information to whomever they pleased. Further, Joffre did not have the right to disobey a cabinet directive. Therefore, Joffre would have to inform Millerand and himself of the statistics in question before the beginning of the offensive in Champagne, at the latest on 24 September.[94]

In the same letter, Poincaré registered a second complaint about Joffre's conduct. He advised Millerand that Joffre had forbidden the transmission of orders to Paris concerning operations, which prevented him and Viviani's ministry from becoming involved in them. Joffre, Poincaré lamented, always acted on his own initiative. Regrettably, his solitary style had resulted in numerous serious mistakes. Consequently, Poincaré felt that the time had come for him and Viviani's cabinet to insist on being informed so that they could have some input into GQG's planning.[95]

Poincaré's letter offers several insights into the negative state of French civil-military relations in the early autumn of 1915: Joffre had never complied with the government's request of 27 August to submit a plan for his next offensive to them; Poincaré was attempting to exercise government authority over Joffre with regard to receiving information of a military nature; Poincaré's desire for political involvement in operations indicated a lack of confidence in Joffre's generalship; and Poincaré still entertained hopes of stopping the offensive in Champagne and Artois.

French politicians were not the only ones diverting Joffre's attention from the Western Front. The French government's plan, as detailed in the next chapter, to mount an expedition to Salonika to come to the aid of the Serbs, whom they thought were soon to be attacked after Bulgarian mobilization on 21 September, set off a whole train of events. On 23 September, Kitchener suggested sending 300,000 Allied troops to Serbia. Joffre rejected his proposal the following day. He claimed that reports of 450,000 German and Austro-Hungarian troops in Bulgaria were highly exaggerated, and therefore the Anglo-French force sent to Salonika could be much smaller than 300,000. In addition, the Allies did not have enough men and matériel to maintain three fronts simultaneously. Consequently, formations transferred to Salonika would have to come from the Dardanelles rather than from the Western Front.[96]

Kitchener was but one of the several members of Asquith's cabinet who advocated an eastern strategy. Wilson, a committed westerner, wrote in his diary on 25 September: "A long letter from a prominent Unionist about the flutter in cabinet about Bulgaria mobilizing. L[loyd] George says an invasion of Egypt and Asia Minor by [Germans] is imminent; Winston [Churchill] wants to send everyone to Smyrna; others want to send large forces to Salonika. Were there ever such fools?"[97]

If Joffre did not agree with the letter of Wilson's argument, he certainly concurred with its spirit. On 3 October – during the lull between the first and second phases of his offensive on the Western Front – Joffre briefly turned his attention to events in the Balkans. He acknowledged, in a letter to Millerand, that the Allies had a responsibility to prevent the Germans, Austro-Hungarians, and Bulgarians from crushing Serbia. Joffre even admitted that the men and matériel needed to achieve this objective would have to come from the Western Front. But he went on to say that the number of troops and munitions would have to be kept to a minimum. Most importantly, the resources could not be French.[98]

Joffre argued instead that the British should come to the rescue of Serbia, for they had large reserves of manpower and the industrial capacity to increase munitions production on a grand scale. Finally, British troops, Joffre reasoned, displayed less aptitude for offensive action and, for that reason, would be better suited for a defensive role in a secondary theatre of operations. Joffre concluded his letter with a sop to the British and to Viviani's cabinet: he offered to send one or two divisions from France (presumably from the zone of the interior) to Greece.[99]

PERFORMANCE IN THE FIELD

Joffre's offensive went ahead as scheduled on 25 September, in spite of Poincaré's opposition to it. The weather turned out to be even worse than Robertson had feared. Heavy rain began falling during the night of 24–25 September, which stopped only at brief intervals until the skies cleared somewhat on the 29th. In Champagne, French artillery opened fire at 09:00 hours. The infantry rushed forward fifteen minutes later. The Second Army captured the first line of German trenches north of the village of Perthes. By sunset on 26 September, the Second and Fourth armies had advanced four kilometres before being stopped in front of the second line of trenches by units of the German Fifth Army. The promising start to the offensive came to an abrupt halt the following day, and repeated attacks produced few results. The French called off their offensive on 30 September, with little to show for their strenuous efforts.[100]

In Artois, the Allied infantry soon seized most of the first band of German trenches on 25 September. D'Urbal's French Tenth Army made significant gains north of Arras. Haig's British First Army on d'Urbal's left did the same south of Loos.[101] The use of poison gas facilitated the

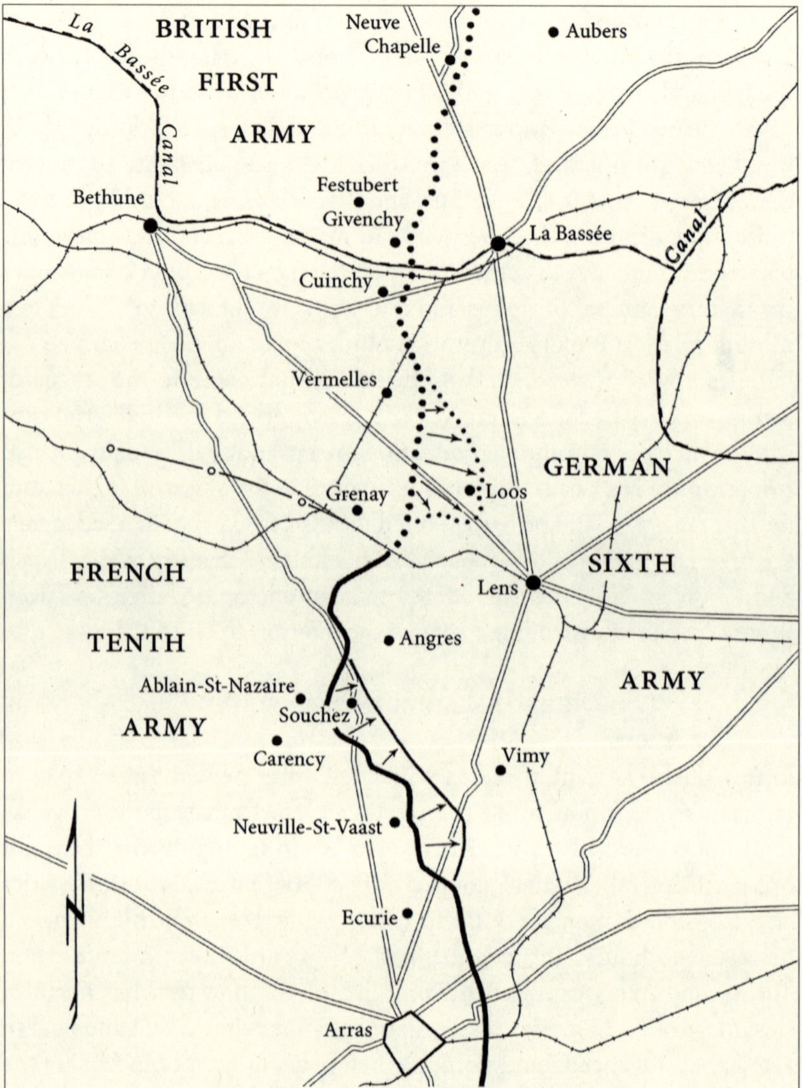

ANGLO-FRENCH OFFENSIVES,
SEPTEMBER/OCTOBER 1915

Line at the start of battle British • • • • • • French ——

Line at the close of battle British • • • • • • • • • French ——

0 1 2 3 4 5
miles

Stuart Daniel, 2013

progress of the First Army.[102] But Sir John French's failure to make adequate reserves available to Haig to exploit this initial success would lead to his recall, as discussed in chapter 12.

Sir John confronted an immediate challenge: inadequate Anglo-French cooperation on the battlefield. On 26 September, the right flank of Haig's army came under a furious German counter-attack. An angry Sir John advised Joffre that, unless the left wing of d'Urbal's army attacked energetically and without delay, he might have to order Haig's right wing to retreat.[103]

Joffre and Foch held an urgent meeting at Drury the same afternoon. The wily Joffre tried to make the best of a bad situation. He instructed Foch to halt d'Urbal's attack while giving Sir John the impression that the French Army was not letting the BEF down. Joffre believed that d'Urbal's attack would succeed if GQG sent more formations and artillery to him. But Joffre had no intention of reinforcing d'Urbal and, by extension, Sir John, if this meant putting the offensive in Champagne at further risk.[104]

On the morning of 27 September, d'Urbal promised Haig that the Tenth Army would attack vigorously.[105] It did not perform with enough energy to suit Sir John, who notified Joffre that he would be obliged to suspend the offensive by Haig's dangerously exposed right wing unless d'Urbal put more energy into his own attack.[106] Joffre, however, wanted to focus his attention on events in Champagne without being distracted by Sir John's problems in Artois. Consequently, he instructed Foch to speak to Sir John as soon as possible, telling him that the instructions he had given at Drury two days earlier remained in effect. Joffre in effect "passed the buck" to Foch, who, he observed, was the only one in a position to decide how d'Urbal could best assist Sir John.[107] Foch and Sir John met again on 28 September. Foch made three promises: one of d'Urbal's divisions would relieve one of Haig's divisions; d'Urbal would attack more forcefully; and he would provide more artillery support to Haig. Foch reported optimistically that these measures satisfied Sir John,[108] signalling a relaxation in their relationship.

The acrimonious nature of the conflict before this easing of tensions was revealed in Robertson's letter to the king's secretary on 28 September, in which he expressed his opinion on why the French and British had such difficulty coordinating their efforts. Robertson attributed it primarily to the national character of the French, offering an assessment of the French that was even less flattering than the French staff's evaluation of

British soldiers: "The French are a queer people and difficult to understand," Robertson wrote. "They make excellent promises and write splendid orders, but nothing happens very often. They have the peculiar practice of never beginning their fights until one or two o'clock … and it is now quite dark by six o'clock, therefore very little can be done. They seem to like to have their déjeuner first."[109] At this point in his letter, Robertson changed tack, laying most of the blame at Foch's door. "Yesterday the Chief [Sir John] wired to Joffre saying Foch really must be more vigorous in his action and dependable upon his promises. Foch came to see us this morning and seemed to feel he should do more. He is rather a flatcatcher, a mere professor, and very talkative. He compares ill with Joffre and Castelnau in the confidence he gives one."[110]

Happily, Foch made a better impression on Sir John than on Robertson. On 29 September, Foch paid another visit to Sir John's headquarters. The two field commanders agreed to attack the Germans' second line of trenches "shoulder to shoulder" on 2 October.[111]

Rain coupled with Haig's desire to capture an important piece of terrain to the left of his army led to several delays in the resumption of the Anglo-French offensive in Artois.[112] On 5 October, Sir John finally decided that Haig's attack would begin five days hence, on 10 October; an ill-humoured appeal from Joffre to advance the date of Haig's assault to 9 October elicited only a non-committal response from Sir John.[113] Foch stated that Joffre had declined further delay for the resumption of his offensive in Champagne beyond 6 October. Therefore, Foch pointed out the necessity of the BEF advancing the date of its attack toward Loos to 7 or 8 October.[114]

The following day, Sir John advised Foch that Haig's attack could not begin until 10 October owing to muddy terrain and mist.[115] This was not a case of stalling by the British, as d'Urbal was experiencing delays for the same reasons.[116] Nevertheless, Millerand placed the entire blame for the postponement on the British.[117]

Under Joffre's direction, the Centre Army Group commander, Castelnau, resumed his offensive in Champagne on 6 October. Joffre's motive for renewing it is puzzling. Three days earlier, he had written a letter to Millerand stating that his goal was to "rupture" the second band of German trenches. Yet Joffre also admitted that doing so would not be enough to achieve a breakthrough. Instead, he now envisaged ultimate victory through a series of small-scale battles and attrition.[118] Castelnau's offensive was even less successful than his offensive of 25–29 September. Joffre called a halt to the operation the following day.[119]

The end of the French offensive in Champagne did not alter Allied plans for an attack toward Loos. On 7 October, Foch and d'Urbal agreed to coordinate the resumption of the Tenth Army's offensive with that of the BEF on 10 October.[120] But a strong German counter-attack against Haig on 8 October persuaded Sir John to postpone the British assault until 12 or 13 October.[121] On the 11th, Sir John postponed Haig's attack until the 13th. Wilson, ardent in his francophilia, reacted with a considerable degree of sarcasm: "So we [have] gone from 5th to 9th to 10th to 12th to 13th. Not bad considering we were working, or supposed to be, with the French!"[122]

In spite of the delay by the British, Foch ordered d'Urbal to attack on 10 October. Thick fog forced a delay of twenty-four hours. D'Urbal's attack went ahead on the 11th. It achieved almost nothing. D'Urbal ordered an end to the attack that evening. Haig moved forward at last on 13 October. His efforts also failed.[123] Although Joffre had limited French support for Haig to artillery fire from the IX Corps of the Tenth Army,[124] Foch pressed for the resumption of d'Urbal's attack, in the name of Allied solidarity. However, Joffre instructed Foch to order d'Urbal to entrench, in spite of the Tenth Army being situated a mere three hundred to four hundred and fifty feet below the crest of Vimy Ridge.[125]

Joffre had three reasons for his decision: operations showed that d'Urbal's troops, after nearly three weeks in combat, no longer had the capacity to succeed in a new large-scale action; he did not have any fresh units to send to d'Urbal; and his supply of munitions had dwindled, compelling him to stop major operations on the Western Front.[126] The much-vaunted Loos-Champagne offensive had come to a miserable conclusion.

The Allies achieved little in Champagne and Artois in September and October 1915, despite the high cost in blood and treasure. The French Second, Third, Fourth, and Tenth armies suffered more than 190,000 casualties, including over 80,000 dead or missing. As for the expenditures of munitions, the four armies fired more than 830,000 rounds of heavy shells and nearly 4,400,000 rounds of light shells.[127] The British First Army suffered approximately 62,000 casualties at Loos, including 26,000 dead or missing.[128]

Joffre nonetheless blamed the setback on a lack of artillery. In a more honest evaluation, realizing that his exhausted army required a long period of recuperation and reconstitution, he decided to eschew offensive operations during the winter of 1915–16. The year of large-scale offensives in France had ended in failure. The French staff would henceforth have to seek other strategic and operational alternatives in its quest for victory.[129]

NEW INITIATIVES

More prone than other Allied leaders to see the need for closer integration in marshalling the resources of the Entente coalition, Joffre came to the conclusion that success against the Central Powers would depend largely on coordination in the major theatres of war. A flurry of activity aimed at improving Allied coordination was thus undertaken as the offensive in France petered out. On 1 October, General Albert d'Amade, GQG's liaison with Russian Army headquarters, submitted Joffre's proposal to Czar Nicholas II that he send a highly qualified representative to GQG. The Russian representative would be charged with the task of informing Joffre of the intentions of the imperial government and helping to coordinate the movements of the French and Russian armies. Nicholas accepted Joffre's proposal with alacrity. In addition, d'Amade broached the subject of the Russians creating an organization similar to the Section d'Etudes de la Défense nationale. Nicholas immediately perceived the advantage of this type of organization being formed in all Allied countries. He ordered his General Staff to create its Russian equivalent. Finally, Nicholas said that the Austro-German offensive had been stopped. The Russian Army, he concluded, would be able to launch its own offensive by the middle of November.[130] Regrettably, that date was six weeks too late to assist the French and British armies on the Western Front.

Sometime on or before 11 October, Joffre apprised Millerand of his desire to organize an Allied conference. On the 11th, Millerand suggested that Joffre create a permanent organization (presumably at GQG) consisting of officers of the Allied armies, whose role would be the same as that of Section d'Etudes de la Défense nationale.[131] The following day, Joffre informed Millerand that he had sent a note to the military attachés of the Allied armies with regard to a meeting of the commanders-in-chief of these armies (or their representatives) at Chantilly sometime in November. The meeting would be similar to the one held there on 7 July. The commanders-in-chief would discuss the situation in all theatres of operations, how best to coordinate an offensive in 1916, and Millerand's suggestion of the previous day for creation of a permanent Section d'Etudes. Joffre openly asserted what Millerand had implied: the "study section" would be established at Chantilly.[132] The Allied conference took place at Chantilly on 6–8 December 1915.

In Britain, Esher wanted to go beyond Allied cooperation among the military leaders. Wilson, who wisely chose to remain anonymous, gave Esher his written appraisal of the current Allied modus operandi, of which he disapproved. He called instead for a small Allied body of the foremost politicians and military officers to run the war effort. Esher himself thought that Joffre's broad concept too difficult to implement. But he saw an Anglo-French coordination body as feasible. This entity would do away with the frequent meetings and conferences that accomplished little. Esher concluded with the warning that the Allies had to set up such an organization in the near future or risk losing the war.[133]

Allied cooperation at the political level, however, depended on the present political and military leaders in each country staying in their posts. In Russia, the entire political system was slowly crumbling, although the fall of the Romanov dynasty was still seventeen months in the future. In France, Viviani's cabinet had only two more weeks to live. If Millerand was forced out of the War Ministry, Joffre, even assuming he remained in his post, might have to acquiesce to more ministerial involvement and parliamentary oversight of his operations.

In Britain, King George V surmised that Kitchener, Sir John, and Hamilton were in danger of being removed.[134] The king's supposition was not long in becoming fact. Kitchener had to deal with sniping from adversaries within the cabinet. Asquith's coalition government faced increasing criticism from inside and outside the House of Commons. Moreover, the Dardanelles Committee was too large to prosecute effectively an all-out war in an era of mass mobilization and industrialization. On 7 October, King George suggested that the committee be limited to four men: Asquith, Kitchener, Balfour, and Grey.[135] This number was even smaller than the French super cabinet of five that Joffre had suggested earlier to Poincaré.

Five days later, on 12 October, Esher assessed the system of cabinet governance in Britain as unsuitable in a time of full-scale warfare, a point he had made earlier in a paper printed for the War Council in May 1915. Esher offered his solution: formation of a small body of politicians and military officers to direct the British war effort.[136] Esher's proposed entity resembled Joffre's super cabinet, but it presumably would be a little larger. This was essentially the model Lloyd George adopted later.

But Asquith, a diehard Liberal unwilling to alter the structure of government, preferred the king's suggestion rather than Esher's and replaced the Dardanelles Committee with a much smaller War Committee of six key ministers in early November.[137] Meanwhile, the prime minister had to survive politically. Already, on 17 August, he had appealed to Kitchener for his support in the critical situation then facing the government. Asquith warned that the attacks on him by Lloyd George and Carson were actually indirect attacks on Kitchener, whom they wanted removed from the War Office. Asquith concluded with the observation that he and Kitchener had to stand together in order to make sure the British war effort was prosecuted to the fullest extent possible.[138]

CONCLUSION

The preparation and conduct of the combined Loos and Champagne offensive was a bittersweet chapter in the story of Anglo-French command relations. Even after Kitchener's intervention at the end of August compelling Sir John French to engage at Loos according to the French strategic plan, numerous difficulties arose in the planning process, occasioning many delays as Joffre attempted to maximize his resources in men and munitions for what he hoped would be the great breakthrough battle.

With the advent of the Sarrail Affair and the French government's effort to mount a reinforced expedition on the Asian coast of the Dardanelles, the conflict then shifted from the relationship between the commanders on the Western Front to their mutual resistance to the politicians. In a long-running bout, Joffre successfully warded off the demands of his political masters for an additional four divisions for the Dardanelles, persuading them to accept his position that such a move should await the conclusion of his fall offensive. But the collapse of the French government was already imminent – in part, at least, as a result its inability to stand up to Joffre.

The first day of the offensive on 25 September seemed to augur well for both the British and the French as both armies scored initial successes. But Sir John and Roberston's lingering suspicions of the French and the sheer difficulty of trying to coordinate detailed action between Allied forces at Loos and Arras, under conditions of growing failure and bad weather, led to very strained interactions between the two allies. This, however, would be Sir John's last grand battle, as accumulated blotches on his record, triggered by his failure to bring up the reserves in time in the initial success at Loos, would prompt his recall. The entire British political-military structure would be overhauled at the same time, giving the government a much more martial allure.

For Joffre and his staff, the failure of the combined battle signalled that yet other initiatives would have to be taken to assure that the full weight of the Entente coalition would be brought to bear on the Central Powers. In the meantime, a great imbroglio would unfold as the two allies tried to mount an expedition to Salonika in aid of the Serbs.

Like the Artois offensive, the failure of the joint Loos and Artois-Champagne offensive demonstrated the bankruptcy of existing political-military structures in France, just as it did in Britain, and would lead at year's end to a major overhaul redefining Joffre's command and his relationship with the government. Building on the success of his July initiative and the ever-growing need for closer Allied coordination, Joffre would assume the role of effective coordinator in the second Allied military conference at Chantilly on 6–8 December 1915.

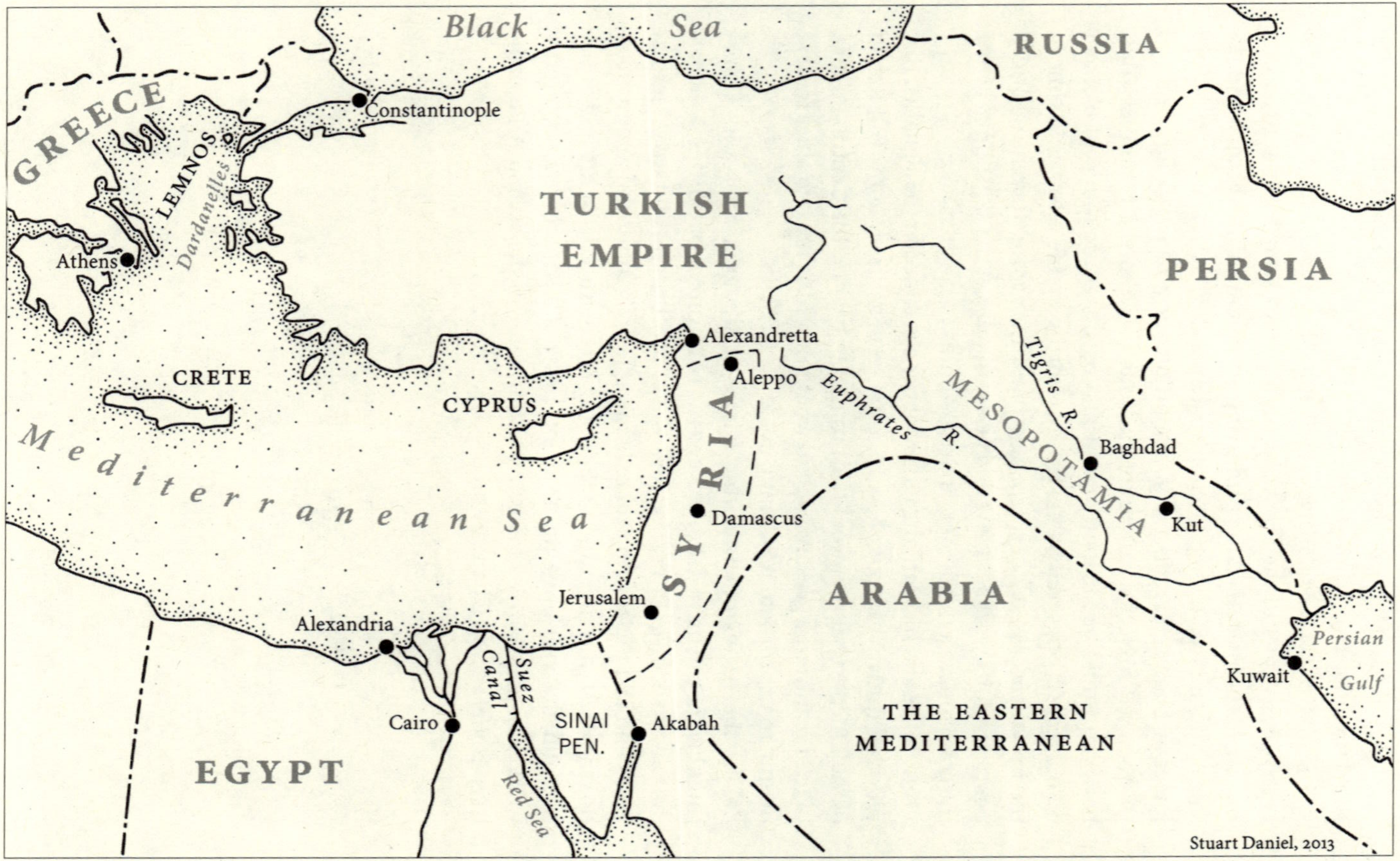
Black Sea
RUSSIA
GREECE
Constantinople
LEMNOS
Dardanelles
Athens
TURKISH EMPIRE
PERSIA
CRETE
CYPRUS
Mediterranean Sea
Alexandretta
Aleppo
SYRIA
Damascus
Jerusalem
Euphrates R.
Tigris R.
MESOPOTAMIA
Baghdad
Kut
ARABIA
Persian Gulf
Kuwait
Alexandria
Cairo
Suez Canal
SINAI PEN.
Akabah
Red Sea
EGYPT
THE EASTERN MEDITERRANEAN
Stuart Daniel, 2013

CHAPTER ELEVEN

Salonika, Egypt, and the Western Front, September–December 1915

EVEN THOUGH MORE THAN a century has come and gone, various aspects of Anglo-French interaction relating to the mounting of the Salonika expedition in 1915 and its competition with the Allied campaign on the Western Front have remained obscure.[1] The multifaceted tug-of-war between the British and French governments, which attempted to mount an expedition to Salonika, and the conflict of these two governments with the field commanders on the Western Front over available forces during the heat of the Loos and Artois-Champagne offensive, bear closer examination.[2] Inevitably, Joffre was drawn into a wider and wider field of involvement as the interests of the Western Front, in which Sir John French also had a vital stake, conflicted with those of the new expedition.

Intertwined with the tangled and conflicting Anglo-French positions on the future of the expedition was the British desire to send eight divisions from the Western Front to Egypt as a necessary defence against the Turks in the event of a final evacuation of the Dardanelles. Also, the confusing and ever-changing interplay of opinion within the British government on the proposed withdrawal from the Dardanelles, and the repercussions of that on the French government and the two commands on the Western Front, deserve further enquiry. Happily for the Allies, the withdrawal from the Dardanelles proceeded systematically and without loss.

The Anglo-French experience in mounting the Salonika expedition in the heat of the fall offensive in France is a powerful example of how coalitions should *not* function. Indeed, seldom have coalitions functioned so poorly. The two governments, both weak and divided, and the two commands, at loggerheads with their governments over strategy, worked at cross-purposes in a confused series of ad hoc political and military consultations. The machinery of traditional diplomacy proved totally inadequate for the task. The result was that "too little, too late" was sent to be of any practical help to the Serbs, who succumbed to a combined German, Austro-Hungarian, and Bulgarian offensive.

The chief benefit of the experience was to underline the need for an effective Allied body to prepare for and coordinate diplomatic and military initiatives. A first tentative step was taken in the establishment of a loosely structured joint committee in January 1916 to include the prime ministers and the chief political and military leaders of the two countries as required. But the exercise accomplished little more than to set up regular consultations. The formation of an Allied Supreme War Council would have to wait for an even worse crisis, the Italian collapse at Caporetto in 1917.

BACKGROUND

The Salonika expedition was the linear successor of the Dardanelles expedition, which likewise had proven highly divisive in Anglo-French relations.[3] As we have seen, with the Dardanelles operation floundering and consideration being given to withdrawal, the British government was quite surprised at the end of August 1915 when the French made a proposal for the deployment of four additional French divisions on the Asiatic side of the Straits to bolster the campaign.[4] While some French cabinet ministers, leftist politicians, and a handful of generals had long favoured the deployment of larger forces in the Near East, the catalyst for the new venture came from the need for the French government to find a command for General Maurice Sarrail, whom Joffre had peremptorily sacked on 22 July. The French had little choice but to cater to Sarrail and his Socialist supporters since their backing was necessary to avoid a breakdown of the delicately balanced *union sacrée*.[5]

But numerous issues remained unresolved, such as how this deployment could be reconciled with the forthcoming fall offensive, who would supply the troops and from where, and what shipping arrangements would be required. To address these and other issues, Kitchener met Alexandre Millerand, the French war minister, Sir John, Joffre, and Sarrail, designated for the new French eastern command, in a political-military conference at Calais on 11 September 1915.[6] The major fall offensive in Champagne and Artois was about to begin in less than two weeks, and Joffre continued to adamantly oppose any diversion of troops from the Western Front. All agreed that the Allied offensive in France should take immediate priority. Only very reluctantly did Joffre agree to make available four divisions from his front for the expedition – after 10 October, when it was presumed the fall offensive would be over. While Kitchener favoured the new initiative, Sir John French lined up in support of Joffre's position and likewise resisted any redeployment of British troops from the Western Front to the Dardanelles.[7]

These lines of cleavage remained unaltered when, on 21 September 1915, news of the intended mobilization of Bulgaria and its likely entry into the war on the side of the Central Powers arrived in Paris and London. Political and military leaders on both sides of the Channel, as a result, redirected their attention from the enlargement of the Dardanelles venture to the need for an expedition to Salonika in support of the Serbs.[8] The mobilization of Bulgaria and eventual collapse of Serbia changed the strategic equation dramatically.

With the wide range of sources now available in British and French archives, it is possible to trace the involvement of both powers in ensuing events, and to provide a fairly clear view of what happened at each step of the way.

DIPLOMATIC ORIGINS

The opaque and complicated web of Balkan diplomacy that provides the background to the Salonika expedition is beyond the scope of this volume. What the British failed to realize was that, for the French, Greece represented a foothold in the eastern Mediterranean for the preservation of French interests in Syria and Lebanon. The French considered the entire eastern rim of the Mediterranean their sphere of influence. Their presence in Greece would serve as a counterweight to the Allied commitment to allocate the Straits to Russia at the end of the war, as well as to the ever-present British presence in Egypt and elsewhere in the region.[9] While Serbia was the diplomatic protégé of imperial Russia in the prewar period, the small state had also been the military client of the French, obtaining loans and military training and equipment from them.[10]

The legacy of the two Balkan Wars of 1912–13 weighed heavily in Balkan politics. Suffice to say that Greece and Serbia emerged from the

Second Balkan War in 1913 as allies bound together in an alliance of mutual assistance in which Serbia promised to aid Greece with an army of 150,000 men in the event of a new war against Bulgaria.[11] The Triple Entente, in its quest for new allies in the Balkans in 1915, was unable to offer Bulgaria adequate compensations to assure either intervention or neutrality because of Serbian unwillingness to make concessions. The Central Powers were bound by no such restriction. Generous offers of compensation to Bulgaria by the Central Powers at the expense of Serbia and their victories over Russia on the battlefield in the summer of 1915 tipped the scales in favour of Bulgarian intervention on their side in September 1915. As a result of Bulgarian mobilization, the Greek premier, Eleutherios Venizelos, always pro-British and pro-French in his orientation (contrary to the pro-German attitude of Constantine, the Greek king), immediately offered Greek intervention on the Allied side on 22 September, but on condition that the Allies provide a force of 150,000 men to compensate for the promised Serbian force, no longer available because of the war.[12]

The French response was immediate, if ill-advised. On 21 September the French cabinet was still largely concerned with how to counteract Joffre's stiffening opposition to the proposed Dardanelles Asiatic landing, and, specifically, how to prevent him from welching on his promise to deliver four divisions from his front for the venture by 10 October.[13] The Dardanelles operation, Joffre had argued in a letter the day previous, had to be subordinated to the forthcoming offensive on the French front, and it needed to be thoroughly studied in advance and not undertaken without adequate means in order to succeed, so as not to damage French prestige.[14] Thus, in light of Bulgarian mobilization and possible intervention into the war on the side of the Central Powers, the cabinet took only tentative steps toward shifting the proposed expedition from the Dardanelles to Greece. Foreign Minister Théophile Delcassé's advice was to reflect and "to consult our allies." [15]

That sage advice was disregarded by Poincaré, the president, who, the next day, forced the hand of his government by advising Delcassé to accept immediately the Greek offer, before the French cabinet had a chance to deliberate further. Although the cabinet unanimously endorsed the measure the following day, the British had not been consulted in advance of French acceptance of the Greek offer.[16]

From the outset, the British government was much less keen on the Greek offer than the French. The British cabinet, which deliberated on the matter on 22 September, decided to wait until Kitchener's return from a trip to France before reaching a conclusion.[17] The Dardanelles Committee turned its attention to the subject after Kitchener's return the next day. The committee was doubtful of its course, mainly because of its concern with regard to the impact of the new deployment on the Dardanelles expedition; and should that fail, the ultimate safety of Egypt and India. The committee was badly divided on whether to take troops from Suvla Bay in the Dardanelles for the venture or to start anew. Joffre's opposition to sending four divisions from his front in support of the Dardanelles Asiatic initiative was a major factor. The day before he had confided to Kitchener his opinion that "the French divisions should not be sent."[18]

Kitchener, whom the committee asked to study the military question, argued that at least 300,000 men would be required to save the Serbs from the expected combined Central Power and Bulgarian onslaught, and in his view it was "no use" going to their aid with anything less.[19] But Joffre, whom he consulted on the issue, considered Kitchener's estimate of enemy forces much exaggerated and recommended that the new expedition be composed of Anglo-French troops, beginning with two British and two French divisions, drawn from the Dardanelles.[20] Thus, in a meeting of the British Dardanelles Committee on 24 September, Kitchener's plan for an Allied force of 300,000 was sidelined in favour of the French plan to send 150,000 men, for which he would withdraw two British divisions from Suvla Bay as an initial instalment on the Salonika venture. As the French had already accepted the Greek offer, the British felt obliged to participate on French terms.[21] Opponents of the expedition in Britain thereafter complained that they had been dragged into the venture by the French, who, in not consulting them in advance, had not played the game according to the agreed-on rules.[22] The British clearly had not appreciated the extent of French interests in Greece.

DIVIDED ALLIES, INEFFECTUAL GOVERNMENTS, UNWILLING FIELD COMMANDERS

The difficulties of mounting a new expedition to Greece, just as Joffre and French had begun the fall offensives in Champagne and Artois on 25 September, would have been a daunting task had the Allies governments been united in their views on the new expedition, and had there existed an effective Allied council to coordinate their efforts. But, not only were the Allies not united in their views and lacked any agency for coordinating their efforts, their respective governments were also sharply divided within and ineffectual.

On the British side, the coalition government of H.H. Asquith lacked the essential unity and cohesion necessary for decisive action, and was marked, in the eyes of one astute observer, by "grave ... indecision and weakness."[23] The Dardanelles Committee, which had replaced the War Council when Asquith formed his coalition government in May, was intended to guide the government's footsteps strategically, but it had inadequate staff advice and, like its predecessor, was too large to be effective. Though the committee was not devoid of talent, its several participants, in the absence of thorough and reliable professional opinion, engaged in acrimonious and confused discussion reflecting their own preconceptions and party biases.[24] In addition, again like its predecessor, it lacked executive authority as all its decisions had to be debated and ratified by the full cabinet.[25]

While Kitchener was still dominant in strategic matters, his authority and judgment were frequently challenged. To reinforce the General Staff, Sir Archibald Murray, a new chief of staff, was thrust upon him in his absence at a cabinet meeting on 22 September.[26] And, to make matters worse, Kitchener himself showed a growing uncertainty with regard to what course to follow amidst the various options of Middle Eastern strategy and their relationship to the Western Front.[27] The fast-moving evolution of the diplomatic situation, for which the Foreign Office was unprepared, meant that British strategy was entirely reactive since no proper contingency plans had been worked out for the unfolding drama or any of it scenarios.

The French government under Viviani was an even weaker coalition in which Poincaré, the president of the republic, often made important decisions in consultation with ministers without a full discussion in cabinet. The government had weathered the crisis in the spring over its conduct of the war[28] but was under severe attack from the parliamentary commissions, notably the Army, Navy, and Foreign Affairs Commissions of the Chamber of Deputies, which, in the absence of regular parliamentary sittings, took on the essential task of watchdog of the government. These commissions were dominated by "easterners" who demanded a major commitment of men and resources to the Eastern Front, accentuating the pressure from leftist groups to find a command for Sarrail.[29] In opposition stood Joffre, the beleaguered master of French strategy, who was inflexible in his resistance to any diversion from the French front and, as events would show, was subject to almost no persuasion except that resulting from a decline in his own military and political fortunes.

GREEK EQUIVOCATION AND THE ALLIED LANDING

The Anglo-French decision to send forces to Greece according to the Greek request and to draw forces initially from the Dardanelles for the venture was made with relative celerity. But Venizelos's offer turned out to be largely an internal political manoeuvre to force his own government's intervention in the conflict. On 26 September he had to report that an Allied landing in Greece had not been officially approved, but expressed the view that Allied support staff could proceed to make arrangements in Salonika provided they did not come in uniform.[30] The British balked at this suggestion, refusing any action without official approval of the Greek government,[31] and it was not until 27 September that Venizelos indicated that a landing could proceed officially, though it would be accompanied by a protest of the king for the sake of form.[32] The French immediately made specific plans for the Salonika expedition.[33] The British followed suit, despite grave misgivings over the Greek attitude, for, as Asquith told the king, "it was impossible for us in the circumstances to hold back."[34]

On 28 September the French government ordered the withdrawal of the 156th French Division from Cap Helles and its transport to Salonika. Two regiments of spahis (colonial cavalry) in Egypt and a mixed brigade from the French front, which Joffre gave up in protest, would make up a second division. Sarrail was instructed to go to Salonika with this brigade.[35] The British 10th Division from Suvla Bay was also re-embarked and ordered to Moudros with the intention of landing later in Salonika.[36] Two small British contingents totaling 11,000, originally intended as reinforcements for the Dardanelles, were also rerouted to Salonika.[37]

The difficulty was in the details.[38] Joffre, who had barely completed the first phase of his Champagne offensive, complained that the one brigade given up had been intended for the next attack.[39] To persuade Joffre to give up forces from his front, Millerand had been obliged to remind him very firmly that the five new divisions formed in the spring were only on loan to him.[40]

Kitchener's base of support in the cabinet was also beginning to erode. Exhausted, angry, and in a state of near collapse on 30 September, after a week of wrangling with "irresponsible" ministers in meetings of the cabinet and Dardanelles Committee,[41] he found that while he was away reviewing troops with the king, the committee had ordered a division from Suvla Bay to Salonika.[42] Clearly losing grip on the strategic direction of the war, he threatened resignation.[43]

Freeing the French 156th Division from Cap Helles meant that it had to be replaced by British forces, which occasioned delay and misunderstanding. Sir Ian Hamilton, the commander of British forces in the Dardanelles, protested that he could not relieve more than a brigade of French troops from Cap Helles with available forces, and when the French government unilaterally ordered the 156th Division withdrawn, he had to redirect his 53rd Division from Suvla Bay to Cap Helles rather than to Salonika.[44]

The British Dardanelles Committee wished to have British and French troops land simultaneously.[45] That was in fact realized, with the first elements of both arriving in Salonika on 5 October, but only after another delay. The new delay was occasioned by further Greek hesitation in their authorization for Allied forces to land, following a speech by British Secretary of State Sir Edward Grey in the House of Commons on 2 October which gave the Greek government the impression that the Allied powers still favoured ceding parts of Macedonia to Bulgaria.[46] The expedition got off to a very jerky and inauspicious start, to say the least.

THE CALAIS CONFERENCE, 5 OCTOBER 1915

From the outset, the merits of the Salonika expedition, the future of the Dardanelles expedition, the defence of Egypt and India, and the availability of forces weighed heavily in British considerations.[47] As the Salonika expedition got underway, Kitchener was anxious that specific issues be resolved, such as how was the balance of the Salonika force committed by each ally to be made up, when it could be ready, and what instructions were to be given to the first arrivals. He also wanted to know the aims and objectives of the larger expedition envisaged, and how a force of 300,000 to 400,000 might be constituted if necessary against a combined Austro-Hungarian-German and Bulgarian assault against Serbia. In particular, Kitchener wished to have the opinion of Joffre, whom he acknowledged as the real master of French strategy. Thus, on 1 October, Kitchener proposed a *conférence contradictoire* with his French allies to deal with the issues arising from the new expedition.[48] The conference met at Calais on 5 October.

The French government's position at the conference was shaped largely by prior consultation with Joffre, who, whether as a result of the grave military situation of the Serbs or the prospect of the fall of the government if he did not cooperate, had now come to the conclusion that Serbia needed to be assisted. But he was prepared to assist only with a minimum of French forces, given the vital nature of the French front and the growing shortage of French manpower. Accordingly, he proposed that the British carry the greater weight of the enterprise – with forces not then in France.

Now that the fall offensive had begun to wind down, Joffre was prepared to release from his front one and a half more infantry divisions and a cavalry division, making a total, with forces already deployed, of approximately 60,000. The British, he argued, had greater manpower resources than the French, and divisions already formed in Britain could easily raise the balance of the promised 150,000. The strategy should be largely defensive – to occupy Macedonia and assure the railway connection with the Serbs on the line up the Vardar, the sole railway linking Salonika with Uskub and Nish. The main purpose would be for the French to show the flag in Greece as at Gallipoli. The need for an Allied force of 300,000–400,000 men would arise only in what he deemed the unlikely event of a combined Central Powers and Bulgarian attack on Serbia and Greece. In that case, he thought the British should make up the additional requirement.[49] In an interview with Poincaré, Viviani, and Millerand on 4 October, Joffre conceded one additional division of cavalry (5,000 men) and agreed that British divisions in France might be sent to Salonika providing they were replaced "by new divisions coming from England."[50]

The British Dardanelles Committee, which staked out the British position on 4 October, was very mistrustful of French intentions in view of the known divergence between the French government and the General Staff on the question of sending troops out of France. The French needed "to put their cards on the table," observed Asquith. Kitchener, for his part, "doubted if the French really intended to send troops" as "the French Ministry had made the promise and had always acted from purely political motives." He thus was "anxious to reach a decision on the matter in conjunction with the French Staff" in order to assure that France honoured its commitment. Most agreed with Lloyd George that "the real director of French policy was General Joffre." Kitchener, moreover, continued to believe that the force of 150,000 men envisaged was too small to save the Serbs and that "if a serious offensive was found to be necessary in Serbia or Bulgaria, 300,000 to 400,000 men would be required." On his advice, Arthur Balfour, first lord of the Admiralty, was added to the conference to confer on shipping requirements with his French counterpart, Victor Augagneur.[51]

The Calais Conference held on 5 October 1915 was a meeting of the war and naval ministers of the two countries and, for reasons that are not clear, did not include Joffre or French. Kitchener's concern relative to the composition of a combined force of 131,000 was fairly easily resolved. To forces already committed, Millerand said that Joffre would add from the French front one brigade immediately and another infantry division and two divisions of cavalry after the current offensive, which would bring the French total to 64,000. Since Joffre had no objection to the deployment of British forces from France providing they would be replaced by British troops from England, Kitchener agreed to send three divisions from Sir John French's forces, bringing the British contingent up to 67,000. The French would be able to provide shipping for their entire force except for the two divisions of cavalry, which the British agreed to transport.[52]

The question of raising the additional 20,000 promised the Greeks was unresolved since the French, citing their shortage of manpower, were unwilling to commit another 10,000 men and Kitchener was unwilling to commit extra British troops from the Western Front. He expressed grave concerns, moreover, that the enterprise was an *engrenage*, a meat grinder, likely to involve larger and larger forces, and raised the idea of 400,000 men being required eventually. The real difference occurred, however, when the discussion shifted to the orders to be given the Salonika force. Divergent diplomatic appreciations of the situation immediately came to the fore. For the French, since the expedition was to go to the aid of the Serbs, their plan was to advance along the railway line into Serbia toward Nish; in contrast, because the British considered their intervention to be on behalf of Greek intervention in support of Serbia, Kitchener indicated that British troops would not move from Salonika until Greece entered the war. This contentious issue remained unresolved, underscoring a fundamental difference between the two allies.[53]

GREEK NEUTRALITY, BRITISH EQUIVOCATION

The French government was fearful that the British attitude would immobilize British forces at Salonika and imperil the whole operation, a

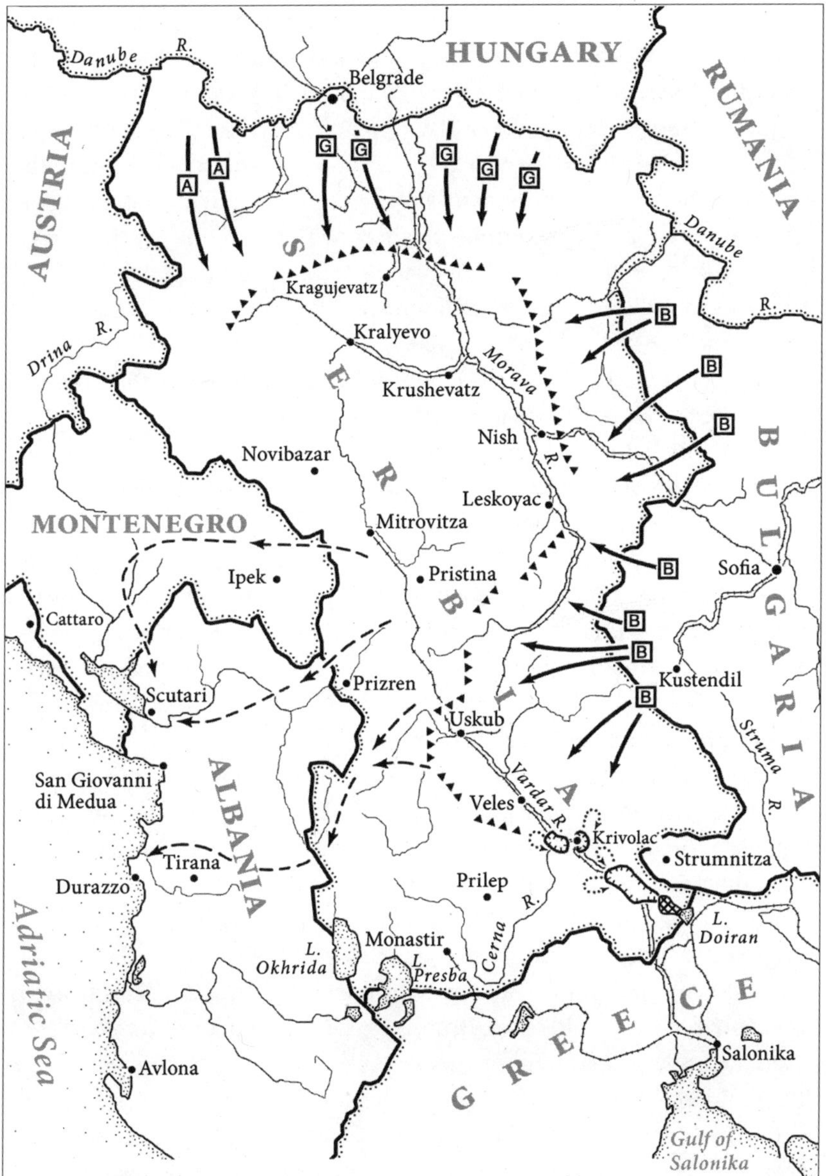

THE DEFEAT OF SERBIA, 1915

Austrian Armies -A→
German Armies -G→
Bulgarian Armies -B→
British positions, 29 Oct.
French positions, 29 Oct.
French movements, 1 and 2 Nov.
Serbian positions, 29 Oct.
Serbian retreat end of Nov.
Railways

S. Daniel, Starshell Maps, 2013

matter all the more urgent as an attack on Serbia by the Central Powers and Bulgaria was now deemed imminent. The differing stances of the two allies were accentuated by the fact that, on 5 October, King Constantine of Greece forced the resignation of Venizelos, following a speech in the Greek Parliament which the king thought would compromise the country's neutrality by promising assistance to Serbia against its enemies. The French government responded sharply. In a meeting on 6 October, the French cabinet judged the British attitude toward the purpose of the Salonika expedition, and its resultant strategy as expressed at the Calais Conference, to be totally unacceptable. In a dramatic move, Viviani and Augagneur were dispatched to London that night to clarify the situation and bring the British to their line of thinking.[54]

On the British side, indeed, the fall of Venizelos and the consequent unwillingness of the Greeks to intervene in the conflict put the whole Salonika expedition in jeopardy since Grey, the foreign secretary, was adamant that the British ought not intervene unless invited by the Greeks.[55] When Augagneur and Viviani arrived in London on 7 October, Viviani vigorously presented to Asquith, Grey, Balfour, Kitchener, and Lloyd George the French position that Allied intervention in Greece was absolutely necessary: from the political point of view, to prevent the loss of prestige in the Near East and in Islamic countries; and from the strategic point of view, to prevent the collapse of Serbia and the arrival of the Germans in Constantinople. While Grey continued to speak against an unauthorized intervention, Kitchener argued that the 150,000 men intended by the joint arrangement was not sufficient to resist the Austro-Hungarian-German-Bulgarian assault which now appeared very likely. (It had, in fact, been launched the day previous.) It was his belief that 250,000 men would be required to stand on the defensive and 400,000 to take the offensive. Britain, he said, would be prepared to provide the bulk of the force for the expedition provided Joffre would free the required British troops from France. An easterner at heart, Viviani immediately accepted Kitchener's scheme, the one he had really favoured from the beginning. But, as Joffre had French forces on the Western Front under his control, Kitchener considered it essential to get his approval before proceeding. Dramatically, Kitchener thus agreed to accompany Viviani and Augagneur on their return to France that evening for a consultation with Joffre.[56]

Kitchener's meeting with Joffre at French headquarters at Chantilly on 8 October, which included Viviani, Millerand, and Pellé, Joffre's chief of staff, was a major disappointment for Kitchener. While Joffre continued to argue for the necessity of the Salonika expedition, he still opposed giving it more than a limited, defensive role: to keep the railway open to Uskub and to hold the Bulgarians at bay, and in the worst case to provide an escape route for the Serbs. Deployment of the quantity of men required either to lead a strong defensive or to take the offensive he considered an impossibility. The meeting broke down into an acrimonious exchange between him and Kitchener over the use of British troops in France. Kitchener chided Joffre for his unwillingness to release any British troops for service elsewhere even though he had sent him fourteen divisions since the beginning of July, when the British decided to send their New Armies to France, and the Germans were weaker now than they were then. He angrily threatened not to send more troops, and if the necessity should arise, to withdraw ten divisions of those already there. Clearly, the question of alliance obligations was beginning to grate on the British chief, who longed for a freer rein on the disposition of his forces and a more independent role in the alliance, something he was not likely to achieve while Joffre remained in effective control of French strategy. The final conclusion of the meeting was to stick with the previous plan of sending 150,000 men to Salonika, and Kitchener now agreed to send an additional 20,000, which, adding to forces already committed by the British and the French, would make up the required 150,000.[57]

FRENCH OPPOSITION TO THE BRITISH DECISION TO REINFORCE EGYPT

Piqued by the situation in France, Kitchener found much consolation among the members of the Dardanelles Committee, which met on 11 October, upon his return to England. Unsure whether the French would really send troops to Salonika, and in view of the Greek attitude, the committee did not wish to proceed with the Salonika expedition. But, greatly concerned about the situation in the Dardanelles and British control over Islamic territories should the Central Powers arrive at Constantinople, the committee took the dramatic decision to transfer eight divisions from France to Egypt. From there they could be deployed as circumstances required. These would be replaced in France but not immediately, as Kitchener's Fourth New Army was not yet ready for field service and would require a further four months' training.[58] As an immediate measure, Kitchener asked Joffre on 13 October to relieve the two British divisions under General Charles Monro on the Somme for movement to Egypt.[59] This time it was Sir John's turn to be piqued by not being included in discussions which affected his forces.[60]

In France the demands of the field took priority. An amazing exercise in military foot dragging followed, as Joffre and Sir John jostled with each other over who was to take up the line of the departing troops. Joffre's immediate response was to refuse the required reliefs on the basis that he still had operations in Champagne to finish and, fearing a counter-offensive, he had no available troops to relieve British forces. Given the critical state of the Serbian Army now under attack, he urged that British troops should depart at once, as had French troops already, and not delay. But, while he was agreeable that the British suspend their current offensive operations if need be, he urged that, in view of the more favourable ratio of British reserves to those of the French, the British provide the required troops on their own. To Wilson, Joffre confided that he did not plan to relieve any British troops.[61] The British, he observed, with 36 divisions held a front of 100 kilometres while the French with 90 divisions held a front of 650 kilometres. Moreover, there had been no agreement, he said, regarding the dispatch of additional English divisions to Egypt. In a letter to Kitchener, Millerand endorsed Joffre's views and expressed his own concern that British troops were being directed to Egypt rather than Salonika.[62]

In this fracas between the field commanders, Kitchener sustained Sir John French, who claimed that he had no available forces even after suspending current operations. On 16 October, Kitchener insisted once again that Joffre relieve at once the two British divisions on the Somme, arguing that refusal by Joffre to relieve them would prevent the British from keeping their promise relative to the 150,000 pledged for the expedition. At the same time, Kitchener downplayed the fact that the two divisions were destined for Egypt, saying they would have to go to Alexandria to pick up equipment for mountain warfare, which would entail little delay, and was evasive about whether the ultimate destination of the other British divisions to leave France would be Salonika or Egypt.[63]

Concerned that the British had in effect dropped the Salonika venture in favour of a major troop build-up in Egypt, the French government dispatched Millerand to London on 17 October to urge again full British compliance with the earlier agreement. Millerand's trip to the British capital, which stretched to the 20th, produced some results, first in identifying the reluctance of public opinion and a faction in the cabinet to send British forces against the wishes of the Greeks. He also learned of Sir John's resistance to deployment of troops from his front. Both he and Kitchener agreed on the urgency of supporting the Serbs.[64] But Millerand was only partially able to counteract the stance of Grey and two Unionist ministers, the Marquess of Curzon and the Earl of Selborne, that British involvement in Greece should be subordinated to Greek participation in the conflict. With typical ambivalence, Asquith's cabinet agreed in a written text to continue the Salonika expedition in view of the needs of the Serbs, but it reserved the right to re-examine the military situation when British troops arrived in Egypt.[65]

Millerand's intervention did help to break the log-jam between Joffre and Sir John French on the question of reliefs. On 17 October, without waiting for the results of the conference, Millerand instructed Joffre that in the event of Sir John's refusal to send his reserve forces to Salonika, he should relieve the two British divisions on the Somme at once, on a temporary basis. In a meeting the next day, Joffre and Sir John French worked out an amiable arrangement. In the interest of time, the British would dispatch their 28th Division in reserve immediately and another division from the Somme as the two British divisions on the Somme were replaced by French divisions. The arrangement, said Joffre, was made only because of the urgency of the situation in Serbia and on the understanding that the two British divisions go directly to Salonika and not to Egypt or the Dardanelles.[66] Before the conflict over who would relieve the trenches had been resolved, it had delayed the deployment of the two British divisions by four or five days. Millerand's seeming triumph in bringing the field commanders together and in getting renewed British commitment (albeit qualified) for the Salonika expedition would be his last before the fall of the Viviani government.

BRITISH EQUIVOCATION AND JOFFRE'S TRIP TO LONDON

Divided counsels in Great Britain meant that the concession reluctantly extracted by Millerand for the British to support the Salonika expedition was only temporary. Following the Bulgarian occupation of Uskub on 22 October, cutting off French contact with the Serbs, the entire Near Eastern situation was reviewed in the Dardanelles Committee on 25 October. Despite the special pleading of Sir John French, called in from the field for the occasion, not to take troops from his front, it was decided to maintain the decision to dispatch a total of eight divisions from the

French front to Egypt. Uncertain of the future of either the Dardanelles or the Greek venture, and with the prospect of the Germans at Constantinople, the British wished to take precautions to protect their interests in the Near East by a troop build-up in Egypt. The committee also came to the conclusion that the two British divisions recently freed from France should go to Egypt and not Salonika as the French desired. On 25 October the British cabinet ordered Sir John to dispatch four more divisions from the Western Front to Egypt. Along with the two British divisions rerouted to Egypt and two Indian divisions previously designated, these latest transfers raised the number of divisions heading for Egypt to eight. Wilson, a staunch westerner, feared that the eight divisions would sit in Egypt doing nothing.[67]

The next day, the British advised the French that they considered it was already too late for troops sent to Greece to be of any help to the Serbs. To make their point, they dispatched the director of military operations, Charles Callwell, and Sir Archibald Murray, the recently appointed chief of the Imperial General Staff, to France on 27 October to talk with Joffre to present the British point of view.[68]

The resultant meeting at Joffre's headquarters on 28 October produced no tangible results. The two British officers, lacking executive authority, could do little more than raise technical difficulties associated with the operation, such as the limited port capacity of Salonika and the inadequate capacity of Greek railways. The meeting had one beneficial effect, however, which was to convince Joffre of the need for high-level representation to persuade the British to keep their original agreement.[69] Indeed, as of the day previous, three French divisions were engaged in Salonika as far north as Veles, while the one British division remained behind in Salonika and the other two were at Marseille in transit.[70]

The role of Joffre in the Salonika expedition was also changing. Until early October he had been very resistant to any deployment of troops outside of France but had given in to government pressure to allocate a limited number of divisions to the Salonika enterprise. Unbeknownst to the British, his attitude began to shift in early October as the Central Powers' attack on Serbia became imminent. During a visit of Poincaré, Viviani, and Millerand to Chantilly on 4 October, Joffre acknowledged the "need to act in the Balkans."[71] On 14 October, as the joint Austro-Hungarian-German and Bulgarian campaign got underway, Joffre came to Poincaré's office and, in the presence of Millerand and Augagneur, "repeated several times, with great insistence, that he considered the Balkans operation as essential." It would prevent the Serbian Army from being cut off, surrounded, and taken prisoner, assure its supply in foodstuffs and munitions, and maintain an Eastern Front, which he deemed "necessary for general operations." He then indicated to Millerand the instructions he thought should be given to Sarrail to ensure the protection of the railway and the cooperation of French troops with the Serbian Army.[72] Joffre's sense of Allied solidarity and the need to maintain the Serbs in a multifront war thus gained ground as the Bulgarian offensive got under way.

Just over a week later, on 22 October, in a three-hour consultation with Poincaré, Viviani, and Millerand, Joffre underlined the importance of the expedition to Greece and the need for the British to continue sending troops. On this occasion, Viviani spoke at length on the critical situation of the cabinet and obtained Joffre's approval of Gallieni as the new minister of war in a reconstituted ministry.[73] In addition to the grave military situation in Serbia, Joffre's greater awareness of the fragility of the Viviani government underscored the necessity for Allied intervention, if only in a limited way, with full British participation.

As a result, Joffre himself, accompanied by Sir William Robertson, Sir John French's chief of staff, went to London on 29–30 October to get the British to agree to support the expedition.[74] "Super-Frog," as Asquith dubbed Joffre,[75] was more effective in personal communication than his political predecessors. Reassuring the British about the capacity of the port of Salonika and the ability of the Uskub railway to sustain eight divisions, Joffre countered the claim that it was too late to help the Serbs. The loss of Veles could be reversed, he stated. His plan was for the British to maintain the railway as far as Krivolak and to allow the French to penetrate farther north.[76] Not only did Joffre make a good impression on Asquith at the dinner table,[77] but his energetic argumentation swept away all lingering doubt about French intentions raised by his earlier reluctance to support the enterprise. The clincher was his appraisal of the political situation. Privately, he indicated that his own position was at risk, and the alliance in danger, if the British did not send their forces as originally agreed.[78]

Under these conditions, the Grey faction was temporarily overridden and the British decided to give vigorous support to the Salonika expedition.[79] The 22nd Division at Marseilles was ordered to go directly to

Salonika, the 28th Division was instructed to move from Egypt to Salonika at once, and Sir John French was ordered to free two more divisions for the enterprise. British forces at Salonika would now cooperate fully with the French plan.[80] On 6 November, Kitchener was able to report to Joffre that all these decisions were being executed to the full.[81]

But here, as on numerous occasions earlier and later, the British gave support to what they deemed a doubtful enterprise only for the sake of the alliance.[82] It was merely a temporary resolution as the future of the expedition was soon brought into question when British and French operations failed to save the Serbs in mid-November. By that time, the Serbian Army, faced with an attack from Bulgaria that cut its lines of communication to the south, and the Austro-Hungarian-German assault from the north, had been pushed to its last defences. Cut off from their Anglo-French allies, the Serbs were forced into a disastrous retreat westward over the mountains in Albania to the seacoast, and what was left of their force was transported by Allied ships to the Island of Corfu. It was indeed a question of "too little, too late," the result, in large part, of the failure of the Allies to coordinate their efforts.

The irony of it is that for Joffre, apparently recognizing that the survival of his government and even his own depended on the success of the new venture, the measures taken were also "too little, too late" to have any effect. His earlier stalling and British equivocations resulted in his government falling on the issue on 29 October. In a reversal of roles, it was then Joffre who took up the cudgel on behalf of Aristide Briand's new government, in order to get British support for the expedition.

THE COLLAPSE OF THE VIVIANI GOVERNMENT

By the fall of 1915, the French government and command were having serious trouble justifying to the public their performance in the conduct of the war. The basic problem was the continuing failure to achieve victory and the heavy costs involved in pursuing a costly war with no visible end in sight. Despite his titanic reputation as "Victor of the Marne," Joffre was coming under severe criticism. His initial strategy in early 1915 of wearing down the enemy with partial offensives following the onset of trench warfare in November 1914 not only led to great losses in life and resources but achieved little. His major offensives in spring and fall of 1915, despite the mobilization of material resources to produce more guns and shells, similarly produced no tangible results.[83] By the end of 1915, France, which had carried the major burden of the war on the Western Front, had already suffered losses of nearly 2,000,000 – of whom 1,000,000 were dead.[84]

The sequence of events that brought down the Viviani government, nonetheless, was triggered not only by failure on the Western Front but also by the difficulties and delays in mounting a joint Anglo-French expedition to Salonika. When Sarrail arrived in Salonika on 12 October, he had at his disposal one French division, advance units of another, and a British division, the latter under an entirely independent command. His daunting mission, with the one British division in place not having immediate approval for its advance, was to "cover the lines of communication between Salonika and Serbia against the advance of Bulgarian forces."[85]

On the same day, in the wake of the fall offensive and the launching of the Salonika expedition, an important vote of confidence was held in the Chamber of Deputies. The deputies now voted 372 to 9 to support the government, but the large number of abstentions signalled that Viviani's *union sacrée* coalition was in big trouble.[86]

The Viviani ministry had been under attack for its conduct of the war since the failure of the spring offensive. The brunt of parliamentary criticism fell on Millerand, who, despite his considerable contribution to the mobilization for industrial warfare, was considered little more than the mouthpiece of Joffre in the cabinet and a reluctant supporter of the eastern strategy.[87] The ministry began to totter following the resignation of Delcassé, the foreign minister, on 9 October, who, although ill with fatigue and dizziness, resigned, in large part, owing to his opposition to the Salonika venture.[88] Following Delcassé's resignation, Viviani, who still had a majority in the Chamber, wished to restructure his ministry, but he was unable to do so as several candidates refused to enter the cabinet unless Millerand was removed as minister of war. On 25 October, Viviani announced to Poincaré his intention to resign.[89]

The opposition of the left had crystallized against the government when, as a result of Bulgarian occupation of Uskub on 22 October, French forces in Serbia lost contact with the Serbs. Viviani, Millerand, and Augagneur were asked to account for their ineptitude in mounting the Salonika expedition before a joint meeting of the Army and Navy Commissions of the Chamber on 26 October.[90] The Army Commission found their explanations inadequate and drafted a letter to that effect the next day,[91] closing the noose on the beleaguered ministry.

While Viviani had decided to resign before the commissions pronounced on the performance of his ministry, their assessment is a fair indicator of the dissatisfaction of the Chamber. The government officially fell on 29 October.[92] René Viviani's *union sacrée* government thus collapsed ostensibly because of the failure of its Balkan policy but in reality because of its inability to deal with the broader issues of the war.

THE GOVERNMENT OF ARISTIDE BRIAND

Under the watchful eye of Poincaré, Aristide Briand, after four days of intense negotiation with members of Parliament, managed to constitute a new *union sacrée* coalition that assumed office the same day as the Viviani government fell.[93] Briand, a devoted easterner, a skilled politician and recognized orator, and a centre-left independent, had been premier in two prior ministries since 1909. His government, under Poincaré's urging, contained representatives of all political groupings from the far right to the Socialists on the left. Unlike the pliant Viviani, Briand functioned much more independently of the president of the republic and less frequently sought his advice, to Poincaré's chagrin.[94]

Several members of the previous government continued in their posts. Alexandre Ribot remained as minister of finance, Louis-Jean Malvy as minister of the interior, Gaston Doumergue as minister of colonies, and Albert Thomas as War Ministry under-secretary for artillery and munitions. Briand became his own foreign minister. Viviani became deputy premier and swapped places with Briand as minister of justice. As a symbol of national unity, the cabinet was enlarged to include several "old guard politicians" from a wide spectrum of ideologies, and five of them, Charles de Freycinet, Emile Combes, Léon Bourgois, Jules Guesde, and Denys Cochin, were elevated to the prestigious post of minister of state.[95]

Those who felt France needed a change of military leadership, such as Georges Clemenceau, Charles Humbert, and Paul Doumer, favoured General Joseph-Simon Gallieni as a replacement for Joffre. Before the Viviani ministry fell, it had been agreed that Gallieni (with Joffre's prior assent) would be the minister of war and Admiral Lucien Lacaze would replace Augagneur as minister of marine.[96] Criticism of Joffre's command would be blunted in the new ministry with the installation of Gallieni as the minister of war to exercise closer supervision of Joffre.

left A skilful politician, Aristide Briand succeeded Viviani as French premier on 29 October 1915, forming a *union sacrée* government representing all political groupings, and remained in power until 20 March 1917. A devoted "easterner" and ardent supporter of greater Allied coordination, Briand made Joffre commander-in-chief of all French armies to assure support for the Salonika expedition and to raise his stature in the eyes of France's allies, but limited his powers by reinforcing the Conseil supérieur de la Défense nationale to provide greater political direction. (Library of Congress)

right Joseph-Simon Gallieni, Joffre's commanding officer in Madagascar prior to the war and more recently military governor of Paris, was brought into Briand's government to better manage the High Command. Gallieni soon fell into conflict with Joffre, whom the cabinet supported against him, and resigned in March 1916 because of ill health. He died shortly thereafter. (*THW*, 1:242)

The Conseil supérieur de la Défense nationale was strengthened to provide more unified direction of the war. The membership of this inner cabinet consisting of key ministers – the prime minister, the war minister, the navy minister, and others as required – remained unchanged, except that both service chiefs (not just Joffre) were now included. The council was still presided over by the president of the republic, but its role in military matters was expanded. All the French staff's plans for major offensives and for Allied coordination would be now be subject to prior approval by the council.[97] Joffre's powers were curtailed under the new ministry and the French government assumed a greater role in the overall direction of the war, since all of Joffre's plans for major operations and also for coordination of the Allies required governmental approval.

Briand was a strong proponent of Allied coordination and gave Joffre full support in his initiatives in that regard. In the previous cabinet, the easterners – Briand and several ministers – felt that France needed a new strategy to focus on external theatres. The installation of the Briand government resulted in little immediate change in Anglo-French relations relative to the Salonika expedition, however, as it continued along the path of its predecessor, but the new ministry provided a breath of fresh air in terms of the overall management of the war.

IMPACT OF THE BRITISH DIVERSION OF TROOPS TO EGYPT ON SIR JOHN'S RELATIONS WITH JOFFRE

The tug-of-war between Joffre and Sir John for troops on the Western Front continued with the British diversion of troops from France to Egypt. On 1 November, Joffre indicated to Foch that the six British divisions leaving France for the eastern theatre would be replaced by divisions coming from Britain. Joffre asked Foch if he thought it possible to ask Sir John to extend the BEF's front around Loos and south of the River Somme, which the French Tenth and Sixth Armies respectively had relieved earlier.[98] Foch thought it was possible to ask. But a week later Robertson noted: "We can make no statement about [further reliefs] of French troops at present."[99]

While Robertson was reticent, Sir John, in marked contrast, had much to say on the subject to the British government in a memorandum in mid-November. He strongly protested the previous diversion of ten British divisions from the Western Front to the eastern theatre. Sir John claimed that if these ten divisions, along with French divisions, had not been transferred to the east, the Allies could have transformed their outstanding tactical achievements on 25–26 September into decisive tactical successes in Champagne and Artois. The British government, Sir John complained, was now ordering him to send eight more divisions to the Mediterranean. He observed that the cabinet revealed insufficient understanding of the BEF's situation in France, and that it was also issuing directives that would result only in a waste of manpower. Finally, Sir John warned that, if the government persisted in its present course, he would "refuse any longer to be responsible for the conduct of the campaign."[100]

Sir John also sent his memorandum to GQG. Joffre, no stranger to threatening his own government with resignation, welcomed receipt of the memorandum. In his reply, Joffre praised Sir John, indicating that the latter's memorandum offered new proof of the cordiality and mutual respect with which they had always dealt with military problems. He added that the two of them considered that the French and British armies actually formed one army, whose principal reserve of manpower was the British New Armies, that the Western Front was the decisive theatre of operations, and that secondary theatres must therefore receive only a minimum of manpower and matériel.[101] The warm feelings between the two men, however, would only endure for a month, until Sir John's removal from office on 19 December 1915 and replacement by Sir Douglas Haig as commander-in-chief.[102]

KITCHENER'S TRIP TO THE DARDANELLES

On 5 November 1915 Kitchener conferred with key ministers in Paris en route to the Middle East. Only days before, Asquith had persuaded him to undertake a fact-finding tour of the eastern theatre. His motive was to keep his restive cabinet from fracturing over the question of whether Kitchener should be removed as secretary of state for war. Asquith hoped that getting rid of Kitchener temporarily would give his ministers time to calm down, thereby preserving his government.[103]

Kitchener conversed with Briand and Gallieni about the eastern theatre in Paris on 5 November. The dispatch of eight divisions from the Western Front for the defence of Egypt remained a sore spot with the French. While Briand and Gallieni fully recognized the potential danger to Egypt, they expressed their desire to have the eight British divisions sent to Salonika to rescue the Serbian Army and to persuade Greece and Romania to join the Allies.[104]

Kitchener arrived in Mudros on 10 November. He immediately consulted with Charles Munro and other leading army and navy officers. They favoured the evacuation of Gallipoli. Kitchener accepted their assessments, and the newly formed War Committee, which replaced the

Conference of Anglo-French political leaders (with the addition of Joffre) meeting at the Quai d'Orsay in Paris, 17 November 1915, in one of the several conferences called to resolve issues related to the Salonika expedition. British ministers, left side of the table (left to right): Grey, Asquith, Balfour, Lloyd George; French representatives, right side of the table (left to right): Briand, Gallieni, Joffre, and Admiral Lacaze, French naval minister. (*THW*, 7:258)

Dardanelles Committee in early November, took the momentous decision less than two weeks later to pull out of Gallipoli.[105]

Meanwhile, to everyone's surprise, Kitchener adopted the suggestion of Lieutenant-General Sir John Maxwell that a landing at Alexandretta precede the withdrawal from the Dardanelles. This operation would protect British interests in the Middle East and North Africa, and allow Britain to evacuate Gallipoli, if necessary, without losing too much prestige.[106] On 11 November, Kitchener asked the government to dispatch two divisions in Egypt and two divisions in Gallipoli to Alexandretta.[107]

Briand's cabinet reacted with dismay to the news that Kitchener, without consulting them, was reneging on his promise to send the two divisions in question to Salonika.[108] On the 13th, members of the Conseil supérieur de la Défense nationale – Poincaré, Briand, Gallieni, Joffre, and Lacaze – united in opposition to Kitchener's project at Alexandretta on the grounds that it would dissipate the strength of Allied forces in the eastern theatre and that the force would encounter not only Turks but also 45,000 German troops. Seeing the proposed Alexandretta expedition as unfeasible, the French insisted that the British government reject it.[109] Although the Conseil supérieur did not say so in communications to the British, its members also opposed the projected landing because Alexandretta was located close to Syria, France's traditional sphere of influence in the region.[110]

The reaction in Britain to the proposed landing at Alexandretta was equally cold. The General Staff of War Office rejected the project because it would require more troops than Kitchener considered adequate.[111] On 15 November, the new, smaller War Committee (Asquith, Bonar Law, Lloyd George, Reginald McKenna, and Balfour) expressed its strong disapproval of the Alexandretta expedition owing to its unwillingness to undertake a "new military commitment in the Near East" that would open a "new line of naval communication" and engage in yet one more dispute with the French government and army.[112]

On 17 November, the foremost French and British politicians and military leaders held a conference in Paris to discuss events in the entire eastern theatre. Briand, Gallieni, Joffre, and Lacaze represented France. Asquith, Grey, Balfour, and Robertson represented Britain. The two governments concluded that difficulties in logistics and transportation precluded the launching of another military operation in the eastern theatre.[113] Kitchener's Alexandretta project was dead.

REACHING A COMPROMISE ON SALONIKA

On 4 December, the Allied leaders again met at Calais. Briand, Gallieni, and Joffre represented France. Asquith, Kitchener, and Murray (Sir John resigned his command on 4 December) represented Britain. They discussed the situation in the Balkans. The British advocated leaving the region. The French wanted to maintain troops there. Since the British remained adamant, Briand finally agreed to pull French troops out of Greece.[114]

The French government repudiated the agreement the following day.[115] Its decision angered the British.[116] But at the Allied military conference held at Chantilly from 6 through 8 December, the Russian, Italian, Belgian, and Serbian representatives sided with the French, while the British persisted in their objection to maintaining an Allied presence in Salonika.[117] The impasse clearly revealed the gravity of the tensions between the British and French.

Hoping to reconcile the differences between the two governments over Greece, Asquith sent Kitchener and Grey to Paris for talks with Briand and Gallieni. During meetings on 9 and 11 December, Kitchener and Grey reversed course and decided to collaborate with French plans. The two armies would adopt a defensive stance around Salonika. But neither government stated how long it would keep troops in Greece.[118] These meetings, although not totally satisfactory, eased strained relations between London and Paris. But the issue of what to do with the Salonika expedition, whether to withdraw, stand pat, or attack, would bedevil Anglo-French relations throughout 1916 and well beyond.

THE COMMITTEE OF SIX

By mid- to late October, criticism was widespread in influential circles in both countries over the inability of the Allies to work together in an efficient manner to mount an expedition to Salonika; the "frittering of energy"[119] and the "continued and continuing 'misunderstandings,'" it was argued, were "gravely imperiling the relations between the two counties."[120] The traditional practice of diplomatic relations with exchange of missives and political-military conferences had proven totally inadequate for the coordination of Allied efforts. As early as March 1915, Esher had begun advocating an Allied committee to manage joint affairs. Behind the scenes, Wilson vigorously promoted a proposal to set up such a committee, which eventually gained ground. In Wilson's plan, the coordinating body would consist of a committee of six: the prime ministers and the war and navy ministers of the two countries.[121]

The failure of Kitchener to inform the French in advance about his plan on 11 November to divert British troops to Alexandretta in preparation for an offensive there underscored the urgent need for closer Anglo-French cooperation. As William Philpott has pointed out, by this time, various schemes for coordination were put forth; some proposed a body that would include military representatives to guide the alliance strategically, some advocated a closer link between general staffs in the two countries, and others favoured a vehicle consisting mainly of politicians and focused on the oversight of grand strategy. Still others thought the joint council should include prominent political and military leaders from both countries. There was considerable discussion on whether the body should have executive authority or be purely advisory.[122]

Apart from the lack of agreement on the form and powers of the new coordinating body, the troubled nature of divergent policies in the Mediterranean and the lack of certainty while Kitchener's fate was being determined created obstacles to the quick resolution of the issue. A staunch advocate of a tighter link between military staffs in London and Paris, Esher embraced a proposal by Selborne, a member of the British cabinet, for a joint "Bureau de Guerre" (War Office) to manage the war, and promoted this proposal with French leaders Briand and Gallieni and with Asquith, Kitchener, and the king on the others side of the Channel from late October throughout November. But Joffre's initiative in calling a new Allied military conference undercut Esher's proposal and focused attention on the political side of the discussion.[123]

Focusing on the need for political coordination, Wilson, the driving force behind the idea of a Committee of Six, became even more forceful in his advocacy of it. On 19 November, he wrote a letter to Andrew Bonar Law, the Unionist leader in Asquith's coalition, insisting that the Allies were "courting disaster in not establishing the Committee of Six."[124] In his reply to Wilson four days later, Bonar Law stated that he was reluctant to broach the subject of the Committee of Six with Asquith because the friendship between Bonar Law and Wilson (who was persona non grata with the Liberal Party since the Curragh affair in 1914) might automatically prejudice Asquith against it.[125] Briand and Gallieni, on the other hand, were ardent supporters of the new structure.[126] On 26 November, Wilson received word that Briand had sent Jules Cambon, the last pre-war French ambassador to Germany, to London to ask the British to agree to form the Committee of Six. Wilson welcomed this good news. But, when Cambon pushed Grey on the matter, Grey replied that he had already submitted proposals to Paul Cambon, the French ambassador. This positive news was followed soon afterwards by a minor setback. Joffre, who had promised Wilson that he would raise the subject of the Committee of Six with the British War Committee in late November, was unable to do so because the scheduled meeting had been postponed until 2 December. To Wilson, "these delays [were] terrible."[127]

Much further discussion followed. Neither side wanted to tie its hands by creating a body with executive powers. As proposed by the French and endorsed by Asquith, on 19 January 1916, an Allied committee, serving as an advisory body and bringing together political and military leaders of each country, was officially constituted. In the final analysis, the permanent members of the committee were limited to the two prime ministers, with other ministers and military authorities to be added as deemed necessary. Provision was made for a regular secretariat but only for irregular meetings, as required.[128] Though largely ineffective owing to the looseness of its structure and the absence of a fixed schedule of meetings, the committee marked a new step in the direction of Allied planning. Its main accomplishment was to provide a written statement of a desire for closer collaboration. Nonetheless, it may also be seen as a forerunner of the Supreme War Council that was formed after the Italian Caporetto defeat of 1917.

CONCLUSION

The operation of a coalition is never an easy matter. As Gordon Craig pointed out in regard to the 1813 coalition against Napoleon, differing political objectives, heightened civil-military conflict, and lack of unity of command are likely to place stress on allied relations and any attempt at a concerted effort.[129] All of these elements were observed as the British and French attempted to mount the Salonika expedition in late September and October 1915. Sir Edward Grey, the British secretary of state for foreign affairs, and those who supported him, adamantly resisted British intervention in Greece without Greek approval and intervention in the war on behalf of Serbia. This stance brought his government into continual conflict with France, which was more interested in an eastern expedition and saving the Serbs than in diplomatic niceties. Underlying these conflicts was a basic difference of political objectives. For the French, Greece and saving the Serbs represented a more vital interest than Egypt, whereas, for the British, Egypt and the defence of British interests in the Middle East had a higher priority. The British plan for a build-up of troops in Egypt, as a guarantee of British interests should the Dardanelles venture fail, seemed to the French like a contravention of joint agreements and a betrayal of the immediate need to aid the Serbs.

Lack of unity of command was also manifest in the extreme as the two most powerful military personalities of the alliance clashed. Kitchener, with real prescience, favoured sending a large expedition of 300,000–400,000 men to Salonika or none at all, which brought him into direct conflict with Joffre, who wanted a smaller expedition and was loath to release either French or British troops from the Western Front for the purpose. In addition, civil-military conflict was heightened as both Joffre and Sir John French were in fundamental disagreement with the strategy of their governments from the outset, and worked together, or at cross-purposes in the case of reliefs, to thwart the desires of the two governments to send troops to Salonika.

But, in the case of the Salonika expedition, the problem of Allied coordination was exacerbated by further conditions unique to the Anglo-French Entente. The lack of pre-war planning and the absence of any mechanism for dealing with issues beyond the traditional methods of diplomacy meant that the process was very slow and uncertain, at best. The old diplomacy was hardly able to deal with the fast-moving contingencies of war. In the absence of any joint body with an established framework and procedure to resolve issues and make plans, the only recourse was a confused and confusing series of Allied conferences – six in less than four weeks – to deal with political, diplomatic, and military issues as they arose. Such proved to be wholly inadequate to deal with the complex issues of the region.[130] The proposed Committee of Six was a first step in the right direction, but hardly an adequate response.

The lack of any joint agency was further exacerbated by the relative weakness of the instruments of government and control in each country. The French government, suffering from serious division, was unable to impose its will on the French command until the ministry was about to be swept aside by the parliamentary opposition. The British government, lacking adequate staff advice from the two services, was fractured on the issue of how best to defend British interests. While Kitchener and Joffre were the dominant players, their authority was on the wane. Under these conditions, given the differing attitudes of the two governments toward Greek neutrality, and their divergent priorities in the region, it was impossible for any of the consultations to be durable and binding. In the absence of any Allied machinery, a frenzied series of conferences and consultations was unable to arrive at firm decisions, so that action dragged and the expedition failed to bring effective aid to the Serbs. It is clear that, for Allies to coordinate effectively, they must first put their own houses in order.

How serious were the consequences of the Allied imbroglio in attempting to mount the Salonika expedition? From the military point of view, given the overwhelming numerical superiority of the combined German,

Austro-Hungarian, and Bulgarian forces engaged,[131] it is doubtful that the French plan of deploying 150,000 men, had it been carried out with celerity, would have been able to do much more than provide the Serbs with a safe escape route into Greece. To have taken the offensive against such large numbers would have undoubtedly required the 300,000 to 400,000 Allied troops for which Kitchener, probably the most far-sighted of the Allied military leaders in terms of his calculation of what forces would be required to render effective aid to the Serbs, had repeatedly pressed. But dispatching such a considerable force would have meant suspending or scaling down dramatically the fall offensive in France, a major strategic adjustment that Joffre was not prepared to countenance. That the expedition failed to accomplish even its limited objective of maintaining the railway to Uskub and joining hands with the Serbian army, and was, as a result, unable to prevent the destruction of a large part of the Serbian Army, was a major setback.

Diplomatically, the consequences were also serious. The inability of the two governments to come to anything like a consensus on the issue led even Joffre to wonder whether the alliance was not in question. Feeling that they had been dragged into a doubtful military exercise because of the demands of French politics, and that they had been obliged to infringe on the rights of a neutral state, the British, over the next two years, would try almost continuously either to get out of the venture or to limit its scope. Their unwilling participation proved to be a running sore in their relationship with the French throughout the period of Robertson's tenure as chief of the Imperial General Staff and engendered much acrimony. The wisdom of Allied intervention into Greek politics, which ultimately led to the overthrow of the Greek dynasty, and the maintenance of a large force at Salonika in relative inactivity, over a long period of time, is still a matter of debate more than a century later.

CHAPTER TWELVE

Preparation for 1916: Leadership Changes and Strategic Coordination

THE ANGLO-FRENCH COALITION embarked in several new directions at the end of the 1915 campaign season in an effort to better prosecute the war effort in 1916.[1] In France, an important political-military readjustment took place. Aristide Briand, the prime minister since October, was an "easterner" and proponent of greater Allied cooperation, and less beholden to Poincaré, the president of the republic, than his predecessor. In response to Joffre's repeated requests, Briand enlarged the scope of Joffre's control by his appointment as commander-in-chief of the armies of France both on the Western Front and in the Middle East, which was intended to achieve a balance between the two fronts and also raise his stature in dealing with French allies. But Joffre was subjected to much closer governmental supervision by the reinforcement of the Conseil supérieur de la Défense nationale. All the French staff's plans for Allied cooperation and for major offensives would now need to be subjected to prior government approval. Joffre's powers at GQG were also eroded in that Castelnau was appointed as his chief of staff.

British leadership was likewise strengthened with the replacement of Sir John French as commander-in-chief of the BEF with Sir Douglas Haig, and the appointment of Sir William Robertson as chief of the Imperial General Staff, whose powers were greatly enhanced in the process. Following closely on the evolution of British strategy in 1915 toward a fuller commitment to the French, the new leaders would serve as guarantors of the strict application of the "western" strategy in 1916.

As soon as the Anglo-French fall offensives in Champagne and Loos had run their course, Joffre and his staff began to plan for the 1916 campaign season. With his government's approval, Joffre assumed the new role of Allied coordinator and, building on the initiative of the first Allied military conference under his auspices held on 7 July, called another such meeting at Chantilly for 6–8 December to plan the 1916 campaign season. In addition to assuring coordinated offensives, this conference would also give him a stronger hand in dealing with the British in terms of Middle Eastern strategy and the planning of joint operations in France. The political-military framework provides the background to these changes.

The first full year of trench warfare, 1915, as indicated, was a formative one, with major new challenges for armies in the field and the political and military leaders. This was a new kind of war, the industrialized total war of the twentieth century, for which neither the generals nor the politician were prepared by their previous training and experience. As the war dragged on with no appreciable Allied success, the public's confidence in its political and military leaders began to falter.

Both Entente governments by mid-1915 were coalitions with inherent elements of instability. In the French case, the *union sacrée* government of René Viviani rested on shifting political groupings and interests, whose strategic demands had to be considered. In Britain, the coalition government of H.H. Asquith, formed in May 1915, rested on the support of an unhappy amalgam of Liberals and Unionists, without strong central leadership. Moreover, the high commands and their staffs, who made the military plans, had varying degrees of latitude and enjoyed differing degrees of support from their governments.[2] By the end of 1915, in both countries, significant changes were undertaken in the political-military leadership and the institutional framework, altering overall perceptions of the war. The Entente political-military context thus set the stage as the third campaign season of the war approached.

FRENCH GOVERNMENT AND COMMAND

Aristide Briand, who succeeded Viviani as French prime minister on 29 October, formed a cabinet that excluded Millerand as minister of war. Before the Viviani ministry fell, it had been agreed that General Joseph-Simon Gallieni, a high-ranking military officer, would be the minister of war and that Admiral Lucien Lacaze, a naval officer, would replace Augagneur as minister of marine.[3] Installing Gallieni as the minister of war, with a view to his exercising a closer supervision of Joffre, would blunt criticism of Joffre's command within the new ministry and in the Chamber of Deputies. Additionally, the Conseil supérieur de la Défense nationale was given new powers as an inner cabinet for the direction of the war. This body would provide closer coordination of political-military planning, since, by government direction, the French staff's plans for major offensives and Allied coordination would now be subjected to prior council approval.[4] As a result, Joffre's powers were curtailed, while the French government assumed a greater role in planning operations on the Western Front and in Allied coordination.

As war minister in Briand's cabinet, Gallieni, Joffre's former chief in Madagascar, soon found himself embroiled in conflict with Joffre. The French commander-in-chief resisted the war minister's attempt to impose tighter control of his command. At the same time, Joffre renewed his request, dating from July, that, for the sake of unity of action, he be placed in charge of all operations – not only in France but also in the Middle East, where the Salonika expedition had assumed greater proportions.[5]

In Gallieni's clash with Joffre, the government ultimately sided with Joffre. It agreed on the need for unity of action but rejected a plan to install Gallieni as commander-in-chief on all fronts, for fear of involving the Parliament, to which he would be accountable, in strategy.[6] Thus, on 2 December, to the consternation of some Socialists, who were still stinging under Joffre's heavy-handed dismissal of Sarrail, Joffre was made commander-in-chief of all armies in France and in the Middle East. And eight days later, General Édouard de Curières de Castelnau, a recognized staff officer (then in command of the Second Army Group), was installed as Joffre's chief of staff to anchor him with high-level professional advice.[7]

Briand was a devoted easterner who was able to obtain leftist support in the Parliament. While the extension of Joffre's jurisdiction may have been a ploy by Poincaré and Briand to bind Joffre to an eastern strategy and oblige him to divert resources to Sarrail, it also had the effect of giving him a lever to maintain the Salonika expedition as limited in scope and subordinate to operations on the Western Front.[8] On 4 December 1915, in a meeting with Anglo-French political and military leaders at Calais, Joffre and Briand argued – in the face of adamant British opposition –

for the necessity of a military presence in Greece, even though it was too late to come to the assistance of the Serbs. Retaining a small Allied force of 150,00 men in the region, they argued, would pin down 400,000 enemy troops.[9] In 1916 Joffre would ardently defend the continuation of the Salonika venture, to the great ire of the British generals and politicians, but, despite the call for more British troops and repeated demands for joint offensives in the region, he would never assign these more than a secondary role.

The extension of Joffre's command as commander of all French forces, including those in the Middle Eastern theatre, raised Joffre's stature and, in so doing, improved his position in dealing with the Allies in matters of military planning.[10] All of Joffre's plans, however, now had to be approved by the newly reconstituted Conseil supérieur de la Défense nationale. While Joffre's overall jurisdiction in the direction of the war had been considerably broadened, his liberty of action had been undermined and the government's role enhanced.[11] The long process of the reassertion of civilian authority over the High Command was well under way as the French government assumed a more aggressive role in Allied coordination. But, ironically, as the sole technical military adviser to the government, Joffre was generally able to hold his own with the ministers and have his point of view prevail.

SIR JOHN FRENCH'S COMMAND

The changing of the guard in the top military leadership of the British Expeditionary Force in France and the Imperial General Staff in London at the end of 1915 had major implications for the future conduct of the war. Indeed, the replacement of Sir John French by Sir Douglas Haig as commander of the BEF was significant both for the future of the campaign in France and for relationships with French Army Commander Joseph J.-C. Joffre. The appointment of Sir William Robertson as chief of the Imperial General Staff involved not only a change of personnel but also a transformation of power relationships within the British government and a change of strategy in favour of full commitment to the Western Front.[12] These two developments were interrelated and stemmed more than heretofore known from the blueprint laid down by Robertson following the failed Artois offensive in May–June 1915.

Known as a "Thruster" from his exploits in the Boer War, Sir John French had assumed the command of the BEF in 1914 with a certain number of liabilities. While he had the support of the Prime Minister H.H. Asquith and the majority of his cabinet, some of his subordinates, including Sir Douglas Haig, the commander of the British First Corps, had doubts about his capacity to lead a great army in a great war. French's biographers have noted his prickly sensitivity to his superiors and others as well as his mercurial temperament, while praising his attempt to interact with his men and the warmth of his personality.[13] But his style of personal leadership, based on a network of personal relations rather than solid staff planning, proved inadequate for the direction of large units under the stress of battle.[14] A recent biographer has concluded that Sir John was not fully qualified for the job.[15]

At the outset, as he took to the field in August 1914, grave conflict developed within his staff, exacerbated by the volatile nature of his character. Though Sir Archibald Murray, Sir John's chief of staff, was a capable officer, he was wanting in emotional resilience and his suspicions of the French made him unduly cautious. The subchief of staff, Sir Henry Wilson, was "more French than the French" and an advocate of offensive action, creating an ongoing conflict in Sir John's headquarters.[16]

Sir John faced a difficult command, given the narrow range of his discretionary authority and his need to coordinate with the French.[17] His efforts were frequently circumscribed in the field by the imperious leadership of Kitchener, the secretary of state for war, the great soldier appointed by Asquith to give his government a more martial appearance.[18] At the same time, Sir John had to deal with Joffre, who, realizing immediately that Sir John's command was independent, resorted to a number of measures in the 1914 campaign to have the British send a maximum of forces to France, to have them engage fully in the field, and to gain strategic control of the BEF. These included, among others things, appealing to the British government over Sir John's head, enclosing British with French forces, and attempting to effect favourable leadership changes at British headquarters.[19]

One should not be surprised, therefore, that the rigours of the battlefield, particularly in light of initial Allied defeats on the frontiers in August 1914, led to a series of leadership crises in the field. One of these, the October-November command crisis, involving both Joffre and

Kitchener, challenged Sir John's continuation in office as commander of the BEF. Even though the sequence of crises in 1914, summarized in the first chapter of this study, were eventually resolved, they left a sense of rancour on a number of scores.

In early January 1915, with very considerable difficulty, Sir John was able to get the approval of Kitchener and the British government for a combined military and naval attack on the coastal ports, Zeebrugge and Ostend, which he and Churchill had worked up. Joffre seemed to give his support to the project for a time, ostensibly as a ruse to get the maximum of British troops in France. The project was then undercut when Joffre revealed his true strategy for a combined Anglo-French attack in Artois and Kitchener withdrew his support of the coastal operation in favour of the Dardanelles expedition instead.

The British government's decision to send the 29th Division to the Dardanelles rather than to the Western Front led to a breakdown in French's relationship with Joffre at the end of February 1915, as Sir John refused to replace French troops in the line. The result was that Joffre withdrew French support for the British attack at Neuve Chapelle on 10–13 March 1915, leaving the small British force to attack the German Army virtually unaided.[20] This marked the lowest point in Anglo-French military relations in 1915. Relations were also very strained following the German assault on Ypres in April. which led Sir John to believe that he had not been sufficiently supported by the French. There was also considerable acrimony in July and August over the desirability of the Loos offensive.

One might anticipate that Joffre, given his attempt at the beginning of November 1914 to have Sir John French replaced, and his later representations to have Archibald Murray, Sir John's chief of staff, replaced with Wilson, would play a significant role in Sir John's ultimate replacement. But such does not appear to have been the case. The French had apparently learned their lesson following the failure of the Wilson intrigue to replace Murray and thus resorted to other methods to gain strategic control of the British forces in France. Following the Neuve Chapelle incident, Joffre lobbied consistently for the subordination of the British command, which Kitchener finally granted in a formula for partial subordination in August before the Loos offensive. Joffre also began a series of Allied military conferences in an attempt to coordinate the alliance and gain strategic control. The first, on 7 July 1915, was sufficiently successful that Joffre followed it up with another military conference at Chantilly in early December 1915 in which the Allies agreed to the French plan for a coordinated Allied attack in 1916.[21] In this way, Joffre became the effective coordinator of the Allied military effort and was able to exert additional pressure on the British, both in France and in the Balkans, to have them conform to his strategic approach.

Though Joffre apparently was not unhappy with Sir John's replacement in December 1915, the record shows no further attempt on his part to effect personnel changes at British headquarters. While severe conflict between the two had arisen in 1915 on various operational matters, they had been able to collaborate effectively on pressing the British government for more troops and countering British peripheral strategy in the Dardanelles.

Kitchener's role was likewise not the key element in Sir John's recall. One highly regarded historian has characterized the relationship between French and Kitchener as one of continuous conflict following Kitchener's September 1914 visit to Paris.[22] This needs to be qualified, however, with the observation that there were moments of at least partial reconciliation in the relationship. Despite his awareness that Kitchener had been engaged in a discussion with the French for his replacement at Dunkirk on 1 November 1914, Sir John, in his memoirs, speaks of very cordial relations between himself and Kitchener when they met with Asquith at Walmer Castle on 20 December 1914 to discuss, among other things, the shortage of ammunition and the danger of invasion in the event of a feared German build-up on the Western Front.[23] In the weeks that followed, there was sharp disagreement between the two over the employment to be made of the New Armies,[24] and, throughout much of 1915, there was considerable tension over Kitchener's support of the Dardanelles expedition. But it should be noted that relations between the two men began to improve markedly in the spring of 1915. A series of four secret meetings between them over the seven-week period from 23 March to 6 May[25] marked the easing of tensions and led to a more satisfactory meeting of the minds. With growing confidence, Sir John laid out fully for Kitchener during their 6 May meeting his plans for the immediate combined Anglo-French Artois offensive, having indicated previously that his stock of artillery shells was satisfactory. Kitchener was sufficiently impressed that he dropped his earlier condition of success in the field before sending major reinforcements and promised Sir John the deployment to France of all six divisions of his First New Army.[26] The Artois offensive, however, would shatter these cordial relations and lay the basis for Sir John's eventual recall, but remarkably, not at Kitchener's hand, despite the ensuing Shells Crisis.

ARTOIS AND LOOS: SIR JOHN'S RECALL, BRITISH MILITARY RESTRUCTURING, AND WESTERN STRATEGY

From a number of points of view, the Artois offensive was the main factor in Sir John French's fall. Still reeling from the German gas attack at Ypres and a severe quarrel with the French over plugging the gap in the line,[27] Sir John suffered a major setback in his unsuccessful attack on Aubers Ridge on 8 May. With only a limited artillery barrage of forty minutes, British troops advanced and were cut down without success. The French, with a more ample supply of artillery, launched a one-and-a-half-day artillery attack and scored an initial victory on 8 May, advancing as much as three miles north and east of Arras.[28]

Smarting from his failure in the face of French success, Sir John initially blamed hostile machine-gun fire.[29] Eventually, however, he came to believe that the problem had been his lack of heavy artillery, which the French had in greater abundance. Deflecting the responsibility from himself to his political masters, Sir John broke the normal convention of military subordination and appealed directly to the British press and the Opposition rather than his government, citing the shortage of high-explosive shells as the reason for his failure.[30] Putting the blame on Kitchener, who as secretary of state for war was responsible for munitions production, French hoped for his replacement.[31] Not fully understanding the nuances of the British cabinet system, he failed to realize that the prime minister would have to accept ultimate responsibility.

The Shells Crisis that followed had major ramifications. Feeling bereft over the loss of a lady friend's attention, Asquith was faced both with the revolt of Jackie Fisher, the first sea lord, over his Dardanelles policy and with criticism of his management of the production of shells. To counter these attacks and to provide a broader base of support, he called in the Unionists to form the first coalition government on 25 May 1915.[32] Lloyd George was placed in charge of shell production in the new Ministry of Munitions, which cut into powers previously wielded by Kitchener.[33] The new government maintained the strategic policy of the old in supporting the Dardanelles operation.

Kitchener, also under personal attack, played a curious role in the Shells Crisis. Imperious by nature and always desirous to gain the upper hand over an opponent, Kitchener immediately countermanded the transport of the remaining five divisions of the First New Army to France. Only one division had already arrived. His argument to Sir John was that there was no use sending further forces to him, since he did not have adequate artillery for those already in place.[34] Only under special pleading by Sir John that more troops were required to meet promises made to the French did Kitchener relent and send two additional divisions, sending instead the remaining three divisions to the Dardanelles.[35] But on the question of Sir John's replacement, Kitchener took a measured approach. After lecturing Sir John on the limits of a field commander's role with regard to overall strategy, he stood behind his beleaguered chief rather than seeking his dismissal.[36] Kitchener's "position in the country" was still "very strong";[37] hence, no change in personnel was made in the military leadership.

Several historians have left the story there, thinking that the next step leading to Sir John's replacement was his failure to bring up reserves after an initial advance in the Loos offensive, and that Haig's intervention with the king, along with some critical comments by William Robertson, was the major cause of his replacement.[38] Roberston's blistering letter to the king's secretary on 23 June 1915, however, would suggest that there were serious fallouts from the Artois offensive, and that Robertson played a much more active role in Sir John's replacement and the military restructuring that took place in December 1915 than is generally believed. Indeed, Robertson, in his letter to the king's secretary, Lord Stamfordham, on 23 June 1915, after commenting on the recent campaign and the general strategic situation,[39] launched a broadside against Sir John.[40] In addition to underscoring Sir John's unhappy relationship with Joffre, Robertson blasted his chief for not fully representing his views to the government. The government, he opined, did not listen to him because he was a "disgraced non-entity." "If they do *not* trust him they should replace him," he said. He also argued that the British Imperial General Staff should be restructured with a "trusted & competent head" to provide effective staff work and strategic control of the war, which Kitchener had not been able to perform for want of staff advice.[41] An amazing document for the time, this letter was not only a major attack against Sir John French by his closest adviser, but also the blueprint for the entire staff reorganization that would later take place in December.

The decision, moreover, made in June at Roberston's suggestion, that all communications between Sir John in the field and Kitchener in London pass through the hands of Sir John's staff marked a major step in Robertson's rise to power. Thereafter, numerous weighty staff memos written by Robertson provided the basis for analysis of strategy, including a major review on 10 June of the shells situation.[42] By subjecting all of Sir John's communications to his review, Robertson gained the upper hand in the control and management of Sir John's staff, much as he would of the strategic policy of the government as chief of the Imperial General Staff.

The personally troubled nature of the French-Kitchener relationship thereafter became less visible, though not sufficiently to prevent a major dispute in July 1915 between Sir John and Kitchener over the British attack at Loos proposed by the French as part of the fall offensive, with Sir John initially supporting the French plan. But in this Kitchener had the advantage, given the shaky standing of Sir John following the Artois offensive. Sir John thus trimmed his sails to the wind first by following Kitchener's lead in resisting the proposed French offensive, basing his case on the unfavourable terrain of the proposed operation at Loos and the shortage of munitions; and then by giving it his full support, because Kitchener, struck by the weakness of the French government and the fall of Warsaw, "told him to." Kitchener also acceded to the French formula for Sir John's partial subordination to Joffre.[43]

The Loos offensive was the last chance for Sir John to show his mettle and revive his fortunes. But his unfortunate denial of reserves to Haig prior to the offensive, leading to their delay in exploiting the initial victory at Loos on 25 September, and the latter's referral of the matter to the king, was the last straw. Predictably, Robertson again made unfavourable comment on Sir John's generalship which further undermined his position.[44]

It was not Kitchener, however, who fired Sir John. Indeed, Kitchener's own position was seriously threatened during the last four months of 1915. Authoritative and secretive by nature, Kitchener was no match for the wily politicians who accused him of withholding and falsifying information. The looming failure of the Dardanelles strategy and his inability to chart a firm course in the Salonika venture in October weakened his standing in the government. Kitchener had begun to lose his way. His strategic clairvoyance in establishing the New Armies, and his clear-sightedness in understanding the need to sustain British allies, now gave way to an ad hoc approach and an uncertain and variable strategy in the Mediterranean.[45] Mounting the Salonika expedition posed additional problems. Unable to persuade Joffre or his colleagues to send a major expedition to save the Serbs, he ultimately convinced the Dardanelles Committee and the War Committee, which replaced the former in early November, to send eight divisions to Egypt to protect British interests in the Mediterranean should the Central Powers forge a link to Constantinople. A growing chorus of criticism arose over the inability of the French and British to come to a consensus regarding the Salonika expedition.[46]

To the British cabinet, it had already become clear in September that Kitchener lacked adequate staff advice. As a first step to strengthening the Imperial General Staff, the cabinet appointed Sir Archibald Murray as chief of staff on 22 September, while Kitchener was in France. In the management of the Dardanelles expedition and coordination with the French over the newly mounted Salonika expedition, Kitchener had lost the confidence of his cabinet colleagues. In November, rumours circulated in official circles that he would be replaced as secretary of state for war.[47]

The rising star was Sir William Robertson, whose well-reasoned staff documents on a variety of subjects attracted the attention of the Dardanelles Committee and its successor in London. It could not have escaped their attention that Robertson was a committed westerner and much opposed to diversionary deployments outside of Europe. His uncompromising demand that the Imperial General Staff be the sole British adviser on strategy should he be appointed chief was first resisted and then largely met as he finally worked out an arrangement with Kitchener on 10 December which would provide a nominal role for the latter.[48] Asquith and his cabinet, in appointing Robertson chief of the Imperial General Staff on 23 December 1915, had agreed not only to a new institutional framework but also to a new strategy. Robertson was thus one of the principal beneficiaries of Sir John's growing weakness and the foibles of Kitchener's superior conduct of the war in London. The other beneficiary was Sir Douglas Haig, whose role in undermining French's position following the Loos offensive is well known.

left Douglas Haig was appointed commander-in-chief of the British Expeditionary Force in December 1915, replacing Sir John French. In 1915, as commander of the First British Army, Haig objected to the terrain prior to the Loos offensive in September 1915 but was compelled for political reasons to attack in force. His report to the king, stating that Sir John French had failed to place reserves at Haig's immediate disposal in order to exploit an initial breakthrough, was a factor in Sir John's recall. (*THW*, 1:129)

right William Robertson, a highly competent staff officer, rose from the ranks to become, in succession, quartermaster-general of the British Expeditionary Force, chief of the General Staff (1915), and, at the end of 1915, chief of the Imperial General Staff. Since he was a "westerner," with a dominant voice in strategy, his appointment assured that the British would commit their resources almost entirely to the Western Front in 1916. (*THW*, 7:289)

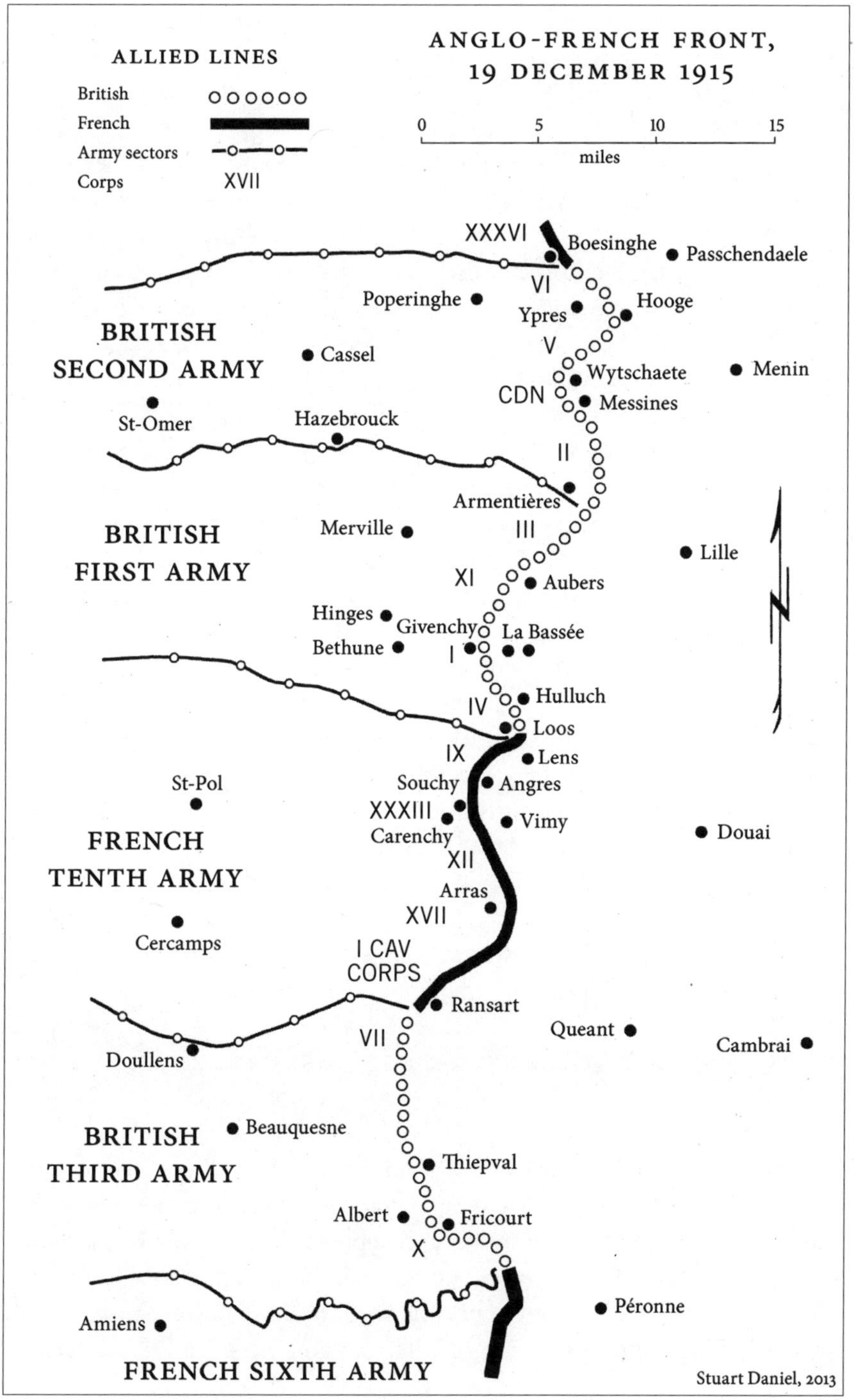

ANGLO-FRENCH FRONT,
19 DECEMBER 1915
ALLIED LINES
British
French
Army sectors
Corps
XVII
0
5
10
15
miles
XXXVI
Boesinghe
Passchendaele
VI
Poperinghe
Ypres
Hooge
BRITISH
SECOND ARMY
Cassel
V
Wytschaete
Menin
CDN
Messines
St-Omer
Hazebrouck
II
Armentières
BRITISH
FIRST ARMY
Merville
III
Lille
XI
Aubers
Hinges
Givenchy
La Bassée
Bethune
I
Hulluch
IV
Loos
IX
Lens
St-Pol
Souchy
Angres
XXXIII
Vimy
Douai
Carenchy
FRENCH
TENTH ARMY
XII
Arras
XVII
Cercamps
I CAV
CORPS
Ransart
Queant
Cambrai
VII
Doullens
BRITISH
THIRD ARMY
Beauquesne
Thiepval
Albert
Fricourt
X
Amiens
Péronne
FRENCH SIXTH ARMY
Stuart Daniel, 2013

But it was upon the repeated urging of the king that Asquith, undoubtedly remembering what the Shells Crisis had done to his government, ultimately decided – with the knowledge of a few close advisers – to replace Sir John French. Asquith entrusted the delicate mission of advising French that it was time for him to give up his command to Esher, who attempted to persuade Sir John, in successive visits, that it was now time to "change the bowler," and offered him the position of chief training officer in the United Kingdom to soften the blow.[49] The best-qualified replacement as commander of the BEF was the ponderous and inarticulate Haig, who took up the post on 19 December. Thus was installed the Robertson-Haig team that would dominate British strategic direction of the war for the next two and a half years.

Robertson's vision of the structure of the Imperial General Staff and his undermining of the position of French as commander of the BEF after the Artois offensive played a significant role in the ultimate outcome. While using his conduit with the king, as did Haig, for influencing affairs, Robertson grew in stature with the cabinet in the last months of 1915, preparing the way for his elevation. The changing of the guard in British military leadership and the emergence of new institutional and strategic imperatives was a delayed response to the failed Artois offensive.

In short, neither Joffre nor Kitchener, who had earlier tried to fire French during the October-November command crisis in 1914, played any role in his dismissal. Rather, it was Asquith, whose Liberal government had been toppled by the Shells Crisis in May, who "blew the whistle" on Sir John French following the advice of Robertson, Haig, and the king, and appointed Robertson chief of a revitalized Imperial General Staff. Robertson's role in both developments following the failed Artois offensive was more significant than heretofore realized.

FRENCH GRAND STRATEGY: BACKGROUND TO ALLIED COORDINATION

Joffre's consistent operational goal, determined by the political and physical realities of the situation, was to beat the German Army and drive it out of France and to aid and support the Russians in the process.[50] Failure of the costly, ever-larger offensives launched in 1915 was blamed on the lack of heavy artillery and munitions. The response was to order massive amounts of heavy artillery and shells, which French industry provided in remarkable quantities. Though it was not unresponsive to the tactical needs of the new conditions of trench warfare, the French staff's re-evaluation of tactics proceeded methodically but slowly under central control.[51]

The French staff believed that the experiences of 1915 demonstrated that French troops could always penetrate the German trenches. The problem was not how to breach the trenches but how to exploit victory. In this analysis, the Artois offensive in the spring of 1915 failed because of the narrowness of the attack, which exposed their forces' flank to enemy counter-fire, and because of the availability of German reserves. The 1915 fall offensives were thus launched on two fronts, with an attack by the British and French at Loos and Arras to draw in enemy reserves followed by the main French attack in Champagne to make a breakthrough.[52] But, in the French view, the availability of German reserves proved decisive, leading to the failure of both attacks. To win the war, the French concluded, the Allies would have to use up available enemy reserves on all fronts before engaging the decisive battles. Joffre's growing concept of the need for the attrition of the enemy prior to ultimate victory formed the backdrop to his plans for the coordination of Allied military operations in the fall of 1915.[53]

French grand strategy prior to 1914 had relied not only on French military strength but also on the support of French allies, of which Russia, deemed a faithful partner, was the chief cornerstone. From the time of his appointment as French chief of staff in 1911, Joffre had recognized fully that the next war would be a coalition war, which could be won only by the concerted action of allies. One of his first moves, therefore, was to ascertain the nature of the diplomatic setting, and then to enter into closer collaboration with Russia, France's principal ally.[54]

On the other hand, repeated attempts by the French government to draw the British, linked only by the tenuous Entente Cordiale, into a firmer commitment prior to 1914 had failed. While staff and naval conversations laid down a contingency plan, the arrangement contained no firmer assurance than the promise to consult in time of crisis and, as a result of the 1912 naval accords, a British commitment to defend the French northern sea coast. The apocryphal story of a conversation between Major-General Henry Wilson and General Ferdinand Foch in 1910 contains the germ of the relationship. "What would you say was the smallest British military force that would be of any practical assistance to you?" Wilson queried. "One single private soldier," replied Foch, "and we would take good care that he was killed."[55] To draw the British deeper in their commitment to French defence was a major French goal from the outset of the war. Joffre's consistent objective was to obtain a maximum participation from his British allies and to submit them to French strategic control.[56]

The goal of fully involving French allies had been pursued with at least a modicum of success in 1914, the initial Russian offensive in 1914 having contributed significantly to the Battle of the Marne by the diversion of German forces to the Eastern Front, and the British having played an ever-increasing and significant role in all the left-wing battles from the outset of the war.[57] The Russian attack in Galicia in March 1915 had led the Germans to withdraw eight divisions from the Western Front and ultimately to choose the Eastern Front for their 1915 offensive.[58]

As a military man possessed of a strong sense of Allied solidarity, Kitchener was motivated by concerns for the overall effectiveness of the coalition earlier than many others.[59] As early as March 1915, he had suggested to the French that Joffre ought to play a larger role in the overall coordination of the coalition with a view to simultaneous attacks on both Eastern and Western Fronts.[60]

By mid-1915, the seeming unity of Allied efforts had broken down as the Russians retreated before the combined might of the German and Austro-Hungarian forces and the British pursued a competing policy of peripheral operations in the Dardanelles offensive. The addition of Italy into the war at the end of May added another reason for Allied coordination. The French staff came to the conclusion in June 1915, following successive Russian reversals on the Eastern Front, that the war was without direction and that lack of coordination was a major weakness of the coalition. Consequently, France, as the lynchpin of the coalition, ought to take the initiative in Allied strategic planning. In addition to the British, the Italians seemed agreeable to the French taking the lead.[61] Unfortunately, a plan to create a more permanent central organ for the coordination of Allied operations was dropped in the haste to convene the July conference to deal with the immediate situation.[62]

Joffre's first attempt at Allied military coordination thus began in the summer of 1915. The coordination of Allied military efforts depended on the realization by the respective governments and commands that the war could not be won by a series of isolated actions, and that the Allies would have to cooperate to produce the desired effect. Because of his prestige as Victor of the Marne and the central role of France in the coalition, the French commander, though lacking any official mandate, had the tacit support of the Allies for taking the initiative in calling the first Allied military conference, which met at French headquarters at Chantilly on 7 July 1915.[63]

The day previous, as de facto coordinator on the Western Front, Joffre scored a major coup in his attempt to draw the British further into the war. The failed Battle of Artois in the spring of 1915 had convinced him and his staff that the French could not win the war without massive British assistance and that, in particular, British forces must serve as the reserve of the French Army. Accordingly, Joffre requested repeatedly the deployment of twenty divisions of Kitchener's New Armies to France. After a full review of British strategy involving the field commander and staff, the British cabinet decided to send the "New Armies" to France, rather than deploy them elsewhere, cognizant of the need to support the hard-pressed Russians and fearful that the French would wobble without maximum British support.[64] And so, when the highest-ranking French and British political and military leaders met at Calais on 6 July for the first time in a political-military conference to resolve basic issues of strategy and resource allocation, the British promised to deploy their New Armies in France while also encouraging a defensive-offensive strategy on the shared front. Having retained the right to determine the scope of operations, Joffre promptly ignored this counsel the next day in planning his fall offensive.[65]

With British support assured, Joffre was able to take the initiative at the Chantilly Allied military conference the next day in arranging coordinated offensives for the fall of 1915, on both the Western and Italian fronts, in order to take the pressure off their Russian allies. These offensives, though not fully coordinated and only partially attaining their goal, were sufficiently successful to vindicate Joffre's initiative in Allied military planning. The process of Allied coordination, moreover, in this case abetted by Russian weakness, had provided Joffre with a further lever for extracting stronger participation from the British at Loos against the will of Sir John French. As a result, always concerned that the British would either not engage fully or divert forces to other theatres, the French staff was doubly encouraged to take on a greater role in Allied coordination by calling another major Allied military conference at Chantilly on 6–8 December 1915 to prepare for coordinated Allied offensives in 1916.[66]

In this initiative, Joffre had the full endorsement of Briand, who, in addition to being an easterner, was a firm believer in the need for Allied coordination at all levels.[67] One week before the conference, Joffre presented his plan for Allied coordination to key ministers for consideration by the Conseil supérieur de la Défense nationale.[68] The French staff plan for Allied coordination was now the French government's plan as well.[69]

While the need for closer coordination of Allied efforts, particularly on the Western Front, had long been apparent, the imbroglio attending the mounting of the Salonika expedition in September–October 1915 made it abundantly clear that such a need was paramount.[70] By the end of October, various plans were being discussed between political and military leaders of the two countries for a body (similar in intent to later Supreme War Council set up in November 1917) to determine the best way to coordinate both the political and military aspect of the coalition. As support coalesced around Joffre's initiative for military coordination of the coalition, the most promising idea for political coordination was the proposed "Committee of Six," to include the prime ministers and the war and navy ministers of both allies. But the realization of this project was still in the future – it was only partially implemented in January following long discussions – and its scope was limited to include the two prime ministers with a permanent secretariat and additional ministers as needed.[71]

In terms of the overall coalition, the concept of Allied military coordination was entirely sound, and Joffre was correct in assuming that under existing conditions – in the absence of any other coordinating instrument – he was the only Allied leader with enough stature to make it effective.[72] He therefore pressed forward with his plan for an Allied military conference to lay the foundation for Allied coordination in 1916.

As the 1916 campaign season approached, the prospects looked promising to the French staff. True, Britain was lagging in the "production of needed war material," but, with nearly seventy divisions now mobilized with the Kitchener New Armies, "it had not yet put into the balance the maximum of its power." If the Russians could be properly supplied, they too would be able to attack, as would the Italians. If all of the Allies could attack simultaneously in a coordinated way, the Central Powers would not be able to use their interior lines to meet one attack after another, and once their reserves were used up, the Allies would drive on to victory. Joffre, ever optimistic, believed, as he had at the beginning of campaign season in 1914, and again in 1915, that in 1916 he was going to win the war.[73]

But behind his optimism there lay a deep anxiety with regard to the state of French arms. On 7 October 1915, as the fall offensive was grinding to its conclusion, the French staff had begun to assess the situation and future possibilities. The failure of the current operation to obtain more than tactical success it blamed largely on lack of artillery munitions. The French Army's offensive capacity had been blunted, as had that of its British allies, and it was anticipated that the army would have to go on the defensive for several months while its artillery stocks were replenished and its effectives reconstituted. The main concern was lack of effectives. Noted the French staff: "We are coming to the end of our resources in men, and … the 1916 and 1917 classes (about 270,000 total) constitute the only reserve with which we can undertake the 1916 campaign."[74] "From the beginning of the campaign," Joffre wrote the same day, "France has carried the greater weight of the war," but "it cannot continue to do so without compromising her future." French allies, particularly the Russians and British, with their large manpower reserves, must now carry the "main effort, which will result in the definitive attrition of the adversary." France, he concluded, "must keep its last troops intact for the final exploitation of victory; it must not waste [*user*] them prematurely."[75] Here indeed was Joffre's "hidden" agenda for Allied coordination.

ALLIED MILITARY PLANNING AT CHANTILLY, 6–8 DECEMBER 1915

The second Allied military conference met under French auspices at French headquarters at Chantilly on 6–8 December 1915. The decisions taken at the three-day military conference, to which all the Entente allies sent military representatives, were far-reaching and decisive. It is much to Joffre's credit that, among Allied generals and politicians, he had the greatest vision of the need for Allied coordination and the stature, energy, and drive to seize the initiative to bring it to pass.

The Allied military conference, held at Chantilly, 6–8 December 1915, under Joffre's leadership, made plans for coordinated Allied offensives in 1916. Front row (left to right): General Pellé, French chief of staff, General Carlo Porro, representing Italy, Marshal French, representing Britain, General Joffre, French commander-in-chief, General Gilinsky, representing Russia; second row (left to right): General Wielemans, representing Belgium, General Huguet, liaison officer at British headquarters, and four unidentified officers. (*L'Illustration*, 11 December 1915)

At the Chantilly Conference, having already brushed aside a Russian proposal for a massive offensive in the Balkans,[76] Joffre rallied the military representatives of all the Allies – Russia, Great Britain, Italy, Belgium, and Serbia – to his plan, which had the prior approval of his government. Decidedly offensive in conception, the French plan was to launch major coordinated offensives against the principal forces of the enemy and destroy the main enemy armies in the field. The military delegates of the several Allied armies thus agreed with the French that the Dardanelles should be evacuated. But the French, for political reasons, and in order to placate the easterners in the cabinet and buttress their Balkan policy, wished to maintain the expedition to Salonika. Already at loggerheads with the British, who wished to withdraw from Salonika, the French used the occasion to isolate the British and, with the united support of the Italians, Serbs, and Russians, who wanted to maintain an Anglo-French presence in the area, Joffre gained general support for the French Balkan policy. With the exception of the British delegation weakly led by Sir John French, approaching the end of his tenure as commander-in-chief of the BEF in France, and Sir Archibald Murray, a stop-gap appointee as chief of the Imperial General Staff in London, all of the delegates agreed that the Allies should remain at Salonika.[77] This put renewed pressure on the British government to stay at Salonika, despite their having extracted a promise from the French two days previous at Calais to evacuate.[78]

The major result of the conference was unanimous endorsement of the principle that "the decision must be sought by concerted offensives on the main theatres where the enemy maintains the greater part of his forces, that is to say, on the Russian, Anglo-French and Italian fronts."[79] The specifics of these attacks were left for later discussion, but the concept that they should take place as soon as possible, and not later than March 1916, was endorsed by all, so as not to leave the initiative to the enemy. In the event that one of the major armies was attacked before the plan came into effect, the others were to come to its aid. The Russians, who had been sorely taxed by Central Power offensives in 1915 and had felt largely deserted by their allies, had this mutual-assistance clause inserted.[80]

A crucial issue associated with the French plan, later to become a serious bone of contention, was the question of preliminary "wearing" operations. As indicated, the French, who had borne the brunt of the fighting on the Western Front to that point, were seriously beginning to feel the shortage of effectives by the close of the 1915 campaign season. As their low birthrate provided no surplus of available men, they now began to look to their allies (the British in particular), with their immense reserves of manpower, to carry a greater portion of the burden.[81] Thus, argued Joffre, those powers with the greater reserves of manpower, that is to say, Russia, Britain, and Italy, should proceed with a series of wearing operations, pending the major offensives, in order to draw in and use up enemy reserves. The conference delegates agreed to this proposal,[82] which was to prove the thorniest of all as both the British command and the government in London later took umbrage at large isolated British wearing operations in which the French were not involved.[83]

The basis had been laid for a concerted military effort, with provisions for a variety of contingencies. So far as the coordination of the coalition was concerned, this was Joffre's greatest achievement. For the first time, the Allies had a plan by which they would all march together and prevent the Germans from using their interior lines to their advantage in engaging them one at a time.[84] The difficulty, of course, lay in the plan's execution. But that is a subject for another volume, yet to appear.

CONCLUSION

The issues of 1916 in Anglo-French command relations would be quite different from those of 1915. In 1915 the British were compelled by the urgent needs of a seemingly faltering coalition to put their major effort into the war in France. In 1916, with that strategy and a new leadership team in place, the main British strategic aim in their dealings with the French was to limit their involvement in the Salonika expedition. A western strategy prevailed, leading to the great bloodletting on the Western Front at Verdun and in the Battle of the Somme in 1916. With advent of the Lloyd George government at the end of the year, the British resumed their push for a stronger peripheral strategy, which again embroiled them in conflict with the generals in the field and the French government.

While the appointment of Robertson and Haig gave greater scope to the generals in the British war effort, the changes in the French political-military and command structure gave greater control to the French cabinet but also enhanced Joffre's role as Allied coordinator. He was therefore able at Chantilly to carry the several Allies with him in working up a joint plan for 1916, and later to coordinate with the British in planning for a massive joint offensive on the Somme. The real problem arose when the Germans pre-empted French plans with their Verdun offensive in February 1916. The relationship between the Verdun battle and the planning and execution of the Somme offensive occupied centre stage in Anglo-French command relations in 1916, while the future of the joint expedition in Salonika remained a bone of contention on both sides.

CHAPTER THIRTEEN

Reflections and Conclusions

THE POLICIES AND STRATEGIES OF France and Britain in 1915 played a decisive role in shaping Anglo-French command relations on the Western Front. The British, still focused largely on the defence of the empire, were torn between the pursuit of the war in France and the allocation of British resources elsewhere. Following flirtation with an initiative to defend immediate British interests on the Channel Coast, the British pressed forward with the Dardanelles expedition, peripheral to the Western Front, while France's strategy, largely under Joffre's control, focused on winning the war at home and giving aid to its principal ally, Russia. The tug-of-war between these strategies had a major impact on the two commands, pitting them against each other until they learned, after the isolated British action at the Battle of Neuve Chapelle, that their common interest was best served by pulling together in pressing their demands for the growing British New Armies and in resisting the Dardanelles strategy.

The course of the war then obliged a change in British strategy. The weakness of the Russians after the Gorlice-Tarnów breakthrough on 2 May and the perceived instability of the French political system after the failed Battle of Artois in the spring of 1915 led the British government on 6 July at Calais – in the first high-ranking Anglo-French military-political conference of the war – to commit its New Armies to France. In doing so, it obtained an assurance that these armies were to be used in a defensive-offensive role until furnished with adequate munitions. Joffre, however, pressed forward with his plans for massive offensives, despite Sir John French's misgivings about the role assigned him, that of attacking in the difficult and highly fortified terrain about Loos. Again, Russian weakness and a governmental crisis in France prompted Britain to give full support to Joffre's fall offensives in Artois and Champagne.

Ironically, in late summer, with the British shift in policy toward less equivocal support of the Western Front and questioning the merits and future of the Dardanelles expedition, the French government pressed first for a strengthened French operation on the Asiatic side of the Dardanelles, a demand growing out of French domestic politics. Then, at the end of September, the French championed an expedition to Salonika, Greece, to shore up Serbia, now threatened by a joint Austro-Hungarian-German and Bulgarian attack as Bulgaria entered the war on behalf of the Central Powers. This French shift in policy reversed the roles, with the French demanding a Salonika expedition (largely with British forces) and Britain, resistant to the venture, sending troops from the Western Front to safeguard Egypt in preparation for evacuation of the Dardanelles.

In these successive quests for peripheral operations, first by the British and then by the French government, Joffre, with the support of Sir John French, opposed any diversion of troops from the main theatre of war on the Western Front. As the "Victor of the Marne," he remained largely in control of French strategy in 1915 and, in fact, stymied all attempts to send more than limited forces for external operations, which in retrospect denied them the chance of more than limited success. In his focus on offensive strategy on the Western Front, Joffre was the main stabilizing influence in the Anglo-French alliance throughout 1915, particularly as the two governments scrambled incoherently to put together the Salonika expedition. In the meantime, following the failed Artois offensive and Italian entry into the war, Joffre assumed the larger role of coordinating the military strategy of the several Entente belligerents, an endeavour in which, in successive military conferences, he was quite successful.

MULTIPLE FACTORS AFFECTING COMMAND RELATIONSHIPS

Admittedly, there are many factors that may affect relationships between commanders of national armies in the field. The command relations between Joffre and Sir John French in 1915 reflect several of these, which had a bearing on their relationship and the conduct of joint operations.

The relative size of each army and its material preparation had a significant impact on command relations. It was a foregone conclusion from the outset of the war in August 1914 that Joffre, who commanded a force many times greater than that of the British, would take the lead in coordination of Anglo-French forces on the Western Front. The British were not necessarily always amenable to that formulation. Sir John French, in particular, was very protective of the independence of his command. As his army grew in size, he became progressively more assertive of his independent rights and stoutly resisted a unified command under French leadership.

Preconceived strategies played a significant role. As William J. Philpott has demonstrated, Sir John French, prior to the outbreak of war, had a predilection for a northern strategy to clear the Channel ports, which he put on a backburner for the sake of the alliance as the 1914 campaign began. His strategic preferences, nonetheless, re-emerged in several instances later, particularly in his desire to have the BEF transported from the Aisne to the French left wing in October 1914, and in his subsequent forward movement in Flanders, the failure of which denied him the dream of rolling up the German flank. In January 1915 his proclivity for a northern strategy was abundantly apparent in the coastal operation planned with Churchill, the first lord of the Admiralty, in which the Royal Navy would effect a landing at Zeebrugge and Ostend in conjunction with a military attack on the German right flank. When that operational plan was squelched by Joffre's lack of support and the British launching of the Dardanelles offensive, the coastal operation was adjourned, as a second-stage operation, in favour of the main offensive in Artois which Joffre envisaged. The northern strategy was never entirely out of view to British military leaders, however, and resurfaced in Haig's 1917 Passchendaele offensive.[1]

On the French side, Joffre was imbued with the doctrine of the offensive and, in spite of lack of adequate munitions, forged ahead with offensive actions for the course of 1915 – with partial offensives in the first months of 1915 and intermittently thereafter – and major joint offensives in the spring and fall. In Joffre's mind, the only road to victory was to beat the main German Army on the Western Front. Aimed at liberating French soil and assisting the Russians, Joffre's offensive doctrine and focus on the Western Front frequently created frictions in his relationship with Sir John and the British government. But, as de facto coordinator of Anglo-French forces, Joffre, with the help of Kitchener, generally got his way.

Personal interactions and the level of trust between commanders was also a factor.[2] In temperament, Joffre and Sir John were quite different. Sir John was highly mercurial and prickly about any form of higher direction, whether from his own government or the French High Command. Joffre, on the other hand, was the epitome of stolid steadfastness but was equally jealous of his personal authority, particularly with regard to his government; and, imperious by nature, he tended to treat the BEF like any other army under his command.

While there was a fair level of accommodation between Joffre and Sir John in 1915, especially in planning future offensives, in requesting more troops from Britain, and in resisting peripheral operations that detracted from the Western Front, there was always a considerable element of distrust in the background. Sir John, in particular, based on his 1914 experiences, including being unsupported in a forward position at Le Cateau in August 1914 and the lack of French support during the Second Battle of Ypres in April 1915, was afraid that Joffre would not provide him with adequate reinforcements in time of need. After what he deemed insufficient French assistance during the Second Battle of Ypres in April 1915, he thus demanded the stationing of three French divisions on the British front as a condition for his participation in the spring offensive. Nor was he in the least willing to submit himself to a unified command under French direction. While Wilson had a close relationship with Foch, who after 4 October 1914 was Joffre's hands-on coordinator of Allied operations for the northern front, Sir John was often wary of Foch's promises and proposals. The instruction given to Sir John French in August 1914 that his was an independent command and that he was to cooperate with the French, but not engage in major operations without French participation, remained in effect. This suited Sir John, who could hide behind these instructions to justify his independent-mindedness.

Joffre, for his part, was often impatient with Sir John and his seeming lack of aggressiveness. From the outset of the war, Joffre's main objective, for which he had the unstinted support of his government, was to have greater British participation on the Western Front. His constant refrain was to have the British government send more troops. In 1914 Joffre, in order to have the British assume a more aggressive stance, had appealed to the two governments, appointed Foch as coordinator of French, British, and Belgian forces in the northern theatre, encased British troops with French troops, and attempted to have first Sir John and then his chief of staff, Archibald Murray, replaced by Wilson.

In 1915, by a variety of tactics, Joffre attempted to have Sir John take over longer stretches of the trenches and to engage his forces with greater vigour. To obtain these objectives, he sought a unified command on the Western Front under French direction. In addition, he undertook coordination with all the Entente powers, with the intent of having greater control of Allied strategy on the Western Front and drawing in the British more fully under French strategic control. These 1915 tactics were partially effective, giving Joffre increased influence over British strategy on the Western Front.

Pre-war stereotypes, seemingly reinforced by the experience of battle, played a significant role in Entente military relations. The French staff perceived the British as "slow and late" and as unaggressive warriors – and hence, better suited for trench warfare. Joffre's assessment of the British and their level of performance was partly related to this stereotype. The British, on the hand, favoured offensive action to guarding the trenches and considered the French generals as shifty and unreliable.

At the political level, the French, with the concept of "perfidious Albion" not far from the surface, were wary of British imperial designs in the Middle East, which caused rancour in planning the Dardanelles expedition. The British, following their pre-war assessment, had severe doubts concerning the stability of the French government and French public opinion. Responding to indications of French governmental instability, the British government decided in June 1915 to send the New Armies to France to aid both the French and the Russians; and for similar reasons, it agreed in August to full British engagement in the joint fall offensive in Artois in conjunction with the French attack in Champagne.

Language barriers were also a consideration. In the nineteenth century, French was the universal language, similar to English in our time. None of the French political and military leaders spoke English, except Foch, who had limited skills in the language. Among the British military leaders, Sir John French had a very fragmented knowledge of French and relied on a translator, generally Wilson, in his communications with Joffre. Among British governmental leaders, Kitchener had an excellent command of French and, as a result, often dominated joint councils, while Asquith's French was only passable.[3] The most visible example of language serving as a barrier to communication occurred in the first Anglo-French political-military conference held at Calais on 6 July 1915, at which, inexplicably, interpreters were excluded. While Kitchener made an eloquent presentation and Asquith was able to chair the meeting, give an opening statement in French, and summarize what others had said, Sir John French, presumably, as a result of his limited skills in the language, made minimal comments. These were in support of Joffre's offensive plan as opposed to Kitchener's defensive-offensive strategy.

The conditions of trench warfare were of major significance in shaping the discussion between military chiefs. The lack of munitions and heavy artillery was a focus of numerous discussions in 1915 and, in particular, contributed to British unwillingness on several occasions to engage in full-fledged offensive operations on the Western Front. The inadequate supply of guns and munitions was a burning issue between the military leaders and the civilian chiefs in 1915, and it was always a factor in any discussion of operational strategy for the Western Front and grand strategy for the entire Entente coalition.

Despite these considerations, some of which had considerable influence on Anglo-French command relations, the argument presented in this volume, and in the one preceding it, is that the main determinant of command relations on the Western Front was the political and strategic aims of the two belligerent governments. This derives from the fact that the military commanders, despite their independent-mindedness, were, in the final analysis, dependants of the civil authority. Even though the commanders of the two armies sometimes functioned independently, in a general way they carried out (or were affected by) the policy and strategy of their respective countries. A brief review of the events of 1915 will show that, at each stage, the strategic objectives of the two governments and their relationships with their own military chiefs provided the backdrop to the interaction of the field commanders.

DIFFERING POLITICAL-MILITARY STRUCTURES

But to understand fully the impact of British and French strategy on the field commanders, one must first appreciate the power structure and decision-making process in each country, which set the stage for civil-military interactions in each. In the British case, Parliament had granted a wide range of discretionary powers to the cabinet in August

1914 for the conduct of the war. But the freedom of action of Sir John French, the commander of British Expeditionary Force, was narrowly circumscribed by Lord Horatio H. Kitchener, British secretary of state for war, who initially shared the strategic direction of the war with Winston Churchill, first lord of the Admiralty. Sir John's main recourse for the redress of grievances was to appeal to Churchill, the prime minister, and the cabinet; and, as in the extreme case of the Shells Crisis in May 1915, the parliamentary opposition and the press. After Churchill was cashiered as first lord of the Admiralty with the fall of the Asquith government, Kitchener remained the effective voice of British strategy for the rest of 1915. While Sir John had a substantial range of discretion in the command of the armies in the field, Kitchener (to the extent that he was informed) kept a fairly close watch on the intended operations of British forces. Kitchener, with a strong sense of Allied solidarity, often sided with Joffre, the effective master of French strategy, rather than Sir John, in a bid to sustain the French and Russian allies.

After the Shells Crisis, Asquith formed a coalition government with Lloyd George as minister of munitions, curtailing to some degree Kitchener's dominance over strategy. As the misadventures of the Dardanelles expedition accumulated, British cabinet ministers began to lose confidence in Kitchener's strategic direction and, at year's end, brought in Sir William Roberston as chief of the Imperial General Staff, making him the effective master of British strategy.

The French power structure was quite different from the British in that, at the outset of the war in 1914, the French Parliament, the true centre of power in the Third Republic, had delegated immense powers to the cabinet for the conduct of the war. But, in view of the short war anticipated, the government had granted sweeping powers to General Joseph J.-C Joffre, the commander-in-chief of the French armies of the northeast, for the conduct of operations. Because of his immense reputation as the "Victor of the Marne," Joffre acquired ascendancy over the government in the formulation and execution of French strategy. In this, he had a consistent ally in Alexandre Millerand, the French war minister, who considered it his duty to advocate Joffre's ideas to the government and to shield him from the ministers and the Chamber of Deputies.

Joffre's offensive operations on the Western Front were conducted with the objective of driving the Germans out of France and supporting the Russian ally. He and the French government viewed the war as a multi-front one from the outset and put a priority on sustaining their allies, particularly the Russians. Their concerted actions often reflected this appreciation. Millerand, moreover, often served as Joffre's mouthpiece in dealing with the British.

But, with the advent of trench warfare at the end of 1914 and the huge losses sustained in Joffre's continued partial offensives in early 1915, with little ground gained, discontent mounted within the government. While Joffre was able to withstand the government's proposal for a major Salonika expedition in early January 1915 and thereafter that year, in favour of offensive action on the Western Front, the heavy losses and lack of success in the Artois offensive heightened the pressure for alternative fronts. A significant part of the government's effort in 1915, especially after the Artois offensive, was aimed at wresting power from Joffre in order to forestall very costly attacks on the Western Front and to divert more of French resources to actions in the Mediterranean.

Restive over the heavy losses sustained in operations with little tangible success, the Chamber also sought to reassert its authority. Working largely through its commissions, it criticized both Millerand for his administration of the war effort and Joffre for his conduct of operations. After Joffre's dismissal of Sarrail at the end of July, the Chamber, responding more fully to Socialist pressure, came out strongly in favour of an eastern strategy. This development, compounded by the accumulation of discontent over the mismanagement of the Salonika expedition, led to the fall of the Viviani government at the end of October 1915.

The new French prime minister, Aristide Briand, restructured the French command structure, giving Joffre a broader jurisdiction by appointing him commander-in-chief of all French armies, which would oblige him to give support to the Salonika expedition. At the same time, he limited Joffre's powers by appointing Gallieni as minister of war and subjecting Joffre to greater government control in the newly strengthened Conseil supérieur de la Défense nationale.

IMPACT OF DIFFERING POLICIES AND STRATEGIES ON COMMAND RELATIONS

The differing policies and strategies of the two governments had an immediate impact in 1915 on Anglo-French command relations. In January, the initial conflict between Joffre and Sir John French was over operational strategy on the Western Front. Sir John, in cooperation with Churchill, wanted to pursue a combined naval and military operation at Ostend and Zeebrugge to roll up the German flank in Belgium. Faced first with support, then resistance, and finally acceptance by the British government, Sir John's plan was undermined by Joffre, who withdrew reserve forces from the sector. Joffre wanted to follow the basic operational strategy of smashing in the big bulge of the German lines in France by attacking from Artois in the west and Champagne on the south. In his plans to drive the Germans out of France, Joffre also had in mind the need to provide assistance to the Russians on their front. His strategy for liberating France clashed with Sir John's northern strategy, which seemingly had the support of the British government.

The British government, however, had recently done a strategic review, which, in light of the deadlock on the Western Front, came out in favour of peripheral actions to take advantage of British sea power, rally the Balkan states, and, where possible, extend the empire. Ultimately, Kitchener, with his eyes on mounting a Dardanelles expedition, and concerned about Russian weakness, sided with Joffre's strategy for a joint Anglo-French offensive in Artois, to the deep disappointment of Sir John French. The coastal operation was postponed *sine die*. British government policy and strategy thus had a significant impact on command relations in the field, obliging Sir John to submit himself to French operational strategy.

The Dardanelles offensive created a more significant problem for Sir John. As the British built up their New Armies, they looked for other places for their deployment rather than facing the impasse in France, and also for theatres that would enhance their situation in the empire once the war had concluded. Despite the European war, imperial defence remained a primary British objective, and it was not by chance that the Dardanelles was the location of the first British foray outside of Europe. The initial plan, as George Cassar had shown, was not only to force the Straits but also to mount a military expedition from Alexandretta to Mosul to secure the oil wells and create a defensive zone against the Russians and the French in the post-war world. It was the French government, suspicious of British aims, that put a stop to the Alexandretta proposal.

The British diversion of forces intended for the Western Front, notably the 29th Division, to the Mediterranean led to a renewed conflict between Joffre and Sir John. Sir John was unwilling to relieve trenches held by the

French Tenth Army, and Joffre, without the freeing up of new forces, was unwilling to join what was intended as a joint attack. The result was that the British attacked alone at Neuve Chapelle on 10–13 March 1915. This marked the nadir of Anglo-French cooperation on the Western Front in 1915. British peripheral strategy had had, in this instance, a major repercussion on Sir John's relationship with Joffre.

However, the common enemy brought them back together, and a visit by Kitchener to France and a conference with Joffre and Sir John on the 29 March patched over the difference temporarily. Kitchener promised two territorial divisions to allow Sir John French to relieve the necessary trenches. British government intervention played a key role in resolving the dispute following the Neuve Chapelle low point.

Overly optimistic, Joffre, with an increment of manpower and more adequate munitions, was able to launch a big Allied offensive in Artois between 9 May and 25 June. Yet the Artois offensive was preceded by another irritation in Anglo-French command relations: John French was very unhappy with the French retreat north of Ypres on 22 April as a result of the German gas attack intended to mask the deployment of German troops to the east. He blamed the French retreat not on the gas attack but on the fact that Joffre had withdrawn major reinforcements from the theatre. Sir John was even more upset when the French made only a half-hearted attempt to regain the lost terrain and he had to retreat to straighten out his line north of Ypres. To assure British security in the north, he demanded that three French regular divisions be stationed in the region. Suspicions were much elevated at this juncture.

None of this, however, prevented him and Joffre from cooperating in the preparation and execution of the Artois offensive. Critical of Joffre's partial offensives in early 1915, the French government now favoured the larger Artois operation in order to buoy up public opinion. But, in the event, this offensive failed miserably, with huge losses to both the French and British armies. Military relations during the offensive soured as Sir John's participation fell short of French expectations.

The failed offensive had a decisive impact politically and in strategic planning in both countries. The ensuing Shells Crisis in Britain brought down Asquith's Liberal administration and led to the formation of a coalition government with Lloyd George as minister of munitions. Arthur Balfour, a prominent Unionist, replaced Churchill, who, as first lord of the Admiralty, was tarred with responsibility for the Dardanelles fiasco. And Sir John French nearly became "unstuck"; his firing in December was only a delayed reaction. The restructuring of the Imperial General Staff at the end of 1915 with Sir William Robertson at its head, as new research has shown, also proceeded from recommendations engendered by the failed offensive.

On the French side, Millerand was obliged to relinquish some of his powers to four under-secretaries, including Albert Thomas as under-secretary of munitions. Pressured by Poincaré, Joffre, who was criticized for being autocratic and not listening to his subordinates, was obliged to consult periodically with his army group commanders.

At the same time, Joffre became convinced that he could not win the war on the Western Front without massive British assistance and therefore demanded that twenty divisions of the British New Armies be dispatched to France in order to engage in yet bigger battles at two locations. In his bid to have these armies sent to France, his resistance to the Dardanelles campaign, and his proposal for major new offensives, Joffre had the support of Sir John French as the two banded together for the common cause. In this case, their joint resistance to British strategy was a key factor in their renewed cooperation.

Joffre's plan led to a major conflict between the French High Command and the British government. Kitchener, in a further strategic re-evaluation, regarded the Artois offensive as proof that breaking through the German trenches was impossible, and therefore, given the limited supply of British ammunition, he favoured a defensive-offensive stance on the Western Front until the British New Armies were fully equipped.

At this point, the larger aims of alliance policy intervened as the British received various bits of information that the French government and people were starting to wobble. Russia also was yielding rapidly to an Austro-Hungarian-German offensive on the Eastern Front after the Gorlice-Tarnów breakthrough. Therefore, in a strategic review at the end of June 1915, the British government decided to send the New Armies to France. The initial British imperial stance, with the priority it placed on defending the empire, could not be maintained because of the weakness of their continental allies, and therefore the British government was obliged to commit major forces to the Western Front. Only the nature of their employment was in doubt.

In a major conference, the first such Allied political-military meeting, that took place at Calais on 6 July 1915, the politicians of both countries agreed – even though French politicians advised prudence in the use of available forces and Kitchener urged a defensive-offensive strategy – to allow Joffre liberty of action for coming offensives. With the promise of six divisions of the British New Armies and the support of Sir John French, Joffre continued with his plan for a joint offensive at Loos and Arras and a larger French attack in Champagne.

Soon thereafter a conflict arose in the field as Sir John French, responding at least in part to his government's imperative to take a defensive-offensive posture, expressed his unhappiness, in line with Haig's concerns, over the heavily fortified terrain at Loos, scarred with slag heaps, that Joffre had given him for the big fall attack. This terrain, Sir John urged, was especially unsatisfactory in view of his lack of munitions.

But Kitchener again sided in August with Joffre to have Sir John participate to the fullest. The French government, according to information he had received, was in the midst of a ministerial crisis and Warsaw had fallen to the Germans at the end of August. There was a great need to prop up the continental allies. Thus, at the end of August, Kitchener obliged Sir John French to attack at Loos according to Joffre's requirements. He also approved a French plan for the partial subordination of Sir John French. Joffre would determine objectives and resources to be committed and set the date for future attacks. In short, the policy and strategy of the British government determined the outcome of the dispute.

Having promoted the spring offensive in Artois, the French cabinet resisted Joffre's Artois-Champagne offensive in the fall owing to lack of sufficient heavy artillery. After the Sarrail affair, the Viviani government, under pressure from the Chamber, favoured first a strengthened Dardanelles operation and then an expedition to Salonika to assist the Serbs. Given the dire state of the Russian front after the fall of Warsaw in August 1915, and with support from Kitchener who now supported the offensive, Joffre managed to withstand pressure from his government and to get his way with regard to the fall offensive.

An additional conflict developed over the deployment of French and British troops at Salonika to save the Serbs. The Serbs, following Bulgarian mobilization on 22 September, were attacked by the combined forces of Austria-Hungary, Germany, and Bulgaria. Six major conferences between the French and the British political and military leaders ensued in less than four weeks on the subject of an Allied expedition to Salonika, but with limited results. Joffre was willing to send only minimal forces and the British government, resistant to the Salonika expedition, had their eyes on defending Egypt in view of their withdrawal from the Dardanelles. Some British and French divisions from the Dardanelles and some French forces went to Salonika to aid the Serbs, but that, of course, was "too little, too late." The Serbian Army was ultimately forced over the mountains to Durrazo and was ultimately evacuated by Allied shipping and reinstalled in Corfu.

The British caused much consternation in the French government and at French headquarters when they diverted eight divisions from the Western Front to Egypt to ward off potential Turk attacks following the evacuations of the Dardanelles. The French were suspicious of British intentions in the Mediterranean and very unhappy about such a large diversion of troops from the Western Front. The field commanders, both French and British, were equally distraught by the diversion of troops from their front. There was, as a result, major jostling between Sir John and Joffre as to who was to take up which trenches as both moved to protect their interests. The strategies of the two governments were again responsible for renewed friction between the commanders in the field.

In sum, the policies and strategies of the two governments played a decisive role in determining most of the conflictual relationships between Sir John French and Joffre. They also played a dominant role in persuading the field commanders to coordinate their efforts in the quest for more troops for the Western Front and in their resistance to the Dardanelles and Salonika expeditions.

PREPARING FOR 1916

The lack of overall direction of the war sparked a new French initiative. In June 1915, following the Artois offensive and Italian entry into the conflict, Joffre and his staff were deeply concerned about the incoherence of Allied military effort. Reasoning that the French were best situated to coordinate the work of the Entente coalition, Joffre took the initiative by calling the first Allied military conference at Chantilly on 7 July 1915, which succeeded in planning coordinated fall offensives to assist the Russians.

The concept of Allied coordination was bolstered by Aristide Briand, who succeeded Viviani as prime minister at the end of October. While limiting Joffre's powers in a newly reconstituted Conseil supérieur de la Défense nationale, Briand appointed him commander-in-chief of all French armies, which would give him political capital with Sir John French in his endeavour to coordinate the actions of all the Allied armies for 1916.

Building on the success of his July initiative, Joffre followed up by calling a second Allied military conference at Chantilly on 6–8 December 1915, with military representatives from each of the Allied powers. Under Joffre's direction, the conference managed to hammer out a plan for a joint, coordinated attack on all fronts for 1916. Needless to say, Joffre was able to use demands from the Italian and Russian allies to put pressure on the British not to scuttle the Salonika expedition.

Joffre's initiative to coordinate the military actions of the Entente powers must be recognized as one of his greatest achievements. His failure to create an institutional structure in the form of an Allied supreme council, however, as suggested in his original proposal but not followed up on, meant that the conference system of coordinating Allied operations would last only as long as Joffre was in command of the French armies.

The incoherence of Allied policy in the Balkans in the last months of 1915 with regard to mounting the Salonika expedition was all too apparent. The dizzying round of Anglo-French conferences and the inability in these meetings to arrive at binding decisions clearly demonstrated the need for some sort of joint political body, with binding authority, to coordinate Anglo-French strategy. Early in the new year, a joint committee consisting of the two prime ministers, with other ministers to be added as needed, was set up with a permanent secretariat, but beyond providing for regular consultations, it proved largely ineffective. Still, in facing the challenges of 1915, the French and the British governments, despite a painfully slow and hesitant approach, must be given at least some credit in their efforts to devise appropriate agencies to deal with Allied coordination.

With a recently appointed cabinet under Briand, with Gallieni as war minister and Joffre as commander-in-chief of French armies, and with a revitalized Conseil supérieur handling political-military coordination, the French were better positioned for the conduct of the war in 1916. In the wake of the failed fall offensives, the British also made major changes. Sir John French, who had visible flaws in his leadership, was replaced as commander-in-chief of the British Expeditionary Force by Sir Douglas Haig, a sturdy warrior and devout westerner. At the same time, in light of the incoherence of Kitchener's strategic initiatives, Sir William Robertson was appointed chief of the Imperial General Staff, with effective control of British strategy. The appointment of the Robertson-Haig team assured that a western strategy would prevail in 1916 and that the bulk of British resources would be committed to the war in France.

In sum, Joffre played a dominant role in 1915 in his attempt to coordinate the Anglo-French alliance on the Western Front and the overall Entente coalition. Amid the swirl of competing military objectives and the incoherence of intergovernmental planning, he was an anchor of stability. In 1914 Joffre's main objective with regard to the British was to have them send a maximum of forces to France, and to have these make an unmitigated military effort under French strategic control. This continued in 1915, and despite the many conflicts in his relationship with Sir John French and Kitchener, he succeeded remarkably well in his endeavour to draw the British fully into the war on the Western Front. In his relationship with the British government, Joffre could always rely on the unstinted support of Millerand.

A republican general with no apparent political ambitions, Joffre showed an uncanny capacity to profit from the looseness of the coalition in winning support for his plans. Very shrewd politically, Joffre frequently managed to align in his favour three of the four main powerbrokers in major disputes. In squelching Sir John's coastal operation, he had the support of his own government and Kitchener. In his opposition to reinforcing the Dardanelles operation and the call for the dispatch of the New Armies to France, he had the support of Sir John French, the British commander, and the French government. In preparation for the fall offensive, after getting Kitchener's support for the action at Loos, he used the support of both Sir John and the Kitchener to pressure his own reluctant government to give the offensive its backing. But the chief motivation behind full British commitment to the continental war in the course of 1915 was not the strength either of French military leadership or of their army, but the perceived weakness of their French and Russian allies in what, militarily, was a very bad year for the Entente.

Projecting pre-war policy and practice, in the first two years of the war, Joffre, possessing an adroit appreciation of the international situation, worked hand in glove with his government in the conduct of what was perceived as a multi-front war, giving full support to the Russians and drawing in the British. Broadening the concept, in the Allied military conference at Chantilly in December 1915, he used the support of the Russian and Italians to thwart the British plan to withdraw from Salonika. The hope for the future lay in better coordination of the Entente coalition, and the further mobilization of men and resources.

MILITARY EFFECTIVENESS

Joffre's relationship with Sir John French was much less successful. The term "bittersweet" probably best describes it. While there were periods of unified action, relating to resistance to peripheral operations and the request for more and more British troops on the Western Front, their cooperation in joint planning and the execution of operations on the battlefield field had many ups and downs that detracted from the military effectiveness of their joint endeavours.

While the on-the-ground process of joint coordination between Foch and Wilson was generally beneficial, Foch's occasional dissimulation of his true intentions, as in the promise to retake lost French trenches at Ypres, sometimes backfired. Wilson, on the other hand, played a major role in smoothing over joint command relations after the Battle of Neuve Chapelle and on other occasions. Many of Sir John's initiatives to collaborate with Joffre in requests for British troops and resistance to the Dardanelles venture originated with Foch and Wilson. Recognizing, as he had in 1914, that British participation in the absence of a defined formula depended on goodwill, Joffre and members of his staff met periodically with Sir John French and his staff, both at Sir John's headquarters and at GQG. These meetings, along with joint political-military gatherings, helped to smooth over differences and reaffirm solidarity against the common enemy.

While the two chiefs showed considerable goodwill, even enthusiasm, in military planning, and made efforts to cooperate in joint operations, a sufficient level of trust in the relationship was never present for effective military cooperation and a number of issues remained unresolved. Not the least of these was the occupation of the trenches, a continual bone of contention. The question of having the British take up a more equitable length of trenches loomed large in 1915 and in subsequent years. Based on the deeply entrenched stereotype of the British as "slow and late" and unaggressive, the French command mischaracterized their ally as better suited for trench duty than offensive warfare – hence, the usual request before battles to have the British take over more of the trenches to free French troops for the offensive. The British command, on the other hand, much preferred fighting in the field to guarding the trenches. Sir John's resistance to repeated French demands to take over more of the trenches was a significant component of underlying conflict in the relationship.

While the British did not occupy their fair share of the trenches in 1915 proportionate to that of the French – never more than half as much, according to Joffre's reckoning – there were mitigating factors. As Robertson explained, these included delayed troop arrivals and the varying quality of troops, such as territorials and partially trained troops not ready for trench warfare. Given the lack of trust between the two commands, a major British concern as an independent force was to have an adequate reserve on hand in the event of a strong German attack. Another British objective was to have a sufficient reserve available in order to maintain their offensive capability. Although the British did not carry a proportionate length of trenches, their losses were very high in 1915, especially given the penury of British munitions. High British casualties in 1915, including heavy losses in the Second Battle of Ypres, would suggest that the British, especially when framed against their overall contribution to the war effort, may have carried a more or less equal share of the burden in 1915.[4]

After the battle of Neuve Chapelle, the two commands did show solidarity in attempting to coordinate their joint operations, but these operations tended to be ill-coordinated and lacking in overall directions, particularly when they became bogged down after the first attacks. The question of a unified command had much more appeal to the French as a means of resolving these issues than it did for the British, who, for a number of reasons, resisted its application. The advantages in establishing more effective planning and better integration of military efforts were all too apparent to Kitchener. But Kitchener was not inclined to tie his hands to French strategy on the Western Front in the spring and summer of 1915, a time when he was pursuing the Dardanelles offensive and disagreed with French offensive strategy in France. Sir John French resisted a unified command, in large part, to preserve the independence of his command.

To surrender the command of a national army, the ultimate symbol of national sovereignty, to another state, is an act of faith for which there was not sufficient trust in 1915. Joffre did get Kitchener to agree in August to a formula for partial subordination of Sir John to the French command, but there is reasonable doubt that Kitchener ever shared it with Sir John French or his government. In a nutshell, the British cherished their independence of action in 1915, as they had in 1914, and were not sufficiently trusting of the French to embrace fully the idea of a unified command.

The Russian theorist of coalition warfare, N.P. Mikhnevich, presented the "axiom that in armed coalitions actual military force is always less than the sum of component armies." One of the causes he identified was "diversity of aim."[5] This was certainly true with regard to the overall functioning of the Anglo-French coalition in 1915. While Anglo-French collaboration on the Western Front achieved a moderate level of success, it fell well below the level of military efficiency of a national force. It is doubtful, however, whether greater unity of action would have tipped the scales in 1915 in favour of Allied victory, given the strength of German trenches and German resistance.

There can be no doubt that in 1915, while the British mobilized and the Russians were beaten back, the French carried the main burden of the war. The traditional criticism that Joffre paid too high a price, while attacking with limited supplies of ammunition, may be mitigated by the realization that Joffre's repeated offensives, large and small, in 1915 were always geared toward aiding the Russians. Yet the loss of life was very heavy, so much so that, by the end of 1915, France had come to the limit of its manpower resources, with major consequences in Allied planning for the 1916 campaign season. French and British offensive actions in 1915 were sufficient, nonetheless, to relieve pressure on the beleaguered Russians and to redirect German attention to the Western Front in 1916.

PAST AND FUTURE

In retrospect, 1915 proved to be a less than satisfactory year for the Allies militarily, in which many of the stresses of differing policies were reflected in the conflict between the commanders-in-chief on the Western Front. Joffre and Sir John were always united with regard to the request for the dispatch of all available troops to the front and their opposition to the Dardanelles enterprise and the launching of the Salonika expedition in September. While they almost always engaged in a tug-of-war over their respective occupation of trenches, they were generally able to manage at least a modicum of cooperation in the planning and conduct of operations. Their greatest quarrels arose when the peripheral strategy of the British government conflicted with the Western Front strategy of the French field commander. In most instances, their relationships reflected the strategic decisions of their respective governments.

At the end of 1915, with Sir Douglas Haig as commander-in-chief of the British Expeditionary Force and Sir William Robertson as chief of the Imperial General Staff, both of whom were committed westerners, the path for the next year was clear. The British government, having both sent its New Armies to France and engaged them at Loos, now found itself committed to the Western Front strategy of the new leaders. Under Joffre's direction, the Allied military conference at Chantilly in December put in place a plan for a joint, coordinated attack on all fronts for 1916. The year closed on a positive note as the Allies moved toward a more focused and coordinated prosecution of the war effort.

The stage was thus set for a new kind of war in 1916, that of attrition warfare, which included the great bloodletting battles of Verdun and the Somme, the magnitude of which still boggles the mind. While the French, in fact, suffered heavier losses in 1914 than they would at Verdun, the huge British losses on the Somme, with nearly 50,000 casualties on the first day, was a new experience for the British and left a mark on the national psyche that endures to this day. The tangled and painful experiences of 1915 in Anglo-French military and political relations are the vital link between the high expectations of 1914 and the slogging match and attritional warfare of 1916. The path to that outcome was a tortuous one, and the consequent losses excessively high, but no one could yet come up with a better alternative.

NOTES

PREFACE

1 See, for example, Stevenson, *Cataclysm*; Strachan, *First World War*; Doughty, *Pyrrhic Victory*; Greenhalgh, *Victory through Coalition* and *Foch in Command*; Foley, *German Strategy*; Goya, *La chair et l'acier*; Cassar, *Kitchener's War*; French, *Strategy of the Lloyd George Coalition*; Cassar, *Lloyd George at War*; McCrae, *Coalition Strategy*.

2 Saboul, "Editorial," 1–2; Bell, *Churchill and the Dardanelles*; Greenhalgh, *French Army*; Porte, *Joffre*.

3 See "Centenary News First World War Books" at www.centenarynews.com/allbooks (consulted 3 September 2019).

4 See Gardner, *Trial by Fire*; Herwig, *The Marne*.

5 Greenfield, *Baptism of Fire*; Cassar, *Hell in Flanders Fields* and *Trial by Gas*; Christie, *The Canadians in the Second Battle of Ypres*.

6 Krause, *Early Trench Tactics in the French Army*.

7 Lloyd, *Loos, 1915*; Cherry, *Most Unfavourable Ground*; Corrigan, *Loos 1915*.

8 Sheldon, *The German Army on the Somme*; Gilbert, *The Somme*; Prior and Wilson, *The Somme*; Philpott, *The Sacrifice of the Somme* and *Three Armies on the Somme*; Hart, *The Somme*.

9 Sheffield and Bourne, *Haig: War Diaries and Letters*; Reid, *Architect of Victory*; Harris, *Douglas Haig and the First World War*; Sheffield, *The Chief* and *Douglas Haig*; Ryan, *The Chief*.

10 See Greenhalgh, *Foch in Command* and *French Army*; Doughty, *Pyrrhic Victory*.

11 For example, Hart, *The Somme*; St Clair, *The Road to St. Julien*, supplementing earlier works, such as Macdonald, *1915*.

12 See these standard works: Philpott, *Anglo-French Relations and Strategy on the Western Front*; Greenhalgh, *Victory through Coalition*.

13 Doughty, *Pyrrhic Victory*, 2.

14 See Neilson, *Strategy and Supply*, viii–ix, 305–11, and *Britain and the Last Tsar*, xi–xiv, 371.

15 See Travers, *Killing Ground*.

16 On comparative troop strengths of belligerents in August 1914, see Royde-Smith and Showalter, "World War I, 1914–1918" (last updated 1 November 2019), "Forces and Resources of Combatant Nations in 1914," www.britannica.com/event/World-War-I/Forces-and-resources-of-the-combatant-nations-in-1914. Against the 198 divisions of the Entente coalition, the Central Powers fielded 146 divisions, 98 by Germany and 48 by Austria, but had the obvious advantage of interior lines of communication (ibid.). For the expansion of British forces and British contribution to the 1914 campaign, see Prete, *Strategy and Command, 1914*, 74–183, 196–200.

17 See Philpott, "Kitchener and the 29th Division," 375–407.

18 Cf. Prete, "Le conflit stratégique franco-britannique," 17–49.

19 Wallach, *Uneasy Coalition*.

20 See Philpott, *Anglo-French Relations and Strategy on the Western Front*.

21 See Prete, *Strategy and Command, 1914*, xv.

22 For a fuller treatment, see ibid., 74–183.

23 *Department of Defense Dictionary of Military and Associated Terms* (August 2017 edition), www.jcs.mil/Portals/36/Documents/Doctrine/pubs/dictionary/pdf; also, Joint Publications 3–0, www.jcs.mil/Portals/36/Documents/Doctrine/pubs/jp3_0_ 20170117.pdf (brought to my attention by Brigid Dooley-Tremblay).

CHAPTER ONE

1 Quotations: Hackett, *Profession of Arms*, 49–50. For the best recent histories of the First World War, see Strachan, *The First World War*; Stevenson, *Cataclysm*; Beckett, *The Great War*. Cruttwell, *The Great War*, though older, is still useful on operations.

2 See treatment in Prete, *Strategy and Command, 1914*, 3–43.

3 Doughty, *Pyrrhic Victory*, 2–3; Prete, *Strategy and Command, 1914*, 3–12.

4 Prete, *Strategy and Command, 1914*, 9–10.

5 Ibid., 3–8.

6 For a detailed treatment of the development of the Entente Cordiale after 1904, see Williamson, *Politics of Grand Strategy*.

7 Prete, *Strategy and Command, 1914*, 9, 11–12.

8 Ibid., 5–8. For illuminating insight on Joffre's relationship with the politicians, see Varillon, *Joffre*, 357–420. Varillon, alone, has had access to Joffre's private papers.

9 Doughty, *Pyrrhic Victory*, 2–3. For an overview of French military relations with their allies under Joffre, see Joffre, *Mémoires*, 2 vols.; Desmazes, *Joffre*.
10 For the relationship between Millerand and Joffre, see Farrar, *Principled Pragmatist*, 15–92.
11 Lloyd George, *War Memoirs*, 1:66–7; Wilson, *The Myriad Faces of War*, 28–31.
12 Joffre, *Mémoires*, passim.
13 See ibid., 1:352, 482–3.
14 See Prete, "War of Movement," 130–8; Prete, "French Strategic Planning," 42–62.
15 Prete, "War of Movement," 502–6.
16 See French, *British Strategy and War Aims*, 1–19; Otte, "'A Fair Equilibrium?'"
17 See Howard, *The Continental Commitment*; Kennedy, *The Rise of the Anglo-German Antagonism, 1860–1924*.
18 For a critique, see Donald M. Schurman, Keynote Address, Military History Symposium, Royal Military College of Canada, Kingston, ON, 24 March 1994; for a reappraisal, see Neilson, *Britain and the Last Tsar*.
19 Williamson, *Politics of Grand Strategy*, 227–99.
20 Philpott, "British Military Strategy on the Western Front," 1–77.
21 French, *British Strategy and War Aims*, 20–8.
22 Philpott, "British Military Strategy," 1–161 and passim.
23 Great Britain, Historical Section of the Committee of Imperial Defence, *HGW* (1914*)*, vol. 1, appendix 8, 498–500.
24 French, *British Strategy and War Aims*, 25.
25 Prete, "The War of Movement," 248–55, 271, 368–9, 449–53.
26 See Neilson and Prete, eds., *Coalition Warfare*; Colloque, *Forces armées et systèmes d'alliances*, 3 vols. For a classic appraisal, see Craig, *Problems of Coalition Warfare*.
27 See Greenhalgh, *Victory through Coalition*, 281–5.
28 McCrae, *Coalition Strategy*.
29 Kennedy, "Military Coalitions," in Prete and Neilson, eds., *Coalition Warfare*, 3.
30 As cited in "Lord Palmerston Quotes," at www.thinkexist.com/quotes/lord_palmerston/ (consulted 28 November 2011).
31 See chapter 3.
32 See Albrecht-Carrié, *A Diplomatic History of Europe*, 334–9. For an in-depth study, see Nevakivi, *Britain, France and the Arab Middle East, 1914–1920*.
33 Erickson, "*Koalitsionnaya Voina*: Coalition Warfare in Soviet Miltary Theory, Planning, and Performance," in Neilson and Prete, eds., *Coalition Warfare*, 88.
34 Prete, "French Strategic Planning," 42–62.
35 For a fuller treatment, see Prete, "War of Movement," 144–324.
36 Philpott, *Anglo-French Relations and Strategy on the Western Front, 1914–1918*, 1–14. See also Philpott, "The Strategic Ideas of Sir John French," 458–78.
37 Philpott, *Anglo-French Relations and Strategy on the Western Front, 1914–1918*, 31–50.

38 Philpott, "British Military Strategy," 115–61.

39 For a fuller treatment, see Prete, *Strategy and Command, 1914*, 149–83.

40 Prete, "The Anglo-French Command Crisis of October–November 1914," 112–26.

41 Prete, *Strategy and Command, 1914*, 176.

42 Keiger, *Poincaré*, 187–90; Prete, *Strategy and Command, 1914*, 48; Godfrey, *Capitalism at War*, 44–6.

43 Messimy, *Souvenirs*, 231–3; King, *Generals and Politicians*, 15–16.

44 Keiger, *Poincaré*, 205–6.

45 Ibid., 164–90.

46 See Wright, *Raymond Poincaré and the French Presidency*, 1–6ff.; Keiger, *Poincaré*, 122, 146, 150–2; also, ibid., 201–2, for Poincaré's guidance of the Viviani ministry despite his frustration with the limitations of his office.

47 Prete, *Strategy and Command, 1914*, 51–2.

48 Paul Cambon to Delcassé, 27 August 1914, Delcassé Papers, AE, vol. 3, 326–38.

49 For Poincaré's role in the pre-war crisis and as wartime leader, see Keiger, *Poincaré*, 163–239.

50 See ibid., 204–21; Wright, *Raymond Poincaré and the French Presidency*, 142–59.

51 See Godfrey, *Capitalism at War*, 44–52; Joffre, *Mémoires*, 1:429–30.

52 See King, *Generals and Politicians*, 34–191.

53 Poincaré, Notes Journalières, XXXIX, BN, NAF (16030), 27 April, 25, 27, 29 May, 20 June 1915; Prete, "Le conflit stratégique franco-britannique," 25–6.

54 See Greenhalgh, *Foch*, 45–7, 51ff.; Prete, *Strategy and Command, 1914*, 150–4.

55 See Greenhalgh, *Foch*, 46–90; Prete, *Strategy and Command, 1914*, 151–83.

56 Prete, *Strategy and Command, 1914*, 189–92.

57 Rocolle, *L'hécatombe*, 262; Doughty, *Pyrrhic Victory*, 59–60, 85, 110–11.

58 Greenhalgh, *The French Army*, 72.

59 Greenhalgh, *Foch*, 121.

60 Berthelot, *Diary*, 1:232, 244–5, 16, 22, 24 November 1914. "Sidney Clive up & tells me Gen: Berthelot (the Fat Boy) has been 'dégommé'd,'" wrote Wilson, with wry humour (Wilson Diaries, V, IWM, DS/Misc/80, 24 November 1914). For a full discussion, see Torrey, *Berthelot*, 74–81.

61 Pichot-Duclos, *Réflexions*, 189, 193; Gamelin, *Manoeuvre*, 92–3, 62–6, 106–7, 181–4; Joffre, *Mémoires*, 1:239–40, 379–86.

62 Berthelot, *Diary*, 1:235, 17 November 1914; note from Field Marshal French to Foch, 16 November 1914, France, Ministère de Guerre, *AFGG*, II A(I), no. 132; no. 835, Foch to GQG, 16 November 1914, *AFGG*, II A(I), no. 131.

63 Prete, *Strategy and Command, 1914*, 41, 189.

64 Ibid., 40–2.

65 French, *British Strategy and War Aims*, 9–10.

66 Clive Diaries, II/I, LHMA, 27 November 1914; see *AFGG*, X (1), 5; cf. "Memorandum [of the 3rd Bureau] on the Subject of Relieving the VIIIth Army by the English Army," 21 December 1914, *AFGG*, II A(I), no. 426.

67 See Prete, "Coalition Warfare," 497–8.

68 On the 1917 crisis, see Guinn, *British Strategy and Politics*, 211–12; King, *Generals and Politicians*, 143–4. For a sample of the conflict in 1915, see no. 6365, Joffre to French, 19 February 1915, *AFGG*, II A(II), no. 927; Memorandum OA613, French to Joffre, 23 February 1915, *AFGG*, II A(I), no. 979; CT no. 2395, Joffre to Foch, 7 March 1915, *AFGG*, III A(I), no. 16. Haig, *Private Papers*, 129–34ff., points out similar difficulties prior to the Battle of the Somme.

69 Hankey, *The Supreme Command*, 1:233.

70 See Cassar, *Kitchener*, 259–60; Hankey, *The Supreme Command*, 1:223–33, 237; K.G. Robbins, "Foreign Policy, Government Structure and Public Opinion," in Hinsley, ed., *British Foreign Policy under Sir Edward Grey*, 533–54.

71 Guinn, *British Strategy and Politics*, 34, 42; Hankey, *The Supreme Command*, 1:237–55; Cassar, *Kitchener*, 259–60ff.; Asquith, *Memories and Reflections*, 2:64–75ff. For a critique of the War Cabinet, see Taylor, *English History*, 74–7.

72 Weygand described Murray as "negation made man" (Weygand, *Mémoires*, 1:303; cf. Joffre, *Mémoires*, 1:422).

73 For a full account, see Prete, *Strategy and Command, 1914*, 189–96.

74 Ibid., 35–6, 191–2.

75 Clive Diaries, II/I, LHMA, 21 January 1915.

76 Millerand, handwritten notes of his trip to London, 22 January 1915 (also in typescript), Millerand Papers, AN, 470AP15. On 10 January 1915 Asquith noted in his diary that he thought both Kitchener and Churchill "agree to advise French to take Haig in place of Murray" (Asquith, *Memories and Reflections*, 2:65).

77 French to Kitchener, 23 January 1915, Kitchener Papers, NA, 30 57/50 WA/70; Lambton to Kitchener, 25 January 1915, Kitchener Papers, NA, 30 57/50 WA/71.

78 French to Kitchener, 25 January 1915, Kitchener Papers, NA, 30 57/50 WA/72. Nine months later, however, when Kitchener enquired about the possibility of Murray's assuming a command in France, Sir John was of the opinion (as he would be at a later date) that "his health would not stand the strain." Murray to Kitchener, 12 July 1915, Kitchener to French, 14 September 1915, French to Kitchener, 14 September 1915, Kitchener Papers, NA, 30 57/50 WA/10, 123, 126; cf. French, *1914*, 108, who cites the breakdown of Murray's health as the sole reason for his recall.

79 Asquith, *Memories and Reflections*, 2:69 (diary entry of 26 January [1915]); Haig, *Private Papers*, 26 January [1915], 85.

80 Joffre, *Mémoires*, 1:422.

81 Foch to Joffre, 26 January 1915, Correspondance Foch (10 octobre 1914–21 janvier 1916), AG, no. 30.

82 Haig, *Private Papers*, 31 January [1915], 85; *HGW* (1915), 1:363. Clark, *The Donkeys*, 31, erroneously claims that Wilson retained his position as subchief of the General Staff.

83 Foch to Joffre, 26 January 1915, Correspondance Foch, AG, no. 30.

84 Haig, *Private Papers*, 26 January [1915], 85.
85 See Wilson Diaries, V, IWM, DS/Misc/80, 20, 21 February 1915; Clark, *The Donkeys*, 32.
86 See DeWeerd, "Churchill, Lloyd George, Clemenceau," in Earle, ed., *Makers of Modern Strategy*, 298–9.
87 Clive Diaries, II/I, LHMA, 31 January, 8 February 1915.
88 See Clark, *The Donkeys*, 31.
89 Ibid. See Wilson Diaries, VI, IWM, DS/Misc/80, 1915, passim.
90 There is no indication in the documents of Joffre having been involved in the events leading to Sir John's recall at the end of 1915.

CHAPTER TWO

1 See French, *British Strategy and War Aims* and *Strategy of the Lloyd George Coalition*; Neilson, *Strategy and Supply*; Burk, *Britain, America, and the Sinews of War*; Greenhalgh, *Victory through Coalition*.
2 See King, *Generals and Politicians*, 34–5, 41–2, 67–8ff.; also, Poincaré, *Au service*, 6:18–19.
3 See Hankey, *The Supreme Command*, 1:242–3, and Trumpener, *Germany and the Ottoman Empire*, 21–60, for the circumstances surrounding Turkish entry into the war. The Turks had already closed the Straits in September, following the arrival of the *Goeben* and *Breslau*.
4 Lowe and Dockrill, *The Mirage of Power*, 2:185–6.
5 Asquith, *Memories and Reflections*, 2:58, 28 November 1914; Lowe and Dockrill, *Mirage of Power*, 2:183–6; Guinn, *British Strategy and Politics*, 44.
6 Guinn, *British Strategy and Politics*, 44.
7 Doughty, *Pyrrhic Victory*, 116–20. See Godfrey, *Capitalism at War*, for an assessment covering the entire war.
8 Doughty, *Pyrrhic Victory*, 115.
9 Foch to Joffre, 19 November 1914, Correspondance Foch, AG, no. 11. For an English translation, see Foch, *Memoirs*, 80–3. Foch expected the Germans to withdraw to a more defensible line.
10 Weygand, *Mémoires*, 1:209.
11 Foch to Joffre, 19 November 1914, Correspondance Foch, AG, no. 11.
12 Falkenhayn, *General Headquarters*, 34–5. For an account of the campaign in Poland, see Stone, *Eastern Front*, 92–121.
13 Berthelot, *Diary*, 1:20, 21, 22 November 1914, 238–9; Joffre to Foch, 20 November 1914, *AFGG*, II A(I), no. 167; Foch to Joffre, 20 November 1914, *AFGG*, II A(I), no. 168.
14 French to Kitchener, 1, 3 December 1914, Kitchener Papers, NA, 30 57/49 WA/51–2.
15 Wilson Diaries, V, IWM, DS/Misc/80, 7 December 1914; cf. CT, 1530, Joffre to Foch, 7 December 1914, *AFGG*, II A(II), no. 266; *AFGG*, II, 243; Yarde-Buller to Kitchener, 10 December 1914, Kitchener Papers, NA, WO/159/9.

16 No. 1725, Instruction générale no. 8 pour les généraux commandant les armées, 8 December 1915, AFGG, II A(I), no. 280.

17 Doughty, *Pyrrhic Victory*, 112–14. The quotation (on 112) is from a report by Sir John French to the British War Council on 13 January 1915 (Secretary's Notes of a Meeting of the War Council, January 1915, 7, PRO CAB 42/1/16). See also, Greenhalgh, *French Army*, 71–2.

18 See Ferro, *Great War*, 63; cf. Joffre, *Mémoires*, 2:1–2.

19 Doughty, *Pyrrhic Victory*, 113.

20 Ibid., 108–9; Cassar, *The French and the Dardanelles*, 35–6.

21 Poincaré, Notes Journalières, XXXVIII, BN, NAF (16029), 1 January 1915. See above for a fuller account of the French political-military situation in early 1915.

22 Lloyd George, *War Memoirs*, 1:219–29.

23 Poincaré, *Au service*, 6:7–8; King, *Generals and Politicians*, 41.

24 Poincaré, Notes Journalières, XXXVIII, BN, NAF (16029), 9 January 1915; Poincaré, *Au service*, 6:8–10. According to Herbillon, Joffre threatened to resign rather than countenance a diversion. (Herbillon, *Souvenirs*, 1, 9 January 1915.)

25 Joffre, *Mémoires*, 2:70.

26 William Philpot, "The Strategic Ideas of Sir John French," 458–77.

27 See above; also, French, *1914*, 303.

28 Churchill to French, 22 November 1914, French Papers, IWM, 75/46/11; French, *1914*, 303–5.

29 French Diaries, G, IWM, 75/46/2, 5, 7 December 1914; Wilson Diaries, V, IWM, DS/Misc/80, 8, 10 December 1914; French, *1914*, 305; cf. Cassar, *Kitchener*, 261; Philpott, *Anglo-French Relations and Strategy on the Western Front*, 53–4.

30 Churchill to French, 8 December 1914, French Papers, IWM, 75/46/11; Kitchener to French, 9 [December 1914], French Papers, IWM, 75/46/11; Wilson Diaries, V, IWM, DS/Misc/80, 10 December 1914.

31 Churchill to French, 8 December 1914; French Papers, IWM, 75/46/11.

32 No. 2128/g, War [Ministry] to General Commander-in-Chief, 9 December 1914, AG, Fonds Buat, Ordres généraux du GQG, December 1914; reproduced in AFGG, II(A), no. 291.

33 David French, *British Strategy and War Aims*, 24–5.

34 Esher, *Journals and Letters*, 3:58, 6 September 1911; cf. Magnus, *Kitchener*, 279.

35 Cassar, *Kitchener*, 256–7.

36 Qtd. in Keith Neilson, "Kitchener: A Reputation Refurbished?" 208.

37 Poincaré, Notes Journalières, XXXVI, BN, NAF (16028), 1 November 1914, 142.

38 French to Kitchener, 1, 3 December 1914, Kitchener Papers, NA, 30 57/49 WA/51–2.

39 Wilson Diaries, V, IWM, DS/Misc/80, 7–10 December 1914; French Diaries, G, IWM, 75/46/2, 10 December 1914.

40 French Diaries, G, IWM, 75/46/2, 8 December 1914; Wilson Diaries, V, IWM, DS/Misc/80, 8 December 1914.

41 Wilson Diaries, V, IWM, DS/Misc/80, 8 December 1914.

42 Churchill to French, 13 December 1914, French Papers, IWM, 75/46/11.

43 See Wilson Diaries, V, IWM, DS/Misc/80, 7–17 December 1914; French Diaries, G, IWM, 75/46/11, 8, 15, 17, 18 December 1914.

44 No. 2234, Commander-in-Chief to Minister of War, Bordeaux, 10 December 1914, Fond Buat, AG, GN7, dossier [hereafter dos.] Ordres généraux du GQG, December 1914, printed in *AFGG*, II A(I), no. 303.

45 No. 2128/9, CT War to Commander-in-Chief, 9 December 1914, *AFGG*, II A(I), no. 291.

46 Foch to Joffre, 10 December 1914, Correspondance Foch, AG, nos. 13, 14; cf. Wilson Diaries, V, IWM, DS/Misc/80, 11 December 1914.

47 No. 4838, Commander-in-Chief to Foch, 19 December 1914, *AFGG*, II A(I), no. 406.

48 No. 5499, Commander-in-Chief to Foch, 21 December 1914, and "Note relative to the Relief of the VIIIth Army by the English Army," 21 December 1914, *AFGG*, II A(I), no. 462.

49 Ibid.

50 CT no. 1014, Foreign Minister to French Ambassador, London, 21 December 1914, AE, "Guerre 1914–1918," no. 534, 176.

51 Bertie to Grey, 26 December 1914, NA, WO/800/166, no. 108.

52 Foch wrote a personal letter to Joffre once or twice a week, sometimes daily, occasionally two or more in a day. See Correspondance Foch, AG, many letters of which have been reproduced in *AFGG*.

53 See reference to his communications, CT no. 68, Cambon to Foreign Minister, 14 January 1915, AG, "Guerre 1914–1918," no. 535, 19.

54 Poincaré, Notes Journalieres, XXXVIII, BN, NAF (16029), 22 February 1915.

55 CT no. 3373, Commander-in-Chief to the Military Mission, at Saint-Omer, 11 January 1915, AG, 16N1676, "Ordres et Instructions relatifs aux Opérations," dos. 25, doc. 2319, reproduced in *AFGG*, II A(I), no. 588; no. 3123, Commander-in-Chief to Minister of War, 12 January 1915, AE, "Guerre 1914–1918," 535, 18.

56 Poincaré, Notes Journalières, XXXVIII, BN, NAF (16029), 12 January 1915.

57 Kitchener to French, 11 December 1914, and attached letter, Kitchener to Churchill, 10 December 1914, French Papers, IWM, 75/46/11.

58 Churchill to Sir J. French, 10 December 1914, French Papers, IWM, 75/46/11, and attached letter, B.B. Corbett, Military Secretary of the Admiralty, 3 December 1914, French Papers, IWM, 75/46/11.

59 Churchill to Asquith, 2 January 1915, Asquith Papers, 14, Bodleian Library, Oxford.

60 Asquith to Kitchener, 18 December 1914, Asquith Papers, 13/237–8, Bodleian Library, Oxford; Cassar, *Kitchener*, 261–2.

61 Wilson Diaries, V, IWM, DS/Misc/80, 19 December 1914; Kitchener to French, 18 December 1914, French Papers, IWM, 75/46/11.

62 Asquith to Churchill, 18 December 1914, Asquith Papers, 13/237–8, Bodleian Library, Oxford.

63 Asquith, *Memories and Reflections*, 2:61; Cassar, *Kitchener*, 62–3.
64 See Churchill to French, 8, 9, 11 January 1915, French Papers, IWM, 75/46/11.
65 Neilson, "Kitchener: A Reputation Refurbished?" 210.
66 Kitchener to French, 18 [December 1914], French Papers, IWM, 75/46/11.
67 Asquith, *Memories and Reflections*, 2:59–60.
68 Ibid.
69 Wilson Diaries, V, IWM, DS/Misc/80, 25 December 1914.
70 Letter no. 57, Huguet to Joffre, 25 December 1914, *AFGG*, II A(I), no. 461.
71 French Diaries, G, IWM, 75/46/2, 27 December 1914.
72 CT no. 2574, Kitchener to French, 26 December 1914, French Papers, IWM, 75/46/6.
73 French Diaries, G, IWM, 75/46/2, 27 December 1914. Note given by Joffre to French, 27 December 1914, *AFGG*, II A(I), no. 480; French to Kitchener, 28 December 1914, Wilson's Notes on "Meeting of Field Marshal and General Joffre at Chantilly, 27.12:14," French Papers, IWM, 75/46/5.
74 Cf. French Diaries, G, IWM, 75/46/2, 18 December 1914.
75 Ibid., 27 December 1914.
76 Dispatch no. 7003, Commander-in-Chief to Foch, 28 December 1914, *AFGG*, II A(I), no. 492.
77 French, *1914*, 331.
78 Wilson Diaries, V, IWM, DS/Misc/80, 28 December 1914.
79 Ibid., 29 December 1914.
80 French Diaries, G, IWM, 75/46/2, 31 December 1914; cf. French, *1914*, 344–5.
81 Kitchener to French, 29 [December 1914], Murray Papers, NA, WO 7963.
82 Wilson Diaries, V, IWM, DS/Misc/80, 31 December 1914.
83 French Diaries, G, IWM, 75/46/2, 2 January 1915.
84 Ibid.; Wilson Diaries, VI, IWM, DS/Misc/80, 2 January 1915.
85 See above.
86 See Cassar, *Kitchener*, 264–5.
87 French, *1914*, 33.
88 Kitchener to French, 29 [December 1914], Murray Papers, NA, WO 79/63.
89 Kitchener to French, 2 January 1915, Murray Papers, NA, WO 79/63.
90 French Diaries, G, IWM, 75/46/2, 2 January 1915; Wilson Diaries, VI, IWM, DS/Misc/80, 2 January 1915.
91 See French to Asquith, 4 January 1914, Asquith Papers, 26/206–7, Bodleian Library, Oxford; French Diaries, G, IWM, 7546/2, 2 January 1915.
92 Kitchener to French, 6 January 1915, French Papers, IWM, 75/46/11.
93 French to Kitchener, 8 January 1915, French Papers, IWM, 75/46/11.
94 Churchill to French, 1 January 1915, French Papers, IWM, 75/46/11.
95 See Memorandum, Churchill to Asquith, 29 December 1914, in Gilbert, *Churchill*, vol. 3, *Companion*, 1:343; cf. Asquith, *Memories and Reflections*, 2:62–3 (29, 31 December [1914]).

96 See French, *British Strategy and War Aims*, 1–29, 52.
97 Neilson, "Kitchener: A Reputation Refurbished?" 211–12.
98 See Cassar, *Kitchener*, 268; Guinn, *British Strategy and Politics*, 44–5; Cruttwell, *The Great War*, 32–3.
99 Lowe and Dockrill, *Mirage of Power*, 2:xii.
100 Asquith, *Memories and Reflections*, 2:61–2 (diary, 29 December [1914]); see also Lieutenant-Colonel Hankey, Memorandum, 29 December 1914; Winston S. Churchill to H.H. Asquith, 29 December 1914, in Gilbert, *Churchill*, vol. 3, *Companion*, 1:337–45.
101 Churchill to Asquith, 29 December 1914, Asquith Papers, 13/242–3, Bodleian Library, Oxford.
102 Cassar, *Kitchener*, 260; Churchill to Asquith, 29 December 1914, Asquith Papers, 13/242–3, Bodleian Library, Oxford.
103 Bell, *Churchill and the Dardanelles*, 118–19, 150.
104 Asquith, *Memories and Reflections*, 2:62 (29 December [1914]).
105 Ibid., 64 (1 January [1915]); David Lloyd George, Memorandum, 31 December 1914, in Gilbert, *Churchill*, vol. 3, *Companion*, 1:350–6.
106 Asquith, *Memories and Reflections*, 2:62, 64 (29, 31 December [1914], 1 January [1915]).
107 Cassar, *Kitchener*, 268.
108 Kitchener to French, 2 January 1915, Kitchener Papers, NA, 30 57/50, WA/64.
109 [Memorandum, 3 January 1915], Sir John French to Kitchener, Kitchener Papers, NA, 30 57/50.
110 Asquith, *Memories and Reflections*, 2:57.
111 Churchill to French, 8 January 1915, French Papers, IWM, 75/46/11; also, Kitchener to French, 9 January 1915, French Papers, IWM, 75/46/11.
112 Churchill to French, 8 January 1915, French Papers, IWM, 75/46/11.
113 Churchill to French, 1, 11 January 1915, French Papers, IWM, 75/46/11; CT no. 2632, Kitchener to French, 2 January 1915, French Papers, IWM, 75/46/6.
114 Kitchener to French, 9 January 1915, French Papers, IWM, 75/46/11.
115 Kitchener to French, 7 January 1914, French Papers, IWM, 75/46/11.
116 Asquith to French, 8 January 1915, IWM, French Papers, 75/46/11; cf. Churchill to French, 5 January 1915, French Papers, IWM, 75/46/11.
117 Wilson Diaries, VI, IWM, DS/Misc/80, 13 January 1915, in conversation with Lansdowne, a member of the Opposition, who already knew of the conflict. Sir Francis Bertie, the British ambassador in Paris, wrote to Sir John on 13 January decrying "interference with the man on the spot by those who think that they know everything better than he" (French Papers, IWM, 75/46/11). Walter Long, another prominent Conservative, wrote to Sir John's secretary, Brimsley Fitzgerald, on 4 January 1915 reaffirming his support for Sir John. "There is nothing which we will not do, in or out of Parliament, to secure the removal of any

obstacle which may exist to his unfettered control of the campaign," he vowed. (B. Fitzgerald Papers, IWM, PP/MCR/118.)

118 French Diaries, H, IWM, 75/46/2, 13 January 1915; Cassar, *Kitchener*, 276–7. On 11 January, Churchill wrote to Sir John: "I favour remaining in the Northern theatre [in France], but endeavoring, as our numbers & resources increase, to lengthen the German line & compel him to expose new surfaces to the waste of war." Churchill thus favoured an attack on the Island of Borkum in March or April, to be followed by the offer to Holland of 700,000–800,000 men to induce it to join the Allies. "One of the reasons I favour the coast operation [in Belgium] is that it is a step in the direction of Holland, & that every yard of Belgian soil cleared shows the Dutch that England never deserts her friends." (French Papers, IWM, 75/46/11.) Churchill could never be faulted for lack of imagination!

119 CT no. 404–NO93, Cambon to Foreign Affairs (from the military attaché for the minister of war), 18 January 1915, *AFGG*, II A(I), no. 662.

120 Wilson Diaries, VI, IWM, DS/Misc/80, 17 January 1915; see also Cassar, *Kitchener*, 276.

CHAPTER THREE

1 Neilson, "Kitchener: A Reputation Refurbished?" 214; Cassar, *Dardanelles*, 46–7; Cassar, *Kitchener*, 276–7.

2 "Observations sur l'Appréciation Anglaise des Forces Allemandes," 7 January 1915, AG, 16N1675, dos. 25, doc. 2286 bis.

3 French Diaries, H, IWM, 75/46/2, 17 January 1915.

4 Wilson Diaries, VI, IWM, DS/Misc/80, 17 January 1915; French Diaries, H, IWM, 75/46/2, 17 January 1915.

5 General Commanding-in Chief to Field Marshal French, 19 January 1915, French Papers, IWM, 75/46/5.

6 French Diaries, H, IWM, 75/46/2, qtd. in Gerald French, ed., *War Diaries*, 74.

7 No. 63H, Huguet to General-in-Chief, 19 January 1915, *AFGG*, II A(I), no. 678.

8 French to Joffre, [20 January 1915], *AFGG*, II A(I), no. 692; Wilson Diaries, V, IWM, DS/Misc/80, 20 January 1915.

9 French Diaries, IWM, PP/MCR/C32, reel 2, 20 January 1915.

10 Ibid., 20, 23 January 1915.

11 Ibid.

12 Agreement between Joffre and French, 21 January 1915, *AFGG*, II A(I), no. 702; Wilson Diaries, VI, IWM, DS/Misc/80, 21 January 1915.

13 French Diaries, IWM, PP/MCR/C32, reel 2, 22, 23 January 1915.

14 French to Kitchener, 23 January 1915, Kitchener Papers, NA, 30 51/50.

15 CT no. 8, Cambon to Foreign Minister, 14 January 1915, AE, "Guerre 1914–1918," no. 535, p. 19.

16 CT no. 74, Cambon to Foreign Minister, 15 January 1915, ibid., 20.

17 See no. 5442, "Note for the Minister," 17 January 1915, signed by Pont, head of the Third Bureau, *AFGG*, II A(I), no. 650; Herbillon, *Souvenirs*, 1:95–6, 17, 18 January; also, no. 5869, "Note for the Minister," 20 January 1915, *AFGG*, II A(I), no. 690, in which Joffre requests the two territorial divisions earlier turned down by Sir John in favour of twenty-four battalions.

18 Millerand, handwritten notes of his trip to London, 22 January 1915 (also in typescript), Millerand Papers, AN, 470AP15.

19 "E. [Esher], Jan. 22/15," Kitchener Papers, NA, 30 57/57. The document begins, "Lord K told me …" Esher had, in fact, told Kitchener informally of Joffre's objection to the coastal operation in a previous interview. (Ibid.)

20 "E. [Esher], Jan. 22/15," Kitchener Papers, NA, 30 57/57.

21 Millerand, handwritten notes of his trip to London, 22 January 1915 (also in typescript), Millerand Papers, AN, 470AP15.

22 Ibid.

23 Ibid.

24 Poincaré, Notes Journalières, XXXVIII, BN, NAF (16029), 26 January 1915.

25 Millerand, handwritten notes of his trip to London, 22 January 1915 (also in typescript), Millerand Papers, AN, 470AP15.

26 Ibid.; French Diaries, IWM, PP/MCR/C32, reel 2, 24 January 1915; Foch to Joffre, 26 January 1915, Correspondance Foch, AG, no. 30.

27 Churchill to French, 24 January 1915, French Papers, IWM, 75/46/11.

28 Churchill to French, 11 January 1915, ibid.

29 Cassar, *Kitchener*, 280–2.

30 See Neilson, "Kitchener: A Reputation Refurbished?" 214–15.

31 Lloyd George to Churchill, 29 January 1915, Churchill Papers, CA, 26/2/47.

32 Cassar, *Kitchener*, 281–2.

33 French Diaries, IWM, PP/MCR/C32, reel 2, 29 January 1915.

34 French Diaries, IWM, PP/MCR/C32, reel 2, 30 January 1915.

35 Poincaré, Notes Journalières, XXXVIII, BN, NAF (16029), 2–4, 13 February 1915.

36 Cassar, *Kitchener*, 287.

37 Poincaré, Notes Journalières, XXXVIII, BN, NAF (16029), 7 February 1915. Poincaré claimed that Millerand obtained this concession from Joffre "without difficulty." Ibid.

38 Foch to Joffre, 26 January 1915, Correspondance Foch, AG, no. 30; French Diaries, IWM, PP/MCR/C32, reel 2, 26 January 1915.

39 CT no. 1363, French to Kitchener, 1 February 1915, IWM, French Papers, 75/46/6.

40 CT no. 2937, Kitchener to French, 1 February 1915, IWM, French Papers, 75/46/6.

41 CT no. F1368, Kitchener to French, 1 February 1915, IWM, French Papers, 75/46/6.

42 French Diaries, IWM, PP/MCR/C32, reel 2, 5 February 1915.

43 Wilson Diaries, VI, IWM, DS/Misc/80, 5 February 1915.

44 French Diaries, IWM, PP/MCR/C32, reel 2, 6, 9 February 1915.

45 Wilson Diaries, VI, IWM, DS/Misc/80, 5 February 1915.

46 The Third Bureau memorandum, which Joffre took to the meeting, indicates that the French General Staff had again come to the conclusion that the British Expeditionary Force was not carrying its fair share of the load. The complaints against the British were twofold: first, that the terms of the agreement of 21 January on the relief of the French IX and XX corps, conditional on the relief of the British I Corps north of La Bassée, brought minimal advantage to the French and, therefore, the British should be made to effect the required reliefs while maintaining their entire line; and secondly, that the British had made plans to begin the relief of the French IX Corps only upon 10 March, while the four divisions promised by Kitchener were to have arrived in France by the 15th or at the latest the 20th of February. What was the cause of the delay? These forces, it was argued, would suffice to relieve the French IX and XX Corps without French relief of the British I Corps. ("Note sur la relève de la VIIIe Armée par l'Armée Anglaise," 3 February 1915, AG, 16N1905, 3e Bureau, Armée anglaise, no. 4, reproduced in *AFGG*, II A(II), no. 791. See n.1 in particular.) Many of these complaints would be expressed later, but their presentation at this point would have been strongly resented by the British, who attended the meeting, and would have been reflected in their diary accounts.

47 No. 2319, Commander-in-Chief to Minister of War, 8 February 1915, *AFGG*, II A(II), no. 826.

48 French to Kitchener, 6 February 1915, Kitchener Papers, NA, 30 57/50; French Diaries, IWM, PP/MCR/C33, reel 2, 6 February 1915.

49 French Diaries, IWM, PP/MCR/C33, reel 2, 8 February 1915 (printed in Gerald French, ed., *War Diaries*, 178).

50 French Diaries, IWM, PP/MCR/C32, reel 2, 9 February 1915.

51 Ibid.

52 Cassar, *Kitchener*, 288; Neilson, *Strategy and Supply*, 69.

53 War Council meeting of 13 January 1915, NA, CAB 42/1/16; Churchill to Kitchener, 20 January 1915, in Gilbert, *Winston S. Churchill*, vol. 3, *Companion*, vol. 1, *Documents July 1914–April 1915*, 433.

54 For problems related to the use of Archangel through May 1916, see Neilson, *Strategy and Supply*, 176–82.

55 War Council meeting of 10 March 1915, 663–73; Jukka Nevakivi, "Lord Kitchener and the Partition of the Ottoman Empire," 316–29.

56 Cassar, *The French and the Dardanelles*, 54.

57 Ibid., 51–9.

58 Bell, *Churchill and the Dardanelles*, 100–4; Nevakivi, "Lord Kitchener and the Partition of the Ottoman Empire," 289–90.

59 Asquith to the King, 17 February 1915, NA, CAB 41/36/5.

60 Cassar, *Kitchener*, 288–90; Philpott, "Kitchener and the 29th Division," 388–95.

61 Poincaré, Notes Journalières, XXXVIII, BN, NAF (16029), 18 February 1915.

62 Cassar, *The French and the Dardanelles*, 73–4.

63 Poincaré, Notes Journalières, XXXVIII, BN, NAF (16029), 18 February 1915; Minister of Foreign Affairs to Embassy, 18 February 1915, Kitchener Papers, NA, 30 57/59.

64 Commander-in-Chief to Minister of War, 1 March 1915, AG, 16N1905, dos. 1, Armée Anglaise, no. 13 bis; Philpott, "Kitchener and the 29th Division," 389–90.

65 Senator Boudenoot, Vice-President of Senate Army Commission, to Millerand, 2 February 1915, Millerand Papers, AN, 470AP28.

66 Millerand to Kitchener, 2 March 1915, Millerand Papers, AN, 470AP28.

67 Philpott, "Kitchener and the 29th Division," 394.

68 No. 6364, Commander-in-Chief to Minister of War, 19 February 1915 (carried by Penelon on the morning of the 20th), AG, 16N1905, dos. 1, Armee Anglaise, no. 10, reproduced in *AFGG*, III A(I), no. 10. See below regarding the conflict with Sir John.

69 Esher to Kitchener, 21 February 1915, Kitchener Papers, NA, 30 57/59.

70 Cassar, *Kitchener*, 291–3; no. 626, Colonel de la Panouse, Military Attaché in London, to Minister of War, Paris, 20 February 1915, AG, 7N700, Section Anglaise, "Correspondance de l'attaché Militaire à Londres," dos. Février 1915, reproduced in *AFGG*, VIII A(I), no. 1.

71 No. 626, de la Panouse to Minister of War, 20 February 1915, AG, 7N700, Section Anglaise, "Correspondance de l'attaché Militaire à Londres," dos. Février 1915, reproduced in *AFGG*, VIII A(I), no. 1.

72 Kitchener to Esher, 22 February 1915, Kitchener Papers, NA, 30 57/59.

73 Churchill to French, 11 January 1915, French Papers, IWM, 75/46/11.

74 French Diaries, IWM, PP/MCR/c33, reel 2, 7 February 1915.

75 Ibid., 14 February 1915.

76 Ibid., 15 February 1915; Wilson Diaries, VI, IWM, DS/Misc/80, 15 February 1915; no. 5213, Joffre to French, 15 February 1915, *AFGG*, II A(I), no. 890.

77 French to Mrs Bennett, 19 November 1914, 18 January 1915, 24 February 1915, 16 March 1915, French Papers, IWM, PP/MCR/C33, reel 1.

78 See in particular ibid., French to Mrs Bennett, 27 February 1915.

79 No. 5213, Joffre to French, 15 February 1915, *AFGG*, II A(I), no. 890; French Diaries, IWM, PP/MCR/C32, reel 2, 18 February 1915. Regarding Foch's role, see no. 5210, Commander-in-Chief to Foch, 16 February 1915, AG, 16N1905, dos. 1, Armée Anglaise, no. 5.

80 French Diaries, IWM, PP/MCR/C32, reel 2, 18 February 1914; no. 0158, French to Joffre, 18 February 1915, *AFGG*, II A(II), no. 916.

81 OA58/2, French to Joffre, 18 February 1915, *AFGG*, II A(II), no. 917.

82 Ibid.

83 Clive Diaries, II/I, LHMA, 18 February 1915.

84 French Diaries, IWM, PP/MCR/C32, reel 2, 3, 19 February 1915.
85 No. 6365, Commander-in-Chief to Marshal French, 19 February 1915, *AFGG*, II A(II), no. 927.
86 Bertie to French, 13 January 1915, IWM, French Papers, 75/46/11.
87 No. 6365, Commander-in-Chief to Marshal French, 19 February 1915, *AFGG*, II A(II), no. 927.
88 Wilson Diaries, VI, IWM, DS/Misc/80, 20, 21 February 1915.
89 French Diaries, IWM, PP/MCR/C32, reel 2, 21 February 1915.
90 Wilson Diaries, VI, IWM, DS/Misc/80, 21 February 1915; French Diaries, IWM, PP/MCR/C32, reel 2, 21 February 1915. "I fancy Joffre hardly saw this letter & it was probably written by some young upstart French Staff officer," concluded Sir John French in his diary (French Diaries, ibid.) The original of the letter, conserved in the National Archives, was in fact signed by Joffre in his own hand. (No. 6365, Commander-in-Chief to Marshal French, 19 February 1915, NA, WO 158/13, 194–6.)
91 Wilson Diaries, VI, IWM, DS/Misc/80, 23 February 1915.
92 Ibid., 21, 23 February 1915. "In order to show strength he is intensely secretive, suspicious & jealous. I don't know if I can work with him," wrote Wilson (ibid., 23 February 1915).
93 OA613, Memorandum of Field Marshal … to Commander-in-Chief of the French Army, 23 February 1915, *AFGG*, II A(II), no. 979.
94 Wilson Diaries, VI, IWM, DS/Misc/80, 23 February 1915; Foch to Joffre, 23 February 1915, Correspondance Foch, AG, no. 32; no. 7966, Commander-in-Chief to Foch, 24 February 1915, AG, 16N1905, dos. Armée Anglaise, no. 13.
95 Wilson Diaries, VI, IWM, DS/Misc/80, 23 February 1915; Joffre's marginalia on OA613, French to Joffre, 23 February 1915, *AFGG*, II A(II), no. 979, p. 328, n.2.
96 No. 7966, Commander-in-Chief to Foch, 24 February 1915, AG, 16N1905, dos. Armée Anglaise, no. 13; Wilson Diaries, VI, IWM, DS/Misc/80, 23, 24 February 1915.
97 CT no. 3231, Kitchener to French, 24 February 1915; CT, French to Kitchener, 24 February 1915, Kitchener Papers, NA, 30 57/57 5, WH 16, 17.
98 French Diaries, IWM, PP/MCR/C32, reel 2, 24 February 1915.
99 CT no. 1536, French to Kitchener, 24 February 1915, Kitchener Papers, NA, 30 57/5, WH 17.
100 Doughty, *Pyrrhic Victory*, 208; Poincaré, *Au service*, 6:81.
101 French Diaries, IWM, PP/MCR/C32, reel 2, 28 February 1915; Wilson Diaries, VI, IWM, DS/Misc/80, 27 February 1915.
102 Wilson Diaries, VI, IWM, DS/Misc/80, 23 February 1992.
103 Ibid., 28 February 1915; French Diaries, IWM, PP/MCR/C32, reel 2, 28 February 1915.
104 French to Mrs Bennett, 27 February 1915, IWM, MM/MCR/C33, reel 1.
105 Wilson Diaries, VI, IWM, DS/Misc/80, 28 February 1915.
106 Ibid.

107 Wilson Diaries, VI, IWM, DS/Misc/80, 28 February 1915.
108 Foch to Joffre, 28 February 1915, Correspondance Foch, AG, no. 34.
109 Commander-in-Chief to Minister of War, 1 March 1915, AG, 16N1905, dos. 1, Armée Anglaise, no. 13 bis, reproduced in *AFGG*, II A(II), no. 1041.
110 Poincaré, Notes Journalières, XXXVIII, BN, NAF (16029), 2 March 1915.
111 Minister of War to Minister of Foreign Affairs, 2 March 1915, AE, "Guerre 1914–1918," no. 35, p. 130; Millerand to Kitchener, 2 March 1915, Millerand Papers, AN, 470AP15.
112 Millerand to Kitchener, 2 March 1915, Millerand Papers, AN, 470AP15.
113 Kitchener to French, 5 March 1915, IWM, French Papers, 75/46/11.
114 Ibid.
115 French to Kitchener, 7 March 1915, Kitchener Papers, NA, 30 57/50 Erd/1259.
116 Ibid.; Asquith to French, 8 March 1915, IWM, French Papers, 75/46/11.
117 French Diaries, IWM, PP/MCR/C32, reel 2, 19 February, 1 March 1915.
118 CT no. 39, Cambon to Minister of Foreign Affairs, 5 March 1915, AE, "Guerre 1914–1918," no. 535, p. 144.
119 Kitchener to Millerand, 4 March 1915, Millerand Papers, AN, 470AP15.
120 Ibid.
121 Ibid.
122 Ibid.
123 Poincaré, Notes Journalières, XXXVIII, BN, NAF (16029), 9 March 1915.
124 CT no. 726, Minister of Foreign Affairs to French Ambassador, London, 7 March 1915, AE, "Guerre 1914–1918," no. 535, p. 152.
125 No. 512, 854, Joffre to Foch, 2, 3, March 1915, *AFGG*, II A(II), nos. 1050, 1056.
126 Wilson Diaries, VI, IWM, DS/Misc/80, 1 March 1915.
127 Ibid., 5 March 1915.
128 Clive Diaries, II/I, LHMA, 6 March 1915; Wilson Diaries, VI, IWM, DS/Misc/80, 5 March 1915.
129 No. 2266, Commander-in-Chief to Field Marshal French, 7 March 1915, *AFGG*, II A(II), no. 1108.
130 Wilson Diaries, VI, IWM, DS/Misc/80, 8 March 1915.
131 Commander-in-Chief to Minister of War, 7 March 1915, Millerand Papers, AN, 470AP15.
132 No. 6315, Commander-in-Chief to Marshal French, 19 February 1915, *AFGG*, II A(II), no. 927.
133 French Diaries, IWM, PP/MCR/C32, reel 2, 23 February 1915.
134 French to Mrs Bennett, 2 March 1915, French Papers, IWM, PP/MCR/C33, reel 1.
135 French Diaries, IWM, PP/MCR/C32, reel 2, 8 March 1915.
136 Ibid., 7 March 1915.
137 No. 2686, Joffre to Foch, 8 March 1915, *AFGG*, II A(II), no. 1116; Foch to Joffre, *AFGG*, II A(II), no. 1143.
138 French Diaries, IWM, PP/MCR/C32, reel 2, 11, 13, 19 March 1915; cf. Cruttwell, *The Great War*, 149–51.

CHAPTER FOUR

1 No. 4681, General, Commander-in-Chief, to Sir John French, 14 March 1915, AG, 16N1905, dos. 1, Armée Anglaise, no. 25.
2 French Diaries, IWM, PP/MCR/C32, reel 2, 16 March 1915.
3 Foch to Joffre, 16 March 1915, Correspondance Foch, AG, no. 39.
4 French Diaries, IWM, PP/MCR/C32, reel 2, 16 March 1915; Foch to Joffre, 16 March 1915, Correspondance Foch, AG, no. 39.
5 Clive Diaries, II/I, LHMA, 23 March 1915.
6 See Doughty, *Pyrrhic Victory*, 115–20; Joffre, *Mémoires*, 2:7–50. See below.
7 Greenhalgh, *The French Army*, 59.
8 Doughty, *Pyrrhic Victory*, 107.
9 See ibid., 154.
10 Neilson, *Strategy and Supply*, 71; Gilbert, *First World War*, 138.
11 See Bell, *Churchill and the Dardanelles*, 103, 105–6, 120–3, 131–4, 137–41.
12 Neilson, *Strategy and Supply*, 71–3.
13 Cf. Doughty, *Pyrrhic Victory*, 169.
14 Ibid., 155.
15 No. 5668, Commander-in-Chief to Minister of War, 17 March 1915, and annex, *AFGG*, II A(II), no. 1205.
16 Poincaré, Notes Journalières, XXXVIII, BN, NAF (16029), 18 March 1915.
17 Ibid., 21 March 1915.
18 Doughty, *Pyrrhic Victory*, 153–4.
19 Poincaré, Notes Journalières, XXXVIII, BN, NAF (16029), 18, 21 March 1915.
20 Prete, "French Military War Aims," 890–1.
21 Poincaré, Notes Journalières, XXXVIII, BN, NAF (16029), 18, 21 March 1915.
22 Ibid.
23 Joffre's conversation with Wilson, Wilson Diaries, IWM, DS/Misc/80, reel 6, 23 March 1915.
24 Poincaré, Notes Journalières, XXXVIII, BN, NAF (16029), 21 March 1915.
25 Wilson Diaries, IWM, DS/Misc/80, reel 6, 23 March 1915.
26 Clive Diaries, II/I, LHMA, 15 March 1915 (interview of Clive with Pellé, French chief of staff).
27 No. 4797–1/II, Minister of War to Commander-in-Chief, Armies of the North-East, 1 April 1915, *AFGG*, II A(II), no. 1282; Poincaré, Notes Journalières, XXXVIII, BN, NAF (16028), 1 April 1915.
28 Clive Diaries, II/I, LHMA, 15, 17 March 1915; see no. 690, Colonel de la Panousse to the Minister of War, 16 March 1915, with marginal note, "copie au GQG 1829–2/11 22 mars," AG, 7N700 EMA, Section Anglaise, Entrées: Correspondance de l'attaché militaire à Londres, dos. Mars 1915 (referring to earlier dispatch).
29 Foch to Joffre, 14, 16 March 1915, Correspondance Foch, AG, nos. 38, 39.
30 French Diaries, IWM, PP/MCR/C32, reel 2, 18 March 1915.

31 Wilson Diaries, IWM, DS/Misc/80, reel 6, 21 March 1915.

32 Wilson Diaries, IWM, DS/Misc/80, reel 6, 13 March 1915; French Diaries, IWM, PP/MCR/C32, reel 2, 13 March 1915; Poincaré, Notes Journalières, XXXVIII, BN, NAF (16029), 15 March 1915.

33 Wilson Diaries, IWM, DS/Misc/80, reel 6, 19 March 1915.

34 OA767, Robertson to Huguet, 20 March 1915; 1111/SC, Foch to Huguet, 20 March 1915, *AFGG*, II A(II), nos. 1234, 1235. Wilson, however, reproached Robertson for having addressed Foch through Huguet and not Wilson. According to Wilson, Robertson "climbed down." (Wilson Diaries, IWM, DS/Misc/80, reel 6, 21 March 1915.)

35 Ibid., 22 March 1915.

36 Ibid.; Foch to Joffre, 22 March 1915, Correspondance Foch, AG, no. 40 and attached CT 290, Etat-Major St Omer à General Foch, Cassel, 22 March 1915.

37 French to Mrs Bennett, 17 March 1915, IWM, PP/MCR/C33, reel 1; Wilson Diaries, IWM, DS/Misc/80, reel 6, 17, 18, 22 March 1915.

38 Wilson Diaries, IWM, DS/Misc/80, reel 6, 20, 22 March 1915 and passim until the coalition government was formed on 26 May 1915. How much impact these initiatives had remains to be assessed.

39 Wilson Diaries, IWM, DS/Misc/80, reel 6, 22, 23 March 1915.

40 Clive Diaries, II/I, IWM, 22 March 1915.

41 Wilson Diaries, IWM, DS/Misc/80, reel 6, 23 March 1915.

42 Ibid.

43 Ibid.

44 Wilson Diaries, IWM, DS/Misc/80, reel 6, 24 March 1915; no. 8451, Joffre to Marshal French, 24 March 1915, *AFGG*, II A(II), no. 1249.

45 Wilson Diaries, IWM, DS/Misc/80, reel 6, 25 March 1915.

46 OA792, Robertson to Wilson, 26 March 1915, *AFGG*, II A(I), no. 720.

47 French Diaries, IWM, PP/MCR/C32, reel 2, 25 March 1915; French to Joffre, 26 March 1915, *AFGG*, II A(II), no. 1256.

48 Cf. French, "The Military Background to the 'Shell Crisis,' of May 1915," 192–205.

49 French to Churchill, 3 September 1914, in Gilbert, ed., *Churchill*, vol. 3, *Companion*, 1:79–80.

50 "Memorandum, prepared in answer to Lord Kitchener's private letter to Sir John French, dated 2–1–15 on the subject of the employment of British troops elsewhere than in the present theatre," 2 January 1915, Kitchener Papers, NA, 30/57/50.

51 Foch to Joffre, 13 March 1915, AG, 16N1905, dos. 1, Armée anglaise, no. 22 (reproduced in *AFGG*, II A(II), no. 1177); Foch to Joffre, 14 March 1915, Correspondance Foch, AG, no. 38. Ammunition deliveries were cut from 18 to 13.5 rounds per day (ibid.).

52 Asquith to Venetia Stanley, 18 March 1915, in Brock and Brock, eds., *Letters to Venetia Stanley*, 487–8.

53 Ibid., 507n.11.

54 Minutes of War Council, 19 March 1915, NA, CAB 42/4/14.
55 French Diaries, IWM, PP/MCR/C32, reel 2, 23 March 1915.
56 French to Churchill, 24 March 1915, in Gilbert, ed., *Churchill*, vol. 2, *Companion*, 1:724; French Diaries, IWM, PP/MCR/C32, reel 2, 18 March 1915.
57 Ibid., 23 March 1915.
58 Asquith to Venetia Stanley, 24 March 1915, in Brock and Brock, eds., *Letters to Venetia Stanley*, 506.
59 French Diaries, IWM, PP/MCR/C32, reel 2, 23 March 1915.
60 Ibid.
61 Ibid.
62 Asquith to the King, 17 March 1915, NA, CAB 41/36/11, no. R/213.
63 French Diaries, IWM, PP/MCR/C32, reel 2, 23 March 1915.
64 Asquith to Venetia Stanley, 24 March 1915, in Brock and Brock, eds., *Letters to Venetia Stanley*, 506.
65 French Diaries, IWM, PP/MCR/C32, reel 2, 23 March 1915. This opinion was gleaned from a private letter of Hamilton, who believed that the Royal Navy relied too hastily on the destructive power of their big guns. (Asquith to Venetia Stanley, 18 March 1915, in Brock and Brock, eds., *Letters to Venetia Stanley*, 487–8.)
66 French to Churchill, 24 March 1915, in Gilbert, ed., *Churchill*, vol. 2, *Companion*, 1:728.
67 CT no. 414, Cambon to Minister of Foreign Affairs, 9 March 1915, Millerand Papers, AN, 470AP15.
68 Fleuriau (French Embassy) to Grey, 14 March 1915, Kitchener Papers, NA, 30 57/77.
69 "Note pour M. le Ministre of R. D[oumayrous]" of his interview with Esher, Paris, 23 March 1915, Millerand Papers, AN, 4705AP15.
70 CT no. 12, Military Attaché in London to Minister of War, 22 March 1915, Millerand Papers, AN, 4705AP15.
71 Churchill to Kitchener, 20 January 1915, Fisher to Churchill, 9 March 1915, Asquith to the King, 9 March 1915, Secretary's Notes of Meeting of War Council, 10 March 1915, in Gilbert, ed., *Churchill*, vol. 3, *Companion*, 2:433, 659–60, 663–73.
72 No. 690, de la Panouse to Ministry of War, 16 March 1915, AG, 7N700, "EMA, Section Anglaise: entrées … mars 1915"; also, TC 510–11, Cambon to Minister of Foreign Affairs, 22 March 1915, Millerand Papers, AN, 470AP15; also in AE, "Guerre 1914–1918," no. 535, pp. 204–5. See Jukha Nevakivi, "Lord Kitchener and the Partition of the Ottoman Empire," in Bourne and Watt, eds., *Studies in International History*, 316–29; Memorandum by Lord Kitchener, "Alexandretta and Mesopotamia," 16 March 1915, Memorandum by the Admiralty, "Alexandretta and Mesopotamia," 17 March 1915, NA, CAB 42/2/10–11.
73 Poincaré, Notes Journalières, XXXVIII, BN, NAF (16029), 20 March 1915. That British forces had not left Egypt and that the British had requested that the

French division under d'Amade at Lemnos return to Alexandria helped foster this suspicion. (Ibid.)

74 Asquith to Venetia Stanley, 22 March 1915, in Brock and Brock, eds., *Letters to Venetia Stanley*, 497.

75 Asquith to Kitchener, 22 March 1915, Kitchener Papers, NA, 30/57/74.

76 For the French account of the interview, see TC 510–11, Cambon au Ministre des Affaires Etrangères, 22 March 1915, Millerand Papers, AN, 470AP15.

77 No. 681, de la Panouse to the Minister of War, 11 March 1915, Millerand Papers, AN, 470AP15.

78 TC 510–11, Cambon to Minister of Foreign Affairs, 22 March 1915, Millerand Papers, AN, 470AP15.

79 T no. 523, Cambon, London, [to Minister of Foreign Affairs], 23 March 1915, Millerand Papers, AN, 470AP15; also in AE, "Guerre 1914–1918," 208.

80 Ibid.

81 Note pour le Ministre, Etat-Major de l'Armée, 3e Bureau, 23 March 1915, Millerand Papers, AN, 470AP15.

82 Memento préparé en vue de l'entrévue du 29 mars 1915 … original remis au Col Pellé, 28 March 1915, "Subordination du Maréchal French au Général Joffre," AG, 16N1905, no. 33, March 1915.

83 "Relations entres les Commandements Français et Anglais …," March 1915, AG, 16N1905, dos. Armée Anglaise, no. 34.

84 Esher, Journals, 22 January 1915, *Journals and Letters*, 3:209.

85 "Secretary's Notes of a Meeting of a War Council," 28 January 1915, NA, CAB 42/1/26.

86 Ibid.

87 France, Ministère de la Défense, Etat-Major de l'Armée, Service Historique, *Inventaire Sommaire des Archives de la Guerre Serie N 1872–1919*: by Guinard, Devos, Nicot, 83–4.

88 Esher, Journals, 23 January 1915, *Journals and Letters*, 3:210.

89 See letter to Venetia Stanley, 18 March 1915, in Brock and Brock, eds., *Letters to Venetia Stanley*, 488.

90 Rhodri Williams, "Lord Kitchener and the Battle of Loos," in Freedman, Hays, and Obernul, *War Intelligence and Security*, 121–2.

91 Esher to Kitchener, 21 March 1915, Kitchener Papers, NA, 30 57/59.

92 Ibid.

93 Esher, Journals, 18 March 1915, *Journals and Letters*, 3:222.

94 Esher to Kitchener, 21 March 1915, Kitchener Papers, NA, 30 57/59.

95 Esher, Journals, 20 March 1915, *Journal and Letters*, 3:223.

96 "Note pour M. le Ministre," of R. D[oumayrou] of his interview with Esher, Paris, 23 March 1915, Millerand Papers, AN, 470AP15.

97 Wilson Diaries, VI, IWM, DS/Misc/80, 28 March 1915.

98 Ibid.

99 "Notes remises au Commandant en Chef en vue de la visite de Lord K," March 1915, "Entrevue avec Lord Kitchener," "Gal Pellé," AG, 16N1905, dos. 1, Armée anglaise, no. 35.

100 Bertie to French, 13 January 1915, French Papers, IWM, 75/46/11.

101 Millerand's notes, "Sa visite à Londres," 22 January 1915, Millerand Papers, AN, 470AP15; Poincaré, Notes Journalières, XXXVIII, BN, NAF (16029), 26 January 1915.

102 No. 9.751 D.A., Commander-in-Chief to Minister of War, 21 February 1915, AE, "Guerre 1914–1918," no. 535 (contains previous communications); Minister of War to Minister of Foreign Affairs, 28 February 1915, 304 and attachment CT no. 3006–4/11, [Millerand to] Military Attaché.

103 Bertie, British Ambassador in Paris, to the French Foreign Ministry, AE, "Guerre 1914–1918," no. 535. The note mistakenly asserted that Millerand and Kitchener had come to an agreement on the subject and expressed concern that the French military authorities had been unwilling to make the necessary technical arrangements with Sir John French.

104 No. 9.751 D.A., Commander-in-Chief to the Minister of War, 21 February 1915, AE, "Guerre 1914–1918," no. 535.

105 De Margerie [Political Director, French Foreign Office] to Buat [Chief of Staff to Millerand], AG, Fond Buat 6N29, "Angleterre et Portugual …," dos. mars 1915; Bertie to Grey, 2 March 1915, Bertie Papers, NA, 800/167.

106 Kitchener to Millerand, 4 March 1915, Millerand Papers, AN, 470AP15.

107 No. 4534, Secret, Personal, General Commander-in-Chief to Minister of War, 13 March 1915, AG, 16N1905, dos. 1, Armée Anglaise, no. 23.

108 Prete, "French Military War Aims," 887–91.

109 Ibid.

110 Ibid.

111 See above.

112 "Note pour M. le Ministre of R D[oumayrou]" of interview with Esher, 23 March 1915, Millerand Papers, AN, 470AP15.

113 Asquith to Kitchener, 22 March 1915, Kitchener Papers, NA, 30/59/74.

114 French Diaries, IWM, PP/MCR/C32, reel 2, 23 March 1915.

115 Wilson Diaries, IWM, DS/Misc/80, reel 6, 24 March 1915.

116 CT no. 8413, General Commander-in-Chief to the War Ministry, 24 March 1915, AG, 16N1905, dos. 1, Armée Anglaise, no. 28; CT no. 911, Minister of Foreign Affairs to French Ambassador, London, 24 March 1915, AE, "Guerre 1914–1918," no. 535, p. 21; also in Kitchener Papers, NA, 30/57/77, WU28; CT no. 538, Cambon to Minister of Foreign Affairs, 25 March 1915, Millerand Papers, AN, 470AP15.

117 French Diaries, IWM, PP/MCR/C32, reel 2, 26, 28 March 1915; Wilson Diaries, VI, IWM, DS/Misc/80, 28 March 1915.

118 Wilson Diaries, VI, IWM, DS/Misc/80, 28 March 1915.

119 The most extensive accounts of the conference are those of Sir John French, Diaries, IWM, PP/MCR/C32, reel 2, 29 March 1915, and [Procès-verbal de la] Confer-

ence du 29 mars [1915], AG, 16N1905, dos. 1, Armée Anglaise, no. 32, of which a portion is reproduced as an "Extract" in *AFGG*, III A(1), no. 23. Wilson's briefer account, Wilson Diaries, IWM, DS/Misc/80, 29 March 1915, is reproduced with minor adjustments in Callwell, ed., *Wilson*, 1:218–19. Only Yarde-Buller indicates that Kitchener chaired the meeting (Yarde-Buller to Kitchener, 4 April 1915, Kitchener Papers, NA, WO 159/10 Erd/2219).

120 Gilbert, ed., *Churchill*, 3:373–5, 377–9.

121 Wilson Diaries, IWM, DS/Misc/80, reel 6, 29 March 1915; Gilbert, ed., *Churchill*, 3:373–5, 377–9.

122 French Diaries, IWM, PP/MCR/C32, reel 2, 29 March 1915.

123 Wilson Diaries, IWM, DS/Misc/80, reel 6, 29 March 1915; French Diaries, IWM, PP/MCR/C32, reel 2, 29 March 1915; [Procès-verbal de la] Conférence du 29 Mars [1915], AG, 16N1905, dos. Armée Anglaise, no. 32.

124 French Diaries, IWM, PP/MCR/C32, reel 2, 29 March 1915; [Procès-verbal de la] Conférence du 29 mars [1915], AG, 16N1905, dos. Armée anglaise, no. 32.

125 Wilson Diaries, IWM, DS/Misc/80, reel 6, 29 March 1915.

126 French Diaries, IWM, PP/MCR/C32, reel 2, 29 March 1915.

127 Ibid.; [Procès-verbal de la] Conference du 29 mars, AG, 16N1905, dos. 1, Armée Anglaise, no. 32.

128 French Diaries, IWM, PP/MCR/C32, reel 2, 29 March 1915; [Procès-verbal de la] Conférence du 29 mars, AG, 16N1905, dos. 1, Armée Anglaise no. 32.

129 French Diaries, IWM, PP/MCR/C32, reel 2, 29 March 1915. Kitchener also agreed to supply 100 tons of toluol, explosive required in shell production, to the French, in exchange for the French supplying 52,000 rounds of ammunition for the 52 Portuguese guns in British employ. [Procès-verbal de la] Conférence du 29 mars, AG, 16N1905, dos. 1, Armée Anglaise, no. 32. Ultimately the French modified their request to 200 tons of tolite, nitrified toluol, and 100 tons of pieric acid. (See de la Panouse to Kitchener, 2, 9, 10 April 1915, Kitchener Papers, NA, 30 57/57 WH 21, 22; Yarde-Buller to Kitchener, 4 April 1915, Kitchener to Yarde-Buller, 9 April 1915, Kitchener Papers, NA, WO 159/10 Erd/2219.

130 French Diaries, IWM, PP/MCR/C32, reel 2, 29 March 1915.

131 [Procès-verbal de la] Conférence du 29 mars, AG, 16N1905, dos. 1, Armée Anglaise, no. 32. The British accounts do not mention this aspect of the discussion.

132 Ibid.; French Diaries, IWM, PP/MCR/C32, reel 2, 29 March 1915.

133 T, Millerand to Minister of Foreign Affairs for Paul Cambon, 29 March 1915, Millerand Papers, AN, 470AP15; see also "Visite du 29/3/15" [Millerand's handwritten notes on the conference of 29 March 1915] in ibid.

134 Poincaré, Notes Journalières, XXXVIII, BN, NAF (16029), 30 March 1915.

135 T, Millerand to Minister of Foreign Affairs for Paul Cambon, 29 March 1915, Millerand Papers, AN, 470AP15; see also "Visite du 29/3/15" [Millerand's handwritten notes on the conference of 29 March 1915] in ibid.

136 Poincaré, Notes Journalières, XXXVIII, BN, NAF (16029), 30 March 1915.

137 Ibid.
138 "Visite du 29/3/15" [Millerand's handwritten notes on conference of 29 March 1915], Millerand Papers, AN, 470AP15.
139 Ibid.
140 Ibid.
141 Ibid.
142 Esher to Kitchener, 31 March 1915, Kitchener Papers, NA, 30 57/59.
143 Poincaré, Notes Journalières, XXXVIII, BN, NAF (16029), 30 March 1915.
144 French Diaries, IWM, PP/MCR/C32, reel 2, 31 March 1915 (conversation with Kitchener).
145 Asquith to Venetia Stanley, 30 March 1915, in Brock and Brock, eds., *Letters to Venetia Stanley*, 520.
146 Robertson to Callwell, 31 March 1915, LHMA, Robertson Papers, 1/8/17a–b.
147 French Diaries, IWM, PP/MCR/C32, reel 2, 29 March 1915.
148 Wilson Diaries, IWM, DS/Misc/80, reel 6, 30 March 1915.
149 Clive Diaries, II/I, LHMA, 1 April 1915.
150 French to Kitchener, 8 April 1915, Kitchener Papers, NA, 30 57/50 Erd/1259.
151 French Diaries, IWM, PP/MCR/C32, reel 2, 30 March 1915.
152 Foch to Joffre, 3 April 1915, Correspondance Foch, AG, no. 43.
153 Callwell to Robertson, 5 April 1915, Robertson Papers, LHMA, I/8/18a–b.
154 Callwell, ed., *Wilson*, 1:222.
155 OAM 808, French to Joffre, 1 April 1915, *AFGG*, II A(I), no. 1283.
156 French Diaries, IWM, PP/MCR/C32, reel 2, 29, 30, 31 March 1915.
157 Ibid., 31 March 1915; cf. French, ed., *War Diaries*, 188.
158 Ibid., 5 April 1915; Wilson Diaries, IWM, DS/Misc/80, reel 6, 5 April 1915.
159 French to Mrs Bennett, 5 April 1915, IWM, PP/MCR/C33, reel 1.
160 Callwell to Robertson, 5 April 1915, Robertson Papers, LHMA, I/8/18a–b.
161 French to Kitchener, 2 April 1915, Kitchener Papers, NA, 30 57/50 Erd/1259.
162 French to Kitchener, 8 April 1915, Kitchener Papers, NA, 30 57/50 Erd/1259. The king, however, was informed.
163 French Diaries, IWM, PP/MCR/C32, reel 2, 14 April 1915. "He told me he had certain knowledge that Italy and Romania were coming in," Sir John recorded. (Ibid.)
164 Kitchener to Asquith, 14 April 1915, Asquith Papers, 14/25, Bodleian Library, Oxford.
165 French to Mrs Bennett, 2 April 1915, French Papers, IWM, PP/MCR/C33, reel 1.
166 French to Mrs Bennett, 16 April 1915, IWM, PP/MCR/C33, reel 1.
167 CT no. 588, Cambon to Ministère des Affaires Etrangères, 31 March 1915, Millerand Papers, AN, 470AP15.
168 Poincaré, Notes Journalières, XXXVIII, BN, NAF (16029), 1 April 1915; cf. Millerand to Cambon, 14 April 1915, Millerand Papers, AN, 470AP15.
169 Esher Journals, CA, 2/14, 1 April 1915.
170 Ibid.

171 Ibid.
172 French Diaries, IWM, PP/MCR/C32, reel 2, 29 March 1915.
173 Wilson Diaries, IWM, DS/Misc/80, reel 6, 1, 2 April 1915.
174 Esher Journals, CA, 2/14, 2 April 1915.
175 Esher to French, 3 April 1915, French Papers, IWM, 75/46/11, reported in Esher, *Journals and Letters*, 3:226–7.
176 French Diaries, IWM, PP/MCR/C32, reel 2, 4 April 1915; Esher Journals, CA, 2/14, 4 April 1915; see Esher, *Journals and Letters*, 3:228.
177 Esher to French, 12 April 1915, Esher, *Journals and Letters*, 3:228.
178 Ibid.; also Asquith to Esher, 14 April 1915, ibid., 230.
179 See Fonds Joffre, AG, 1K268, dos. 2 (4 November 1914–26 May 1915).
180 Millerand to Cambon, 14 April 1915, Millerand Papers, AN, 470AP15.
181 Wilson Diaries, IWM, DS/Misc/80, reel 6, 1 April 1915.
182 Foch to Joffre, 3 April 1915, Correspondance Foch, AG, no. 43.
183 S/C460, Secret Note to Marshal French, 6 April 1915, *AFGG*, III A(II), no. 32; French Diaries, 5 April 1915, IWM, PP/MCR/C32.
184 Wilson Diaries, IWM, DS/Misc/80, reel 6, 7 April 1915.
185 French Diaries, IWM, PP/MCR/C32, reel 2, 8 April 1915.
186 Ibid., 10 April 1915. See OAM 857, Robertson to Wilson, 9 April 1915, *AFGG*, III A(I), no. 39.
187 Foch to Joffre, 11 April 1915, Correspondance Foch, AG, no. 45.
188 French Diaries, IWM, PP/MCR/C32, reel 2, 19 April 1915.
189 Wilson Diaries, IWM, DS/Misc/80, reel 6, 10 April 1915.
190 Ibid.

CHAPTER FIVE

1 Portions of this chapter were previously published in Roy A. Prete, "Les relations franco-britanniques et l'attaque au gaz allemande à Ypres, avril 1915," under the direction of Roch Legault and Jean Lamarre, in *La Première Guerre mondiale et le Canada: Contribution sociomilitires québécoises* (Montreal: Méridien 1999), 225–40. All efforts have been made to secure the necessary rights to publish previously published material, but without results in this case, the publisher having reportedly ceased publication in 2007. If the need arises to make any corrections or additions, this will be done in future editions.
2 See Rothfels, "Clausewitz," in Earle, ed., *Makers of Modern Strategy*, 107.
3 See Trumpener, "The Road to Ypres," 461–2.
4 See Swettenham, *Canada and the First World War*, 8–9; Godspeed, *Les Forces Armées du Canada*, 33–5; Nicholson, *Official History: Canadian Expeditionary Force*, 49–92; Cassar, *Hell in Flanders Fields*.
5 See Greenhalgh, *Foch*, 105–10.
6 See Trumpener, "The Road to Ypres," 461, 470, 474–8; "Sketch 9, Ypres 1915, the First Gas Attack, 22 April," *HGW*, *France and Belgium (1915)*, 1:176–7.

7 See Prete, *Strategy and Command, 1914*, 163–4, 172. Cf. Cassar, *Trial by Gas*, 9–11.

8 Foch to Joffre, 23 April 1915, Correspondance Foch, AG, no. 46.

9 French Diaries, IWM, PP/MCR/C33, reel 3, 22 April 1915.

10 Nicholson, *Official History: Canadian Expeditionary Force*, 60–1; *HGW, France and Belgium, 1915*, 1:163–6. For a Belgian bulletin warning of the impending use of gas, see no. 247, "Bulletin d'information," 16 April 1915, AFGG, II A(II), no. 1392.

11 French to Mrs Bennett, IWM, PP/MCR/C33, reel 1, 20 [23 or 24] April 1915. Although the German Fourth Army had launched sixty gas shells on 20 April at the hotly disputed Hill 60, on the southern arc of the Ypres salient, the effect was minimal. (*HGW, France and Belgium, 1915*, 1:169n.1.) Sir John's statement to Mrs Bennett that the use of gas had "only happened on French troops" indicates that he was not referring to the Hill 60 incident, as only British troops were involved there, and also places his observation prior to the German gas attack on the Canadians on 24 April. The letter therefore should be dated 23 or 24 April 1915.

12 *HGW, France and Belgium, 1915*, 1:178–87; Nicholson, *Official History: Canadian Expeditionary Force*, 61–71.

13 Foch to Joffre, 23 April 1915, Correspondance Foch, AG, no. 46, reproduced in AFGG, II A(II), no. 1422.

14 French Diaries, IWM, PP/MCR/C32, reel 3, 23 April 1915; cf. Foch to Joffre, 23 April 1915, Correspondance Foch, AG, no. 46, reproduced in AFGG, II A(II), no. 1422, in which Foch indicates that two battalions of Zouaves and a group of artillery were sent from Nieuport and the 153 Division with two groups of artillery from the French Tenth Army.

15 Foch to Joffre, 23 April 1915, Correspondance Foch, AG, no. 46, reproduced in AFGG, II A(II), no. 1422.

16 French Diaries, IWM, PP/MCR/C32, reel 3, 24 April 1915; cf. Foch to Joffre, 24 April 1915, Correspondance Foch, AG, no. 48, reproduced in AFGG, II A(I), no. 1334. Huguet, for his part, was "annoyed" that Foch had not kept him properly informed. Clive Diaries, II/I, LHMA, [24] April 1915.

17 Clive Diaries, II/I, LHMA, [24] April 1915.

18 French to Kitchener, 24 April 1915, Kitchener Papers, NA, 30 57/50 WA/84.

19 Yarde-Buller to Kitchener, 24 April 1915, Kitchener Papers, NA, WO 159/10, no. 35. Working from German sources, Ulrich Trumpener has confirmed that the loss of life due to the gas attack was light. Trumpener, "Road to Ypres," 460n.1.

20 See *HGW, France and Belgium, 1915*, 2:214–39; Nicholson, *Official History: Canadian Expeditionary Force*, 71–83.

21 Wilson Diaries, IWM, DS/Misc/80, reel 6, 25 April 1915.

22 Ibid., 24 April 1915.

23 Robertson to Callwell, 25 April 1915, Robertson Papers, LHMA, I/8/22a–b.

24 Ibid., 25 April 1915.

25 Erickson, "*Koalitsionnaya Voina*: Coalition Warfare in Soviet Miltary Theory, Planning, and Performance," in Neilson and Prete, eds., *Coalition Warfare*, 88.

26 Robertson to Callwell, 25 April 1915, Robertson Papers, LHMA, I/8/22a–b.
27 French Diaries, IWM, PP/MCR/c32, reel 3, 25 April 1915.
28 Ibid., 26 April 1915.
29 Ibid., 27 April 1915; Wilson Diaries, IWM, DS/Misc/80, reel 6, 27 April 1915; Cassar, *Trial by Gas*, 11, 78–80.
30 French Diaries, IWM, PP/MCR/C32, reel 3, 7 May 1915.
31 French Diaries, IWM, PP/MCR/C32, reel 2, 22 April 1915.
32 Foch to Joffre, 22 April 1915, Correspondance Foch, AG, no. 47.
33 Ibid.
34 CT no. 8469, Joffre to Foch, 23 April 1915, *AFGG*, II A(II), no. 1417.
35 Clive Diaries, II/I, LHMA, 25 April 1915.
36 French Diaries, IWM, PP/MCR/C32, reel 3, 26 April 1915 (see a shortened version in French, ed., *War Diaries*, 195). Cf. Wilson Diaries, VI, IWM, DS/Misc/80, 26 April 1915.
37 French Diaries, IWM, PP/MCR/C32, reel 3, 26 April 1915. Cf. Wilson Diaries, VI, IWM, DS/Misc/80, 26 April 1915.
38 Wilson Diaries, VI, IWM, DS/Misc/80, 26 April 1915.
39 Wilson Diaries, VI, IWM, DS/Misc/80, reel 6, 27 January 1919. Cf. Foch to Joffre, 27 April 1915, Correspondance Foch, AG, no. 49. For a French account of the battle, see *AFGG*, II, 699–719.
40 See Robertson to Callwell, 26 April 1915, Robertson Papers, LHMA, I/8/221a–b.
41 Clive Diaries, II/I, LHMA, 26 April 1915.
42 See Wilson Diaries, IWM, DS/Misc/80, reel 6, 27, 28 April 1915.
43 Ibid., 27 April 1915.
44 Ibid.
45 Ibid.
46 Wilson Diaries, IWM, DS/Misc/80, reel 6, 28 April 1915.
47 French Diaries, IWM, PP/MCR/C32, reel 2, 28 April 1915; "Resumé de la conversation du 28 avril 1915, 11 h entre le général Foch et le maréchal French," *AFGG*, II A(II), no. 1465.
48 "Resumé de la conversation du 28 avril 1915, 11 h entre le général Foch et le maréchal French," *AFGG*, II A(II), no. 1465.
49 Foch to Joffre, 28 April 1915, *AFGG*, II A(II), no. 1466; Note pour Monsieur le maréchal French, 28 April 1915, *AFGG*, II A(II), no. 1467.
50 Dufieux [liaison officer to Foch] to Joffre, 28 April 1915, *AFGG*, II A(II), no. 1468.
51 French Diaries, IWM, PP/MCR/C32, reel 3, 28 April 1915.
52 Wilson Diaries, IWM, DS/Misc/80, reel 6, 28 April 1915.
53 French Diaries, IWM, PP/MCR/C32, reel 3, 29 April 1915.
54 Foch to Joffre, 29 April 1915, Correspondance Foch, AG, no. 55; Dufieux to Joffre, 29 April 1915, *AFGG*, II A(II), no. 1479; Wilson Diaries, IWM, DS/Misc/80, reel 6, 28, 29 April 1915; French Diaries, IWM, PP/MCR/C32, reel 3, 29 April 1915 (see French, ed., *War Diaries*, 195). Foch thus did not carry out the ruse he and

Wilson had concocted of offering to take over the British salient with French troops only to feign that Joffre had refused. (Foch to Joffre, 29 April 1915, Correspondance Foch, AG, no. 52; Wilson Diaries, IWM, DS/Misc/80, reel 6, 28, 29 April 1915.)

55 Kitchener to French, 28 [April 1915], IWM, French Papers, 75/46/11.

56 Wilson Diaries, IWM, DS/Misc/80, reel 6, 30 April 1915.

57 French to Kitchener, [30] April 1915, Kitchener Papers, NA, 30 57/50 WA 82. The date of this is confirmed by French Diaries, IWM, PP/MCR/C32, reel 3, 30 April 1915.

58 French to Kitchener, [30] April 1915, Kitchener Papers, NA, 30 57/50 WA 82; Wilson Diaries, IWM, DS/Misc/80, reel 6, 30 April 1915.

59 French Diaries, IW, PP/MCR/C32, reel 3, 1 May 1915; Wilson Diaries, IWM, DS/Misc/80, reel 6, 1 May 1915; *HGW, France and Belgium, 1915*, 1:86–7, claims the decision to withdraw to the new line had been made before the results of the fighting came in. According to the Official History, Joffre instructed Foch to share a note with the British, which he did during a visit earlier in the day. In that note Joffre indicated his intention to go on the defensive about Ypres "in view of the planned joint offensive on the front Neuve Chapelle-Ypres." Foch, moreover, was to reduce forces about Ypres, engaging only in partial offensives, until the date of the big attack. Neither Wilson nor French, in their diaries, however, mention any earlier visit by Foch or the note from Joffre. The issue of reduction of the French force in the salient did not arise until the next day, which is probably when Foch delivered the note. (See below.)

60 French Diaries, IWM, PP/MCR/C32, reel 3, 1 May 1915. See Foch to Joffre, 1 May 1915, Correspondance Foch, AG, no. 53, reproduced in *AFGG*, II A(II), no. 1488, in which he suggests to Joffre that he does not think the British retreat to this new line will have serious consequences in view of the forthcoming attack.

61 See *HGW, France and Belgium, 1915*, 1:287–97.

62 French to Kitchener, 2 May 1915, Kitchener Papers, NA, 30 57/50 Erd/1259.

63 Wilson Diaries, IWM, DS/Misc/80, reel 6, 2 May 1915; French to Kitchener, [30] April 1915, Kitchener Papers, NA, 30 57/50 WA 82 (see n.56 above).

64 French to Kitchener, [30] April 1915, Kitchener Papers, NA, 30 57/50 WA 82.

65 French Diaries, IWM, PP/MCR/C32, reel 2, 2 May 1915; Wilson Diaries, IWM, DS/Misc/80, reel 6, 2 May 1915.

66 OAM62, French to Foch, 3 May 1915, *AFGG*, III A(I), no. 106.

67 No. 1877, Joffre to French, 5 May 1915, *AFGG*, III A(I), no. 121.

68 Cassar, *Trial by Gas*, xi–xii.

69 Wilson Diaries, IWM, DS/Misc/80, reel 6, 2 May 1915.

70 Ibid. See also 6 May 1915. Even Sir John, who rarely turned on Wilson, "was quite distant" with him on 3 May, when Wilson attempted to discuss with him British relations with the French. (Ibid., 3 May 1915.)

71 Ibid., 1, 2 May 1915.

72 Ibid., 6 May 1915.

73 Cassar, *Trial by Gas*, xi–xii; Greenhalgh, *Foch*, 108; Cherry, *The Battle of Loos, 1915*, 304.

74 Cf. Greenhalgh, *Foch*, 108–10.

75 No. 1877, Joffre to French, 5 May 1915, *AFGG*, III A(I), no. 121; Wilson Diaries, IWM, DS/Misc/80, reel 6, 5 May 1915.

76 No. 2043, Joffre to King of the Belgians, 5 May 1915, *AFGG*, III A(I), no. 122; no. 8520 P.L. Col. Genie to Commander in Chief, 7 May 1915, *AFGG*, III A(I), no. 137.

77 Poincaré, Notes Journalières, XXXIX, BN, NAF (16029), 6 May 1915.

78 Wilson Diaries, IWM, DS/Misc/80, reel 6, 6 May 1915.

79 French Diaries, IWM, PP/MCR/C32, reel 3, 7 May 1915.

80 Wilson Diaries, IWM, DS/Misc/80, reel 6, 7 May 1915; Foch to Joffre, 7 May 1915, Correspondance Foch, AG, no. 58.

81 Foch to Joffre, 7 May 1915, Correspondance Foch, AG, no. 58.

82 Wilson Diaries, IWM, DS/Misc/80, reel 6, 5–7 May 1915.

83 Asquith to Venetia Stanley, 6 January 1915, in Brock and Brock, eds., *Letters to Venetia Stanley*, 361–2.

84 French Diaries, IWM, PP/MCR/C32, reel 2, 23, 29–31 March 1915, 14 April 1915.

85 French Diaries, IWM, PP/MCR/C32, reel 2, 6 May 1915; French to Kitchener, 2 May 1915, Kitchener Papers, NA, 30 57/50. See no. 857, de la Panouse to Minister of War, 8 May 1915, AG, 7N700, Section Anglaise, dos. Mai 1915.

86 No. 889, de la Panouse to the Minister of War, 14 May 1915, AG, Section Anglaise, dos. Mai 1915.

87 Wilson Diaries, IWM, DS/Misc/80, reel 6, 4, 5–7 May 1915 (from interview with Joffre).

88 French Diaries, IWM, PP/MCR/C32, reel 3, 8 May 1915.

89 Clive Diaries, II/I, LHMA, 5 May 1915.

90 French Diaries, IWM, PP/MCR/C32, reel 3, 8 May 1915; Herwig, *The First World War*, 139.

91 French Diaries, IWM, PP/MCR/C32, reel 3, 8 May 1915.

CHAPTER SIX

1 See Greenhalgh, *French Army*, 90–3, 95, and *Foch in Command*, 110–12; Doughty, *Pyrrhic Victory*, 158–61.

2 French Diaries, IWM, PP/MCR/C32, reel 3, 9 May 1915; CT no. 452, Etat-Major St Omer à Général Foch, Cassell, GQG, 9 May 1915.

3 Wilson Diaries, IWM, DS/Misc/80, reel 6, 8 May 1915.

4 French Diaries, IWM, PP/MCR/C32, reel 3, 10 May 1915.

5 Wilson Diaries, IWM, DS/Misc/80, reel 6, 10 May 1915.

6 Ibid.

7 Ibid.
8 Ibid., 11 May 1915.
9 Ibid.
10 French Diaries, IWM, PP/MCR/C32, reel 3, 11 May 1915, printed somewhat out of context in French, ed., *War Diaries*, 198.
11 Ibid.
12 Ibid.
13 Ibid., 12 May 1915.
14 Ibid.
15 Cassar, *Kitchener*, 354.
16 Greenhalgh, *French Army*, 92–3, and *Foch in Command*, 111–13; Doughty, *Pyrrhic Victory*, 160–3.
17 French Diaries, IWM, PP/MCR/C32, reel 3, 12 May 1915; cf. Wilson Diaries, IWM, DS/Misc/80, reel 3, 12 May 1915.
18 Wilson Diaries, IWM, DS/Misc/80, reel 3, 12 May 1915.
19 Ibid.; French Diaries, IWM, PP/MCR/C32, reel 3, 12 May 1915.
20 Ibid., 16 May 1915.
21 Esher Journals, CA, 2/14, 15 and about 21 May 1915.
22 Wilson Diaries, IWM, DS/Misc/80, reel 3, 17 May 1915.
23 Secretary's Minutes of War Council, 14 May 1915, NA, CAB 42/1; Esher Journals, CA, 2/14, 14 May 1915; Hankey Papers, Diary, CA, 1/1, 14 May 1915.
24 French to Asquith, 20 May 1915, Bodleian Library, Asquith Papers, 26/226–31, Bodleian Library, Oxford.
25 T no. Y97, French to Kitchener, 15 May 1915, NA, WO 33/739/2465.
26 French Diaries, IWM, PP/MCR/C32, reel 6, 16 May 1915.
27 CT no. 4694, Kitchener to French, 16 May 1915, NA, WO 33/739/2470.
28 T no. Y100, French to Kitchener, 16 May 1915, NA, WO 33/739/2472.
29 T no. Y105, French to Kitchener, 16 May 1915, NA, WO 33/739/2474.
30 T no. Y108, French to Kitchener, 17 May 1915, NA, WO 33/739/2480. This was followed by a carefully reasoned letter, French to Secretary, 17 May 1915, NA, WO 33/739/2481; Robertson Papers, LHMA, I/5/1a–c.
31 CT no. 4719, Kitchener to French, 17 May 1915, NA, WO a33/739/2481.
32 Wilson Diaries, VI, IWM, DS/Misc/80, 17 May 1915.
33 Ibid., reel 6, 21 May 1915.
34 Ibid., 22 May 1915.
35 Wilson Diaries, IWM, DS/Misc/80, reel 6, 18–21 May 1915.
36 French Diaries, IWM, PP/MCR/C32, reel 3, 21 May 1915.
37 Doughty, *Pyrrhic Victory*, 162.
38 Wilson Diaries, IWM, DS/Misc/80, reel 6, 25 May 1915.
39 French Diaries, IWM, PP/MCR/C32, reel 3, 25 May 1915.
40 Ibid., 26 May 1915.
41 Doughty, *Pyrrhic Victory*, 163.

42 Wilson Diaries, IWM, DS/Misc/80, reel 6, 27 May 1915.
43 French Diaries, IWM, PP/MCR/C33, reel 3, 30 May 1915.
44 Wilson Diaries, IWM, DS/Misc/80, reel 6, 30 May 1915.
45 T no. 12127, Joffre to French, 30 May 1915, *AFGG*, III A(I), no. 425; Weygand to Huguet, 5 June 1915, NA, WO 158/26, Foch Correspondence with British General Headquarters, 141; Foch to Joffre, 6 June 1915, AG, Correspondence Foch (10 octobre 1914–21 janvier 1916), no. 61; Wilson Diaries, IWM, DS/Misc/80, reel 6, 8 June 1915; no. 266/pc, Weygand to Wilson, 10 June 1915, NA, WO 158/26, Foch Correspondence with British Headquarters, 136.
46 No. 197 p.c., Foch to French, 31 May 1915, NA, WO 158/26, Foch's Correspondence with British Headquarters, 146–7; ibid., Robertson to Wilson, 7 June 1915; Wilson Diaries, IWM, DS/Misc/80, reel 6, 8 June 1915.
47 French Diaries, IWM, PP/MCR/C33, reel 3, 12 June 1915.
48 No. 297/pc, Foch to Wilson, 13 June 1915, NA, WO 158/26, Foch Correspondence with British Headquarters, 133.
49 Foch to Joffre, 13 June 1915, Correspondence Foch, no. 63.
50 See next chapter.
51 Poincaré, Notes Journalières, XXXIX, BN, NAF (16030), 13 June 1915.
52 Ibid.
53 Ibid.
54 No. 85H, Huguet to Joffre, 10 June 1915, AG, 16N1905, 3e Bureau, Armée anglaise, no. 48.
55 Wilson Diaries, IWM, DS/Misc/80, reel 6, 14 June 1915.
56 Wilson Diaries, IWM, DS/Misc/80, reel 6, 9 June 1915.
57 CT no. Y140, Chief to Proemial, 16 June 1915, French Papers, IWM, 75/46/6.
58 Wilson Diaries, IWM, DS/Misc/80, reel 6, 16 June 1915; Doughty, *Pyrrhic Victory*, 161–2.
59 Doughty, *Pyrrhic Victory*, 163–4; Greenhalgh, *Foch in Command*, 114–15, and *French Army*, 93–5.
60 Poincaré, Notes Journalières, XXXIX, BN, NAF (16030), 18 June 1915. See below for details.
61 Ibid., 25 June 1915. See below.
62 Esher to French, 19 June 1915, French Papers, IWM, 75/46/11.
63 No. 374, Foch to French, 19 June 1915, NA, Foch's Correspondence with British General Headquarters. Regarding the discussion of the new offensive, see "Notes from Conversations 4th June" (approved by Joffre 5 June) by G.S. Clive, British Liaison Officer, 4 June 1915, Robertson Papers, I/5/13a-c, LHMA; Wilson Diaries, IWM, DS/Misc/80, reel 6, 5, 6 June 1915.
64 Esher Journals, 15, 19 June 1915, CA, 2/14; Callwell, *Wilson*, 1:252, diary entry, 22 June 1915.
65 See chapter 7 for a fuller treatment of this request.
66 Kitchener to French, 15 June 1915, French Papers, IWM, 75/46/11.

67 Callwell, *Wilson*, 1:252, diary entry, 22 June 1915; French Diaries, IWM, PP/MCR/C33, reel 3, 22 June 1915.

68 Clive Diaries, II/II, LHMA, 22 June 1915.

69 French to Kitchener, 23 June 1915, Robertson Papers, LHMA, 1/5/2a–2f.

70 No. 9.860, Joffre to Millerand, 24 June 1915, AG, Fonds Joffre, 14N10, 1, annexe no. 2.

71 Foch to Joffre, 18 June 1915, Correspondance Foch, AG, no. 65; Note de Foch sur une Conversation avec le Général Wilson, 20 June [1915], *AFGG*, III A(I), no. 693.

72 Minutes of the Meeting at Chantilly 24 June 1915, Robertson Papers, LHMA, 1/5/14a-yd.

73 Ibid.

74 Robertson to Wigram, 24 June 1915, Royal Archives, Geo. V. Q 2522/3/184.

75 No. 10.159, Joffre to Millerand, 24 June 1915, Millerand Papers, AN, 470AP15, dos. "Con[cernant] Millerand-Joffre."

76 French to Mrs Bennett, 21 May 1915, French Papers, IWM, PP/MCR/C33, reel 1.

77 Doughty, *Pyrrhic Victory*, 164–5.

78 "The Great War," "Battles of the Western Front," and "Allied Offensive in Artois," at www.greatwar.co.uk/battles/ (consulted 19 July 2013).

79 CT no. 544, French to Kitchener, 26 June 1915, Asquith Papers, 14/45, Bodleian Library, Oxford.

80 T, Huguet to Joffre, 29 June 1915, *AFGG*, III A(I), no. 788.

81 Joffre to Millerand, 30 June 1915, Millerand Papers, AN, 470AP15, dos. "Con[cernant] Millerand–Joffre."

82 See chapter 8.

CHAPTER SEVEN

1 No. 10159, Joffre to Minister of War, 24, 29 June 1915, *AFGG*, III A(I), nos. 743, 787.

2 French, *1914*, 356–7.

3 Churchill to French, 13 May 1915, French Papers, IWM, 75/46/11. See Koss, *Asquith*, 178–81, 192–3, for an account of the rumour that in April "Churchill had combined with Balfour, Lloyd George & [J.L.] Garvin [editor for both the *Observer* and the *Pall Mall Gazette*] in an effort to overthrow Asquith and Grey ... To this end they enlisted the support of Sir John French" (193). Both Repington and Churchill were at British headquarters at the same time, but Churchill's role remains obscure.

4 French, *1914*, 357.

5 Ibid.

6 See Cassar, *Kitchener*, 354.

7 French, *1914*, 357.

8 French to Mrs Bennett, 21 May 1915, French Papers, IWM, PP/MCR/C33, reel 1.

9 French Diaries, IWM, PP/MCR/C32, reel 3, 9 May 1915.

10 His account of the meeting with Kitchener on 1 September 1914, in which none of Kitchener's instructions is recorded, is a case in point.

11 Wilson Diaries, IWM, DS/Misc/80, reel 6, 9 May 1915, qtd. in Callwell, ed., *Wilson*, 2:226.

12 French Diaries, IWM, PP/MCR/C32, reel 6, 11 May 1915; Clive Diaries, II/I, LHMA, 9 May 1915.

13 Ibid.; French Diaries, IWM, PP/MCR/C32, reel 3, 11 May 1915.

14 French Diaries, IWM, PP/MCR/C32, reel 3, 11 May 1915, printed somewhat out of context in French, ed., *War Diaries*, 198.

15 Ibid.

16 Ibid., 12 May 1915.

17 Ibid.

18 Cassar, *Kitchener*, 354.

19 Cf. "Need for Shells," *The Times*, 14 May 1915, 1.

20 For interpretations of the May cabinet crisis and Asquith's formation of the coalition government, see Jenkins, *Asquith*, 349–70; Koss, *Asquith*, 175–98; Cassar, *Asquith*, 91–110.

21 Asquith to Sylvia Henley, 12 May 1915, MSS, Eng. Lett., C542/1/1–6, Bodleian Library, Oxford.

22 Ibid.

23 Asquith to Henley, 13 May 1915, MSS, Eng. Lett., C542/1/10–11, Bodleian Library, Oxford.

24 For a judicious appraisal of the issue, see Levine, *Politics, Love and Religion*, 292–300. See also, Cassar, *Asquith*, 99–100.

25 Asquith to Henley, 4–18 June 1915, MSS, Eng. Lett., C542/1/49–134, Bodleian Library, Oxford. Romantic, even poetic, in his letters to Sylvia, craving of her attention and interest, regaling in long afternoon motor rides in the countryside and other social interactions with her, Asquith, however, appears to have stopped short of sexual relations, maintaining a platonic hand-holding relationship as he had with her younger sister, Venetia. (See Brock and Brock, eds., *Letters to Venetia Stanley*, "Introduction," 3; Asquith to Henley, 18–20 June 1915, MSS, Eng. Lett., C542/1/141–6, Bodleian Library, Oxford.)

26 Cassar, *Kitchener*, 361–5.

27 See Esher to Bertie, 5 May 1915, NA, FO 800/167/Fr/15/33, for a contemporary opinion.

28 Fraser, "The British Shells Scandal of 1915," 69–86.

29 Cabinet Circular, 17 May 1915, Kitchener Papers, NA, 30 57/74 WR/16. Cf. Koss, *Asquith*, 183–5.

30 See Levine, *Politics, Religion and Love*, 765n.41. The reference is to Adelman, *Decline of the Liberal Party*, 14.

31 Cassar, *Kitchener*, 370–1.

32 Ibid., 373–4, 519n.6.

33 Ibid., 370, 524n.25. For Churchill's role in the Dardanelles Committee until his resignation, see, Bell, *Churchill and the Dardanelles*, 188–203.

34 See Fraser, "The British Shells Scandal of 1915," 69–86; French, "The Military Background to the 'Shell Crisis' of May 1915," 192–205; Cassar, *Kitchener*, 331–60.

35 Cassar, *Kitchener*, 359.

36 Ibid., 331–2.

37 See Neilson, *Strategy and Supply*.

38 Fraser, "The British Shells Scandal of 1915," 69–86.

39 Cassar, *Kitchener*, 336.

40 French, "The Military Background to the Shells Crisis," 192–205.

41 Esher Journals, 15 and about 21 May 1915, CA, 2/14.

42 Wilson Diaries, IWM, DS/Misc/80, reel 3, 17 May 1915.

43 Secretary's Minutes of War Council, 14 May 1915, NA, CAB 42/1; Esher Journals, 2/14, CA, 14 May 1915; Hankey Papers, Diary, 1/1, CA, 14 May 1915.

44 See previous chapter for details of this discussion.

45 French Diaries, IWM, PP/MCR/C32, reel 6, 16 May 1915.

46 Esher Journals, CA, 2/14, 14 May 1915, printed in part in Esher, *Journals and Letters*, 2:233.

47 Cited in Cassar, *Kitchener*, 354–5.

48 Cited in ibid., 355.

49 French to Asquith, 20 May 1915, Asquith Papers, 26/226–31, Bodleian Library, Oxford.

50 Lloyd George to Asquith, 19 May 1915, Asquith Papers, 14/36, Bodleian Library, Oxford.

51 Cassar, *Asquith*, 102–3. In this scheme, Kitchener was to become commander-in-chief (Hankey Papers, Diary, CA, 1/1, 17–18 May 1915), a proposal urged by Esher on the War Council and the king, to achieve unity of command ("Unity of Command," by Lord Esher, 12 May 1915, Royal Archives, GV, Q765/2); Esher Journals, 14 May 1915, CA, 2/14). On Esher's urging, Kitchener momentarily fell in line with this plan, which had the support of the king (Esher Journals, 16, 21 May 1915, CA, 2/14), but the succession of events rendered it nugatory.

52 Cassar, *Kitchener*, 357–8.

53 Asquith to French, 21 May 1915, French Papers, IWM, 75/46/11.

54 Asquith to Henley, 30 May, 2 June 1915, MSS, Eng. Lett., C542/1/27–30, 41–6, Bodleian Library, Oxford.

55 Esher Journals, CA, 2/14, 21 May 1915.

56 Esher Journals, CA, 2/14, 22 May 1915; Esher to Fitzgerald, 24 May 1915, Kitchener Papers, NA, 30 57/59 W1/48.

57 Esher to Kitchener, 23 May 1915, Kitchener Papers, NA, 30 57/59 W1/44.

58 Esher to Fitzgerald, 23 May 1915, Kitchener Papers, NA, 30 55/59 W1/48. Robertson's role in suggesting this to Sir John is elaborated in Esher Journals, CA, 2/14, 22 May 1915.

59 For interpretations of the May cabinet crisis and Asquith's formation of the coalition government, see Jenkins, *Asquith*, 349–70; Koss, *Asquith*, 175–98; Cassar, *Asquith*, 91–110.

60 For a judicious appraisal of the issue, see Levine, *Politics, Love and Religion*, 292–300. See also Cassar, *Asquith*, 99–100.

61 Cabinet Circular, 17 May 1915, Kitchener Papers, NA, 30 57/74 WR/16. Cf. Koss, *Asquith*, 183–5.

62 French to Asquith, 20 May 1915, Asquith Papers, 26/226–31, Bodleian Library, Oxford; French to Mrs Bennett, 21 May 1915, French Papers, IWM, PP/MCR/C33, reel 1.

63 See Fraser, "The British Shells Scandal," 69–86.

64 Cassar, *Asquith*, 135–6.

65 See, for example, Woodward, *Great Britain and the War of 1914–1918*, 137–99; Cassar, *French*, 270–82.

66 Robertson to Stamfordham, 23 June 1915, Robertson Papers, LHMA, 1/12/2a–2c.

67 Robertson Papers, LHMA, 1/12/3a–3e.

68 Pamela Clark, Deputy Registrar, Royal Archives, to author, 10 February 1993.

69 Robertson to Stamfordham, 23 June 1915, Robertson Papers, LHMA, 1/12/2a–2c, 1/12/3a–3e; cf. letter, Robertson to Esher, 23 June 1915, CA, Esher Papers, 5/48.

70 Poincaré, *Au service*, 6:196, 204, 207, 211, 134; Doughty, *Pyrrhic Victory*, 165–6.

71 Yarde-Buller to Kitchener, 16 May 1915, Kitchener Papers, NA, WO 159/10/45.

72 Poincaré, Notes Journalières, XXXIX, BN, NAF (16030), 3 June 1915.

73 Francis Bertie, British Ambassador in Paris, to Grey, Secretary of State for Foreign Affairs, 9 June 1915, Bertie Papers, NA, FO 800/1671/Fr/15/34.

74 Poincaré, Notes Journalières, XXXIX, BN, NAF (16030), 3 June 1915.

75 For the evolution of parliamentary inspection in 1915, see King, *Generals and Politicians*, 36–66.

76 King, *Generals and Politicians*, 58–9.

77 Poincaré, *Au service*, 6:196, 204, 207, 211.

78 Greenhalgh, *French Army*, 100; King, *Generals and Politicians*, 63–4; Doughty, *Pyrrhic Victory*, 166; Godfrey, *Capitalism at War*, 52–4.

79 Doughty, *Pyrrhic Victory*, 115–20.

80 Joffre, *Mémoires*, 2:28–31.

81 Poincaré, Notes Journalières, XXXIX, BN, NAF (16030), 27 April, 25, 27, 29 May, 18, 19, 20 June 1915.

82 Doughty, *Pyrrhic Victory*, 166–7.

83 Poincaré, Notes Journalières, XXXVIII, BN, NAF (16029), 18 March 1915.

84 Troisième Bureau, "Note (à propos de la visite du lord K)" by Pont, 27 March 1915, AG, 16N1905, dos. Armée Anglaise, no. 35.

85 Troisième Bureau, "Note au sujet des conditions générales de la guerre sur le front occidental," 25 May 1915, *AFGG*, III A(II), no. 360.

86 Ibid.; no. 109, PCS, Commander-in-Chief to Minister of War, 27 May 1915, *AFGG*, III A(I), no. 380.

87 French Diaries, IWM, PP/MCR/C32, reel 3, 6 May 1915; no. 857, de la Panouse, military attaché in London, to Minister of War, 8 March 1915, AG, EMA, Section Anglaise, Entrées, correspondance de l'Attaché militaire à Londres, dos. mai 1915.

88 Philpott, "Kitchener and the 29th Division," 396; Buat Papers, no. 968, de la Panouse to Ministre de la guerre, 5 June 1915, AG, 6N29, dos. Angleterre et Portugal, Documents Divers, dos. juin 1915.

89 Session of War Council, 14 May 1915, NA, CAB 42/2/19; Hankey Papers, Diary, CA, 1/1, 14 May 1915.

90 Philpott, "Kitchener and the 29th Division," 397.

91 Session of War Council, 14 May 1915, NA, CAB 42/2/19.

92 Prete, "War of Movement," 364–7, 448–54; CT no. 1014, Ministre des Affaires Etrangères to l'Ambassadeur (Paul Cambon) in London, 21 December 1914, AE, "Guerre 1914–1918," 534:176; no. 3123, Commandant en chef to Ministre de guerre, 12 January 1915, AE, "Guerre 1914–1918," 535:18; incidents cited supra.

93 No. 109, PCS, Lettre du Général Commandant en chef au Ministre de la guerre, 27 May 1915, *AFGG*, III A(I), no. 380.

94 Note verbale du Général Joffre, Commandant en chef des Armées françaises, pour son Excellence lord Kitchener, Ministre de la guerre, 27 May 1915, *AFGG*, III A(I), no. 381.

95 Ibid.

96 Maurice Hankey, Secretary of War Council, to the Prime Minister, 29 May 1915, Asquith Papers, 27/247–50, Bodleian Library, Oxford.

97 Ibid. For 18-pound guns, the British could only supply 10–12 rounds per day, as opposed to the 17 rounds per day that Joffre considered essential during the conference on 29 March 1915. (Ibid.)

98 Ibid.

99 Asquith to Henley, 30, 31 May, 1, 2, 3 June 1915, MSS, Eng. Lett., C542/1/27–48, Bodleian Library, Oxford.

100 Wilson Diaries, VI, IWM, DS/Misc/80, 2 June 1915; French Diaries, IWM, PP/MCR/C33, reel 3, 2 June 1915.

101 Hankey to Prime Minister, 29 May 1915, Asquith Papers, 27/247–50, Bodleian Library, Oxford.

102 French Diaries, IWM, PP/MCR/C33, reel 3, 2 June 1915; Wilson Diaries, VI, IWM, DS/Misc/80, 2 June 1915.

103 Poincaré, Notes Journalières, XXXIX, BN, NAF (16029), 3 June 1915.

104 Asquith to Henley, 2 June 1915, MSS, Eng. Lett., C542/1/41–6, Bodleian Library, Oxford.

105 Poincaré, Notes Journalières, XXXIX, BN, NAF (16029), 3 June 1915. Poincaré, who received his information from Millerand, gives the impression that Asquith made greater commitments than the British participants reported. He recorded: "It was agreed between Asquith, Millerand, Joffre and French, that they would send 5 or 6 new divisions to France, in the near future" (ibid.).

106 Foch, "Journées," AFF, 414AP10, 2 June 1915.

107 Asquith to Henley, 2 June 1915, MSS, Eng. Lett., C542/1/41–6, Bodleian Library, Oxford.

108 "Note prepared after visit to Sir J. French, June 1915 (copy to Lord K.)" (in Asquith's hand), Asquith Papers, 27/266, Bodleian Library, Oxford.

109 "Notes from Conversations 4th June" (approved by Joffre 5 June) by G.S. Clive, British Liaison Officer, 4 June 1915, Robertson Papers, I/5/13a-c, LHMA; Wilson Diaries, IWM, DS/Misc/80, reel 6, 5, 6 June 1915.

110 Charles Callwell (Imperial General Staff, London) to Wilson, 4, 7 June 1915, Wilson Papers, IWM, 2/75/42, 43; Esher Journals, CA, 2/14, 11 June 1915.

111 Rapport sur la Mission Buat, 8 [11] June 1915, *AFGG*, III A(I), no. 550; Compte-rendu de la mission du Lieutenant-Colonel Renouard au Maréchal Kitchener, 11 June 1915, *AFGG*, III A(I), no. 552.

112 Esher Papers, *Journal*, CA, 2/14, 2 June 1915.

113 Callwell to Wilson, 10 June 1915, IWM, H.H.W. 2/75/44.

114 Wilson Diaries, IWM, DS/Misc/80, reel 6, 11 June 1915.

115 French to Kitchener, 11 June 1915, Kitchener Papers, NA, 30 57/50 Erd/1259.

CHAPTER EIGHT

1 Significant portions of this chapter (and a small segment of the last chapter) were previously published in French in "Le conflit stratégique franco-britannique sur le front occidental et la conférence de Calais du 6 juillet, 1915," *Guerres mondiales et conflits contemporains* 186 (April 1997): 17–49; reprinted with permission of the publisher.

2 See *HGW*, addendum to "1915," vol. 2; Cassar, *Kitchener*, 381–2; French, *British Strategy*, 107–8.

3 Rapport sur la Mission Buat, 8 [11] June 1915, *AFGG*, III A(I), no. 550.

4 Minutes de télégrammes à chiffrer, no. 1269, et suite au no. 1269, Cambon à Diplomatie, Paris, 15, 17 June 1915, Papiers Cambon, AE, Minutes de la Correspondance officielle, vol. 7, dos. no. 22, pp. 20, 21.

5 Minute de Cambon, 24 June 1915, Cambon Papers, AE, Correspondances et Papiers Divers, V Londres, 1912–16, vol. 13, no. 3; Minute de télégrammes chiffrés nos. 1347, 1348, Cambon à Diplomatie, Paris, 24 June 1915, Cambon, AE, Correspondance officielle, 1914–20, vol. 7, dos. no. 22, pp. 22–3; Bertie to Crewe (temporary replacement for Grey at the Foreign Office), 17 June 1915, Bertie Papers, AN, FO 800/167/Fr/15/37.

6 Minute du télégramme no. 1396, Cambon à Diplomatie, Paris, 29 June 1915, AE, Paul Cambon Papers, Correspondance Officielle, vol. 7, dos. 22, pp. 25, 26.

7 OAM 446, Commandant-in-Chief, British Army in the Field, to the Secretary of State for War, London, 23 June 1915, NA, WO 158/21 Erd/2197; Procès-verbal de la réunion tenue à Chantilly, 24 June 1915, *AFGG*, III A(I), no. 736.

8 Foch to Joffre, 18 June 1915, Correspondance Foch, AG, no. 65; Note de Foch sur une Conversation avec le Général Wilson, 20 June [1915], *AFGG*, III A(I), no. 693.
9 French Diaries, IWM, PP/MCR/C33, reel 3, 19 June 1915; dépêche no. 89/t, Huguet à Joffre, 20 June 1915, *AFGG*, III A(I), nos. 691, 692.
10 Procès-verbal de la réunion tenue à Chantilly, 24 June 1915, *AFGG*, III A(I), no. 736.
11 Note of Bertie (on recent interviews of LeRoy Lewis, Military Attaché in Paris), 5 July 1915, Bertie Papers, NA, FO 800/167/Fr/15/40.
12 Poincaré, Notes Journalières, XXXIX, BN, NAF (16030), 29 June 1915.
13 Ibid., 20, 23 June 1915.
14 Poincaré, *Au service*, 6:275–8, 283–7.
15 Note of Bertie (on the interviews of LeRoy Lewis), 5 June 1915, Bertie Papers, NA, FO 800/167/Fr/40.
16 Williams, "Lord Kitchener and the Battle of Loos," 117–31.
17 Memorandum, "Reasons for the Offensive in Flanders," 12 June 1915, Kitchener Papers, NA, 30/57/58 Erd/1316.
18 Esher to Kitchener, 20 June 1915, Kitchener Papers, NA, 30/55/59.
19 AM 446, Commander-in-Chief, British Army in the Field to Secretary of State for War, 23 June 1915, NA, WO 159/21 Erd/2199.
20 Haig to Asquith, 25 June 1915, Asquith Papers, 14/70–4, Bodleian Library, Oxford.
21 Asquith to Henley, 29 June 1915, MSS, Eng. Lett., C542/1/171–4, Bodleian Library, Oxford.
22 T, Bertie to Crewe, 4 July 1915, Bertie Papers, NA, FO800/167/Fr/115/39.
23 Note of Bertie (on the interviews of LeRoy Lewis), 5 June 1915, Bertie Papers, NA, FO 800/167/Fr/40. Cf. Williams, "Lord Kitchener and the Battle of Loos," 125–7, who makes a distinction between the pessimism of Esher and the optimism of Bertie and claims that Bertie did not believe there to be a true public-opinion crisis in France during the summer of 1915.
24 French, *British Strategy*, 106; Cassar, *Kitchener*, 378.
25 Casser, *Kitchener*, 378; Esher Journals, CA, 2/14, 29 June 1915.
26 Esher Journals, CA, 2/14, 29 June 1915.
27 Wilson Diaries, IWM, DS/Misc/80, reel 6, 29 June 1915.
28 Wilson Diaries, IWM, DS/Misc/80, reel 6, 30 June 1915.
29 Ibid., 1 July 1915.
30 French Diaries, IWM, PP/MCR/C32, reel 3, 30 June, 1 July 1915; Asquith to Henley, 2 July 1915, MSS, Eng. Lett., C542/1/189–94, Bodleian Library, Oxford.
31 Asquith to Henley, 2 July 1915, MSS, Eng. Lett., C542/1/189–94, Bodleian Library, Oxford.
32 French Diaries, IWM, PP/MCR/C32, reel 3, 2 July 1915.
33 Wilson Diaries, VI, IWM, DS/Misc/80, 3 July 1915; Asquith to the King, 3 July 1915, with "Cabinet Minute," NA, CAB 41/36/31 and 41/37R/235.

34 Note of Bertie (on the recent interviews de Leroy Lewis), Bertie Papers, British Library, London, 63038/18–27, 5 July 1915.

35 Asquith to the King, 3 July 1915, and "Cabinet Minute," NA, CAB 41/36/31, 41/37R/234, and 41/37R235.

36 Esher Journals, CA, 2/14, 2 July 1915.

37 Williams, "Lord Kitchener and the Battle of Loos," 117–32.

38 Quoted in Becker, *Les Français dans la Grande Guerre*, 102–3.

39 Asquith, notes on the Calais Conference, 6 July 1915, MSS, Eng. Lett., C542/1/212–16, Bodleian Library, Oxford.

40 Esher Journals, CA, 2/14, 7 July 1915.

41 Hankey Papers, Diary, CA, 1/1, 6 July 1915.

42 Ibid.

43 Ibid.; Wilson Diaries, VI, IWM, DS/Misc/80, 6 July 1915.

44 Asquith, *Memories and Reflections*, 2:127–8.

45 French, *British Strategy*, 107.

46 Hankey Papers, Diary, CA, 1/1, 5, 6 July 1915; Wilson Diaries, VI, IWM, DS/Misc/80, 5, 6 July; Clive Diaries, II/II, LHMA, 6 July 1915; Esher, *Journals and Letters*, 3:252–3.

47 "Lt. Col. Hankey's draft of conclusions of Anglo-French Conference held at Calais Tuesday July 6th 1915," NA, CAB 28/9 (discovered in the above-cited 1917 file by Keith Neilson, my distinguished colleague at the Royal Military College of Canada, who, regrettably, died in 2015).

48 Asquith to Henley, 5 July 1915; Notes on the Calais Conference, 6 July 1915, MSS, Eng. Lett., C542/1/ 205–8, 218–23, Bodleian Library, Oxford.

49 French Diaries, IWM, PP/MCR/C32, reel 3, 6 July 1915; French to Mrs Bennett, ibid., 6 July 1915.

50 Millerand Papers, Notes, Calais, 6 July (in Millerand's hand); Procès-verbal, "Conférence de Calais," 6 July 1915, AN, 470AP15, dos. "Conf 2/6/15 ... Calais 11/9."

51 Wilson Diaries, VI, IWM, DS/Misc/80, 5 July 1995.

52 CT no. 3667, chef Mission Militaire Française à St. Omer au Grand Quartier Général, AG, 17N338, dos. MMF/A Brit., dos. Juillet, 5 July 1915.

53 See, for example, Cassar, *Kitchener*, 381 and 520nn.; Cf. Philpott, "Kitchener and the 29th Division," 399 and 407n.147.

54 Cassar, *Kitchener*, 381 and 520n.30, based on "Note written under the direction of Field Marshal Kitchener, 6 July 1915, England," box 59, AG, which appears in French translation as "Note au sujet de l'arrivée en France des divisions anglaises (écrite sous la dictée du maréchal Kitchener)," 6 July 1915, *AFGG*, III A(II), no. 856.

55 Procès-verbal de la Conférence des représentants des différentes armées alliées tenue à Chantilly, 7 July 1915, *AFGG*, III A(II), no. 860.

56 Cassar, *Kitchener*, 381, and Philpott, "Kitchener and the 29th Division," 399, claim that the two chiefs agreed that if a later offensive was necessary, it would be carried uniquely by French forces.

57 Procès-verbal, "Conférence de Calais," 6 July 1915, Millerand Papers, AN, 470AP15.

58 Asquith's notes on the Calais Conference, 6 July 1915, MSS, Eng. Lett., C542/1/218–23, Bodleian Library, Oxford. As these notes indicate, Asquith was careful to suppress from his original text any discussion apt to ruffle French susceptibilities with regard to the British naval contribution, the Dardanelles expedition, and the limitations of British participation generally (ibid.). Cf. Procès-verbal, "Conférence de Calais," 6 July 1915, Millerand Papers, AN, 470AP15.

59 Procès-verbal, "Conférence de Calais," 6 July 1915, Millerand Papers, AN, 470AP15.

60 Ibid.; Note de Millerand, Calais, 6 July 1915, Millerand Papers, AN, 470AP15; Cf. "Note au sujet de l'arrivée en France des divisions Anglaises (écrite sous la dictée du maréchal Kitchener)," 6 July 1915, *AFGG*, III A(II), no. 856.

61 Procès-verbal, "Conférence de Calais," 6 July 1915; Note de Millerand, Calais, 6 July 1915, Millerand Papers, AN, 470AP15.

62 See French, "The Origins of the Dardanelles Campaign Reconsidered."

63 Procès-verbal, "Conférence de Calais," 6 July 1915; Note de Millerand, Calais, 6 July 1915, Millerand Papers, AN, 470AP15.

64 Procès-verbal, "Conférence de Calais," 6 July 1915; Note de Millerand, Calais, 6 July 1915, Millerand Papers, AN, 470AP15.

65 Asquith's notes on the Calais Conference, 6 July 1915, MSS, Eng. Lett., C542/1/218–23, Bodleian Library, Oxford.

66 Note de Millerand, Calais, 6 July 1915, Millerand Papers, AN, 470AP15.

67 Ibid. On Balfour's strategic views, see Balfour to Kitchener, 10 June 1915, Kitchener Papers, NA, 30 57/78, Erd/1297.

68 Procès-verbal, "Conférence de Calais," 6 July 1915, Millerand Papers, AN, 4705AP15.

69 Ibid.

70 Note de Millerand, Calais, 6 July 1915, Millerand Papers, AN, 470AP15.

71 Procès-verbal, "Conférence de Calais," 6 July 1915, Millerand Papers, AN, 470AP15.

72 Ibid.

73 Ibid.

74 Ibid.

75 Ibid.

76 Ibid.

77 Ibid.

78 Ibid.

79 Taylor, *Politics in Wartime*, 15.

80 Asquith's notes on the Calais Conference, 6 July 1915, MSS, Eng. Lett., C542/1/218–23, Bodleian Library, Oxford.

81 Procès-verbal, "Conférence de Calais," 6 July 1915, Papiers Millerand, BN, carton 26, dos. "Opérations B." On Delcassé's insistence on the importance of Romanian entry into the war, it was agreed that the Allied diplomatic effort would

focus on Romania rather than Bulgaria. (Asquith's notes on the Calais Conference, 6 July 1915, MSS, Eng. Lett., C542/1/218–23, Bodleian Library, Oxford; French Diaries, IWM, PP/MCR/C32, reel 3, 6 July 1915; Hankey Papers, Diary, CA, 1/1, 6 July 1915.)

82 Hankey Papers, Diary, CA, 1/1, 6 July 1915.

83 Esher Journals, CA, 2/14, 7 July 1915.

84 Hankey Papers, Diary, CA, 1/1, 6 July 1915.

85 Esher Journals, CA, 2/14, 7 July 1915.

86 French to Mrs Bennett, 7 July 1915, French Papers, IWM, PP/MCR/C33, reel 1.

87 Robertson to Clive Wigram, 19 July 1915, LHMA, Robertson Papers, 13 July 1915.

88 Hankey Papers, Diary, CA, 1/1, 6 July 1915.

89 "Lt. Col. Hankey's draft of conclusions of Anglo-French Conference held at Calais Tuesday July 6th 1915," NA, CAB 29/9/1–2; Hankey Papers, Diary, CA, 1/1, 6 July 1915.

90 French Diaries, IWM/PP/MCR/C32, reel 3.

91 French to Mrs Bennett, 6 July 1915, French Papers, IWM/PP/MCR/C33, reel 1.

92 Ibid.

93 Procès-verbal de la Conférence des représentants des différentes armées alliées tenue à Chantilly, 7 July 1915, *AFGG*, III A(II), no. 860.

94 Ibid.; "Note au sujet de l'arrivée en France des divisions anglaises (écrite sous la dictée du maréchal Kitchener)," 6 July 1915, *AFGG*, III A(II), no. 856.

95 Procès-verbal de la Conférence des représentants des différentes armées alliées tenue à Chantilly, 7 July 1915, *AFGG*, III A(II), no. 860.

96 Poincaré, *Au service*, 6:253, 257.

97 No. 10486, Extracts of Minutes of Meeting of Kitchener, Millerand, French, Joffre, [29] March 1915, AG, 16N1905, dos. 1, Armée Anglaise, no. 31.

98 "Note sur la situation générale," 21 June 1915, *AFGG*, III A(I), no. 702.

99 No. 9861, Commander-in-Chief to Minister of War, 24 June 1915, *AFGG*, III A(I), no. 701.

100 McCraie, *Coalition Strategy*, 14–17.

101 No. 10159, Joffre to Minister of War, 24, 29 June 1915, *AFGG*, III A(I), nos. 743, 787.

102 Joffre to Minister of War, 29 June 1915, *AFGG*, III A(I), no. 787.

103 T no. 1396, Cambon to "Diplomatie," Paris, 29 June 1915, Paul Cambon Papers, Official Correspondence, 3:22, 25–6; "Historique, Direction de la Guerre Européenne, I," Fonds Joffre, AG, 14N10, 7.

104 Procés-verbal de la conférence des représentants des différentes armées alliées tenue à Chantilly, 7 July 1915, *AFGG*, III A(II), no. 860.

105 Ibid.

106 Keagan, *First World War*, 228.

107 Procés-verbal de la conférence des représentants des différentes armées alliées tenue à Chantilly, 7 July 1915, *AFGG*, III A(II), no. 860; Wilson Diaries, VI, IWM, DS/Misc/80, 1 July 1915.

108 "Procès-verbal de la conférence qui eut lieu à Saint-Omer au quartier général de l'armée anglaise dans la matinée du 11 juillet," *AFGG*, III A(II), no. 889.

109 Wilson Diaries, IWM, DS/Misc/80, reel 6, 15, 19 July 1915; no. 174518, Foch to Joffre, 17 July 1915, *AFGG*, III A(II), no. 954.

110 "Historique – Direction de la Guerre Européenne," 1:7-8, AG, Fonds Joffre, 14N10.

CHAPTER NINE

1 "Note au sujet de l'arrivée en France des divisions anglaises, 6 juillet 1915 (écrite sous la dictée du maréchal Kitchener)," *AFGG*, III A(II), no. 856. See also chapter 8.

2 Minutes of meeting at Chantilly, 24 June 1915, Robertson Papers, LHMA, I/5/14a.

3 "Procès-verbal de la conférence des représentants de Différentes armées Allieés tenue à Chantilly, le 7 juillet, 1915," *AFGG*, II A(II), no. 860. For a fuller discussion of Joffre's attempt to coordinate Allied efforts in 1915 and 1916, see Roy A. Prete, "Joffre and the Question of Allied Supreme Command," 329–37.

4 "Procès-verbal de la Conférence des représentants des différentes armées alliées tenue à Chantilly, 7 juillet 1915," *AFGG*, III A(II), no. 860.

5 "Procès-verbal de la conférence qui eut lieu à Saint-Omer au quartier général de l'armée anglaise dans la matinée du 11 juillet," *AFGG*, III A(II), no. 889.

6 Wilson Diaries, IWM, DS/Misc/80, reel 6, 15, 19 July 1915; no. 174518, Foch to Joffre, 17 July 1915, *AFGG*, III A(II), no. 954.

7 Wilson Diaries, IWM, DS/Misc/80, reel 6, 15, 19 July 1915; no. 174518, Foch to Joffre, 17 July 1915, *AFGG*, III A(II), no. 954.

8 French Diaries, IWM, PP/MCR/C32, reel 3, 20, 22, 23, 24 July 1915; Sheffield, *Haig*, 123. The description of the terrain is from French to Joffre, 29 July 1915, Joffre's Correspondence with British Headquarters, NA, WO 158/13, 152–5.

9 Clive Diaries, II/II, LHMA, 17 July 1915.

10 Esher Journals, CA, 2/14, 15 July 1915.

11 Esher Journals, CA, 2/14, 17 July 1915.

12 Esher Journals, CA, 2/14, 15 July 1915.

13 French Diaries, IWM, PP/MCR/C32, reel 3, 20 July 1915.

14 French Diaries, IWM, PP/MCR/C32, reel 3, 24 July 1915.

15 Clive Diaries, II/II, LHMA, 25, 26 July 1915.

16 Wilson Diaries, VI, IWM, DS/Misc/80, 24 July 1915.

17 Robertson to Wigram (assistant secretary to the king), 27 July 1915, Robertson Papers, LHMA, I/12/19a.

18 Wilson Diaries, IWM, DS/Misc/80, 24 July 1915.

19 Report of a meeting between Field-Marshal Sir John French and General Foch, Frévent, 27 July 1915, Foch Correspondence with British Headquarters, NA, WO 158/26, 107–11; no. 97/8, A.M., le général commandant en chef à titre de compte

rendu [interview between French and Foch, 27 July 1915], *AFGG*, III A(II), no. 1026.

20 Ibid.; Ferdinad Foch, Journées, AFF, 11 August 1915.

21 Foch to Joffre, 27 July 1915, AG, 16N1905, 3e Bureau, Armée anglaise, no. 72.

22 Wilson Diaries, IWM, DS/Misc/80, reel 6, 27 July 1915.

23 Ibid., 28 July 1915.

24 French Diaries, IWM, PP/MCR/C32, reel 3, 28 July 1915.

25 Clive Diaries, II/II, LHMA, 28 July 1915.

26 French to Foch, 29 July 1915, Joffre's correspondence with British Headquarters, NA, WO 158/13, 152–5; French Diaries, IWM, PP/MCR/C32, reel 3, 29 July 1915.

27 Clive Diaries, II/II, LHMA, 28 July 1915.

28 No. 16481, Joffre to French, 31 July 1915; no. 16482, Pellé [for Joffre] to Foch, 31 July 1915; no. 2138, Joffre to Foch, 3 August 1915; no. 60/9, Foch to Joffre, 3 August 1915; no. 2874, Joffre to French, 5 August 1915, *AFGG*, III A(II), nos. 1055, 1056, 1082, 1089, 1102.

29 French Diaries, IWM, PP/MCR/C32, reel 3, 1–5, 6 August 1915. See French to Kitchener, 8 August 1915, Kitchener Papers, NA, 30 57/50, in which Sir John French complains to Kitchener of no improvement in munition deliveries.

30 French Diaries, IWM, PP/MCR/C32, reel 3, 7 August 1915; see also Robertson to Wigram, Robertson Papers, LHMA, I/12/20/1a, 6 August 1915.

31 OAM 694, French to Joffre, 10 August 1915, *AFGG*, III A(II), no. 1143; no. 8384, Joffre to Foch, 12 August 1915, *AFGG*, III A(II), no. 1155; no. 8385, Joffre to French, 12 August 1915, Joffre's correspondence with British Headquarters, NA, WO 158/13, 136–7 (reproduced in *AFGG*, III A(II), no. 1156).

32 Rawlinson Diary, CA, 1/3, 13, 14 August 1915.

33 OAM 718, French to Joffre, 14 August 1914, *AFGG*, III A(II), no. 1174.

34 French Diaries, IWM, PP/MCR/C32, reel 3, 15, 16 August 1915.

35 Poincaré, *Au service*, 7:11, 14, 16, 25–9; King, *Generals and Politicians*, 40–80.

36 Joffre, *Mémoires*, 2:104–20; see Tanenbaum, *Sarrail*, 56–7.

37 Prete, *Strategy and Command, 1914*, 31.

38 Tanenbaum, *Sarrail*, 56–7; Doughty, *Pyrrhic Victory*, 211–12.

39 Tanenbaum, *Sarrail*, 57–9.

40 Ibid., 61; Doughty, *Pyrrhic Victory*, 212.

41 Poincaré, *Au service*, 7:11, 14, 16, 25–30.

42 Poincaré, *Au service*, 7:31–4; Millerand Papers, dos. "Conseil des ministers 4/8/15 Notes de Millerand," AN, 470AP18.

43 Poincaré, *Au service*, 7:39, 44–8, 59–60.

44 Poincaré, *Au service*, 7:9, 11–13; no. 1389, Commander-in-Chief to Millerand, 2 August 1015, dos. "Con[cernant] Millerand-Joffre," Millerand Papers, AN, 470AP15.

45 Poincaré, *Au service*, 6:314–15, 7:9, 11–14. See also Poincaré's interview with General Philippe Pétain on 6 July, in which Pétain decried the lack of artillery preparation before attacks. Pétain was unfavourable to new offensives, believing the

war would be prolonged and that it was necessary to husband French forces and, before attacking, to first procure heavy artillery and munitions. (Ibid., 6:311–12.)

46 Foch, Journées, AFF, 11 August [1915]; Meeting of Army Group Commanders, 11 August 1915, *AFGG*, III A(II), no. 1150, 554–8.

47 Meeting of Army Group Commanders, 11 August 1915, *AFGG*, III A(II), no. 1150, 554–8.

48 Ibid.; Foch, Journées, AFF, 11 August [1915].

49 Ibid.

50 Ibid.

51 Poincaré, Notes Journalières, XXXVIII, BN, NAF (16031), 14 August 1915; Poincaré, *Au service*, 7:31, 34–7.

52 Poincaré, *Au service*, 7:37–8.

53 Poincaré, Notes Journalières, XXXVIII, BN, NAF (16031), 14 August 1915.

54 Poincaré, *Au service*, 7:38.

55 Ibid., 40, 49.

56 Memorandum, Joffre to Millerand, 20 August 1915, *AFGG*, III A(II), no. 1209.

57 Ibid.; no. 6320–3/11, Millerand to Delcassé, 27 August 1915, no. 1264.

58 "Note au sujet des Dardanelles" prepared by Section d'Etudes de la Défense Nationale, 31 August 1915, AG, Fonds Joffre, 14N10, dos. no. 1, annexe no. 10; Ibid., 10 September 1915, doc. no. 14.

59 Poincaré, *Au service*, 7:49.

60 Ibid., 64, 66–70, 78–9, 153–5, 177–8, 186–8, 192–3.

61 Poincaré, Notes Journalières, XXXVIII, BN, NAF (16029), 30 March 1915, 194; Millerand's handwritten notes of conference of 29 March 1915, Millerand Papers, AN, 470AP15.

62 CT no. 588, P. Cambon to Ministère des Affaires Etrangères, 31 March 1915, Millerand Papers, AN, 470AP15.

63 Copy of personal letter, Millerand to Paul Cambon, 14 April 1915, Millerand Papers, AN, 470AP15; Poincaré, Notes Journalières, XXXVIII, BN, NAF (16029), 1 April 1915.

64 Callwell, *Wilson*, 1:232, diary entry of 23 June 1915.

65 No. 15682, Général Commandant en chef au Ministre de la Guerre, 30 July 1915, *AFGG*, III A(II), no. 1044.

66 Ibid. Cf. Poincaré, *Au service*, 7:45.

67 No. 1738, Cambon to Diplomacy, Paris, 9 August 1915, Cambon Papers, AE, "Correspondance officielle," VII/22/53; no. 4395, Minister of Foreign Affairs to Minister of War, 11 August 1915, Fonds Buat, AG, 6N7, file "Correspondance … formule de commandement."

68 Wilson Diaries, VI, IWM, DS/Misc/80, 16 August 1915.

69 Bertie to Grey, 1, 3, 4, 6 August, NA, FO 800/58/56–8, 59–61, 119–22, 64–9.

70 Bertie to Grey, 14 August 1915, NA, FO 800/58/80–2; Bertie to Grey, 12, 14 August 1915, Bertie Papers, FO 800/167/Fr/15/62,64.

71 Callwell, ed., *Wilson*, 1:242–4.

72 Wilson Diaries, IWM, DS/Misc/80, reel 6, 9 August 1915.

73 Wilson Diaries, IWM, DS/Misc/80, reel 6, 16 August 1915.

74 Wilson Diaries, IWM, DS/Misc/80, reel 6, 19 August 1915.

75 "Programme du voyage de Lord K," August 1915 [between 8 and 11 August 1915 in the file], dos. "Conf 2/15 … Calais 11/9," AN, Millerand Papers, 470AP15; CT, Military Attaché, London [translation] to War Minister and General Joffre, 11 August 1915, dos. "Conf 2/15 … Calais 11/9," AN, Millerand Papers, 470AP15; Wilson Diaries, IWM, DS/Misc/80, reel 6, 9 August 1915.

76 Foch, Journées, AFF, 16 August [1915].

77 Wilson Diaries, IWM, DS/Misc/80, reel 6, 16 August 1915.

78 No. 101H, Huguet to Joffre, 19 August 1915, *AFGG*, III A(II), no. 1205; Poincaré, Notes Journalières, XL, BN, NAF (16031), 19 August 1915; no. 8551-D, Minister of War to Ministry of Foreign Affairs, 20 August 1915, Millerand Papers, AN, 470AP15; Kitchener to Millerand, 20 August 1915, Kitchener Papers, NA, 30 57/57 Erd/1268.

79 No. 101H, Huguet to Joffre, 19 August 1915, AG, 16N1905, 3e Bureau, Armée anglaise, no. 82; also in *AFGG*, III A(II), no. 1205.

80 Asquith to the King, 20 August 1915, NA, CAB 41/36/40 R/244.

81 Ibid.

82 Asquith to Henley, 20 August 1915, MSS, Eng. Lett., C547/2/369–72, Bodleian Library, Oxford.

83 Ibid.; Asquith to the King, 20 August 1915, NA, CAB 41/36/40 R/244.

84 Kitchener to Millerand, 20 August 1915, Kitchener Papers, NA, 30 57/57 Erd/1268; French, *British Strategy*, 111.

85 Cassar, *Kitchener*, 389.

86 Becker, *Les Français dans la Grande Guerre*, 125–32.

87 Greenhalgh, *Foch*, 296–310. The quotation is on 310.

88 Erickson, "*Koalitsionnaya Voina*: Coalition Warfare in Soviet Miltary Theory, Planning, and Performance," in Neilson and Prete, eds., *Coalition Warfare*, 88.

89 Quoted from Foch, AFF, 17–18, in Prete, *Strategy and Command, 1914*, 176; see also 254n.122.

90 129H, Huguet to General Commander-in-Chief, 17 December 1915, *AFGG*, IV A(I), no. 62.

91 No. 101H, Huguet to Joffre, 19 August 1915, AG, 16N1905, GQG, 3e Bureau, Armée anglaise, no. 82.

92 Poincaré, *Au service*, 7:46–50.

CHAPTER TEN

1 Cassar, *Dardanelles*, 41–80.

2 For an analysis of literature on the Dardanelles expedition, see Spiers, "Gallipoli," in Bond, ed., *The First World War and British Military History*, 165–88.

3 Hankey, *Supreme Command*, 1:390–412; Poincaré, Notes Journalières, XXXX, BN, NAF (16031), 28 August 1915.

4 Asquith to the King, 3 September 1915, NA, CAB 41/36/42, no. R266; no. 1.306, Colonel de la Panouse, French Military Attaché in London, to Minister of War, Paris, 3 September 1915; no. 1590, Pellé, Chief of Staff, to Minister of War, 3 September 1915, Millerand Papers, AN, 470AP15; T no. F.346, French to Kitchener, 2 September 2015, French Papers, IWM, 75/14/6.

5 "Compte Rendu de la séance tenue à Calais le 11 septembre 1915," Joffre Papers, AG, 14N10, dos. I, pièce annexe no. 12; French to Mrs Bennett, 11 September 1915, French Papers, IWM, PP/MCR/C33, reel 1; Wilson Diaries, VI, IWM, DS/Misc/80, 11 September 1915.

6 See Pellé, Chief of Staff, to Joffre, 21 September 1915, Joffre Papers, AG, 1K268, dos. 3/27; "The position in the Balkans. Note by the Secretary [Hankey], prepared by the direction of the Prime Minister," 21 September 1915, NA, CAB 42/3/26.

7 Ibid., 56–61.

8 Proceedings of a meeting held at Chantilly, 22 August 1915, NA, WO 158/3, Joffre Correspondence with British Headquarters, 112.

9 Doughty, *Pyrrhic Victory*, 188.

10 French to Kitchener, 23 August 1915, Kitchener Papers, NA, 30 57/50 WA/121.

11 Poincaré, Notes Journalières, XL, BN, NAF (16031), 28 August 1915.

12 Ibid., 1 September 1915.

13 Proceedings of a meeting held at Chantilly, 22 August 1915, NA, WO 158/3, Joffre Correspondence with British Headquarters, 112; no. 1459/9, Foch to French, 11 September 1915, *AFGG*, III A(II), no. 1380; OAM, IAO, French to Foch, 11 September 1915, *AFGG*, III A(II), no. 1381.

14 Robertson to Wigram (the king's assistant secretary), 12 January 2017, LHMA, I/12/31A. This is Robertson's reflection "on what happened on every occasion when I was in France." (Ibid.)

15 Wilson Diaries, IWM, DS/Misc/80, reel 6, 20 August 1915.

16 Proceedings of a meeting held at Chantilly on 22 August 1915, NA, WO 158/3, Joffre Correspondence with British Headquarters, 113.

17 Ibid.; no. 799, Joffre to French, 1 September 1915, NA, WO 158/13, Joffre Correspondence with British Headquarters, 106.

18 Doughty, *Pyrrhic Victory*, 188.

19 No. 799, Joffre to French, 1 September 1915, NA, 158/13, Joffre Correspondence with British Headquarters, 106.

20 Ibid.; OAM 870, French to Joffre, 3 September 1915.

21 No. 110/H, Huguet to Joffre, 7 September 1915, *AFGG*, III A(II), no. 1349.

22 OAM 812, Sir John to Joffre, 12 September 1915, NA, WO 158/13, Joffre Correspondence with British Headquarters, 103.

23 Wilson Diaries, IWM, DS/Misc/80, reel 6, 12 September 1915.

24 Greenhalgh, *French Army*, 111; cf. Wilson Diaries, ibid.

25 French to Kitchener, 23 August 1915, Kitchener Papers, NA, 30 57/50 WA/121.

26 French to Mrs. Bennett, 12 September 1915, French Papers, IWM, PP/MCR/C33, reel 1.

27 Wilson Diaries, IWM, DS/Misc/80, reel 6, 14 September 1915.

28 Asquith to King George V, 10 September 1915, NA, CAB/37/8, p. 4.

29 Doughty, *Pyrrhic Victory*, 190.

30 Lambton to King George V, 28 August 1915, RA, GV Q832/235; ibid., Robertson to Stamfordham, 19 September 1915, RA, GV 0832/280.

31 Fitzgerald Diary, IWM, PP/MCR/118, reel 1, 14 September 1915.

32 Proceedings of a meeting held at Chantilly, 22 August 1915, NA, WO 158/3, Joffre Correspondence with British Headquarters, 112.

33 Fitzgerald Diary, IWM, PP/MCR/118, reel 1, 12 September 1915.

34 Clive Diaries, II/II, LHMA, 20 September 1915; Cassar, *Kitchener's War*, 120, 205.

35 Rawlinson Diary, CA, 1/3, 17 September 1915.

36 Wilson Diaries, IWM, DS/Misc/80, reel 6, 19, 20 September 1915.

37 Ibid.

38 Kitchener to French, 1 September 1915, French Papers, IWM, 75/46/11.

39 Personal letter no. 4/266, Asquith to King George V, 3 September 1915, NA, CAB 41/36/42.

40 Wilson Diaries, IWM, DS/Misc/80, reel 6, 10 September 1915.

41 Ibid., 27 August 1915.

42 No. 23, de la Panouse to Joffre, 14 September 1915, AG, Fonds Joffre, 1K268, dos. 3.

43 Poincaré, Notes Journalières, XL, BN, NAF (16031), 21 August 1915; Doughty, *Pyrrhic Victory*, 212.

44 No. 17.839, Joffre to Millerand, 24 August 1915, *AFGG*, III A(II), no. 1240.

45 No. 1264–01/11, Millerand to Joffre, 27 August 1915, *AFGG*, III A(II), no. 1262.

46 Note, 17 or 18 September 1915, Millerand Papers, AN, 470AP16, file "Exposé d'ensemble," subfile "Notes."

47 Ibid., 4705AP16, Chamber of Deputies to Viviani, 26 August 1915, dos. "D II."

48 Ibid., 470AP16, Painlevé to Millerand, 30 August 1915, file "Dardanelles II."

49 No. 4878, Millerand to Delcassé, 31 August, *AFGG*, VVV(I) A(I), no. 331.

50 Poincaré, Notes Journalières, XL, BN, NAF (16031), 28 August 1915; 28 August 1915, Millerand Papers, AN, 470AP16, dos. II, Millerand's notes on the meeting at the Elysée Palace; Poincaré, *Au service*, 7:64, 68.

51 Poincaré, Notes Journalières, XL, BN, NAF (16031), 28 August 1915; 28 August 1915, Millerand Papers, AN, 470AP16, dos. II, Millerand's notes on the meeting at the Elysée Palace; Poincaré, *Au service*, 7:64, 68–9.

52 Poincaré, Notes Journalières, XL, BN, NAF (16031), 1 September 1915.

53 No. 31, Joffre to Millerand, 1 September 1915, *AFGG*, III A(II), no. 1308.

54 Millerand to Joffre, 3 September 1915, Millerand Papers, AN, 470AP16, dos. "Dardanelles II."

55 Ibid., no. 13324–1/11, Millerand to Joffre, 7 September 1915, *AFGG*, III A(II), no. 1345.
56 Ibid., no. 4667, Joffre to Millerand, 8 September 1915, *AFGG*, III A(II), no. 1354.
57 Ibid., no. 9558D, Millerand to Joffre, 14 September 1915, *AFGG*, III A(II), no. 358.
58 No. 12.119, Joffre to Millerand, 20 September 1915, Millerand Papers, AN, 470AP15, dos. "Concernant Millerand – Joffre."
59 Poincaré, Notes Journalières, XL, BN, NAF (16031), 21 September 1915.
60 "Note au sujet des Dardanelles," prepared by Section d'Etudes de la Défense Nationale, 31 August 1915, AG, Fonds Joffre, 14N10, dos. no. 1, annexe no. 10. p. 11.
61 Kitchener to French, 1 September 1915, French Papers, IWM, 75/46/11.
62 CT no. 1978, Cambon to Delcassé, 5 September 1915, Millerand Papers, AN, 470AP15.
63 Poincaré, Notes Journalières, XL, BN, NAF (16031), 14 September 1915.
64 Wilson Diaries, IWM, DS/Misc/80, reel 6, 9 September 1915.
65 Hankey Papers, Diary, CA, 1/1, 7 September–14 September 1915, Calais Conference, 11 September 1915.
66 Millerand to Sarrail, 14 September 1915, Millerand Papers, AN, 470AP16.
67 Wilson Diaries, IWM, DS/Misc/80, reel 6, 11 September 1915.
68 Poincaré, Notes Journalières, XL, BN, NAF (16031), 28 August 1915.
69 Wilson Diaries, IWM, DS/Misc/80, reel 6, 14 September 1915.
70 Poincaré, Notes Journalières, XL, BN, NAF (16031), 28 August 1915.
71 Ibid., 26 August 1915.
72 Memorandum, Joffre to Millerand, 20 August 1915, *AFGG*, III A(II), no. 1209; Millerand to Delcassé, 27 August 1915, *AFGG*, III A(II), no. 1264.
73 See Cassar, *Asquith*, 147–69, 108.
74 Hankey Papers, Diary, CA, 1/1, 7 September–14 September 1915, Calais Conference, 11 September 1915.
75 Esher to French, 14 September 1915, French Papers, IWM, 75/46/11.
76 Wilson Diaries, IWM, DS/Misc/80, reel 6, 17 September 1915.
77 Ibid.
78 No. 207, Esher [?] to Kitchener [?], n.d. [about 19 September 1915 in the file], Kitchener Papers, NA, 30/57/59/1–E.
79 No. 23, de la Panouse to Joffre, 14 September 1915, AG, Fonds Joffre, 1K268, dos. no. 3.
80 Treated in detail in the next chapter.
81 French Diaries, IWM, PP/MCR/C32, reel 3, 22 August 1915.
82 Doughty, *Pyrrhic Victory*, 188
83 Wilson Diaries, IWM, DS/Misc/80, reel 6, 9 September 1915.
84 Joffre, *Mémoires*, 2:127–8.
85 No. 8565, Note for the General Officers Commanding Army Groups, 14 September 1915, NA, WO 158/13, Joffre Correspondence with British Headquarters, 88–9.
86 Doughty, *Pyrrhic Victory*, 189.

87 Wilson Diaries, IWM, DS/Misc/80, reel 6, 14 September 1915.
88 Doughty, *Pyrrhic Victory*, 189.
89 Radiotélégramme allemande, 3 October 1915, Millerand Papers, AN, 470AP14, dos. "Opérations militaries France-Nord, Janvier Mai/Juin Octobre 1915."
90 Robertson to Wigram, 10 September 1915, LHMA, Robertson Papers, I/12/26a.
91 No. 8565, Note for the General Officers Commanding Army Groups, 14 September 1915, NA, WO 158/13, Joffre Correspondence with British Headquarters, 88–9.
92 Doughty, *Pyrrhic Victory*, 190, 196.
93 Poincaré, Notes Journalières, XL, BN, NAF (16031), 23 September 1915.
94 Ibid.
95 Ibid.
96 No. 14542, Note au sujet du télégramme en date du 23 Septembre 1915 de l'attaché militaire à Londres, *AFGG*, VII(I) A(II), no. 43.
97 Wilson Diaries, IWM, DS/Misc/80, reel 6, 25 September 1915.
98 No. 1352, Joffre to Millerand, 3 October 1915, *AFGG*, III A(III), no. 2543.
99 Ibid.
100 Doughty, *Pyrrhic Victory*, 190–4.
101 Ibid., 196–7.
102 Wilson Diaries, IWM, DS/Misc/80, reel 6, 25 September 1915.
103 Clive Diaries, II/II, LHMA, 26 September 1915.
104 "Résumé des directives données à Foch par Joffre," 26 September 1915, *AFGG*, III A(III), no. 1797.
105 Ibid.; no. 16205, d'Urbal to Haig, 27 September, *AFGG*, III A(III), no. 1995.
106 OAM 987, Sir John to Joffre, 27 September 1915, NA, WO 158/13, Joffre Correspondence with British Headquarters, 75.
107 T no. 17146, Joffre to Foch, 28 September 1915, *AFGG*, III A(III), no. 2085.
108 Ibid.; CT no. 1978, Foch to Joffre, 28 September 1915, *AFGG*, III A(III), no. 2101.
109 No. 282, Robertson to Stamfordham, 28 September 1915, RA, GV, Q832/282, no. 282.
110 Ibid.
111 French Diaries, IWM, PP/MCR/C32, reel 3, 29 September 1915.
112 Doughty, *Pyrrhic Victory*, 199.
113 French Diaries, IWM, PP/MCR/C32, reel 3, 5 October 1915.
114 No. 2122, Foch to French, 5 October 1915, *AFGG*, III A(III), no. 2628; ibid., "Extrait du Journal des marches et operations du GAN," 5 October 1915, *AFGG*, III A(III), no. 2629.
115 OAM 41, Sir John to Foch, 6 October 1915, NA, WO 158/26, Foch Correspondence with British Headquarters.
116 "Extrait du Journal des marches et opérations du GAN," 5 October 1915, *AFGG*, III A(III), no. 2675.
117 Papiers Poincaré, Notes Journalières, XL, BN, NAF (16031), 7 September 1915.
118 No. 1352, Joffre to Millerand, 3 October 1915, *AFGG*, III A(III), no. 2543.

119 Doughty, *Pyrrhic Victory*, 194–5.
120 Ibid., 200.
121 French Diaries, IWM, PP/MCR/C32, reel 3, 8 October 1915.
122 Wilson Diaries, IWM, DS/Misc/80, reel 6, 11 October 1915.
123 Doughty, *Pyrrhic Victory*, 200–1.
124 No. 8034, Joffre to Foch, 14 September 1915, *AFGG*, III A(III), no. 2935.
125 Doughty, *Pyrrhic Victory*, 201.
126 Ibid.
127 Ibid.; Greenhalgh, *The French Army*, 116–17.
128 Cherry, *The Battle of Loos, 1915*, 304.
129 Doughty, *Pyrrhic Victory*, 202.
130 T, d'Amade to Joffre, 3 October 1915, *AFGG*, III A(III), no. 2541.
131 Ibid., telephone message, Penelon to Gamelin, 11 October 1915, *AFGG*, III A(III), no. 2872.
132 Ibid., no. 6471, Joffre to Millerand, 12 October 1915, *AFGG*, III A(III), no. 2898.
133 Note by Esher, 12 October 1915, NA, CAB 37/136/4.
134 Report, Stamfordham to King George V, 7 October 1915, RA, GV, K, 873/2.
135 Ibid.
136 Note by Esher, 12 October 1915, NA, CAB 37/136/4.
137 Cassar, *Kitchener*, 421–2, 524n.25.
138 Asquith to Kitchener, 17 October 1915, Kitchener Papers, NA, 30/57/74 WR25.

CHAPTER ELEVEN

1 Significant portions of this chapter were published in Roy A. Prete, "*Imbroglio par Excellence*": Mounting the Salonika Campaign, September–October 1915," *War & Society* 19, no. 1 (May 2001): 47–70; reprinted by permission of the publisher (Taylor and Francis, www.tandfonline.com).
2 On Anglo-French politics in the Balkans, see Dutton, *Politics of Diplomacy*; on the Salonika expedition, Cassar, *Reluctant Partner*, 186–214. For the diplomacy of the First World War by an informed insider, see Pingaud, *Histoire diplomatique de la France pendant la Grande Guerre*, 3 vols. On French logistics, see Bernède, "'The Gardiners of Salonika,'" 43–58.
3 See Cassar, *Reluctant Partner* and *The French and the Dardanelles.*
4 Hankey, *Supreme Command*, 1:390–412; Poincaré, Notes Journalières, XXXX, BN, NAF (16031), 28 August 1915.
5 Tanenbaum, *Sarrail*, 55–65.
6 Asquith to the King, 3 September 1915, NA, CAB 41/36/42, no. R266; no. 1.306, Colonel de la Panouse, French Military Attaché in London, to Minister of War, Paris, 3 September 1915; no. 1590, Pellé, Chief of Staff, to Minister of War, 3 September 1915, Millerand Papers, AN, 470AP15; T no. F346, French to Kitchener, 2 September 1915, French Papers, IWM, 75/14/6.

7 "Compte Rendu de la séance tenue à Calais le 11 septembre 1915," Joffre Papers, AG, 14N10, dos. 1, pièce annexe no. 12; French to Mrs Bennett, 11 September 1915, French Papers, IWM, PP/MCR/C33, reel 1; Wilson Diaries, VI, IWM, DS/Misc/80, 11 September 1915.

8 See Pellé, Chief of Staff, to Joffre, 21 September 1915, Joffre Papers, AG, 1K268, dos. 3/27; "The position in the Balkans. Note by the Secretary [Hankey], prepared by the Direction of the Prime Minister," 21 September 1915, NA, CAB 42/3/26.

9 Dutton, "The Balkan Campaign and French War Aims in the Great War," 97–113; Cassar, *Reluctant Partner*, 187. Also, Nevakivi, *Britain, France and the Arab Middle East*.

10 Brought to my attention by Samir Saul, who critiqued an earlier version of my article, "*Imbroglio par Excellence*," at a meeting of the Western Society for French History held at Asilomar, California, 31 October–3 November 1999; also, Cassar, *Reluctant Partner*, 187.

11 Joffre Papers, AG, 14N10, "Historique – Direction," 1:18–21.

12 For details, see Renouvin, *La crise européenne*, 314–17. For the political origins of the Salonika expedition, see Dutton, *Politics of Diplomacy*, 17–48.

13 Poincaré, Notes Journalières, XXXX, BN, NAF (16031), 21 September 1915.

14 No. 12119, Joffre to Minister of War, 20 September 1915, Millerand Papers, AN, 4705AP16, dos. "Dardanelles II."

15 Poincaré, Notes Journalières, XXXX, BN, NAF (16031), 22–23 September 1915.

16 Ibid.

17 Asquith to the King, 23 September 1915, NA, CAB 41/36/45, no. R/249.

18 Hankey Papers, Diary, CA, 1/1, 23 September 1915; Secretary's Notes of a Meeting of the Dardanelles Committee, 23 September 1915, NA, CAB 42/3/28.

19 Hankey Papers, Diary, CA, 1/1, 23 September 1915.

20 T no. 6770, Military Attaché in London [Colonel de la Panouse] to Foreign and War Office, 23 September 1915, Millerand Papers, AN, 470AP16, dos. "Dardanelles 24 sept.–3 oct. 1915"; no 14.548, Note by Joffre [for Minister of War], 24 September 1915, Millerand Papers, AN, 470A17, dos. "Notes."

21 Secretary's Notes of a Meeting of the Dardanelles Committee, 24 September 1915, NA, CAB 42/3/30; Hankey Papers, Diary, CA, 1/1, 24 September 1915.

22 This was the constant refrain of Sir William Robertson, later chief of the Imperial General Staff, who spent two years trying to have the expedition withdrawn. (Cf. Dutton, *Politics of Diplomacy*, 49–166.)

23 Reginald Viscount Esher to Sir J. French, 14 September 1915, French Papers, IWM, 75/46/11.

24 See, for example, Secretary's Notes of a Meeting of the Dardanelles Committee, 23 September 1915, NA, CAB 42/3/28; also, Asquith to Kitchener, 23 September 1915, Kitchener Papers, NA, 30 57/71 WR/21.

25 See Hankey, *The Supreme Command*, 2:439–42.

26 Asquith to Kitchener, 23 September 1915, Kitchener Papers, NA, 30 57/71 WR/22.

27 See Spiers, “Gallipoli,” in Bond, ed., *First World War*, 183–6.
28 See Prete, “Le conflit stratégique franco-britannique sur le front occidental et la conférence de Calais du 6 juillet 1915,” 17–49.
29 See, for example, sittings of 23 September, 11 October 1915, Chamber Commission of the Army, vol. 2, 1915, AN, C7494.
30 T, French Military Attaché in London to Foreign Ministry, Paris, for the Minister of War, 26 September 1915, *AFGG*, VIII(I) A(II), no. 57.
31 T, French Military Attaché in London to Minister of War via Foreign Ministry, 27 September 1915, *AFGG*, VIII(I) A(II), no. 60.
32 Committee of Imperial Defence, Précis of Documents and Proceedings ... Prepared by the Secretary, 1–28 September 1915, 10, NA, CAB 42/14/21.
33 Poincaré, Notes Journalières, XXXX, BN, NAF (16031), 28 September 1915.
34 Asquith to the King, 2 October 1915, NA, CAB 37/135/1.
35 Poincaré, Notes Journalières, XXXX, BN, NAF (16051), 28 September 1915; Joffre Papers, “Historique – Direction,” 1:17–19, AG, 14N10.
36 Asquith to the King, 2 October 1915, NA, CAB 37/135/1.
37 T, no. 2226, Paul Cambon, French Ambassador in London, to Ministry of Foreign Affairs, 30 September 1915, Delcassé Papers, AE, vol. 24, no. 261.
38 For French and British accounts of Allied deployment and field operations with detailed maps, see the official histories: *AFGG*, VIII(I), 126–64, Cartes, 1–64; *HGW*, 1:22–63 and “Macedonia, Maps.”
39 T no. 17.782, Commander in Chief to Minister of War, 29 September 1915, *AFGG*, VIII(I) A(II), no. 74.
40 No. 9854.D, War Minister to Commander in Chief, 21 September 1915, Millerand Papers, AN, 4705AP16 (reproduced in *AFGG*, VIII(I) A(II), no. 35, indicating it was remitted 25 September 1915). Cf. Joffre Papers, “Historique – Direction” 1:19, AG, 14N10.
41 Hankey Papers, Diary, CA, 1/1, 30 September 1915.
42 Esher Journals, CA, 2/15, 1 October 1915. The reference is apparently to the substitution of the 53rd Division for the 11th Division (a move for which *HGW*, *Macedonia*, 1:40, indicates that the field commander, Sir Ian Hamilton, had taken the initiative).
43 Esher Journals, CA, 2/15, 1 October 1915.
44 Telegrams, French Military Attaché in London to Minister of War, 27 September 1915, *AFGG*, VIII(I) A(II), nos. 60, 61; Poincaré, Notes Journalières, XXXX, BN, NAF (16031), 28, 29 September 1915; Committee of Imperial Defence, Précis of Documents and Proceedings … Prepared by the Secretary, 29 September–5 October 1915, 4, NA, CAB 42/14/21.
45 Secretary’s Notes of a Meeting of the Dardanelles Committee, 30 September 1915, NA, CAB 42/3/35.
46 Committee of Imperial Defence, Précis of Documents and Proceedings … Prepared by the Secretary, 29 September–5 October 1915, 4–19, NA, CAB 42/14/21; Joffre Papers, AG, 14N10, “Historique – Direction,” 1:18.

47 Secretary's Notes of a Meeting of the Dardanelles Committee, 23 September 1915, NA, CAB 42/3/28.

48 T, Military Attaché, London, to War [Ministry], 1 October 1915, for French Headquarters, *AFGG*, VIII(I) A(II), no 88.

49 No. 1357, "Note au sujet du télégramme no. 129 du lord Kitchener," 3 September 1915, *AFGG*, III A(III), no. 2544; no 1352, Commander in Chief to Minister of War, 3 September 1915, Millerand Papers, AN, 470AP16, dos. "Dardanelles 24 sept.–30 oct./15."

50 Poincaré, Notes Journalières, XXXX, BN, NAF (16031), 4 October 1915.

51 Secretary's Notes of a Meeting of the Dardanelles Committee, 4 October 1915, NA, CAB 42/4/2.

52 "Compte rendu de la conférence tenue à Calais le 5/10/15," *AFGG*, VIII(I) A(II), no. 108. As the Allied contingent was to go to the aid of the Serbs, it was agreed that it should be under the direction of a Serb general. (Ibid.) The question of command and Sarrail's role would become a serious issue later.

53 Ibid.; Minutes of Calais Conférence, 5 Octobre 1915, Millerand Papers, AN, 470AP15 [kept by Captain Doumayrou]. The handwritten copy of the minutes indicates that Millerand cited the strain on French manpower resources as a reason they could not send an additional 10,000 men, to which Kitchener replied, "Ah, I did not know." This passage was struck out in the typescript; also, the French intention to advance "toward Nish" was replaced in the typescript by "toward the north." See also Millerand's handwritten notes, "Calais 5/10 15," AN, 4705AP15. Joffre was unhappy that he had not been included in the consultation with Kitchener, and told Henry Wilson that he had let additional forces go to Salonika only in order to squelch the Asia Minor landing (Wilson Diaries, IWM, DS/Misc/80, reel 6, 6 October 1915).

54 Poincaré, Notes Journalières, XXXX, BN, NAF (16031), 5–6 October 1915; Millerand Papers, AN, 4705AP17, Section d'Etudes de la Défense Nationale, Rapport au sujet de la situation crée par les derniers événements d'Athènes, 6 October 1915.

55 Secretary's Notes of a Meeting of the Dardanelles Committee, 6 October 1915, AN, CAB 42/4/3; Lord Bertie, British Ambassador in Paris, to Delcassé, 7 October 1915, Delcassé Papers, AE, t.24, no. 273.

56 Cipher telegrams, 2309–11, Président du Conseil au Ministre des Affaires étrangères, 7 October 1915, Delcassé Papers, AE, t.24, no. 274.

57 Minute of Chantilly Conference, 8 October 1915, Millerand Papers, AN, 470AP15. Cf. Millerand's handwritten notes of meeting of 8 October 1915, AN, 470AP/16, dos. "Dardanelles, 24 sept.–30 oct.1915."

58 Secretary's Notes of a War Council held 11 October 1915, NA, CAB 42/4/6. Meantime, Delcassé resigned as foreign minister on 9 October 1915 owing to ill health and his opposition to the Salonika expedition. Viviani temporarily assumed the portfolio. Poincaré, Notes Journalières, XXXX, BN, NAF (16031), 9 October 1915.

59 Copy of letter, Kitchener to Millerand, 13 October 1915, French Papers, IWM, 75/46/5; "Message téléphoné au GQG" 14 October 1915, *AFGG*, VIII(I) A(II), no. 58.

60 See supra, 121.

61 French Diaries, IWM, PP/MCR/C32, reel 3, 14 October 1915.

62 Millerand to Kitchener, 15 October 1915, with attached letter no. 8324, Joffre to Millerand, 15 October 1915, Millerand Papers, AN, 470AP15, dos. "1915 relations franco-anglais[es]"; no. 8302, Commander in Chief to War Ministry, 15 October 1915, *AFGG*, VIII(I) A(II), no.171. See translated copies in Asquith Papers, 120/151–4, Bodleian Library, Oxford. To Millerand, Joffre argued that, since the British only held 3.5 kilometres of trenches per division compared to 7.5 for the French, and since they had eleven divisions in reserve on their front, they could easily spare all the required troops without French reliefs and even the eight divisions for Egypt if necessary. (Joffre [to Millerand], "Note au sujet des forces britanniques disponibles en France pour un autre théâtre d'opérations," 15 October 1915, Millerand Papers, AN, 470AP15, dos. "1915 relations franco-anglais[es].")

63 CT no. 2.400, Military Attaché, London, to War Minister, 16 October 1915, *AFGG*, VIII(I) A(II), no. 185. The two Indian divisions, he said, would go back to India. (Ibid.)

64 T, Minister of War to President of Council, 18 October 1915, Millerand Papers, AN, 470AP15.

65 Telegrams, Minister of War to President of Council, 18 (no. 2421), 19 October 1915, Millerand Papers, AN, 470AP15.

66 Proceedings of a Meeting held at Chantilly, 18 October 1915, French Papers, IWM, 75/4615. On the evening of 18 October, Millerand again instructed Joffre, in the event of Sir John's refusal to send his reserves to Salonika, to relieve the two British divisions on the Somme. (T no. 142, War Minister to General Commander in Chief, 18 October 1915, Millerand Papers, AN, 470AP15.) But the arrangement had already been worked out by then.

67 Wilson Diaries, IWM, DS/Misc/80, reel 6, 27 and 29 October 1915.

68 Secretary's Notes of a Meeting of the Dardanelles [War] Committee held 25 October 1915, NA, CAB 42/4/17; T, Military Attaché in London to War, Diplomacy, Paris, 26 October 1915, *AFGG*, VIII(I) A(II), no. 275.

69 No. 15.005, Commander in Chief to Minister of War, n.d. [26 or 27 October 1915], Millerand Papers, AN, 470AP/18, dos. "Doc. pour le conseil des ministres"; Joffre Papers, AG, 14N10, " Historique – Direction," 1:23–4; Millerand Papers, Notes on "Conférence du 28/10 15 à Chantilly," AN, 470AP18.

70 T, General Commander in Chief to Colonel Fournier [with the Serb Army], 27 October 1915, *AFGG*, VIII(I) A(II), no. 289.

71 Poincaré, *Au service*, 7:154.

72 Ibid., 7:177; Cf. Poincaré, Notes Journalières, XXXX, BN, NAF (16031), 14 October 1915.

73 Poincaré, *Au service*, 7:192–3.
74 Joffre Papers, AG, 14N10, " Historique – Direction," 1:24.
75 Asquith to Sylvia Henley, 28 October 1915, MSS, Eng. Lett., c542/2/396–9, Bodleian Library, Oxford.
76 Note remise à Kitchener 28 [29] octobre 1915; T no. 17382, Commander in Chief to Minister of War, 31 October 1915, *AFGG*, VIII(I) A(II), nos. 305, 327.
77 Asquith to Sylvia Henley, 29 October 1915, MSS, Eng. Lett., c542/2/400–1, Bodleian Library, Oxford.
78 Hankey Papers, Diary, CA, 1/1, 29–30 October 1915.
79 "Décision du Gouvernement Anglais," 30 October 1915 [signed by Kitchener], *AFGG*, VIII(I) A(II), no. 312.
80 Secretary's Notes of a Meeting of the Dardanelles Committee, 30 October 1915, NA, CAB 42/4/20; T no. 9356, Secretary of State to Field Marshal Commanding in Chief, France, 30 October 1915, NA, WO 33/739/3315; *AFGG*, VIII(I), 163–4.
81 *AFGG*, VIII(I), 163–4.
82 See, for example, Prete, "Le conflit stratégique," 33–49.
83 See Varillon, *Joffre*, 357–420.
84 Woodward, *Great Britain and the War*, 143.
85 Tanenbaum, *Sarrail*, 75–6; Doughty, *Pyrrhic Victory*, 220, 222–3ff. The quotation is taken from Sarrail's instructions (Général Bailloud, Salonique via Moudros, 12 October 1915, *AFGG*, 812–144, 180; À Consul France Salonique pour gal Sarrail, 13 October 1915, *AFGG*, 812–191, 180), cited in Doughty, *Pyrrhic Victory*, 223.
86 Doughty, *Pyrrhic Victory*, 228–9.
87 For an appraisal of Millerand's tenure as war minister and the mounting tensions that led to his fall, see Farrar, *Principled Pragmatist*, 157–92.
88 Poincaré, Notes Journalières, XXXX, BN, NAF (16031), 9 October 1915; Poincaré, *Au service*, 7:127, 130, 134, 136–7, 139, 142, 148, 159, 162–3, 165–8, 175.
89 Poincaré, *Au service*, 7:167–8, 174–8, 180–8, 190–8.
90 Minutes of a joint meeting of the Army and Navy Commissions of the Chamber, 26 October 1915, BN, c7494, vol. 2, "1915 4 août–28 octobre."
91 Minutes of the Army Commission of the Chamber, 27 October 1999, AN, c7494, vol. 2, "1915 4 août–28 octobre."
92 On 29 October 1915, during the ministerial crisis, Poincaré was made aware that on the day previous King George V had fallen from his horse and had been injured while reviewing British troops. Having sent his good wishes, Poincaré was pleased to learn in a telegram from the king that he had not broken any bones and looked forward to a "speedy recovery" (Poincaré, *Au service*, 7:210).
93 Ibid., 7:196–9, 201, 203–11.
94 King, *Generals and Politicians*, 83; Keiger, *Poincaré*, 222–4.
95 Keiger, *Poincaré*, 221–2; Poincaré, *Au service*, 7:210–11.
96 Poincaré, *Au service*, 7:193, 195, 198, 210–11.
97 See Prete, "Joffre and the Question of Allied Supreme Command, 1914–1916," 333.

98 No. 661, Joffre to Foch, 1 November 1915, *AFGG*, III A(IV), no. 3039.
99 Notes on the "Memorandum for a Conference of representatives of the Allied Powers," 8 November 1915, French Papers, IWM, 75/46/5, Correspondence/ Memos b/w GQG 8 GQG, August 1914–December 1915.
100 Memorandum, French government to British government, mid-November 1915, AG, 16N1905, 3e Bureau, Armée anglaise, no. 111.
101 No. 10549, Joffre to French, 19 November 1915, *AFGG*, III A(I), no. 3089.
102 See Sheffield, *Haig*, 131.
103 Cassar, *Kitchener's War*, 252.
104 Kitchener to Asquith, 5 November 1915, NA, Kitchener Papers, 30/57/74 WR76.
105 Cassar, *Kitchener's War*, 252–3.
106 Ibid.
107 Girondon to [Guerre?], 11 November 1915, *AFGG*, VIII(I) A(I), no. 383.
108 Poincaré, Notes Journalières, XXXX, BN, NAF (16032), 12 November 1915.
109 Ibid., 13 November 1915.
110 Cassar, *Asquith as War Leader*, 135.
111 Ibid.
112 Conclusions of a Meeting of the War Committee, 15 November 1915, NA, CAB 37/137/23.
113 Conférence tenue au Ministère des Affaires Etrangères à Paris, 17 November 1915, AE, "Guerre 1914–1918," no. 988, Conférences: I: novembre 1915–avril 1916.
114 "Conseil Franco-Anglais tenu à Calais," le 5 [le 4] Décembre 1915, AG, Fonds Joffre 14N10, dos. III, annexe 54.
115 Doughty, *Pyrrhic Victory*, 234.
116 Secretary's Notes of a Meeting of the War Committee held … [on] December 8, 1915, NA, CAB 42/6/6.
117 Doughty, *Pyrrhic Victory*, 235–6.
118 Conference between Sir E. Grey and Lord Kitchener and M. Briand and General Gallieni at Paris, 9 December 1915, AE, "Guerre 1914–1918," Opérations Stratégiques: dos. "Général III: octobre 1915–janvier 1916," no. 981.
119 [Major] Vivian Gabriel to Lord Stamfordham [secretary to the king], 15 October 1915, RA, GV, Q688.
120 Reginald Lord Esher to MP A.H. Hankey [secretary to the Dardanelles Committee], 25 October 1915, Hankey Papers, CA, 4/7.
121 For a detailed treatment, see Philpott, "Squaring the Circle," 875–98.
122 Ibid., 881–5.
123 Ibid., 885–96; Esher, *Journals and Letters*, 3:272–7, 288–9.
124 Wilson Diaries, IWM, DS/Misc/80, reel 6, 19 November 1915.
125 Ibid., 23 November 1915.
126 Philpott, "Squaring the Circle," 884.
127 Wilson Diaries, IWM, DS/Misc/80, reel 6, 26 November 1915.
128 See Philpott, "Squaring the Circle," 895–6.
129 Craig, *Problems of Coalition Warfare*.

130 Cf. Keith Neilson, “The Anglo-Russian Alliance 1914–17: Lessons for the Present?” Unpublished paper presented to the United States Air Force Academy conference, Boulder, CO, 22 October 1998.

131 See *HGW*, *Macedonia*, 1:22–37.

CHAPTER TWELVE

1 Portions of this chapter were published in Roy A. Prete, “Joffre and the Origins of the Somme: A Study in Allied Military Planning,” *Journal of Military History* 73, no. 2 (April 2009): 420–30; reprinted with permission of the publisher.

2 On the British side, see Woodward, *Great Britain and the War of 1914–1918*; on the French, Jere Clemens King, *Generals and Politicians.*

3 Poincaré, *Au service*, 7:193, 195, 198, 210–11.

4 See Prete, “Joffre and the Question of Allied Supreme Command,” 333.

5 Poincaré, *Au service*, 3:277–80; Doughty, *Pyrrhic Victory*, 229–30.

6 Poincaré, Notes Journalières, XLI, BN, NAF (16038), 1, 2 December 1915, 189, 193; Doughty, *Pyrrhic Victory*, 231–2.

7 See Poincaré, *Au service*, 3:168–70, 9, 10 October 1915.

8 Doughty, *Pyrrhic Victory*, 232–3.

9 Ibid., 233–4.

10 Prete, “Joffre and the Question of Allied Supreme Command,” 333.

11 There is at least a grain of truth in A.J.P. Taylor’s pithy statement that “the French, who had little faith in Joffre, kept him as Commander-in-Chief because they thought that this would please the Allies, and the Allies, who also had no faith in Joffre, conformed to his wishes, because they thought that this would please the French” (Taylor, *Illustrated History of the First World War*, 82–3).

12 See French, *British Strategy and War Aims*, 159–63; Guinn, *British Strategy and Politics*, 159–63.

13 Holmes, *The Little Field Marshal*; Cassar, *The Tragedy of Sir John French.*

14 Gardner, “Command in Crisis,” 13–31.

15 See Cassar, *French*, 83.

16 Prete, “Coalition Warfare,” 105–6.

17 Hankey, *Supreme Command*, 1:188–9.

18 Prete, “Coalition Warfare,” 95–7.

19 Ibid, 503–4.

20 Philpott, “Kitchener and the 29th Division,” 375–407.

21 Prete, “Joffre and the Question of Allied Supreme Command,” 329–38.

22 Holmes, “Sir John French and Lord Kitchener,” 113–39.

23 French, *1914*, 329–35.

24 Asquith to Venetia Stanley, 6 January 1915, in *Letters to Venetian Stanley*, 361–2.

25 French Diaries, IWM, PP/MCR/C32, reel 2, 23, 29–31 March, 14 April, 6 May 1915.

26 French Diaries, IWM, PP/MCR/C32, reel 2, 6 May 1915; French to Kitchener, 2 May 1915, Kitchener Papers, NA, 30/57/50. See no. 857, de la Panouse, French

Military Attaché to Minister of War, 8 May 1915, AG, 7N700 Section Anglaise …, dos. Mai 1915.

27 Prete, "Les relations franco-britanniques et l'attaque au gaz allemande à Ypres."

28 Wilson Diaries, IWM, DS/Misc/80, reel 6, 8 May 1915; French Diaries, IWM, PP/MCR/C32, reel 3, 9 May 1915.

29 French Diaries, ibid., 9 May 1915.

30 French, *1914*, 356–7.

31 French to Asquith, 20 May 1915, Asquith Papers, 26/226–31, Bodleian Library, Oxford; French to Mrs Bennett, 21 May 1915, French Papers, IWM, PP/MCR/C33, reel 1.

32 Asquith, Memo to Cabinet, 17 May 1915, Kitchener Papers, NA, 30 57/74. For details, see Cassar, *Asquith as War Leader*, 91–102.

33 On the formation of the new cabinet, see ibid., 101–10.

34 T no. Y97, French to Kitchener, 15 May 1915, NA, WO/739/2465, T no. 4694, Kitchener to French, 16 May 1915, NA, WO 33/739/2470.

35 T Y100, French to Kitchener, 16 May 1915, T no. 4719, Kitchener to French, 17 May 1915, French Papers, IWM, 75/46/6; French Diaries, 16, 18 May 1915, IWM, PP/MCR/C32; cf. Wilson Diaries, VI, IWM, DS/Misc/80, 17 May 1915; 190 herein.

36 Esher Journals, CA, 2/14, 21 May 1915; Esher to Kitchener, 23 May 1915, NA, 20 57/59.

37 Wilson quoting Esher, Wilson Diaries, 25 May 1915, IWM, DS/80, reel 6.

38 See, for example, Woodward, *Great Britain and the War*, 137–99; Cassar, *French*, 270–82; cf. Sheffield, *The Chief*, 128–31.

39 Robertson to Stamfordham, 23 June 1915, Robertson Papers, LHMA, 1/12/2a–2c.

40 Robertson Papers, LHMA, 1/12/3a–3e; Pamela Clark, Deputy Registrar, Royal Archives, to Roy A. Prete, 10 Feb 1993.

41 Robertson to Stamfordham, 23 June 1915, Robertson Papers, LHMA, 1/12/2a–2c, 1/12/3a–3e; cf. Robertson to Esher, 23 June 1915, Esher Papers, CA, 5/48.

42 OA 2/118D, French to Secretary, War Office, 10 June 1915, with attached "Memorandum on the Supply of Artillery Ammunition to the Army in the Field," Lloyd George Papers, PA, D/17/6/16.

43 See Prete, "Le conflit stratégique franco-britannique sur le front occidental et la conférence de Calais du 6 juillet, 1915," 17–49, esp. 48–9.

44 Cassar, *French*, 270–82; Woodward, *Great Britain and the War*, 137–99.

45 See Prete, "*Imbroglio par Excellence*," 47–70.

46 Ibid.

47 See Cassar, *Kitchener's War*, 235–52.

48 See Woodward, *Field Marshal Sir William Robertson*, 17–25.

49 Cassar, *French*, 269, 287.

50 Joffre, *Memoirs*, 1:327.

51 Doughty, *Pyrrhic Victory*, 105–6, 113–25; Hogue, "André Laffargue and the Birth of Infiltration Tactics."

52 "Note au sujet des conditions générales de la guerre sur le front occidental, 25 mai 1915," *AFGG*, II A(II), no. 360.

53 "Note sur l'emploi des forces anglaises pendant la campagne d'hiver 1915–1916, le 7 octobre 1915," 3e Bureau, *AFGG*, III A(III), no. 2792; Doughty, *Pyrrhic Victory*, 250–2.

54 Joffre, *Memoirs*, 1:36–42, 55–61.

55 Callwell, *Wilson*, 1:28–9; Williamson, *Politics of Grand Strategy*, though somewhat dated, remains the best account.

56 See Prete, "Coalition Warfare," 502–6.

57 Philpott, *Anglo-French Relations and Strategy on the Western Front*, 15–50.

58 See Foley, *German Strategy and the Path to Verdun*, 126–55.

59 See Prete, "War of Movement," 100–1, 135–8, 250–5, 265–70; Neilson, *Strategy and Supply*, 7–11.

60 Prete, "Joffre and the Question of Allied Supreme Command," 332.

61 Ibid.

62 Ibid. For later attempts at forming such a coordinating body, see William Philpott, "Squaring the Circle," 875–98.

63 Prete, "Joffre and the Question of Allied Supreme Command," 332.

64 Prete, "Le conflit stratégique," 26–37.

65 Ibid., 38–46.

66 Ibid., 232–3.

67 See Suarez, *Briand*, 3:217–37.

68 See no. 16650, Commander-in Chief to Minister of War, 30 November 1914, AG, 16N3014, 1/40.

69 Poincaré, *Au service* (1 December 1915), 3:296–301.

70 Prete, "*Imbroglio par Excellence*," 47–70.

71 Philpott, "Squaring the Circle, 881–96.

72 Cf. Joffre, *Memoirs*, 2:407–8.

73 Ibid., 411–12.

74 "Note au sujet des conditions générales de la guerre (début octobre 1915), le 7 octobre 1915," 3e Bureau, *AFGG*, III A(III), no. 2793.

75 "Notes sur l'emploi des forces anglaises pendant la campagne d'hiver 1915–1916, le 7 octobre 1915," 3e Bureau, *AFGG*, III A(III), no. 2792.

76 Joffre, *Memoirs*, 2:413–14.

77 No. 5441, Conference between the Representatives of the Allied Armies (held at Chantilly, 6–8 Dec. 1915), Fonds Joffre, AG, 14N10 11/42, reproduced in *AFGG*, IV(I) A(I), nos. 46–7, 69. On the background to the Anglo-French conflict over the Salonika expedition, see Cassar, *The French and the Dardanelles*; Suarez, *Briand*, 3:115–49, 179–216; Tanenbaum, *Sarrail*, 82–3; Dutton, *The Politics of Diplomacy*; Prete, "*Imbroglio par Excellence*," 47–70.

78 [Procès-verbal du] Conseil Franco-Anglais tenu à Calais le 4 décembre 1915, Fonds Joffre, AG, 14N10, dos. 3, pce annexe no. 54; Dutton, "The Calais Conference of December 1915," 143–56; Cassar, *Asquith as War Leader*, 141–2.

79 "La Bataille de la Somme, I: Préparation des offensives de 1916, La conférence de Chantilly" [a contemporary staff study, n.d.], AG, 16N2062, 1.

80 #5441, "Conference … (Chantilly, 6–8 Dec. 1915)," *AFGG*, IV(I) A(I), nos. 46–7, 69.

81 Ibid.; "Notes sur l'emploi des forces anglaises pendant la campagne d'hiver 1915–1916, le 7 octobre 1915," 3e Bureau, *AFGG*, III A(III), no. 2792.

82 No. 5441, "Conference … (Chantilly, 6–8 Dec. 1915)," *AFGG*, IV(I) A(I), nos. 46–7, 49; Neilson, *Strategy and Supply*, 123.

83 Prete, "Joffre and the Origins of the Somme," 437–41.

84 Desmazes, *Joffre*, 180–1.

CHAPTER THIRTEEN

1 See Philpott, *Anglo-French Relations and Strategy on the Western Front.*

2 See Wallach, *Uneasy Coalition.*

3 See Prete, *Strategy and Command, 1914*, 71–2.

4 A more definitive appraisal awaits an appreciation of all the relevant factors.

5 Erickson, "*Koalitsionnaya Voina*: Coalition Warfare," 88.

BIBLIOGRAPHY

ARCHIVAL SOURCES

Manuscripts

FRANCE

Archives des Affaires Etrangères, Paris

Série "Guerre 1914–1918"

Vol. 535. Grande Bretagne. Dossier Général. II. 1915, janvier–mars.

Vol. 979. Opérations Stratégiques Militaires. Dossier Général I. Novembre 1914–mars 1915.

Service historique de la Défense (Archives de Guerre), Vincennes

16N1675–6. GQG. EM. 3e Bur. Sorties: Ordres et instructions relatifs aux opérations; dos. 11–25, 14 septembre 1914–13 janvier 1915.

16N1728. GQG. EM. 3e Bur. Sorties: Renseignements au Ministre, dos. 1–4, 14 octobre 1914–[illegible].

16N1903. GQG. 3e Bur. Messages téléphonés et télégrammes reçus de l'Armée Britanniques 8 août 1914–16 mars 1915 (12 dossiers).

16N1905. GQG. EM. 3e Bur. Comptes rendus au ministre du 29 août au 14 octobre 1914; Dos. 1. Armée anglaise 19 août 1914–20 janvier 1915; Ordres et instructions relatifs aux opérations.

17N338. Mission M[ilitai]re F[rançai]se près l'Armée Britannique. Section d'Etat-Major. Entrées et sorties. C Coopération Franco-Britannique.

Correspondance secrète entre le GQG et le GHQ, septembre 1914–décembre 1916. Dos. 1: Coopération Britannique et Interalliée, septembre 1914–déc[emb]re 1915.

Archives nationales

C7494, Chambre, Commission de l'Armée.

BRITAIN

National Archives (formerly Public Record Office), London

CAB 41/35. Cabinet Papers. Letters of Asquith to the King.

CAB 42/1. Cabinet Papers. War Council, 1914.

WO 158, War of 1914–1918. Correspondence and Papers of Military Headquarters.

Royal Archives, Windsor Castle, Windsor

Private Papers and Diaries

FRANCE

General Berthelot Diary. "Souvenirs de la Grande Guerre: Notes extraites de mon Journal de Guerre." Vol. 1: "Au Grand quartier general: la guerre de movement de la déclaration de guerre au 24 novembre 1914." Unpublished typescript held by the general's nephew, Jean-Claude Dubois, Cressely, St. Rémy-les-Chevreuses, France.

Edmond Buat Papers. Service historique de la Défense (Archives de Guerre), Vincennes.

Paul Cambon Papers. Archives des Affaires Etrangères, Paris.

George Clemenceau Papers. Service historique de la Défense (Archives de Guerre), Vincennes.

Théophile Delcassé Papers. Archives des Affaires Etrangères, Paris.

Paul Deschanel Papers. Archives nationales, Paris.

Ferdinand Foch, Correspondance Foch. 10 October 1914–21 January 1916. Service historique de la Défense (Archives de Guerre), Vincennes.

Ferdinand Foch Papers. "Journées," Archives of Fournier Foch (private collection, courtesy of Henri-Fournier Foch, now located in Archives nationales, Paris).

Joseph J.-C. Joffre Papers. "Dossiers strictement personnels de M. Le Général Joffre." 1K268, Service historique de la Défense (Archives de Guerre), Vincennes.

Alexandre Millerand Papers. Archives nationales, Paris.

Maurice Pellé Papers. Bibliothèque de l'Institut de France, Paris.

Raymond Poincaré. Notes Journalières. Bilbliothèque nationale, Paris.

Raymond Poincaré Papers. Archives nationales, Paris (formerly in Bibliothèque nationale).

Marcel Sembat Papers. Office universitaire de recherche socialiste, Paris.

Albert Thomas Papers. Archives nationales, Paris.

BRITAIN

H.H. Asquith Papers. Bodleian Library, Oxford.
Arthur Balfour Papers. British Library, London.
Francis Bertie Papers. British Library, London.
Francis Bertie Papers. National Archives (formerly Public Record Office), London.
Andrew Bonar Law Papers. Parliamentary Archives, London.
Robert Cecil Papers. National Archives, London.
Austen Chamberlain Papers. Birmingham University Library, Birmingham.
Winston Churchill Papers. Churchill Archives Centre, Cambridge University, Cambridge.
Sydney Clive Diaries. II/I. B.H. Liddell Hart Centre for Military Archives, King's College, London.
Reginald Esher Papers. Churchill Archives Centre, Cambridge University, Cambridge.
Brimsley Fitzgerald Papers. Imperial War Museum, London.
John French Papers. Imperial War Museum, London.
King George V Papers. Royal Archives, Windsor Castle, Windsor.
Edward Grey Private Papers. National Archives, London.
Douglas Haig Papers. National Library of Scotland, Edinburgh.
Maurice Hankey Papers. Churchill Archives Centre, Cambridge University, Cambridge.
Horatio Kitchener Papers. 30/59. National Archives, London.
Horatio Kitchener Private Office Papers. WO/159. National Archives, London.
David Lloyd George Papers. Parliamentary Archives (formerly House of Lords Record Office), London.
Walter Long Papers. British Library, London.
Archibald Murray Papers. National Archives, London.
Henry Rawlinson Papers. Churchill Archives Centre, Cambridge University, Cambridge.
William Robertson Papers. B.H. Liddell Hart Centre for Military Archives, King's College, London.
Henry Wilson Papers. Imperial War Museum, London.

Government Publications and Official Histories

Britain. Historical Section of the Committee of Imperial Defence. *History of the Great War Based on Official Documents*. Compiled by Brig.-Gen. Sir James E. Edmonds et al. [1st ed., except *France and Belgium, 1914*, vol. 1, and maps in 3rd ed. (1933).] 14 vols. London: Macmillan 1922–47.
Canada. Col. G.W.L. Nicholson. *Official History of the Canadian Army: Canadian Expeditionary Force, 1914–1919*. Ottawa: Queen's Printer 1962.

France. Ministère de la Défense. État-Major de l'Armée, Service Historique. *Inventaire Sommaire des Archives de la Guerre Série N 1872–1919: Introduction: organization de l'Armée Française, Guide des Sources Bibliographie.* Col. Pierre Guinard, Jean-Claude Devos, Jean Micot. Troyes: Imprimerie des Renaissance 1975.

France. Ministère de la Guerre. Etat-Major de l'Armée: Service Historique. *Les Armées Françaises dans la Grande Guerre.* 105 vols. Paris: Imprimerie Nationale 1923–39.

PRINTED SOURCES

Adelman, Paul. *The Decline of the Liberal Party, 1910–1931.* London, New York: Longman 1982.

Albrecht-Carrié, René. *A Diplomatic History of Europe since the Congress of Vienna.* New York, Evanston, and London: Harper and Row 1958.

Alexandre, Général R[ené]. *Avec Joffre d'Agadir à Verdun: Souvenirs, 1911–1916.* Paris: Berger Levrault 1932.

Allain, Jean-Claude. *Joseph Caillaux: Le défi victorieux 1863–1914.* Paris: Imprimerie Nationale 1978.

Amson, Daniel. *Poincaré: L'Acharné de la politique.* Paris: Tallandier 1997.

Andrew, Christopher M. *Théophile Delcassé and the Making of the Entente Cordiale: A Reappraisal of French Foreign Policy 1898–1905.* New York: St Martin's Press 1968.

Arnold, Joseph C. "French Tactical Doctrine, 1870–1914." *Military Affairs* 42 (April 1978): 61–7.

Arthur, Sir George. *The Life of Lord Kitchener.* 3 vols. London: Macmillan 1920.

Asquith, Earl of Oxford and Asquith [H.H.]. *Memories and Reflections, 1852–1927.* 2 vols. London: Cassell 1928.

Audoin-Rouzeau, Stéphane, and Annette Becker. *14–18: Understanding the Great War.* Trans. Catherine Temerson. New York: Hill and Wang 2000.

Auphan, Amiral [G.A.J.P.]. *La Marine dans l'histoire de la France.* Paris: Librairie Plon 1955.

Autin, Jean. *Foch ou le triomphe de la volonté.* 2nd ed. Paris: Perrin 1998.

Barnett, Correlli. *Britain and Her Army, 1509–1970: A Military, Political and Social Survey.* London: Allen Lane 1970.

– *The Swordbearers: Studies in Supreme Command in the First World War.* London: Eyre and Spottiswoode 1963.

Baumont, Michel. "Abel Ferry et les étapes du contrôle aux armées, 1914–1918." *Revue d'histoire moderne et contemporaine* 15 (1968): 162–208.

Beaverbrook, Lord. *Politicians and the War, 1914–1916.* Garden City, NY: Doubleday 1928.

Becker, Jean-Jacques. *1914: Comment les Français sont entrés dans la guerre.* Paris: Presses de la Fondation Nationale des Sciences Politiques 1977.

– *Les Français dans la Grande Guerre*. Paris: Robert Laffont 1980.

– "Les 'Trois Ans' et les débuts de la Première Guerre mondiale." *Guerre mondiales et conflits contemporains* 145 (January 1987): 7–26.

– "Union Sacrée et ideologie bourgeoise." *Revue Historique* 164 (1980): 65–74.

Beckett, Ian, and John Gooch, eds. *Politicians and Defence: Studies in the Formulation of British Defense Policy 1845–1970*. Manchester, UK: Manchester University Press 1981.

Beckett, Ian F.W. *The Great War, 1914–1918*. Harlow, UK: Pearson Education 2001.

Bell, Christopher M. *Churchill and the Dardanelles*. Oxford: Oxford University Press 2017.

Ben-Moshe, T. "Churchill's Strategic Conception during the First World War." *Journal of Strategic Studies* 12, no. 1 (1989): 5–21.

Bernède, Allain. "'The Gardiners of Salonika': The Lines of Communications and the Logistics of the French Army of the East, October 1915–November 1918." *War & Society* 16, no. 1 (May 1998): 43–58.

Bertie of Thame, Viscount. *The Diary of Lord Bertie of Thame, 1914–1918*. Ed. Lady Algernon Gordon Lennox. Vol. 1. London: Hodder and Stoughton 1924.

Blake, Robert. "Great Britain: The Crimean to the First World War." In Michael Howard, ed., *Soldiers and Governments: Nine Studies in Civil-Military Relations*. London: Eyre and Spottiswoode 1957.

Bond, Brian. *France and Belgium, 1939–1940*. London: Davis Paynter 1975.

– ed. *The First World War and British Military History*. Oxford: Clarendon Press 1991.

Bond, Brian, and Nigel Cave, eds. *Haig: A Re-Appraisal 70 Years On*. Barnsley, UK: Leo Cooper 1999.

Boulding, Kenneth E. "National Images and International Systems." *Journal of Conflict Resolution* 3 (1959): 120–31.

Bourget, J.-M. *Gouvernement et commandement*. Paris: Payot 1930.

Bourne, J.M., *Britain and the Great War 1914–1918*. London: Arnold 1989.

Brock, Michael, and Eleanor Brock, eds. *H.H. Asquith, Letters to Venetia Stanley*. Oxford: Oxford University Press 1982.

Broussilov, Général. *Mémoires du Général Broussilov: Guerre 1914–1918*. Paris: Hachette 1929.

Bruntz, George G. *Allied Propaganda and the Collapse of the German Empire in 1918*. Stanford, CA: Stanford University Press 1938.

Burk, Kathleen. *Britain, America and the Sinews of War, 1914–1918*. London: Allen and Unwin 1985.

Cahisa, Raymond. "Le double roman d'amour de Joffre le pyrénéen." *Miroir de l'histoire* 7 (1956): 337–42.

Callwell, Maj.-Gen., Sir C.E. *Experiences of a Dug-Out 1914–1918*. London: Constable 1920.

– ed. *Field Marshal Sir Henry Wilson. His Life and Diaries*. 2 vols. London: Cassell 1927.

Cambon, Henri, ed. *Paul Cambon: correspondance 1870–1946*. Vol. 3: (1912–1924), *Les Guerres Balkaniques, La Grande Guerre, L'Organisation de la Paix*. Paris: Grasset 1946.

Campbell, John P. "Refighting Britain's Great Patriotic War." *International Journal* [Canada] 26 (autumn 1971): 686–705.

Cassar, George H. *Asquith as War Leader*. London: Hambledon Press 1994.

– *The French and the Dardanelles: A Study of Failure in the Conduct of War*. London: George Allen and Unwin 1971.

– *Hell in Flanders Fields: Canadians at the Second Battle of Ypres*. Toronto: Dundurn Press 2010.

– *Kitchener: Architect of Victory*. London: William Kimber 1977.

– *Kitchener's War: British Strategy from 1914 to 1916*. Washington, DC: Brassey's 2004.

– *Lloyd George at War, 1914–1916*. London, New York, Delhi: Anthem Press 2009.

– *Reluctant Partner: The Complete Story of the French Participation in the Dardanelles Expedition of 1915*. Warwick, UK: Helion and Company 2019.

– *The Tragedy of Sir John French*. Newark: University of Delaware Press 1985.

– *Trial by Gas: The British Army at the Second Battle of Ypres*. Lincoln, NE: Potomac Books 2014.

"Centenary News First World War 1914–1918." "Centenary News First World War Books" at www.centenarynews.com/allbooks.

Challener, Richard D. *The French Theory of the Nation in Arms, 1866–1939*. New York: Russell and Russell 1965.

Chastenet, Jacques. *Histoire de la Troisième Republique*. 6 vols. Vol. 4: *Jours inquiets et jours sanglants, 1906–1918*. Paris: Hachette 1952–63.

Cherry, Niall. *Most Unfavourable Ground: The Battle of Loos 1915*. Solihull, UK: Helion and Company 2005.

Chickering, Roger, and Stig Forster. *Great War, Total War: Combat and Mobilization on the Western Front, 1914–1918*. Washington, DC: German Historical Institute / Cambridge: Cambridge University Press 2000.

Christie, N.M. *Canadians in the Second Battle of Ypres, April 22nd – 26th, 1915: A Social History and Battlefield Tour*. Ottawa: CEF Books 2005.

Churchill, Winston S. *The World Crisis, 1911–1918*. 4 vols. New York: Charles Scribner's Sons 1923–29.

Clark, Alan. *The Donkeys*. London: Hutchinson 1961.

Clausewitz, Carl von. *On War*. Ed. and trans. Michael Howard and Peter Paret, commentary Bernard Brodie. Princeton, NJ: Princeton University Press 1976.

Clayton, Anthony. *Paths of Glory: The French Army 1914–18*. London: Cassell 2003.

Clemenceau, Georges. *Grandeurs et misères d'une victoire*. Paris: Plon 1930; trans. as *Grandeur and Misery of Victory*. London: George G. Harrap 1930.

Collier, Basil. *Brasshat: A Biography of Field Marshal Sir Henry Wilson*. London: Secker and Warburg 1963.

Colloque international d'histoire militaire et d'études de défense nationale, Montpellier 2–6 septembre. *Forces armées et systèmes d'alliances.* 3 vols. Montpellier: Les Sept Epées 1983.

Conte, Arthur. *Joffre.* Paris: Oliver Orban 1991.

Corbett, Sir Julian Stafford. *Some Principles of Maritime Strategy.* London: Longmans Green [1938].

Corrigan, Gordon. *Loos 1915: The Unwanted Battle.* Stroud, UK: Spellmount 2006.

Corvisier, André. "Aspects divers de l'histoire militaire." *Revue historique moderne et contemporaine* 20 (January–March 1973): 1–9.

Craig, Gordon A. *Problems of Coalition Warfare: The Military Alliance against Napoleon, 1813–1814.* Colorado Springs, CO: United States Air Force Academy 1965.

– "The World War I Alliance of the Central Powers in Retrospect: The Military Cohesion of the Alliance." *Journal of Modern History* 37 (1965): 336–44.

Cruttwell, C.R.M.F. *A History of the Great War, 1914–1918.* Oxford: Clarendon Press 1934.

Dallas, Gregor. *At the Heart of a Tiger: Clemenceau and His World 1841–1929.* London: Macmillan 1993.

Danilov, Youri. *La Russie dans la guerre mondiale (1914–1917).* Trans. Alexandre Kaznakov. Paris: Payot 1927.

David, Edward, ed. *Inside Asquith's Cabinet: From the Diaries of Charles Hobhouse.* London: John Murray 1977.

Department of Defence Dictionary of Military and Associated Terms (August 2017 edition), www.jcs.mil/Portals/36/Documents/Doctrine/pubs/dictionary/pdf.

Department of Defence Joint Publications 3–0, www.jcs.mil/Portals/36/Documents/Doctrine/pubs/jp3_0_ 20170117.pdf.

Desmazes, Général [René]. *Joffre: La victoire du caractère.* Paris: Nouvelles Editions Latines 1955.

D'Esme, Jean. *Gallieni, destin hors série.* Paris: Plon 1965.

– *Le Père Joffre.* Paris: Éditions France-Empire 1962.

D'Esperey, Franchet, Maréchal. "Notes sur la conduite supérieure de la guerre de 1792 à 1797 et de 1914–1918." *Revue militaire générale,* 2nd Series, 2 (1938): 137–52.

DeWeerd, Harvey A. "Churchill, Lloyd George, Clemenceau: The Emergence of the Civilians." In Edward Mead Earle, ed., *The Makers of Modern Strategy.* New York: Atheneum 1967.

Doughty, Robert A. "French Strategy in 1914: Joffre's Own." *Journal of Military History* 67 (April 2003): 427–54.

– *Pyrrhic Victory: French Strategy and Operations in the Great War.* Cambridge, MA: Belknap Press of Harvard University Press 2005.

Druène, B. "De la guerre de mouvement à la guerre de tranchées." *Revue historique de l'Armée* 20 (1964): 173–80.

Duroselle, Jean-Baptiste. *Clemenceau.* Paris: Fayard 1988.

– "Strategic and Economic Relations during the First World War." In Neville Waites, ed., *Troubled Neighbours: Franco-British Relations in the Twentieth Century.* London: Weidenfeld and Nicholson 1971.

Dutton, David. "La Grande Bretagne, la France et la campagne de Salonique en 1917: l'alliance mise à l'épreuve." *Guerres mondiales et conflits contemporains* 180 (October 1995): 29–45.

Dutton, D.J. "The Balkan Campaign and French War Aims in the Great War." *English Historical Review* 94, no. 370 (January 1997): 97–113.

– "The Calais Conference of December 1915." *Historical Journal* 21 (1978): 143–56.

– *The Politics of Diplomacy: Britain and France in the Balkans in the First World War.* London: I.B. Taurus 1998.

Ehrman, John. *Cabinet Government and War, 1890–1940.* Cambridge: Cambridge University Press 1958.

Erickson, John. "*Koalitsionaya Voina:* Coalition Warfare in Soviet Military Theory, Planning and Performance." In Keith Neilson and Roy A. Prete, eds., *Coalition Warfare: An Uneasy Accord.* Waterloo, ON: Wilfrid Laurier Press 1983.

Esher, Viscount Oliver, ed. *Journals and Letters of Reginald Viscount Esher.* Vol. 3. London: Ivor Nicholson and Watson 1938.

Esher, Viscount Reginald. *The Tragedy of Lord Kitchener.* London: John Murray 1921.

Falkenhayn, General Erich von. *General Headquarters 1914–1916 and Its Critical Decisions.* London: Hutchinson and Company [1924]. [Trans. from 1919 German edition.]

Falls, Cyril. *The Great War.* New York: G.P. Putnam's Sons 1959.

Farrar, Marjorie. "Politics versus Patriotism: Alexandre Millerand as French Minister of War." *French Historical Studies* 11, no. 4 (1979–80): 577–605.

– *Principled Pragmatist: The Political Career of Alexandre Millerand.* New York: Berg 1991.

Farrar-Hockley, Anthony. *Death of an Army.* London: Barker 1967.

Feldman, Gerald D. *Army, Industry and Labour in Germany, 1914–1918.* Princeton, NJ: Princeton University Press 1966.

Ferguson, Niall. *The Pity of War.* London: Allen Lane 1998.

Fergusson, James. *The Curragh Incident.* London: Faber and Faber 1964.

Ferro, Marc. *The Great War.* London and New York: Ark Paperbacks 1987.

Ferry, Abel Jules Edouard. *Carnets secrets, 1914–1918.* Paris: B. Grasset [1957].

Fischer, Fritz. *Germany's Aims in the First World War.* London: Chatto and Windus 1967.

Foch, Maréchal Ferdinand. *Mémoires pour servir à l'histoire de la Guerre de 1914–1918.* 2 vols. Paris: Librairie Plon 1931.

– *The Memoirs of Marshal Foch.* Trans. Col. T. Bentley Mott. Garden City, NY: Doubleday Doran and Company 1931.

Foley, Robert T. *German Strategy and the Path to Verdun: Eric von Falkenhayn and the Development of Attrition, 1870–1916*. Cambridge: Cambridge University Press 2005.

Fraser, Peter. "The British Shells Scandal of 1915." *Canadian Journal of History / Annales canadiennes d'histoire* 18, no. 1 (April 1983): 69–86.

– *Lord Esher: A Political Biography*. London: Hart-Davis MacGibbon 1973.

French, David. *British Economic and Strategic Planning 1905–1915*. London: G. Allen and Unwin 1982.

– *British Strategy and War Aims, 1914–1916*. London: Allen and Unwin 1986.

– "The Dardanelles, Mecca, and Kut: Prestige as a Factor in British Eastern Strategy, 1914–1916." *War and Society* 5, no. 1 (1987): 45–62.

– "Sir John French's Secret Service on the Western Front, 1914–15." *Journal of Strategic Studies* 7, no. 4 (1984): 423–40.

– "The Meaning of Attrition, 1914–1916." *English Historical Review* no. 412 (April 1988): 385–403.

– "The Military Background to the 'Shell Crisis' of May 1915." *Journal of Strategic Studies* 2, no. 2 (September 1979): 192–205.

– "The Origins of the Dardanelles Campaign Reconsidered." *History* 68, no. 223 (1983): 210–24.

– *The Strategy of the Lloyd George Coalition 1916–1918*. Oxford: Clarendon Press 1995.

French, Field Marshal Viscount [John], Earl of Ypres. *1914*. London: Constable and Company 1919.

– *Some War Diaries, Addresses, and Correspondence of Field Marshal the Right Honourable Earl of Ypres*. Ed. Gerald French. London: Herbert Jenkins 1937.

French, Gerald. *The Life of Field-Marshal Sir John French, First Earl of Ypres*. London: Cassell and Company 1931.

Gallieni, General [Joseph S.]. *Les Carnets de Gallieni*. Ed. Gaetan Gallieni. Paris: Albin Michel, Éditeur 1932.

– *Mémoires du Maréchal Gallieni*. Paris: Payot 1926.

Gamelin, General M[aurice]. *Manœuvre et victoire de la Marne*. Paris: Bernard Grasset 1954.

Gardner, Nikolas. "Command and Control in the 'Great Retreat' of 1914: The Disintegration of the British Cavalry Division." *Journal of Military History* 63 (January 1999): 29–54.

– "Command in Crisis: The British Expeditionary Force and the Forest of Mormal, August 1914." *War & Society* 16, no. 6 (October 1998): 13–31.

– *Trial by Fire: Command and the British Expeditionary Force in 1914*. Westport, CT: Prager 2003.

Gibbs, Norman. "British Strategic Doctrine, 1918–1939." In Michael Howard, ed., *The Theory and Practice of War: Essays Presented to Captain B.H. Liddell Hart*. London: Cassell 1965.

Gilbert, Bentley B. "Pacifist to Interventionist: David Lloyd George in 1911 and 1914. Was Belgium an Issue?" *Historical Journal* 28, no. 4 (1985): 863–85.

Gilbert, Martin, ed. *A Century of Conflict: Essays for A.J.P. Taylor.* London: Hamish Hamilton 1966.

– *First World War.* London: Weidenfeld and Nicolson 1994.

– *The Somme: Heroism and Horror in the First World War.* New York: Henry Holt and Company 2006.

– ed. *Winston S. Churchill.* Vol. 3: *1914–1916.* London: Heinemann 1971.

– ed. *Winston S. Churchill.* Vol. 3: *Companion, 1: Documents, July 1914–April 1915.* London: Heinemann 1972.

Girardet, Raoûl. *La société militaire dans la France contemporaine (1815–1939).* Paris: Librairie Plon 1953.

Godfrey, John F. *Capitalism at War: Industrial Policy and Bureaucracy in France 1914–1918.* Leamington Spa, UK, Hamburg, Germany, New York: Berg 1987.

Godspeed, D.J. *Les Forces Armées du Canada: Un siècle de grandes réalisations.* Ottawa: Direction des Services Historiques, Quartier Général des Forces Canadiennes, 1967.

Goguel, François. *La politique des partis sous la IIIe République.* Paris: Seuil 1946.

Gooch, John. *The Plans of War: The General Staff and British Military Strategy c. 1900–1916.* New York: John Wiley and Sons 1974.

– "Soldiers, Strategy and War Aims in Britain, 1914–1918." In Barry Hunt and Adrian Presto, eds., *War Aims and Strategic Policy in the Great War 1914–1918.* London: Croom Helm 1977.

Gorce, Paul Marie de la. *The French Army: A Military-Political History.* Trans. Kenneth Douglas. New York: George Braziller 1963.

Görlitz, Walter. *The German General Staff: Its History and Structure 1657–1945.* Trans. Brian Battershaw. London: Hollis and Carter 1953.

Gottleib, W[olfram] W[ilhelm]. *Studies in Secret Diplomacy during the First World War.* London: Allen and Unwin 1957.

Goya, Michel. *La chair et l'acier: L'invention de la guerre moderne (1914–1918).* Paris: Tallandier 2004.

Greenfield, Nathan M. *Baptism of Fire: The Second Battle of Ypres and the Forging of Canada April 1915.* Toronto: HarperCollins 2007.

Greenhalgh, Elizabeth. *Foch in Command: The Forging of a First World War General.* Cambridge: Cambridge University Press 2011.

– *The French Army and the First World War.* Cambridge: Cambridge University Press 2014.

– *Victory through Coalition: Britain and France during the First World War.* Cambridge: Cambridge University Press 2005.

Grey of Fallodon, 1st Viscount Edward. *Twenty-Five Years, 1892–1916.* 2 vols. New York: Frederick A. Stokes 1925.

Guillen, Pierre, ed. *La France et l'Italie pendant la Première Guerre mondiale.* Grenoble: Presses Universitaires de France 1976.

Guinn, Paul. *British Strategy and Politics, 1914–1918*. Oxford: Clarendon Press 1965.

Hackett, [J.W.] *The Profession of Arms*. London: Times Publishing 1963.

Haig, Douglas. *The Private Papers of Douglas Haig, 1914–1919*. Ed. Robert Blake. London: Eyre and Spottiswoode 1952.

– *Douglas Haig: War Diaries and Letters, 1914–1918*. Eds. Gary Sheffield and John Bourne. London: Weidenfeld and Nicolson 2005.

Halpern, Paul G. *The Naval War in the Mediterranean, 1914–1918*. Annapolis, MD: Naval Institute Press 1987.

Hamer, W.S. *The British Army: Civil-Military Relations, 1885–1905*. Oxford: Clarendon Press 1970.

Hankey, Sir Maurice P.A.H. *The Supreme Command, 1914–1918*. 2 vols. London: George Allen and Unwin [1961].

Hardach, Gerd. *The First World War 1914–1918*. London: Allen Lane 1977.

Harris, J.P. *Douglas Haig and the First World War*. Cambridge: Cambridge University Press 2008.

Hart, Peter. *The Somme: The Darkest Hour on the Western Front*. New York: Pegasus Books 2008.

Hazelhurst, C. "Asquith as Prime Minister, 1908–1916." *English Historical Review* 85, no. 336 (1970): 502–31.

Helmreich, Jonathan E. "Belgian Concerns over Neutrality and British Intentions, 1906–14." *Journal of Modern History* 36, no. 4 (December 1964): 416–27.

– *Belgium and Europe: A Study of Small Power Diplomacy*. The Hague: Mouton 1976.

Herbillon, Colonel [Émile]. *Souvenirs d'un officier de liaison pendant la guerre mondiale: Du général en chef au gouvernement*. Vol. 1: *Sous le commandement du général Joffre*. Paris: Éditions Jules Tallandier 1930.

Herwig, Holger H. "Estranged Bedfellows: Germany and Austria Hungary, 1914–1918." In Dennis E. Showalter, ed. *Future Wars: Coalition Operations in Global Strategy*. Chicago: Imprint Publications 2002.

– *The First World War: Germany and Austria-Hungary 1914–1918*. London: Arnold 1997.

– *The Marne, 1914: The Opening of World War I and the Battle That Changed the World*. New York: Random House 2009.

Hinsley, F.H., ed. *British Foreign Policy under Sir Edward Grey*. Cambridge: Cambridge University Press 1977.

Holmes, Richard. "Sir John French and Kitchener." In Brian Bond, ed., *The First World War and British Military History*. Oxford: Clarendon Press 1991.

– *The Little Field-Marshal: Sir John French*. London: J. Cape 1981.

Horn, Martin. "Alexandre Ribot et la coopération financière anglo-française 1914–1917." *Guerres mondiales et conflits contemporains* 180 (October 1995): 7–28.

– *Britain, France and the Financing of the First World War*. Montreal and Kingston: McGill-Queen's University Press 2002.

– *The Continental Commitment: The Dilemma of British Defence Policy in the Era of the Two World Wars.* London: Temple Smith 1972.

– ed. *The Theory and Practice of War: Essays Presented to B.H. Liddell Hart on His Seventieth Birthday.* London: Cassell [1965].

Howard, Michael E. *The Continental Commitment: The Dilemma of British Defence Policy in the Era of the Two World Wars.* London: Temple Smith 1972.

Huguet, General [Victor Jacques-Marie]. *Britain and the War: A French Indictment.* Trans. H. Cotton Minchin. London: Cassell and Company 1928.

Hull, Isabel V. *Absolute Destruction: Military Culture and the Practices of War in Imperial Germany.* Ithaca, NY: Cornell University Press 2005.

L'Illustration. 1915.

Jeffery, Keith. *Field Marshal Sir Henry Wilson: A Political Soldier.* Oxford: Oxford University Press 2006.

Jenkins, E.H. *A History of the French Navy, From Its Beginning to the Present Day.* London: Macdonald and Company 1973.

Jenkins, Roy. *Asquith.* London: Collins 1978.

Jevons, Brian Andrew. "'*La politique de la guerre*': French Civil-Military Relations, 4 August 1914–12 January 1915." PhD thesis, University of New Brunswick 2000.

Joffre, Maréchal [Joseph J.-C.]. *Mémoires du Maréchal Joffre, 1910–1917.* 2 vols. Paris: Librairie Plon 1932; trans. by Col. T. Bentley Mott as *The Memoirs of Marshal Joffre.* 2 vols. London: Geoffrey Bles 1932.

Johnson, Hubert C. *Breakthrough!: Tactics, Technology, and the Search for Victory on the Western Front in World War I.* Novato, CA: Presidio 1994.

Keegan, John. *The First World War.* Toronto: Vintage Canada 2000.

Keiger, John F. *Raymond Poincaré.* Cambridge: Cambridge University Press 1997.

Kennedy, Paul F. "Military Coalitions and Coalition Warfare over the Past Century." In Keith Neilson and Roy A. Prete, eds., *Coalition Warfare: An Uneasy Accord.* Waterloo, ON: Wilfrid Laurier Press 1983.

– *The Rise of the Anglo-German Antagonism 1860–1924.* London: George Allen and Unwin 1980.

King, Jere Clemens. *Generals and Politicians: Conflict between France's High Command, Parliament and Government, 1914–1918.* Berkeley: University of California Press 1951.

Kluck, Général. *La Guerre de 1914–1918: Les opérations militaires.* Paris: Éditions Sirey 1966.

Koss, Stephen. *Asquith.* London: Allen Lane 1976.

Krause, Jonathan. *Early Trench Tactics in the French Army: The Second Battle of Artois, May–June 1915.* Surrey, UK: Ashgate Publishing 2013.

Kuhl, Général [Hermann Joseph] von. *Le grand Etat-Major allemand avant et pendant la guerre mondiale.* Trans. from German. Paris: Payot 1922.

Lahaie, Olivier. "Les dividendes de l'Entente cordiale: Les accords militaires franco-britanniques avant 1914." *Revue historique des Armées* 237, no. 4 (2004): 1–15.

Lasswell, Harold C. *Propaganda Technique in the World War*. London: Kegan, Paul, Trench, Trubner and Company 1927.

Lennox, Lady Algernon Gordon, ed. *The Diary of Lord Bertie of Thame, 1914–1918*. 2 vols. London: Hodder and Stoughton 1924.

Levine, Naomi B. *Politics, Love and Religion: The Story of H.H. Asquith, Venetia Stanley and Edwin Montagu, Based on the Life and Letters of Edwin Samuel Montagu*. New York and London: New York University Press 1991.

Liddell Hart, Basil Henry. *Foch: The Man of Orleans*. London: Eyre and Spottiswoode 1933.

– *A History of the World War, 1914–1918*. 2nd ed. London: Faber and Faber [1934].

– *Reputations Ten Years After*. Boston: Little, Brown and Company 1928.

– *Strategy: The Indirect Approach*. 3rd ed. rev. London: Faber and Faber [1954].

Liska, George. *Nations in Alliance: The Limits of Interdependence*. Baltimore, MD: Johns Hopkins University Press 1962.

Lloyd, Nick. *Loos 1915*. Stroud, UK: History Press 2008.

Lloyd George, David. *War Memoirs of David Lloyd George*. 6 vols. London: Ivor Nicholson and Watson 1933–36.

Lowe, C.J. "The Failure of British Diplomacy in the Balkans, 1914–1916." *Canadian Journal of History* 4, no. 1 (1969): 73–99.

– "Italy and the Balkans, 1914–1915." In F.H. Hinsley, ed., *British Foreign Policy under Sir Edward Grey*. Cambridge: Cambridge University Press 1977.

Lowe, C.J., and M.L. Dockrill. *The Mirage of Power*. Vol. 2: *British Foreign Policy, 1914–22*. London: Routledge and Kegan Paul 1972.

Lowry, Bullitt. "French and 1914: His Defense of His Memoirs Examined." *Military Affairs* 45, no. 2 (April 1981): 79–83.

Lyautey, Pierre. *Gallieni*. Paris: Gallimard 1959.

Magnus, Sir Philip. *Kitchener: Portrait of an Imperialist*. London: Grey Arrow Editions 1961.

Marder, Arthur J. *From the Dreadnought to Scapa Flow: The Royal Navy in the Fischer Era, 1904–1919*. 5 vols. London: Oxford University Press 1961–70.

Maurice, Sir Frederick. *Lessons of Allied Co-operation: Naval, Military and Air, 1914–1918*. London: Oxford University Press 1942.

Maurin, Jules, and Jean-Charles Jauffret, eds. *La Grande Guerre 1914–1918: 80 ans d'historiographie et de représentations*. Montpellier: UMR 5609 du CNRS-ESID 2002.

Mayeur, Jean-Marie, and Madeline Rebérioux. *The Third Republic from Its Origins to the Great War, 1871–1914*. Trans. J.R. Foster. Cambridge: Cambridge University Press 1984.

McCrae, Meighen. *Coalition Strategy and the End of the First World War: The Supreme War Council and War Planning, 1917–1918*. Cambridge: Cambridge University Press 2019.

McEwen, J.M. "'Brass-Hats' and the British Press during the First World War." *Canadian Journal of History / Annales canadiennes d'histoire* 11, no. 1 (April 1983): 43–67.

Messimy, Adolphe-Marie. *Mes souvenirs*. Paris: Plon 1937.

Millett, Allan R., and Murray Williamson, eds. *Military Effectiveness*. 3 vols. Boston: Unwin Hyman 1988.

Monteilhet, J. *Les institutions militaires de la France, 1814–1932*. Paris: Librairie Félix Alcan 1932.

Neiberg, Michael S. *Foch: Supreme Allied Commander in the Great War*. Washington, DC: Brassey's 2003.

Neilson, Keith. "The Anglo-Russian Alliance, 1914–1917: Lessons for the Present?" In Dennis E. Showalter, ed., *Future Wars: Coalition Operations in Global Strategy*. Chicago: Imprint Publications 2002.

– *Britain and the Last Tsar: British Policy and Russia, 1894–1917*. Oxford: Clarendon Press 1995.

– "'Greatly Exaggerated': The Myth of the Decline of Great Britain before 1914." *International History Review* 13, no. 4 (November 1991): 695–725.

– "Kitchener: A Reputation Refurbished?" *Canadian Journal of History* 15, no. 2 (August 1980): 207–27.

– "Kitchener, Russia and British Strategy, 1914–1915." Unpublished paper 1979 [courtesy of the author].

– *Strategy and Supply: The Anglo-Russian Alliance, 1914–17*. London: Allen and Unwin 1984.

Neilson, Keith, and Greg Kennedy, eds. *Far Flung Lines: Studies in Imperial Defence in Honour of Donald Mackenzie Schurman*. London: Frank Cass 1997.

Neilson, Keith, and Roy A. Prete, eds. *Coalition Warfare: An Uneasy Accord*. Waterloo, ON: Wilfrid Laurier Press 1983.

Neustadt, Richard E. *Alliance Politics*. New York and London: Columbia University Press 1970.

Nevakivi, Jukha. *Britain, France and the Arab Middle East 1914–1920*. London: Athlone 1969.

– "Lord Kitchener and the Partition of the Ottoman Empire, 1915–1916." In K. Bourne and D.C. Watt, eds., *Studies in International History: Essays Presented to W. Norton Medlicott*. London: Longmans 1967.

Otte, T[homas] G. "'A Fair Equilibrium'? Britain and the Origins of the First World War." Paper presented at the 27th RMC Military History Symposium, Royal Military College of Canada, Kingston, Ontario, 22–23 March 2007.

Palmerston, Henry. "Lord Palmerston Quotes," at www.thinkexist.com/quotes/lord_palmerston/ (consulted 28 November 2011).

Paret, Peter. "Clausewitz." In Peter Paret, ed., *Makers of Modern Strategy from Machiavelli to the Nuclear Age*. Princeton, NJ: Princeton University Press 1986.

Pedroncini, Guy. *Les Mutineries de 1917*. Paris: Presses Universitaires de France 1967.

– "Remarques sur la décision militaire en France pendant la grande guerre." *Revue d'histoire moderne et contemporaine* 20 (January–March 1973): 139–52.

– "Trois Maréchaux, Trois Stratégies." *Guerres mondiales et conflits contemporains* 145 (January 1987): 45–62.

Philpott, William James. *Anglo-French Relations and Strategy on the Western Front, 1914–1918*. London: Macmillan 1996.

– *Bloody Victory: The Sacrifice on the Somme and the Making of the Twentieth Century*. London: Little, Brown 2009.

– *Bloody Victory: Three Armies on the Somme: The First Battle of the Twentieth Century*. New York: Alfred H. Knopf 2010.

– "Britain and France Go to War: Anglo-French Relations on the Western Front, 1914–1918." *War in History* 2, no. 1 (March 1995): 43–64.

– "British Military Strategy and the Western Front: Independence or Alliance, 1904–1918." D.Phil. thesis, Oxford University, 1991.

– "The General Staff and the Paradoxes of Continental War." In David French and Holden Reid, eds., *The General Staff: Reform and Innovation, 1890–1939*. London: Frank Cass 2002.

– "Kitchener and the 29th Division: A Study in Anglo-French Strategic Relations, 1914–1915." *Journal of Strategic Studies* 16, no. 3 (September 1993): 388–94.

– "Origines et signification de la stratégie britannique du 'flanc nord.'" *Guerres mondiales et conflits contemporains* 180 (October 1995): 47–63.

– "Squaring the Circle: The Higher Co-ordination of the *Entente* in the Winter of 1915–16." *English Historical Review* 114, no. 458 (September 1999): 873–98.

– "The Strategic Ideas of Sir John French." *Journal of Strategic Studies* 12, no. 4 (December 1989): 458–78.

Pichot-Duclos, Général [R.A.]. *Réflexions sur ma vie militaire. Au G Q.G. de Joffre*. Paris: B. Arthaud 1947.

Pierrefeu, Jean de. *GQG, secteur 1: Trois ans au grand quartier général par le rédacteur du 'communiqué.'* 2 vols. Paris: l'Édition Française Illustrée 1920.

Pingaud, Albert. "L'Entente et la conduite de la guerre." *Revue d'histoire de la Guerre Mondiale* 13 (1935): 224–56.

– *Histoire diplomatique de la France pendant la Grande Guerre*. 3 vols. Paris: Éditions "Alsatia," 1938–40.

Pirenne, Henri. *La Belgique et la Guerre mondiale*. Paris: Presses Universitaires de France 1928.

Poincaré, Raymond. *Au service de la France: Neuf années de souvenirs*. 10 vols. Paris: Plon-Nourrit 1925–33.

Porch, Douglas. "The French Army in the First World War." In Allan R. Millett and Murray Williamson, eds., *Military Effectiveness*. 3 vols. Boston: Unwin Hyman 1988.

– *The March to the Marne: The French Army, 1871–1914*. Cambridge: Cambridge University Press 1981.

Porte, Remy. *Joffre*. Paris: Perrin 2016.

Prete, Roy A. "The Anglo-French Command Crisis of October–November 1914." *Research Studies* 51, nos. 3/4 (September/December 1984): 112–26.

– "The Artois Offensive and the British Changing of the Guard in December, 1915." Unpublished paper, Conference of the Western Society for French History, Los Angeles, 8–11 November 2000.
– "Le conflit stratégique franco-britannique sur le front occidental et la conférence de Calais du 6 juillet, 1915." *Guerres mondiales et conflits contemporains* 186 (April 1997): 17–49.
– "Dossier l'alliance Franco-britannique pendant la Grande Guerre." *Guerres mondiales et conflits contemporains* 180 (October 1995): 3–5.
– "French Military War Aims, 1914–1916." *Historical Journal* 28, no. 4 (1985): 887–99.
– "French Strategic Planning and the Deployment of the B.E.F. in France in 1914." *Canadian Journal of History* 24, no. 1 (April 1989): 42–62.
– "*Imbroglio par Excellence*: Mounting the Salonika Campaign, September–October 1915." *War and Society* 19, no. 1 (May 2001): 47–70.
– "Joffre and the Origins of the Somme: A Study in Allied Military Planning," *Journal of Military History* 73, no. 2 (April 2009): 417–48.
– "Joffre and the Question of Allied Supreme Command, 1914–1916." *Proceedings of the Annual Meeting of the Western Society for French History* 16 (1989): 329–38.
– "Objections to Loos: A Case Study in Anglo-French Command Relations on the Western Front, 1914–1915." Unpublished paper, Conference of the Western Society for French History, Newport Beach, CA, 31 October–1 November 2003.
– "The Preparation of the French Army Prior to World War I: An Historiographical Reappraisal." *Canadian Journal of History* 26, no. 2 (August 1991): 241–66.
– "Les relations franco-britanniques et l'attaque au gaz allemande à Ypres, avril 1915." In Roch Legault and Jean Lamarre, eds., *La Première Guerre mondiale et le Canada: Contribution sociomilitaires québécoises.* Montreal: Méridien 1999.
– *Strategy and Command: The Anglo-French Coalition on the Western Front, 1914.* Montreal and Kingston: McGill-Queen's University Press 2009.
– "The War of Movement on the Western Front, August–November, 1914: A Study in Coalition Warfare." PhD dissertation, University of Alberta, 1979.
Prior, Robin. *Churchill's 'World Crisis' as History.* London: Croom Helm 1983.
Prior, Robin, and Trevor Wilson. *Command on the Western Front: The Military Career of Sir Henry Rawlinson, 1914–1918.* Barnsley, UK: Pen and Sword Books 2004.
– *The First World War.* London: Cassell 1999.
– *The Somme.* New Haven, CT: Yale University Press 2005.
Pul, Paul Van. *In Flanders Flooded Fields: Before Ypres There Was Yser.* Barnsley, UK: Pen and Sword Military 2006.
Ralston, David B. *The Army of the Republic: The Place of the Military in the Political Evolution of France, 1871–1914.* Cambridge, MA: MIT Press 1967.

Read, James Morgan. *Atrocity Propaganda, 1914–1919*. New Haven, CT: Yale University Press 1941.

Recouly, Raymond. *Le Mémorial de Foch: Mes entretiens avec le Maréchal*. Paris: Ed. De France 1929.

Reid, Walter. *Architect of Victory: Douglas Haig*. Edinburgh: Birlinn 2006.

Renouvin, Pierre. *Les formes du gouvernement de guerre*. Paris: Presses Universitaires de France 1925.

– "Histoire de la Guerre." *Revue historique* 167 (1931): 344–71.

– "Le problème du commandement unique." *Revue d'histoire de la Guerre Mondiale* 11 (1933): 339–51.

– *Peuples et civilisations*. Vol. 19, *La crise européene et la première guerre mondiale (1904–1918)*. 5th ed. Paris: Presses Universitaires de France 1969.

Repington, Lieut.-Col. C. à Court. *The First World War, 1914–1918*. 2 vols. London: Constable 1920.

Ribot, Alexandre. *Journal d'Alexandre Ribot et correspondances inédites, 1914–1922*. Paris: Plon 1936.

Rich, Norman. *Great Power Diplomacy, 1814–1905*. New York: McGraw-Hill 1992.

Ritter, Gerhard. *The Sword and the Scepter: The Problem of Militarism in Germany*. Vol. 2: *The European Powers and the Wilhelmian Empire, 1890–1914*. Trans. Heinz Norden. Coral Gables, FL: University of Miami Press 1970.

Robbins, K.G. "Foreign Policy, Government Structure and Public Opinion." In F.H. Hinsley, ed., *British Foreign Policy under Sir Edward Grey*. Cambridge: Cambridge University Press 1977.

Rocolle, Pierre. *L'hécatombe des généraux*. Paris: Editions Lavauzelle 1980.

Robertson, Field Marshal Sir W.R. *From Private to Field Marshal*. London: Constable 1921.

– *Soldiers and Statesmen*. 2 vols. London: Cassell 1926.

Roskill, Captain S.W. *The Strategy of Sea Power: Its Development and Application*. London: Collins 1962.

Roskill, Stephen. *Hankey: Man of Secrets*. Vol. 1: *1877–1918*. London: Collins 1970.

Rothfels, H. "Clausewitz." In Edward Mead Earle, ed., *Makers of Modern Strategy: Military Thought from Machiavelli to Hitler*. New York: Atheneum 1967.

Rothwell, V.H. *British War Aims and Peace Diplomacy 1914–1918*. Oxford: Clarendon Press 1971.

Royde-Smith, John Graham, and Dennis E. Showalter. "World War I, 1914–1918" (last updated 1 November 2019), "Forces and Resources of Combatant Nations in 1914," www.britannica.com/event/World-War-I/Forces-and-resources-of-the-combatant-nations-in-1914 (consulted 11 December 2019).

Royle, Trevor. *The Kitchener Enigma*. London: Michael Joseph 1985.

Ryan, A.P. *The Chief: Douglas Haig and the British Army*. London: Aurum Press 2012.

– *Mutiny at Curragh*. London: Macmillan 1956.

Saboul, Steven. "Editorial: A Brief Note from the Editor." *First World War Studies* 1, no. 1 (March 2010): 1–2.

Schor, Ralph. *La France dans la première Guerre Mondiale*. Paris: Nathan 1997.

Schurman, Donald M. "Keynote Address." [Unpublished typescript] Military History Symposium, Royal Military College of Canada. Kingston, ON, 24 March 1994.

Semmell, Bernard. *Liberalism and Naval Strategy: Ideology, Interest and Seapower during the Pax Britannica*. Boston: Allen and Unwin 1986.

Sheffield, Gary. *The Chief: Douglas Haig and the British Army*. London: Aurum Press 2011.

– *Douglas Haig: From the Somme to Victory*. [c. 2011], rev. ed. London: Aurum Press 2016.

Sheldon, Jack. *The German Army on the Somme, 1914–1916*. Barnsley, UK: Pen & Sword Books 2005.

Showalter, Dennis E., ed. *Future Wars: Coalition Operations in Global Strategy*. Chicago: Imprint Publications 2002.

Silberstein, Gerard E. *The Troubled Alliance: German-Austrian Relations, 1914 to 1917*. Lexington: University Press of Kentucky 1970.

Simkins, Peter. *Kitchener's Army*. Manchester, UK: Manchester University Press 1988.

Sixsmith, Maj.-Gen. Eric R.L. *British Generalship in the Twentieth Century*. London: Arms and Armour Press 1970.

Smith, C. Jay, Jr. *The Russian Struggle for Power, 1914–1917: A Study of Russian Foreign Policy during the First World War*. New York: Philosophical Library 1956.

Smith, Leonard V., Stéphane Audoin-Rouzeau, and Annette Becker. *France and the Great War, 1914–1918*. Cambridge: Cambridge University Press 2003.

Smith-Dorrien, Horace. *Memories of Forty-Eight Years' Service*. London: John Murray 1925.

Soutou, Georges-Henri. *L'or et le sang: Les buts de guerre économiques de la première Guerre Mondiale*. Paris: Fayard 1989.

Spiers, Edward. "Gallipoli." In Brian Bond, ed., *The First World War and British Military History*. Oxford: Clarendon Press 1991.

St. Clair, William. *The Road to St. Julien: The Letters of a Stretcher-Bearer from the Great War*. Ed. John St. Clair. Barnsley, UK: Leo Cooper 2004.

Stevenson, D. "Belgium, Luxembourg and the Defence of Western Europe, 1914–1920." *International History Review* 4, no. 4 (1982): 504–23.

Stevenson, David. *Armaments and the Coming of War: Europe 1904–1915*. Oxford: Oxford University Press 1996.

– *Cataclysm: The First World War as Political Tragedy*. New York: Basic Books 2004.

– *French War Aims Against Germany, 1914–1919*. Oxford: Clarendon Press 1982.

Stone, Norman. *The Eastern Front, 1914–1917*. London: Hodder and Stoughton 1975.

Strachan, Hew. "The Continental Commitment, 1904–14." In David French and Brian Holden Reid, eds., *The General Staff: Reform and Innovation, 1890–1939*. London: Frank Cass 2002.

– *The First World War*. New York: Viking 2004.

Suarez, Georges. *Briand: Sa vie – son oeuvre avec son journal et de nombreux documents inédits*. Vol. 3. Paris: Plon 1939.

Sumida, Jon Tetsuro. *In Defence of Naval Supremacy: Finance, Technology and British Naval Policy, 1889–1914*. Boston: Unwin Hyman 1989.

Swettenham, John. *Canada and the First World War*. [Ottawa]: Canadian War Museum, n.d.

Tanenbaum, Jan Karl. *General Maurice Sarrail, 1856–1929: The French Army and Left-Wing Politics*. Chapel Hill: University of North Carolina Press 1974.

Taylor, A.J.P. *English History, 1914–1945*. Oxford: Oxford University Press 1965.

– *The First World War: An Illustrated History*. London: Hamish Hamilton 1963.

– *Politics in Wartime and Other Essays*. London: Hamish Hamilton 1964.

Thomson, David. *Democracy in France*. 5th ed. Oxford: Oxford University Press 1969.

The Times. "Need for Shells." 14 May 1915, 1.

The Times History of the War. Vols. 1–17. London: The Times 1914–16.

Travers, Timothy. *Killing Ground: The British Army, the Western Front, and the Emergence of Modern Warfare, 1900–1918*. Barnsley, UK: Pen & Sword Military 2009.

Trumpener, Ulrich. *Germany and the Ottoman Empire, 1914–1918*. Princeton, NJ: Princeton University Press 1968.

– "The Road to Ypres: The Beginnings of Gas Warfare in World War I." *Journal of Modern History* 47, no. 3 (September 1975): 460–80.

Varillon, Pierre. *Joffre*. Paris: Librairie Arthème Fayard 1956.

Wallach, Jehudah. *Uneasy Coalition: The Entente Experience in World War I*. Westport, CT: Greenwood Press 1993.

Wanty, Emile. *L'art de la guerre*. Vol. 2: *De la guerre de Crimée à la blitzkrieg hitlerienne*. Verviers, France: Marabout Université 1967.

Weygand, Maxime. *Mémoires*. Vol. 1: *Idéal Vécu*. Paris: Flammarion 1953.

Williams, Rhodri. *Defending the Empire: The Conservative Party and British Defence Policy 1899–1915*. New Haven, CT: Yale University Press 1991.

– "Lord Kitchener and the Battle of Loos: French Politics and British Strategy in the Summer of 1915." In Lawrence Freedman, Paul Hays, and Robert Obernul, eds., *War Intelligence and Security*. Oxford: Oxford University Press 1992.

Williamson, Samuel R., Jr. *The Politics of Grand Strategy: Britain and France Prepare for War, 1904–1914*. Cambridge, MA: Harvard University Press 1969.

Wilson, Trevor. *The Myriad Faces of War: Britain and the Great War, 1914–1918*. Cambridge: Polity Press 1986.

Woodward, David. *Field Marshall Sir William Robertson, Chief of the Imperial General Staff in the Great War.* Westport, CT: Praeger 1998.

– *Lloyd George and the Generals.* Newark: University of Delaware Press 1983.

Woodward, Llewellyn. *Great Britain and the War of 1914–1918.* London: Methuen and Company 1967.

Wright, Gordon. *Raymond Poincaré and the French Presidency.* Stanford, CA: Stanford University Press 1942.

Young, Brig. Peter. *The British Army, 1642–1970.* London: William Kimber 1967.

Young, Robert J., ed. *Under Siege: Portraits of Civilian Life in France during World War I.* New York: Berghahn Books 2000.

INDEX

Page numbers in italics indicate references to illustrations.

29th Division (British): to go to Dardanelles, 78, 98, 306, 332–3; to go to Salonika, 77, 78; planned for trench relief, 60–1, 62, 76; trench relief cancelled, 66, 73, 78–80, 81, 86, 88–93, 97–8

Alexandretta, 77–8, 86, 110, 293–5, 332; Kitchener's November 1915 plan for, 293–5. *See also* Turkey
Allenby, Edmund, 160, 181
Allies. *See* Entente coalition
Anglo-French commands relations. *See* high commands' relations
Army Commissions of the Chamber and Senate (France), 21–2, 33, 79, 165, 185–6, 198, 226, 228, 251, 276, 289–90; political-military structure, 331
Army of the Near East (Armée d'Orient), 227, 251–5. *See also* Sarrail, Maurice
Arras: fall 1915, 215–16, 261–3; planning after Second Battle of Ypres, 141, 142–3; spring 1915 planning, 55, 63, 68, 75, 82, 84–5, 90, 93; spring success brief, 164, 168, 185. *See also* Loos fall offensive
Artois offensive, fall 1915: battles, 261–6; political-military structures' impact on, xviii, 333–4; Salonika conflicting needs, 271–2; Sir John's fall, 308–11, 314. *See also* Champagne offensive; Loos fall offensive
Artois offensive, late 1914, 41
Artois offensive, spring 1915: Anglo-French planning and expectations, 107, 149–50, 152, 163–4, 169; Aubers Ridge attack, 155–7, 170, 172, 175, 179, 183, 308; catalyst for strategy changes, 194; Festubert, 156–8, 161, 170; Givenchy, 156–8, 160, 161, 164, 174, 180, 184, 192; June attacks, second phase, 161–4; last-minute glitches, 147–9; losses, 168, 170, 173–4; political-military consequences, 152–3, 165–6, 170–2, 185–8; Vimy Ridge attacks, 84, 153–5, 161–2, 165, 167, 192. *See also* Shells Crisis

Asquith, Herbert Henry, *17*, *207*, *294*; Anglo-French pressure for troops to front, 166–8; attacks on, 268; characterizations of French, 287; coordinated/unified command, 89–93, 129; French language, 328–9; the great arbiter, 51–2; Kitchener and, 60, 110; Kitchener-Sir John feud, 181–3; mistresses, 175–6, 181–2, 204; Murray-Wilson intrigue, 31–3; note to king re. New Armies, 202–3; public opinion in France, 199; Salonika expedition, 76–7, 279, 295–6; Shells Crisis and fall of, 175–9; Sir John's removal, 314; War Committee, 295. *See also* policy and political leadership
– meetings: 2 June 1915, with French, 191–2, 196; 6 July 1915, Calais Conference, 196–7, 203, 205–6, 211–12; 7 Oct. 1915, Viviani and Augagneur, 282; 17 Nov. 1915, Paris Conference, 295; 20 Dec. 1914, Walmer Castle, 52, 55; 22 Jan. 1915, with Millerand, 71; 22 March 1915, Kitchener visit to France, 110–11; 29 March 1915, Chantilly Conference, 123; 29–30 Oct. 1915, Joffre to London, 287
Aubers Ridge, 155–7, 170, 172, 175, 179, 183, 308. *See also* Artois offensive
Augagneur, Victor, *207*; 5 Oct. 1915 Anglo-French Conference, 280; 6 July 1915, Calais Conference, 203, 210; 7 Oct. 1915 trip to London, 282; Alexandretta, 78, 110; Briand government, 290; Conseil supérieur, 232; Salonika expedition, 286–7, 289–90
Australian divisions, 78, 208

Balfour, Arthur, 62, *207*, *294*; Asquith's Unionist coalition, 177; Shells Crisis, 157, 173, 175; War Committee, 295
– meetings: 5 Oct. 1915, Anglo-French Conference, 280; 6 July 1915, Calais Conference, 203, 208–10, 212; 7 Oct, 1915, Viviani and Augagneur, 282; 17 Nov. 1915, Paris Conference, 295
Balkan offensive: eastern-western strategic debate, 34–5, 42–3, 57–8, 73–4, 260–1, 282; French strategy, 42–3, 337. *See also* Salonika expedition
Battle of Artois. *See* Artois offensive
Battle of Aubers Ridge, 155–7, 170, 172, 175, 179, 183, 308. *See also* Artois offensive
Battle of Festubert, 156–8, 161, 170
Battle of Neuve Chapelle: ammunition used, 108; Anglo-French conflict over, 66, 82–5, 99, 306, 340; French planning for attack, 90; Joffre's analysis of, 101; origins of battle, 81–2; political-military structures' impact on, 333; results of battle, 96, 98; Sir John's decision to proceed, 94, 96–7
Battle of the Falklands, 35
Battle of the Masurian Lakes (February 1915), 77
Battle of the Somme, xxi, 135
Battle of Ypres, First, 3
Battle of Ypres, Second: Anglo-French joint-offensive planning and, 140–1; as attack on "centre of gravity," 134–5, 137; gas attack, 135–7; losses, 147; recriminations among Allies, 137–40; reserve forces for future, 145–7, 151; shortening the line, 141–5
Becker, Jean-Jacques, 237
Belgium: 6–8 Dec. 1915, Chantilly Conference, 319–22; Anglo-French relations and, 48–9, 53–4, 66, 116–17; British coastal strategy,

54–7, 62–4, 69, 72, 97; defence of Antwerp (1914), 13; German invasion (August 1914), 5, 8. *See also* Ostend and Zeebrugge
Belin, Émile, 84
Benazet, Paul-Louis, 42
Bennett, Winnifred (Mrs): correspondence with Sir John, 82, 87, 94, 126–7, 137, 167–8, 173, 204, 248
Berthelot, Henri, 23, 27, 33
Bertie, Francis, 48, 114–15, 123–4, 199–200, 234
Birdwood, William, 89
Bonar Law, Andrew, 157, 173, 175, 295, 297
Boulogne Conference on munitions, 200
Breganze, Giovanni di, 215
Briand, Aristide, *291*, *294*; Committee of Six, 297; coordinated/unified command, 318, 337; Joffre, commander-in-chief, 336–7; Millerand's government, 234; political-military structure, 331; Salonika expedition, 295–6, 303–4; strategy debate, 34–5, 41–3; *union sacrée*, 19, 290–2
– meetings: 7 Jan. 1915, Elysée Palace, 43; 17 Nov. 1915, Paris Conference, 295
Bridges, Tom, 53, 54–5
Britain. *See* high commands' relations; policy and political leadership; *individual leaders*
British empire: Dardanelles operation, 78–9, 110, 240–1, 249; defence of, 7, 9; empires competing, 78–9, 240–1, 273; Entente Cordiale and, 5. *See also* Egypt
British Expeditionary Force (BEF): 1914 campaign, 12–15; Belgian Army incorporation, 54–5; pre-1914 strategy, 8. *See also* high commands' relations; policy and political leadership; *individual leaders*
British War Council. *See* War Council
Buat, Edmond, 193
Bulgaria: joined Germany, 246, 250, 260–1, 273–4; neutrality of, 72, 74, 77; Uskub occupation, 285, 289

Caillaux, Joseph, 234–5
Calais, 115–17, 120, 123
Calais Conference, 6 July 1915, *206*; aftermath, paradoxical, 211–13, 219–21, 229; Asquith's conclusion, 211; coordination of command issue, 317; French public opinion, 198–203; Kitchener-Joffre private meeting, 205; Kitchener's preparation for, 200–2; language barriers, 204, 328–9; military-political divide, 210–11, 220, 334–5; minutes and notes of, 195, 204–5, 208, 211; origins of, 189, 196–8; turning point in war, 203–11; Wilson's preparation for, 200–1
Calais meeting, 5 Oct. 1915, 278–80
Callwell, Charles, 123, 125, 286
Cambon, Jules, 297
Cambon, Paul, 19, 85–6, 111, 127, 129, 196–7, 297
Canadian Division: arrival as trench reliefs, 76, 83, 85; gas attack on, 138; Ypres, 137, 139
Carson, Edward, 255
Cassar, George, 205, 332
Castelnau, Édouard de Curières de, 23, 42, 187–8, 229–30, 264–5, 303
Cavendish, Frederick, 146
"centre of gravity," 134–5, 216
Champagne offensive, early 1915, 41, 42, 88, 101, 102
Champagne offensive, fall 1915: Anglo-French joint offensive, 216, 246–7, 248; battles, 261–6; French internal relations, 229–32, 250, 251–5, 335; Joffre's optimism, 258–9; losses, 265; Salonika conflicting

needs, 271–2. *See also* Artois offensive
Chantilly Conferences: 6–8 Dec. 1915, 267, 318, 319–22, 337, 342; 7 July 1915, 213–16, 220, 336; 22 Aug. 1915, 246–7; 29 March 1915, 117–23
Churchill, Winston, *20*; 1914 campaign, 29–30; 22 Jan. 1915, Millerand meeting, 70–2; Asquith's Unionist coalition, 177; coastal strategy, 44–5, 47, 50–4, 58, 62–3, 73; creativity of, 51; Dardanelles, 65, 80, 105, 333–4; Holland, offensive in, 124; Kitchener and, 51–2; political-military structure, 330, 333–4; Salonika expedition, 260; trench-warfare deadlock, 36, 58, 60–1, 64, 72
class of 1915 (double cohort), 79, 100, 102, 153. *See also* trench warfare
Clausewitz, Carl von, 102, 134, 216
Clive, Sidney, 93, 104, 138, 140, 221–2
coalitions, nature of, 9–11, 139, 341. *See also* Entente coalition
Comité des Forges, 187
commissions. *See* Army Commissions of the Chamber and Senate (France)
Committee of Six, *297*, 297–8, 318
communications: Joffre with Russia, 41; Kitchener-Joffre direct line, 249, 256; Kitchener-Sir John through Robertson, 182, 310; Kitchener's misstep (February 1915), 85–6; Kitchener's unofficial network, 87, 113; military-political during battle, 259–61; Sir John to government lacking, 70–2, 91; Ypres as communication centre, 135, 137
conscription (Britain): poster, *19*
Conseil supérieur de la Défense nationale, 231–2, 251, 255; Briand government, 291–2, 294–5, 303–4, 318, 331, 336–7; political-military structure, 331
Cowans, John, 120, 123
Craig, Gordon, 297
Crewe, Lord, 203, *207*, 211–12
Curzon, Marquess of, 285

Daily Mail, 179, 181
d'Amade, Albert, 89, 266
Dardanelles Committee (Britain), 177, 267–8, 275, 283–6
Dardanelles operation: 5 Nov. 1915, Kitchener trip to, 293–5; 11 Sept. 1915, Calais, 245–6, 248–9, 253, 254, 273–4; Allied evacuation agreement, 321; Anglo-French military opposition to, 166, 167, 172, 173–4, 176, 198, 215, 334, 338; British political plan for, 65, 77–8, 105, 121, 124, 133, 249–50; coordinated/unified command, 89, 253–4; French political plan for, 86, 227–9, 231, 242–3, 243–6, 250, 251–5; Gallipoli withdrawal, 293–4; New Armies, 164–5, 166, 190, 207–8; political-military structures' impact on, 332–6; Salonika, diversions to, 277–8, 279. *See also* Turkey
de Broqueville, Charles, 87
de la Panouse, Arthus, 49, 250
Delcassé, Théophile, *207*; 7 March letter, unified command, 93; 13 June 1915, Elysée Palace, 163; Conseil supérieur, 232; coordinated/unified command, 127, 129; as foreign minister, 19; Salonika expedition, 74, 274; *union sacrée*, 19; Viviani government collapse, 289
Derby, Lord, 199
d'Espèrey, Louis Franchet, 42, 43
Doughty, Robert A., xiv, 101
Doumer, Paul, 185
Doumergue, Gaston, 101–2, 185, 228, 290

Dubail, Auguste, 226–7
Dubail, Yvon, 23, 175, 187–8
Dubois, Pierre, 185
DuCane, J.P., 156–7
Dunkirk: Kitchener requests as base, 91–2, 103; rejected as British base, 114–17, 120–1, 123
Dunkirk Conference (November 1914), 46
d'Urbal, Victor, 137–8, 140, 164; Arras, fall 1915 battle, 261–5; Artois, May 1915; Vimy Ridge, 153, 161–2

Egypt: Anglo-French divide, 273, 283–5, 336; Britain's defence of, 35, 57, 200–1, 260; British protectorate over, 5, 45; forces in, 78, 92, 207, 271, 277, 285–8
Elysée Palace meetings: 7 Jan. 1915, 43; 13 June 1915, 163–4; 21 March 1915, 101–2
Entente coalition: 6–8 Dec. 1915, Chantilly Conference, 319–22, 337–9; competing strategies, 35–6, 240–1, 341; conflicting interests' resolutions, 10–11; coordination and growth of, 213–16, 336–9; divisions fielded, xvi–xvii, 344n16; eastern-western strategic debate, 34–5, 42–3, 73–4, 338, 342; French Balkan policy, late 1915, 321; guns and munitions supply, 329; nature of coalitions, 9–11, 139, 341; as not functioning, 271–2; roots of Anglo-French strategic conflict, 4–5. *See also* high commands' relations; policy and political leadership; *individual members*
Entente Cordiale, 5, 315
Esher, Reginald: Artois failure and consequences, 165–6; coordinated/unified command, 112–14, 127–9, 166, 267–8, 297; Dardanelles operation, 80–1; Kitchener-Sir John feud, 182; Sir John, 221, 314; various, 179, 199, 200, 255–6
– meetings: 2–3 July 1915, cabinet sessions, 203; 6 July 1915, Calais Conference, 204, 213–14; 8–9 June 1915, French officers in London, 193

Falkenhayn, Eric von, 37
Ferry, Abel, 186
Festubert. *See* Battle of Festubert
Fisher, John (Jackie), 29, 124, 176
FitzGerald, Brindsley, 157, 173, 175
Foch, Ferdinand, 25, *40*; 1914 command adjustments, 22–8, 33; Anglo-French pressure for troops to front, 167; Anglo-French relations, 223–6, 339; Arras plans, 93, 125; Artois, eve of battle relations, 149–50; Artois, Givenchy attack, 156–8, 174; Artois failure and consequences, 165–6; Artois glitches, 147–9; Artois initial success, 155; Artois trench negotiations, 161–2; British coastal strategy, 48–9, 54; British troops needed, 315–16; on Dardanelles operation, 254; Egypt, movement of troops to, 292; fall 1915 offensive, 223–6, 229–32, 248, 263–5; guns and ammunition for British, 105; Kitchener and, 52, 87; Kitchener-Sir John feud, 161; shortening the line at Ypres, 142–5; Sir John and, 47; spring 1915 joint offensive, 125, 131, 140–1, 143; trench warfare, 37, 69, 84–5; Vimy Ridge attacks, May 1915, 161–2; Ypres recriminations, 137–40, 147, 150–1; Ypres reserve forces for future, 145–7
– meetings: 2 June 1915, with British, 191–2; 11 July 1915, Anglo-French command, 215–16; 12 May 1915, with Sir John, 157–8; 16–19 Aug. 1915, Kitchener visit, 235–40; 22 Aug. 1915, Anglo-French, 246–7; 23 June

1915, with group commanders, 187; 24 April 1915, with British, 140–1; 27 July 1915, with Sir John, 221–3; 28 April 1915, with Sir John, 142–3; 28 Sept. 1915, with Sir John, 263–4

Formidable: sinking of, 61

France. *See* Army Commissions of the Chamber and Senate (France); Conseil supérieur de la Défense nationale; high commands' relations; policy and political leadership; *individual leaders*

French, David, 8

French, John (Sir John), *25*, *207*, *320*; 1914 campaign, 12–15, 23; analysis of his command, 304–8; Anglo-French pressure for troops to front, 166–8; artillery, role of, 107–9; Churchill and, 51–2; coastal strategy, 44–5, 47, 50–7, 60–4, 66, 68, 69–70, 72–3, 97, 326, 332; coordinated/unified command, 89–93, 112, 113–14, 127–31, 232–4, 238, 326, 327; Dardanelles operation, 78, 79–80, 121, 306; Egypt, movement of troops to, 284–6; Foch and, 47, 52, 327; French, distrust of, 47, 238, 327, 340; French language, 328–9; guns and ammunition from French, 105; Haig and, 305; independence of command, 11, 29; mistress's correspondence, 82, 87, 94, 126–7, 167–8, 173, 204, 248; Murray and, 30–3; offensive/defensive strategy, 221; political-military structure and impact, 329–30, 331–6; preconceived strategies, 326; on public opinion in France, 199; replacement of, 301, 308–11, 314, 333–4; Robertson and, 182, 183–5, 309–11, 314; Salonika expedition, 74–5, 76–7, 280, 311; Shells Crisis, 172–3, 179

– Artois offensive: Aubers Ridge failure, 155–7, 183; failure and consequences, 155, 165–6; glitches, 147–9; inadequate coordination, 263–5; June delays, 162–3; Loos, objections to, 221–6, 236, 310; offensive assessment by French, 68; relations, eve of battle, 149–50; strained relations, 223–6, 239–40, 248–9; strategy (Calais Conference), 210, 212–13; trench negotiations, 161–2

– Joffre: concealed purpose of demands for troops, 70–2; correspondence (February 1915), 82–4; Egypt, troops to, 292–3; impact of relationship with, 339–41; meetings with, 53–4, 66, 69, 75; rank compared to, 122; reconciliation with, 99–100, 105–7; relationship with, xv–xvi, 50, 79–80, 87–8, 90–1, 93–4, 97

– Kitchener: fall offensive relations, 249–50; letter from (2 Jan. 1915), 58–61; relationship with, 55–7, 61, 86–8, 97, 108–9, 124–6, 132–3, 193; secret meetings with, 108, 149; Shells Crisis, 159–61, 172–4, 177, 179–83, 310

– meetings: 2 June 1915, with French, 191–2; 2–3 July 1915, cabinet sessions, 201–2; 6 July 1915, Calais Conference, 196–7, 203, 205, 210, 212–13; 6–8 Dec. 1915, Chantilly Conference, 321; 7 July 1915, Chantilly Conference, 215; 9 May 1915, with Joffre, 173–4; 11 July 1915, with command, 215–16; 11 Sept. 1915, Anglo-French, 245–6, 248–9; 12 May 1915, with Joffre and Foch, 157–8; 22 Aug. 1915, Chantilly, 246–7; 24 April 1915, with Joffre, 140–1; 24 June 1915, with Joffre, 167–8, 198, 219–20; 27 July 1915,

with Foch, 221–3; 28 April 1915, with Foch, 142–3; 28 Sept. 1915, with Foch, 263–4; 29 March 1915, Chantilly Conference, 117–23
– spring offensive: Neuve Chapelle decision, 94, 96–7; offensive expectations, 124–6, 131; offensive planning, 140–1, 143–4; relationship with men in trenches, 81; trench-warfare strategy, 36, 39, 69, 80, 81–5; Ypres gas attack, 137; Ypres recriminations, 137–40, 150–1; Ypres reserve forces for future, 145–7, 151; Ypres shortening the line, 141–5. *See also* trench warfare
French empire: Dardanelles operation, 78–9; empires competing, 78–9, 240–1, 273; pre-1914 strategy, 4, 5
French left wing: Briand government, 290, 303; Socialists and Radical Socialists (France), 15, 19, 22, 171, 185–6, 219, 226–8, 234, 254, 272, 290, 303, 331; Viviani government's collapse, 289

Galicia, 135, 185, 190, 316
Gallieni, Joseph-Simon, *291*, *294*; 17 Nov. 1915, Paris Conference, 295; re. Champagne offensive, 42; Committee of Six, 297; Joffre, clash with, 303; Millerand, proposed to replace, 185; minister of war, 287, 290; political-military structure, 331; Salonika expedition, 295–6
Gallipoli, 139. *See also* Turkey
Gamelin, Maurice, 23
gas and chemical warfare, 261–3. *See also* Battle of Ypres, Second
George V (British head of state): 23 June 1915, Robertson letter to, 183–5, 309–11; Allied coordination, 297; Asquith's communications with, 202–3, 236, 248, 277; Dardanelles Committee size, 267; Haig's intervention, 309, 310; late 1915 assessment of government, 267; Robertson assessment of Loos, 222; Sir John's removal, 183, 314
Germany: Allied fall offensive intelligence, 258–9; British intelligence on, 131; French assessment of, 70–1; gas attack on Ypres, 135; invasion of Belgium (August 1914), 5, 8; Joffre's assessment of, 102; Kitchener's assessment of, 45–7, 50, 61, 71, 159, 180, 210; Sir John's under-evaluation of, 99–100, 125, 164
Gilinsky, General, *320*
Givenchy, 156–8, 160, 161, 164, 174, 180, 184, 192. *See also* Artois offensive
government. *See* policy and political leadership; *individual members*
Grand Quartier Général (GQG; French headquarters), 23, 28. *See also* High Command (France)
grand strategy: Allied coordination, 214–16; eastern-western debate, 34–5; terminology, xx–xxi. *See also* strategy
grand strategy – Britain: 1914 campaign, 11–15; early changes to, 8–9; trench-warfare context, 35, 57–61
grand strategy – France, 308–11, 314; 1914 campaign, 12–15; coordinated/unified command, 314–19
Graziani, Jean César, 119
Greece: diplomatic ties to Serbia, 273–4; Lemnos, 78–9; offer to Allies, 274–5, 277, 300; Venizelos fall, 282. *See also* Balkan offensive; Salonika expedition
Greenhalgh, Elizabeth: *Victory through Coalition*, 9
Grey, Edward, *294*; 1914 campaign, 29, 31; 7 Oct. 1915, Viviani and

Augagneur, 282; 17 Nov. 1915, Paris Conference, 295; Committee of Six, 297; coordinated/unified command, 233–4, 238; Egypt, movement of troops to, 285, 287–8; January 1915, Millerand meeting, 70–2
Guesde, Jules, 19, 227–8, 290
Guest, Frederick, 157, 173, 175
guns and munitions. *See* war matériel

Haig, Douglas, 31–2, *312*; Artois, fall 1915 battle, 261–5; Artois, holding attack, 161–2; Aubers Ridge, 9 May 1915, 155; coordinated/unified command, 239; future scholarship on, xxi; Givenchy attack plan, 155–6, 164, 174; Loos, objections to, 221, 222, 224; on public opinion in France, 199; Sir John, replacement, 301, 314; Sir John and, 305, 309, 310
Hamilton, Ian, 139, 190, 250, 253–4, 278; 1914 campaign, 14, 55
Hankey, Maurice, 29, 58, 177, 212
Harcourt, Robbie, 256
Harmsworth, Alfred. *See* Northcliffe newspapers
Henley, Sylvia, 175–6, 181–2, 204
high commands' relations – Allies: 6–8 Dec. 1915, Chantilly meeting, 295–6, 318, 319–22, 337, 342; 7 July 1915, Chantilly Conference, 213–16, 336; coordinated/unified command, 216–17, 218, 237–40, 266–8, 318–19, 336–9
high commands' relations – Anglo-French: 1914 campaign, 11–15, 22–8, 55; 1915 as transitional year, xiv; British shortage of shells, 157–8; British troops as reserves for French, 314–19, 321–2; characterizations and stereotypes, 27–8, 113, 138–9, 237, 263–4, 287, 328, 339–40; cooperation breakdown (January-February), 72, 96–8, 132–3; coordinated command background, 314–19, 336–9, 340–1; coordinated/unified command, 89–93, 111–14, 127–33, 218–19, 232–3, 236–40, 266–8; December 1914, closer liaison between, 53–4; eastern-western strategic debate, 260–1, 282–3, 337–8, 341–2; force British troops to front, 166–8; Kitchener-Sir John feud, effect on, 161; multiple factors affecting, 325–9; political leadership as primary in, xix–xx; political-military point of view, 92, 240–1; political-military structures' impact on, xvii–xix, 331–6; Robertson-Wilson conflict, 146–7; Salonika, divided, ineffectual and unwilling, 74–7, 275–7, 298–300; secret treaties among Allies, 10; Sir John letter, 20 Jan. 1915, 69; trench-reliefs conflict, 82–5, 105–6, 108–9; trust, lack of, 340; war matériel, differences in use of, 155; Wilson's intrigue, 30–3. *See also* Calais Conference; policy and political leadership; Shells Crisis; trench warfare
– fall offensive: command issues, 232–4, 263–6; delays, 247–50; French government's objection, 228–32; planning, 213–16, 219–21; strained relations, 223–6, 234–40, 248–9. *See also* Artois offensive, fall 1915
– meetings: 4 Dec. 1915, Calais, 295; 7 July 1915, Chantilly Conference, 213–16, 336; 11 July 1915, of commands, 215–16, 220–1; 11 Sept. 1915, Calais, 245–6, 248–9, 253, 254, 273–4; 12 May 1915, 157–8; 21 Jan. 1915, Chantilly, 68, 69, 72, 83, 85; 23 March 1915, Wilson and Joffre,

105–7; 24 June 1915, Chantilly, 167–8, 198, 219–20; 27 July 1915, Sir John and Foch, 221–3; 27 Dec. 1914, Chantilly, 53; 29 March 1915, Chantilly Conference, 117–23, 333; 29–30 Oct. 1915, Joffre to London, 287
– spring offensive: Artois, on eve of, 149–50; Artois battle, 152–3; Artois glitches, 147–9; Givenchy attack, 156–8, 161, 174; joint planning, 140–1; reserve forces at Ypres for future, 145–7, 151; Ypres, shortening the line, 141–5. *See also* Battle of Ypres, Second
High Command – Britain: analysis of Sir John's command, 304–8; artillery, role of, 107–9; blueprint for staff reorganization (Robertson), 183–5, 304, 309–11; competing strategies for deadlock, 57; division with government, 70–2, 79, 91; Givenchy attack, 161; Kitchener and Sir John, 210; Kitchener-Sir John, 23 March 1915 meeting, 108–9; Loos offensive objections, 221–3; northern strategy, 326; political-military structure, impact of, xvii–xix, 331–6; Robertson and Wilson conflict, 146–7, 149. *See also* policy and political leadership; *individual leaders*
High Command – France: 1914 adjustments, 22–8; 1914 relations with government, 15, 19–22; Allied troops as reserves, 314–19; on British-Belgium relations, 66, 69; British coastal strategy, 52–4, 73, 332, 338; characterizations and stereotypes, 339–40; dissatisfaction with British command, 93–4; division with government, 79; eastern-western strategic debate, 34–5, 42–3, 73–4, 226, 250, 337–8; fall offensive, political challenges, 259–61; General Order no. 8, 39; Kitchener's assessment of, 45–7; parliamentary commissions' role, 185–6; political-military structure, impact of, xvii–xix, 331–6. *See also* policy and political leadership; *individual leaders*
HMS *Attention:* Kitchener-Sir John meeting, 108, 149
Holland, 119, 124
Huguet, Victor, *320*; 1914 command adjustments, 27; Anglo-French command conflict, 94; on Dardanelles operation, 254; trench-reliefs conflict, 84; trench-warfare strategy, 69; Ypres recriminations, 137–8
– meetings: 6 July 1915, Calais Conference, 204; 11 July 1915, Anglo-French command, 215–16; 12 May 1915, with British, 158; 22 Aug. 1915, Anglo-French, 246–7; 24 April 1915, with British, 140–1; 24 June 1915, with British, 167; 28 April 1915, with British, 142–3; 29 March 1915, Chantilly Conference, 119

Ignatieff, Paul, 215
Imperial General Staff: restructuring of, 184–5
Indian troops (28th Division), 83
Italy: 6–8 Dec. 1915, Chantilly Conference, 319–22, 337; 7 July 1915, Chantilly Conference, 215; Allied 1915 fall offensive and, 258; Allied coordination, 213, 316, 318–19; Entente expectations of, 100, 141, 157; French opinions of, 209; Isonzo River offensive, 215, 217

Joffre, Joseph J.-C., *24*, *40*, *118*, *206–7*, *294*, *320*; 25 May 1915 memo, 188;

1914 relations with British command, 12–15, 22–3, 28, 33, 53–4, 55; 1914 relations with government, 5–7, 15, 21–2; Allied troops as reserves, 317–19; Anglo-Belgian relations, 66, 69; Anglo-French pressure for troops to front, 166–8; British coastal strategy, 48–50, 62–4, 66–72, 332, 338; British New Armies, appeal for, 188–94, 247–8; commander of all fronts, 303–4; Committee of Six, 297; conscription double cohort, 79; Conseil supérieur, 255; coordinated/unified command, 89–93, 113–14, 127–9, 166, 232–4, 266–8, 328, 336–9, 340–1; coordinator for Allies, 121, 214–15, 266–8, 302, 319–22, 320, 336–9; coordinator for Allies, hidden agenda, 319; Dardanelles operation, 79–80, 338; dissatisfaction with British command, 93–4; on Dunkirk as British base, 116–17, 120–1; Egypt, movement of troops to, 284; Gallieni, clash with, 303; re. government war management, 231–2; grand strategy, xxi; Millerand and, 254–5; offensive strategy, 34–6, 39–43, 47, 100–4, 124–5, 131, 163, 231, 326–7; offensive strategy (Calais Conference), 209, 210; Poincaré, clash with, 103; political-military structure, 330–1; political-military structure, impact on, 331–6; preconceived strategies, 326–7; Russians, loyalty to, 68, 161, 163, 167, 231, 341; Salonika, diversions to, 277; Salonika expedition, 74–5, 261, 286–8, 295–6, 298–300; Sarrail Affair, 226–7, 231; trench reliefs, 81–5; Viviani government collapse, 288–92. *See also* high commands' relations; trench warfare

– fall offensive: battle coordination, 263–6; government objections, 229–32; political-military conflicts, 259–61; political-military relations, 251–5; strained relations, 223–6, 239–40, 249

– Kitchener: 27 May 1915, note to, 190–1; direct communication with, 249; Kitchener-Sir John feud, 88–9, 161; relationship with, 87, 94

– meetings: 2 June 1915, with British, 191–2; 5 Oct. 1915, Anglo-French Conference, 278–80; 6 July 1915, Calais Conference, 196–7, 203, 205, 209, 210, 212; 6–8 Dec. 1915, Chantilly Conference, 319–22, 337; 7 Jan. 1915, Elysée Palace, 43, 63; 7 July 1915, Chantilly Conference, 215, 220, 336; 8 Oct. 1915, with Kitchener, 282–3; 9 May 1915, with Sir John, 173–4; 11 July 1915, with commands, 215–16, 220–1; 11 Sept. 1915, Anglo-French, 245–6, 248–9, 253; 12 May 1915, with Sir John, 157–8; 16–19 Aug. 1915, Kitchener visit, 235–40; 17 Nov. 1915, Paris Conference, 295; 22 Aug. 1915, Chantilly, 246–7; 23 June 1915, with group commanders, 187–8; 24 April 1915, with Sir John, 140–1; 24 June 1915, with Sir John, 167–8, 198, 219–20; 29 March 1915, Chantilly Conference, 117–23, 122; 29–30 Oct. 1915, London, 287

– Sir John: Egypt, troops to, 292–3; February 1915 correspondence, 82–4; impact of relationship with, 339–41; meetings with, 53–4, 75; rank compared to, 122; reconciliation with, 99, 105–7; relationship, xv–xvi, 50, 79–80, 87–8, 90–1, 93–4, 98, 306–7; strains on relations, 327–8

– spring offensive: Arras plans on hold, 93; Artois, eve of battle relations, 149–50; Artois initial success, 155; failure and consequences, 165–6, 185–90; Givenchy attack, 156–8, 174; glitches, 147–9; joint planning, 140–1, 143; June delays, 162–3; scaled-down expectations, 163–4; Ypres, reserve forces for future, 145–7, 151; Ypres, shortening the line, 143–5; Ypres recriminations, 137–40

Kennedy, Paul, 10

Kitchener, Horatio Herbert, *18–19*, *118*, *206–7*; 1914 campaign, 12, 14, 29–30; Anglo-French alliance as primary, 80; Anglo-French pressure for troops to front, 166–8; artillery, role of, 107–9, 119; Artois, eve of battle relations, 149–50, 159; Churchill and, 51–2; coastal strategy, 48, 50–4, 55–6, 62–4, 332; coordinated/unified command, 89–93, 111–13, 121–2, 127–30, 232–4, 236–40, 306–7, 316, 340–1; coordinator for Allies, Joffre as, 121, 336–9; Dardanelles operation, 80, 121, 249–50, 253–4, 293–5; defensive posture advocated, 200–1, 208, 210, 219; deployment miscommunication, 85–6; Dunkirk, requests as base, 91–2, 103, 114–17, 120–1; Egypt, movement of troops to, 284; fall offensive command issues, 234–40; French language, 328–9; French troop strength, 79; on German and French strength, 45–6; German strategy, assessment of, 45–7, 50, 61, 71, 159, 180; government, opinion of, 255; imperialism of, 78, 79, 240–1; Joffre and, 70–2, 249; Loos, support for, 236; Millerand, reply to (4 March 1915), 91–3; New Armies creation, xvii; political-military structure, 330; pre-1914 strategy, 8–9; on public opinion in France, 199; Salonika expedition, 71, 72–3, 260–1, 275–8, 295–6, 298–300, 311; secretary of state for war appointment, 8; Shells Crisis, 177–9, 309; spring 1915 joint offensive, 124–6, 130, 143–4; trench-warfare deadlock, 36, 39, 58–61; troop deployment, 80; waging war as we must, 235, 246; Ypres, 138, 144–5. *See also* New Armies; policy and political leadership

– meetings: 5 Oct. 1915, Anglo-French Conference, 278–80; 5 Nov. 1915, to Dardanelles, 293–5; 6 July 1915, Calais Conference, 196–7, 203, 205–12; 7 Oct. 1915, Viviani and Augagneur, 282; 8 Oct. 1915, with Joffre, 282–3; 8–9 June 1915, French officers in London, 193; 11 Sept. 1915, Anglo-French, 245–6; 16–19 Aug. 1915, visit to France, 234–40; 22 Jan. 1915, with Millerand, 70–2; 29 March 1915, Chantilly Conference, 117–23; March 1915 visit to France, 109–14; visits to France, 238–9

– Sir John: 2 Jan. 1915, letter to, 58–61; fall of, 305–8, 308–11; fall offensive relations, 249–50; relationship, 55–7, 61, 66, 86–8, 108–9, 124–6, 132–3; secret meetings with, 108, 149, 307; Shells Crisis and, 159–61, 172–4, 177, 179–83

La Bassée. *See* Battle of Neuve Chapelle

Lacaze, Lucien, 290, *294*, 295

language barriers, 204, 328–9

Lanrezac, Charles, 185

Lemnos. *See* Greece

Lewis, LeRoy, 199–200
Lloyd George, David, *178*, *294*; 7 Oct. 1915, Viviani and Augagneur, 282; Boulogne Conference on munitions, 200; coordinated/ unified command, 112; Millerand meeting (January 1915), 70–2; political-military structure, 330; Salonika expedition, 72–3, 76–7, 260, 279; Shells Crisis, 173, 175, 181; War Committee, 295; Western Front deadlock, 42, 58
Loos fall offensive: 22 Aug. 1915, Chantilly meeting, 246–7; ammunition for, 248; Anglo-French coordination, 215–16, 243, 248, 338; Anglo-French strained relations, 223–6, 232–4, 236–7, 248–9; battle and losses, 236, 261, 264, 265, 268–9; Sir John/government divide, 221–6, 335; Sir John's fall, 309. *See also* Arras; Artois offensive; Champagne offensives
losses, 100, 147, 168, 170, 173–4, 289, 340, 342
Lowe, C.J., 58

Malvy, Louis-Jean, 290
Maud'huy, Louis, 82
Maxwell, John, 123, 294
McCrae, Meighen, 9–10
McKenna, Reginald, 295
Messines and Warneton offensive (December 1914), 47, 48, 57
Messimy, Adolphe, 6, 19
Mikhnevich, N.P., 11, 139, 238, 341
Millerand, Alexandre, *17*, *118*, *206–7*; 1914 power relations, 19–22; Anglo-French pressure for troops to front, 167–8; Artois failure and consequences, 165, 185–8, 334; British New Armies, appeal for, 193; Conseil supérieur, 232; coordinated/unified command, 89–93, 121–2, 127–9, 232–3, 266–7; on Dunkirk as British base, 115–16; Egypt, movement of troops to, 284; fall 2015 offensive, 229–32, 250, 251–5, 259–61; High Command mouthpiece, 6, 43; Joffre and, 254–5; Joffre's spring 1915 offensive plans, 104; Kitchener, 4 March 1915 reply from, 91–3; Kitchener, notes on visits of, 239; Kitchener-Sir John dispute, 88–9; offensive strategy (Calais Conference), 208–9; political-military structure, 330–1; production of war matériel, 100; on public opinion in France, 200; Salonika expedition, 74, 279, 286–7, 289–90; strategy debate, 34–5; Surrail Affair, 227–8; troop deployment, 80; troops in depots, 79; Viviani government's collapse, 289–90
– meetings: 2 June 1915, with British, 191–2; 5 Oct. 1915, Anglo-French Conference, 280; 6 July 1915, Calais Conference, 196–7, 203, 212, 229; 6 July 1915, Calais Conference notes, 205, 208–9, 211, 239; 7 July 1915, Chantilly Conference, 215; 8 Oct. 1915, with Kitchener, 282–3; 11 Sept. 1915, Anglo-French, 245–6; 13 June 1915, Elysée Palace, 163; 16–19 Aug. 1915, Kitchener visit, 235–40; 17–20 Oct. 1915, to London, 284–5; 22 Jan. 1915, to London, 70–2; 23 June 1915, with group commanders, 187; 29 March 1915, Chantilly Conference, 119
Monro, Charles, 283–4
Montagu, Edwin, 76
Morocco, 5
Munro, Charles, 293
Murray, Archibald, 23, 30–3, 49, 68, 276; 6–8 Dec. 1915, Chantilly

Conference, 321; assessment of, 305; Salonika expedition, 286, 295–6
Murray, Wolfe, 108

navy. *See* Royal Navy
Neilson, Keith, 57
Neuve Chapelle. *See* Battle of Neuve Chapelle
New Armies (Britain): 6 July 1915, Calais Conference, 200–2; 8–9 June 1915, French officers in London, 193; Anglo-French military pressure for, 167–8; Artois offensive plans, 103, 163–4; coastal operation and, 69–70; conflicting strategies for, 57–61, 240–1; for continental defence, 202; creation of, xvii, 8–9; fall offensive arrival schedule, 207–8, 219, 247–8; Joffre's post-Artois appeal for, 188–94; Kitchener-Joffre Calais meeting, 205; Kitchener-Sir John feud, 56–7, 159–61, 179–80; Loos attack planning, 216; as reserves to French, 317–19; Salonika expedition, 282–3; Sir John's requests for, 144, 168, 197–8. *See also* Calais Conference, 6 July 1915; Kitchener, Horatio Herbert
New Zealand Divisions, 78
Nicholas Nikolaevich (grand duke), 41, 102
Nieuport, 69
Nobel, *chef de cabinet*, 193
Northcliffe newspapers, 76, 175, 179, 181. See also *Times*
Nudant, Alphonse, 28

omnibuses as military transport, 51
operational level: terminology, xx–xxi. *See also* strategy
Ostend and Zeebrugge: British coastal strategy, 44–5, 47, 51, 60–1, 62–4, 71–4, 97, 332; literature on, xvii–xviii; operation postponed, 68

Paget, Arthur, 193
Paléologue, Maurice, 41
Palmerston, Henry Lord, 10
Pellé, Maurice, *320*; 7 July 1915, Chantilly Conference, 215; 8 Oct. 1915, meeting with Kitchener, 282–3; 22 Aug. 1915, Anglo-French meeting, 246–7; 24 June 1915, meeting with British, 167, 198; 29 March 1915, Chantilly Conference, 119; coordinated/unified command, 114; relations with British, 28
Penelon, Marie-Jean, 165, 231
Pétain, Henri-Philippe, 153, 235, 247, 385n45
Philpot, William, 44
Philpott, William J., 296, 326
Plumer, Herbert, 139–40
Poincaré, Raymond, *16*; re. 4 March letter from Kitchener, 92–3; 7 Jan. 1915, Elysée Palace meeting, 43, 63; 13 June 1915, Elysée Palace meeting, 163; 23 June 1915, meeting with group commanders, 187, 198; 1914 power relations, 14–15, 19–22; Artois failure and consequences, 165; Briand government, 290–2; coordinated/unified command, 127, 213; fall 1915 offensive, 229–32, 251–5, 259–61; Greek offer to Allies, 274–5; Joffre, clash with, 103; Joffre-Sir John-Kitchener dispute, 89; Salonika expedition, 74, 279, 286–7; spring 1915 offensive plans, 101–3, 110, 163; strategy debate, 34–5, 41–3; Surrail Affair, 228. *See also* policy and political leadership
policy and political leadership – Allies: Anglo-French command relations and Western Front, 324–5,

341–2; trench-warfare conditions, 329; "wearing" operations, 321–2
policy and political leadership – Anglo-French: 1914 campaign, 12–15; Artois failure and consequences, 165–6, 170–2, 188–94; Artois joint offensive, 140–1, 143–5, 169; basic conflict with military, 92; characterizations and stereotypes, 27–8, 113, 138–9, 237, 263–4, 287, 328; command relations as primary, xix–xx; cooperation breakdown (January-February) and restoration, 96–8, 109–11; coordinated/unified command, 296–8, 302, 314–19, 340–1; Dardanelles becomes joint offensive, 243–6; eastern-western strategic debate, 282–3, 301, 337–8, 341–2; empires competing, 78–9, 240–1, 273; Greek offer to Allies, 274–5; political-military structures, impact of, xvii–xix, 331–6; political-military structures of, 329–31; public opinion in France, 198–203; Salonika expedition, 74–7, 275–7, 280–3, 298–300; strategic policy review, 195–6; trench-warfare competing strategies, 35–47, 82–5; Ypres, shortening the line, 143–5. *See also* Artois offensive; Calais Conference, 6 July 1915
– meetings: 2 June 1915, at French front, 191–2; 2–3 July 1915, cabinet sessions, 200, 201–2; 4 Dec. 1915, Calais, 295; 5 Oct. 1915, Anglo-French Conference, 278–80; 8–9 June 1915, French officers in London, 193; 11 Sept. 1915, Calais, 245–6, 253; 17 Nov. 1915, Paris Conference, 294; 17–20 Oct. 1915, Millerand to London, 284–5; 22 Jan. 1915, Millerand to London, 70–2; 29 March 1915, Chantilly Conference, 117–23, 333; 29–30 Oct. 1915, Joffre to London, 287; Kitchener's visits to France, 238–9. *See also* Calais Conference, 6 July 1915
policy and political leadership – Britain: analysis of Sir John's command, 304–8; Asquith's Unionist coalition, 177; before 1914, 7–9; blueprint for staff reorganization (Robertson), 183–5, 304, 309–11; coastal-strategy opposition, 50–4, 60–1, 72–3; coordinated command background, 236–40, 336–9; Dardanelles Committee, 177, 267–8, 275, 283–6; dissatisfaction with French, 72; eastern-western strategic debate, 260–1, 301, 337–8; Kitchener and Sir John, 149–50, 152; March 1915 power relations, 110; Millerand exposes Joffre's demands, 70–2; New Armies for continental defence, 202; New Armies to Dardanelles, 164–5, 166, 249–50; political-military structure, impact of, xvii–xix, 331–6; political-military structure of, 329–30; public opinion in France, 198–203; Salonika, divided and ineffectual, 275–7, 287–8; trench-warfare deadlock, 35–6, 42, 43–7, 57–61; "wearing" operations, 321–2. *See also* Calais Conference, 6 July 1915; Shells Crisis; War Council
– fall offensive: fall 1915 instability, 267; internal conflicts, 255–6; munitions demands, 221–5
– spring offensive: Aubers Ridge, 155, 183; expectations of, 125, 131, 133; failure and consequences, 170–1, 175–9, 194. See also Artois offensive; Shells Crisis
policy and political leadership – France: 1914 and before, 4–7, 15, 19–22, 33; Anglo-French pressure

for troops to front, 167–8; Artois, Joffre's spring offensive, 101–3, 131, 133, 163–4; Artois failure and consequences, 165–6, 171–2, 185–8, 194, 198; British coastal- strategy reception, 48–50; conflict with military, 210–11, 250; coordinated command and grand strategy, 314–19; coordinated/unified command, 336–9; eastern-western strategic debate, 226, 250, 292, 301, 303, 337–8; fall offensive, conflict with military, 259–61; fall offensive, internal conflicts, 219, 228–32, 251–5; Kitchener-Sir John dispute, 88–9; Near East expeditionary force, 86–7; parliamentary commissions and inspections, 185–6, 226; political-military structure, impact of, xvii–xix, 331–6; political-military structure of, 330–1; public opinion in France, 198–203; Salonika, divided, 276–7, 299; Sarrail Affair, 226–7, 243–6; trench-warfare deadlock, 34–43, 57; *union sacrée*, 15, 19, 227; Viviani government collapse, 226, 228, 288–90. *See also* Artois offensive; Conseil supérieur de la Défense nationale; High Command (France); trench warfare

– meetings: 13 June 1915, Elysée Palace, 163–4; 21 March 1915, Elysée Palace, 101–2; 23 June 1915, with group commanders, 187–8, 198; 28 Aug. 1915, cabinet, 251

Porro, Carlo, *320*

Prete, Roy: *Strategy and Command, 1914*, 4

Putz, Henri-Gabriel, 139

Ragueneau, Camille, 120

Rawlinson, Henry, 113

Renouard, Colonel, 193

Repington, Charles à Court, 157, 172–3, 175, 180–1

Ribot, Alexandre, 19, 238, 290

Robertson, William, *312*; blueprint for staff reorganization, 183–5, 304, 309–11; characterizations of French, 263–4; chief of the Imperial General Staff, 301, 304–8, 334; Egypt, movement of troops to, 292; Kitchener-Sir John communications, 182, 184; letter to king (23 June 1915), 183–5; Loos, objections to, 222–3, 224; Murray-Wilson intrigue, 31–3; political-military structure, 330; proposal for future action, 81, 83; Sir John's removal, 183–5, 308–11, 314; trench-reliefs conflict, 84–5, 105, 107; Wilson and, 146–7

– meetings: 2–3 July 1915, cabinet sessions, 200, 201–2; 7 July 1915, Chantilly Conference, 215; 11 July 1915, Anglo-French command, 215–16; 17 Nov. 1915, Paris Conference, 295; 22 Aug. 1915, Anglo-French, 246–7; 24 June 1915, with French, 167, 198; 28 April 1915, with French, 142–3; 29–30 Oct. 1915, Joffre to London, 287; 29 March 1915, Chantilly Conference, 123

– spring offensive: Aubers Ridge failure, 156, 157; eve of battle relations, 149–50; expectations of, 125, 131; French offensive assessment, 68; Ypres, shortening the line, 141–3; Ypres recriminations, 138–9

Romania, 141

Rousset, Léonce, 42

Royal Navy (Britain): 6 July 1915, Calais Conference, 197; blue water strategy, 44; French undervalue of, 5; pre-1914 reliance on, 7; resignation of Fisher, 176; trench-warfare deadlock, 58

Russia: 6–8 Dec. 1915, Chantilly Conference, 319–22, 337; Allied 1915 fall offensive and, 258; Allied coordination, 266, 318–19; Allies need to rescue, 215, 235, 246–7; Anglo-French divergent assessments of, 68; attack in Galicia, 135, 185, 190, 316; British expectations of, xv, 57, 150, 159; Carpathian offensive, 100, 102–3, 135, 150, 157; French loyalty to, xiv, xvi–xvii, 5, 6, 41, 57, 163, 315, 341; Joffre communication with, 41; reversals of, 80, 97, 161, 235; Salonika diplomatic origins, 273–4; transporting war matériel, 77–8

Salonika expedition: 5 Oct. 1915, Calais Conference, 278–80; Allied agreement on, 321; Anglo-French disagreements, 260–1, 303–4, 321, 323; Anglo-French equivocation, 277–8, 280–3, 286–8, 325, 335–6; background, 272–3; British abortive plan, 72–4; British support of Serbs, 71, 246; diplomatic origins, 273–5; divided, ineffectual, and unwilling, 275–7, 298–300, 318, 337; Egypt, movement of troops to, 283–5; Entente coalition decision, 295–6, 338–9; in French strategy debate, 34–5, 42, 303–4; governments versus commands, 74–7; Greek neutrality, 280–3, 298; Serbian troops retreat, 288; Viviani government's collapse, 289–90; Western Front conflicting needs, 271–2. *See also* Balkan offensive

Sarrail, Maurice, 185, 219, 227, *244*, 250, 251–5; 11 Sept. 1915 Anglo-French meeting, 245–6; diverted to Salonika, 277, 289

Sarrail Affair (France), 226–7, 243–6

Sarraut, Albert, 101–2

Second Battle of Ypres. *See* Battle of Ypres, Second

secret treaties among Allies, 10

Section d'Etudes de la Défense nationale, 232, 255

Selborne, Earl of, 285, 297

Sembat, Marcel, 19, 227–8

Serbia: 6–8 Dec. 1915, Chantilly Conference, 319–22, 337; 7 July 1915, Chantilly Conference, 215; Allied fall offensive and, 258; British support of, 71; Bulgarian mobilization, 246; coordination with Allies, 213; diplomatic ties to Greece, 273–4; troop retreat, 288. *See* Salonika expedition

Serbian-Austro-Hungarian front, 42

Shells Crisis: Asquith ministry's fall, 175–9; Kitchener and Sir John relations, 159–61, 172–3, 177–83; overview, 155, 156–7, 172–5; Sir John's fall, 308

Smith, F.E., 124

Smith-Dorrien, Horace, 137, 139–40, 141

Socialists and Radical Socialists (France), 15, 19, 22, 171, 185–6, 219, 226–8, 234, 254, 272, 290, 303, 331

South Midlands Division, 104. *See also* trench warfare

Stamfordham, Lord, 184, 309

Stanley, Venetia, 175–6

Stephanovitch, Colonel, 215

stereotypes and characterizations (Anglo-French), 27–8, 113, 138–9, 237, 263–4, 265, 287, 328, 339–40

Straits Agreement with Russia (March 1915), 10

strategy: eastern-versus-western debate, 34, 42–3, 73–4, 226, 250, 282–3, 337–8, 341–2; terminology, xx–xxi

strategy (Britain): 1915 as transitional year, xiv–xviii; political-military structure, 329–30
strategy (France): 1915 as transitional year, xiv–xviii
Strategy and Command, 1914 (Prete), 4
Sykes-Picot Agreement (1916), 10

tactics: terminology, xxi
terminology, British versus American, xx–xxi
Thomas, Albert, *206–7*; 6 July 1915, Calais Conference, 203; Boulogne Conference on munitions, 200; Briand government, 290; munitions crisis, 171, 186–7, 334
Three Year Law (1913, France), 79; class of 1915 (double cohort), 79, 100, 102, 153. *See also* trench warfare
Times: Shells Crisis, 157, 159, 172–3, 175, 180–1. *See also* Northcliffe newspapers
trench warfare: 1915 transitional year, xvi; Anglo-French competing demands, 96–8; characterizations and stereotypes, 339–40; commands' relationship with troops, 81; explanation re. not sending 29th Division, 92; French strategic response, 36–43; Joffre-Sir John-Kitchener dispute, 88–9; losses 1915, 100, 147, 168, 170, 173–4, 289, 340, 342; role of munitions and heavy artillery, 107–9, 329; shortening the line at Ypres, 141–5; territorials or untrained troops, 79, 85, 91, 104. *See also* Shells Crisis; war matériel
– trench reliefs: 21 Jan. 1915 agreement, 69–70; Anglo-French April 1915 compliance, 124; Anglo-French disputes, 74–6, 82–5; Artois attack, 161–2; British agreement for (March 1915), 104–5, 120; British change plans for, 73; British mistrust of French, 238, 340; British plan to send, 60–1; British troops' arrival schedule, 62; British troops' non-arrival, 66, 73, 78–80, 81, 86, 88–93, 97–8; British troops to Egypt, 292–3; class of 1915 (double cohort), 79, 100, 102, 153; fall offensive 1915 plans, 215–16, 220, 247–8. *See also* New Armies
– Western Front deadlock: Artois offensive expectations, 103–4, 124–6; post-Artois, 188–94; background to, 3–33; Boulogne Conference on munitions, 200; British change of strategy, 57–61, 63–4; British troops to Egypt, 283–6; coordination of Allies needed, 328, 341–2; eastern-western debate, 34–6, 42–3, 337–8, 341–2; French change of strategy, 41–3, 63–4; French expectations of British, xvi–xvii; non-arrival of 29th Division, 98
Turkey: Alexandretta, 77–8, 86, 110, 293–5, 332; British strategy discussions, 57–8; entry into war, 29, 35. *See also* Dardanelles operation

Unionist Party (Britain), 29, 157, 173, 260, 284–5, 297, 333; coalition government, 153, 177, 181, 302, 308. *See also individual members*

Valois group, 235
Venizelos, Eleutherios, 274, 282
Vimy Ridge attacks, 84, 153–5, 161–2, 165, 167, 192, 265. *See also* Artois offensive
Viviani, René, *16*, *207*; 1914 power relations, 15, 19–21; Anglo-French pressure for troops to front, 168; Artois failure and consequences,

165; Briand government, 290; coalition government, 6; Conseil supérieur, 232; expectations of war's progress, 150; fall 1915 offensive, 230–1, 251–5, 259–61; government collapse, 226, 228, 288–90; Salonika expedition, 279, 286–7; strategy debate, 34–5, 41–3
– meetings: 6 July 1915, Calais Conference, 197, 203, 206, 209, 210; 7 Jan. 1915, Elysée Palace, 43; 7 Oct. 1915, trip to London, 282; 8 Oct. 1915, with Kitchener, 282–3; 13 June 1915, Elysée Palace, 163; 23 June 1915, with group commanders, 187

Walmer Castle meeting (20 Dec. 1914), 52, 55
War Committee (British): formation, 268; Gallipoli withdrawal, 293–4
War Council (British): 7–8 Jan. 1915, 50, 60–1; 9 Feb. 1915, Sir John, 76–7; 13 Jan. 1915, 62–3, 65; 14 May 1915, 159, 180, 189–90; 28 Jan. 1915, 72–3; deficiencies, 59; formation, 29–30, 33; replaced by Dardanelles Committee, 177. *See also* Dardanelles Committee; policy and political leadership
war matériel: Allied assessment of Russian supplies, 52–3; Anglo-French differences in use of, 155, 156–7; Boulogne Conference on munitions, 200; British production of, 177–9; British request for French, 191–2; British shortage of, 104–5, 119–20, 123, 152, 164–5, 221–5; coordinated Allied command, 318–19; Dardanelles/front division of, 108–9, 172–4, 176, 179, 193, 199, 202, 218–19, 221, 249–50; failure due to lack of, 41, 102; fall 1915 offensive statistics, 265; French production of, 37, 53, 100, 187, 319; French shortages, 229–30, 319; Loos offensive ammunition, 248; omnibuses as military transport, 51; transporting to Russia, 77–8; trench warfare and role of artillery, 107–9, 223. *See also* Shells Crisis
War of Movement (1914), xiv, 3, 21
"wearing" operations, 321–2
Wedgwood, Josiah, 256
Western Front deadlock. *See* trench warfare
Weygand, Maxime, 85–6, 142, 158
Wielemans, Félix, 215, *320*
Williams, Hanbury, 161
Williams, Rhodri, 203
Wilson, Henry, *26*; 1914 campaign, 14, 23, 55; Anglo-French command conflict, 94; Anglo-French pressure for troops to front, 166–8, 200–1; Belgian Army and coastal strategy, 54; characterizations of French, 265; Committee of Six, 297; coordinated/unified command, 114, 128, 131, 233, 267, 297; on Dardanelles operation, 250, 254; Egypt, movement of troops to, 284, 286; fall 1915 Anglo-French offensive, 265; French need for British troops, 315–16; guns and ammunition from French, 105; intrigue by, 30, 31–2, 105; Joffre and, 49; Kitchener and Sir John, 85–8; liaison with French, 53, 339; Millerand's government instability, 234–5; Murray and, 30–3; opinion of government, 255–6; Robertson and, 146–7; Russian situation, 161; Salonika expedition, 260–1; Sir John and, 47, 305; spring 1915 joint offensive, 131, 143–4; spring offensive, Artois, 68, 93, 141–3, 149–50, 156, 161–2; trench-reliefs conflict,

84–5; trench-warfare strategy, 69; Ypres recriminations, 138–9. *See also* Calais Conference, 6 July 1915; War Council

– meetings: 2–3 July 1915, cabinet sessions, 200, 201–2; 6 July 1915, Calais Conference, 204; 7 July 1915, Chantilly Conference, 215; 9 May 1915, with Joffre, Sir John, 173–4; 11 July 1915, Anglo-French command, 215–16; 12 May 1915, with French, 158; 16–19 Aug. 1915, Kitchener visit to France, 235–40; 22 Aug. 1915, Anglo-French, 246–7; 24 April 1915, with French, 140–1; 24 June 1915, with French, 167, 197–8; 28 April 1915, with French, 142–3; 29 March 1915, Chantilly Conference, 119

Woevre offensive, 120

Yarde-Buller, Henry, 79, 138, 190–1, 249

Ypres. *See* Battles of Ypres, First and Second

Zeebrugge and Ostend. *See* Ostend and Zeebrugge